A PERSONAL NOTE FROM HARLEY HAHN

The Internet is, by far, the greatest and most significant achievement in the history of mankind. What? Am I saying that the Internet is more impressive than the pyramids? More beautiful than Michelangelo's David? More important to mankind than the wondrous inventions of the industrial revolution?

Yes, yes and yes.

Do I expect you to believe this? Of course not—not right now anyway. However, for years now, people have been connecting computers into networks, and now we have the Internet: a worldwide network connecting millions of computers and millions of people. What is amazing is that, within a few short years, the Internet has changed our civilization permanently and has introduced us to two completely unexpected ideas.

First, hundreds of thousands of people have been laboring to build the Internet. They have worked alone, in small groups, and within organizations, like so many ants in a global anthill. Many of these people are only doing their jobs but, just like the ants, they serve the common good while having no conception of the order and of the compelling forces that drive their work.

Deep inside us, there is an irresistible genetic program to follow. There is a voice that we hear only subconsciously and only as a species. A voice that commands us to take our computers, connect them into networks and... communicate.

This leads to the second great idea: When we connect computers we invariably create something that is well beyond the sum of its parts. Although there are millions of computers on the Internet, the computers are important only in that we use them to follow our instructions and to store our data. What is more important is something we cannot yet understand: the answer to the question, what happens when millions of people gather in a safe place to talk and to share? That is what the Internet is about, and that is what we are just beginning to find out.

I sense we are near the beginning of a great and important change in human affairs. There is a reason we built the Internet and, as human beings, we have an obligation to learn how to use it and to participate.

Now, about this book.

Before we start—you and I—I want to make sure you understand an important point: the Internet is easy to use, but is difficult to use well. I have filled this book with technical details, important details you must understand and master in order to use and enjoy the Internet. Still, don't for a moment think that you need to be a computer expert. The Internet is not for nerds, but just as surely it is not for dummies: it is for those people who are willing to think and to learn and to contribute.

If you ever have one of those days where everything seems to go wrong, and the computer just won't cooperate, and you can't understand what is happening, take a moment and try to see things in a larger sense. As a human being, you share the birthright of intelligence, curiosity and, above all, the ability to learn. However, these gifts are not free. By your very nature, you can not only learn, you are compelled to learn if you are to remain happy and fulfilled. Still, as the saying goes, there is no royal road to knowledge.

To use the Internet, you will have to expend some time and some effort (actually, a great deal of time and effort). But if you do, here is what I promise you:

- I promise I will stay with you.
- I promise I will guide you.
- I promise I will teach you the new words and the new ideas and the new skills you need to use the Internet well.

I have taken a great deal of time to organize this book so as to lead you from one topic to another in a way that will make sense to you (at least, in retrospect). However, you do not need to read everything from start to finish (although I think you should). Actually, this book comes with only two simple instructions:

1. Start by reading chapter 1.
2. When in doubt, do something enjoyable that requires effort.

I know what it is like to be faced with a large, inconceivable mass of unknowable information. What you are holding in your hand is much more than a computer book. It is a connection—a real connection—between you and me. Your job is to put in the effort and the time. My job is to open the doors.

I wrote this book to be your companion and, I promise you, it will be a good one. Take a few moments and skim through the pages. This is not your ordinary computer book, not by a long shot. There is a long journey ahead of you, and I will be with you every step of the way.

Buy this book. I am on your side.

Harley Hahn

Harley Hahn's

The Internet Complete Reference, Second Edition

Harley Hahn

Osborne **McGraw-Hill**

Berkeley New York St. Louis San Francisco
Auckland Bogotá Hamburg London Madrid
Mexico City Milan Montreal New Delhi Panama City
Paris São Paulo Singapore Sydney
Tokyo Toronto

Osborne **McGraw-Hill**
2600 Tenth Street
Berkeley, California 94710
U.S.A.

For information on translations or book distributors outside the U.S.A., or to arrange bulk purchase discounts for sales promotions, premiums, or fundraisers, please contact Osborne **McGraw-Hill** at the above address.

The Internet Complete Reference, Second Edition

567890 DOC 9987

ISBN 0-07-882138-X

Executive Editor Scott Rogers	**Indexer** Wendy Murdock
Editorial Assistant Daniela Dell'Orco	**Computer Designer** Richard Whitaker
Project Editor Janet Walden	**Quality Control Specialist** Joe Scuderi
Copy Editor Lunaea Hougland	**Illustrator** Marla J. Shelasky
Proofreader Pat Mannion	**Cover Design** Compass Marketing

The Unisphere logo and the name "Harley Hahn" *HARLEY HAHN*™ are trademarks of Harley Hahn.

About the Author

Harley Hahn is an internationally recognized writer, analyst and consultant. He is the author of fourteen books, including the best-selling *The Internet Complete Reference* and *The Internet Yellow Pages*, and the highly regarded *Assembler Inside & Out*. His Unix books include *The Unix Companion*, *A Student's Guide to Unix*, *Peter Norton's Guide to Unix* and *Mastering Xenix on the IBM PC AT*.

Hahn has a degree in Mathematics and Computer Science from the University of Waterloo, Canada; and a graduate degree in Computer Science from the University of California at San Diego. Before becoming a professional writer, he studied medicine at the University of Toronto Medical School.

Hahn enjoys writing computer books, because "I get to sleep in, and I like telling people what to do."

Hahn does not live in a converted farmhouse in Connecticut with his wife, three children, and a Labrador Retriever named Rolf. Nor does he commute frequently to New York.

His favorite pajamas are green.

To Wendy

Contents at a Glance

Contents

List of Figures

Acknowledgments

My favorite part of writing a book comes at the end, when everything else is finished, and all I have to do is write the final section: the acknowledgments. However, it occurs to me that it may not be as interesting for you to read these acknowledgments as it is for me to write them. After all, I know all these people and you don't.

"Why," I can hear you say, "should I care about all the people who helped you? What is it to me that Joe Such-and-such from the Acme Computer Company gave you a Personal Widget System to use with your research?"

Good point. So, to make it more interesting and rewarding for you to read this section, I have decided to hold a contest. Here is how it works.

From now on, wherever you go—to the supermarket, to school, to a business conference, for a workout at the health club—carry this book with you. Whenever you meet a new person, check to see if his or her name is mentioned in this section. If so, have the person sign the page on which the name appears. Once you have collected the signatures of everyone in this section, send your book to me. The first person to send me a full list of all the signatures will win a nice prize. (Of course, the validity of the signatures will have to verified.)

So, now that it is worth your while to read these acknowledgments, let's push on. To start, I would like to thank my chief researcher, Wendy Murdock. Wendy knows more about the Internet than anybody I know. Moreover, she is talented, hard-working and smart as the dickens. It might be possible to write an Internet book without Wendy's help, but I certainly wouldn't want to try.

Next, I thank my four technical reviewers: John Navarra (Chicago, Illinois), Eric Johannsen (Germany), Peter ten Kley (Holland) and Kenn Nesbitt (Beaverton, Oregon). These four people spent large amounts of time reading each chapter to help me make everything as perfect as possible. John, Eric, Peter and Kenn are all highly accomplished people in their own right. So much so, that if you ever meet one of them, you should make a point of asking them to shake hands with you. I know I do whenever I get a chance.

For special technical assistance, I thank Carrie Campbell, for commenting on the IRC and mud chapters, and George Reese for expert information about muds. I also thank Mark Schildhauer for help in setting up my Sun workstation; Patrick Linstruth for help with networking; Allan Kent for help getting SLIP running under OS/2; Robert Manning at IBM and Douglass Anderson at Microsoft for high-quality tech support; Hal Lenox at Pacific Bell for information about ISDN; and Michael Grobe for information about the Lynx browser.

For Internet access, I thank Timothy Tyndall and Marcy Montgomery of the Regional Alliance for Information Networking.

For equipment and support, I thank the IBM PC Company (James Adkins and Guy Tanzer), Sun Microsystems (Laura Sardina, Ranjini Mehdi and Wayne Gramlich), and Apple (Keri Walker, Tina Rodriguez and Doedy Hunter). For PPP software and support, I thank Morning Star Technologies (Jamey Laskey and Ashley Burns).

To access the Internet, I use a high-speed line from my network to the outside world. At various times, this line encountered serious technical problems. Solving these problems required a massive undertaking on the scale of the Manhattan Project.

Eventually, the problems were fixed and, in gratitude, I would like to the thank numerous engineers and technicians at GTE who worked on the problem for weeks, at times sacrificing their evenings and weekends: K.C. Abbott, Mark Duvall, Lorne Gadway, Jose Gomez, Louis Gonzalez, Henry Kroepel, Gil Leon, Bob Malloy, Roger Putnam and Mike Underwood. In addition, I would like to thank Gary Foshee and Bobby Duke of Adtran, who flew all the way to the West Coast from Alabama to lend their assistance. I know it seems hard to believe, but it really did take all these people to solve the problem.

Finally, there are the large number of people who actually produce the book. These people work under enormous deadlines and pressures that you and I, as civilians, can only imagine.

To start, I thank my copy editor Lunaea Hougland. Lunaea read every word in every chapter, laboring to make everything flawless and clear.

The bulk of the production work takes place at the publisher, Osborne McGraw-Hill. The most difficult job fell to Janet Walden. Nominally, Janet is the Project Editor. In reality, she is the person whose job it is to make sure everything happens correctly or to die in the process. Although comparatively few Project Editors actually pass away, most of them are severely damaged during production. The fact that Janet made it through this book virtually unscathed, I can only attribute to her experience as a mother of young children, which leaves her uniquely qualified to deal with writers and other inhabitants of the publishing industry.

Along with Janet, there are several other people—in what is euphemistically referred to as "Editorial"—who worked on this book. These people are Pat Mannion (proofreading), Cindy Brown and Claire Splan (line corrections) and Terese Tatum (assisting Janet).

In the production department, I thank the following people: Deborah Wilson (Director of Manufacturing and Production); Marcela Hančík (Production Manager); Peter Hančík (page layout), Lance Ravella (illustrations); Jani Beckwith, Roberta Steele, Richard Whitaker, and Leslee Bassin (page layout); Joe Scuderi (quality control) and George Anderson (Manufacturing/Inventory).

With respect to marketing, I thank Kendal Andersen (Marketing Manager), Claudia Ramirez (International Marketing), Polly Fusco (Special Sales), Anne Ellingsen and Patty Mon (Public Relations), and Allan Benamer (Internet Marketing). In addition, Patrick Hansard and Gemma Velten in the McGraw-Hill New York office helped Claudia with the international marketing. (If you are reading this book outside of the United States or Canada, you can thank Claudia, Patrick and Gemma.)

Finally, I thank Scott Rogers, the Osborne McGraw-Hill Executive Editor, and Daniela Dell'Orco, his talented and hard-working assistant. Scott and Daniela have labored for months on end hoping that, one day, I would stop writing books long enough for them to take a vacation.

We will see.

—Harley Hahn

Chapter One

Introduction

In this chapter, I will introduce you to the Internet and describe my intentions as to the nature of this book and how you and I will spend our time together.

I will start by asking the seminal question, "What is the Internet?" From there, I will advance from the philosophical to the practical by offering suggestions on how to best use and enjoy this book.

Finally, I will answer an oft-asked query, "Do I need to learn Unix?" (as well as the only slightly less-asked query, "What is this Unix thing anyway?).

What is the Internet?

The INTERNET is the name for a vast, worldwide system consisting of people, information, and computers. The Internet is so large and complex as to be well beyond the comprehension of a single human being. Not only is there no one who understands all of the Internet, there is no one who even understands most of the Internet.

The roots of the Internet lie in a project called the ARPANET which was sponsored by the United States Department of Defense Advanced Research Projects Agency (ARPA). The Department of Defense was interested in building a network that could maintain itself under adverse conditions. (A NETWORK is simply two or more computers connected together.) The original idea was to build a network capable of carrying military and government information during a "nuclear event".

The project was started in 1968 and soon evolved into a more general goal of developing techniques to build a large-scale network. The Arpanet continued for years and was gradually phased out after having officially been declared completed. By then, the technology to connect computers reliably and economically had been developed, and today the Arpanet's spiritual descendents form the global backbone of what we call the Internet.

HINT

How old is the Internet? If you are interested in the Internet's birthday, I can give you four choices:

(1) The first Arpanet working group met at Stanford Research Institute on October 25 and 26, 1968.

(2) The original Arpanet used special-purpose communication computers called IMPs (Interface Message Processors). The IMPs acted as the interface between regular computers and the Arpanet. The first IMP was delivered to a lab at UCLA in Los Angeles on September 1, 1969.

(3) The first connection between two distant IMPs was established on November 21, 1969. IMP #1 was in Los Angeles. IMP #2 was at the Stanford Research Institute in Menlo Park, California.

(4) Finally, on Dec 5, 1969, the Arpanet was officially established by connecting four IMPs at Los Angeles, Menlo Park, Santa Barbara (U.C. Santa Barbara), and Utah (the University of Utah).

INTERNET RESOURCE *Look in the catalog under Internet Resources for*
Internet Timeline

At first, the goal of the Arpanet researchers was to develop one large network to connect computers over long distances. However, by the mid-1970s, it became clear that no single network was going to be able to serve everyone's needs. The researchers saw it would be far more useful to develop a technology that could connect various types of networks into a single large system. This led to the concept of an "internetwork" or "internet".

Thus, today's Internet is not really a single large computer network. It is actually a collection of tens of thousands of networks spanning the globe.

Perhaps the best way to understand the organization and importance of the Internet is to compare it to the two other great worldwide communication systems: the postal system and the telephone system. Both of these consist of many, many smaller parts, connected together into a large international organization. The great advantage of the Internet, though, is it is much more flexible and a lot faster.

Although the Internet is newer than the postal and telephone systems, it has found a permanent place in our society and our economy. Indeed, the world is now so dependent on the Internet, we could not get by without it. (If you have not yet used the Internet, you may find it difficult to believe how important it is. All I can say is, just wait until you have used the Internet for a few months, and you will see for yourself.)

It would be a mistake, though, to think of the Internet as a computer network, or even a group of computer networks. From our point of view, the computer networks are simply the medium that carries the information. The beauty and utility of the Internet lie in the information itself and in the people who participate. As we start to work together, this is how I want you to think of the Internet: not as a computer network, but as a huge source of practical and enjoyable information.

But this is only the beginning. I would also like you to develop an appreciation of the Internet as a people-oriented society. Put simply, the Internet allows millions of people, all over the world, to communicate and to share. You communicate by either sending and receiving electronic mail, or by establishing a connection to someone else's computer and typing messages back and forth. You share by participating in discussion groups and by using the many programs and information sources that are available for free.

In learning how to use the Internet, you are embarking upon a great adventure. You are about to enter a world in which well-mannered people from many different countries and cultures cooperate willingly and share generously. They share their time, their efforts, their knowledge and their products. (And you will too.)

Every resource on the Internet exists because a person or a group volunteered their time. They had an idea, developed it, created something worthwhile, and then made it available to anyone in the world.

Thus the Internet is much more than a computer network or an information service. The Internet is living proof that human beings who are able to communicate freely and conveniently will choose to be socially cooperative and selfless.

The computers are important because they do the grunt work of moving all the data from place to place, and they execute the programs that let us access the information. The information itself is important because it offers utility, recreation and amusement.

But, overall, what is most important is the people. The Internet is the first global forum and the first global library. Anyone can participate, at any time: the Internet never closes. Moreover, no matter who you are, you are always welcome. You will never be excluded for wearing the wrong clothes, having the wrong colored skin, being the wrong religion, or not having enough money.

A cynic might say the reason the Internet works so well is that there are no leaders. Actually, there is some truth to this. As unbelievable as it sounds, nobody actually "runs" the Internet. Nobody is "in charge" and no single organization pays the cost. The Internet has no laws, no police and no army. There are no real ways to hurt another person, but there are many ways to be kind. Perhaps, under the circumstances, it is only natural for people to learn how to get along. (Although, this does not stop people from arguing.)

What I choose to believe is, for the first time in history, unlimited numbers of people are able to communicate with ease, and we are finding that it is in our nature to be communicative, helpful, curious and considerate.

My suggestion is to think about the Internet as an entity in its own right: a worldwide organism consisting of countless numbers of people, information sources, and computers joined in a symbiotic confluence. At first, the term "organism" may seem a bit strange but, as you start using the Internet, you will see it very much has a life of its own beyond the machines and the individual people.

What's in a Name?

The Net

The Internet is often referred to as THE NET. This conjures up an image of a mysterious something-or-other that magically connects people, information, and computers from all over the world.

Actually, this is a pretty good way to think of the Internet and, in this book, I will use the terms "Internet" and "the Net" interchangeably.

Although there is plenty of room on the Internet for technical thinking, much of what happens really does fall into the category of magic. What do I mean by this? I mean that now that the people, the information, and the computers have come together, we human beings find ourselves with something more wonderful than we have ever imagined, something that transcends anything we have ever created.

Someday, I am sure, we will have a name for this wonderful thing. For now, we just call it "the Net".

Joining the Internet allows you to become part of a complex system with millions of components that, taken as a whole, is nothing less than the next great step in human evolution.

That is the Internet.

⚑ HINT

The Internet is like Life, only more fun.

Using the Internet

Using the Internet means sitting at your computer screen and using a program to perform some task. You might be at work, at school, or at home, using virtually any type of computer, such as a PC or a Macintosh.

A typical session might begin with you checking your electronic mail. You can read your messages, reply to those that require a response, and perhaps send a message of your own to a friend in another city.

You might then read a few articles in some of the worldwide discussion groups: perhaps jokes from one of the humor groups, or recipes for a dinner that you are planning for the weekend. Maybe you are following a discussion about Star Trek or philosophy or literature or aviation.

After leaving the discussion groups, you might play a game, or read an electronic magazine, or search for some information on a computer in another country. You might then spend a half hour or so looking around for interesting things. On the Internet, it is easy to move from one place to another as your mood takes you.

This is what using the Internet means and this is what I will show you how to do in this book.

How to Use This Book

The title of this book contains the word "Complete" so let's take a minute to discuss exactly what I mean by that.

I promise to teach you everything you need to know to be able to use the Internet and its basic resources. Within the catalog at the end of this book, you have a list of Internet resources. If you would like a much larger catalog of resources of all types, look at my book *The Internet Yellow Pages* (Osborne McGraw-Hill). Still, my intention is that for most people, most of the time, this book will be all you need.

Since the purpose of this book is to show you how to understand and use the Internet, I will start by providing the proper background and by teaching you some technical details. This is what I will do in Chapters 2 through 6. These chapters explain the basics: how the Internet is organized, how you connect to the Internet and, most important, how to understand Internet addressing and directory structures.

As you know, when you use a telephone you need a number to dial, and when you mail a letter you need a postal address. Similarly, the Internet has its own official "addresses". Each person and each computer has its own address, and Chapter 6 explains how the system works. Almost everything you do is built around these addresses, so it is crucial that you read this chapter at the beginning of your Internet career.

Once you have read Chapters 2 through 6, you can go wherever your interests take you. If you want to explore the Internet by using the World Wide Web, read Chapters 9 through 12. If you want to send electronic mail, start with Chapters 7 and 8. If you want to participate in a Usenet discussion group, read Chapters 13 through 15. Once you understand the basics, there is no special order for learning.

If you are using this book to teach a course, you can follow the chapters in order. I have carefully designed the material to cover the most important topics first. You can start from the beginning and teach your students (or yourself) as much as you want, leaving the rest for another day.

If you have never used the Net before, it is tempting to want to rush right in and explore, especially if someone shows you how to use a "browser" to access the World Wide Web. It's possible you are used to using "user friendly" programs, say, on a Macintosh or under Microsoft Windows. If so, you may be in the habit of using a program immediately without spending any time reading the documentation.

This may have worked for you in the past, but the Net is a complex place, and I do want to encourage you to take some time at the beginning and let me teach you the basics. In my experience, if you don't really understand what you are doing, you can go only so far, and it is best to learn the fundamental concepts properly at the start of your Internet career.

So please, take some time to read through the beginning chapters, and give me a chance to show you how it all works. I promise you, by the time you finish this book, you will agree it is more fun to understand the details of what you are doing than to rush in blindly with no preparation.

HINT

Computers in general—and the Net in particular—are powerful, complex tools. It is not reasonable to expect you can start using such tools effectively without some careful preparation. Although it is possible to start using your Internet programs right away, your overall enjoyment and long-term satisfaction will be greatly diminished. Using the Internet well requires you to learn the basic principles, and that takes some time and some effort. In my book, anyone who says differently is selling something. (This is my book.)

Do You Need to Know Unix?

The answer is no, but read on.

UNIX is a family of operating systems (master control programs) used to control computers. Virtually all types of computers can run Unix. Conversely, there are many variations of Unix for all sizes of computers.

When I use the word "Unix" as a general term, I mean more than an operating system. I am actually referring to an entire culture with its own language, technical terms, conventions, traditions and a wide variety of computer-oriented facilities. To many people, the Unix culture is intimately connected to the Internet. Some people consider the Internet to be part of the Unix culture. Other people consider Unix to be part of the Internet culture.

The truth of it is the Internet has a life of its own. Although many of the Internet's computers use Unix, the details are hidden from you. Thus, you do not need to learn Unix *per se* in order to use the Internet.

However, you do need to understand the rudiments of using your own computer system. You must know how to start the system, enter commands, use the keyboard (and mouse if you have one) and shut down the system when you are finished. It is also helpful—almost indispensable—to be able to manipulate data files, so you can save and retrieve information, and so you can create and edit your own information. For example, when you send someone a message using electronic mail, it is convenient to be able to use a text editing program to compose the message.

When you use a Unix system to access the Internet, it is often difficult to say where Unix ends and the Internet begins. Some of the programs you will be using will be Unix programs, perhaps not built-in to the operating system itself but very much a part of the Unix culture. For example, many people read their electronic mail using the Unix mail program.

However, you are perfectly justified in keeping your knowledge of Unix to a practical minimum and spending your time, instead, exploring and using the Internet. There is no need for you to become a Unix expert.

Should You Learn Unix?

Having just told you that you do not need to become a Unix expert in order to use the Internet, I am now going to tell you, yes, I do recommend you learn Unix. You do not need to, but you ought to, and here is why:

As I mentioned earlier, Unix is a lot more than an operating system. It is actually a large, worldwide culture, intimately connected to the Internet. On its own, Unix has a lot to offer and hence, is worth learning.

Moreover, if you are using Unix to access the Internet, there are a great many advantages to having some technical knowledge of the underlying system. For example, you will probably want to send messages, either to another person or to a discussion group. To compose such messages, you should be able to use one of the Unix text editing programs.

As you work with the Internet, you may also want to collect information you find on computers around the world. This means you will need to know how to create and to manipulate data files. There are many such examples and they all illustrate the fact of life that, regardless of what anyone tells you, it is always a good idea to learn something about the technical details of your computer system.

Wait a minute, you may be saying, this might be okay for the people who are using Unix-based systems, but I use a PC (or a Macintosh or some other fine non-Unix system) to access the Internet, and the people who set up everything promised it would be "user friendly". They told me I could select anything I wanted from a menu and I wouldn't have to spend any time learning anything as evil and horrible as Unix commands. Besides, computers scare me.

Well, far be it from me to deny you the comfort and security of your own fears. Moreover, the last thing I would do in a family-oriented book like this would be to disagree contentiously with those misguided souls who firmly believe that the future of computing lies in the populace-at-large selecting items from menus.

Suffice to say, as you use the Internet, you will, from time to time, connect to remote computers that will be running Unix. At such times, a basic knowledge of the Unix culture and its tools can provide practical benefits.

In order to help you, I recommend my book *The Unix Companion* (Osborne McGraw-Hill). That book and this Internet book complement one another nicely.

⚑ HINT

Learning the fundamentals of Unix will make your work with the Internet more comfortable and will expand your possibilities.

Chapter Two

Understanding the Internet

In order to use the Internet well, you need to understand something of what it is and how it works. In this chapter, I will start with the idea of computer networks, cover a few basic concepts and terms, and then move quickly to the Internet itself.

The most important ideas I will discuss are clients and servers, and then hosts and terminals. These concepts are central to appreciating the Net and, by the time you finish this chapter, you will start to understand the Internet and how it works.

The last idea I will cover is one you will hear people talk about all over the Net: the mysterious TCP/IP. TCP/IP is nothing less than the glue that holds the Internet together and, by the time you finish this chapter, you will know what it is and why it is so important.

Our Friend the Network

The term NETWORK refers to two or more computers connected together. There are a number of reasons to connect computers into networks, but the two most important (from our point of view) are:

- to allow human beings to communicate
- to share resources

As an Internet user, there are a number of ways you can communicate with people. The most important are sending electronic mail, and typing messages back and forth in real time using your keyboard and screen.

Network users can also share resources. Indeed, computer managers often arrange networks so resources that are expensive or difficult to maintain can be used by anyone on the network. For instance, a manager might attach a costly printer to a network so everybody who needs it can use the same printer. On the Internet, we share information resources rather than pieces of hardware.

A LOCAL AREA NETWORK, or LAN, is a network in which the computers are connected directly, usually by some type of cable. When we connect LANs together, we call it a WIDE AREA NETWORK or WAN. Most wide area networks are connected via some type of telephone line, although a variety of other technologies, such as satellite links, are used as well. The wide area connections for most of the Internet travel over some telephone system or another. Indeed, the bottleneck in establishing Internet service within developing countries is usually the lack of a reliable phone system.

Here is a typical example of a network: Imagine yourself sitting in a room full of computers in the Social Sciences Computing Facility at a major university. (The weather outside happens to be cold and rainy but, since it has nothing to do with the example, I won't mention it.) Your computer is connected in a LAN to all the other computers in the room and to the computers within people's private offices throughout the building. This arrangement is shown in Figure 2-1.

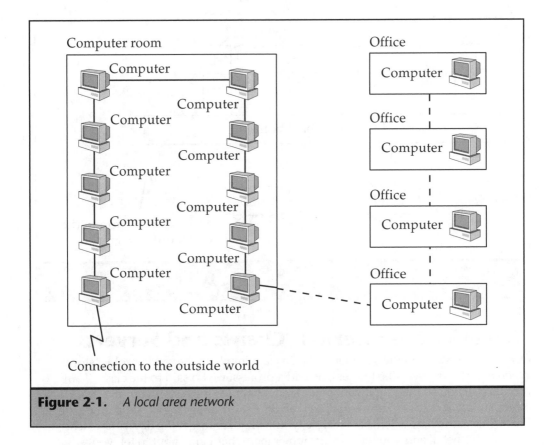

Figure 2-1. *A local area network*

There are a number of other LANs on the campus. For example, the psychology department has its own network of computers, as does the math department, the computer science department, and so on. Each of these LANs is connected to a high-speed link, called a BACKBONE, to form a campus-wide WAN. This is shown in Figure 2-2.

Although I have used a university as an example, many types of organizations use similar arrangements: companies, governments, research facilities, other types of schools, and so on. If an organization is small, it may have only a single LAN. Large organizations may have multiple LANs connected into one or more complex WANs. Such organizations usually have a full time staff to care for and feed the networks.

How are the LANs connected? By special-purpose computers called ROUTERS. The job of a router is to provide a link from one network to another. We use routers to connect LANs (to form WANs) and to connect WANs to form even larger WANs. In other words, you can consider the computers within the Internet to be connected into LANs and WANs by a large number of routers. However, there is more to the picture that I need to explain. But first, let's take a moment to talk about clients and servers.

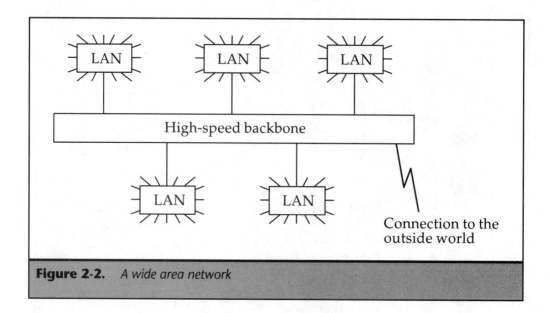

Figure 2-2. *A wide area network*

The Secret of the Internet: Clients and Servers

Once, when I was a medical student, I had a class in which the teacher told a story. When he was a student (he told us), he had a professor who said to the class: "I am about to tell you something I want you to remember for the rest of your medical career. In fact, it is so important that, as I tell it to you, I am going to stand on my head. This will ensure that, as long as you live, you will never forget the day your teacher stood on his head, and you will always remember what I am about to tell you."

Well, what I am going to tell you right now is that important. It is the main secret to understanding the Internet, and it is something I want you to internalize until it becomes second nature. Unfortunately, I can't be with you in person, so I am not able to stand on my head as you read this. You will just have to pretend. (Imagine me standing on my head.)

Here it is: The secret to understanding the Internet is that the Net is populated by two types of computer programs: servers and clients. SERVERS are programs that provide resources. CLIENTS are programs that you use to access those resources.

As you know, the Internet contains millions of computers, as well as a lot of wires, cables, telephone lines, satellite links, and so on. And the whole purpose of all of this equipment is simply to let the clients and the servers talk to one another. In other words, the Internet was constructed so client programs (which you use) can talk to server programs (which provide resources).

HINT

Learning how to use the Internet means learning how to use the client programs that run on your computer.

For example, to read electronic mail, you use a mail client program to send and receive messages. The mail server maintains an electronic "mailbox" and makes sure outgoing mail is delivered correctly. The mail client acts as your interface. It gets the messages, shows them to you, helps you write replies, maintains an address book for you, and so on. To send and receive mail, you don't need to know anything about the mail server: it does its job behind the scenes. All you need to learn is how to use the mail client.

Here is another example. The Internet supports a large system called the World Wide Web, often referred to as "the Web". I discuss the Web in detail in Chapters 9 through 12. For now, here are the highlights:

The Web consists of a great many web servers scattered all around the Net. These web servers can respond to requests for information organized into "pages". A web page can contain text, pictures, or even sounds. To access a web page, you use a web client that calls upon the appropriate web server to send you the page. Your client then displays the page for you on your screen. If necessary, your client will call upon an auxiliary program to show you a picture, or to play a sound.

What makes web pages special is they can contain links to other web pages. As you use your web client to read a page, you can tell it to follow a particular link. Your client will then jump to whatever web page the link points to, even if it is on an entirely different computer (sort of like jumping through hyperspace).

To make the jump, your client will send a message to the server that controls the new page, requesting a copy of that page. The server will send it to your client, which will then display the page for you. Thus, as you use the Web, you can jump from one server to another, all around the Net without having to know any of the technical details. Your client (which runs on your computer) takes care of everything.

In web language, a client program is called a "browser". Thus, I can say, in order to access the Web, you use a client called a browser to request and display information from one of the many web servers situated around the Net.

Throughout this book, I will be discussing all the important services the Internet has to offer. Each service has its own clients and, to utilize a service, you will have to learn how to use the appropriate client. For example, to access the Web, you will have to learn how to use a web client. To send and receive electronic mail, you will have to learn how to use a mail client.

Each Internet service has a variety of clients available. For example, when it comes to using the Web, there are browsers for Microsoft Windows, browsers for OS/2, browsers for the Macintosh, browsers for X Window, and browsers for plain Unix. Moreover, most services have more than one client available for a particular system. For instance, when you set up a Windows or Macintosh system, you will find you can choose from a number of different browsers.

It is not necessary for you to learn how to use all the possible clients. You really only need to learn one client for each service. However, you will find most clients for a particular service work more or less the same way and, although there are differences, it is not too hard to move from one client to another. Indeed, many people like to switch clients every few months as better programs become available.

X Window and X Clients

In the previous section, I explained how we use client programs to access Internet services. Each type of service has its own client. The job of the client is to communicate with a server that allows you to use the service. For example, to access the Web, you use a web client to fetch and display information from a web server.

As you would imagine, each type of computer has its own set of Internet client programs. If you use a Macintosh, you will run Macintosh clients. If you use a PC with Windows, you will run Windows clients. Later in this chapter, you will see how some people use a phone connection to utilize a Unix computer. In this case, you would run Unix clients.

The idea here is straightforward: Mac people run Mac programs, Windows people run Windows programs, and Unix people run Unix programs. These are three of the most common systems. However, there is a fourth system, called X WINDOW, which is also used widely. If your computer uses X Window, this section will explain the basic concepts you should understand. As you will see, X Window gives you certain advantages when you use the Internet.

If you are not an X Window user, feel free to move on to the next topic. Still, a lot of people use X Window, and you may want to skim this section, just to see what all the fuss is about.

HINT

If you are using a Unix workstation (such as a Sun computer), there is a good chance you can use X Window. If you are not sure, ask your system administrator.

X Window is used with systems that support graphical user interfaces. A GRAPHICAL USER INTERFACE, or GUI, allows you to use, not only your keyboard, but a mouse or some other type of pointing device. With the help of your mouse, you select items from menus and manipulate objects on the screen. You can also run more than one program at the same time, each of which can reside in its own rectangular area called a WINDOW. Of course, the idea of a GUI (pronounced "goo-ey") is nothing new. If you have ever used a Macintosh, or a PC with Windows or OS/2, you have used a GUI.

Most of the time, X Window is run on a Unix system. However, with the proper software, you can also run it on a PC or a Mac.

INTERNET RESOURCE *Look in the catalog under Internet Resources for* *X Window Software*

In the world of personal computers, there is not a lot of choice for graphical operating systems. There is really only one main type of Microsoft Windows, OS/2, or Macintosh operating system. New versions do come out from time to time—such as Windows 95 replacing Windows 3.1—but you don't need to get a special version of the operating system for each brand of computer. For example, Windows is designed to run on any IBM-compatible PC.

Unix is different. There are many types of Unix for many different brands of computer systems. X Window was developed in order to provide a common GUI for all such systems. X Window offers a set of tools for programmers who develop graphical applications, as well as a standard interface for users to interact with those applications. Although there is nothing in the design of X Window that says it must be used with Unix, in practice, this is often the case.

For convenience, X Window is usually referred to as X. For example, if a friend tells you he has a program you might want to use, you can ask him, "Does it run under X?"

What's in a Name?

X Window

At one time, an operating system named V (the letter "V") was developed at Stanford University. To work with V, the programmers created a windowing system which they named W. Later, the W system was sent to someone at MIT who used it as the basis for a new windowing system which he named X.

The modern X Window system, first developed in 1984, grew out of this initial effort. Today, the current version of X Window is version 11 release 6, usually written as "X11R6".

Note that the official name of this system is the singular "X Window", not the plural "X Windows".

In X terminology, the three devices you use to interact with your computer—the keyboard, the screen and the mouse—are referred to as a DISPLAY. X lets you run more than one program at the same time on a single display. As part of the graphical user interface, each program resides in its own window on the screen. To switch from one program to another, you use the mouse to move from one window to another.

When you use X, the details of maintaining the GUI for all the programs that are running are handled by a single program called a DISPLAY SERVER or an X SERVER.

For example, say you have four programs running at the same time, each of which resides in its own window. As you work, you can move the windows or even change their size. Now, suppose one of the programs needs to draw a circle on the screen. Rather than doing the work itself, it sends a message to the X server—the program controlling the screen—telling it to draw a circle of a particular size at a particular location. The X server actually does the work.

This division of labor has several important advantages. First, it means the entire GUI is controlled by a single program that ensures everything works as it is supposed to. For example, the window in which a program is running may be partially obscured by another window. The program itself does not need to know this, nor does it care. The X server will handle the details.

Second, when a programmer designs a new program, he or she does not have to worry about the user interface, the hardware or the operating system. All that is necessary is for the program to call on X in the standard way whenever such work needs to be done. This makes for smaller, more reliable programs which are portable from one X system to the next.

Since all X servers provide the same functions, a program written to depend upon an X server will run under any X system. You can, for instance, find an X program anywhere on the Internet, copy it to your computer, and run it under your own graphical user interface. Once you learn how to use the Internet file transfer service, you will be able to acquire many such graphical programs for free.

The third advantage of X is that graphical user interfaces are more or less standard.

The part of the system that provides the look and feel of your interface is called the WINDOW MANAGER. (Technically, the window manager is itself a program running on top of X.) There are two widely used window managers, named Motif and Open Look. There are differences between the two, but they are not pronounced.

If you saw identical programs running on two computer screens, one using Motif and one using Open Look, the main thing you would notice is the appearance of the windows and other graphical elements would be somewhat different. In addition, you would use the mouse and the menu system slightly differently.

However, the basic concepts are the same no matter which window manager you use. Certainly, the programs inside the windows would not change. Basically, if you know how to use one X system, you know how to use them all.

Figure 2-3 shows an X display in five different programs running at the same time, each one in its own window. Notice that, as these programs execute, they depend on a single X server program to maintain the user interface.

By now, this should all remind you of the client/server relationship I discussed in the previous section. Indeed, this is the case. The programs you run are clients and, as such, are referred to as X CLIENTS. They request services—managing the user interface—from the X server program you run on your own computer. In other words, the term "X client" is a synonym for any program running under the auspices of X Window.

The most powerful feature of X Window is that X clients do not have to run on the same computer as the X server. When you use X, the X server program will always run on your computer, the one in front of you. However, the X clients can run on any computer connected to your computer via the network. In Figure 2-3, you can see five X clients. Of these, two are running on remote computers.

If you are an X user, the Internet is important to you in two ways. First, as I mentioned above, there are many X clients available for you to copy and use for free.

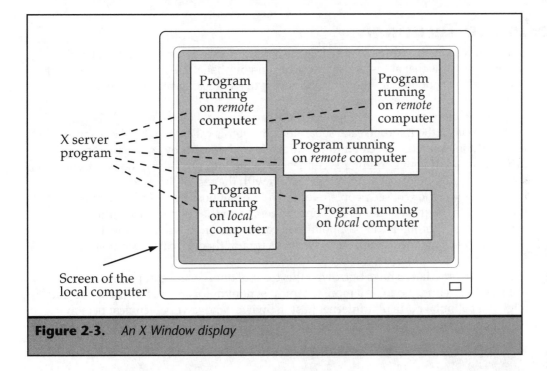

Figure 2-3.   *An X Window display*

Second, you can use the Internet to connect to another computer and run an X program that will be displayed on your screen. (However, if the remote computer is far away, the response may be too slow for your liking.)

⚑HINT

Some people will tell you the X Window system is confusing because the server program runs on your computer, while the client programs may run on remote computers. Such people maintain this is the opposite of what you might expect.

As you now know, the idea behind X is simple, so don't let silly people confuse you. When you meet such a person, be graceful and remind yourself, "There but for the grace of God, go I."

Explain to this person that you already understand X just fine, thank you. If he looks disappointed at not being able to mix you up with a lot of unnecessary technical details, you might gently suggest he use his time to perform some socially useful function like writing a letter to the editor or learning a new Unix command.

Hosts and Terminals

So far, I have talked about servers (programs that provide Internet resources) and clients (programs that access those resources on your behalf). As you use the Internet, you will also encounter another important pair of technical terms I want you to understand: host and terminal.

To start, there are two meanings for the word "host" you should know about.

First, within the Internet, each separate computer is called a HOST. For example, you might tell someone he can find the information he wants by connecting to a host in Switzerland. If your computer is connected to the Internet, then it too is a host, even though you may not be sharing any resources with the rest of the world.

Sometimes, you will see people refer to an Internet host as a NODE. Here is why: If you draw a diagram of points and lines to represent the connections within a network, each computer will be a point and each connection will be a line. In the part of mathematics that deals with such diagrams (graph theory), each such point is called a "node".

Network specialists have borrowed this term to refer to any computer connected to a network. Thus, "node" is a more technical synonym for "host". So where you and I might talk about a particular Internet host in Switzerland, a very technical person would talk about a node in Switzerland.

⚑HINT

If you are trying to see if someone is a nerd, ask him, "What is the technical term for a computer attached to the Internet?" If he says "node", chances are he is a nerd.

The second meaning of the word "host" has to do with how certain computer systems are set up.

In general, there are two ways you might use a computer: you might have it all to yourself, or you might share it. For example, only one person at a time can use a PC running Windows or a Macintosh. Single-user computers, especially the more powerful ones, are sometimes called WORKSTATIONS.

Some computers, however, are made to support more than one user at the same time. These multiuser systems are often referred to as HOST computers.

For example, a powerful computer—perhaps looking no larger than a PC—can act as a host for hundreds of users at the same time. The Unix operating system, which I discussed earlier, is a multiuser system. Although some people use a Unix computer as a personal workstation, many Unix computers are used as hosts and support multiple users.

When you have your own computer, you interact by using the keyboard, screen, and mouse. These devices are part of the computer. With a multiuser computer, each person has his or her own TERMINAL to use. A terminal has a keyboard, screen, perhaps a mouse. All of the terminals are connected to the host, which provides the computing power for everybody. This arrangement is called a TIMESHARING SYSTEM, and is shown in Figure 2-4.

Thus, there are two meanings for the word "host". Within the Internet, each computer is called a host (or node). Within a timesharing system—such as Unix—the

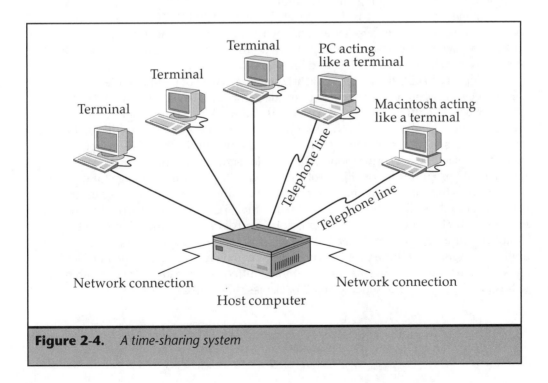

Figure 2-4. *A time-sharing system*

main computer, which supports each user on a separate terminal, is also called a host. Of course, if such a computer were connected to the Internet, it would be both a timesharing host and an Internet host.

Later in the chapter, I will discuss various ways in which you can access the Internet. One way is for you to arrange for your computer to connect right to the Net. In this case, your computer—the one sitting in front of you—becomes an actual Internet host (at least during the time you are connected).

A second way to access the Net is to use the services of a remote timesharing host connected to the Internet (usually a Unix system). Instead of connecting your computer directly to the Internet, you use your computer to access the timesharing host which is already on the Net. Your computer pretends it is a terminal, and you use your keyboard and screen to run programs on the host, sort of like remote control.

Don't worry about the details: I will discuss them later. For now, just think about the idea of hosts and terminals and be glad you were not the person who had to figure all of this out in the first place.

What Is TCP/IP?

Now that you know about clients and servers, and about hosts and terminals, there is one more fundamental technical term I would like to explain: TCP/IP.

As you know, the Internet is built on a collection of networks covering the world. These networks contain many different types of computers and somehow, something must hold the whole thing together. That something is TCP/IP.

The name is pronounced as five separate letters: "T C P I P". If you want to sound like a pro, practice saying these letters so they roll off your tongue quickly, like one long slurred word—"tee-see-pee-eye-pee"—with the accent on the last syllable. (Don't pronounce the slash, or you will sound like a goof.)

The details of TCP/IP are highly technical and are well beyond the interest of almost everybody, but there are a few basic ideas I would like you to understand.

To ensure that different types of computers can work together, programmers write their programs using standard PROTOCOLS. A protocol is a set of rules describing, in technical terms, how something should be done. For example, there is a protocol describing exactly what format should be used for sending a mail message. All Internet mail programs follow this protocol when they prepare a message for delivery.

TCP/IP is the common name for a collection of more than 100 protocols used to connect computers and networks. The actual name, "TCP/IP", comes from the two most important protocols: TCP (Transmission Control Protocol) and IP (Internet Protocol). Although you don't need to know the details, it is useful to have an appreciation for what these protocols are and how they hold together the Internet.

Within the Internet, information is not transmitted as a constant stream from host to host. Rather, data is broken into small packages called PACKETS.

For example, say you send a mail message to a friend on the other side of the country. TCP will divide the message into a number of packets. Each packet is marked with a sequence number, the address of the recipient, and the address of the sender. In addition, TCP inserts some error control information.

The packets are then sent over the network, where it is the job of IP to transport them to the remote host. At the other end, TCP receives the packets and checks for errors. If an error has occurred, TCP can ask for that particular packet to be resent. Once all the packets are received correctly, TCP will use the sequence numbers to reconstruct the original message.

In other words, the job of IP is to get the raw data—the packets—from one place to another. The job of TCP is to manage the flow and ensure the data is correct.

Breaking data into packets has several important benefits. First, it allows the Internet to use the same communications lines for many different users at the same time. Since the packets do not have to travel together, a communication line can carry all types of packets as they make their way from place to place. Think of a highway in which separate cars all travel on a common road even though they are headed for different destinations.

As packets travel, they are sent from host to host until they reach their ultimate destination. (The actual route is chosen by special-purpose computers called routers.) This means the Internet has a lot of flexibility. If a particular connection is disrupted, the computers controlling the flow of data can usually find an alternate route. In fact, it is possible that, within a single data transfer, the various packets might follow different routes to the same destination.

This also means that, as conditions change, the network can use the best connection available at the time. For example, when a particular part of the network becomes overloaded, packets can be routed over other, less busy, lines.

Another advantage of using packets is that, when a small transmission error occurs, only a single packet will need to be resent rather than the entire message. This greatly increases the overall speed of the Internet.

All of this flexibility makes for high reliability: one way or another, TCP/IP makes sure the data gets through. In fact, the Internet runs so well that a file may be sent from one host to another in only a few seconds, even though they are thousands of miles apart and all the packets must pass through multiple computers.

Thus, there are two answers to the question, "What is TCP/IP?" The technical answer is TCP/IP is a large family of protocols used to organize computers and communication devices into a network. The two most important protocols are TCP and IP. IP (Internet Protocol) transmits the data from place to place, while TCP (Transmission Control Protocol) makes sure it all works correctly.

The best answer, though, is the Internet depends on thousands of networks and millions of computers, and TCP/IP is the glue holding it all together.

HINT

If you wonder what the route looks like from your computer to another, you can use the **traceroute** program.

This command is not available on all systems. If your computer does have this program, you can use it to check on the route to an Internet host by specifying the address of that host. (I discuss Internet addresses in Chapter 6.)

For example, on a Unix system, you would enter the following command to see the current route from your computer to the host whose address is **rtfm.mit.edu**:

```
traceroute rtfm.mit.edu
```

The output will show you each step in the path between the two computers. If you try this command at various times, you may see different routes as conditions change.

Chapter Three

A Tour of the Internet

Having covered the basic framework of the Internet, let's take a look at what it has to offer. In this section, I will discuss all of the important Internet resources. In later chapters, I will discuss each service in detail, at which time I will show you how it works and the best way to use it. Figure 3-1, at the end of the chapter, contains a summary of each of the Internet resources and shows you which chapters to read for more details.

Mail

As an Internet user, you can send and receive messages from anyone else on the Internet. Moreover, you can communicate with people who use other systems—such as Compuserve, Prodigy, America Online or MCI Mail—which have connections with the Internet.

However, mail does not mean simply personal messages. Anything that can be stored in a text file can be mailed: pictures, computer programs, announcements, electronic magazines, and so on.

Indeed, this service is so important that, when Internet people talk about "mail", you can always assume they mean "electronic mail". (You will also hear the word "email".) When Internet people need to refer to regular post office mail, they will do so explicitly. Such mail is often referred to as "snail mail", as it takes much longer to arrive than Internet mail.

The Web

The Web is a large system of servers which offers all kinds of information to anyone on the Net. The information can be in the form of regular text, as well as pictures, sounds, and other types of data. To access this information, you use a client program called a browser.

There are two reasons why the Web is so popular. First, it is easy to use. Second, it is easy to create your own web information to share with people all over the Net. Indeed, you will find many of the Web resources are maintained by individuals for their own pleasure.

Within the Web, information is stored in pages. (This is just a name: it has nothing to do with pages in a book.) Each page can hold, not only information, but links to other pages. As you read a page, you can follow a link to jump from one page to another.

The remarkable thing is that the various pages can be on any computer on the Net. When you want to follow a link, your browser will find out where it is, contact the web server at that location, request the new page, and then display it on your screen. All of this happens automatically. All you need to do it tell your browser what you want.

The idea of data containing links to other data is called hypertext. Thus, we can say the purpose of the Web is to fetch and display pages of hypertext. This simple idea has proved to be so useful and enjoyable, within a short time, that the Web has grown to be one of the three most popular Internet services (the other two being electronic mail and the Usenet discussion groups).

Web Search Engines

Nobody really knows how many web servers there are in the world. Suffice to say there are a great many, all of which have their own series of pages offering information and services. Many of these pages are constructed by individuals.

If you know where something is on the Web, all you have to do is tell your browser the address. However, what do you do if you want to find something and you have no idea where to look?

The solution is to use one of the web search engines. These are tools that keep track of many web sites around the world and let you search for particular items whenever you want. The result of a search is a custom list of links, pointing to whatever items the search engine found that met your criteria. To check out an item, all you need to do is select a link and your client will connect you to the appropriate web server, wherever it may happen to be. In fact, unless you specifically ask, you will not even know what computer you are using or what country it is in. Amazing.

Usenet

Usenet is a system of discussion groups in which individual articles are distributed throughout the world. Usenet has literally thousands of different discussion groups, so there is definitely something for everyone. Just about any topic you can think of is discussed in some Usenet group. Moreover, Usenet is really the only place on the Net where you can address the population at large.

For example, say you want to find a copy of an old Freddy the Pig book for your uncle Fred's birthday. The thing to do would be to send a request to the appropriate Usenet group to see if anyone knows where you can find the book.

As with other Internet resources, Usenet is free (once you have Net access), and you can participate in as many groups as you want. Until you have used Usenet for awhile, it is hard to understand why it is so popular and so important. Suffice to say, for now, that Usenet is one of the main reasons why people use the Internet.

The name Usenet is a contraction of "User's Network" (although Usenet is not actually a network, it is a system of discussion groups). Originally, Usenet was set up to provide an electronic bulletin board service on which news articles were posted. For this reason, many of the words used to talk about Usenet refer to news. For example, discussion groups are often referred to as newsgroups, and many people refer to Usenet itself as Netnews.

To participate in Usenet, you use a client program called a newsreader. Using your newsreader, you can select articles to read, save articles to a file, respond to an article, or send in an article of your own.

HINT

Reading Usenet articles—especially the jokes—is a good way to spend time which would otherwise be wasted on work.

Gopher

The gopher system is similar to the Web, in that you use a client to connect to servers all over the world, one at a time. The totality of all the information available via this system is called gopherspace. The difference between gopherspace and the Web is in the way in which information is organized.

Within gopherspace, information is presented as a series of simple menus. Each gopher server has a main menu, and a series of sub-menus. To use a gopher, all you need to do is select the menu item you want, and your client will fetch it for you.

Menu items can point to a number of different types of resources: files, pictures, other Internet resources, and so on. When you select a menu item, your client will do whatever is appropriate. For example, if you select a file, your client will contact the gopher server containing that file and request a copy. When the file arrives, your client will display it for you on your screen.

The power of the gopher is that menu items can point to other menus. A single item on a particular menu can point to the main menu of a completely different gopher server. Thus, it is a simple matter for you to zip around from one gopher server to another—all over the Net—just by selecting items from menus. Your gopher client handles all of the details behind the scenes. This arrangement also means any organization can create its own gopher server and then link it with other gophers all over the world.

How does gopherspace compare to the Web? The gopher technology is older and is not as rich as the web technology. However, gophers are simpler to use, fast, and ubiquitous. Moreover, there are high quality text-based gopher clients that—unlike the popular web browsers—do not require a graphical user interface. (I discuss this idea in Chapter 5.)

HINT

To use the Net well, you have to be familiar with both the Web and gopherspace.

Veronica and Jughead

Like the Web, gopherspace is large and full of more items than you could ever find on your own. To help you find things in gopherspace you can use veronica: a tool that keeps track of an enormous number of gopher menu items from all over the Net. You can use veronica to perform a search and look for all the menu items in gopherspace containing certain keywords. A related tool, jughead, does the same thing for a specific group of gopher menus: say, all the menus at a particular university.

After veronica or jughead finishes searching, you will be presented with a new menu containing the names of whatever items were found. To access one of these items, all you need to do is select it, and your gopher client will connect you to the appropriate gopher server automatically. The results of a typical veronica search will be items from around the Net, but you won't need to know any of the details: your client will take care of everything for you.

Anonymous ftp

The ftp service allows you to copy files from one computer to another. (The name ftp stands for "file transfer protocol", one of the many protocols that are part of the TCP/IP family.)

For security reasons, you cannot copy files between two computers unless you can log in to the remote computer. For example, say you have an account on two computers that are both on the Internet. You decide you want to copy some files from one computer to the other. From the first computer, you use an ftp client program to connect to the second computer. When you do, you are asked to enter a userid and password for the second computer. Once your password is validated the connection is established. You can now use your ftp client to copy files in either direction.

This service is handy for people with accounts on more than one computer (like I described above for telnet). Such people can use ftp to copy files from one computer to another as the need arises. However, many Internet sites have files of public interest they would like to make available to anyone on the Net. To do so, they use a system called anonymous ftp. This system allows anyone to use a guest account to connect to the computer. Once the connection is made, the person can copy only those files that are stored in a special public area.

By convention, when you use your ftp client to connect to a public site, you can access the system by using a userid of **anonymous**. (Hence the name, anonymous ftp.) In such cases, you do not need a regular password.

Anonymous ftp is one of the most important Internet services. Virtually every possible type of data is stored somewhere, on some computer, and it is all available to you for free. For example, many of the programs used on the Internet are created and maintained by certain individuals who then distribute the programs worldwide via anonymous ftp. You can also find electronic magazines, archives of Usenet discussion groups, technical documentation, and much, much more. As a full-fledged Internet user, you will come to depend heavily on anonymous ftp.

What's in a Name?

Downloading, Uploading

When you copy files from a remote host to your computer, we say you are DOWNLOADING the files. When you copy files from your computer to a remote host, you are UPLOADING.

An easy way to remember the difference is to imagine the remote host floating above you in the sky. You send files up, and you ask for files to be sent down.

Archie

There are thousands of anonymous ftp servers around the world offering more files than you can imagine. The role of archie is to make the whole system manageable by helping you find what you need. There are a number of archie servers around the Net, each of which contains a database of most of the files that are publicly available via anonymous ftp.

Suppose you want a particular file—for instance, a program a friend has told you about—but you don't know which anonymous ftp server has the file. You use an archie client to connect to an archie server. You can have your client ask the server to search for files that have the same name as the program you want. After a short wait, the server will send back a list of addresses of some of the Internet sites that have files with that name. Once you know where to look, it is a simple matter to use ftp to download the file.

If you consider the world of anonymous ftp as an enormous, worldwide library which is constantly changing, you can think of the archie servers as the catalog. Indeed, without the archie servers, most of the anonymous ftp resources would be impossible to find.

The name "archie" was chosen to express the idea of an "archive server". In deference to the well-known propensity of computer people to engage in whimsical personification, we usually refer to archie as if it were human. For example, you might ask someone, "Do you know which anonymous ftp sites carry the such-and-such electronic magazine?". "No, I don't," replies your friend, "Why don't you ask archie?"

You may have noticed that, conceptually, archie provides a service for anonymous ftp similar to what veronica and jughead do for the gopher system. Actually, anonymous ftp and archie came first. When a program was designed to search gopherspace, the programmers chose the name "veronica" because, in the Archie comic books, Veronica was Archie's girlfriend. Similarly, Jughead was Archie's best pal. You might wonder if any other search programs are named after Archie characters. The answer is, not yet (although I expect it won't be long before we see such programs).

Mailing Lists

A mailing list is an organized system in which a group of people are sent messages pertaining to a certain topic. The messages can be articles, comments, or whatever is appropriate to that topic. As with other Internet services, mailing lists are free services.

All mailing lists—and there are thousands of them—have someone in charge who administers the list (although the details will probably be handled by a computer program). You can subscribe or unsubscribe to a list by sending a message to the appropriate address. Some mailing lists are moderated, which means someone decides which material will be accepted. Other lists will accept and send out messages from anybody.

If you feel lonely and ignored, subscribing to just a handful of mailing lists is guaranteed to keep your electronic mailbox filled to the Plimsoll line.

Telnet (Remote Connection)

With some computer systems, you need to enter a user name and a password in order to start a work session. We call this process logging in. For example, you may have to log in to a computer in order to establish your connection to the Internet.

One of the original reasons why the Internet was set up was to allow people to work on remote computers. For instance, a scientist who works at one university might, for some reason, also have an account on a host computer on the other side of the country. If he were actually there, he could log in by typing his user name and password. However, with the Internet, he can connect to the remote host, log in, and start work just as if he were there in person.

The service allowing you to log in and use a remote computer is called telnet. To utilize this service, you use a telnet client to make the connection and then provide the services of a terminal. (We say the client emulates a terminal.) Thus, using a telnet client is just like using a terminal to work with a remote host; it's just that the host can be anywhere on the Net.

You will find the word "telnet" is often used as a verb. For example, you might tell someone, "If you telnet to this computer, you will be able to display a weather report for any region in the country."

Most Internet computers to which you might log in use Unix, and so we borrow the terminology for logging in from Unix itself. The name by which an account is known is called a userid (pronounced "user-eye-dee"). Using telnet, you can log in to any computer on the Internet that supports remote users (as long as you have a valid userid and password for that computer).

Unless you have a special need, you will probably never have an account on a remote computer. However, as a public service, many Internet hosts are set up to allow anybody to log in using a special guest account. When you log in with such an account, you will have restricted privileges: usually you will be able to run one specific program.

For example, in the United States, there is a remote host to which you can telnet in order to display weather reports from around the country. Anyone can log in to this system and check out the weather without using a password.

Talk Facilities

A talk facility allows you to communicate with other people on the Net in real time, either by typing messages back and forth or by actual voice conversation. (Or course, to use voice transmission, you need a computer with a microphone and sound capability.)

There are a large variety of talk facilities available on the Net, all of which are set up as client/server systems. Once you have the proper client program, you can talk to anyone else who is using the same system.

Just about every variation you can imagine exists somewhere on the Net. You can talk to one person at a time in complete privacy, you can have a group discussion in private, or you can have public conversations with whoever happens to drop into the talk facility. If you are bored or lonely, you can connect to a talk system anytime you want and see what is happening.

Although typing can be slower than real talking, you can have a conversation with anyone on the Net, no matter how far away he or she is, with no long distance phone charges at the end of the month. Moreover, you can make friends with people all over the world: people you would otherwise never meet in person.

Internet Relay Chat

Internet Relay Chat, usually called IRC, is a public talk facility which can be used by anyone on the Net at any time. Within IRC, there are many, many conversations going on at any time, many of which are organized around a particular topic or idea.

Each IRC conversation is carried on a channel. To join an existing conversation, all you need to do is tell your IRC client you want to join such-and-such channel. You can create a new channel whenever you want and use it for as long as you want. Once the last person leaves a particular channel, it vanishes automatically.

As you might imagine, IRC is widely used by a great many people around the world. Indeed, there are many people who have made IRC friends they talk to regularly. In general, IRC conversations are public, however you can arrange to have a private conversation with people of your own choosing, much like a telephone conference call.

HINT

If you find yourself spending large amounts of time using IRC, remind yourself you are talking to the type of people who spend a large amount of time using IRC.

Muds and Other Imaginary Places

The Internet supports a wide variety of interactive virtual environments. These are places in which you can interact with people and situations which offer an imaginary setting of some type.

For example, you might spend some time exploring a countryside based on the myth of King Arthur and his knights. During your visits, you would use various commands to walk around the town, visit the pubs, talk to other people, get into fights, look for treasure, and so on. Some of the time, the people you encounter will be real people who have adopted a particular persona. For instance, you may encounter someone who is a wizard like Merlin, or a rogue who sneaks around stealing things, or a giant who runs around killing monsters. You yourself might be a traveling knight who visits various towns, looking for adventure.

Aside from real people who are pretending, you may also find characters—even whole villages of people—which are completely created by the computer. For example, there may be a gremlin who teleports himself around stealing things from you. Or you might enter an area based on Alice in Wonderland or The Wizard of Oz where you can meet all the characters from the book.

If you have ever played a role-playing game, such as Dungeons and Dragons—or spent any time in a singles' bar—you will already be familiar with environments in which people adopt an imaginary identity. However, visiting a computerized facility can be a much richer experience. Although you don't get to see the other people in person, this can be an advantage: you won't find yourself distracted by the reality of the actual people (who often do not resemble their imaginary counterparts).

The first such computerized environment was modelled after Dungeons and Dragons and became known as a "Multiple User Dungeon" or a Mud. Eventually, the name "mud" caught on as a word in its own right. Some people say "mud" stands for the more generic "Multiple User Dimension" or "Multiple User Dialogue" but it really doesn't matter: a mud is a mud.

There are now a large number of muds on the Net, as well as variations called MUSHs, MOOs, MUSEs and MUCKs. In addition, there are several types of muds. Each of these environments has its own characteristics and its own band of enthusiasts, and there are all manner of variations. Some muds are based on action: solving puzzles, fighting other characters, and so on. Other muds are more for conversation: there will be an imaginary environment, but its main purpose is to provide a place to meet other people and talk.

If you become a mud fanatic, it is easy to spend all your spare time on the Net. Moreover, all muds are constructed to be expandable, and many people spend time improving and enhancing their favorite virtual home away from home.

⚑ HINT

Join a mud and hide from reality. Forget to graduate. Lose your job. Ignore your friends, family and loved ones.

In other words, lots of good, clean fun.

Chapter	Name	Description
7,8	Mail	send and receive messages
9,10,11,12	The Web	multi-linked information
10	Web Search Engines	search the Web
13,14,15	Usenet	vast system of discussion groups
16,17	Gopher	menu-based information
16	Veronica and Jughead	search gopherspace
18,19	Anonymous ftp	public access to data archives
20	Archie	search anonymous ftp archives
22	Mailing Lists	discussions/information by mail
23,24	Telnet (Remote Login)	connect to and use a remote host
25,26	Talk Facility	private conversation
27	Internet Relay Chat	public Net-wide conversations
28	Muds	multi-person imaginary environments

Figure 3-1.   *Summary of Internet resources*

Chapter Four

Hardware Requirements to Connect to the Internet

To use the Internet, you need to connect your computer to another computer that is already part of the Net. There are several ways to do this and, in the next two chapters, I discuss the various possibilities. I explain what it means to connect to the Net, and how you can do so with a minimum of fuss. To start, I will discuss what sort of computer equipment you need to use the Internet. I will then discuss the choices you have for connecting to the Net over a telephone line.

What Do You Need to Use the Internet?

As I discuss in Chapters 2 and 3, you access the Internet by using various client programs. Each type of client allows you to use a different Internet resource. For example, for electronic mail, you use a mail client program; for the Web, you use a web client; for anonymous ftp, you use an ftp client; and so on.

So, for example, if you hear someone say he uses the Internet mail system, all it means is he has a mail client that can send and receive messages on his behalf.

Thus, to use the Internet you need three things:

- a computer
- client programs to run on your computer (one client for each type of service you want to use)
- a way to connect your computer to the Net so your clients can service your requests.

Accessing the Internet via Your Local Network

Consider the computing resources at a university. Throughout the campus, there are rooms of computers for people to use. Each of these computers is connected to a local area network; these networks are connected into one large campus network which is itself connected to the Internet.

When someone at a university sits down at one of these computers, he or she has access to whatever programs have been installed on that particular computer. In particular, there will probably be some Internet clients available. Whenever someone uses one of these clients, it accesses the Internet on his behalf by utilizing the connection joining the campus-wide network to the outside world. In such a situation, the person doesn't have to do anything special to get Internet access: it is already there. All the person needs to do is learn how the Internet works and how to use the various client programs.

Many people have access to similar resources. If you work at a university or a large company connected to the Internet, your network probably has Internet access. That means you can use the Internet simply by running an Internet client on your computer. When your client needs access to an Internet service, it will use the network connection automatically.

If this is the case for you, you may feel like skipping this chapter and Chapter 5, because you already have Internet access. Still, there are a number of interesting topics, and I suggest you at least skim most of these chapters before moving on. At the very least, make sure you read the sections in Chapter 5 that explain hosts and terminals, as well as shell accounts and PPP. Understanding those concepts is crucial to using the Net.

Accessing the Internet via the Telephone System

As I explained in the previous section, many people already have access to the Internet because they work at a place where the computers are connected to a network with Internet access. If you use a computer at a university, this will almost certainly be the case. However, most people do not have such facilities. Instead, they use the Internet by connecting to another computer over a phone line.

Knowing how this works is important even if you have direct Internet access. For example, say you are a student and your school has computers connected to the Net. That's fine for when you are at school, but when you get home you will not be able to use the Internet unless you find a way to connect your own computer over a phone line.

Conceptually, it is not a difficult thing to do. You run a communications program on your computer to dial the phone. Another computer answers the phone, and your program talks to a program on the other end and establishes a connection. You can now do whatever work you want, during which the remote computer provides access to the Net. When you are finished, you break the connection by telling your communications program to hang up.

Once a system like this is set up, you can initiate an Internet connection just by starting your program and telling it to dial. Aside from the communications program, you will need a MODEM—a hardware device acting as an interface between your computer and the telephone system—and the telephone line itself.

What's in a Name?

Modem

Data inside a computer is stored in a form that is different from data transmitted over a phone line. Computer data is stored in a DIGITAL format, while phone lines transmit data in an ANALOG format. We say information is digital if it can be represented by discrete numbers. We say data is analog if it is represented by quantities that vary continuously.

For example, an analog watch has a minute hand and an hour hand pointing to the current time. A digital watch only has numbers. At 10:00, an analog watch will have the minute hand on the 12 and the hour hand on the 10. A digital watch will simply say "10:00".

For our purposes, I don't need to be too technical. All you need to understand is that, when we connect two computers over a phone line, the data coming out of the computer is digital and, before it can be transmitted over the phone line, it must be converted to analog data. At the other end, the analog data must be converted back to digital data before it can be accepted by the other computer.

Now, the process of converting from a digital format to an analog format is called MODULATION. And the process of converting analog data back to its digital form is called DEMODULATION. Thus, the device we use to act as an interface between our computer and the phone system is called a "modulator/demodulator" or "modem".

If you have only one phone line, you can certainly use it for Internet access, although you won't be able to talk on it at the same time. For this reason, many people put in a second line just for their computer. That way, they don't tie up their primary line for hours at a time using the Net, and they don't have to worry about someone picking up an extension phone and causing noise that might break the connection.

So, to summarize, to access the Internet over a phone line, you need:

- a computer
- a modem
- an available telephone line
- the appropriate software, including a communications program
- a telephone number to use to connect to a remote Internet computer

In order to help you get started properly, I will talk about each of these items in turn. To start, let's talk about what kind of computer you need.

Choosing a Computer

There are lots of considerations when buying a computer, but it can all be summed up in one short hint.

🏴 HINT

When you buy a computer, don't skimp in order to save money.

In the same way you can't be "too thin or too rich", it is impossible to have a computer that is too fast, and has too much memory or too large a hard disk.

Buying a computer is not like buying most other things. For most purchases, you are usually smart to pick something in the middle. For example, when you buy clothes, the cheapest ones will fit poorly and wear out faster, but it is not really worth it to spend a lot of money for expensive designer items just for the name on the label.

Computers are different. You *do* want the best equipment you can afford. The reason is that today's programs are very sophisticated and demanding. Although you personally might think you do not need a very fast machine, remember you are not buying a computer for yourself: you are buying it to run programs. And modern programs—especially Internet programs—require a lot more speed and memory than you would think. Moreover, you don't want to have to buy a new computer each year. Your purchase should last several years and, unless you buy at the high end now, you will find your machine will become too slow in a short time.

Here is the secret to understanding computer prices:

🏴 HINT

At any time, the computer you should buy will cost between $1500 to $2500 in the United States, and about DM 3000 to DM 4000 in Europe. The only way anyone can offer a computer system for less is to sell you old or inferior technology.

Do your best to resist buying a cheap system just to save money up front. Today's programs require today's computers to run well, and you must plan ahead. The last thing you want is to be running next year's programs using last year's technology.

For example, at the time I wrote this chapter, it was possible to buy a PC that had either a Pentium processor or a 486 processor. (Without getting too technical, the PROCESSOR is the main "brain" of the computer. The Pentium is newer and faster and was designed to replace the 486.) Although you could save money by buying a

486 computer, it would be a foolish choice: no one has any business buying such old technology.

Here is another hint when it comes to salespeople.

HINT

No matter what a salesman may say or do, he is *not* on your side. He is there for one reason: to sell as many computers as possible. Approach a computer salesman as you would a car salesman. Know what you want in advance, and don't let him talk you into anything else. Avoid people who start a conversation by asking you what your budget is.

So here is my advice: buy a fast computer, with lots of memory and a large hard disk. The computer should also have a CD drive, speakers, and a microphone. (Sometimes machines with these items are called MULTIMEDIA computers, because they are suitable for displaying pictures and working with sounds.) Although you may not see the need for all this power and all these options, once you start using the Net for awhile, you will be glad you did not skimp. If anyone ever tells you differently, just remember: they are wrong and I am right.

Last point: the OPERATING SYSTEM is the master control program that runs the computer. Make sure you do not get stuck with an old operating system. For a PC, you want at least Windows 95 or OS/2 Warp. For a Mac, you want at least MacOS System 7.5.

Choosing a Modem

Choosing a modem is easy. All you have to do is make one choice, and then follow a simple guideline.

As I explained earlier, a modem acts as the interface between your computer and the phone line. There are two types of modems: internal and external. An internal modem resides on an adaptor card which fits into an expansion slot inside your computer. An external modem is a small box connected to your computer with a cable.

How do you decide what type of modem to buy? First, forget about price: the price difference between comparable internal and external modems is not significant. To make your choice, use the following guideline. If you understand a lot about modems and you are 100% sure you will only use the modem in one computer, think about getting an internal modem. It will take up less room and be more convenient. Otherwise, get an external modem.

An external modem requires a cable and must be plugged into an electrical outlet. However, you will have the maximum flexibility. It is easy to move an external modem from one computer to another—even from a PC to a Macintosh—and there are indicator lights on the front which are sometimes helpful if something goes wrong. Moreover, when the need arises, it is easy to turn the modem off and on to reset it. With an internal modem, you will have to restart the whole computer.

Choosing between an internal and external modem is the first of two considerations. The other is to make sure you get the right speed. Modem speeds are expressed in BITS PER SECOND, or BPS. There are several standard modem speeds. They are 2400 bps, 9600 bps, 14400 bps and 28800 bps. Sometimes people use the abbreviation "K" (as in the metric system) to stand for "1000". Thus, the last two modem speeds are usually referred to as 14.4 Kbps and 28.8 Kbps.

What's in a Name?

BPS, Baud

Modem speeds are measured in bps, or bits per second. You may also encounter an older term, BAUD, used as a synonym for bps. For example, you might read that a particular modem runs at 28.8K baud (which means 28.8 Kbps).

The term "baud" is named after J. M. Baudot, the inventor of the Baudot telegraph code. The Baudot code represents each character by a specific 5-bit pattern (the modern ASCII code which we use for computers requires 8 bits per character) and was used with a variety of now-obsolete communication devices.

Electrical engineers use the term "baud" to describe modulation rates (don't even ask). Modulation rates are similar to—but not exactly the same as—data transmission speeds. Thus, computer people, who are less precise, use "baud" as a synonym for "bits per second" to describe the speed of a modem.

From time to time, you will encounter the sort of person who will say, "Technically speaking, the baud rate is not the same as bits per second, so it is incorrect to say 'baud'. You should only say 'bits per second'." Such people are necessary to our culture and are to be tolerated—so be polite. (Just be sure not to marry one.)

When it comes to numbers and modems, there is only one important guideline to follow: do not buy any modem that is slower than 28.8 Kbps. Remember, no matter what anyone says—and they may tell you 14.4 Kbps is fast enough, or they may tell you the computer you want already comes with a built-in 14.4 Kbps modem—do not buy anything slower than 28.8 Kbps. Be forewarned, a slower modem will cost less, but this is just about the worst place to try to save money. A slow modem will guarantee your life on the Net will be filled with agonizing minutes of waiting and waiting and waiting. Moreover, if you are paying by the minute for Internet access, a slow modem will force you to pay a lot more for the extra time it takes to download large files.

When you shop for a modem you will encounter a number of technical terms and statistics. First, you will see the official names of the industry standards used for modem communications. Although you really don't need to know about these terms, here they are in case you see them:

One standard defines the basic speed of the modem: 28.8 Kbps uses a standard named V.34 (pronounced "vee dot 34"). 14.4 Kbps uses a standard named V.32bis. The only other important standards are V.42 for error correction, and V.42bis for data compression. Still, as I mentioned, you don't really need to understand the details. If you make sure you get a 28.8 Kbps modem, it will have all the correct standards built into it (V.34, V.42 and V.42bis).

The second type of number you will see has to do with statistics showing how much data a modem can transfer. The V.42bis standard allows a modem to compress data in certain ways so as to raise the effective speed of the modem. In theory, a modem using V.42bis might be able to achieve compression ratios as high as 4 to 1. Thus (in theory), a 9600 bps modem might transmit data at up to 38.4 Kbps; a 14.4 Kbps modem might transmit data at up to 57.6 Kbps; and a 28.8 Kbps modem might hit 115.2 Kbps.

Realize, though, that there are theoretical maximums which are never—repeat, never—achieved in real life. In real life, a 28.8 Kbps modem, even with data compression, will sustain speeds a lot closer to 28.8 Kbps than 115.2 Kbps. Still, you will see all kinds of modem advertisements that boastfully offer the magic speeds of 57.6 Kbps and 115.2 Kbps.

You might ask: The modem companies certainly know what is real and what is not real. Does this mean they are lying? The answer is, yes, of course they are lying. But they all lie in the same way, using the same numbers, so it is okay. Just make sure you get a 28.8 Kbps modem that supports V.34, V.42 and V.42bis (and they all do) and you will be okay.

So, to summarize, choosing a modem is easy. Just decide if you want an external or internal modem, and then make sure you get one that is 28.8 Kbps.

📖 What's in a Name?

Bit, Bits per Second

Within a computer, information is stored as long strings of discrete units called BITS. Each bit represents a tiny entity that can be either "off" or "on". Computer scientists represent the "off" by a 0 and the "on" by a 1. Thus, we can think of computer memory as consisting of long strings of 0's and 1's.

Information is stored according to various codes, so particular patterns of 0's and 1's represent certain values. For example, each character in the alphabet is stored as a unique pattern of 8 bits. For example, the pattern that represents the letter "H" is:

01001000

Here is another example. The word "Harley" contains 6 characters and, hence, is stored in the computer's memory as a string of 48 bits (6 characters x 8 bits per character). In fact, the actual bit pattern for "Harley" is:

010010000110000101110010011011000110010101111001

The important thing to understand is that, since data is stored in bits, it makes sense to measure the speed of a modem in bits per second. For example, a 28.8 Kbps modem transmits data at a basic speed of 28,800 bits per second.

In mathematics, there is a number system—called the BINARY SYSTEM—based entirely on the digits 0 and 1. This is where the name "bit" comes from: it is actually an abbreviation for "binary digit".

ISDN

ISDN is a type of telephone service which is an alternative to a regular phone line. (The name stands for "Integrated Services Digital Network".) The great advantage of ISDN for us is it allows you to connect to another computer at a speed which is much faster than even the fastest modem. If ISDN is available in your area, you should consider it as an alternative to using a modem with a regular phone line. You will find life on the Internet to be a lot more pleasant with a high-speed connection, because you don't have to wait so long for things to happen.

Since ISDN works differently than a regular phone line, let's take a few moments to discuss some of the details.

So far, I have talked about using your computer over a regular phone line. To do so, you use a modem to act as the interface between your computer and the telephone system. At the other end, the remote computer also has a modem to connect to its telephone line.

As I explained earlier in the chapter, computers use digital data, while phone lines carry analog data. The purpose of the modem is to convert the digital signal from the computer into the analog signal used by the phone line, and vice versa.

(You may remember that "digital" refers to a system in which the information can be stored as discrete numbers, and "analog" refers to a system in which the information varies continuously. For example, at 10:00 AM, a digital clock would read "10:00", while an old-style analog clock would have an hour hand pointing at 10 and a minute hand pointing to 12. At one minute past 10, the digital clock changes to "10:01". On the analog clock, the minute hand moves slightly to the right. Where the digital clock changes from one specific number to another, the analog clock moves its hands continuously around the clockface.)

The engineering details regarding digital and analog devices are not all that important right now. For our purposes, you only need to remember two things: First, computers are digital and regular phone lines are analog. Second, when it comes to working with large amounts of information, digital is better than analog. For example, a music CD player (which is digital) has better sound than a cassette tape or an old-style record (both of which are analog).

Thus, if you are using a phone line to connect your computer to the Internet, you are better off with an ISDN connection because it is digital and it is a lot faster. Moreover, a single ISDN line can support up to eight devices and (in theory) up to 64 different telephone numbers.

How ISDN Is Organized

ISDN is a telephone service provided by the phone company. Although ISDN is not new, there are still some places where it is not available, so you will have to check with your local telephone company.

ISDN services are generally delivered in one of two ways: a BASIC RATE INTERFACE (BRI), or a PRIMARY RATE INTERFACE (PRI). The difference is that a PRI is an expensive, large-scale service suitable for a company needing to connect many computers and other devices. For a home or small business, you would use a BRI.

Before I can discuss how ISDN is packaged, I need to mention the idea of BANDWIDTH. This refers to the capacity to transmit information. For example, a modem communicating at 28.8 Kbps (28,800 bits per second) theoretically provides twice the bandwidth of a modem communicating at 14.4 Kbps. (I say, "theoretically", because, in the bandwidth game, there are always a number of variables affecting the total throughput.)

HINT

As a human being and an Internet user, one of your goals should be to get as much bandwidth as possible. Earlier in the chapter, I quoted the saying "you can't be too thin or too rich". Perhaps a more up-to-date axiom would be: "You can't be too thin, too rich, or have too much bandwidth".

A single ISDN line provides a number of CHANNELS, each of which offers a specific amount of bandwidth. A BRI (Basic Rate Interface) provides three channels: two B channels and one D channel. The B CHANNELS carry the bulk of the data: computer connections, voice conversations, fax transmissions, and so on. The name "B channel" is short for "bearer channel", because the B channels bear most of the load.

The D CHANNEL is used for the control of ISDN itself. It is used for sending the setup and signalling information back and forth between the telephone system and your devices. In other words, the D channel is used to control the other ISDN channels. The name "D channel" stands for "data channel". This is an unfortunate name, as it implies that the D channel transports your computer data. Actually, the D channel carries the internal ISDN data. *Your* data is actually carried on the B channels.

Within a standard BRI, each of the two B channels offers a bandwidth of 64 Kbps. You can use these B channels in two ways. First, you can combine them into a single large channel and connect it to your computer. This effectively gives you up to 128 Kbps of bandwidth. (Compare this to the fastest modem, which is only 28.8 Kbps.)

Alternatively, you can use one B channel for your computer and another for a telephone. This means you would have only 64 Kbps in bandwidth for the computer, but you would not have to pay for a separate phone line. Moreover, you can use the computer and talk on the phone at the same time and they won't interfere with one another.

Now, what of the D channel? The D channel has 16 Kbps. However, as I mentioned, it is used by ISDN itself and so it is not available for use with a computer or a telephone.

HINT

Not all phone companies offer the full 64 Kbps per B channel. Here is why:

The standard ISDN BRI facility offers two B channels, each with 64 Kbps, and one D channel with 16 Kbps. The D channel is used by ISDN to set up and maintain the other channels and so is not available to carry computer or voice information. One way to look at this is that ISDN requires 8 Kbps (from the D channel) to administer each B channel. Thus, administering the two B channels requires 16 Kbps.

In some places, the ISDN system is not able to use a separate D channel. This means the bandwidth necessary to maintain the B channels must be taken from the B channels themselves. Thus, each B channel must give up 8 Kbps to overhead. So, where a standard B channel has 64 Kbps, a B channel in such a situation will only have 56 Kbps.

If this is the case where you live, you will have to make do with less than the maximum ISDN bandwidth. Of course, this is still a potential of 112 Kbps (56 Kbps + 56 Kbps), which is four times the bandwidth of the fastest modem (28.8 Kbps).

This loss of bandwidth will most likely be a temporary problem. Eventually, most companies will offer the complete implementation of ISDN, and everyone will be able to get the full 128 Kbps.

What Do You Need in Order to Use ISDN?

When you use your computer with a modem and a regular phone line, the modem acts as the interface between the computer and the telephone system. With ISDN, you need two different interfaces.

First, you need a special device called an NT-1 to act as the interface between all of your equipment and the outside ISDN line. You connect devices to the NT-1, and the NT-1 connects to the ISDN wall jack. The NT-1 requires its own power supply.

One way to understand an NT-1 is with an analogy. Think about how electricity enters your house or apartment. Your wall outlets do not connect right into the raw power lines. Rather, they connect to a circuit breaker box or fuse box which lies between the household wiring and the outside world. This box acts as the interface between the raw electricity and your home wiring system. An NT-1 provides a similar function for ISDN service.

The second ISDN interface you need is called a TERMINAL ADAPTOR. Its job is to convert signals from your computers, telephones, and fax machines into ISDN data. The terminal adaptor connects to the NT-1. For example, a typical setup might involve a computer connected to a terminal adaptor. The terminal adaptor connects to an NT-1, which connects to the ISDN wall jack.

What's in a Name?

NT-1

The NT-1 interface acts as the bridge between the phone company's ISDN network and your personal equipment. In the language of ISDN, the connection between your equipment and the ISDN wall jack is called "layer 1". The name "NT-1" actually stands for "network terminator for layer 1".

Now, let's discuss the details. First, the NT-1. In some countries (throughout Europe and Japan, for example), the NT-1 interface is provided by the telephone company. You don't have to do anything special: when you order ISDN service, the phone company installs the NT-1 when they bring in the ISDN line. The cost is passed on to you as part of your service charge.

In other countries (such as the United States and Canada), you need to provide your own NT-1, which means you must pay for it and install it yourself.

Why is this? In the U.S. and Canada, the federal communication authorities deliberately decided to remove the NT-1 from the control of the local phone companies. Although it means more bother for you, it also means you can buy your NT-1 at a fair market price. (You may have noticed the tendency for phone companies to charge exorbitant amounts for services over which they hold monopolies.)

Moreover, making the NT-1 a separate requirement opens the market to competition and encourages other companies to innovate. For example, you can buy ISDN devices with built-in NT-1s, or you can buy a separate NT-1 and connect multiple devices to it directly. Remember, ISDN was designed, not only for the home user, but for large companies requiring many devices, terminal adaptors, and ISDN channels. By retaining control of their NT-1s, such companies have more flexibility and less dependence on the local phone company.

The terminal adaptor acts as the interface between a communication device and the NT-1. In particular, you will use a terminal adaptor to connect your computer to the NT-1. If you are using a computer designed to be "ISDN-ready", you will not need a terminal adaptor; this functionality is built into the computer. For example, some Sun workstations come ready to connect to an NT-1. If you have a PC or a Mac, though, you will probably need a terminal adaptor to act as your ISDN interface.

When you are ready to buy ISDN equipment, you will find a lot of variations. For example, you can buy a separate NT-1, power supply, and terminal adaptor. Or, you can buy a single card for your computer combining the NT-1, power supply, and terminal adaptor in one package.

The advantage of separate components is you have more flexibility to connect other devices. For example, you may want to connect more than one computer, some telephones, or a fax machine to your ISDN line. (Remember, a single ISDN connection can handle up to eight different devices.)

The advantage of a single adaptor card is it makes life simpler (and less expensive). All you need to do is install the card and its software, and then use a modular plug to connect the computer to the ISDN wall jack.

One type of ISDN device you may encounter is a so-called DIGITAL MODEM. There is no strict definition of what a digital modem really is, so you will have to check out each type carefully. Generally speaking, these are devices combining several functions into a single adaptor card or a small box.

For example, you can get a digital modem adaptor card which combines an NT-1, power supply and a terminal adaptor, as well as a feature allowing the card to act like a regular modem and fax device. Such an adaptor allows you to do more than ISDN. Since the adaptor can act like a modem, you can use a communications program which works with a regular modem. And since the adaptor can emulate a fax device, you can also use your computer to send and receive faxes.

⚑ HINT

If all you want to do with ISDN is connect a single computer to the Internet at high speed, your best bet is to use an adaptor card combining all the ISDN interfaces into a single package. Once you have installed the card and its software onto your computer, all you will have to do is use a modular plug to connect the computer to your ISDN wall jack.

So, what does this all mean? To use an ISDN connection you will have to get your phone company to install an ISDN line (and then pay the monthly services charges). You will need an adaptor card (or separate devices) to provide the functionality of an NT-1—at least in the United States and Canada—and its power supply, and you will also need a terminal adaptor. Moreover, you will have to find an Internet service provider who will sell you an ISDN connection to the Net. Such a connection will almost certainly cost more than the regular dial-up service. (I discuss Internet service providers in Chapter 5.)

Is ISDN worth all of this trouble and expense? If you can afford it, yes, yes, yes. ISDN offers a huge amount of bandwidth and, on the Net, bandwidth is everything.

HINT

ISDN can be a great way for a business to connect to the Internet. A single ISDN BRI connection can serve an entire local area network and will cost significantly less than other alternatives (such as a leased line). For a bigger company, the larger PRI connection can provide ISDN service to a great many devices and provide as much bandwidth as a high-capacity leased line.

INTERNET RESOURCE *Look in the catalog under Internet Resources for ISDN*

Chapter Five

Software Requirements and Internet Service Providers

In the last chapter, I discussed what type of computer equipment you need to use the Internet. I also talked about the choices you have for connecting to the Net using a telephone line. In this chapter, I will discuss the different types of Internet accounts, the software you need to use the Internet, and how to find and evaluate an Internet service provider. I will also explain why most Internet software is available for free and what this means to you.

Although there are some complex ideas in this chapter, they all involve one-time tasks. Once you get up and running, you can forget about the details.

Hosts and Terminals

In Chapter 4, I talked about the equipment you need to connect your computer to the Internet over a phone line. I explained that you can use either a regular phone line with a modem, or an ISDN line with an NT-1 interface and a terminal adaptor.

To connect to the Net, you run a communications program to dial the number of an Internet service provider. (I will discuss how to choose an Internet service provider later in the chapter.) When the remote system answers the phone, your modem (or ISDN device) talks to the other system and a connection is established.

At this point, there are two possible types of connections: a shell account or a PPP account. Your entire experience on the Internet depends greatly on which type of account you are using. Although both accounts allow you to access the Net, there is a striking difference between them, and your minute-to-minute Internet experience can vary enormously.

Generally speaking, a PPP account is better, but there are times when a shell account has some advantages, so I want to be completely sure you understand the difference. Before I can discuss these ideas, though, I need to spend some time talking about hosts and terminals.

In Chapter 2, I explained that each individual computer on the Internet is referred to as a "host". For example, if you were at a nerd convention, you might overhear someone saying, "I wanted to show my mother how the Internet works, so I used telnet to log into a remote host in Switzerland."

In the same chapter, I also explained multiuser systems and timesharing hosts. To review, a timesharing host is a computer that can be used by more than one person at the same time. For this reason, such computers are often called multiuser systems. To access a multiuser system, you use a device called a terminal. Technically, a terminal is not much more than a keyboard and a display. Some multiuser systems are set up to be used by a large number of people at the same time and, in the olden days, each person would use his or her own terminal to connect to the main computer.

Terminals, however, are relatively simple devices, and they can't really do much on their own. In fact, the only use for a terminal is to connect to a multiuser system. Today, real terminals are not used much anymore because computers are so inexpensive. However, there are still a great many timesharing hosts around that are designed to be accessed via terminals. When you want to use such a host, you run a program on your computer which makes it act just like a terminal. You then connect to the multiuser system, which treats you just as if you were working on a real terminal. In technical terms, we say you use your computer to EMULATE a terminal.

How this is important, you will see in a minute. But first, I need to discuss two important topics: operating systems and Unix.

Unix Hosts, VT-100 Terminals, and Telnet

Every computer has a master control program that manages the resources of the computer. This program is called the OPERATING SYSTEM. The job of the operating system is to make efficient use of the computer hardware, and to act as an interface for the person using the computer and for programs running on the computer.

On a PC, the first major operating system was DOS. (The name stands for "Disk Operating System", which refers to the fact that the entire operating system is so large it cannot all fit in the computer's memory at the same time: much of the operating system is stored on disk and is called into memory as needed.)

Today, the most common PC operating systems are Microsoft Windows 95, and the older Windows 3.1 (which builds on top of DOS to provide a graphical working environment). Other PC operating systems are Windows NT from Microsoft and OS/2 from IBM. (The name "OS/2" refers to the fact that the operating system was originally designed for IBM's PS/2 computers.) On a Macintosh, the operating system is called MacOS.

The reason I mention these names is because I want to spend a few moments talking about another operating system called Unix. Unix is unique in that it is really a family of operating systems that run on just about every type of computer you are likely to see, from PCs to the largest supercomputers.

Unix is important to us because it is used to run many of the computers on the Internet (see Chapter 1). Although most Net users access the Internet with individual PCs and Macintoshes, almost all of the computers that provide Internet services run Unix. This means that, no matter what computer you may be using for yourself, when you connect to another computer to access an Internet resource, it is probably a Unix machine.

For us, as Internet users, the widespread use of Unix on the Net has several important implications. First, many of the conventions that are part of the Internet culture were adopted directly from Unix. As we encounter these ideas, I will be sure to explain them to you. Suffice to say that the Internet owes a large part of its existence to the Unix culture and to the Unix nerds who did the original work to build the Net.

The second important point is that Unix is a multiuser timesharing system designed to work with terminals. This means when we want to work directly with a Unix computer, we must have our computer emulate a terminal. This comes up a lot more often than you might think.

In general, there are two ways to access the Internet over a telephone line: you can have your computer connect right into the Net, or you can use your computer to emulate a terminal and then connect to a timesharing host (usually a Unix system). In the first case, your computer is actually on the Internet (at least during the time your phone connection is active). In the second case, your computer is not on the Internet. It is merely providing a keyboard and display for you to access the remote computer, which is on the Net. (I will discuss the details of such connections in the next section.)

Now, Unix was designed to work with many different types of terminals. However, there is one terminal which has become a de facto standard. It is called the VT-100.

The original VT-100 was an actual hardware device manufactured by the Digital Equipment Corporation. However, it has been years since Digital has made a real VT-100. Instead, it has become the standard for communications programs that emulate a terminal. For example, when you use a communications program on your PC to emulate a terminal—so you can connect to a remote timesharing host—your computer is pretending it is a VT-100 terminal (or some variation, such as a VT-102 terminal).

(I hope you appreciate the irony here, of using a powerful computer—a marvel of modern engineering, complex computer science, and deceptive marketing—to emulate a primitive terminal that was obsolete years before Bill Gates was even a millionaire.)

As a Net user, there is another situation in which the VT-100 terminal will be important to you. As I mentioned in Chapter 3, you can use the telnet service to access a remote Internet host. (I discuss this in detail in Chapter 23.) In most cases, you will need an account on the remote computer. That is, you will need a user name and password. However, many Internet computers provide special services that are available to anyone, via telnet, without a password.

In either case, the telnet client allows you to use the remote computer by emulating a VT-100 computer. Thus, no matter how you connect to the Net with your computer, the idea of terminals and hosts is an important one, and the ubiquitous VT-100 will soon become a small but important part of your life.

Shell Accounts and PPP Accounts

Here is an overview of how you access the Internet via a phone line:

You connect your computer to the telephone system using either a regular phone line (with a modem) or an ISDN line (which requires special equipment). To start work, you run a communications program to dial the phone and establish a connection with a remote Internet host. Once the connection is established, you log in to the system by typing your user name and password. (Your communications program may do this for you automatically, so you won't have to actually type the words yourself.) You are now ready to use the Internet.

One question I have not yet discussed is: What remote computer do you dial to connect to the Internet? In most cases, what you must do is arrange for an account from an Internet service provider. This is a company that sells Internet access to the public. They maintain computers that are connected to the Internet (usually at high speed). When you arrange for an account, the service provider will give you a user name and a password. (Some providers let you choose your own user name. Virtually all providers let you change your password whenever you want.) You will also be told which telephone number your communications program should dial in order to establish an Internet connection.

If you work or study at a university and you have a computer account, there will most likely be a phone number you can use to connect to the university system from home. This might also be the case if you work for a company, connected to the Internet, that has arranged for dial-in access. Regardless, establishing an Internet connection over a phone line will work the same way. The only difference is you won't have to pay for the service.

Later in the chapter, I will discuss the details of getting an account from a public Internet service provider. First, though, I need to talk about the two basic types of Internet accounts.

The first type of Internet account is called a PPP ACCOUNT. This type of account lets you connect your computer right onto the Internet. When you have a PPP account, your computer is a full-fledged Internet host during the time you are connected. With this type of account, your own computer does most of the work, and the remote computer acts mainly as a conduit into the Net.

Here is an example. In Chapter 3, I mentioned Usenet, a worldwide system of thousands of different discussion groups. Say you are using a PPP account, and you want to read the articles in a particular discussion group. To do so, you use a Usenet client program that runs on your own computer. Each time you ask to see an article, your client requests the article from the Usenet server. As each article is sent down to your computer, your client program displays it on your screen. If you decide to post your own article to a discussion group, your client program will send out the article on your behalf. Thus, everything happens on your computer.

The second type of Internet account is called a SHELL ACCOUNT. With this type of account, you actually do your work on the remote computer. Your computer is not on the Net itself. Rather, your computer emulates a terminal which allows you to work directly with the remote host. When you use a shell account, the only program that runs on your computer is the terminal emulator. All the Internet clients actually run on the remote computer.

For example, say you want to read an article from a Usenet discussion group. With a shell account, you run a Usenet client program on the remote computer. Although you control the client from your keyboard, and you see the output on your screen, all the processing takes place on the remote computer. Thus, Usenet articles are not actually sent down in their entirety to your computer: the remote Usenet client requests the articles and then displays them for you, one screenful at a time. To post an article on your own, you must first send it to the remote computer. From there, you can have your Usenet client post the article for you.

Unfortunately, the nature of a terminal emulator is that it only supports a text-based interface, not a graphical interface. This is a severe limitation which I will discuss in the next two sections.

To summarize: there are two basic ways to access the Internet over a phone line. You can either connect your computer directly to the Net (with a PPP account), or you can use a terminal emulator and do your work on the remote computer (with a shell account).

The Nature of a PPP Account

I would like to spend just a few more minutes comparing PPP and shell accounts, because the type of account you use will greatly affect your Internet experience. If you have not yet started to use the Net, I want to make sure you understand the alternatives, so you can make a good choice when you choose your Internet service provider and arrange for your account.

When you use a PPP account over a phone line, your computer is connected right onto the Internet. This means that, for the duration of your Internet session, your computer is a part of the Net, just like a computer directly connected with a cable. The only difference is your computer is connected over a phone line. But, as far as the rest of the Net is concerned, you are *on* the Net, and other Internet computers can communicate with your computer directly. In other words, when you use a PPP connection, your computer temporarily becomes an Internet host.

This means the client programs you use to access the various Internet services run on *your* computer. For example, if you use a PC with Microsoft Windows, you would run Windows programs to act as your clients. If you use a PC with OS/2, you would run either OS/2 or Windows programs to act as your clients (OS/2 can run both types of programs). And if you are using a Macintosh, you would use Mac programs. Thus, all your Internet clients will look and act like all the other programs you use on your computer.

For example, in Chapter 3, I explained that you access the Web by using a client program called a "browser". So if you are a Windows person, you will use a browser that works just like all your other Windows programs. If you are a Mac person, you will be using a Mac browser that works like all your other Mac programs. And if you use OS/2, you will have a choice of either an OS/2 or Windows browser, whichever you prefer. The important thing is that, when you use a PPP connection, the clients run on your computer using your particular system.

Perhaps the best thing about a PPP connection is you can use as many clients as you want at the same time. For example, you could start four programs—a web client, a gopher client, a mail client, and an ftp client—and switch back and forth from one to the other. Or you could run two separate web clients at the same time.

The best way to think about a PPP connection is as a tunnel into the Net. You run whatever client programs you want on your computer and, when they need to send or receive information, they use the tunnel. The nature of the tunnel is such that it will support as many clients as you want to use. (Of course, if you make too many demands on the system at the same time, the traffic in the tunnel will increase and everything will slow down.)

HINT

You might ask: If I use a PPP account to connect to the Net, does this mean my computer can offer Internet services to other computers around the world? For instance, could my computer act as a server for the Web, or for anonymous ftp, or for a gopher? The answer is yes, as long as you have the proper software and you know enough about what you are doing to set up and maintain everything. Of course, if you are using a phone line, your services will be available to the Internet only during those times your Net connection is active.

However, if you really want to provide your own information service to the Net—and many people do—it is better to use facilities offered by your Internet service provider. I will discuss such considerations later in the chapter.

The Nature of a Shell Account

A shell account works differently than a PPP account. As I explained, when you use a shell account, the client programs run on the *remote* host, not on your computer. All your computer does is emulate a terminal. This allows you to use your keyboard and display to work with the remote host.

This means you do not run programs on your own computer, so you cannot take advantage of the characteristics of your computer: you are limited to the capabilities of the terminal your computer is emulating. Unfortunately, this means you can use only text-based programs. Here is why this is important.

There are two ways in which information can be presented on a computer screen. With a TEXT-BASED INTERFACE, a program can display only characters: letters, numbers, punctuation, and so on. With a GRAPHICAL INTERFACE, a program can not only use characters, it can also draw shapes (such as rectangles, lines and circles) and display images (such as pictures and drawings).

When you use a PC with Windows or OS/2, or when you use a Macintosh, your system takes full advantage of the graphics capabilities to display windows, scroll bars, dialog boxes, icons, pictures, and all the other elements that give your system its particular personality. This is commonly referred to as a GRAPHICAL USER INTERFACE, or GUI. Aside from the GUI, your programs can also use the multimedia (sound and video) capabilities of your computer.

With a PPP connection, you run the Internet clients on your own computer. This means all your programs use the GUI for your particular system and have full graphical capabilities. For example, if you use a PC with Windows, your Usenet client is a full-fledged Windows program with scroll bars, pull-down menus, pictures, and so on.

With a shell account, your terminal emulator will only support a text interface. This means all your Internet clients can display only characters, giving them a plain appearance. There will be no fancy windows and pull-down menus.

Moreover, since your clients are running on the remote host and not your computer, every time you want to download a file (that is, copy a file from a distant computer), the file will end up on the remote host. You will then have to take an extra step to copy the file to your computer. With a PPP account, your computer is on the Net, and when you download a file it comes directly to you.

Similarly, when you want to upload a file from your computer to a distant computer, you will first have to copy it to the remote host and then upload the file from there. With a PPP account, you can upload a file from your computer to any other Internet computer in a single step.

Another disadvantage to a shell account is that, since you must run your client programs on the remote host, it is not convenient to use multiple client programs simultaneously. With PPP, you can run as many clients as you want on your own computer. With a shell account, you usually work with one client at a time. (Note: If your remote host is a Unix system—which is likely—there are ways you can run more than one program at the same time. However, this calls for some advanced Unix knowledge and is not as convenient as a PPP account.)

So far, I have explained three major disadvantages to a shell account: the interface is text-based, not graphical; your computer is not actually on the Internet; and you are usually limited to running one client at a time. However, there are some advantages to this type of account.

First, to use the Net you must arrange for an account from an Internet service provider. Virtually all of these providers use Unix computers to act as hosts. With a shell account, you are using the remote host directly and, hence, you have access to a Unix computer on the Internet.

Unix is a complex operating system, and I can't go into all the details here. However, I will say Unix is a great system with a large number of wonderful tools and, if you know what you are doing, having an account on a Unix computer can be a great advantage. And, if you have a shell account, you will have access to a Unix system (the remote host).

Second, graphical systems are nice, but they are inherently slower than text-based systems. This is because it takes a lot more information to display pictures and drawings than it does to display simple characters and, whenever you access a remote Internet service, you must wait for that information to be sent back to your client.

For example, when you use the Web with a graphical client, you will spend a *lot* of time waiting unless you have a fast connection (like ISDN). Even with a 28.8 Kbps modem you will spend a lot of time waiting. However, there is a nice text-based web client named Lynx which will run perfectly well on a remote system using a shell account. Although Lynx cannot show you images, it receives and displays text quickly. Thus, if you want to use the Web and you don't really care about seeing pictures (which is the case more often than you might imagine), Lynx and a shell account are just fine.

The same is true for other Internet services. There are text-based clients for every type of service, and they all run more quickly than their graphical counterparts. Moreover, text-based clients are designed for people using Unix systems. Since such people are usually more computer-oriented and—dare I say it?—smarter than normal people, you will find that many of the text-based clients are more powerful than their graphical counterparts, which are designed to be used by any Joe or Jane with a PC or Macintosh. (If you are not a Unix user, please don't be chagrined. The mere fact you are reading this book shows that you are smarter than most people.)

Here is another advantage to a shell account. Say you are visiting a friend or traveling on a business trip, and you want to check your mail. If you only have a PPP account, you are out of luck. You will have to wait till you get home and connect with your own computer. But if you have a shell account, and you can find an Internet connection, you can use telnet to connect to your remote host and check your mail in the regular manner. The telnet client emulates a terminal, just like the communications program on your home computer, and most everything will look and work the same way.

Finally, some people find they cannot get a PPP account (or it is too expensive). For such people, a shell account is just right.

Which Type of Account Is Right for You?

There is no doubt a PPP account is great because it puts you right on the Internet and lets you use graphical programs designed for your particular system. However, a shell account can be faster and does have certain advantages. Thus, I suggest you choose an account according to the following guidelines:

HINT

If a PPP account is available, it should always be your first choice. However, you should also get a shell account if (1) you want to use Unix, or (2) you are generally a smart person, or (3) you plan to travel a fair bit and would like to use the Net while you are away from home.

Some Internet service providers will give you a shell account for free when you pay for a PPP account. Other providers will make you pay extra. I will discuss how to choose a provider later in the chapter.

The True Story of the Three Brothers

Once upon a time, there were three brothers—triplets—named Oscar, Mac and Will. One of the brothers was dropped on his head when he was young and, since then, had trouble concentrating and learning complex ideas. The second brother was smart but strange, and lived in a world of his own. The third brother was also smart, but was a lot more normal, generally going along with everyone else.

Now, I am not going to tell you which brother is which. All I will say is that, when the boys turned 12 years old, their parents decided to buy them computers and allowed each brother to choose whichever computer he wanted. Oscar chose a PC running OS/2. Will picked a PC running Windows 95. And Mac decided upon a Macintosh.

Several weeks later, after the boys had had time to learn how to use their computers, the parents connected the three machines into a small network, and arranged for it to have high-speed ISDN access to the Internet using a PPP account.

The next day, they walked into the computer room and found all three brothers using the Web. To their surprise, the parents saw that, although the boys were all doing the same thing, they were using completely different web clients. Oscar was using an OS/2 browser, Will was using a Windows browser, and Mac was using a Macintosh browser.

"We did the right thing," said the father to his wife. "By letting the boys choose their own computer, they were able to get the system best suited to their own personal abilities and tastes. And by arranging for an ISDN connection, we ensured they all have sufficient bandwidth to use the Internet effectively. But, most important, because we connected their computers to the Net by using PPP, they can all run client programs on their own computers.

"This means the bright but strange boy can use a system that challenges him and forces him to work in a world where he must build many of his own tools. The more normal boy can use a system that has a large supply of publicly accessible software created by other normal boys and girls all around the word. And the boy who was dropped on his head has a computer suited to his abilities and will not frustrate him unnecessarily."

"Yes," said the mother, "each boy can access the same Internet services as his brother by using whatever client programs run on his particular system. If we had got them shell accounts instead of PPP, each brother would have had to use the same limited text-based interface to run clients on the remote host. Truly we have made a wise choice. And arranging for the smart but strange brother to also have a shell account was a good idea as well. He really seems to like Unix."

"I agree," said the father. "We did the right thing. How satisfying it is to be a parent." And they all lived happily ever after.

PPP and SLIP

If you hang around people who talk about PPP, you are bound to encounter the term "SLIP". Here is what it is, and why you don't want to use it.

In the olden days (before the mid-1980s), the main way to access a computer over a telephone line was to use a communications program to emulate a terminal. This was adequate but, as I explained earlier in the chapter, emulating a terminal does not give you the advantages of having an actual network connection. However, even if there had been a way to establish a network connection over a phone line, it would have been unsatisfying because the modems of the time were far too slow. (Network connections require a lot more bandwidth than a simple terminal-host connection.)

With the advent of higher-speed modems (9600 bps, 14.4 Kbps, and now 28.8 Kbps), it became possible to think about supporting a network connection over a phone line. To do this, the network programmers called upon a protocol originally designed to support Internet software running on computers joined by what is called a serial cable.

As I explained in Chapter 2, the family of Internet protocols (technical specifications) is called TCP/IP. The job of IP (Internet Protocol) is to move the raw data from one place to another. Thus, the protocol developed to support TCP/IP over a serial cable was called SERIAL LINE IP, or SLIP. SLIP dates from the early 1980s and was designed to be a simple, but not very powerful method of connecting two IP devices over a serial cable.

In 1984, SLIP was made to work under Unix and, within a few years, people began to use SLIP extensively around the world. In the early 1990s, as the Internet started to grow quickly, a lot of people started to use SLIP to connect computers to the Net over a phone line. This meant you could have a real Internet connection even when your computer was not part of a local area network.

By the late 1980s, it had become clear that SLIP was lacking in a number of important ways. I won't go into the technical details as they would only bore you (as they bored just about everyone in the Internet community who was not a serious nerd). The important thing is that a replacement for SLIP, called PPP, was created. The catchy name PPP stands for POINT-TO-POINT PROTOCOL. (In nerd-speak, a "point-to-point link" is the same thing as a serial connection.)

In November of 1989, the first paper was circulated proposing PPP as an official Internet standard. This paper described PPP's advantages over SLIP: PPP is more powerful (it works with other systems and not just TCP/IP), more dependable, more flexible, and is a lot easier to configure when you need to get it up and running on a new system.

Today, PPP has replaced SLIP as the protocol of choice for connecting to the Net over a phone line. Although some Internet service providers still support SLIP, just about everyone has moved to PPP.

HINT

If you ever have to choose between a PPP or a SLIP connection, choose PPP. Unless someone else does everything for you, getting SLIP to work will drive you crazy. PPP is a lot easier to install and configure.

> ## HINT
>
> Some people use the word "SLIP" as a generic term to refer to both SLIP and PPP. No doubt this is because the word "SLIP" is a lot easier to pronounce than "PPP". For example, some Internet service providers say they offer "SLIP accounts". However, when you check into it, you will probably find they actually offer both SLIP and PPP. Nobody who knows what he is doing will use SLIP if PPP is available.

Internet Service Providers

An INTERNET SERVICE PROVIDER is an organization or business offering public access to the Internet. Although there are a number of community-oriented providers (usually called FREENETS) that offer free access, most providers are businesses that charge money. Some providers are large, national or multi-national companies serving hundreds of cities. Other providers are small, perhaps run by a single person and serving only one area.

> ## HINT
>
> If you have any trouble finding an Internet service provider in your area, there are lists of providers you can download for free from the Internet. If you do not already have Internet access, you will have to ask a friend to help you download the list.

In order to access the Internet using your phone line, you will need to establish an account with an Internet service provider. To start service, you will have to register with that provider and choose either a PPP or shell account (or both). This may involve giving them a credit card number so they can bill you each month.

Once you register, your provider will give you a user name (called a userid), a password, and a phone number to dial. To establish an Internet connection, you have your communications program dial the number. You then log in using your particular userid and password.

What's in a Name?

Userid, Log in, Log out

Much of the Internet was developed by people using Unix computers. Even today, many of the computers providing Internet services run Unix. For example, when you dial an Internet service provider, chances are the computer at the other end will be a Unix system. For this reason, a lot of Internet terminology is borrowed from Unix. In particular, we use the terms "userid", "log in" and "log out".

Each time you call the remote host that provides your Internet connection, you must LOG IN to start a work session. To do so, you type your user name and password. In Unix, a user name is referred to as a USERID (pronounced "user-eye-dee"), and we use the same term on the Internet. When you are finished and you break the connection, we say you LOG OUT. If you use a shell account, you will actually type the userid and password yourself. If you use a PPP account, your PPP program will log in for you automatically.

How does the PPP program know your userid and password? Before you can use PPP, you must configure the program. At that time, you tell PPP your userid, password, and other important information (such as the phone number to dial). This information is stored in a configuration file that PPP calls upon each time you tell it to establish a connection with your Internet provider.

Choosing an Internet service provider is an important decision, so I want to spend some time talking about the possibilities and showing how to make a wise decision. There are a lot of different Internet service providers you can consider, from large companies covering the entire United States or much of Europe, to small local providers who service a single city or town. The first thing to decide is whether you want to use only the Internet, or an online information service as well as the Net.

Online Information Services

There are a number of large companies offering their own information and online resources as well as access to the Internet. For example, in the United States there are America Online, Compuserve, Prodigy, and others.

The advantage to an information service is you will be able to use a variety of resources that do not exist on the Internet. For example, you may have access to stock market quotations, an airline reservation system, electronic versions of popular magazines, and so on. In addition, such systems tend to have well-developed resources for allowing people to talk with one another. Although there are ways to talk with people over the Internet, people who love to talk to other people have a lot more fun using, say, America Online.

Another advantage is most information services offer some sort of technical support. Although they may encourage you to read the documentation first, or to listen to a large number of pre-recorded "tips", eventually, if you are persistent enough—and you don't mind waiting—you can usually get a real live person to help you (either on the phone or online).

Finally, information services are a lot more than computerized libraries: they are communities, each with its own atmosphere, traditions, language, and environment. Once you become an experienced member of America Online, Compuserve, Prodigy, or whatever, it's like living in a small town where you can develop a sense of belonging. It is true many people feel this same sense of community on the Internet. However, the Internet is not run by a central authority, and if you like to live with order and security, you will probably be more comfortable with a well-organized online information service.

However, there are three important disadvantages to an information service. First, it will probably cost you more than will simple Internet access. This only makes sense, as you are getting a lot more than the Internet for your money. However, many people (including me) are perfectly happy with the Net and feel no need to pay extra for anything else.

Second, the Internet access provided by such services is not always that good. For example, you may not be able to utilize the full set of Internet resources. Moreover, you will probably be forced to use a standard one-size-fits-all interface that is dumbed down to ensure that anyone, no matter how clueless, will be able to use the Internet. You may find, for example, you can't just download the latest web browser from the Net and be able to use it with your information service. If you are the least bit savvy as an Internet user, you will likely find general-purpose Internet interfaces to be awkward, incomplete, and frustrating.

Third, I mentioned that information services are organized and administered by a central authority. This is good in the sense that organization and administration are good. However, when you use these services, there is very much a sense that somebody is "in charge". To many people, the best thing about the Internet is no one is in charge, and the vast majority of Internet users enjoy the anarchy. To Internet people, a huge network free of censorship and silly procedures is much more valuable and stimulating than a well-managed community where you are forced to behave according to somebody else's rules.

⚑ HINT

Take some time and investigate the information services. Read their literature and see if anything looks good to you. Usually, you can arrange to try a service for a short time for free. Check out their Internet access by trying it for yourself and by comparing notes with experienced Internet people.

My personal preference is to go with straightforward Internet access and skip the information services. (But then, I am the type of person who doesn't like to follow the rules.)

Choosing an Internet Service Provider

There are probably more Internet service providers in your area than you would expect. For example, in the United States and Europe, there are a variety of companies in the business of selling Internet access throughout the entire country. There are also local companies and organizations providing more regional access.

As you look for an Internet service provider, here is a technical term you will encounter: Each local facility you can dial to connect to an Internet service provider is called a POINT OF PRESENCE or a POP. Some companies have hundreds of POPs throughout the U.S., Canada and Europe. This means you can connect to the service via a local phone call from many different places. A small local organization might have only a single POP. However, if this POP is a local phone call for you, the local provider may be the better choice.

Why? Because as an Internet user, you want only one thing: a phone number to have your computer dial in order to connect to the Net. And what do you require from your provider? Three things: a reasonable price, enough phone lines so you aren't always getting a busy signal, and a well-run service from people who know what they are doing.

What I suggest is you gather some information about the providers in your area and make an informed decision. Here are some things to investigate:

- Can you access the service with a local phone call?

Some providers have a toll-free number you can call if there is no local number. However, although you won't have to pay a long distance fee to the phone company for the call, the provider will probably charge you extra to use the toll-free number. (Remember, nothing in business is free. If they have to pay for the toll-free number, they are going to find a way to pass on that cost to you.)

HINT

Be careful that you evaluate the costs of using an 800 (toll-free) number. When you use such a number to access the Internet, it is not "toll-free": it is really a collect call that automatically reverses the charges to you. The only difference is the Internet service provider will send you the bill, not the telephone company.

When you look at the costs carefully, you will usually find the extra money you pay to use a "toll-free" number are more than it would cost to dial an actual long distance call, especially in the evening or on the weekend. Thus, you may find it less expensive to dial directly to your favorite Internet service provider, even if their number is not a local call.

Toll-free numbers are best used when you are traveling and you need to log in for a few minutes to check your mail. Such numbers are too expensive to use on an ongoing basis.

- Can you get a flat monthly rate?

Some providers will sell you all the connection time you want for a fixed monthly fee. In the United States and Europe, a typical fee would be $20-$30 U.S. a month. Other providers, though, will charge you a monthly fee plus a surcharge by the minute. Beware of such charges: they can add up a lot quicker than you would think, especially if you are already paying extra to dial in on a toll-free number. In addition, some providers add an extra charge based on how much information is transmitted to your computer. This too can add up quickly.

    Personally, I would like you to be able to use the Internet as much as you want in an enjoyable manner, and it's hard to enjoy yourself if you are always worrying about the connection cost. So go for the flat fee.

- Does the provider have sufficient phone lines?

Many providers are seriously oversold. This means during peak hours, you will have to dial over and over to get through to the system. Don't depend on the provider's advertising propaganda. Ask people who use the service what it is like.

- What type of accounts does the provider offer?

Make sure you get a PPP account. (If they are backwards enough to only offer SLIP, that will do as a second choice, but you should definitely get one or the other.) Ask if you have to pay extra for a shell account. Some providers will give you a free shell account when you pay for a PPP account. As I discussed earlier in the chapter, a shell account can be a good thing to have.

- Does the provider have ISDN and fast modems?

As I explained earlier, you should be using either ISDN (if it is available and if you can afford it) or, at the very least, a 28.8 Kbps modem. Don't accept anything slower. And, if you get an ISDN connection, find out if you supply your own equipment or if you must rent it from the service provider.

- Can you use any Internet clients you want, or must you use the provider's software?

Once you get on the Net, you will find it is easy to download all sorts of free Internet clients. For example, if you are a Windows or Macintosh user, there are a large number of web clients (browsers) you can get for free. Some Internet service providers have set up their systems so you must use only their software. They may give you the software for free, but you will be limited as to what clients you can use. Unfortunately, many of these "complete" Internet software packages use clients significantly inferior to what you can get on the Net for free. Go for a provider who can sell you a generic PPP connection that will allow you to use any client you want.

- Does the service provider offer full Internet access?

Some services (especially online information services) do not allow you to access all the Internet services. Look at the list in Chapter 3, and make sure you can use each of the resources I discussed. As a general rule, a company primarily in the business of offering Internet service will have better access than an information provider that has added Internet service to remain competitive. Be careful. The definition of "Internet access" can be amorphous.

- Can you put up your own web page for free?

In Chapters 9 through 12, I will discuss the Web in detail. At that time, you will see that web information is organized into "pages", and many people have their own web pages, called "home pages". Having a home page means you can create your own presence on the Internet and share whatever you want with everyone else. Some Internet service providers will allow you to put up your own home page for free. Other providers will sell you this service as an extra feature (usually for too much money). Some providers won't do it at all. But be sure to ask. Making your own home page can be a lot of fun, especially if you are at all creative.

Finally, here are two limitations I want to make sure you understand. First, some providers make it very easy to choose their service. For example, some companies literally give away the software you need to access the Internet using their service (and their service only). Other well-known companies include Internet software built-in to their computer systems.

Microsoft, for instance, includes their own Internet software with Windows 95, and IBM includes their own Internet software with OS/2. I guess it will come as no surprise to you to find that Windows 95 makes it easy to sign up with the Microsoft Network, and OS/2 makes it simple to sign up with the IBM Global Network. All you need to do is click on a couple of buttons and type in your credit card number.

My advice to you is to be choosy. These vendors have gone to great trouble to make it easy for you to buy their Internet services, but that doesn't mean that they are the best ones for your needs. Follow the criteria that I explained above, and you will make the right decision.

HINT

Although Windows 95 and OS/2 steer you toward Microsoft's and IBM's own Internet services, you do not have to use them. The built-in software will work with any Internet service provider that you choose. Moreover, both Windows 95 and OS/2 will allow you to use your own Internet clients. You don't have to use the ones that come with the system.

The final limitation that I want you to understand is that, for the amount per month that you pay for service, you cannot expect good-quality technical support. The profit margin for an Internet account is too low (there is a lot of competition in the market), and companies do not make enough money to pay someone to spend a lot of time talking with you. This isn't bad: Computer products are a commodity these days and few companies can afford the high labor costs that go with excellent support.

There are some providers that offer help (over the telephone or online), but don't expect a huge amount of personal attention. In particular, it is unrealistic to expect your Internet service provider to teach you all about the Internet and how to use it. (That's what this book is for.)

HINT

To summarize, here is what you want from an Internet service provider:

- access via a local phone call
- a flat monthly fee
- an ISDN or fast (28.8 Kbps) connection
- a PPP account
- a shell account at no extra charge
- the ability to use whichever Internet clients you want
- full Internet access to all resources
- the capability of having your own web home page

 **INTERNET RESOURCE**   *Look in the catalog under Internet Resources for*
Internet Service Providers

What Software Do You Need?

To access the Internet by telephone you will need various computer programs. Basically, you will need TCP/IP, PPP, and a collection of Internet clients. (Note: If you use a shell account, you don't need any of this. All you need is a communications program that can dial the phone and emulate a terminal.)

TCP/IP and PPP software is easy to find, often in one complete bundle. There are three ways you can get what you need.

First, most or all of what you need may be packaged for free with your operating system. For example, if you use Windows 95 or OS/2 Warp, the system comes with TCP/IP, PPP and a collection of Internet clients.

Second, you can buy a commercial Internet software package containing everything you need to get up and running. Such packages are usually for Windows or for Macintosh.

Finally, most Internet service providers offer a free bundle containing all the software you need. Large national or multi-national providers will usually give you a slick software kit that installs with a minimum of trouble. Smaller, regional providers will put together a number of free (or shareware) programs configured to access their particular system.

These bundles are nice, but I want you to be aware of how they are packaged. The money in this business is made, not by selling the software, but by selling Internet access. Thus, IBM, Microsoft, and all the other large Internet service providers are more than glad to give you the software for free in the hope that you will sign up for their service (and pay them money, month after month after month). Before you commit yourself to a particular software package, ask the following questions:

- Will the software work with any Internet service provider?

For example, the Windows 95 package steers you toward the Microsoft Network and the OS/2 Warp Internet package steers you toward the IBM Global Network. Similarly, other packages (some free, some you pay for) are set up to work primarily with one particular service provider. Investigate and you will find this provider may not be your best choice. (See the discussion earlier in the chapter about choosing an Internet service provider.)

With Windows 95 and OS/2, by the way, you can use any provider you want, although that fact is not stressed by IBM and Microsoft.

- Will the software allow you to use any Internet clients you want?

Some software packages are complete in the sense that they contain everything you need to use the Net. However, they will not let you use whichever Internet clients you want; you must use the ones that come with the package. This is especially true with service providers that furnish you with proprietary software used only for their system.

Although such providers will say their clients are as good as any others, the fact is new clients are developed all the time and distributed for free over the Net. If your Internet software is inflexible, you will be stuck with an old package long after everyone else has moved on to the newest web browser or mail program.

Finally, not everyone likes the same type of software, and it is nice to have a choice of Internet clients. "One size fits all" isn't even a good idea for clothes. It certainly doesn't work well with Internet client programs.

HINT

Windows users: make sure your software is "Winsock compliant". (This is explained in the next section.)

TCP/IP and PPP Software

Some people find all the Internet software they need in a single bundle. Others must find the various pieces and install them one at a time. For that reason, I would like to talk for a moment about some of the specific concepts. Even if you do plan on using a pre-packaged bundle, these are ideas I would like you to understand.

In Chapter 2, I explained that TCP/IP is the name of the family of protocols (technical specifications) used to organize the computers and communications devices making up the Internet. When you use PPP, your computer is actually part of the Internet during the time you are connected. This means your computer—like all the computers on the Net—needs to be able to support TCP/IP.

Think about it as follows: PPP connects your computer to a remote Internet host. TCP/IP uses the PPP connection to make your computer part of the Net. And your client programs use TCP/IP to send and receive information from other Internet hosts.

As you might imagine, the details are complex. However, all you need to do is make sure the PPP and TCP/IP software is installed on your computer. You can then use PPP to call the remote computer and (as long as the programs are set up properly) everything else is automatic. Once the PPP connection is established and TCP/IP is running, your client programs will access the Net, as the need arises, in order to carry out your requests.

You will sometimes see the TCP/IP software referred to as a STACK. Here is what the word means. Networking people often draw diagrams in which several network components are shown in layers. Your TCP/IP software will perform functions on several of these layers. Hence, the idea of a "stack" of components, one per layer, that together provide the entire TCP/IP functionality. Actually, the idea of a stack is just a metaphor (and a confusing one at that), so don't worry about it. Just install the program.

For a Macintosh, you will use a program called MacTCP. This program comes free with the Mac operating system (MacOS) as long as you have System 7.5 or later. If you have an earlier version of MacOS, you can get MacTCP from various sources. Before System 7.5, it was Apple's intention that their users should buy MacTCP from a third party vendor who licensed it from Apple. Most people obtained MacTCP in a bundle with other Internet Mac programs.

If you are using a version of MacOS older than System 7.5, I suggest you upgrade. There are a number of important advantages to having a newer operating system, and upgrading is generally a good idea. However, if you have an old MacOS and you don't want to upgrade, you should not just copy MacTCP from a friend. Legally, you should find someone to pay for it. (Yeah, right.)

If you use a PC with Microsoft Windows, you will encounter another technical term: WINSOCK. This is short for "Windows socket interface". SOCKETS are a facility that programs can use to communicate with one another while they are running. Winsock is what your Internet clients will use to talk to TCP/IP. For convenience, TCP/IP and Winsock usually come in a single package. Sometimes, PPP is even included. If so, all you need to do is install Winsock on your machine.

Winsock will be included in any Windows Internet software package you buy (or receive free from your Internet service provider). In addition, there is also a well-known version of Winsock, called Trumpet Winsock (developed by Peter Tattam), available as shareware. You can either download it from the Net or get a copy from someone.

If you use a PC with Windows 95 or OS/2 Warp, life is easier: TCP/IP and PPP come built into the system. All you have to do is configure it.

 **INTERNET RESOURCE**   *Look in the catalog under Internet Resources for*
      TCP/IP Software
      PPP Software

nstalling and Configuring TCP and PPP

As part of the research for this chapter, I installed and configured TCP/IP, PPP and SLIP on:

- a PC using Windows 95
- a PC using Windows 3.1
- a PC using OS/2
- a Macintosh
- a Sun workstation using Unix (PPP only)

After hours of intensive work and experimentation, I can summarize the whole thing for you in one concise hint:

HINT

The very best way to install and configure PPP or SLIP is to find someone else who has already done it, and get him or her to do it for you.
(I am serious.)

You may remember that, earlier in the chapter, I advised you to stay away from SLIP and use PPP. One reason I told you this is PPP is a lot easier to get running.

For example, when a SLIP program makes a connection, it uses a SCRIPT as part of the login procedure. This script contains instructions for typing your userid and password, and then establishing the SLIP connection. It is up to you to furnish the script. Unless you are a programmer, believe me, you will not enjoy messing about with SLIP scripts. (The only practical procedure in such a situation is to find someone who uses the same system and get a script that already works.) PPP, however, is more sophisticated and requires less help from you.

Perhaps the most complex part of installing TCP/IP, PPP and SLIP (aside from scripts) is CONFIGURING the program. This process requires you to tell the program all the information it needs to connect to the Internet. For example, you will need to specify your userid, your password, and what phone number to dial.

Unfortunately, there is no standard configuration procedure: each program does it differently. If you use an Internet software package, things are a lot easier. Most of them come pre-configured for one particular Internet service provider and, if you use that provider, there will be very little for you to specify to get started. (Although you can be sure the program will ask for your credit card number.)

To help you, I will explain some of the terminology you may encounter as you configure TCP/IP and PPP. However, you will probably have to read the documentation that comes with your software (however obtuse it may seem). You should also check to see if the configuration program has any online help.

Before I start, I would like to mention two important terms I discuss in more detail in Chapter 6. The first is DOMAIN NAME. A domain name is a standard Internet address. For example, `rtfm.mit.edu` is the domain name of a particular computer at MIT. (Each separate part of the name is called a "domain".)

The second term is IP ADDRESS. Underneath the calm, cool veneer of the Internet as we see it lie millions of computers. Many of these computers have domain names but, technically, all Internet computers are actually known by their IP address, which is a series of four numbers. For example, the IP address of `rtfm.mit.edu` is `18.181.0.24`.

The numeric IP addresses are the "official" addresses of the Net. Domain names are only for the convenience of human beings. This means that, before a domain name can be used, it must be translated into a numeric IP address. All of this is done automatically by an Internet service called DOMAIN NAME SYSTEM, or DNS.

So why am I telling you this? Because every time your client programs need to connect to another computer, they will have to call upon a special server, called a DNS SERVER, to translate a domain name into an IP address. The DNS server your computer uses will probably be the remote host that provides your Internet connection. To make sure this all works, you will have to specify the IP address of your DNS server as part of the PPP configuration.

Here now are some of the terms you may encounter as you configure TCP/IP and PPP. The exact wording will differ from one program to another, but the general idea will be the same. Most of the information I mention here will be given to you by your Internet service provider when you get an account. All you need to do is make sure it is specified properly when you configure the software.

First, you will have to specify your userid (which may be called a "Login ID" or something similar) and your password. You will also have to specify the phone number of the remote host. As I mentioned earlier, if you have a choice between a local number and a toll free number, choose the local number. There will probably be a special charge to use a toll free number.

Next, you will also be called upon to give the IP address of your DNS server, as well as the domain name of your remote host.

Once you make the connection to the Net, your computer is a bona fide Internet host. Like all Internet hosts, your computer will need to have its own IP number. Some providers will assign you a permanent IP number to use each time you log in. (This is called a STATIC IP ADDRESS.) If so, you will have to specify this number as part of the configuration.

With other providers, the remote host will assign a different IP number each time you connect. (This is called a DYNAMIC IP ADDRESS.) If your system uses dynamic IP numbers, PPP will take care of the details automatically, and there is nothing special for you to do.

Aside from Internet-type information, you will also have to tell your software something about your own computer. You may have to tell it what kind of modem you are using and if that modem requires any special initialization commands.

For a Mac, you will also have to specify whether your modem is connected to the modem port or the printer port. (A PORT is a plug on the computer to which you can attach a device.) For a PC, you will have to specify the number of the "comm port" (communications port) to which your modem is attached.

Finally, you will have to choose the speed for your modem. (See Chapter 4 for a discussion of modem speeds.) Remember, you may see the word "baud" used as a synonym for "bps".

HINT

With most communications programs, the speed you will be asked to choose specifies the maximum rate at which data can be transmitted between your computer and the modem. This is not the same as the basic speed of the modem itself. For example, a 28.8K bps modem can compress data as it is transmitted, which means it can handle more than 28.8K bps of data from the computer. As a general rule, you would normally set the computer/modem transmission speed to be 2-4 times greater than the basic modem speed.

My advice is to start by setting the speed to the highest possible value. If the modem doesn't respond, work your way down through the list of possible values until you find the highest computer/modem speed that functions properly.

These then are the most important quantities you will have to specify in order to configure your TCP/IP and PPP software. If your particular software requires other information, you should ask your Internet service provider which are the appropriate values to use. Such questions are common, and they may provide you with a document that walks you through the installation step by step.

Where to Get Internet Client Programs

Most of what I have talked about so far has to do with getting you up and running on the Internet. However, these are all one-time considerations. Once you have your computer, your modem (or ISDN equipment), and your phone connection, and once you have a PPP or shell account with TCP/IP and PPP installed, you can spend all your time using the Net. And using the Net means using your Internet client programs.

Thus, most of this book deals with what you will be doing from day to day: learning about and using your Internet clients. Still, the question arises, where do you get client programs? As I explained in Chapter 2, you use a different client for each Internet service. For example, to use the Web, you need a web client (called a browser); to send and receive mail, you need a mail client; to participate in the Usenet discussion groups, you need a Usenet client (called a newsreader); and so on. Where do these clients come from?

There are several answers. First, if you use an Internet software package to get started, it will already have some client programs as part of the package. This is also true if you are using an operating system—like Windows 95 or OS/2 Warp—that comes with built-in Internet software.

However, the very best place to get clients is on the Net itself. There are literally tens and tens of different clients you can download and use for free. Some of these programs are SHAREWARE (which means if you like them, you are supposed to pay a small registration fee), but you can certainly try everything for free.

HINT

Most shareware programs will work just fine, even if you don't pay the registration fee. However, if you end up using such a program regularly, there are two reasons why I suggest you pay the fee.

First, I am a well-known Internet author, and well-known Internet authors are supposed to tell their readers to pay for shareware.

Second—and this really is important—most of what is worthwhile on the Net was put there by individual people who created something they were willing to share. If it were left up to the large companies whose names I won't mention (such as Microsoft, IBM, Compuserve, Prodigy and America Online), the quality of your Net experience would be much, much different. The small, independent programmers and the small software houses provide an important service, and we should support them.

You will remember that, earlier in the chapter, I advised you to go with an Internet service provider that has set up their system so you can use any clients you want. (For Windows, their software should be Winsock compliant.) The reason I made this suggestion is there are so many free Internet clients on the Net—with more being offered all the time—that if you use a provider who requires you to use their proprietary software, you may not be able to use other clients.

This is a lot more important than you might think, because the quality and features of the different clients vary greatly, and I want you to have the freedom to choose whichever programs are best for you.

HINT

Once you get used to using the Net and you know how to download programs, spend some time checking out the various clients that work with your system. (If you are a Macintosh or Windows user, you will have a lot of choices.) Don't necessarily go with whatever was given to you: pick the clients you like the best.

There are many places on the Net where you can get free client software. For your convenience, I have listed some of these places in the catalog at the end of the book. There is nothing wrong with changing from one client to another every few months as new programs become available. One of the things that makes the Internet such a wonderful place to be is the large amount of wonderful new software continually being offered for free.

INTERNET RESOURCE   *Look in the catalog under Internet Resources for*
Windows 95 Internet Client Programs
Windows 3.1 Internet Client Programs
Macintosh Internet Client Programs
OS/2 Internet Client Programs

Chapter Six

Internet Addressing

Whatever you do, make sure that you read this chapter. Here is why: Every computer that is on the Internet has its own unique address. Likewise, every person who uses the Internet has his or her own address. You must learn how to understand such addresses.

In the non-computer part of your life, you need to remember different types of information to be able to communicate with someone: a postal address, perhaps a separate street address, a home telephone number, a business telephone number, a fax number, and so on.

On the Internet, there is only one type of electronic address. Once you know someone's Internet address, you can send mail, transfer files, have a conversation, and even find out information about that person. Conversely, once you start to use the Internet, you will need to give other people only one simple address in order for them to be able to communicate with you. Moreover, when someone wants to tell you where on the Internet certain information or a particular resource is to be found, they do so by giving you the address of a computer.

For these reasons, understanding the Internet addressing system is crucial to using the Internet. In this chapter, I will show you everything you need to know.

Standard Internet Addresses

On the Internet, the word ADDRESS always refers to an electronic address, not a postal address. If someone asks for your "address", he wants your Internet address.

All Internet addresses follow the same form: the person's user name, followed by an **@** character (the "at" sign), followed by the name of a computer. (Every computer on the Internet has a unique name.) Here is a typical example:

harley@fuzzball.ucsb.edu

In this case, the user name is **harley**, and the name of the computer is **fuzzball.ucsb.edu**. As this example shows, there are never any spaces within an address.

Each person has a user name called a USERID (pronounced "user-eye-dee"). It is this userid that we use as the first part of someone's address. If you access the Internet via a Unix system, your userid will be the name you use to log in.

The part of the address after the **@** character is called the DOMAIN. In this case, the domain is **fuzzball.ucsb.edu**. Thus, the general form of all Internet addresses is:

userid**@**domain

As you might imagine, a userid by itself is not necessarily unique. For instance, within the entire Internet, there are probably a number of people lucky enough to have a spiffy userid like **harley**.

What must be unique is the combination of userid and domain. So, although there may be more than one `harley` on the Internet, there can be only one such userid on the computer named `fuzzball.ucsb.edu`.

If you read an Internet address out loud, you will see that using the **@** character is appropriate. For example, let's say you use your mail program to send a message to the following address:

```
mail harley@fuzzball.ucsb.edu
```

As you type the address, you can say to yourself, "I am sending mail to Harley, who is at the computer named `fuzzball.ucsb.edu`".

Understanding a Domain Name: Sub-Domains

In the last section, I used `harley@fuzzball.ucsb.edu` as an example of an Internet address. I explained that `harley` is the userid and `fuzzball.ucsb.edu` is the domain. Each part of a domain is called a SUB-DOMAIN. As you can see, sub-domains are separated by periods. In our example, there are three sub-domains: `fuzzball`, `ucsb` and `edu`.

The way to understand a domain name is to look at the sub-domains from right to left. The name is constructed so that each sub-domain tells you something about the computer. The rightmost sub-domain, called the TOP-LEVEL DOMAIN, is the most general. As you read to the left, the sub-domains become more specific.

In our example, the top-level domain `edu` tells us that the computer is at an educational institution. (I will explain the meanings of the various top-level domains in a moment.) The next sub-domain, `ucsb`, tells us the name of this institution (the University of California at Santa Barbara). Finally, the leftmost sub-domain is the name of a specific computer named `fuzzball`. Thus, when you send mail to the following address

```
mail harley@fuzzball.ucsb.edu
```

you can say to yourself, "I am sending mail to Harley, at a computer named `fuzzball`, at the University of California at Santa Barbara, which is an educational institution".

In computer terminology, we use the terms LOWERCASE to refer to small letters, and UPPERCASE to refer to capital letters. When you type an address, you can mix upper- and lowercase letters however you want. To describe this idea, we say addresses are CASE INSENSITIVE. (In situations where upper- and lowercase do matter, we say the spelling is CASE SENSITIVE.)

Since addresses are case insensitive, the following two addresses are equivalent:

```
mail harley@fuzzball.ucsb.edu
mail harley@FUZZBALL.UCSB.EDU
```

With respect to using uppercase letters, you will see two other common address variations. First, some people type only the top-level domain in uppercase:

```
mail harley@fuzzball.ucsb.EDU
```

Other people like to emphasize the site of the computer:

```
mail harley@fuzzball.Ucsb.Edu
```

Remember, though, addresses are always case insensitive and the uppercase letters are optional.

HINT

As a general rule, use all lowercase for Internet addresses. There is really no need to mix in uppercase letters.

If you see an address in which some of the letters are uppercase, it is always safe to change them to lowercase.

If you do decide to use some uppercase letters, it is best not to change the userid. On some systems, it may make a difference (although it's not supposed to).

Variations on the Standard Internet Address Format

All Internet addresses follow the standard format:

userid@domain

However, there are several variations you may encounter. The example I have been using has three sub-domains:

```
harley@fuzzball.ucsb.edu
```

You will often see addresses that have more sub-domains in order to be more specific. Here is an example:

```
scott@emmenthaler.cs.wisc.edu
```

In this case, the userid is **scott**. The domain refers to a computer **emmenthaler** that is part of the computer science (**cs**) department at **wisc**, the University of Wisconsin (presumably, an educational institution).

Many Internet sites use patterns to name their computers. For example, you might see computers named after cartoon characters, mythical heroes, local landmarks, or whatever. At the University of Wisconsin, many computers are named after types of cheese.

HINT

As all students of world geography know, it is the custom, within the United States, for each state to have its own nickname. For example, California is the Golden State. New York is the Empire State. The reason there are so many "cheese" computers at the University of Wisconsin is that Wisconsin is known as the Dairy State.

(In other words, by the time someone got around to Wisconsin, all the good nicknames were already taken.)

INTERNET RESOURCE *Look in the catalog under Internet Resources for* ***Computer Names (Strange and Interesting)***

Some Internet addresses have only two sub-domains (the minimum). Here are three examples:

```
wendy@muffin.com
billg@microsoft.com
randall@ucsd.edu
```

When you see an address with only two sub-domains it can mean two things. First, it might mean the organization is so small that it only has one computer on the Internet. In the first example, this is the case. The top-level domain **com** tells us that this is a commercial organization. (More about top-level domains in a moment.)

The second and third examples are from organizations that have a great many computers. In such organizations, one computer is usually used to send and receive all the outside mail. In our example, the names of these computers are **ucsd.edu** and **microsoft.com**. The system administrators for these organizations have simplified the mailing addresses by arranging for everyone to be able to receive mail addressed to **ucsd.edu** and **microsoft.com**. Here is how it works:

In general, the term GATEWAY refers to a link between two different systems. In this case, we have a **MAIL GATEWAY**. The computers **ucsd.edu** and **microsoft.com** act as the mail link between the internal network and the outside world. The mail gateway has a list of userids and local addresses. When a message arrives, the gateway can check the list and forward the message to the appropriate local computer.

For example, say a person has a userid of **melissa** on a computer named **misty** within the **ucsb.edu** domain. Normally, her address would be:

```
melissa@misty.ucsd.edu
```

However, in order to make her mail address simpler, she registers with the mail gateway. From then on, she can receive mail at **melissa@ucsd.edu**. When mail arrives, the gateway will automatically forward it to the **misty** computer.

So, as you can see, an address with only two sub-domains usually means that the organization is very small (like **muffin.com**) or very large (like **ucsd.edu** or **microsoft.com**).

I am explaining this in detail because there may be times when you need a person's exact address, for example, to contact him or her using a **talk** program (which I discuss in Chapter 25). In such cases, the simplified mail address may not work and you will have to ask for a longer, more specific one.

To conclude this section, I will discuss one final form of Internet addressing that you will sometimes see in a mail address. In this form, a **%** (percent) character is used as part of the address. In such addresses, the **%** character will be to the left of the **@** character. For example:

```
melissa%misty@ucsd.edu
```

The idea is that the computer receiving the message (in this case, **ucsd.edu**) will look at everything to the left of the **@** character (in this case, **melissa%misty**) and try to make sense out of it.

Usually, the **%** character will separate a userid from the name of a local computer. In this example, userid **melissa** uses a local computer named **misty**. Within the local network, there may be several different connections from the mail gateway to that computer. At the time the message is received, the mail gateway will choose the best path to use to deliver the mail.

HINT

Many people know their Internet address, even though they don't understand it. Some organizations have more than one way to address mail, and the system managers will usually tell their users which address works best.

So don't worry too much about the variations. When you send mail to someone, just use whatever address the person gave you.

Top-Level Domains

The way to understand an address is to read it from right to left. The top-level domain will be the most general specification. In the following example, the top-level domain of **edu** tells us the computer is at an educational institution:

```
mail harley@fuzzball.ucsb.edu
```

In the next example, a top-level domain of **com** indicates a commercial organization:

```
billg@microsoft.com
```

In general, there are two types of top-level domains. The old-style ORGANIZATIONAL DOMAINS (as in these two examples) and the newer GEOGRAPHICAL DOMAINS.

The organizational domains are based on an addressing scheme developed before the days of international networks. It was intended to be used mainly within the United States.

The idea was that the top-level domain would show the type of organization responsible for the computer. Figure 6-1 shows the various categories. All of these categories have been around since the beginning of the Internet except **int**, which is a relatively recent addition for certain organizations that span national boundaries (such as NATO).

Once the Internet expanded internationally, new, more specific top-level domains became necessary. To meet this need, a new system of geographical domains was developed in which a two-letter abbreviation represents an entire country. There are many such top-level domains—one for every country on the Internet—and they are all listed in Appendix A. For quick reference, Figure 6-2 shows a representative sample.

As an example, take a look at the following address:

```
michael@music.tuwien.ac.at
```

Domain	Meaning
com	commercial organization
edu	educational institution
gov	government
int	international organization
mil	military
net	networking organization
org	non-profit organization

Figure 6-1.   *Organizational top-level domains*

Domain	Meaning
at	Austria
au	Australia
ca	Canada
ch	Switzerland ("Confoederatio Helvetica")
de	Germany ("Deutschland")
dk	Denmark
es	Spain ("España")
fr	France
gr	Greece
ie	Republic of Ireland
jp	Japan
nz	New Zealand
uk	United Kingdom (England, Scotland, Wales, Northern Ireland)
us	United States

Figure 6-2.   *Examples of geographical top-level domains*

Here we have a computer at the Technical University of Vienna in Austria (top-level domain of **at**).

Some countries use a sub-domain, just to the left of the top-level domain, to divide it into categories. For example, you might see **ac** to refer to an academic organization or **co** to indicate a commercial company. In our example, we see that the Austrian address uses **ac**.

For the most part, the geographical domains are simply the standard two-letter international country abbreviations. (The ones that everybody in the world knows about except the Americans.) The exception to this scheme is Great Britain. Its international abbreviation is **gb**, but it also uses a domain name of **uk** for "United Kingdom".

This makes sense when you remember Great Britain includes only England, Scotland and Wales, while the United Kingdom also includes Northern Ireland. (Evidently, the English use some alternative meaning of the word "united" that nobody else understands.)

As you can see from Figure 6-2, the United States does have a geographical domain name (**us**), although it is not used much. Outside the U.S., though, geographical names are used almost exclusively. However, regardless of what type of top-level domain your organization uses, you can communicate with any address on the Internet. Both types of top-level domains are recognized everywhere.

HINT

Within Britain and New Zealand, the order of domains is sometimes reversed. For example, you may see an address like:

```
peirce@uk.ac.oxford.compsci
```

The mailing system is supposed to reverse the domains in order to communicate with the outside world. However, occasionally, a reversed address will escape from one of these countries, like a bad table wine exported for foreign consumption. If you need to use such an address outside its native environment, be sure to reverse the sub-domains:

```
peirce@compsci.oxford.ac.uk
```

so they form a standard address.

 INTERNET RESOURCE *Look in the catalog under Internet Resources for*
Top-Level Domains

Pseudo-Internet Addresses

There are many organizations that would like to be on the Internet but who do not have the time or the money to maintain a permanent Internet connection. As an alternative, they make an arrangement with a nearby Internet site that agrees to act as a mail gateway for them. For example, a small company could make such an arrangement with an Internet access provider.

With such an arrangement, the organization can be given a mailing address that looks just like a standard Internet address. However, such organizations are not really on the Internet.

For example, say the Marlinspike Consulting Company would like an Internet address. It contracts with SnowyNET, a local Internet access provider, to handle its mail. As part of the arrangement, the company is given the name **marlin.com**, which is registered with the Internet addressing system.

Any mail sent to **marlin.com** is automatically routed to the SnowyNET gateway computer. At certain times, the **marlin.com** computer connects over a telephone line with the SnowyNET computer and picks up its mail. At the same time, any mail from **marlin.com** that is being sent outside the company is passed to the SnowyNET computer.

A user at a company with such an arrangement will use an address that looks just like a standard Internet address. For example, someone might tell you that his address is:

`tintin@marlin.com`

When you see such an address, there is no way of knowing whether or not it represents a real Internet address. In other words, there is often no way to tell, from the address alone, if a computer is actually on the Internet. If you see a name like:

small-company-name.**com**

you might be suspicious. However, even some large companies use a gateway rather than a real Internet connection. If it is important that you know for sure if a computer is on the Internet, you can use the **host** command, described in the next section.

 **INTERNET RESOURCE** *Look in the catalog under Internet Resources for* ***Domain Name Registration***

IP Addresses and DNS

So far, I have talked about Internet addresses in which each sub-domain is a name. However, underneath the socially-acceptable veneer of this system lies a typical computer trick: the real Internet addresses are actually numbers, not names. For example, the computer **ucsd.edu**, which I mentioned earlier, is actually called **128.54.16.1**.

Names, of course, are easier for people to use, but every time you use a domain address, your system has to turn it into a number, although the details are hidden from you. You will recall in Chapter 2, I explain that the part of the Internet that moves data packets from one place to another is called IP (Internet Protocol). For this reason, the numeric version of an address is called an IP ADDRESS (pronounced "eye-pee address"). For example, the computer **ucsd.edu** has an IP address of **128.54.16.1**.

As you can see, an IP address looks something like the domain addresses I have already discussed in that there are several parts separated by periods. However, the parts of an IP address do not correspond directly to sub-domain names, so don't read too much into the pattern.

You can use an IP address anywhere you would use a regular address. For example, the following two addresses are equivalent:

`randall@ucsd.edu`
`randall@128.54.16.1`

The part of the Internet that keeps track of addresses is called the DOMAIN NAME SYSTEM or DNS. DNS is a TCP/IP service called upon to translate domain names to and from IP addresses. Fortunately, it is all done behind your back, and there is no reason to bother with the details.

In rare cases, it may be that your system has trouble understanding a domain address. If this happens, the IP address may work better (as long as it is correct).

If you have a shell account (see Chapter 5) and you would like to test DNS, you can use the **host** command. There are two formats:

```
host standard-address
host IP-address
```

HINT

The **host** command is not available on all systems. If your system does not have **host**, try the **nslookup** or **traceroute** programs. If none of these are available, you can try using **telnet** (Chapter 23) to see if you can at least connect to the remote computer. If a connection is established, you can then quit **telnet**.

If you specify a standard address:

```
host ucsd.edu
```

DNS will display the IP address. If you specify an IP address:

```
host 128.54.16.1
```

DNS will display the standard address.

HINT

Only real Internet hosts have IP addresses. Thus, you can use the **host** command to check if a computer is on the Internet. If **host** displays an IP address, the computer you specified is on the Internet. If you specify an address that is not on the Internet, you will see:

```
Host not found.
```

If this happens, be sure to check your spelling.

UUCP

Once you have read the previous sections of this chapter, you have learned just about everything you need to know about standard Internet addresses. However, I do want to spend a little time discussing the addressing schemes used by a few other networks. As an Internet user, you can exchange mail with these networks, and it will help you understand what type of addresses they use.

To start, I will discuss the Unix-based UUCP network. I will then conclude the chapter by explaining what addresses to use to send mail to other popular networks, such as Compuserve, MCI Mail, America Online, and so on.

All Unix systems come with a built-in networking system called UUCP (pronounced "you-you-see-pee"). Although the job of UUCP is to connect Unix computers, it is not as powerful as TCP/IP. For example, UUCP does not provide a remote login facility. Moreover, as you will see in a moment, the UUCP mail facility is slower and more awkward than the TCP/IP-based Internet system. However, UUCP does have an important advantage. It is a standard part of Unix (free with most systems), and it runs cheaply and reliably over dial-up or hardwired connections.

📖 What's in a Name?

UUCP

UUCP is a Unix-based networking facility consisting of a family of programs. Within the UUCP family, there are a number of separate programs, each of which performs a different function. One of the more important programs is named **uucp**. Its job is to copy files from one Unix system to another.

Thus, the UUCP family is named after the **uucp** program, and the name **uucp** stands for "Unix to Unix copy".

You may see a similarity here to the name TCP/IP. As I discuss in Chapter 2, TCP/IP is a large family of protocols named after its two most important members, TCP and IP.

UUCP works by allowing Unix systems to connect together to form a chain. For example, say you are using a computer named **alpha**. Your computer is connected to another computer named **beta**. This computer is connected to **gamma** which is, in turn, connected to **delta**.

You decide to send mail to a person with a userid of **murray**, who uses **delta**. You send the message from your computer, **alpha**. UUCP will pass the message from **alpha** to **beta** to **gamma** to **delta**, where it will be delivered to userid **murray**.

Our example involves four computers and three different connections. It might be these are hardwired connections, in which the computers are joined by a cable. Typically, though, the connections are made over a telephone line. At certain intervals, each computer calls (or is called by) its neighbor. When they connect, they swap whatever mail they have waiting for one another. Some of the mail will be for local users. Other mail will need to be forwarded to another computer.

The system works well in that it provides an economical way to send mail from computer to computer over large distances. However, there is an important limitation: Since many UUCP connections are made over a telephone line at certain predefined times, mail delivery can take hours, or even several days.

Compare this to the Internet, in which connections are permanent and messages are transmitted quickly, often within seconds, almost always within minutes.

UUCP Addresses and Bang Paths

Many sites, which at one time depended on UUCP for mail and file transfer, now use the faster, more dependable Internet. However, there are still a number of UUCP installations, so it is a good idea to know something about their addresses.

To send mail to a UUCP address, you must specify the route you want the message to take. For example, you must say, "I want this message to go to computer **beta**, and from there to computer **gamma**, and from there to computer **delta**. At that point, I want the message delivered to userid **murray**."

To do so, you construct an address consisting of each of these names in turn, separated by **!** (exclamation mark) characters. For example, here is a **mail** command that will send a message to the userid I just described:

```
mail beta!gamma!delta!murray
```

When you create such a message, your system will store it until contact is made with computer **beta**, at which time the message will be sent on its way.

In Unix terminology, one of the slang names for the **!** character is BANG. Thus, a UUCP address that specifies multiple names is sometimes called a BANG PATH. When a Unix person reads such a path out loud, he will pronounce the **!** character as "bang". For example, you might hear someone say, "I tried to send you mail at beta bang gamma bang delta bang murray."

HINT

If you are using a shell account with a Unix system, the program that reads and interprets your commands is called a SHELL. (This is why such accounts are called "shell accounts".) There are various shells you might use, and some of them—in particular, the C-Shell—recognize a ! character as part of a facility called history substitution. This facility allows you to recall and edit previously entered commands. As you might imagine, history substitution can be a real time-saver.

However, this means the ! character has a special meaning, and, when you type this character as part of a UUCP address, it will cause an error. For example, if you enter the command:

```
mail beta!gamma!delta!murray
```

the C-Shell will try to interpret the command as a history substitution request. I won't go into the details here, except to say you will see an error message like this:

```
gamma!delta!murray: Event not found.
```

(The term "event" refers to a previously entered command.)

Thus, if you are using Unix with a shell like the C-Shell, you need to tell it that the ! characters in a UUCP address are to be taken literally. To do so, you preface each ! with a \ (backslash) character:

```
mail beta\!gamma\!delta\!murray
```

The \ characters are not really part of the address. They are there only to tell the shell not to misinterpret the ! characters.

Simplified UUCP Addressing

As I explained in the previous section, UUCP is inexpensive and accessible to anyone with a UUCP software (which comes with all Unix systems), a modem, and another computer to which to connect. Indeed, before the Internet became so popular, many people used to send mail over a large, worldwide UUCP network. Today, many of these people have migrated to the Internet, but there are still a large number of computers out there that are reachable only by UUCP.

One of the problems with UUCP addressing is the addresses can be long. Moreover, you must specify an exact path from one computer to the next. In the last section, we looked at a sample **mail** command that specified a path via three different computers.

```
mail beta!gamma!delta!murray
```

This is okay, albeit inconvenient, as long as you know which path to use. But many UUCP paths are much longer. Moreover, how do you know how to construct the path?

Let us say, for example, you have a friend with a userid of **albert** who uses a computer called **gendeau.com**. If he were connected to the Internet, you would send mail to him by using the command:

```
mail albert@gendeau.com
```

But suppose he is on the UUCP network, not the Internet. How do you have any idea what path to use from your computer to his?

In general, this is a big problem with UUCP because the path to a computer depends very much on where you start. Thus, if your friend wants to correspond with people at different locations, he might have to give each of them a different address. The nice thing about the Internet and the Domain Name System is that all you have to do is specify the address of the destination. The system automatically figures out the best route to take.

To bring the same sort of convenience to UUCP, an undertaking was started called the UUCP MAPPING PROJECT. This project regularly publishes "maps" of data that are sent to many key UUCP computers. When UUCP mail reaches these computers, they can look at the maps and decide the best route to use. In essence, this allows you to use a UUCP address that is similar to an Internet address, and let the system do the work.

Thus, on occasion, you may see an address that uses a top-level domain of **uucp**. For example, a friend might say you can send mail to him at:

```
albert@gendeau.uucp
```

When you use such an address, it is a signal to the mail routing software to find the name in the UUCP mapping data and figure out the best path to use. Your computer may be able to do this itself, or it may send it to another computer to do the job.

In practice, all you have to do is get the address right and it should work. But, if you ever have a choice between a UUCP address and an Internet address, choose the Internet one.

Sending Mail to Other Networks

The Internet has mail gateways to a large number of other networks. As long as you know the right way to address mail, you can send messages to people on these networks via their gateway. Some of these gateways serve commercial networks that charge for their services. Nevertheless, as an Internet user, you can use the gateway for free.

To conclude this chapter, I will discuss a few of the most widely used mail gateways, and I will show you how to use an Internet-style address to send mail to users on these networks.

First, there are the commercial mail systems: America Online, AT&T Mail, Compuserve, MCI Mail, Prodigy, and so on. To send mail to users on these systems, just use one of the following domains:

```
aol.com
attmail.com
compuserve.com
mcimail.com
prodigy.com
```

As a general rule, you can use the standard format: the user name or identification number, followed by an **@** character, followed by the domain. Note: Compuserve uses identification numbers that contain a comma, such as **12345,678**. When you use such a number in an Internet address, you must change the comma to a period. Here are some examples:

```
nipper@aol.com
nipper@attmail.com
123456.789@compuserve.com
nipper@mcimail.com
nipper@prodigy.com
```

Another address you might encounter is one from Fidonet. This is a worldwide network of personal computers that connect via telephone lines. (In principle, Fidonet is not unlike UUCP.) To reach Fidonet, you use a domain name that ends in **fidonet.org**. The name of the actual Fidonet computer is specified as a series of sub-domains. It works like this:

In the terminology of Fidonet, a computer name consists of three parts: a zone number, a net number, and a node number. The zone number is followed by a **:** (colon) character, and the net number is followed by a **/** (slash) character. For example, someone might tell you that his Fidonet computer is:

```
1:234/567
```

In this case, the zone number is **1**, the net number is **234**, and the node number is **567**.

To specify a Fidonet computer name from the Internet, you use these same three numbers, in reverse order, according to the following pattern:

f*node***.n***net***.z***zone***.fidonet.org**

Within Fidonet, users are known by their full names. You separate each part of the name with a period. Thus, a person named Artie Choke will have a user name of **Artie Choke**. For example, to send mail to Artie Choke at the Fidonet computer **1:234/567**, use:

```
mail Artie.Choke@f567.n234.z1.fidonet.org
```

The last type of mail address I will mention is for Bitnet users. Bitnet is a collection of different networks based in the United States, Canada, Mexico and Europe. To send mail to a Bitnet user, you need to know his or her user name and host computer. From the Internet, the address is simple. Use a top-level domain of **bitnet**. To the left, put the name of the Bitnet host.

For example, say you want to send mail to a friend whose Bitnet user name is **lunaea**. The name of her computer is **psuvm**. Use the command:

```
mail lunaea@psuvm.bitnet
```

If you hang around with Bitnet people, you will notice a lot of the computer names end in "vm". This is because they are IBM mainframe computers using the Virtual Machine operating system.

The name **bitnet** is not an official Internet domain and is an example of what is called a PSEUDO DOMAIN. When you use an address with a pseudo domain, the mailing software on your system must recognize the domain, re-write the address, and send the message to a computer that knows how to send mail to that particular network. In this case, your mailing program would have to send the message to a BITNET/INTERNET GATEWAY.

On some systems, this type of address will not work because the local mail software is not set up to recognize a **bitnet** pseudo domain. If this is the case on your system, you can send the message directly to any one of the Bitnet/Internet gateways. Here are several of them:

Bitnet/Internet Gateways

```
brownvm.brown.edu
cunyvm.cuny.edu
pucc.princeton.edu
uga.cc.uga.edu
vm1.nodak.edu
```

There are two addressing formats you can use. The preferable one uses the UUCP bang path notation:

```
gateway!computer.bitnet!userid
```

For example, to send a message to **lunaea** on the Bitnet computer named **psuvm**, you might use the address:

```
brownvm.brown.edu!psuvm.bitnet!lunaea
```

The second format uses the **%** notation I discussed earlier:

userid%*computer*.**bitnet**@*gateway*

For example:

lunaea%psuvm.bitnet@brownvm.brown.edu

Technically speaking, this form of the address is not officially supported by the Internet, although such addresses will usually work.

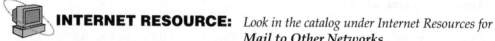 **INTERNET RESOURCE:** *Look in the catalog under Internet Resources for* ***Mail to Other Networks***

Chapter Seven

Mail

By far, electronic mail is used more than any other Internet resource. Indeed, for many people, mail is the only Internet service they use.

In this chapter, I explain the Internet mail system and discuss everything you need to get started. You will learn all about the programs you can use and the techniques you need to send and receive mail. At the end of the chapter, I will give you some hints to make using the Internet mail system as comfortable as possible.

SMTP: The Basis for the Internet Mail System

The Internet mail system is, by far, the most important of the various Internet services. Every day, countless messages are sent from one part of the Internet to another and it is no exaggeration to say the economy of the world is now dependent on Internet mail. As you would expect, many of these messages are personal notes from one person to another. Most messages consist of plain text. However, it is also possible to mail all types of data, such as pictures, computer programs, spreadsheets or word processing documents.

One of the most important uses of the Internet mail system is to allow people who are not near one another to work together. Indeed, it is common for someone to collaborate with a person who is thousands of miles away; someone they may never meet in person.

Here is an interesting example. As I worked on this book in California, I mailed each chapter to reviewers in Holland, Germany, Oregon and Chicago. Each of the reviewers would read the chapter and make comments. Because we used the Internet mail system, it was possible for them to respond quickly even though, physically, none of us were near one another. (In fact, the reviewer from Oregon spent a lot of time in Europe and, as he traveled around, he would find a friendly Internet connection and pick up his mail on the road.)

Whenever I finished a new chapter, I would mail the text to each of the reviewers. Each person would insert his comments right into the text and mail it back to me. Because the Internet is so fast and reliable, it was not uncommon for us to be able to review an entire chapter within a day. If I had had to depend on standard post office mail, processing a chapter might have taken weeks.

A similar procedure is carried out, on a much larger scale, when decisions have to be made that affect the Internet itself. Whenever an idea or a new standard is proposed, people around the world participate in a debate via the mail system (and the Usenet discussion groups). Eventually, the technically-oriented members of the Internet community reach a consensus and, if appropriate, the new standard is propagated throughout the Net.

As you think about all of this, it is natural to wonder what holds the mail system together. After all, the Internet connects hundreds of thousands of networks, each of which has its own mix of computers and software. How can all these different systems work together to exchange mail so quickly and reliably?

The answer is, the delivery of mail is standardized by a system called SMTP. SMTP, which stands for SIMPLE MAIL TRANSFER PROTOCOL, is part of the TCP/IP family of protocols I discussed in Chapter 2. The SMTP protocol describes how mail is to be delivered from one Internet computer to another.

Throughout the Internet, there are millions of computers using SMTP to send and receive mail. The actual work is done by a program called a TRANSPORT AGENT, which functions behind the scenes to ensure that messages are transported in an orderly fashion according to the SMTP protocol. In doing so, the transport agent provides a mail link to the outside world.

Now, as I explained in Chapter 2, many of the host computers on the Internet run Unix. (Indeed, most of the computing that holds the Net together is done by Unix computers.) Thus, of hundreds of thousands of transport agents scattered around the Net, most of them are running under Unix. Specifically, most of these computers use a transport agent called **sendmail**, which runs by itself in the "background", always ready to respond to whatever requests it may receive. In Unix terminology, such a program is called a DAEMON (yes, that is the correct spelling), and every Unix system has various daemons, quietly lurking in the background, waiting to provide services for you.

In theory, it doesn't matter which transport agent your system uses, as long as it knows how to send and receive mail using SMTP. However, it is interesting to know that, somewhere along the line, your mail service probably depends on a Unix machine running a **sendmail** daemon.

Now, am I saying you should understand the technical details of how all of this works? Of course not. However, what I do want you to appreciate is the that Internet mail system works because everybody's network has at least one computer running a transport agent, sending and receiving mail according to the SMTP protocol. Although you will never work directly with your local transport agent, it is useful to know it exists and what it does. (For example, if someone tells you **sendmail** is down temporarily, you will understand why mail cannot move in or out of your network until **sendmail** is restored.)

How You Access the Mail System

In the previous section, I described how the Internet mail system is held together by transfer agents, whose job it is to use the SMTP protocol to send and receive mail behind the scenes. However, how does the mail get from the transfer agent to you?

The usual setup is for the computer that provides your Internet connection to also act as your mail host. Typically, this computer runs a transport agent program which is connected to the Internet 24 hours a day. This means, no matter when mail arrives for you, there is a transport agent available to accept it.

Whenever a message arrives, the transport agent saves it in a file called a MAILBOX. Each person who has an account on the host computer is given his own mailbox file. This allows the host computer to keep everyone's mail organized and to ensure no one is allowed to read anyone else's messages.

How you access your mailbox depends on what type of Internet account you have. If you have a shell account (see Chapter 5), you run all your Internet programs on the host computer. To use the mail system, you run a Unix mail program, called a USER AGENT, on the host computer. The user agent acts as the interface between you and the Internet mail system. The two most popular Unix mail programs are called **pine** and **elm**, and I will discuss them in the next section.

If you have a PPP or SLIP account (also see Chapter 5), you run Internet programs, called clients, on your own computer. These clients carry out your requests by communicating with server programs, somewhere on the Internet. (This is all explained in Chapter 2.)

Thus, with PPP or SLIP you use the mail system by running a MAIL CLIENT on your own computer. Whenever your client needs to send or receive mail, it connects to a MAIL SERVER which runs on the host computer. Together, the mail client (on your computer) and the mail server (on the host computer) provide the functionality of a user agent. The mail client and mail server communicate with one another by using a system called POST OFFICE PROTOCOL or POP. For this reason, a mail server of this type is sometimes referred to as a POP SERVER.

Here is how this all might work. Say you are using a PC with Windows to connect to an Internet host via a PPP connection over a telephone line. To use the Internet mail system, you run a Windows mail client on your own computer. Whenever you need anything, this program uses POP to connect to the mail server program on the host.

For instance, let's say you want to see if any new mail has arrived. You ask your client to check for new mail. To do so, your client connects to the mail server (on the Internet host) and asks it to check your mailbox. If there is no mail, the server tells the client your mailbox is empty. The client will then display a message, telling you there is no mail. If there is mail, the server will send it to the client, which will store it in a local mailbox on your own computer. The client will then show you a list of messages, and wait for you to indicate which one you want to read first.

Now, say you want to send a message to a friend. First, you use your mail client (on your computer) to compose the message. Once it is ready to go, your client contacts the mail server and sends the message out to the Internet host. From there, the server calls upon the transport agent to deliver the message to the appropriate Internet computer.

The nice thing about this system is how smoothly it works. Once everything is set up properly, incoming mail just appears on your own computer (as if by magic), and outgoing mail is automatically sent to the host computer for delivery anywhere in the world.

Which Mail Program Should You Use?

So now you understand how mail is moved around the Internet by transfer agents and how, to send and receive mail, you use a user agent to act as your interface. With a shell account, you use a Unix mail program. With a PPP or SLIP account, you use a mail client on your own computer to communicate with a mail server on the host where your mailbox resides. Thus, learning to use mail really means learning to use one particular mail program. The question is, which one should you use?

If you use a PPP or SLIP account, the mail program runs on your computer. For example, if you use a PC with Windows, you run a Windows mail program. If you use a Macintosh, you run a Macintosh mail program.

There are many different Internet mail clients, some of which are available for free (or as shareware). Most people tend to use whichever mail client came with their Internet software. However, in most cases, there is no reason why you can't try different programs and choose whichever one you like best. Once you are connected to the Net, you can download the various shareware programs and see which one you prefer.

In this chapter, I will show you examples from a mail program called Eudora. I like Eudora because it is both powerful and easy to use. In addition, Eudora is freeware (which means you can use it for free), and there are versions for both Windows and the Macintosh. However, everyone has their own tastes, and you might like a different program better.

If you use a shell account, your clients run on a Unix host computer, so the question is really, which Unix mail program should you use? There are a variety of such programs, but the two most popular are **pine** and **elm**, and I recommend you use one of these two.

pine is best for people who are beginners, or who do not want to spend much time learning a new program. **pine** is easy to learn and comes with its own built-in text editor (called **pico**) for composing messages. However, **pine** is excessively simple and, once you are experienced, is likely to drive you nuts.

elm is a lot more powerful, but it does require more effort to learn. In this book, I will show you how to use **pine** (Chapter 8). However, if you want to learn **elm**—and I encourage you to do so—I suggest you take a look at one of my other books, *The Unix Companion* (Osborne McGraw-Hill). This book covers both mail programs, as well as Unix in general.

HINT

You can choose whichever mail program you like, based on what is available and your particular preferences. However, since everyone on the Internet is part of the same standard mail system, the basic ideas are the same, no matter which mail program you decide to use.

INTERNET RESOURCE *Look in the catalog under Internet Resources for* **Mail Client Programs**

An Example of Moving Mail Around the Net

The rest of the chapter is devoted to teaching you the details of reading and sending mail. However, before I move on, I want to give you one more example to make sure you understand how it all works.

In this example, you are using a PC with Windows which connects to the Internet using PPP. You want to send a message to two of your friends: Peter in Holland and Eric in Germany. Peter uses a Macintosh and also connects to the Net using PPP. Eric uses a shell account by connecting to a Unix host computer. Figure 7-1 illustrates the example.

To compose the message, you use a Windows mail client on your own computer. When you compose the message, you address it to both Peter and Eric. (On the Internet, you can send the same message to as many people as you want.) Once the message is finished, you tell your program to send it on its way. Your client connects to the mail server on your Internet host and, using the POP protocol, sends your message to the server. The server then passes your message to the transport agent.

The transport agent looks at the addresses in your message and connects to the appropriate computers over the Net. First, it connects to a transport agent on the host computer in Holland that receives mail for Peter. Once the connection is made, the two transport agents use the SMTP protocol to relay the message. After the message is sent, your transport agent terminates the connection and forms a new connection with

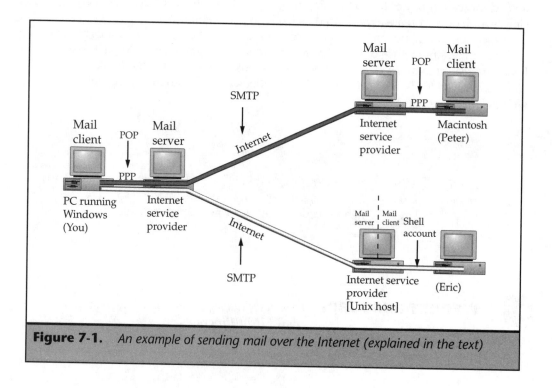

Figure 7-1. *An example of sending mail over the Internet (explained in the text)*

the transport agent on the appropriate computer in Germany. Again, the two transport agents use SMTP to relay the message. Once the message is sent, your transport agent terminates the connection. Its job is finished.

In Holland, Peter decides to check his mail. He tells his Macintosh mail client to see if any new mail has arrived. The mail client connects to the mail server on Peter's host computer and, using the POP protocol, asks the server to check Peter's mailbox. The server finds your message and (using POP) sends it to the client. Peter's Macintosh client places the message in his local mailbox (a file on the Mac) and tells him that new mail has arrived. Peter then tells the program to display the message.

Meanwhile, in Germany, Eric has logged into his shell account on a Unix host. He runs his Unix mail program which checks his mailbox and tells him new mail has arrived. Using the appropriate command, Eric tells the mail program to show him your message.

In this example, both you and Peter used a mail client on your own computer, while Eric used a Unix mail program on the host computer. The important thing to realize is that, even though you all use different computers and different programs, the mail moves smoothly and quickly.

This is the magic of the Internet and SMTP.

Understanding Mail Headers

Whichever mail program you decide to use, there are certain basic concepts you should understand. In the next few sections, I will discuss these ideas so you will have the proper background for learning how to use your particular mail program.

To start, let's talk about what a mail message looks like. All messages have two parts: a header and a body. The HEADER consists of a number of lines of special information at the beginning of the message. This information shows who sent the message, where it is going, what time the message was sent, who should receive copies, and so on. In addition, there may also be lines showing technical information, such as the route the message took as it traveled from one computer to another on its way to the destination.

The second part of the message is the BODY. This is the actual text, whatever you typed when you composed the message.

Figure 7-2 shows a typical message, containing a full header along with the body. Most mail programs will not show you the entire header unless you ask to see it. They will suppress some of the more technical lines as you don't normally want to see them. However, in this example, I have included all the lines so you can see what the complete message looks like.

Mail headers contain a number of standard and non-standard lines, each one containing a particular piece of information. The format of the header may vary on your system, but the general idea will be the same. It is important to understand the most important parts of a header, so let's take a look at the message in Figure 7-2, one line at a time.

```
From harley@nipper.ucsb.edu Thu Dec 21 13:00:56 1995
Return-Path: <harley@nipper.ucsb.edu>
Received: from hub.ucsb.edu by mail.princess.com
    with id QAA01329 SMTP for <melissa@misty.princess.com>
    on Thu, 21 Dec 1995 13:01:10 -0800
Received: from mail.princess.com by misty.princess.com
    with id NAA02881 SMTP
    on Thu, 21 Dec 1995 13:01:10 -0800
Date: Thu Dec 21 13:00:56 1995 -0800 (PST)
From: "Harley Hahn" <harley@nipper.ucsb.edu>
Message-Id: <9504057997.AA799715495@nipper.ucsb.edu>
X-Mailer: Windows Eudora Version 1.4.4
To: melissa@princess.com
Cc: tln@princess,com, randolph@princess.com
Subject: Do you want free money?

They will be giving free money away today at 3 PM.
Can you get the day off?
--Harley
===========================================================
Harley Hahn                         harley@nipper.ucsb.edu
                (202) 456-1414
===========================================================
```

Figure 7-2.   *A typical mail message, showing the full header*

All messages start with a **From:** line showing who sent the message. In our example, the message was sent by userid **harley@nipper.ucsb.edu**. We also see that the message was sent on Thursday, December 21, 1995 at 1:00 PM and 56 seconds. Notice that Unix uses a 24-hour clock, so that 1:00 PM is written as **13:00**.

The rest of the lines do not necessarily come in the same order, nor will they always be present. It depends on how the sending and receiving mail systems are configured and on what options are set with your particular mail program. At the bare minimum, you will always see an initial **From:** line, a **Date:** line, and a **Subject:** line.

In our example, the **From:** line is followed by a **Return-Path:** line. This tells your mail program where to send a reply should you choose to respond to the message.

The following two lines are **Received:** lines. These lines trace the route that the message followed as it was being delivered. **Received:** lines are often long and, as in this example, are usually broken into several parts. So, even though you see six lines in the header (in this example), logically, there are only two long **Received:** lines.

You can usually ignore these lines. However, if you take a moment to look closely, you may see some interesting information. (Well, if you are a nerd it will be interesting.)

Moving on, we see the **Date:** line. This shows the time and the date that the message was sent. Notice the notation **-0800 (PST)** at the end of the line. This is an important convention you should understand.

Since the Internet spans the globe, its users are in many different time zones. It is often important to know what time a message was sent, but the time you see in the header might be confusing. Suppose, for example, that you are in Vienna, Austria, and you receive a message from someone in California. The time on the message is **13:00:56**. How do you know if this is California time or Austrian time?

This same problem arises in many situations so, as a solution, the Internet has adopted Greenwich Mean Time as a standard. Sometimes you will see this written as GMT. You may also see it referred to as Universal Time or UT (which is the newer, more official name). Whatever you see, just remember that whenever a standard reference time is needed, GMT is used.

The line in the example above indicates that a local time is being used but that that local time is 8 hours less than GMT. In other words, the message was sent at 1:00 PM local time, which is 9:00 PM GMT.

Aside from GMT or UT, there are other common abbreviations you will see in North America. These names refer to local North American time zones and are shown in Figure 7-3.

To continue our discussion, the next header line is another **From:** line. This shows extra information about the userid that sent the message. In this case, we can see that this userid is registered to Harley Hahn. This means that either Harley, or someone using his account, sent the message.

Abbreviation	Time Zone
UT	Universal Time (same as **GMT**)
GMT	Greenwich Mean Time
EST	Eastern Standard Time
EDT	Eastern Daylight Time
CST	Central Standard Time
CDT	Central Daylight Time
MST	Mountain Standard Time
MDT	Mountain Daylight Time
PST	Pacific Standard Time
PDT	Pacific Daylight Time

Figure 7-3. *Summary of time zone names*

This is followed by a **Message-ID:** line. Each message that is sent over the Internet is given a unique identification tag. The tag is used internally by the software; you can ignore it.

Next, there is an **X-Mailer:** line. In general, the characters "**X-**" indicate a non-standard header line inserted by the mail program. In this case, the mail program inserted a line identifying itself (version 1.4.4 of the Windows Eudora program). From time to time, you will see an **X-Mailer:** line, although not all mail programs put it in. You may also see other "**X-**" lines, which you can safely ignore.

Following this, we see the **To:** line. This shows the userid to whom the message was addressed. If you are reading a message that was sent to you, this line will contain your address. If the message was also sent to other people, their addresses will appear on this line as well.

The **Cc:** line shows any userids who are to receive copies of this message. (I will discuss this in more detail later in the chapter. Basically, each userid in the **To:** or **Cc:** lines will receive an identical copy of the message.)

Finally, the **Subject:** line shows the subject of the message. This is a short description that is typed by the person who composed the message. If the subject starts with the letters **Re:**, it indicates the message is a response to a previous message. For example, say that you send a friend a message with the following subject:

```
Subject: Do you want free money?
```

If your friend uses his mail program to send a reply to you, the program will automatically insert the characters **Re:** at the beginning of the **Subject:** line. The **Subject:** line of the message you get back will look like this:

```
Subject: Re: Do you want free money?
```

Think of **Re:** as meaning "This is a reply to the previous message with the subject..."

HINT

When you compose a message, give some thought to the subject. At the destination, your recipient's mail program will show him a summary of all the messages waiting to be read. He will probably see the subject of each message, along with the name of the sender.

Some people receive a great deal of mail and, if you want to get their attention, it behooves you to use a short, but intriguing subject. Indeed, some busy people will simply ignore mail that looks unimportant. This is especially true with overworked system administrators who may literally receive more than 100 messages a day.

In general, it is a good idea to be specific in the **Subject:** line. For example, a message with a subject like **"Need to recover lost payroll files"** is more likely to be read immediately than a message with the subject **"Possible problem"**.

In this section, I have covered the most important header lines you are likely to encounter. However, you should understand there is considerable variation in how the lines may be constructed. Moreover, there are other types of header lines that I did not describe, but which you can usually ignore.

HINT

Some mail programs will not show you the full header unless you specifically ask for it. Most of the time, this is okay as you really only need to pay attention to the **From:, Date:, To:, Cc:** and **Subject:** lines.

However, if one of your messages is returned as being undeliverable, you should tell your mail program to show you the entire header. Somewhere along the line, some computer will have inserted a message telling you what went wrong.

Signatures

A SIGNATURE is a group of lines that is automatically appended to the end of every message you send. The custom is for you to use your signature to hold information about yourself. For example, here is a signature that contains a name, a mail address and a phone number. Some people include a postal address, fax number, description of their organization, job title, and so on.

```
===========================================================
Harley Hahn                        harley@nipper.ucsb.edu
        (202) 456-1414
===========================================================
```

Many people use their signatures to be creative. For example, people will often include a witty saying or a small picture drawn with text characters. For instance:

```
=====================        !___!        =======================
Harley Hahn                 / 0 0 \       If growing up was easy,
harley@nipper.ucsb.edu      \  ¦  /       everyone would do it.
=====================        \---/        =======================
```

How do you arrange for your signature to be added to the end of your messages? It depends on what type of program you use. If you use a mail client on a PC or Macintosh (via a PPP or SLIP connection), your program will have some way for you to specify a signature. For example, Eudora allows you to create a signature which it saves for you and lets you change whenever you want. Each time you send a message, the mail program will automatically insert your signature at the end of the message.

If you use a Unix computer (via a shell account), you must use a text editor to create a file named `.signature` in your home directory. (Your home directory is the place set aside for you to store your files.) Whenever you send a message, your mail program will look for a `.signature` file. If it is there, the mail program will automatically append its contents to the end of your message.

(Notice that the name of this file begins with a `.` [period] character. There is a reason for this. Within Unix, you use the `ls` command to display a list of your files. When you do so, names beginning with a `.` character are not listed unless you ask for them specifically by using the `-a` [all files] option. Files that are created to provide a standard function, such as the signature file, will often have names that start with a `.` character and are called DOTFILES. Thus, each time you list your files with `ls`, you won't have to look at the names of your dotfiles. If you want more information about Unix files or mail programs, see my book *The Unix Companion*, published by Osborne McGraw-Hill.)

HINT

As you might imagine, there are a great many creative people who spend a long time working on their signatures, and it is not hard to come up with an elaborate multi-line creation. However, when you receive mail repeatedly from a particular person, it is irritating to have to read the same long signature every time he or she sends you a message. For this reason, it is considered polite to limit your signature to four lines.

Although someone may think it is cool to use a 15-line signature with drawings of boats and seagulls (because he wants everyone in the world to know he lives near the ocean), such extravaganzas are annoying and are considered ill mannered.

It is a real challenge to be creative in a small number of lines. Be polite and keep your signature short.

Mail Addresses

I discussed addresses in detail in Chapter 6. In this section, I will talk a little more about how to specify addresses when you send mail.

To start, I will remind you that, when you see the word "mail", it always means electronic mail, and the word "address" always refers to an Internet address. On those rare occasions when it is necessary to talk about regular post office mail, the reference will be explicit. Thus, if someone on the Net asks "What is your address?", tell him or her your electronic address.

What's in a Name?

Snail Mail

Sometimes, you will see post office mail referred to facetiously as SNAIL MAIL. For example, it is common for people who send articles to Usenet discussion groups to put their street address at the end of the article. You will often see the words "Snail Mail:" followed by a postal address. The name, of course, refers to the fact that post office mail is much slower than Internet mail.

The most common type of address is the full Internet address I discussed in Chapter 6. Here is an example:

```
melissa@misty.acme.com
```

If the recipient is within your local network, you can often leave out part of the address. For example, say your address is **harley@nipper.acme.com** and you are mailing to a friend whose computer is on the same network. Your friend's address is **melissa@misty.acme.com**. You are usually safe in leaving off the part of the address you both have in common: that is, the part of the address describing your local network. So, in this case, you could use:

```
melissa@misty
```

The mail software should be able to figure out this is a local address and deliver the message properly. If you have a problem, you may have to use the full address.

If the person you are sending mail to is on the same computer as you, it is possible to leave out the computer name entirely and just use the userid. For example, if your address is **wendy@misty.acme.com** and you want to send mail to **melissa@misty.acme.com**, you can use:

```
melissa
```

In case you have problems, every Internet system has a userid named **postmaster** to whom you can send queries. For example, say you have trouble finding out the address of someone who uses a computer named `misty.acme.com`. You can send a message asking for the person's mail address to:

`postmaster@misty.acme.com`

HINT

If you have a problem with mail not reaching its destination, try the following (in this order):

1) Check the spelling of the address.
2) Specify the entire address.
3) If the mail is returned to you, examine the full header for error messages.
4) Call the person on the phone and confirm his or her address.
5) Ask an experienced person for help.
6) If all else fails, send a query to the `postmaster` userid.

Sending Mail

(Note: In the next few sections, I will explain how to send and process mail using a mail client program running on your own computer. This will be the case if you use a PPP or SLIP account. If you use a shell account, you will run a Unix mail program on the Unix host. The main ideas will be the same, so you should read through the rest of this chapter anyway. But to learn how to use a Unix mail program, read Chapter 8, in which I explain how to use `pine`.)

To send mail, you need to compose a message, and then tell your mail program (the mail client) to deliver it. Most programs are designed so the whole process is one smooth procedure. After you are finished composing the message, you either press a key, or use your mouse to click on a button or select a menu item. (The details, of course, depend on your particular program.) Your mail client will then contact the mail server on your Internet host and send the message on its way.

There are several ways in which your mail client can handle outgoing mail. First, it might save all your outgoing messages in a QUEUE (that is, a waiting area). Then, at a particular time, your client will contact the mail server and send all the outgoing mail at once. This might happen at regular intervals (say, every half hour). Alternatively, your program might wait until you tell it to send the mail, or until the next time it happens to contact the server to check for new mail. Finally, your program might send each new message immediately, as soon as it is ready.

HINT

Your mail program will have options you can set to tell it when outgoing mail should be sent to the server. If your Internet connection is always available, you may want to have your mail client send all new messages right away. However, if you are paying for Internet or telephone service by the hour or by the minute, it makes more sense to compose all your messages offline (that is, while you are not connected), and then connect for a brief time to send everything at once.

Sending a message means (1) filling out the header, and (2) typing the body of the message. Your program will fill out most of the header lines for you. You will only have to specify the address of the recipient, the subject of the message, and any addresses to which you want to send copies. Figure 7-4 shows what Eudora looks like

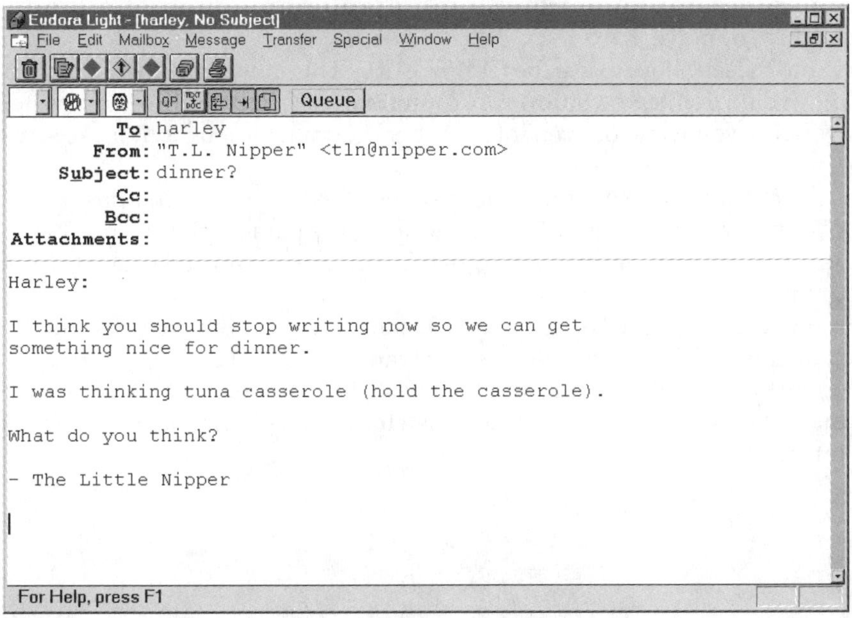

Figure 7-4. *Composing a message with Eudora*

as you compose a message. The header is on the top part of the window, while the bottom part is where you type the actual message (the body).

To make it easy to specify an address, your mail program allows you to maintain a list of names and addresses called an ADDRESS BOOK. The name may differ from one program to another—in Eudora, for example, it is referred to as a list of "nicknames"—but the idea is the same. You can keep a permanent list of all the people to whom you might write, along with their Internet addresses. Then, whenever you need to specify an address, you can simply select it from the list.

There are two ways to get addresses into your address book. First, if someone gives you his or her address, you can manually type it into the address book. Second, whenever you read a message, you can tell your program to copy the address of the person who sent the message right into your address book. This is not only fast, it also ensures the address will be copied correctly with no typing mistakes.

While you are composing a message, there will be a number of key combinations and menu items you can use to edit and to make corrections. These facilities will vary, of course, depending on your particular program. Still, most programs follow the general rules for the system on which they run. For example, Windows and Macintosh programs allow you to use your mouse to select a particular segment of text and then delete it, copy it, or move it.

Make sure to learn how to use the CLIPBOARD. This is an area to which you can copy or move data from any window. Once data is in the clipboard, you can paste it into any window you want, or even into another program (as long as it make sense to do so).

Using the clipboard allows you to move or copy text as you are composing a message. For instance, you may want to move an entire paragraph from one place to another. You can also find information from a different program and bring it into your mail program.

For example, say you are looking at a Web site with your web program, and you encounter an interesting mailing address you want to use. You can copy it to the clipboard, start your mail program, and then paste the address right into a message. Or, you can call up your address book and save the address permanently by pasting it directly into the book.

⚑ HINT

Take some time and teach yourself how to use all the editing keys and menu items for your particular program. There will be shortcuts for common editing functions and, if you don't learn how to use them, you will end up wasting a lot of time. For example, you might end up pressing BACKSPACE 45 times in a row rather than simply selecting a line of text and pressing DELETE.

Sending Copies of a Message

Earlier in the chapter, we saw a **Cc:** line in the header of a message. Here is the actual line:

```
Cc: tln@princess.com, randolph@princess.com
```

It indicates that a copy of the message should be sent, not only to the principal recipient, but to two other userids (**tln@princess.com** and **randolph@princess.com**).

When you compose a message, your mail program will allow you to specify that copies of the message should go to other people. For example, you may want to send a message to your boss, with a copy to his or her assistants. Some people also send copies to themselves so they can keep an archive of all their outgoing mail. (Most programs can be set up to save copies of outgoing mail automatically, so if you really want to save all your mail, you won't have to send copies to yourself.)

HINT

The mail system allows you to send messages to more than one recipient by specifying more than one address in the **To:** line. Alternatively, you can send a message to one person only with copies to other people. For example, you could send a message to userids **curly**, **larry** and **moe**:

```
To: curly, larry, moe
```

or you could send the message to **curly**, with copies to **larry** and **moe**:

```
To: curly
Cc: larry, moe
```

What is the difference? As far as the mail system is concerned, the end result is the same: all three people get the same message. However, you may find that the politics and personalities of the people involved should be considered. If all three people are friends of yours, go ahead and address the message to all of them. However, if **curly** is the big boss and **larry** and **moe** are his assistants, it might be more diplomatic to send the message to **curly** with copies to the others.

Remember, when the messages are delivered, all three people will be able to look at the header and see who was the principal recipient and who received the "copies".

There are two types of copies, regular copies and blind copies. A BLIND COPY is a secret copy that no one else knows about except the person who sent the message. For example, say you are writing an important proposal. You want to send a copy to your boss, whose address is **melissa@princess.com**, and to her two assistants whose addresses are the ones above. However, you also want to send a secret copy to your best friend, whose address is **wendy@muffin.com**. All you have to do is tell your mail program to send a blind copy to that address.

The exact details of sending a regular or blind copy depend on which program you are using. Regardless, your program will make sure the outgoing message contains the appropriate header lines. In this case, they would be:

```
To: melissa@princess.com
Cc: tln@princess.com, randolph@princess.com
Bcc: wendy@muffin.com
```

When the message is delivered, the **Bcc:** line will have been removed automatically. Thus, no one will ever know that a blind copy was sent (except you and the recipient of the blind copy).

HINT

When you receive a message, there is no guarantee that other people have not received blind copies; nor is there any way for you to find out if this was the case. Even if you know that you received a blind copy, you can't tell whether or not anyone else also received one.

So be careful. Even paranoids have real enemies.

What's in a Name?

Cc, Bcc

A long time ago, before there were copy machines and computers, there was only one easy way to send a copy of a typewritten letter to someone: You had to use carbon paper to make an extra copy as you typed the letter. You would send the original copy to the principal recipient and the "carbon copy" to the second person. (In addition, most business people made at least one extra carbon copy for their files.)

When a carbon copy was sent to somebody (say Ben Dover), a notation would be made in the bottom left-hand corner of the first page:

```
cc: Ben Dover
```

This would tell the person reading the letter that Ben Dover also received a copy.

It has been a long time since carbon paper has been used regularly to make copies. Still, the custom is to use **Cc:** in the header to refer to a copy of a message. When the idea of blind copies was invented, the notation was extended to **Bcc:**.

Reading Mail

Before I talk about reading mail, I want to review how new mail gets to your computer. When people send you mail, it does not go right to your computer. After all, you may not be connected to the Internet 24 hours a day. Rather, the messages are stored in a mailbox on your Internet host computer where they wait to be picked up.

To read the mail, you use a mail client program on your own computer. This client contacts the mail server on the Internet host and asks it to check your mailbox for new mail. If there is new mail, the server will send it to the client which will store it in a local mailbox on your computer. Once your client has determined that the messages have arrived intact, it will tell the server to delete them from the host mailbox. The client will then display a summary of the messages in your local mailbox.

Figure 7-5 shows what the message summary looks like with Eudora. Your program may not look identical, but the general idea will be the same. You will see a one-line summary for each message, probably showing the subject of the message, the time and date it was sent, and the name of the person who sent it. You may also see some indication of how big the actual message is.

To read a message, all you need to do is select it. The details may vary depending on your program, but usually you can either move to it and press ENTER, or double-click on it with the mouse. After you have read a message, you should dispose

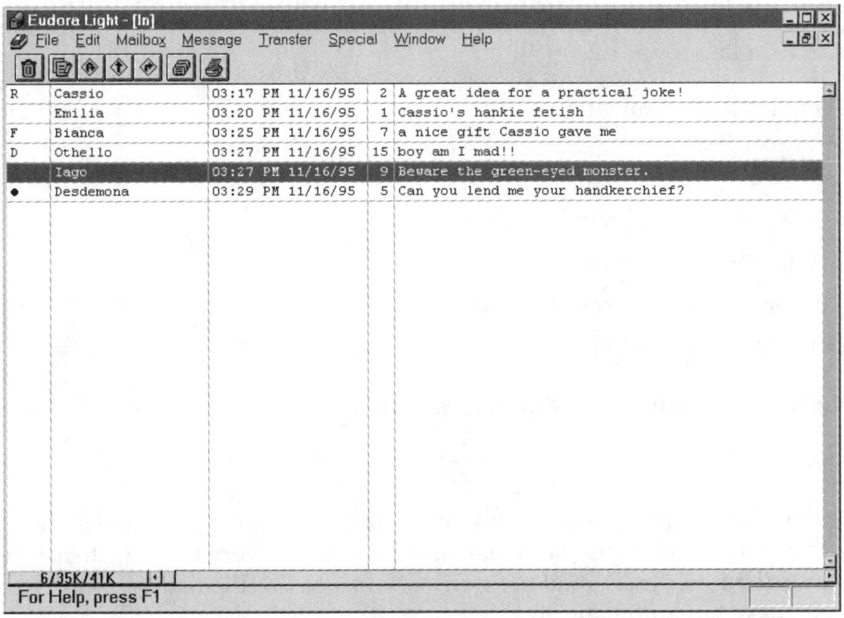

Figure 7-5.   *A summary of incoming mail with Eudora*

of it in some way. Broadly speaking, you have two choices. You can either delete the message, or you can save it. I will discuss these options in the next section.

In addition, you can also send a copy of the message to someone else. The most common way is to reply back to the sender, by including the original message and adding some comments of your own. However, you can also send the message, with or without new comments, to a third person. I will explain how this all works later in the chapter. However, before I do, I would like to take a few moments to talk about managing your mail.

Hints for Managing Your Mail

Once you build up a correspondence, it doesn't take long before you have more messages than you have time to deal with. Many people routinely ignore (or fail to delete) messages, with the result that their mailboxes become clogged past the point of no return.

Most mail programs recognize this problem and have features to help you deal with large amounts of mail. However, the secret of maintaining control over your mailbox is not really what program you use. The secret is to employ a practical approach to managing your mail. All you need to do is use the following guidelines:

- Look at each message only once.
- Reply or save immediately.
- Before you move on to the next message, delete the one you have just read.

Finally, the most important rule of all:

- When in doubt, throw it out.

Thus, a typical session of reading mail should look like this:

1. Start your mail program.
2. Display the first message.
3. Save or reply to the message as you wish.
4. Delete the message and display the next one.

Repeat steps 3 and 4 until all your messages have been read.

5. Quit the mail program.

There is a certain type of person who saves every message that arrives in his or her mailbox. Even worse, some people actually save a copy of every message they send to someone else. (Unfortunately, mail programs encourage this by making it easy to save all outgoing messages automatically.)

Whatever you do, please don't turn into one of these people. Chances are you will rarely have the time or inclination to go through your old messages. All that will happen is that you will amass an ever-growing accumulation of forgotten messages, which you will never have the nerve to delete. Much better to, once in a while, save an important message deliberately and throw away the rest as a matter of course. There is really no need to save everything.

HINT

If you never lie, you will never have to remember what you said.

Replying to a Message

Whenever you read a new message, the first thing you will do is decide if you want to REPLY to it. If you do, your mail program will handle all the details for you. It will create a brand new message already addressed to the person who sent you the original message. (Your mail program will extract the return address from the header of the original message.)

When you reply to a message, you should not assume the person who sent the message remembers every word he or she wrote. Many people send and receive so many messages that they are easily confused when they receive a reply that contains only an oblique reference to an earlier comment. For example, what you would think if you received the following message?

```
Okay, but what about parsnips instead?
I did.  She says she's too busy.
```

Imagine you are overwhelmed with work and you see this message along with 45 others in your mailbox. What does it mean? In this case, the original message was a long note from a friend. At the end of the note were the lines:

```
I am planning a party for next Saturday.
Do you think you will be able to bring some groatcakes?
If you need a lift, ask Wendy to drive you.
```

Wouldn't it have been a lot nicer if the person had included that part of the original message? For example, a better reply would have been:

```
> I am planning a party for next Saturday.
> Do you think you will be able to bring some groatcakes?

Okay, but what about parsnips instead?

> If you need a lift, ask Wendy to drive you.

I did.  She says she's too busy.
```

Although you might think it is easy for everyone to remember every word they write, it is just not so. I strongly encourage you to always include the original message when you compose a reply, and edit out those parts that are irrelevant.

To help you, the mail program will preface each line of the original message with a > (greater-than sign). This is a standard convention that everyone will understand. Thus, when you start typing your reply, you will already have the original message included, each line being marked by a > character. Now all you have to do is delete the superfluous lines and insert new comments as you wish.

Figure 7-6 shows a reply message ready to be edited with Eudora. Notice two things: the original message has been included and marked with > characters, and the characters **Re:** have been inserted at the beginning of the **Subject:** line. This shows that the message is in reply to a previous message.

Forwarding and Bouncing Mail

From time to time, you may want to mail someone a copy of a message you have received. In such cases, you have two choices.

First, you can FORWARD the message: that is, you can send someone a copy along with your own comments. Your mail program helps you do this by creating a new message addressed to that person. Within the new message, your program will copy

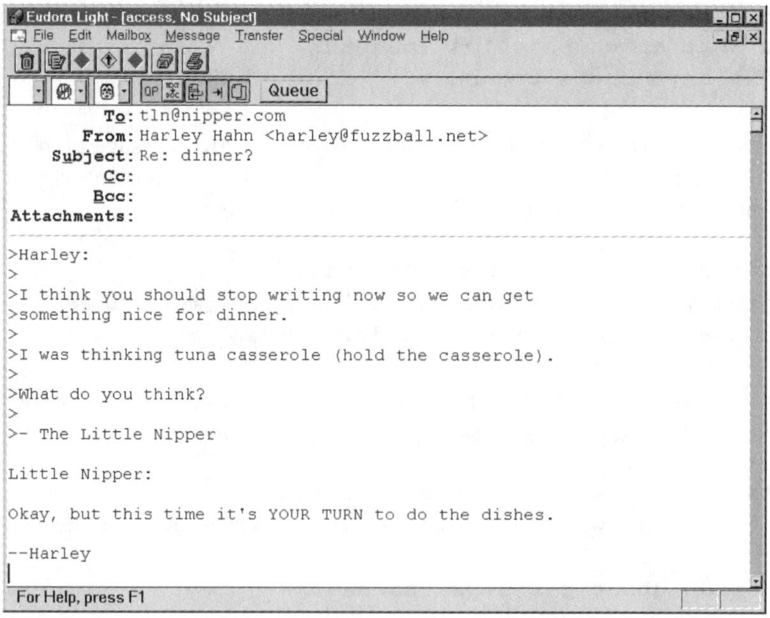

Figure 7-6. *Replying to a message with Eudora*

all the text of the old message. You can then edit it in whatever manner you want before sending it. This allows you to receive a message, insert some comments of your own, and then send the whole thing to someone else.

Alternatively, you can BOUNCE the message to someone: that is, you can send an identical copy without editing it in any way. If all you want to do is send a copy to someone else, bouncing is faster for you than forwarding, because you don't have to edit the message. (Note: Some mail programs use the term REDIRECT rather than "bounce".)

When you receive a forwarded message, it is obvious where it came from. For one thing, the sender's mail program will insert a special character at the beginning of each line of text from the old message. Usually, this will be a > (greater-than) character. Thus, when you read a message in which many of the lines begin with a > character, you can tell that those lines were quoted from a previous message. In addition, the **From:** line will have the address of the person who forwarded the message, not that of the original person. Finally, some mail programs will add a designation like **(fwd)** to the **Subject:** line to let you know you are looking at a forwarded message.

When you receive a bounced message, it will look as if it was sent by the original person, not by the person who did the bouncing. Some mail programs will change the header to indicate the message has been bounced to you. Even so, unless you look closely, you may not notice. And, even more confusing, certain programs will let you change a message before you bounce it to someone else.

Thus, you must be careful. The original person may have no idea you received a copy of the message. And if you reply to it, your reply will go to the original person, not the bouncer. If you have any doubt as to whether or not a message is bounced, take a look at the full header. Within it, there will be enough information to figure out where the message originated.

HINT

Most mail programs do not show you the full header unless you specifically ask for it. Thus, it is easy to assume you are the original recipient of a message which was, in reality, bounced to you by someone else.

For this reason, you should be especially careful before sending a reply that is confidential or personal. Imagine how you would feel if a friend bounced you a love letter from one of his secret admirers, and you replied to it directly, thinking that it was intended for you.

Many people love to share, and they will merrily bounce mail all over the place without telling anybody. Be careful: This happens a lot more than most people imagine, and there is no way for you to know if someone has bounced (or forwarded) one of your messages. I suggest you refrain from using electronic mail for anything that is highly personal or secret.

HINT

If you are ever tempted to be intimate within a mail message, just remember you are only one bounce away from sharing everything with the rest of the world.

HINT

If you are a major celebrity, never send a message to anyone who knows the electronic mail address of the *National Enquirer*.

How Mail Is Stored (Folders)

There will be times when you will want to keep certain messages for future reference. To help you, your mail program allows you to save messages into FOLDERS. A folder is a collection of messages with a particular name. You may want to keep a separate folder for each person with whom you correspond. When you decide to keep a message from someone, you can save it to his or her folder. Alternatively, you might use a different folder for various projects or topics.

Your mail program makes it easy to create and manipulate folders. You can save messages to specific folders and, whenever you want, open those folders and re-read the messages.

However, if you were to look inside a folder, you would not see anything special. A folder is simply a file containing one or more messages. Indeed, if you do look directly into a folder (with some type of word processor or editor), all you will see is one message after another, containing line after line of text. The reason a folder is easier to read with a mail program is the program will look for the **From:** lines at the beginning of each message. This allows the program to separate the various messages and present them to you in a readable manner.

Generally speaking, working with folders is easy. You create them when you need them and delete them when they become unnecessary. If a folder becomes too large and unwieldy, you can organize it better by creating new, smaller folders and rearranging the messages. For example, if you have a folder named "Friends" to hold messages from your friends, you may decide that it is better to have a separate folder for each friend. (Personally, my advice would be to throw out all the old messages, rather than rearranging them.)

The name "folder" is used because it allows you to think of a regular file folder in which you might store separate pieces of paper. However, there is some room for confusion, because the word "folder" is also used in another way.

Outside of the mail program, your operating system (Windows, MacOS or OS/2) allows you to organize files into collections. Often such collections are called directories but, on some systems, they are also called folders.

This means there are two meanings of the word "folder", so don't be confused. In both cases, a folder contains other objects. However, within your mail program, a folder is a single file containing messages. Outside of your mail program, within the operating system, a folder is a directory: a collection of files or even other folders.

The Difference Between Text and Binary Data

In the next section, I will discuss how you can use the Internet mail system to send and receive all types of data—pictures, sound recordings, and so on—and not just simple text. However, before I approach this topic, I need to take a moment and explain to you how computer people classify different types of information.

The term DATA refers to any type of information that might be stored or processed by a computer. It is helpful to consider data as being of one of two basic types: text and binary data.

TEXT consists of ordinary characters: letters, numbers, punctuation and so on. Special characters, such as the space and tab, are also considered to be text. An example of text is a message that you might type at your keyboard and mail to a friend. Within this chapter, all of the data that we have looked at so far is text.

A file that contains such data is called a TEXT FILE. Another name for such a file is an ASCII FILE. (The name comes from the ASCII CODE, a specification that defines how all the various characters are represented as computer data. ASCII stands for "American Standard Code for Information Interchange". I will not go into the details here. If you want more technical information, see my book *The Unix Companion* (Osborne McGraw-Hill).

Any data that is not simple text is referred to as BINARY data. An example of binary data is a file that contains a picture. Such a file does not contain characters. Rather, it contains information that represents the many small dots that make up the image. A file that contains binary data is called a BINARY FILE.

Where does the name "binary" come from? I will show you by means of an example. Imagine an image that you might display on your computer screen. The image consists of many tiny dots. For the sake of this example, let us say that each dot is either black or white.

You might wonder, how are such images stored in files? And, is it possible to mail such a file to a friend so he or she can display the same image on his computer?

A binary file that stores a picture does not contain the actual image in the way that a photograph album might hold a picture. Rather, the binary file stores the data necessary to recreate the image. Here is how it works.

Each individual dot is encoded as one of two numbers, either a **0** or a **1**. In our example, a **0** might represent a white dot; a **1** might represent a black dot. In other words, a file that contains an image actually consists of a long string of **0**s and **1**s. The program that displays the image must be able to read and understand this type of data in order to recreate the picture on your screen.

In computer science terms, an element that can contain either one of two values—such as **0** or **1**—is called a BIT. (The name is an abbreviation for "binary digit".) In technical terms, we can say that our file contains a large number of bits, all of which have a value of either **0** or **1**. Each of these bits represents either a black dot or a white dot.

In this context, the word "binary" indicates that only two different values are used. In computer terms, any data that does not consist of characters and must be represented by sequences of bits is called "binary data".

My example is, of course, simplified to the level of a normal human being. Computer scientists (and other related fauna) recognize many different types of bit patterns and, hence, many different types of binary data. For instance, to store color pictures, you would need to use the **0**s and **1**s differently. To store sound recordings, you need to use yet another method of using **0**s and **1**s.

The important idea is that it is relatively simple for a program to work with text data. With binary data, the information consists of more than simple characters, and manipulating the data becomes more complex.

All Internet mail programs can send and receive textual data: messages you can type at your keyboard and display on your screen as individual characters. However, when it comes to sending binary data, a special system is needed. The special system is called Mime, and I will discuss it in the next section.

HINT

When you transfer data from one computer to another, there will be times when it is necessary to know whether you are working with text or binary data. As a general rule, data consisting only of ordinary characters is text; anything else is binary data. However, there are times when you may be fooled.

It is obvious that a file that holds a picture or a sound recording is a binary file, since such information cannot be represented by ordinary characters. What you may not know is that many common computer tools—such as word processors and spreadsheet programs—also store data as binary files. Although the information may look like characters when it is on your screen, the program puts in special non-character codes when it stores the data in a file. For example, a word processor will use such codes to indicate italics or boldface words. Thus, files such as word processing documents or spreadsheets are stored in a special format and are properly classed as binary files.

sing Mime to Mail Binary Data as an Attachment

In the last section, I explained that binary files contain data that does not consist of simple text. There is a way to mail such files using the Internet mail system. However, it will only work if the mail programs at each end are set up to handle binary data.

In Chapter 2, I explained how the Internet uses a large family of protocols to ensure all the different types of computers and programs can work together. Each protocol is a set of rules and specifications that describes how something should be done. For example, SMTP (Simple Mail Transfer Protocol) describes how mail is transported. Using SMTP, Internet computers can send and receive messages that consist of text.

To enable people to send binary data, another protocol, named MIME, was developed. The name stands for "Multipurpose Internet Mail Extensions". A system using Mime can include binary data along with a regular message. The whole thing is then transported (using SMTP) to the destination computer. At the other end, another Mime system will make the binary data available to the recipient. Of course, everything is automatic so you don't need to care about any of the details.

In order to send or receive binary data, all you need is a mail program that supports Mime. I say this rather glibly but, the fact is, some mail programs cannot make full use of Mime. This is the case, for example, with some of the Unix-based mail programs such as **elm**, which I mentioned earlier in the chapter. However, **elm** is really only used by people with shell accounts. If you have a PPP or SLIP account (see Chapter 5), you will be running a mail program on your own computer and virtually all such programs support Mime.

HINT

If you use a shell account, you may prefer to use **elm** instead of **pine** as your Unix mail program. This is fine and, indeed, I prefer **elm** myself. You will find that **elm** is good at receiving Mime-transported files, but it is not good at sending such files. Thus, my advice is to use **pine** when you need to send files with Mime, and use **elm** for everything else.

Strictly speaking, the Internet mail system can only transport text data, not binary data. This means that, in order to mail a binary file, it must first be converted to a text file. Here is how it works.

A mail program sends a file by ATTACHING it to a message. This means that the file is joined to a regular message and the whole thing is mailed as a complete package. At the other end, the recipient's mail program separates the file from the message. When you send a file in this way, it is referred to as an ATTACHMENT.

To mail a file, all you need to do is tell your mail program that you want to attach the file to a message. You compose the message in the regular manner—typing the address, subject, and so on—but you also specify the name of the file to be attached. Your mail program will read this file and use a special procedure (which is part of Mime) to encode the information in the file as textual characters. It is this encoded data that is attached to the message and mailed to the recipient. (Remember, the Internet mail system can only handle textual data.)

If you were to look at this data, you would see actual characters, but the whole thing would look like gibberish. However, at the other end, the mail program recognizes the data as being an attachment. As long as the program understands Mime, it can decode the data and reconstruct the original file. In this way, you can mail anything to anyone on the Internet.

To attach a file to a message, you do not need to understand how Mime works (although it is interesting). All you need is a Mime-aware mail program to take care of the details. Moreover, it doesn't matter if you and the other person are using different mail programs. All that is necessary is that both programs support Mime.

HINT

If you do not have access to Mime, there is another way to send a binary file via the mail system. You can use a program named **uuencode** to encode the binary data as text. You can then mail this text as part of a regular message. At the other end, the recipient can take the text and, using a program named **uudecode**, convert it back to its original binary format.

The original **uuencode** and **uudecode** were Unix programs, part of the UUCP system I mentioned in Chapter 6, and are still available on all Unix computers. Today, however, versions of both these programs are also available on other systems such as DOS and Windows.

An alternative to **uuencode** and **uudecode** is another pair of programs, **mpack** and **munpack**. (The names stand for "Mime pack" and "Mime unpack".) If these programs are available on your system, you can use them to send and receive Mime-encoded files.

Hints for Practicing Safe Mail

If you have never used electronic mail, it may take you a while to appreciate how different it is from regular mail and from talking on the telephone. To smooth the way, here are a few hints to make life easier.

1. Assume there is no privacy.

Do not send messages that, within the bounds of reason, you would not want everyone to see. Thus, it is a good idea to avoid intimate love letters, temperamental tirades, mean-spirited insults, and so on.

Most mail programs make it easy to forward or bounce a message to another person. Some people love to bounce mail, just as some people like to gossip. So do not assume a message is private just because you send a message to only one person.

HINT

When it comes to private matters, such as love letters, you will find that it is often more romantic—and much safer—to avoid the Internet and send messages by more traditional means (such as using your employer's Federal Express number).

2. Do not assume that a deleted message cannot be restored.

More than likely, the person who manages your Internet host computer (where your mailbox resides) does regular backups of the file system. If you delete a sensitive message on Tuesday, chances are it was preserved as part of the regular Monday night backup. Unix does not have a paper shredder.

3. Be careful what you promise.

It is the nature of electronic mail that people take messages they receive more seriously than messages they send. Because it is so simple to send a quick note anywhere in the world, it is easy to forget how permanent such a note can be.

As a general rule, do not send a message you would not want to see a year from now. It is easy for someone to save one of your messages in a file and then, when you least expect it, dredge it up again. Never let yourself get in a position where someone can say to you, "What do you mean you are too busy to help me paint my house? I have a message right here, which you sent me four years ago, in which you specifically told me to ask if I ever needed any help."

4. Be polite and keep your temper.

One day, someone will send you a stupid message that really bothers you. When this happens, resist the temptation to lash out by sending back an abusive or sarcastic response. Force yourself to wait at least one day before replying to the message.

This is especially important with people you have not met in person and whose motivations may not be clear. It is easy to get angry and send an immediate reply but, I promise you, if you can wait even a single day, you will have better judgment. Remember, once a message is on its way, there is no way to get it back, even if the person has not yet read it.

5. Remember that many Internet people are foreigners.

When you send mail to another country, remind yourself that many people speak English as a second language. If you write metaphorically or use slang, it is easy for someone from another culture to misinterpret what you are saying.

> **HINT**
>
> Sarcasm and irony do not travel well across national boundaries.

Smileys

Before I finish talking about mail, there is one last idea I would like to explain. Electronic mail is a lot like being with someone in person or talking on the telephone. Mail is quick, simple and usually informal. Moreover, electronic messages tend to have a sense of immediacy missing in other types of correspondence. However, there is something missing. When you send mail on the Internet, the other person does not hear the inflections or personality in your voice; nor does he see your facial expressions or your body language.

Because of this, you will find that it is all too easy to misinterpret the informality of the system and insult someone accidentally. A comment which you mean to be humorous might be taken literally and cause offense. For this reason, there is a convention that whenever you write something in jest that might be misunderstood, you should include a SMILEY at the end of the remark.

A smiley is a tiny picture of a smiling face, drawn with punctuation characters. The basic smiley consists of three characters: a colon, a minus sign, and a right parenthesis. It looks like this:

```
:-)
```

Turn your head sideways to the left. See the smiling face?

You use a smiley to indicate irony so subtle your correspondent might miss it. For instance:

```
Are you always such a jerk? :-)
```

Here is an example of how you might use a smiley. Say that a friend has just sent you a message telling, in great detail, how he met the woman of his dreams the night before at a Unix singles club. If he were to tell you this story in person, you could make a funny remark without risking an insult (wink, wink, nudge, nudge). By mail, however, it is easy to be insulting where no offense was meant.

Thus, if you want to reply in a humorous vein, it is best to include a smiley:

```
Oh yes, I know who you mean...
She'll go home with anyone who can write a Unix shell script
:-)
```

This makes it more likely that your friend will be able to appreciate the subtle irony of your comment.

For more information about smileys, see Chapter 14 (in which I discuss the worldwide system of Usenet discussion groups).

 **INTERNET RESOURCE** *Look in the catalog under Internet Resources for* *Smileys*

Chapter Eight

Using Mail from a Shell Account: pine **and** pico

If you use a shell account, you run your Internet client programs on a Unix-based host computer, not on your own computer. Thus, to send and receive mail, you must use a Unix mail program.

There are a variety of such programs, the two most popular being **pine** and **elm**. The **pine** program is designed to be quick to learn and easy to use, and is most suitable for people whose email needs are not demanding. For this reason, **pine** is used widely throughout the Internet by people who do not want to spend a lot of time learning computer commands. **elm**, on the other hand, is better for people who want to take more time to learn to use a better tool.

In this chapter, I will show you how to use **pine**. If you would like to learn **elm**, I suggest you get a copy of my book *The Unix Companion*. In that book, I explain how to use **elm**, as well as everything else you need to know about Unix (such as the **vi** and **emacs** text editors).

Before you read this chapter, it would be a good idea to read Chapter 6 of this book, in which I discuss Internet addresses, and at least skim through Chapter 7, in which I cover the Internet mail system in general.

A Quick History of `pine` and `pico`

pine was developed at the University of Washington in 1989. At the time, the administrative staff used a mail program named "Ben" with a mainframe computer. (Ben had been adapted from a mail program written at UCLA for their mainframe users.) Ben was designed to be easy to learn and easy to use and, as the use of mainframes decreased, there was a need for a similar mail program that would run on the small, less expensive Unix systems.

The solution was for the university programmers to take another Unix mail program, **elm**, which had been written as a replacement for the standard Unix mail program, and modify it appropriately. They did, and the result was **pine**.

Although **pine** was developed for users at the University of Washington (and administrative users at that), with the growth of the Internet, **pine** began to fill an important need for users around the world. Here was a mail program that was so simple, you could sit down and use it with no special training. Today, **pine** is probably the single most widely used Unix mail program in the world.

What's in a Name?

pine, elm

The **pine** program was written as an alternative to **elm**. The creators of **pine** felt that **elm** was a good program, but many people required something simpler. They started with the actual **elm** software, and modified it to make it less powerful and, hence, easier to use. They chose the name **pine** as an acronym for "**pine** is not **elm**" (a wry comment indeed).

(The name **elm**, by the way, stands for "electronic mailer".)

The original version of **pine** still contained a fair bit of the **elm** program. Eventually, all of the original bits and pieces were replaced by all new software. Once this was accomplished, the name **pine** was redefined to mean "**pine** is no longer **elm**".

More recently, the developers of **pine** have extended it to, not only send and receive Internet mail, but to read articles from Usenet newsgroups (discussion groups). Thus, the name has once again been revised. The current official party line is that the name **pine** stands for "program for Internet news and email". (But we know better.)

As **pine** was being developed, the programmers saw the need for a simple text editor to use for composing messages. Most **elm** users used the **vi** editor (a Unix program). However, **vi** is complex and can take a long time to master. The **pine** developers wanted an editor that was as easy to learn as **pine** itself. Their solution was to create their own editor, **pico**.

What's in a Name?

pico

The **pico** editor was designed for people to use when composing messages within **pine**. Thus, the name "**pico**" was chosen to stand for "**pine** composer".

However, the name is appropriate for another reason. The editor was designed to be small—that is, to have a limited number of commands and rules—and the word "pico" suggests the idea of smallness. For example, within the international system of measurement—based on the metric system—the prefix "pico" indicates a million millionth (that is, a trillionth). There are, for instance, one trillion picoseconds in a second.

Using pico by Itself

Although **pico** was designed to be used within **pine**, you can also use **pico** by itself. You can edit any file you want—separately from **pine**—by using the **pico** command. For example, if you want to use **pico** to edit a file named **document**, enter:

```
pico document
```

Once **pico** starts, it works almost the same as it does within **pine** (there are minor differences). I will discuss how to use **pico** later in the chapter.

HINT

If you do not know how to use one of the other Unix text editors (such as **vi** or **emacs**), you can use **pico** to edit those small files that are important to you as a Unix user. For example, you could use **pico** to create a **.signature** file to hold the signature that is appended to the end of all your mail messages (see Chapter 7).

Orientation to pine

The **pine** programmers had a set of goals when they designed the program. Above all, they decided, everything you see should be simple and clear. Although large programs are complex, all the complexity of **pine** should be hidden from the end user. The programmers' idea was that **pine** should contain only a minimum of basic features. It is better to have a few simple commands that can be repeated to achieve some goal, they reasoned, than to have many sophisticated, less general commands.

For example, while you are composing a message, there are commands to move the cursor forward by one character, one word, or one line. However, there is no way to move ahead by, say, six characters, or five words, or a single sentence or paragraph. Nor is there any way to move backward, except one character at a time. This makes for a working environment that, if somewhat tedious, is uniformly comfortable and non-challenging.

These design considerations allowed the programmers to build a unique, self-contained, and easily understood mail program. As a **pine** user, you can do just about anything you want by selecting commands from a set of small, simple and complete menus. All operations have some type of immediate feedback, and nothing that is irreversible can be done without your explicit confirmation. For example, there is no way to press the wrong key and accidentally delete a file.

Such characteristics give **pine** its distinctive feel, a sensibility based on three specific features. First, **pine** is so well designed that you can use it immediately, without having to read a manual or documentation. Second, after only a brief time, the **pine** working environment will become so comfortable that you will never feel lost. Finally, no matter what your level of expertise or motivation, you can explore without fear of causing damage.

Here is a quick summary of what it is like to use pine to send and receive mail. To send a message, you enter the **pine** command followed by the address of the recipient. For example, say that you want to send a message to a friend whose address is **wendy@muffin.com**. At the shell prompt, enter the command:

```
pine wendy@muffin.com
```

This will start the **pine** program in such a way that everything is set up to compose a message. (You will see the details in a moment.) Once you are finished composing, you will tell **pine** to send the message. The program will then finish, leaving you back at the shell prompt.

The first time you use **pine**, it will start by displaying a welcome screen with some general information. After the screen is displayed, **pine** will ask you if you would like to receive a copy of a document called "Secrets of Pine". If you answer yes, **pine** will send a message to a program at the University of Washington, which will respond by mailing you a copy of this document.

Although it seems like an appropriate thing to read if you are a beginner, the document is really more for experienced people. Generally, it describes the new features in the current version of **pine**, along with certain technical considerations. As a beginner, you don't really need to read it.

HINT

How does **pine** know whether or not this is your first time using the program? In order to store certain configuration information from one session to the next, **pine** maintains a file named **.pinerc** in your home directory. The first time you use **pine**, you do not have a **.pinerc** file, so **pine** creates one for you automatically. Whenever you change your configuration (discussed later in the chapter), **pine** updates this file for you.

Thus, it is easy for **pine** to see if you are a first-time user. All it has to do is check if you have a **.pinerc** file.

To read your messages, simply enter the **pine** command by itself:

`pine`

The program will start by showing you a menu of choices. (Again, I will go over the details later.) From this menu, you will tell **pine** to show you a summary of your messages. You will then select which message you want to read first.

After reading the message, you may decide to compose a reply. If so, **pine** will set everything up for you to do so. After you are finished reading (and possibly replying), you will decide how to dispose of the message. In most cases, you will either delete it or save it to a file.

Once you have finished reading all of your messages, you tell **pine** to quit. The program will end, returning you to the shell prompt.

So that's the general idea. Now, let's take a look at the details.

HINT

In the following sections, I will show you how to use the **pine** command with various options. I will be covering the most important of them. Most of the options are specialized and you will never need to use them. However, if you do want more information, enter the **pine** command with the **–h** (help) option:

`pine -h`

This will display a summary of all the options and what they mean. If you want even more details, you can display the page from the online Unix manual by using the command:

`man pine`

This will show you all the technical (nerd-like) information relating to starting the pine program.

Starting pine to Send a Message

To send mail, use the **pine** command with the following syntax:

`pine [-r]` *address*`...`

For example, to send mail to a friend who's address is wendy@muffin.com, enter the command:

```
pine wendy@muffin.com
```

If you want to practice composing mail (or if you want to let someone else practice), you can use the **-r** (restricted) option. This tells **pine** to only send messages to yourself. If you specify **-r** and then try to send a message to someone else, **pine** will refuse to do so. The intention is that, while you are learning, you should start **pine** with the **-r** option until you feel confident in your ability to compose a message. That way, you can't accidentally send someone else a mixed up message. Once you know what you are doing, you can leave out the **-r** and start sending messages to other people.

HINT

The **-r** option is useful if you are teaching someone who is not all that bright, and you want to make sure he or she stays out of trouble.

Composing a Message: The Screen

When you indicate that you want to send a message, **pine** will display a message composition screen. Figure 8-1 shows a typical example. Notice that the screen is divided into four parts. The top line shows general information: what version of **pine** you are using, and which folder (if any) you currently have open. In our example, we are not reading mail, so no folder is open.

Below this line, we see the header (the **To** line, **Cc** line, and so on). This is where you type the subject of the message, and indicate if you want to send a copy or attach a file.

Underneath the header, you see a line that says:

```
----- Message Text -----
```

This line separates the header from the body of the message. Whatever you type below this line becomes the text of your message. (The words **Message Text** are not part of the message.)

The general idea is to fill in the header, then move down below the **Message Text** line and type the body of the message, then give the command to send the message. It all works smoothly, once you get used to it.

Notice that, just below the **Message Text** line, you see the following lines:

```
===========================================================
Harley Hahn                        harley@nipper.ucsb.edu
              (202) 456-1414
===========================================================
```

```
PINE 3.91    COMPOSE MESSAGE                    Folder: (CLOSED) 0 Messages
To       : wendy@muffin.com
Cc       :
Attchmnt :
Subject  :
----- Message Text -----



==========================================================
Harley Hahn                    harley@nipper.ucsb.edu
            (202) 456-1414
==========================================================








^G Get Help ^X Send      ^R Rich Hdr ^Y PrvPg/Top ^K Cut Line  ^O Postpone
^C Cancel   ^D Del Char ^J Attach   ^V NxtPg/End ^U UnDel Line^T To AddrBk
```

Figure 8-1.   *Composing a message with* `pine`

This is a signature. As I explained in Chapter 7, your signature is a short file that you create to hold information to be included with each message you send. In this case, you see a name, a mail address, and a phone number.

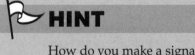

HINT

How do you make a signature file? All you need to do is create a file named `.signature` in your home directory. `pine` will find it and automatically insert the contents into each message you send. To create such a file, you can use any text editor. If you want to use `pico`, move to your home directory and enter the command:

```
pico .signature
```

At the bottom of the screen, there is a list of commands. These are the commands you can currently use. Notice that all of them use the CTRL key. For example, the command to send your message is **^X**; the command to cancel the message, should you decide to not send it, is **^C**. (In the world of Unix, it is the convention to write CTRL key names by using the **^** character. Thus, **^X** means CTRL-X. So when you read **^X**, it means hold down the CTRL key and press **X**.)

There is an important reason why all the commands use the CTRL key. Because you are composing a message, you are going to be typing regular characters: letters, numbers, punctuation, and so on. Thus, **pine** must use commands that you would normally not type as part of the text. For example, you might type the letter "X" as part of a message, but you would never type **^X**. This means that, no matter where you are on the screen, you can use any of the commands by pressing the appropriate CTRL key.

At all times, the summary at the bottom of the screen will show you which commands are available. This list will change as you move from one task to another. For example, when you are editing the header, the list of commands is somewhat different from when you are typing the body of the message.

HINT

If, for some reason, you cannot type a particular CTRL key combination, **pine** will let you substitute ESC ESC followed by the alphabetic key. For instance, you can use ESC ESC **A** instead of pressing **^A**.

Here is an example. Sometimes I use a program called **screen** that allows me to have more than one Unix work session at the same time. **screen** is a handy program indeed, but it does have one drawback: it uses the **^A** key for special purposes. (For instance, to switch from one session to the next, I would press **^A** followed by SPACE.) This means that I cannot use **^A** with **pine**, because the **screen** program will intercept it and everything will be mixed up.

The solution is to press ESC ESC **A** instead. As far as **pine** is concerned, this is the same as **^A**.

Composing a Message: General Commands

Whenever you learn a new program, the most important command is the one that displays help information. With **pine**, while you are composing a message, this command is **^G**. You can think of **^G** as meaning "get help".

The actual help you get depends on what you are doing. If your cursor is within the header, you will get a description of the current header line. If your cursor is within the body of the message, you will get a summary of all the available commands followed by general help in composing a message.

HINT

One way to learn how to compose messages well is to move the cursor into the body of a message, press **^G**, and then take a few moments to read all the help text. This will show you just about everything you need to know.

Composing a message with **pine** is easy. All you have to do is move the cursor wherever you want and type. For example, to create the body of the message, simply move to the beginning of the message area and start typing. When you want to insert something, move to where you want the insertion and type the new material. To delete something, move to that position and use one of the deletion commands (explained later in the chapter).

Aside from **^G**, there are two other general commands you can use with **pine**. First, if for some reason, the information on your screen becomes garbled, you can tell **pine** to redraw the screen by pressing **^L**. Second, if your system has job control, you can suspend **pine** by pressing **^Z**. You will then be at a shell prompt, and you can enter any command you want. To return to **pine**, enter the **fg** (foreground) command.

HINT

Job control is a Unix facility that allows you to put something on hold, do something else, and then return to your original task. I discuss job control in my book *The Unix Companion*. If the whole idea seems foreign to you, don't worry about it.

Note: By default, **pine** does not allow you to use job control. If you do want to use the **^Z** command, you will have to modify the **pine** configuration so that the **enable-suspend** feature is turned on. (I will explain how to do this later in the chapter.)

For reference, Figure 8-2 shows the general commands you can use while composing a message.

Command	Description
^G	(get) help
^L	redisplay the screen
^Z	suspend the program

Figure 8-2.   pine: *Composing a message, general commands*

Composing a Message: Moving the Cursor

The first commands you need to learn are the ones to move the cursor. To start, you can move the cursor one position at a time by using the cursor control keys (the ones with the arrows): LEFT, RIGHT, UP, DOWN. If you prefer to keep your fingers on the main part of the keyboard as you type, there are alternative keys you can use instead.

Cursor Control Key	Alternate Key
LEFT	**^B** (back one position)
RIGHT	**^F** (forward one position)
UP	**^P** (previous line)
DOWN	**^N** (next line)

Aside from moving one position at a time, there are several other commands you can use to make longer jumps. To go to the beginning of the current line, press **^A**. To go to the end of the current line, press **^E**. To go forward to the beginning of the next word, press **^**SPACE (that is, hold down the CTRL key and press SPACE). If this key combination doesn't work properly on your terminal, there is an alternative. You can press **^@** instead. Thus, you can move forward, one word a time, by pressing **^**SPACE (or **^@**) repeatedly.

When you are working with a long message, it is convenient to be able to move down and up in larger jumps. There are three commands to use. To move down one screenful, press **^V**. (In **pine** terminology, we would say that **^V** moves down one "page".) To move up one screenful, press **^Y**.

HINT

You can page down through a long message, one screenful at a time, by pressing **^V** repeatedly. Similarly, if you are near the end of a message, you can page up one screenful at a time by using **^Y**.

These key combinations can be a bit confusing, so here is an easy way to remember which is which. Think of the **V** as representing an arrow pointing downward. And think of the **Y** as standing for "Why did they ever pick this key for moving up?"

The final command to jump long distances is **^W**. This command will search forward for a specific pattern of characters and then jump directly to that point. For example, you might want to jump to the next occurrence of the word "Harley". (Think of **^W** as meaning "Where is the pattern I am looking for?")

When you press **^W**, **pine** will ask you to specify the characters for which you want to search. Type whatever you want and then press RETURN. **pine** will search forward and move the cursor to the next occurrence of that pattern. Unfortunately, **pine** will only search forward, not backward. However, if it gets to the end of the message without finding the pattern, **pine** will automatically wrap around to the top and keep searching.

HINT

When you are searching with **pine**, it does not distinguish between upper- and lowercase letters. Thus, you can search for either **Harley**, **HARLEY** or **harley**, with the same results.

The **^W** command is an important one, as it affords an easy way to jump all around (as long as you know a pattern to search for). In addition, there are several variations of this command that are especially useful.

First, if you press **^W** followed by RETURN, **pine** will search for the previous pattern you specified. Here is an example of how this is handy. Say that you use **^W** to search for the word "Harley" which occurs several times within your message. **pine** moves the cursor to the next occurrence of "Harley", but it is not the one you wanted. Simply press **^W** RETURN and jump to the next one. If this is not the place you wanted, press **^W** RETURN again.

The other variations of **^W** allow you to jump directly to the first or last line of the message. To jump to the last line, press **^W^V**; to jump to the first line, press **^W^Y**.

For reference, Figure 8-3 summarizes the commands used to move the cursor while composing a message.

Composing a Message: Editing Commands

While you are composing a message, there are a number of commands you can use to fix mistakes and move text. Compared to other editors, **pine** (**pico** actually) has only a few such commands. However, as you will see, it is possible to combine these commands to perform various types of tasks.

To start, the simplest operation is to delete a single character. As you are typing, you can delete the last character you typed by pressing either BACKSPACE or DELETE, whichever is the **erase** character for your terminal. For convenience, you can also use **^H** to do the same thing.

Command	Description
LEFT	move cursor one position left
RIGHT	move cursor one position right
UP	move cursor up one line
DOWN	move cursor down one line
^B	(back) same as LEFT
^F	(forward) same as RIGHT
^P	(previous) same as UP
^N	(next) same as DOWN
^A	move cursor to start of current line
^E	move cursor to end of current line
^SPACE	move to start of next word
^@	same as ^SPACE
^V	move down one screenful
^Y	move up one screenful
^W*pattern*RETURN	jump to next occurrence of *pattern*
^WRETURN	jump to next occurrence of previous pattern
^W^V	jump to last line of message
^W^Y	jump to first line of message

Figure 8-3. `pine`: *Composing a message, moving the cursor*

Sometimes it is easier to delete a single character forward rather than backward. You can do this by pressing ^**D**. Thus, you can think of BACKSPACE as deleting to the left of the cursor, and ^**D** as deleting to the right.

For example, say you have typed the word "Harley" and you have moved the cursor so that it is on the "r". If you press BACKSPACE, you will delete the "a". If you press ^**D**, you will delete the "r".

HINT

You can use BACKSPACE and ^D to join separate lines. Simply move to the beginning of the second line and press BACKSPACE, or move to the end of the first line and press ^D.

For example, say that you have typed the following three lines:

```
This is the beginning.
This is the middle.
This is the end.
```

If you move to the beginning of the second line and press BACKSPACE you will have:

```
This is the beginning.This is the middle.
This is the end.
```

If, instead, you had moved to the end of the second line and pressed ^D, you would have:

```
This is the beginning.
This is the middle.This is the end.
```

The next editing command is ^K. This command can be used in two ways to delete text. First, if you use ^K by itself, **pine** will delete the current line (the line in which the cursor lies). Alternatively, you can define a particular region of text and use ^K to delete that text. Here is how it works.

Let's say that you have just typed the following three lines of text:

```
The Internet Complete Reference is
not, by any means,
the best Internet book ever written.
```

You realize that you made a terrible mistake: the second line should not be there. To correct this, move the cursor to any position on the second line and press ^K. **pine** will delete the line and you will be left with:

```
The Internet Complete Reference is
the best Internet book ever written.
```

The second way to use ^K allows you to define a region of text to be deleted. All you need to do is move to one boundary of the region and press ^^ (CTRL-circumflex). (On U.S.-style keyboards, the circumflex character is above the "6".) This will set an invisible mark at that point. Now move the cursor to the other boundary of the text to be deleted. As you do, **pine** will highlight all the characters between the invisible mark and the cursor. When the correct region has been highlighted, press ^K and **pine** will delete the text.

For example, let's say you want to delete all the text from a particular point all the way to the end of the message. Move the cursor to that point. Then press ^^ to set the invisible mark. Next press ^W^V to jump to the end of the message. Finally, press ^K to perform the deletion.

Another example: An easy way to delete all the text in the message is ^W^Y ^^ ^W^V ^K. (Well, it's not easy, but it works.) Let's take this long string of commands apart. The ^W^Y commands jump to the beginning of the message. Next, ^^ sets the mark. Then, ^W^V jumps to the end of the message. Finally, ^K deletes everything.

This last example illustrates an important point: The **pico** editor is not a powerful one and there are a limited number of commands. However, with some ingenuity, you can combine commands to perform tasks that are not built in.

For instance, there is no command to delete from the cursor to the end of the current line. However, you can combine three simple commands to do the job. First, use ^^ to set the mark. Then use ^E to jump to the end of the line. Then use ^K to perform the deletion. After a while, you will get used to thinking like this and typing ^^ ^E ^K will seem easy. Similarly, you will be able to type ^^ ^A ^K without thinking, to delete from the cursor to the beginning of the line.

One last word about the ^^ command. If you set a mark and you decide you do not want it, just press ^^ a second time. It will unset the mark for you.

At any time, you can undo the last ^K deletion by pressing ^U. Use this command when you made a mistake and you need to recall the deleted text. However, **pine** will only remember the last deletion, so you must use ^U to make the correction before you use ^K again. Once you use ^K a second time, the original text is gone forever.

The ^U command is useful for more than error recovery. You can combine it with ^K to move text from one position to another. Use ^K to cut the text, move to a new location, and then use ^U to paste the text. For example, say that you have written:

`I think that word order is important extremely.`

You realize that you need to move "extremely" in front of "important". Here is one way to do the job. First, move the cursor to the space before the word "important". Then press ^^ to set the mark. Now move the cursor to the last letter of "important". Press ^K to delete the text. The line now looks like this:

`I think that word order is extremely.`

Next, move the cursor to the period at the end of the sentence. Now press ^U to insert the deleted text. The final line looks like this:

`I think that word order is extremely important.`

HINT

Once you delete text using ^K, you can use ^U repeatedly to insert the same text at more than one location. **pine** will remember this text until you use ^K again.

For reference, Figure 8-4 summarizes the editing commands I covered in this section.

Composing a Message: Advanced Commands

Aside from the commands I discussed in the previous section, there are three others that are helpful as you compose a message. First, when you move the cursor within a paragraph and press ^J, **pine** will reformat the entire paragraph. This means that the long and short lines will be evened out so that the text is easy to read.

HINT

The ^J command—reformat a paragraph—is the most underutilized of all the **pine** commands. It behooves you to use this simple command every time you add or remove words from a paragraph. Doing so will make your messages a lot more pleasant to read and mark you as a considerate and knowledgeable person.

The second command you should never forget is ^T. This is the command to start the spell checker. Checking your spelling before you send a message is—like formatting your text—considered good manners.

Command	Description
^D	delete a single character forward
BACKSPACE or DELETE	delete a single character backward
^H	same as BACKSPACE
^K	delete current line or marked text
^ ^	set/unset invisible mark
^U	undelete last text deleted with ^K

Figure 8-4.   `pine`: *Composing a message, editing commands*

When you press ^T, **pine** starts a simple Unix spelling check program. This program will read your message and show you those words that are not in the list of correctly spelled words, one word at a time. Each time a word is presented, you have two choices. If you want to leave the word alone, simply press RETURN. If you want to change the word, do so and press RETURN. **pine** will then make the change within the message.

Although the spell check program is rudimentary, it does have two nice features. The first feature is handy when you reply to a message. When you are composing a reply to a message, **pine** automatically inserts a ">" character in front of each line from the original message (as I discuss in Chapter 7). Of course, you will want to check the spelling of your reply before you send it. However, you won't want to bother checking all the words in the original message. For this reason, the spell check program will ignore any lines that begin with a ">" character.

The other handy feature is that, once you correct a word, the spell check program will remember the correction. If the same incorrect word occurs more than once, the program will ask if you want to make the same change. This means that you won't have to type the same correction over and over.

⚑ HINT

Say you are typing a long message that contains many occurrences of a long word that is difficult to type. Do not type the word repeatedly as you compose the message. Instead, type a short meaningless string of characters. Then, after you are finished composing the message, use ^T to start the spell checker and use it to change all the occurrences of the meaningless characters to the word you really want.

For example, say that you need to type a message in which the word "tergiversate" occurs many times. Instead, type "ter" everywhere you want the long word. When you are finished, press ^T. When the spell check program flags the first occurrence of "ter", change it to "tergiversate". Then, each time the program encounters another "ter", tell the program to make the same change.

The final command to use when composing a message is ^R. This will read an existing file and insert it right into your message, below the current line. For example, say you have a file called **statistics** that you want to insert into the middle of a message. Move the cursor to that point and press ^R. **pine** will ask you for the name of the file. Type **"statistics"** and press RETURN. **pine** will insert the contents of the file below the current line.

For reference, Figure 8-5 summarizes the advanced editing commands I discussed in this section.

Command	Description
^J	justify (reformat) a paragraph
^T	spell checker
^R	read in a file

Figure 8-5. pine: *Composing a message, advanced editing commands*

Sending Your Message

Once you are finished composing a message, you can send it by pressing ^X. (If you want to remember the name of this command, imagine it will send your message to eXactly the right person.) When you press ^X, **pine** will ask you for confirmation. You will have three choices: If you press **y** (for "yes"), **pine** will send the message. If you press **n** (for "no"), **pine** will retain the message and put you back into the compose screen, so you can make changes. If you decide to forget about the message, press ^C (for "cancel") and **pine** will discard it.

If you are typing a message and you decide to forget it, there is a shortcut. You do not have to press ^X and then ^C: you can press ^C from within the compose screen. Of course, **pine** will ask you to confirm that you really want to cancel the message.

The last way to stop composing a message is to postpone it. To do this, press ^O. **pine** will save the message, exactly as you left it, for as long as you want. You can even stop **pine** and continue another time. Each time you start to compose a message from the main menu (which I will discuss later in the chapter), **pine** will check to see if you have any postponed messages. (You can postpone as many messages as you want.) If so, **pine** will give you a chance to return to one of them.

For reference, Figure 8-6 summarizes the commands used to send a message.

Command	Description
^X	send the message
^C	cancel the message
^O	postpone the message

Figure 8-6. pine: *Commands to send a message*

Editing the Header

I explained earlier how you move the cursor from one part of the screen to another in order to edit either the header or the body of the message. When the cursor is within the header—above the line that says **Message Text**—you can edit the header. When the cursor is below this line, you can edit and compose the body of the message. When you start to compose a message, **pine** builds an empty header for you. It looks like this. (For a discussion of the various parts of a message header, see Chapter 7.)

```
To      :
Cc      :
Attchmnt:
Subject :
```

To fill in the header, all you need to do is move from one line to another and type what you want. **pine** will help you by starting with the cursor on the first line. Once you fill in a line (or decide to leave it empty), you can move to the next line by pressing the DOWN or RETURN key. If you decide to change a header line, you can return to it by pressing the UP key. If you want to replace the entire line, press **^K** to delete the existing text and then type whatever you want.

You will recognize the **To:**, **Cc:** and **Subject:** lines from our discussion in Chapter 7. (These lines show, respectively, the primary recipients of the message, anyone who should receive a copy, and the subject of the message.) The **Attchmnt:** line, however, is not really a header line. It is put there by **pine** to allow you to specify if you want an attachment.

As I explain in Chapter 7, you use attachments to send files to someone via the mail system. As you compose a message, you can tell **pine** that one or more files are to be attached. The attachments are sent along with the message and, at the other end, your recipient can read the message and save the attachments to files on his or her own computer. Using an attachment is especially handy when you need to send someone a non-textual file (like a picture) that you can't send as part of a regular message.

There are two ways to specify that you want an attachment. The easiest is to press **^J** as you are editing the header. This tells **pine** that you want to attach a file to the message. **pine** will ask you for the name of the file and a comment. (At the other end, your recipient will see the comment when he or she receives the file, so be descriptive.) After you specify the file name and comment, **pine** will automatically add the appropriate information to the **Attchmnt:** line in the header. If you want, you can add more than one attachment to a message and **pine** will construct the **Attchmnt:** line appropriately. Here is an example of a header in which we have specified two files to be attached to the message:

```
To       : harley@nipper.ucsb.edu
Cc       :
Attchmnt : 1. /usr/harley/nipper.gif (87 KB) "The Little Nipper",
           2. /usr/harley/budget.xls (4.6 KB) "budget spreadsheet"
Subject : Here are the files you requested.
```

The second way to specify an attachment is to move to the **Attchmnt:** line and type the name of the file yourself. This works fine except that you won't be prompted to enter a comment. Note: If you want to attach more than one file, you must separate the names by commas.

When you are editing a header, you can use most of the commands I have already discussed. (Remember, the help text at the bottom of the screen will always show you what commands are available.) However, there are two more commands specifically for editing headers.

The first one, **^T**, has two different uses depending on which header line you are typing. When you are typing the **To:** or the **Cc:** lines, pressing **^T** allows you to copy someone's address from your "address book". An address book is a list of names and addresses that **pine** helps you maintain. (I will talk about it later in the chapter.) The idea is, when you need an address, you can press **^T**, upon which **pine** will display your address book. You can then just pick out the address you want and **pine** will insert it right into the header line.

The second use of **^T** is for specifying file names. When you are typing the **Attchmnt:** line, you can press **^T** to display a list of file names. You can then choose the file you want and have **pine** insert the name for you. This is useful when you forget the exact name of a file or when the file name is long and difficult to type.

The last command for editing headers is **^R**. This command allows you to edit extra lines in the header. You can think of the command name, **^R**, as standing for "rich header"; that is, a header that contains extra lines.

When I discussed headers (in Chapter 7), I mentioned the various lines that you might put in a header. In particular, along with the **To:, Cc:** and **Subject:** lines, you can use a **Bcc:** line to send a blind copy of the message to one or more people. (This is a secret copy which no one knows about except the person who receives it.) When you are editing a header and you press **^R**, **pine** will display several other lines, including a **Bcc:** line. Thus, if you want to send a blind copy, all you need to do is press **^R**, and then fill in the **Bcc:** line.

Here is what you would see if you were editing the header in our last example, and you press **^R**:

```
To       : harley@nipper.ucsb.edu
Cc       :
Bcc      :
Newsgrps :
Fcc      : sent-mail
Attchmnt : 1. /usr/harley/nipper.gif (87 KB) "The Little Nipper",
           2. /usr/harley/budget.xls (4.6 KB) "budget spreadsheet"
Subject : Here are the files you requested.
```

Aside from the **Bcc:** line, there are two others, a **Newsgrps:** line and an **Fcc:** line. Like the **Attchmnt:** line, these are not standard mail header lines. They are used within **pine** for special purposes. You fill in the **Newsgrps:** line when you want to use **pine** for posting articles to Usenet discussion groups (which are often called "newsgroups"). The **Fcc:** line is for telling **pine** which folder you want to use to save a copy of your outgoing message. In our example, **pine** has already filled in the name of the **sent-mail** folder, which is the default. Later in the chapter, I will discuss the **Fcc:** header line and how to use it.

For reference, Figure 8-7 contains a summary of the commands used to edit the header.

Starting pine to Read Your Mail

To read your mail, use the **pine** command with the following syntax:

pine [**-iz**] [**-f** *folder*]

Most of the time, you will enter the command without any options:

pine

This will start the program and display the main menu (which I will discuss in a moment).

There are three options you may want to use when you start **pine**. First, you can use the **-i** option to tell **pine** to start with the index rather than the main menu. As you will see shortly, the index is a list of all your messages. The important point is that **-i** allows you to start working with your messages right away, bypassing the main menu.

Command	Description
^T	open address book or open a file list
^J	attach a file
^R	display the full (rich) header

Figure 8-7.   pine: *Commands to edit the header*

The **-z** option enables the suspend feature. This allows you to pause the **pine** program and go to a shell prompt. From the shell prompt, you can issue as many commands as you want. When you want to return to **pine**, you can tell the shell to restart the program. This facility is part of what we call job control, and is covered in detail in my book *The Unix Companion* (published by Osborne McGraw-Hill). For now, here is a quick summary.

Job control is used to pause one program and start another. For example, say that you are reading your mail and you want to know what time it is. You could pause **pine**, enter the **date** command (to display the time and date), and then restart **pine**.

To do this, you press **^Z**. This will pause the current program and start a new shell. You can now enter any Unix command you want. When you are ready to return to **pine**, simply enter the **fg** command at the shell prompt. This tells the shell to bring the suspended program back into the "foreground".

In general, most shells support job control, and being able to press **^Z** to suspend a program is a standard Unix feature. With **pine**, however, this facility is *not* the default. This is to prevent naive users from pressing **^Z** by mistake and ending up confused and disoriented at a shell prompt. If you want to use job control with **pine**, you can do so by starting the program with the **-z** option. (You can see where the name of the option comes from: it reminds you of **^Z**, the suspend key.)

HINT

pine has a facility that allows you to specify various preferences in what is called your "configuration". In particular, you can tell **pine** that you always want to start with the index (so you don't have to use **-i** every time you start the program), or that you always want to use job control (so you don't have to use **-z** every time).

I will discuss how to do this later in the chapter. For reference, though, here are the details. You tell **pine** to start with the index by specifying the "**i**" command on your **initial-keystroke-list**; and you automatically enable job control by turning on the **enable-suspend** feature. (This will all make sense later.)

The last option that you are likely to use is **-f**. This allows you to tell **pine** to start reading a different message folder. (In Chapter 7, I explained how mail programs store messages in folders.) Normally, you would want **pine** to read your default folder: the mailbox in which your incoming mail is stored. However, if you have saved some messages into a particular folder (which you will learn how to do later in the chapter), you can use the **-f** option to read them.

For example, say that you have saved a number of messages from your friend Daniela in a folder named **daniela**. To start **pine** so that it automatically reads this folder, you can use:

```
pine -f daniela
```

If you want **pine** to open this folder automatically as the program starts, you can also use the **-i** option:

```
pine -i -f daniela
```

The **-f** option is only for your convenience. You can read any folder you want without the **-f** option by choosing **FOLDER LIST** from the main menu. This will display a list of your folders, from which you can choose the one you want to open.

The Main Menu

When you start **pine** to read your mail, it begins by displaying the main menu. This is shown in Figure 8-8.

You can see there are a number of commands you can use. Some of them are in the menu itself, others are listed at the bottom of the screen. To use a command, all you

```
PINE 3.91    MAIN MENU                        Folder: INBOX   79 Messages



         ?      HELP            -  Get help using Pine
         C      COMPOSE MESSAGE -  Compose and send/post a message
         I      FOLDER INDEX    -  View messages in current folder
         L      FOLDER LIST     -  Select a folder OR news group to view
         A      ADDRESS BOOK    -  Update address book
         S      SETUP           -  Configure or update Pine
         Q      QUIT            -  Exit the Pine program




    Copyright 1989-1994.  PINE is a trademark of the University of Washington.
                    [Folder "INBOX" opened with 79 messages]
? Help                        P PrevCmd                    R RelNotes
O OTHER CMDS L [ListFldrs] N NextCmd                       K KBLock
```

Figure 8-8.   *The* pine *main menu*

need to do is type the appropriate character, you do not have to press RETURN. For example, to quit the program, simply press **Q**.

HINT

I write the command abbreviations as uppercase letters because they are easier to read. However, you can type in either upper- or lowercase. For example, most people type **q**, rather than **Q**, because you don't have to hold down the SHIFT key. Either one will do.

Let's take a quick tour of these commands and then move on to discuss reading the mail. I will discuss most of these commands later so, for now, don't worry about the details.

To start, the most important commands are **?**, to display help information, and **Q** to quit the program. When you press **Q**, **pine** will ask you if you really want to quit, to make sure that you didn't press **Q** by accident.

If you decide to send a message, press **C**. This will start **pico** and display the compose screen. Everything works just as I described earlier in the chapter. Thus, there are two ways to tell **pine** that you want to compose a message. First, as I discussed earlier, you can enter the **pine** command with the address to which you want to send a message. For example:

pine wendy@muffin.com

Or, you can start **pine** without an address and, from the main menu, press **C** to compose a message. This is handy when you are reading mail and you decide that you want to compose a new message.

To read your mail, press **I**. This tells **pine** to display the index of the current folder. The INDEX is a summary of each message that is waiting for you. Basically, **pine** will show you information about all your incoming messages, and you tell it which ones you want to read.

When you use the **I** command, **pine** shows you the index for the current folder. By default, this is the mailbox in which Unix places all your incoming mail. If you want to switch to another folder, press **L**. This allows you to display a list of all your folders. Choose the one you want, then return to the main menu and press **I** to display the new index.

Here is an example. Say that you have saved all the mail from a friend named Daniela in a folder named **daniela**. When you want to read the messages in this folder, you have two choices. First, you can start **pine** with the **-f** and **-i** options (explained in the previous section). This tells **pine** that you want to open and read a specific folder:

```
pine -i -f daniela
```

Or, you can start **pine** without options and, from the main menu, press **L** to list your folders. Now, all you have to do is select the **daniela** folder and press RETURN to display the index. The **L** command is handy when you want to switch back and forth among several folders.

The next command, **A**, allows you to edit your address book. This is a list of names and addresses that **pine** will maintain for you. When you compose a message, you can select the address from your address book. That way, you don't have to remember and retype addresses that you use all the time.

The final command on the main part of the screen is **S**. This command allows you to set up (customize) various parts of the system to your liking.

At the bottom of the screen, you will see several other commands. This is the usual way for **pine** to tell you which commands are available. As you move from one part of the program to another, the commands at the bottom of the screen will change. For example, when you are looking at the main menu, you will see certain commands. If you press **?** to start the help facility, you will see other commands: those appropriate for the situation.

I won't go over all the commands here. In most cases, they are easy to understand and, as I mentioned earlier, you can't cause any damage by experimenting, so feel free to try a new command every now and then just to see what happens.

HINT

The help facility is always available to explain any command you don't understand.

The one command I do want to mention is **O**. This command is used to list other commands which would not fit into the limited amount of space at the bottom of the screen. In some cases, there are only two sets of commands, so pressing **O** twice brings you back to where you started. In other cases, there are more commands, you may have to press **O** several times to cycle through the entire list.

Regardless of how many times you might have to press **O** to see the full list of commands, all of them are available. If you can remember the name of a command, you can use it even if it is not showing on the bottom menu. For example, if you are looking at the main menu and you press **O**, you will see that there is a **G** command to go to a particular folder. If this command is not showing, you do not have to press **O** and then **G**. Since **G** is a valid command from the main menu, pressing **G** by itself is enough.

At first, this shortcut won't help you much but, as you begin to memorize the commands, you will have less of a need to press **O** to refresh your memory.

The Index

To read mail, start from the main menu and press **I** to display the index. The index is a list of all the messages waiting in your mailbox. Figure 8-9 shows a typical index screen. On the top line, we see the name of the folder, **INBOX**. This is the regular incoming mailbox. We can also see that there are 10 messages.

The information about each message is straightforward. The most important parts are the date, the name of the person who sent the message and, to the far right, the subject. In between there is a number in parentheses. This is the size of the message in bytes. For textual information, one byte holds one character. Thus message #1, for example, is 4,762 characters long.

HINT

The byte count for a message includes the header, not just the body of the message. I ran an experiment to find out exactly how large the header might be. I sent myself two messages. The first had no body whatsoever; the second had a body consisting of only a single character. When the messages arrived, I looked at them in the index and found that they had a length of 360 and 361 bytes respectively. Thus, I could estimate the header was 360 characters long. This number will vary, of course, from one system to another.

```
   PINE 3.91    FOLDER INDEX            Folder: INBOX  Message 1 of 10
 + N 1   Jun 14  The Little Nipper   (4,762) Tuna for dinner?
 + N 2   Jun 14  Andrew Harlan       (3,408) I know who Cooper really is
 + A 3   Jun 15  Kantor Voy          (1,022) re: Reality Change 2456-2781
 + N 4   Jun 17  Educator Yarrow     (1,197) Technician must be dispassionate
   D 5   Jun 16  Noys Lambent        (4,901) re: the Hidden Centuries
 +   6   Jun 16  Laban Twissell      (1,741) don't worry about Noys
 + A 7   Jun 17  Brinsley S. Cooper  (9,552) primitive history
 +   8   Jun 17  Vikkor Mallansohn   (1,665) keep the chain intact
 +   9   Jun 17  August Sennor       (2,399) time paradox: meeting yourself
 +  10   Jun 17  Antoine Lefebvre    (1.924) equations & work of Jan Verdeer



 ? Help       M Main Menu P PrevMsg    - PrevPage    D Delete    R Reply
 O OTHER CMDS V [ViewMsg] N NextMsg   Spc NextPage   U Undelete  F Forward
```

Figure 8-9. *A typical* **pine** *index*

When you display the index, you may see certain codes to the left of the index number. First, you will often see a **+** (plus sign) character. This means the message was sent "directly to you". That is, the message is not a copy of a message sent to someone else; nor was it sent to you as part of a mailing list. There are also several letters you may see: **N** means the message is new and you have not yet looked at it; **D** means the message has been marked for deletion (explained later in the chapter); and **A** means you have already answered the message.

In our example, messages 1, 2 and 4 are new; messages 3 and 7 have been answered already; and message 5 is marked for deletion. The other messages have been read, but not answered or deleted. In addition, message 5 is the only one that was not sent directly. That is, it was a copy of a message or sent as part of a mailing list.

When you quit **pine**, it will ask your permission to delete all the messages that are marked with a **D**. Normally, you would say yes. Be aware, though, once **pine** deletes a message, there is no way to get it back.

Selecting a Message to Read

At all times, **pine** will highlight one particular line of the index. The message on this line is called the CURRENT MESSAGE. When you start, **pine** will set the current message to be the newest unread message.

To display a message, all you have to do is move to it—that is, make it the current message—and then press RETURN. **pine** will then display the message, one screenful at a time.

This seems like a simple process, but there are several ways to move the cursor, and it is convenient to understand them all. First, you can use the UP and DOWN keys to move around the index list. However, if you like to type without moving your hands from the keyboard, you will find it more convenient to use **P** (previous) to move up and **N** (next) to move down. You can also use **V** (view) to look at a message instead of pressing RETURN.

If you have so many messages that the entire index does not fit on a single screen, you can press SPACE or **+** (plus sign) to display the next screenful. To move back one screenful, press **–** (minus sign). You can also press **^V** to move forward and **^Y** to move back, as you do when composing a message.

If you would like to move directly to a particular message, use the **J** (jump) command. Press **J** and **pine** will ask you to type the number of the message you want to read. After you type the number and press RETURN, **pine** will jump to that message. You can now press RETURN or **V** to read it.

A second way to jump from one place to another is to use the **W** (whereis) command. This command will search the index for the next message description containing a particular pattern. For example, to jump to the next message that contains the word "Harley", press **W**, then type **harley** (**pine** does not distinguish between upper- and lowercase), and then press RETURN. If this is not the message you wanted, you can press **W** and then RETURN, and **pine** will search for the same pattern once again.

Two variations of **W** allow you to jump directly to the first or last message in the index. To jump to the last message, press **W^V**; to jump to the first message, press **W^Y**.

Finally, when you are finished with the index, you can return to the main menu by pressing **M**. Alternatively, if you decide to send a new message, you can also move to the compose screen by pressing **C**.

HINT

When you are looking at the index and (as you will see in the next section) reading a message, most of the commands are single letters. For example, you would press **?** to display help information, **W** to search for a pattern, and so on. When you are composing a message, the commands are CTRL combinations. For example, you press **^G** for help and **^W** to search.

There is a good reason for this: Single letter commands are easier to remember and use but, when you are composing, you need to be able to type regular characters as part of the text. Thus, while a **W** is fine when you are reading an index or a message, you need to use **^W** while you are composing.

Now, here is the hint. What few people know is almost all the CTRL commands (for composing) are valid all of the time. For example, when you are reading an index or a message, you can search with either **W** or **^W**; you can display help by pressing either **?** or **^G**; and you can move up and down one screenful at a time by pressing **^Y** and **^V** respectively.

As you get used to the keys, remember: what you learn when composing will often carry over to other parts of the program. For example, you can simply memorize that **^W^V** jumps to the end of whatever you are reading, whether it is a message you are composing, an index, a message you are reading, or some help text. Similarly, no matter what you are doing, **^G** will display help and **^Y** and **^V** will move up and down. A number of other CTRL keys also have universal meanings. Experiment and figure out what works best for you.

For reference, Figure 8-10 summarizes the commands used to move around the index and to select a message to read.

Reading a Message

While you are reading a message, there are several commands to use: to page through the message, search for patterns, and control what you see. Most of these will be familiar as they are also used when composing messages or looking at the index.

The fundamental commands are the ones that move forward and backward within the message. To move forward one screenful, you can press either SPACE or **+** (plus sign) or **^V**. To move backward, you can press either **–** (minus sign) or **^Y**. If you want

Command	Description
DOWN	move to next message
N	same as DOWN
UP	move to previous message
P	same as UP
RETURN	view current message
V	same as RETURN
SPACE	move down one screenful
+	same as SPACE
^V	same as SPACE
-	move up one screenful
^Y	same as -
J*number*RETURN	jump to specified message
W*pattern*RETURN	jump to next occurrence of *pattern*
WRETURN	jump to next occurrence of previous pattern
W^V	jump to last line of message
W^Y	jump to first line of message
M	return to main menu
C	compose a new message

Figure 8-10. `pine`: *Commands for reading a message*

to move up or down a single line, you can use UP and DOWN respectively, but these commands are not all that useful. Usually, it makes sense to move a whole screenful at a time.

To search for a particular pattern, use the **W** (whereis) command. This command works in the same manner as when you are reading the index. You can specify a pattern and then press RETURN, or you can simply press RETURN to search for the previous pattern. You can also use **W^V** to jump to the end of the message, or **W^Y** to jump to the top of the message.

By default, **pine** does not show you the full header. You will see only the **Date:**, **From:**, **To:**, **Cc:**, and **Subject:** lines. If you would like to see the full header, use the **H** command. This tells **pine** to show you all the header lines for all messages until you turn it off by pressing **H** a second time.

Note: In order for the **H** command to work, you need to modify the **pine** configuration so that the **enable-full-header-cmd** feature is turned on. (I will explain how to do this later in the chapter.)

Another item you may wish to view is an attachment. As I explain in Chapter 7, an attachment is a file that is joined to a message. If the file is a binary file, such as a picture, it may not be possible to look at it within **pine**. But if the attachment is a regular text file, there is no reason why you cannot look at it while you are reading the message. If this is the case, you can display such a file by using the **V** (view) command.

The next few commands allow you to jump to a different message. One way to do this is to return to the index by using the **I** command. Then, move to a different message and press RETURN or **V** (view). However, if you know the number of a specific message, you can use the **J** command to jump to it directly. You can also use the **N** command to go to the next message, the **P** command to go to the previous message, or the TAB command to go to the next unread message.

Finally, as in other situations, you can press **M** to go to the main menu, or **C** to compose a new message.

For reference, Figure 8-11 summarizes the commands used to read a message.

Command	Description
SPACE	move down one screenful
+	same as SPACE
^V	same as SPACE
−	move up one screenful
^Y	same as −
DOWN	move down one line
UP	move up one line
W*pattern*RETURN	jump to next occurrence of *pattern*
WRETURN	jump to next occurrence of previous pattern
W^V	jump to last line of message
W^Y	jump to first line of message
H	on/off: display the full header
V	view an attachment
J*number*RETURN	jump to the specified message
N	jump to the next message
TAB	jump to the next unread message
P	jump to the previous message
M	return to main menu
C	compose a new message

Figure 8-11. `pine`: *Commands for reading a message*

Deleting a Message

While you are reading a message, there are a number of things you can do with it: You can delete it, you can reply to it, you can send a copy to someone else, and so on. In the next several sections, I will cover all of these commands along with some hints for managing your mail.

The most important command is **D** (delete). Once you are finished with a message, you can press **D** to delete it. **pine** will then automatically show you the next message.

If you change your mind and decide you really didn't want to delete a message, there are two ways to undelete it. First, you can move back to the message by using the **P** (previous command). Then, press **U** to undelete the message. Alternatively, you can press **I** to return to the index, and then move to the message and press **U**.

The advantage of working from the index is that you can see all the messages at once. To help you, **pine** uses a **D** character at the beginning of the line to mark any deleted messages. When you move to a message and undelete it, the **D** character will disappear.

Replying to a Message

To reply to a message, use the **R** command. When you do, **pine** will display the compose screen so you can type the reply. The address of the recipient will be filled in for you automatically (**pine** will read it from the header). As you are composing, you can use any of the commands I discussed earlier in the chapter. When you are finished, you can tell **pine** to either send or cancel the message. **pine** will then display the next message in the index, so you can continue reading where you left off.

When you use the **R** command to reply to a message, **pine** will start by asking you if you want to include the original message in your response. Almost always, you should say yes. Here is why:

As I discuss in Chapter 7, you should not assume that the person who sent the message remembers every word that he or she wrote. Rather, you should include all or part of the original message within your reply. To help you, **pine** will preface each line of the original with a **>** (greater-than sign). This is a standard convention that everyone will understand. See Chapter 7 for more details and for an example.

HINT

You may find that trying to craft a well-designed reply with **pico** is an awkward and frustrating experience. If so, I encourage you to learn how to use a more powerful text editor (such as **vi** or **emacs**). Don't let the weaknesses of **pico** prevent you from writing well. With a better text editor, it is easy to eliminate superfluous lines and to write better replies.

If you have a signature file (a file named .signature in your home directory), pine will automatically include its contents in each message that you send. This is also true when you compose a reply.

However, by default, pine will insert your signature at the beginning of the reply. This encourages people to type their response above the signature, which makes for confusing replies in which the original message is merely tacked on to the end of the reply. It is much better, as I explained, to delete the irrelevant parts of the original message, and intersperse your reply comments within the text of the original message.

Once you form this habit, it will make more sense to have pine insert your signature at the end of the outgoing message. To do so, you will have to modify the pine configuration so the **signature-at-bottom** feature is turned on. (I will explain how to do this later in the chapter.)

Forwarding and Bouncing a Message

Another way to process a message is to forward or bounce it to someone else. As I explain in Chapter 7, forwarding allows you to modify the message, while bouncing sends a copy identical to the original message. When you forward a message, it will be obvious to the other person that it was you who re-sent the message. When you bounce a message, the other person may not notice it came from you—unless he looks at the header carefully, he may mistakenly assume that the message came from the original sender—so bounce with care.

To forward a message, use the **F** command; to bounce a message, use the **B** command. When you forward, pine will display the compose screen, so you can fill in the recipient's address and then edit the body of the message. This allows you to interpose your own comments within the lines of the original message. When you bounce a message, it goes straight to the recipient with no editing.

Note: By default, pine will not let you bounce messages. If you want to be able to use the **B** command, you will have to modify the pine configuration so that the **enable-bounce-cmd** feature is turned on. (I will explain how to do this later in the chapter.)

HINT

Never assume anything is secret. Some people are habitual bouncers who love resending messages to other people. You have no guarantee that anything you write will not be bounced to another person.

Just as important, when you receive an interesting or startling message, take a moment to check if it was really sent to you or bounced to you by someone else. If you want to look at the full header, you can do so by using the **H** command (discussed earlier in the chapter).

Saving, Printing, and Piping a Message

There are two ways to save a message. First, you can use the **S** (save) command to copy the message to a mail folder. When you use the **S** command, **pine** saves the complete message, including the entire header. This means you can later use **pine** (or another mail program) to read the message from its folder.

When you use the **S** command, **pine** will ask you for the name of the folder in which you want to save the message. By default, **pine** will use a folder called **saved-messages**. You can either press RETURN to use this folder, or type a different name. Unless you tell it to do otherwise, **pine** will automatically create new folders in the **mail** subdirectory within your home directory.

HINT

Rather than save all your important mail to the **saved-messages** folder, create separate folders organized by topic or name. For example, you might save all the mail regarding your homework in a folder named **homework**. Similarly, you might save all the important messages from your friend Harley in a folder named **harley**.

As I mentioned, once you have saved messages in a folder, you can use **pine** (or any mail program) to read them. For instance, say that you have a number of messages in a folder named **harley**. You can read the messages from this folder in two ways. First, you can start **pine** using the **-f** and **-i** options. (The **-i** option tells **pine** to open the index automatically.)

```
pine -i -f harley
```

Alternatively, you can start **pine** in the regular manner and then, from the main menu, use the **L** (list folders) command to select a specific folder to read.

The second way to save a file is to use the **E** (export) command. The difference between the **S** and **E** commands is the **S** command saves the complete header, while the **E** command saves only the most important header lines (**From:**, **To:**, **Date:**, **Cc:** and **Subject:**). Thus, it is usually better to save a message with the **E** command, unless you are deliberately saving it to a folder so you can read it later with a mail program.

An alternative to saving a file is to print it. To do so, use the **Y** command. In most cases, this command will only work if a printer is attached to your computer or your network. If you are reading mail on a remote machine, it is unlikely that you will be able to print a message directly on your own printer. You may have to save the message to a file, and then download the file to your own computer.

The final way to process a message is to pipe it to a filter. To do so, type | (the vertical bar) and the name of the filter. (For more information about piping and filters, see my book *The Unix Companion*.) I won't go into the details here, except to give one example. Say you have a long message and you only want to look at the lines that contain the characters "important". You can pipe the message to the **grep** program to extract and display only those lines:

```
| grep important
```

This is a lot faster than saving the message to a temporary file, using **grep** on that file, and then deleting it.

Note: By default, **pine** will not let you pipe messages to a filter. If you want to be able to use the | command, you will have to modify the **pine** configuration so that the **enable-unix-pipe-cmd** feature is turned on. (I will explain how to do this later in the chapter.)

For reference, Figure 8-12 summarizes the commands (from the last few sections) for processing a message while you are reading it.

Using the Address Book

As you become a veteran mail user, you will find yourself accumulating people's addresses. To help you, **pine** will maintain a file, called an address book, in which you can keep a list of addresses. The idea is that you can assign a nickname to each address and, whenever you need to specify an address, you can use the nickname instead. When you do, **pine** will replace it with the full address automatically.

Command	Description
D	delete current message
U	undelete current message
R	reply to current message
F	forward current message
B	bounce current message
S	save current message to a mail folder
E	save current message as a regular file
Y	print current message
|	pipe a message to a filter

Figure 8-12. pine: *Commands for processing a message*

(Note: The actual information is kept in a file named `.addressbook` in your home directory. Don't edit this file directly, though. Let **pine** maintain it for you.)

Here is an example. Say that you often send mail to a friend whose address is **wendy@muffin.com**. You can store this in your address book under the name **wendy**. Now, whenever you want to send mail to this person, all you need to type is **wendy**.

There are two ways to work with your address book. First, when you are reading a message, you can use the **T** (take address) command to extract the address from the message and copy it to your address book. Second, from the main menu, you can use the **A** command. **pine** will show you the contents of your address book and let you edit, delete, and add new entries.

When you are composing a message, you can make use of the address book either by typing a nickname (**pine** will substitute the full address) or by pressing **^T**. If you are editing the **To:**, **Cc:** or **Bcc:** lines of the header, pressing **^T** will show you the entries in your address book and let you choose the one you want.

For reference, Figure 8-13 summarizes the commands used to work with your address book.

Customizing pine

pine was designed to hide all of its technical details wherever possible. Most of the time, you can use **pine** without any changes and rely on the built-in defaults. However, in certain cases, you may want to control a particular feature. To do so, you can modify the configuration. This is a long list of choices that lets you fine-tune the program to work the way you want.

To change the configuration, select **S** (setup) from the main menu, and then press **C** (config). **pine** will now display all the possible configuration items that you can control. To modify an item, simply move to it and press the appropriate key. (When you move to an item, the menu at the bottom of the screen will show you the allowable commands.)

Note: **pine** keeps the configuration in a file named `.pinerc` in your home directory. I suggest that you do not edit this file by hand. It's a lot easier to let **pine** do it for you.

Command	Description
T	(while reading a message) take address from message
^T	(while composing a header) display address book
A	(from the main menu) edit the address book

Figure 8-13. pine: *Commands for using your address book*

As a general rule, you should not change anything you do not understand. Most of the items have defaults that work fine the way they are. However, there are a few items I do want to talk about, which I think you may want to change. In general, if you are not sure what a configuration item does, all you need to do is move to it and press **?** or **^G** to display help.

HINT

If you want to become a **pine** expert, move to each of the configuration items in turn and read the help text. By the time you finish, I guarantee you will know more than anyone else in your immediate circle of friends. That is how I learned about every single configuration item. (And that is why I get invited to so many parties.)

Here are the configuration items I think you may want to change. These are the items I have chosen to customize. You, of course, will have your own choices. Note: For your convenience, I have listed the items in the order in which they occur in the configuration. However, an easy way to find a particular item is to use either **W** or **^W** to search for the name you want.

- **default-fcc** Within the **pine** header, there is a line named **Fcc:** which shows the folder to which the outgoing message should be saved. (You can display this line by pressing **^R** while you are within the header.) Normally, **pine** will save all messages to a folder named **sent-mail**.

  I think it is a bad idea to save every message automatically. All that will happen is you will end up with a whole lot of messages you will rarely, if ever, want to look at. Much better to save only those messages that are really important. To do so, tell **pine** you do not want to save all outgoing messages. Then, when you do want to save a message, press **^R** to display the full header and fill in the **Fcc:** line with the name of a folder.

  To tell **pine** that you do not want to save outgoing messages automatically, move to the **default-fcc** item. Then press **A** to "add" a value, and press RETURN without specifying anything. This should give the item an "Empty Value", which is what you want.

- **enable-alternate-editor-implicitly** and **editor** You can use an alternate editor instead of **pico** by turning on this setting. Move to this item, and then press **X** to turn it on.

  Now, in order for this to work, you must tell **pine** which editor you want to use. Move to the **editor** item and give it a value of **vi** (or **emacs**, or whatever command you use to start your favorite editor).

- **enable-bounce-cmd** When you are reading a message, it is useful to be able to bounce it to another person. By default, **pine** will only forward messages, not bounce them. To be able to bounce messages, move to the **enable-bounce-cmd** item, and press **X** to turn it on.

- **enable-full-header-cmd** I find it handy to be able to press **H** to display the entire header while reading messages. By default, **pine** will not allow the **H** command. To use it, move to the **enable-full-header-cmd** item, and press **X** to turn it on.

- **enable-jump-shortcut** When you are working with the index or reading a message, you can move to a specific message by typing **J** (the jump command) then typing the message number. It is a lot more convenient to not have to type **J**. To set this up, move to the **enable-jump-shortcut** item, and press **X** to turn it on. Now, when you want to jump to a message, all you have to do is type its number and press RETURN.

- **enable-suspend** It is often convenient to put a program on hold, do something else, and then later return to what you were doing. The standard Unix method for doing this is to press **^Z** (the suspend key) to pause the program. You will now be at a shell prompt. After entering as many commands as you want, you can return to where you were by entering the **fg** (foreground) command.

  All of this is called job control. The point is, within **pine**, you can't use job control unless you turn on the **enable-suspend** item. To do so, move to this item, and press **X** to turn it on.

- **enable-unix-pipe-cmd** As I described earlier in the chapter, it is possible to pipe the contents of a message to a Unix filter. This allows you to have another program read the message and do something with it. To make use of this facility, move to the **enable-unix-pipe-cmd** item, and press **X** to turn it on. Now, you can use the | (vertical bar) command while reading a message.

- **signature-at-bottom** By default, **pine** places the contents of your signature file at the top of each new message. I prefer to have the signature at the bottom. To do so, move to the **signature-at-bottom** item, and press **X** to turn it on.

- **initial-keystroke-list** I find it useful to have **pine** display the index automatically each time I start the program. One way to do this—which I explained earlier in the chapter—is to use the **pine** command with the **-i** option. An easier way is to tell **pine** that you always want to start with the index. To do so, move to the **initial-keystroke-list** item, and press **X** to turn it on.

Chapter Nine

Understanding the Web

The Web is an ambitious client/server system that offers a simple, consistent interface to the vast resources of the Internet. By using the Web, you can access much of what the Internet has to offer. Moreover, getting started is easy, and just about anyone can start enjoying the Web with little preparation.

When you use the Web, you follow your nose: that is, you start anywhere you want, and you jump from one place to another pursuing whatever strikes your fancy. The amazing thing is, with only a few simple commands or mouse clicks, you can jump your way around the Internet like a hyperactive flea at a dog convention.

Intrigued? Read on.

Orientation to the Web

Like parachute jumping, surfing in the ocean, or watching an autopsy, using the Web is something you just can't understand through reading. You have to do it yourself. But there is an important reason for this, as I will explain later in the chapter. What I will do is explain how the Web works and teach you everything you need to use it well. Then you can start using it on your own and, after a while, you will come to really understand the Web.

So, what is this Web thing anyway? In one sense, the Web is the name given to a large collection of information, pictures and other data you can access over the Internet. This information has one important characteristic: A data item can contain a link to another data item.

For example, say you are reading an essay about how to prepare California-style food, and you encounter a reference to a recipe for groatcakes. On the Web, such information can be set up so the word "groatcakes" is displayed in a special color on your screen, and when you click on that particular word with your mouse, you are shown an actual groatcake recipe.

Here is another, more important example. Say you are reading an article about me, Harley Hahn. It mentions that my birthday is December 21. The words "December 21" are displayed in a special color and, when you click on them with your mouse, you are shown a list of suggested presents I might enjoy.

In each case, a particular word or sequence of words is displayed in some special manner. In our examples, the words were displayed in a special color. We say that such words are HIGHLIGHTED. When you select a highlighted item (say, by clicking on it with a mouse), you are shown other information. In such cases, we say there is a LINK between the highlighted item and the other information. For instance, there was a link between the words "December 21" and the list of presents. On the Web, a link can point anywhere else on the Internet. Thus, it is possible to follow one link after another, jumping from one computer to another, all around the Net.

In Web language, any information that contains links to other information or to a service is called HYPERTEXT. This idea, that information can contain links to other information, is an important one, and I will discuss it in detail later. For now, all I want to do is introduce you to the basic idea.

The examples I gave are valid examples of hypertext, although they are not that interesting (unless you have more than a passing interest in either groatcakes or my birthday). At first, you might think I am trying to be cute at the expense of giving you rather dumb examples. The truth is, no matter what examples of hypertext and links I might give you, it would sound pretty lame. Here is why.

When people first hear about hypertext, they tend to think mostly about the idea of links. "Wow," they say, "it's so cool how links within an item of information can point to other information anywhere on the Net." Actually, such people are missing the point. The thing that is cool about hypertext is not the links, but the words *between* the links. And that is why hypertext examples are always so lame: when you talk about the links you are focusing on the wrong part of the Web.

This idea takes some explaining, but before I can do so, I need to spend a few moments discussing the origins of the Web.

How Did the Web Start?

The idea of what we now call hypertext is not a new one. For example, in 1945, an engineer named Vannevar Bush discussed an information machine he called a "Memex". He observed that the amount of information available to our society was increasing rapidly and, in order to cope with such vast resources, readers would need to be able to follow various "trails" as they worked their way through the data. His Memex machine would help people do so.

In 1981, a fellow named Ted Nelson self-published a book called *Literary Machines* in which he coined the word "hypertext". He described a system which he named "Xanadu", that would allow people to create and use hypertext.

The first popular hypertext computer application was not released until 1987. It was called Hypercard and was written for the Macintosh. Hypercard made it possible for Mac users to create and share "stacks" of information. Within each stack, there could be hypertext links from one data item to another.

However, important new ideas are usually developed separately by more than one person at the same time. For example, calculus was developed at roughly the same time (1660-1670) by both Isaac Newton (in England) and the German Gottfried Liebnitz (in France), completely independently of one another. Similarly, in the early 1980s, Tim Berners-Lee, a scientist at CERN in Switzerland, was developing his own idea of linked data independent of Nelson's work.

(CERN is the European Laboratory for Particle Physics, headquartered in Geneva, Switzerland. The word "CERN" is an acronym for the original name of the organization, Conseil Européen pour la Recherche Nucléaire.)

Berners-Lee was a member of the high-energy physics community. (You must have heard of them. They are the guys who spend large amounts of money building powerful machines to smash together small particles so they can see what happens.) These physicists were awash in information and Berners-Lee was trying to invent a method to make it all manageable. In March of 1989, he collaborated with Robert

Cailliau to start work on a project that would provide access over a computer network to what we now call hypertext.

Berners-Lee described what he was creating as a "web" consisting of a "network of links". The name stuck and, in May of 1991, the World Wide Web was released for use at CERN. In August 1991, the World Wide Web was announced on Usenet (the global system of discussion groups). And in January of 1992, the first program to access the World Wide Web was made available to the public via anonymous ftp. This meant that the program to access the World Wide Web was now available to anyone on the Internet.

At first the World Wide Web was only a curiosity, and most of the development remained centered at CERN. However, within a short time, interest in the idea grew and what started as a primitive "World Wide Web" began to evolve into a much more complex idea that we now call "the Web". Berners-Lee and Cailliau had initiated an effort that, in less than two years, would change forever the way human beings create and share information over the Net.

How the World Wide Web Turned into "The Web"

We must be careful of our terminology here. When this whole thing started (at CERN), it was named the World Wide Web, which was often abbreviated as WWW. However, since that time, the World Wide Web has evolved into something much more complex and important. This new thing—which I will describe in a moment—is what we call the Web. In other words, when I refer to "the Web", I mean the modern version of what used to be called the World Wide Web. (Although there are some people who still refer to the Web as the World Wide Web or WWW, that usage is fading.)

Like all the Internet services, the Web is based on a client/server system (see Chapter 2). This means you use a client program (which runs on your computer) to contact a server program (which runs on another computer, somewhere on the Internet). In particular, you use a web client to communicate with a web server.

From the beginning, web clients were called BROWSERS. The name is a good one for two reasons. First, many people use the Web just for browsing, so the name is descriptive. Second, browsers can access a lot more than web servers, and so to call such programs "web clients" would be incorrect. For example, modern browsers can act as web clients, gopher clients, ftp clients, Usenet clients and even mail clients. This means that by using a single program—your browser—you can access different types of Internet services, not just web servers.

Thus, what started as the World Wide Web (a relatively simple client/server system for accessing hypertext from web servers), has grown into THE WEB: an enormous Internet-based information utility encompassing not only web servers offering hypertext data, but all the gopher servers on the Net, all the anonymous ftp sites, all the Usenet discussion groups, and so on.

You might ask, if my browser can access all of these Internet resources, does that mean all the services on the Net are being absorbed into the Web? Might it not be that, one day, the Web and the Net will actually be the same thing? The answer is no, and to explain why, I will have to show you what the Web really is.

What the Web Really Is

In the last 100 years, mankind has developed a number of communication systems—the telephone, the radio, television, modern newspapers, and so on—that have had a significant effect on our society. These systems have changed how we interact as a species by making the mass dissemination of information quick, inexpensive and reliable. This capability has increased the pace of events drastically. As individuals, it seems to us that life is getting faster and faster, and it is becoming more and more difficult to keep up.

However, for all its power, our modern communication media have one important limitation: there is no easy way for large numbers of individuals to participate. For example, although many people may read what is printed in the daily newspaper, there is no way for them to respond to what they read. Nor is there a way for them to contribute information of their own.

The Net has changed all of that. For the first time, mankind has a means of disseminating information quickly, while at the same time allowing people to respond and to contribute. Moreover, the Net allows connections between any two people or among any group of people.

This is important for a reason most people don't yet understand. As a species, it is inherent in our nature to connect to one another. Human beings are nothing if not social. We constantly talk, argue, discuss, trade information and solve problems. Indeed, now that we have the Net (or the beginnings of the Net), it is evident that people have a biological need to connect. The most significant thing about the Net is it gives us the potential to connect any one person, to any other person or group of people, as becomes necessary. For example, you can send mail to one person or to a group of people; you can post an article to a Usenet discussion group; you can create some hypertext and put it on the Web; and so on.

As we consider these points, the true nature of the Web begins to emerge. It is not merely another Internet service or another cool thing to do with a computer. The Web is nothing less than an effort to connect the human species in a significant and powerful way.

Actually, the Web is not even the first such attempt to connect mankind on the Net. It is the fourth such attempt. The other three were mailing lists, Usenet and the gopher.

The Web Is the Fourth Attempt

Sending and receiving electronic mail was one of the first services available on the Internet, and not long after this service became available, a few of the early users set up the Internet's first mailing list (to discuss science fiction). A mailing list is a mechanism by which a message can be sent to a group of people, all at the same time. Mailing lists are important as they allow groups of people to carry out discussions by mail. I discuss mailing lists in detail in Chapter 22. The reason I mention them now is because they represent the first attempt to connect groups of people over the Net.

The second such attempt was the development of Usenet, a system of discussion groups. At first, Usenet contained a handful of groups involving people in only a few locations. However, the idea was a good one, and it wasn't long before more and more discussion groups were formed, and many Internet sites began to connect to the service. Today, there are thousands of Usenet groups, devoted to just about any topic you can imagine. (I discuss Usenet in Chapters 13 through 15.)

Compared to mailing lists, Usenet provided a much better means of connecting people. The discussion groups were a lot more accessible to the general population of the Net than were mailing lists. However, there was still an important limitation. Usenet articles are automatically deleted after a short time and, for this reason, it was difficult to accumulate information on a permanent basis. Usenet was great for discussion and debate, but not much more.

The solution to this problem was the development of the gopher system. Gophers provide information to anyone on the Net, by furnishing menus from which you can choose items. Each item is either another menu or data of some type. When you select an item, your gopher client will fetch it. If the item is a file of text, for example, your client will display it for you. If the item is another menu, your client will show it to you and wait for you to make another selection. (I discuss gophers in Chapters 16 and 17.) Thus, using a gopher is simple. You choose from one menu after another, looking for what you want.

Within a short time, the gopher system became popular, and thousands of organizations around the world created their own gopher servers making vast amounts of information available to anyone on the Net. This system represented the third significant attempt to connect people over the Internet. Indeed, there was a time—for about a year and a half—when gophers (along with Usenet) were the dominant information resource, and the conventional wisdom was that the future of the Net lay with this particular system of menus and data.

The demise of the gopher system as the most popular Internet resource was striking for two reasons. First, no one saw it coming. Second, it happened so quickly. In hindsight, it is possible to see why such a change was inevitable. Gophers require that information be arranged into menus, and people just don't think that way. Gophers are good at presenting well-defined chunks of information in a straightforward manner. This is why the gopher system was an enormous hit within companies, universities and government offices. Such organizations thrive on well-defined chunks of information and, philosophically speaking, have a great need to disseminate it. Individuals, unfortunately, do not communicate in this way.

What was needed was a new Internet system, one that could handle all the information of a gopher, while allowing individual people to create and share in a comfortable manner. The Internet needed something that would let anyone become a creator, while maintaining the order and nurturing environment of a well-defined system. Such a something would encourage millions of new users to connect, induce thousands and thousands of organizations to develop a presence on the Net, and make the Internet a permanent part of the popular culture, changing forever our view of mankind and our role in society.

Such a something was the Web: the fourth great attempt by our species to connect ourselves over the Net.

Why the Web Grew

At first the Web was a curiosity. By 1992, the basic idea of hypertext—data containing links to other data—had been explored and was widely accessible on the Net. However, the number of people using the Web was still small. This was because the principal web client programs ran under text-based Unix systems and were awkward to use.

This all changed in February 1993, when Marc Andreesen, then a student at the University of Illinois, released a new program called Mosaic. Mosaic was the first web client to take advantage of a graphical user interface (windows, scroll bars, mouse clicks, and so on). The first version of Mosaic ran under X Window (see Chapter 2), the graphical user interface for Unix. This restricted the user population to those people who had Unix workstations running X Window. Still, it was enough to show the world what the Web *could* look like with the right interface.

The reason this was significant relates to something I said earlier. The most important aspect of the Web is not the links that connect one data item to another. Rather, it is the text between the links. To see why this is the case, let's compare how a gopher and the Web display information. As an example, Figure 9-1 shows a typical gopher menu, while Figure 9-2 shows some typical Web information.

Gopher information is arranged in menus that are easy to understand and well-ordered. The thing is, people do not think in menus. Web information consists of words, sentences and images, punctuated by links to other information. Although this is not exactly how people think, it is a lot closer. When you use the Web, most screens contain text to read and, possibly, pictures to look at. When you use a gopher, most screens contain choices. To actually get to something interesting to read or look at, you have to navigate your way through a series of menus.

Thus, when you use a gopher, you must separate the acquisition of ideas into two processes: selecting (from menus) and reading (text). When you use the Web, you blend these two processes into one continuous activity, an activity which we might call "browsing". In hindsight, we can see that human beings are more comfortable browsing than selecting and reading.

This observation explains why the Web came to dominate over the gopher system, Usenet and mailing lists, but it doesn't explain why it took a few years to do so. The reason was that, until a web client was developed that could be used by most everyone, the Web was still a curiosity. As I mentioned, Marc Andreesen released the X Window version of Mosaic in February, 1993. This was enough to show people what the Web could be, but not enough to make it popular. After all, relatively few people had access to the Unix workstations necessary to run X Window.

```
            Internet Gopher Information Client v2.0.16

     University of Foobar, Unix Studies Department Gopher Server

->      1.   About the Unix Studies Department.
        2.   Where to Buy the Book "A Student's Guide to Unix".
        3.   Search the Online Unix Manual <?>
        4.   The Internet Studies Department Gopher/
        5.   Gopher Servers at the University of Foobar/
        6.   Other Gopher Servers Around the World/
        7.   University of Foobar Directory <CSO>
        8.   The Unix Daemon <Picture>
        9.   University of Foobar Library Catalog <TEL>
       10.   The Sound of Unix <)
       11.   Fun and Games/

Press ? for Help, q to Quit, u to go up a menu        Page: 1/1
```

Figure 9-1. *A typical gopher menu*

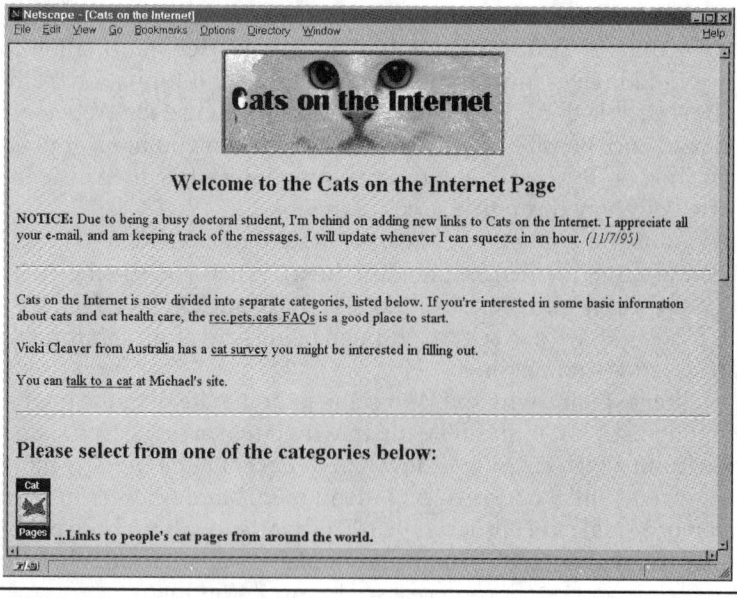

Figure 9-2. *A typical web screen*

However, in the fall of 1993, two new versions of Mosaic were released, one for PCs running Microsoft Windows, the other for the Macintosh. And with the release of Mosaic for Windows and the Mac, everything finally came together:

- an information system that supported words, ideas and pictures
- links that allowed you to jump from one item to another
- a user interface that was familiar and easy to use
- client programs for PCs and Macintoshes, the computers used by most people

Now anyone on the Net could access the Web by starting a program and selecting items with a mouse.

Humanity had created its fourth great attempt to link people together over the Net, and this time it was successful, wildly successful, beyond anybody's expectations.

Chapter Ten

Using the Web

In Chapter 9, I introduced the Web and explained why it is so important and useful. In this chapter, I will show you how the Web works, along with the basic techniques you need to have fun and be productive. I will cover everything you need to understand to use the Web, as well as explain what is involved in having your own web site.

What Is It Like to Use the Web?

In Chapter 9, I explained that the Web is based on hypertext, information that contains links to other information or to services. Underneath, the Web is a huge client/server system (see Chapter 2), with many web servers all over the Internet. To access those servers, you use a client program called a browser that fetches information from a server on your behalf, and then displays the information on your screen. Your browser acts as your interface into the Web, doing whatever is necessary to carry out your requests.

 INTERNET RESOURCE *Look in the catalog under Internet Resources for* ***Web: Browsers***

If you have never used the Web before, the idea of hypertext and using a browser will seem a bit strange, so let's start with a few examples. First, here is an example from regular life. You are reading an encyclopedia, looking at an article with the title "Trees". At the end of the article, you see a reference that says "For related information, see Plants". This last line is a link from the "Trees" article to the "Plants" article. To follow this link, you must fetch the appropriate volume of the encyclopedia and turn to the "Plants" article.

Now, if you were using a browser to read the "Trees" article on the Web, the reference to the "Plants" article would be highlighted in some way. For instance, the actual word "Plants" might be displayed in a different color and underlined. To follow the link, you would use your mouse to click on this word. Your web client program would then fetch the "Plants" article—no matter where it was on the Internet—and display it for you on your screen.

Here is another, more complex example. You have a friend who has set up his own web site. He gives you the address, and you decide to check it out. To do so, you start your browser and tell it to contact the address of your friend's web site. (Don't worry about the details, I will explain later.)

In order to carry out your request, your browser contacts the web server at the address you specified. This server honors the request by sending information to your browser, which displays it on your screen. You see messages and pictures designed by your friend. Within the text, most of the words are black on a gray background. However, there are certain words that are displayed in red and underlined. These words represent links that you can click on at any time.

This web site is shown in Figure 10-1. Here is the first paragraph you read:

```
I am a librarian at Stanford University.  Last year,
I went on a bicycling trip in Holland with my girlfriend
Yolanda.  While we were there, we visited my friends
Peter and Karin and their bunny Pixie.  My hobbies are
photography and collecting Elvis memorabilia.
```

This example contains several links (which I have underlined). The first is **Stanford University**. If you click on this, you will jump to the web site for Stanford University. The next link is **bicycling trip**. Clicking on this will display a long description, written by your friend, of his trip and all the places he visited. The following link is **Yolanda**. Click on this and you will find more information about your friend's girlfriend. First, you will see a picture of Yolanda, followed by the words "For more information about Yolanda, click **here**." If you do click on that link, you will jump to Yolanda's own web site.

Now that you see how this works, you might be able to guess what type of information the rest of the links point to. If you select **Peter and Karin**, you will see a picture of Peter, Karin, Yolanda and your friend, standing beside their bicycles outside a restaurant in Amsterdam. Clicking on **Pixie** shows you a picture of Pixie

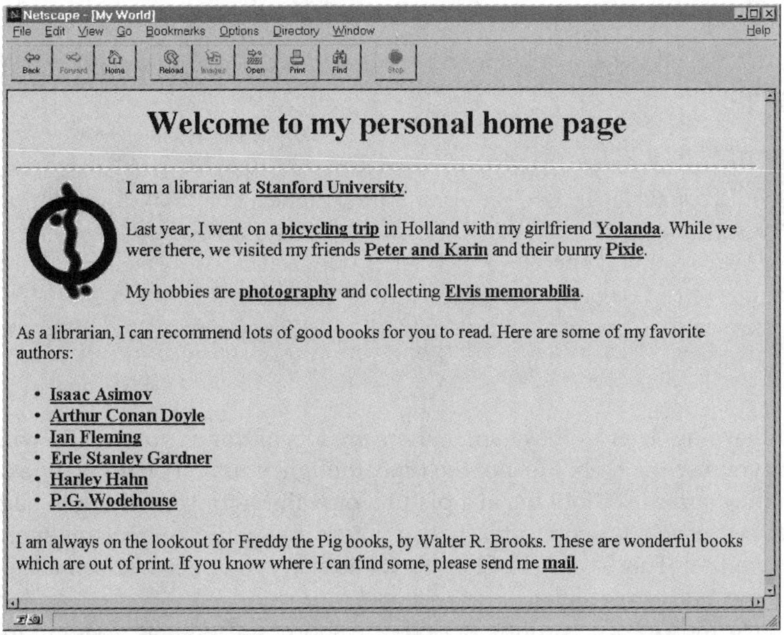

Figure 10-1. *A typical web page*

the Bunny. Clicking on **photography** shows you a small gallery of some of your friend's photos along with a few links pointing to various photographic resources on the Net. Finally, selecting **Elvis memorabilia** takes you to a list of Elvis information sites around the Net, one of which is a guided tour of Graceland (Elvis' home).

Now, the only way to really get a feel for the Web is to use it, but the foregoing example will at least give you an idea of how it works. People create text, and within that text, put links to other text, pictures and various resources. Sometimes links point to something else created by the same person (such as the link to the description of the bicycle trip, or the pictures of Peter, Karin and Pixie). Other links point to resources elsewhere on the Net (such as the links to Yolanda's web site or the Elvis information sites).

This example describes a web site created by one person for his own amusement, and there are many such sites on the Net. However, there are also many web sites created by organizations: companies, schools, government agencies and so on. When you visit such sites, you will find "official" information. For example, the AT&T web site will describe the services and products offered by AT&T. As you might expect, such web sites are better organized, but more formal than the personal ones. For example, the AT&T web site will have slick graphics and all kinds of corporate information. However, what you won't see are descriptions by an AT&T executive of her last trip to Alabama, along with pictures of her family and the pet possum she used to keep as a child.

HINT

The Web is actually a mixture of two very different types of web sites: those created by individuals and those containing information about an organization. This gives the Web a countenance that is unmatched anywhere else in our society. Thus, as you use the Web, you will encounter official, no-nonsense corporate, academic and governmental web sites coexisting peacefully with the highly personal and idiosyncratic creations of people who are free to write and exhibit anything they want.

As I will explain later in the chapter, there are lots of things you can do with your browser as you use the Web. Most of the time, though, you will be doing one of three things: reading some text, looking at a picture, or waiting for something to be copied from a web server to your computer. To be realistic, using the Web means spending a lot of time waiting. This is why, in Chapter 4, I advise you to get yourself as fast an Internet connection as possible.

As you use the Web, the waiting periods are short but frequent. To jump from one web item to another, you use your mouse, click on the next item you want to see, and then wait for it to be loaded. Thus, you will find that you develop a definite rhythm:

click, wait, read... click, wait, read... click, wait, read... The overall timing is affected by what you choose to look at—for example, pictures take much longer to copy than plain text—but just the same, there is a rhythm. If you use the Web during the day when many people are sharing the communication lines, you will wait longer. In the middle of night when there are fewer people, the response times decrease and the pulse of the Web speeds up.

Compare this rhythm (...click, wait, read...) to the rhythm of other popular mental activities. Watching television, for example, is ...click, watch, watch, watch, watch... click, watch, watch, watch, watch. Reading a book is ...turn a page, read, read, read, read... turn a page, read, read, read, read.

HINT

We are shaped by our tools more than we like to admit.

Links, URLs and Hyperspace

Before I discuss the details of using your browser, I would like to explain a few of the important terms and concepts you will encounter as you use the Web.

I have already discussed the idea of hypertext: information that contains links to other information or services. I would like to take a closer look at this idea and answer the question: what exactly is a link?

In the same way that every Internet user has a unique email address, every hypertext item on the Net has an address of its own. This only makes sense. When you tell your browser to fetch and display a particular item, the browser must know where on the Internet that item resides.

The format of such addresses is different from that used for mail addresses. One of the reasons is that the people who first developed the Web wanted it to provide access to all types of information and not just hypertext. Thus, they used an addressing system that is capable of referring to just about any type of Internet information resource. Within this system, we use a special type of address called a UNIFORM RESOURCE LOCATOR, usually referred to as a URL. (The name is pronounced as three separate letters: "U R L".)

Within this system, there is a unique URL for any hypertext item on the Net. Moreover, there are also unique URLs for non-hypertext items from other services, such as gophers, anonymous ftp sites, Usenet newsgroups and wais databases. I discuss these resources in detail in other parts of the book. The important thing to understand here is that, because browsers are designed to access any item that has a URL, you can use your browser to access information from a variety of Internet resources and not just hypertext.

Here are two examples of URLs. (For now, don't worry about the details, I will explain them later in the chapter.)

```
http://www.alan.com/
http://www.bu.edu/Games/games.html
```

Notice that both of these URLs start with **http:**. This means that the URL refers to a hypertext item. (The name **http** stands for HYPERTEXT TRANSFER PROTOCOL, the protocol used to send hypertext data over the Internet.) If a URL refers to a different type of item, you will see a different prefix. For example, a URL that starts with **gopher:** refers to a gopher item, a URL that starts with **ftp:** refers to an ftp resource, and so on. Again, don't worry about the details, I will cover them later.

Each URL refers to one specific Internet resource. To express this idea, we say that the URL POINTS to that resource. For example, the first URL in the above example points to the web site for Alan Colmes, a well-known American radio talk show host. The second URL points to a collection of interactive web games at Boston University.

As you already know, your browser retrieves hypertext data and displays it on your screen. During this process, your browser will recognize the links within the data, and display them so as to make them easy to recognize. For example, your browser may display all the links in a special color, or it may underline each link, or both. (In fact, most browsers give you some choice as to how links are to be displayed.)

Take a look at the following example of hypertext in which the links are underlined.

```
If you want to find out about a real cool guy, check
out Alan Colmes, the famous radio star.  Or, if
you have some extra time, try playing some of
the interactive web games at Boston University.
```

Suppose these two links represent the URLs in our last example. That is, suppose the first link, **Alan Colmes**, corresponds to the URL **http://www.alan.com/**, while the second link, **interactive web games**, corresponds to the following URL: **http://www.bu.edu/Games/games.html**.

If you want to see the information at either of these web sites, all you have to do is select one of the links. (With a mouse, you would click on the actual link.) Your browser will then use the corresponding URL to contact the site and ask for the data to be sent to your computer. When the data arrives, your browser will display it for you on your screen.

HINT

A nice way to think about links is to imagine that underneath each link lies a URL. Thus, each time you select a link, it is as if your browser looks under the link, finds the URL, and does whatever is necessary to fetch the information to which that URL points. With most browsers, you can set an option to have the browser display URLs. Once this option is set, whenever you move your mouse pointer over a link, your browser will show you the corresponding URL. Thus, you can move the pointer around the screen and, each time you pass over a link, your browser will show you the URL that lies "underneath".

When you access a web site by selecting a link, we say that you are FOLLOWING the link. For example, you might follow the **Alan Colmes** link to Alan's web site. Although, technically, it is the browser (a program) that is following the link, we usually talk as if we are performing the action ourselves.

For example, say that you see a guy wearing a T-shirt with a picture of Alan Colmes. You ask, "Where did you get such a radical shirt?" and he says, "I made it from a picture I got from the Web. After I found the picture, I had my browser save it to a file on a floppy disk, which I then took to a place where they printed it on a T-shirt for me." "But how did you ever get the picture in the first place?" you ask. "Oh, that was simple," he responds, "I was looking at a place that had information about talk radio, and I just followed a link to the Alan Colmes web site."

Notice the assumed metaphor. When we use our mouse to select a link, we talk as if *we* are following the link; as if using the Web is like venturing into a foreign land in which we jump from one place to another by following links.

Such observations are more than mere fancy. As human beings we tend to interpret new ideas in light of things we already understand. Thus, it is natural for a human being who is using the Web to imagine himself jumping from one Internet location to another. For this reason, we sometimes talk about NAVIGATING the Web.

The reality of it, though, is that you do not really visit various Internet locations. Each time you follow a link, your browser asks for the information to be sent to *your* computer. Thus, you don't really go anywhere: the various places you "visit" are actually brought to you. Still, if you can suspend belief long enough to think of your screen as a window into the Net, it does seem as if the view changes each time you click on a link.

The word we use to describe all of this is HYPERSPACE. Technically speaking, hyperspace consists of all the possible sites you can access using the Web. Of course, this is a metaphor: hyperspace is not a real place that exists in time and space. Still, it is intriguing to imagine that, in the future, you might connect yourself to the Net in such a way that you actually feel as if you are in a different dimension. And, as you follow the links, you might actually feel as if you are traveling in a strange, alien world. In that sense, hyperspace may one day become a real place in which we may spend all our spare hours. In the meantime, don't forget to stay grounded on Planet Earth and pay your telephone bill.

Words to Avoid

In 1982, William Gibson published a science fiction novel called *Neuromancer* in which he described a futuristic computer-mediated world called "cyberspace". At the time, Gibson was fairly ignorant about computers, so his speculation about computers, humans and the future was both annoying and fascinating.

In the early 1990s, as the Internet and the commercial online services began to grow, people started to refer to these new systems as CYBERSPACE. Later, new expressions for the same idea—the INFORMATION SUPERHIGHWAY, the INFOBAHN, and so on—became popular, especially after they were popularized by the American Senator and Vice-President Al Gore.

Then, in 1992, Jean Armour Polly wrote an article introducing the Internet for a librarians' journal. At the time, Brendon Kehoe had just published a landmark article entitled *Zen and the Art of the Internet* and Polly wanted a title that captured the same tone. She decided to choose something nautical (because the "Net" reminded her of a fishing net). After discarding a number of titles, she came up with one that invoked the idea of "fun, changing conditions, and danger". That title was *Surfing the Internet*.

To Polly (who was a qualified librarian), the word "surfing" captured the essence of using the Internet: "The fun was in trying to find something in the same way that a librarian does research. The danger was that the information might be faulty, old or incorrect. And because conditions on the Internet were always changing, you might have trouble finding your way back to a particular source. Even if you could find your way back, the original information might not be there any longer."

After publishing *Surfing the Internet*, Polly revised it and made it available for free on the Internet. The article quickly became the most popular Internet document of its time. What happened next surprised even Polly. The term SURFING became part of the popular culture, but not as Polly originally intended. Instead, the term came to refer to the activity of browsing the Internet.

Today, Jean Armor Polly is a highly respected Internet expert, sometimes referred to as "Mother Internet". She is, perhaps, the most famous woman on the Internet. (If I weren't so modest, I would tell you who the most famous man is.) However, along with William Gibson and Al Gore, she has the dubious distinction of introducing into the language a word that has become trite and overused.

So here is my advice. I encourage you to tell people that you know how to "navigate the Web" and that you spend time on "the Net". And, if you really want, you can even talk about "hyperspace" (as long as you don't use the word more than once in a single conversation). However, please don't ever let me hear you refer to "cruising the information superhighway", or "surfing the Net" or "hanging out in cyberspace". Such words are to be avoided as they will instantly mark you as someone who has no idea what he is talking about.

⚑ HINT

Stay away from meaningless words and expressions that ignorant people use to describe the Net. Remember, as one of my readers, you are a highly intelligent, knowledgeable and motivated individual—not a clueless goober.

Web Pages and Home Pages

Hypertext information is stored in files, and a URL that points to hypertext is actually the address of a specific file on a particular computer. Each time you select a link that points to a hypertext file, your browser will contact the web server at the appropriate site and request a copy of the file specified in the URL.

The contents of a single file of hypertext is called a PAGE or, more formally, a WEB PAGE. Don't get confused, however, by thinking that a web page is like a page in a book. A web page can be any size at all. Some people will design a web site to consist of a single long page. Other people will break the same information into a number of smaller pages (each in its own file), with links between the pages. Thus, a page may be only a few lines, or it may be so large as to contain many screenfuls of information.

Since pages are the logical units of hypertext, you will often hear people referring to an entire web site as a "page". For example, you might overhear a young child ask his mother, "Is it true that Santa Claus has his own web page?" This is a common way to speak, even though many web sites (including Santa Claus') actually have a number of pages.

When your browser requests and waits for a copy of the page from a web server, we say that the browser LOADS the page. (The term comes from the word "download", which means to copy information from another computer to your computer.) Thus, you might hear someone say, "I'll be with you in a moment, just let me get this web page loading."

Another term you will encounter frequently is HOME PAGE. This term has two distinct meanings. First, a home page is the main page for a particular web site. For example, many people have their own web sites which they maintain for fun. These are called home pages. (Figure 10-2 contains an example of such a home page.) With

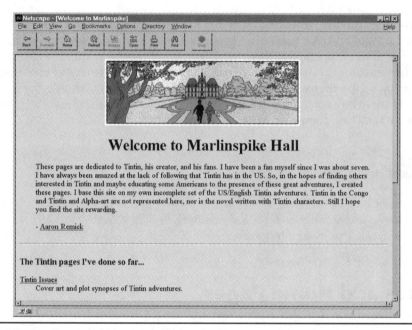

Figure 10-2.   *A personal home page*

an organization (such as a company, university or government department), the home page will be less personal and will act as a main menu from which you can navigate to other pages.

Thus, if you were to take a look at IBM's home page, you would expect to find a main menu pointing to various other pages. If you were to look at Norman Sweetcream's home page, you would expect to find a more personal, idiosyncratic offering, perhaps only a single page.

The second meaning of the term "home page" has to do with your browser. Some people like to start each web session by connecting to the same web page. For example, each time you start your browser, you may want to connect to your favorite humor page to see if there are any new jokes. Most browsers allow you to specify the name of a page that should be loaded automatically each time you start the browser. Within your browser, this page is called your home page.

So don't be confused. To your browser, your "home page" is the page you want to be loaded automatically each time you start the browser. To the Internet community, your "home page" (if you have one) is a specific hypertext page, created by you, as your own personal web site. (I will discuss how to create your own home page later in the chapter.)

 **INTERNET RESOURCE** *Look in the catalog under Internet Resources for* ***Personal Home Pages***

Telling Your Browser Which URL to Use

Each browser works a little differently, but there are certain characteristics that all browsers have in common. As you read the next few sections, follow along with your own browser, so you can see how the details work on your particular system. In the examples, I will mention details pertaining to the Netscape browser, but things should work pretty much the same no matter which browser you are using.

(Note: In the following sections I concentrate on graphical browsers, such as the ones you would use with a PPP account running under Windows, Macintosh, OS/2 or X Window. If you have a Unix shell account, you will probably use the Lynx browser, which I describe separately in Chapter 12.)

Some browsers will automatically load a specific web page for you each time you start the program. This is a feature you can turn off or on and, by default, it may be turned on when you install the program. The web page that is loaded automatically is called your home page. (However, as I explained in the previous section, be sure not to confuse this type of "home page" with a personal home page.) If your program has this feature, and you decide to leave it turned on, you can set your home page to any URL you want. For example, if you have a favorite humor site on the Web, you can have your browser connect to it automatically, so you can check to see if there are any new jokes.

The idea of having a home page from which to start is one that seemed to make sense when browsers first became popular. At the time, the gopher system (see Chapter 16) was widely used and, with a gopher, it makes sense to have a home base. The Web, however, is a lot different and you really don't need to start from the same place each time. For this reason, most people find the auto-loading of a home page annoying and choose to turn off this feature. Still, it is there for you if you want it.

In general, it is up to you to tell your browser where you want to go. You can do this in one of three main ways. First, you can type a specific URL. To do this, you can pull down a menu item that allows you to "open" a new URL. With Netscape, for example, you pull down the "File" menu and choose the "Open Location" item. A dialog box will pop up and wait for you to enter a URL. Alternatively, your browser will have a box, probably near the top of the screen, into which you can enter a URL directly. Simply move your mouse pointer to the box and click the mouse. You can now type a new URL and press ENTER.

Another way to choose a URL is to use one of the built-in features of your browser. Most browsers come with pre-installed URLs to help you connect to a few useful resources. For instance, the Netscape browser has several buttons near the top of the screen. These buttons are assigned to specific resources and, to connect to one of these resources, all you have to do is click on a button. For example, one of the buttons says,

"What's Cool!" When you select it, you will be connected to a list of "cool" web sites maintained by the Netscape company.

The third way in which you can tell your browser what URL to follow is to choose an item from your "bookmark list". A bookmark list is a collection of URLs that you yourself have compiled. As you navigate around the Web, you will encounter sites that are especially interesting to you. Your browser will have an easy way for you to save the URLs of such sites in a special list. At any time, you can recall the list and select any item you want. I will talk about your bookmark list in more detail later in the chapter. For now, I just want you to know you can create such a list and that it is an easy way to jump immediately to a particular web site.

Reading a Web Page

Once you specify a URL, your browser will begin to load the web page at that address. You will find that many web pages contain pictures as well as text and, compared to text, pictures can take a long time to load. For this reason, most browsers will load the text first and then work on the pictures. This allows you to start reading as soon as possible.

If you change your mind about wanting the entire page, you can stop the loading whenever you want. Most browsers have some type of "Stop" button which you can click with your mouse. Alternatively, pressing the ESCAPE key will also work with most programs. If you stop loading a page in this way, your browser will display the parts of the page that were already received, so if you see what you want, there is no need to wait for the entire page to be loaded.

HINT

With most browsers, you do not have to wait until the entire page is loaded to start to select a new link. Even though the current page may still be loading, you can move your mouse pointer to a link and click on it. The browser will stop loading the current page and jump to the new one.

Once a web page is loaded, you can read it at your own speed. If it is too large to fit on your screen, you can move around by using your mouse (click on the scroll bars) or your keyboard (with the PAGEUP and PAGEDOWN keys).

Aside from reading, there are several other things you can do with a page once it is loaded. You can save it to a disk file, print it or mail a copy to someone. You can also save the URL for the page in a special collection of URLs called your "bookmark list" (explained later in the chapter). Saving a URL on your bookmark list allows you to find it again whenever you want. The details of performing these operations vary from one browser to the next. Usually, though, all you will need to do is select an item from a pull-down menu, and specify the appropriate information (file name, mail address and so on).

Links, Forms and Image Maps

Once you have loaded a web page, you can navigate by selecting one link after another. Just move your mouse pointer to a link, click on it, and wait.

HINT

There is an easy way to tell if a word or small picture is a link. Turn on the browser option that tells it to display URLs. Now whenever you move your mouse pointer over a link, your browser will display the corresponding URL. If you are not sure whether or not something is a link, all you have to do is point to it and see if a URL appears.

Most links are simple. They will either be highlighted words or a small graphical element such as a button or a picture. There are, however, two other types of links which are more complex that I want to discuss.

The first type of special link is a FORM. A form is a facility that allows you to enter information to be sent back to the remote web site for processing. For example, say you are visiting the home page of someone who has set up a "guest book". The guest book is set up so anyone who visits the page can leave a personal message, and subsequent visitors can read what other people have written.

When you look at the home page, you will see a box into which you can type a comment. This is the form. Beside the box will be a word or a small picture you can click to send the comment once it is typed. For example, you may see a button that says "Submit". All you have to do is type your comment and then click on the "Submit" button. Figure 10-3 shows a web page that has such a form.

Originally, the idea of a form was developed so that users could submit information which would be sent to the remote web site to be processed, just like a regular form on paper. Although this is still one of the biggest uses for forms, people have found more imaginative ways to use this facility. For example, there are interactive web games in which you can make a move or specify a strategy by filling out a "form" and submitting it.

You might wonder, what happens to the information when it reaches the other end? How is it processed? The answer is, the web server that accepts the information sends it to a special program called a CGI SCRIPT. (The name stands for COMMON GATEWAY INTERFACE.) Thus, whatever you type into the form is sent to a CGI script at the other end that receives the information and processes it in an appropriate manner. This means the person who designed the form must also have set up a CGI script to handle the incoming data. As a user, you do not need to worry about the

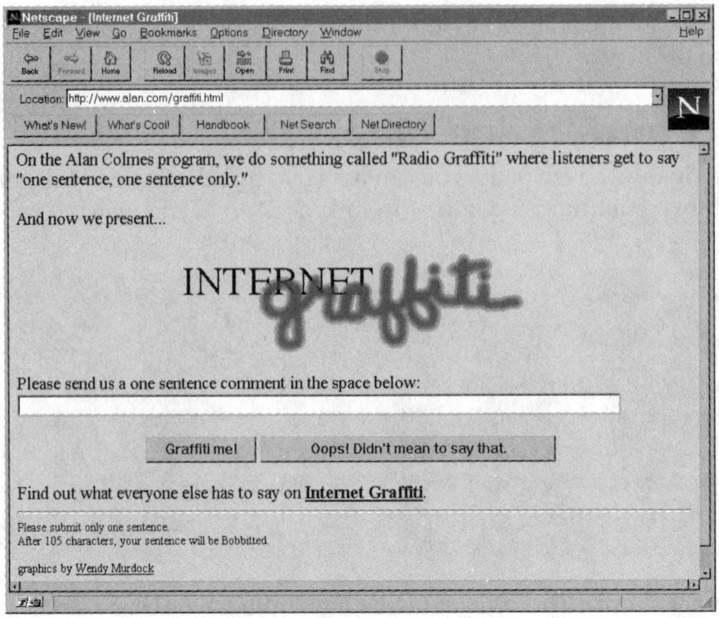

Figure 10-3.   *A web page containing a form*

details. However, if you are developing a home page of your own and you want to use a form, you will have to supply a CGI script to handle the incoming data.

INTERNET RESOURCE   *Look in the catalog under Internet Resources for*
Web: CGI (Common Gateway Interface)

The second type of special link I want to mention is an IMAGE MAP. This is a picture of some type (typically a photo or a drawing) in which the various parts of the image act as separate links. For example, there is a weather report service that will send you a page containing a map of the United States. To request a weather report for any area of the country, all you have to do is click on that part of the map. (Figure 10-4 shows an example.) One common design is to have an image map consisting of several small pictures, each of which is actually a link to a different web page.

How does an image map work? As you move your mouse pointer around the image, your browser keeps track of the coordinates (similar to longitude and latitude on a map). When you click on a particular location, your browser will send the

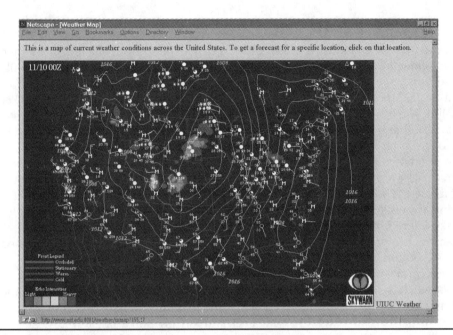

Figure 10-4.   *A web page containing an image map*

coordinates of that location to the remote web server. The web server will then look at the value of the coordinates and send back the appropriate information.

HINT

One problem with image maps is there is no sure way of knowing exactly where the links are. Some browsers will show you the actual coordinates as you move your mouse pointer around the image, but there may be no other clues. Indeed, it can sometimes be hard to recognize a particular picture as being an image map.

For this reason, a good web page designer will put in some text to show you are looking at an image map. For example, you may see something like, "To visit one of our electronic stores, just click on the part of the picture that shows what you want to buy."

INTERNET RESOURCE   *Look in the catalog under Internet Resources for*
Web: Image Map Tutorial

The History List and the Bookmark List

Hyperspace can be a confusing place, and it is easy to jump from one link to another without remembering where you have been. Still, there will be times when you will want to revisit a link you left behind. To help you, your browser keeps a record—called the HISTORY LIST—of the links you have visited. Some browsers keep every link you have visited in the current session, regardless of how much you have branched. Other browsers keep only those links that trace your path from the first page to the current page, with no branching.

There are two ways to use the history list. First, most browsers have an easy way to move backward or forward one link at a time. Typically, there will be two buttons you can press. They will be marked "Back" and "Forward", or have left and right pointing arrows, or something similar. When you click on the "Back" button, your browser will return to the last page you loaded. If you want to move back even further, you can press the button as many times as you want. Once you have pressed the "Back" button, you can press "Forward" to display a subsequent page.

The second way to use the history list is to choose an item from it directly. Your browser will have a way to display the whole history list on your screen. You can then select any item from the list, click on it, and jump to it immediately.

The history list is useful for moving back and forth within a single web session, but there will be many times when you will want to save a web address permanently. For this reason, all browsers have a facility that will save the URL of the current page to a BOOKMARK LIST. Whenever you want, you can display the bookmark list, select an item, and jump to it directly. Unlike a history list, your bookmark list only contains URLs put there by you. Moreover, a bookmark list is permanent. Your browser will automatically save it to a file, so as to be available from one session to the next.

Most browsers have a way for you to edit your bookmark list. At the very least, you should be able to modify the description of any item on the list, as well as delete any unwanted items. Some browsers even allow you to organize the items into categories and subcategories, in the same way that you might organize files into folders or directories.

HINT

As your bookmark list grows, it can become unwieldy and filled with unwanted items. I suggest that you take a few moments every now and then to organize your treasures. You never know what the future holds. If you become famous, a major university may want your bookmark list (along with your papers) after you die. An overgrown, disorganized list will reflect badly on you, serving only to create everlasting embarrassment for your family and friends.

Images

One of the nice things about the Web is there are so many visual images. Broadly speaking, there are two types of pictures: inline images and external images. An INLINE IMAGE is a picture that is a part of a web page. For example, you will often see small pictures or icons loaded along with the text of a page. These are inline images. An EXTERNAL IMAGE is a picture that is a web page in its own right and, when loaded, is displayed in its own window.

Here is an example. Imagine an Internet art gallery which is set up to show you pictures of famous paintings. However, a single picture contains so much data that it would take a long time to load. If the gallery were set up like a real gallery—where you walk in and see all the pictures at once—it might take minutes and minutes to load the gallery home page. The solution is to design the gallery so you can preview the pictures by looking at small images (which load quickly). Then, when you decide which picture you want to see, you can tell your browser to load the full-sized version.

In order to implement this system, the web page designer will create miniature versions of each picture in the gallery. These small pictures will be included on the home page as inline images. Thus, whenever you load the home page, you will see a catalog of what is available in the gallery. Each inline image acts as a link to the file that contains the full-sized picture. So to display a full-sized picture, all you need to do is click on the corresponding small, inline image. When you do, your browser will load the picture and display it in its own window. If you want to look at another picture, you can go back to the home page and click on another inline image.

HINT

If you ever want to use the Web, and you don't care about looking at pictures, your browser will have an option to turn off the automatic loading of images. Setting this option is handy when you want to find something fast, because you don't have to wait for the pictures each time you load a new page.

If you have a shell account (see Chapter 5), another alternative is to use Lynx, a text-only browser. (See Chapter 12 for details on using Lynx.) Personally, when I am doing research and I don't care about images, I often use Lynx because it is much faster than a graphical browser.

Images are stored in various formats, the two most common being GIF and JPEG. For convenience, GIF files are given names that end in `.gif`. Similarly, JPEG files are given names that end in `.jpg`. For example, you might encounter image files named `harley.gif` or `wendy.jpg`. The GIF format was developed by Compuserve. The name GIF stands for "Graphics Interchange Format". JPEG is named after the organization that developed the format, the Joint Photographic Experts Group.

In order to display an image, your browser must be able to understand the format of the data. For example, to display the file **harley.gif**, your browser would have to be able to understand what to do with a GIF file. In web language, a program that can display a particular type of file format is called a VIEWER. Thus, in order to display GIF files, your browser must have access to a GIF viewer. To display JPEG files, your browser needs a JPEG viewer.

It is likely that your browser will have built-in viewers for GIF and JPEG. If it doesn't—or if you want to be able to display other image formats—you can use an external viewer. Simply find an appropriate program (they are readily available on the Net), install it on your computer, and then tell your browser which file formats the new viewer will handle. To do this, use the menu item in your browser that lets you change the configuration or preferences information. This tells your browser which viewer to use when it encounters a particular file format.

Sounds and Video

In addition to images, you will also find many sound and video resources on the Web. Although there are a number of different file formats, only a few are in common use.

The sound formats you are most likely to encounter are AU and WAV. AU was developed by Sun Microsystems; the name stands for "audio file". WAV was developed by Microsoft for Windows; the name stands for "waveform data". There are also other formats (which I will discuss in a minute) that are used for "real-time audio".

For video, there are three common file formats. MPEG was developed by the Motion Picture Experts Group, Quicktime was developed by Apple, and AVI was developed by Microsoft for Windows. The name AVI stands for "Audio/Visual Interleaved data". ("Interleaved" is a technical term indicating that the data is processed in alternating sequences. Don't worry about it.)

As with GIF and JPEG, each of these types of data is stored in files with special names. AU files are given names that end with **.au**; WAV file names end with **.wav**; MPEG file names end with **.mpg**; Quicktime file names end with **.qt** or **.mov** (movie); and AVI file names end with **.avi**. This means that you can tell what format a file uses just by looking at its name. For reference, the most common file formats for images, sound and video are summarized in Figure 10-5.

To listen to audio files or to watch video files, you need programs that can work with the appropriate data formats. With GIF and JPEG files, you use a viewer to display the file. Similarly, we call programs that interpret sound and video files "viewers" (even though you don't really view sound). You may see other names—for example, Netscape calls such programs "Helper Applications"—but the name "viewer" is a generally-accepted generic term.

Although some of the formats in Figure 10-5 were developed by one company or another, they are all in common use, and viewers are available for all types of computers. For example, although the AU format was developed by Sun, you can

Format	Typical File Name	Origin of Name
GIF	filename.gif	Graphics Interchange Format (Compuserve)
JPEG	filename.jpg	Joint Photographic Experts Group
AU	filename.au	Audio file (Sun)
WAV	filename.wav	Waveform data (Microsoft)
Quicktime	filename.qt	Quicktime (Apple)
Quicktime	filename.mov	Quicktime [Movie] (Apple)
AVI	filename.avi	Audio/Visual Interleaved data (Microsoft)
MPEG	filename.mpg	Motion Picture Experts Group

Figure 10-5. *Common file formats for images, sound and video*

listen to AU files on a PC or Macintosh, as long as you have a program that can interpret that file format.

With respect to sounds, there are two types: regular sounds and REAL-TIME SOUNDS. When you listen to a regular sound, the entire file is downloaded to your computer before the sound is played. With a real-time sound, the sound is played as it is being downloaded.

The advantage of a real-time sound is you do not have to wait for the entire downloading process to complete before you can start listening. However, the sound itself is not saved. It is played as soon as it is received, and the data is not retained.

Regular sounds, on the other hand, are stored in a file. Thus, you can keep a copy of a regular sound and replay it whenever you want. Moreover, regular sounds tend to be of higher quality, because in order to make a real-time sound load fast enough, some of the data is discarded.

Real-time sounds are good for transmitting large amounts of data that no one really wants to store permanently. For example, you might listen to a broadcast of a sporting event or a radio program via real-time sound. Regular sounds are used for storing more permanent data. For example, you will find many regular sounds available in web sites and anonymous ftp sites around the Internet.

If your browser does not come with a built-in viewer for any of these formats, external viewers are readily available on the Net. When you install a viewer on your computer, all you need to do is tell your browser where the program can be found, so it knows where to ask for help when it encounters that particular file format. (You set up such information using the configuration or preferences menu.)

Regular sounds use the file formats I mentioned above. Real-time sounds use a variety of different formats. The important thing is to make sure you have the correct viewer—that is, playback program—for the type of sound to which you want to listen.

HINT

Sound and video data takes up a lot of room, even more so than pictures. For this reason, such files tend to be large. Indeed, it is not uncommon to spend minutes and minutes loading a (regular) sound or a video clip, only to have it play back in just a few seconds.

In this way, listening to sounds or watching video on the Web is a lot like Life. People complain that it takes a long time to get what they want and that the quality is poor, and yet the whole thing is over much too soon.

Updating Information Automatically

Once you tell your browser to load a web page, you must wait for the information to be sent from the web server to your computer. As the information arrives, your browser (the web client) displays it for you. However, once the page is displayed, it does not change.

Nevertheless, there are times when it is desirable to display information which can be updated automatically. There are two ways in which this can be done.

First it is possible for a web page to be set up so that it tells your browser to reload itself (or a different web page) automatically. For example, a web page might tell the browser to reload the page every 30 seconds. This facility is called CLIENT PULL, because the client program (your browser) is told to "pull" information from the server without your intervention.

An alternate system allows the server to send new data on its own, without your browser having to make a request. This facility is called SERVER PUSH.

With client pull, the connection between the server and your computer is dropped as soon as the web page is finished loading (which is what happens normally). When your browser is ready to ask for more data, it reconnects to the server and issues the request.

With server push, the connection between the server and your computer is kept open indefinitely. This allows the server to send more data whenever it wants.

Client pull and server push are useful in situations where you are looking at data that changes. For example, a financial service could use server pull to update a stock market report every five minutes. An example of client pull is found with certain web-based talk facilities. (A talk facility lets you use the Web to send messages back and forth to other people.) By using client pull, the talk system can update your window at regular intervals in order to show you any new messages that may have arrived. (For more details about talk facilities, see Chapter 25.)

Client pull and server push will not work with any web page or web server. A web page must specifically request client pull, and a server must be designed to offer server push. In addition, your browser must be aware of these features and must know how to support them. (If your browser does not support these services, the web page will still load, but it will not be updated automatically.)

Web Directories and Search Engines

There are so many items available on the Web, I guarantee you will never run out things to do—as long as you know how to find what you want. However, as I explain in Chapter 1, there is no central authority in charge of the Internet, which means there is no central directory of web sites. Anyone can create (or remove) a web site at any time.

A central directory would be wonderful, as it would allow you to search for anything you want. For example, you might want to look for a certain type of gardening information. Or you might want to get a copy of a free program which is available somewhere on the Net. How do you know where to look?

A good number of people have attempted to solve this problem by compiling a Web directory, and designing a tool to allow users to search the directory for a particular resource. The reason I say "attempted to solve the problem" is that the Web is so huge and so volatile, it is impossible to have a fully comprehensive, up-to-date directory.

Still, web directories do make excellent resources, and if you know how to use them, you can almost always find what you want. This is because web page designers tend to put in links to similar resources. Thus, even if you find only a few resources related to a particular topic, these will often lead you to all the information you want. For example, if you are looking for some specific gardening information, starting with just a few gardening pages will likely lead you to all the links you need.

As you can imagine, it would be a difficult and time-consuming job to compile a comprehensive web directory by hand and to keep it up to date. For this reason, the people who maintain such directories use special programs to do most of the work. These programs search the Web relentlessly, looking for new and updated items. (It is common to see such programs referred to by exotic names, such as "spiders", "worms", "crawlers", "robots" and so on. However, don't worry about the names; they are not important.)

There are a number of free, well-maintained directories available on the Web and, in general, there are two ways to use them. First, some directories have home pages organized into categories. To use such a directory, all you need to do is load the home page and choose the category you want. Within that category, there may be subcategories. Thus, you can select categories and subcategories, until you narrow down your search to find exactly what you want.

Other directories allow you to look for something by using a SEARCH ENGINE. To use a search engine, you use your browser to fill in a form, in which you describe what you are looking for. Once you submit the form, it is sent to the search engine, which quickly looks through the directory, finds what you want (if it exists), and sends back the results.

Regardless of how you access a directory—either by selecting categories or by submitting a request to a search engine—the results are similar: You will end up with a number of links. All you need to do is follow the links to see if, indeed, they contain the information you want.

To help you decide which links are the most useful, the search engine will show you some descriptive information. For example, you will usually see not only a set of links pointing to web pages, but the titles of those web pages as well. Some search engines may also show you part of the actual page. Still others will do their best to rank the results from most to least relevant, based on the search criteria you specified.

Using a search engine for a simple search is easy. Usually, all you have to do is type one or more words into the form, click on the "Submit" button, and wait for the results. However, if you specify a more complex search, you can often get better results.

Most search engines allow you to use various types of search criteria. For example, say you want to find all the web sites that contain a reference to "Harley Hahn". The simplest way would be to search for all the web pages in the directory which contain the two words **Harley Hahn**. However, if this doesn't find what you want, you might want to expand your search by looking for pages that contain either **Harley** or **Hahn**. Or you might want to search for the word **Harley**, followed immediately by the word **Hahn**. Or, perhaps, either the word **Harley** followed by **Hahn**, or the word **Hahn** all by itself. Various search engines allow you to formulate a search in different ways. However, there will be help information, and learning the details for a particular search engine is usually easy.

One set of rules you will often see are those allowing you to combine words using the "and" and "or" operations (like the examples in the previous paragraph). Such searches are often called BOOLEAN SEARCHES.

What's in a Name?

Boolean Search

A boolean search is one that combines search items using "and" and "or" operations. The name originates with George Boole, an English mathematician (1815-1864) who flourished in the mid-nineteenth century. Boole, along with another mathematician, Augustus de Morgan, was one of the chief developers of symbolic logic.

Now, symbolic logic (keep following because I am leading you somewhere) applies mathematical symbols to logic. Using such symbols removes the possibility of verbal ambiguities and simplifies the manipulation of logical relationships. In the history of mathematics, this is considered a big deal. For example, not long after the turn of the century, Bertrand Russell and Alfred Whitehead used and extended Boole's symbolic logic to create the first logical foundation of mathematics. Although this work has since been superseded by more modern analysis, it is considered to be one of the stunning intellectual achievements of the twentieth century.

This same use of logic and symbols was later adapted by computer scientists to create techniques used to design and analyze computing machines. In honor of George Boole, this field of study was called boolean algebra. One important facet of boolean algebra is being able to analyze expressions that involve the "and" and "or" operations. Thus, it has become the custom to use the word "boolean" to describe anything that involves such operations. Hence, it is common for searches defined by "and"s and "or"s to be called boolean searches.

Although many people talk about such searches, few people know what the name means, and even fewer know its origin. (But now you do.)

Aside from simple boolean searches, most search engines allow you to use other, more complex types of search patterns. I suggest you become familiar with three or four different search engines, and take the time to read the help information. With a little practice, you will be able to find just about anything you want.

HINT

Take some time to learn how to use several search engines well. The Web is vast beyond the understanding of any single human being, and being able to search with skill and confidence will open doors which are closed to most everyone else.

INTERNET RESOURCE   *Look in the catalog under Internet Resources for* ***Web: Search Engines***

Customizing Your Working Environment

In general, all browsers have the same purpose in life: to act as a client program—that is, your interface—as you use the Web and other Internet services. There are a great many different browsers, and each one has its own characteristics. Nevertheless, all browsers allow you to customize your working environment to some extent.

In order to use your browser well, you should take some time to explore the program itself and its options; to see what you can change and what choices you have. In most cases, you will access the customization features by using a pull-down menu. Look for a menu or submenu named "Preferences", "Options", "Settings" or something similar.

My advice is to take some time and find out how your particular browser lets you modify your working environment. In general, it is safe to change any of the settings, except those which control your actual network connection.

HINT

As you learn how to use your browser, don't be afraid to experiment. What's the worst that could happen? If you really screw things up, you might need someone else to fix the settings for you, or perhaps even reinstall the software. So what? After all, if Humphrey Bogart had been afraid to experiment with his browser, where would he be today?

To get you started, I will discuss the most common ways to customize your working environment. Your browser will have other settings, but the ones I describe here are generic.

- TEXT AND COLORS: You can specify how text should be displayed (for example, size and typestyle), as long as your system allows such controls. You can also set the background and foreground colors used by your browser.

- LINKS: You can specify how links are to be displayed on your screen. You can change their color, underline them, and so on.

- HOME PAGE: Each time your browser starts, it can automatically load a particular page, called a home page. You can turn this feature off and on, as well as specify a URL for the page to be loaded. (Note: Don't confuse the use of the term "home page" in this context with a personal home page. See the discussion earlier in the chapter.)

- WINDOWS: You can change the size and shape of the various windows used to display information. To experiment, load a page with both text and images, and see what happens to each as you change the size of the window. In general, text will wrap automatically to fit in a newly sized window, while images will not change.

- MANIPULATING WINDOWS: Learn how your particular program and GUI (graphical user interface) let you open, close, iconize (shrink) and move windows. In addition, some browsers will let you open a new window whenever you want, so you can load more than one web page at the same time, each in its own window.

- IMAGE LOADING: You can control whether or not images are loaded automatically. If you turn off this feature, things will move a lot faster, as images can take a long time to load. However, you won't see the pictures unless you ask for them specifically.

- VIEWERS: Your browser already knows how to display certain types of data. However, when you encounter a different data type (image, sound, video), your browser will have to call upon another program, called a viewer, to interpret the data. You can find various types of viewers on the Net and install them on your computer. After you do, you must tell your browser about the new viewer and what data types it handles. (Note: Sometimes viewers are referred to as HELPER APPLICATIONS.)

 INTERNET RESOURCE *Look in the catalog under Internet Resources for*
Web: Helper Applications

- THE TOOLBAR: Some browsers have toolbars (collections of small icons) which allow you to access frequently used operations with a single mouse click. To perform an operation, you can click on one of the small icons, rather than selecting an item from a pull-down menu. If your browser uses toolbars, you will be able to control which toolbars or icons are displayed. Some people like to show all the toolbars all the time. Other people never use them at all.

- BOOKMARK LIST: Your bookmark list is a collection of your favorite links, which you can recall and use whenever you want. Your browser allows you to customize your bookmark list by adding, deleting and editing links. Some browsers even let you organize your bookmark links into folders and subfolders. (For more information about using your bookmark list, see the discussion earlier in this chapter.)

- THE CACHE: Whenever your browser loads a new page, it keeps a copy in a storage area called the CACHE. Using the cache makes it quick to return to a page you have already visited, as your browser can display the data immediately without having to reload it from a distant web server. The cache can be either in memory (which means it disappears when you quit the program) or stored on disk (which means the data is maintained from one work session to the next). If your browser can use both types of cache, you should choose which one you want to use. (A memory cache is faster; a disk cache is more permanent.) You can also control how long items are kept in the cache before they are deleted automatically. (When your browser deletes expired items, we say that it FLUSHES the cache.)

HINT

If your browser uses a disk cache, you may end up accumulating a lot of unused cache files. (Each web page and each external image is kept in a separate file.) For example, as I was writing this chapter, I checked my disk looking for old cache files. One of the browsers I use had created 534 files taking up 4,854,820 bytes of disk space. Another of my browsers had stored 266 files using 1,125,128 bytes. Needless to say, it was the work of a moment for me to delete these superfluous files and reclaim the disk space.

Some browsers allow you to select a menu item to flush the cache immediately. If you are using a disk cache, you should probably do this once in a while, just to get rid of old abandoned files. Alternatively, you can look in the disk directory in which your browser keeps the cache files, and delete all the old files manually. Of course, you should not do this unless you are comfortable with files and directories and know what you are doing.

Distributed Applications: Java

A web page contains information in the form of hypertext, and a web browser displays that information. Once the page is displayed, it doesn't really do anything, it just sits there. However, using special technology, it is possible for web page designers to construct programs that can be sent over the Web along with the regular information. When your browser receives such a program, it can run it while it displays the hypertext. Being able to distribute web programs in this way adds a lot of functionality to the basic system.

For example, a web program might display graphics, or show animation, or perform calculations. In fact, just about anything that can be done with a program can be attached to a regular web page and distributed over the Net. The important thing about these programs is the flexibility they bring. The programs are not installed on your computer permanently. They are loaded and executed dynamically, whenever you select the web page to which they are linked.

Such programs are sometimes referred to as DISTRIBUTED APPLICATIONS ("application" being a synonym for "program"). Distributed applications are written in a computer language that is specifically designed for creating distributed programs. The language design must ensure that it is impossible to write a program that can cause damage on someone's computer. After all, when a program is sent over the Web and executed automatically, you don't have the same level of control as when you download a program and install it yourself.

To distinguish such programs from regular software, we sometimes refer to them as APPLETS. One of the important computer languages for writing web-based applets is named Java. If you are a programmer, you can think of Java as being a lot like C++ without the pointers.

To use a Java applet, all you need is a browser that is Java compatible. If you have such a browser, you do not have to do anything special. When you select a web page that contains a Java applet, your browser will load and execute the applet automatically along with the rest of the page. If you try to load the same web page with a browser that is not Java compatible, it will display the information in the regular manner and ignore the applet.

Chapter Eleven

The Web:
Advanced Topics

In Chapter 9, I talk about the importance of the Web and how it fits into our ideas of the Net. In Chapter 10, I explain how to use the Web. The ideas and techniques in Chapter 10 will be enough for most of your needs, most of the time. However, if you want to use the Web in more advanced ways, you will need to understand a few more ideas, which I will discuss in this chapter. By the time you finish this chapter, you will understand just about everything you need to use the Web well.

URLs and Schemes

Using the Web means having your browser act as a client program on your behalf. In order to fulfill your requests, your browser will contact a server, somewhere on the Net, and ask for either information or a service of some type. How does your browser know which server to contact, and what information or service to request? The details of what to ask for and where to find it are specified by a Uniform Resource Locator or URL.

URLs provide a standard way to specify the exact location and name of just about any Internet resource you can imagine. In Chapter 10, I cover the basic ideas of what is a URL and how to use it. In this section, I would like to provide some more details. I will show you how URLs are constructed, and how you can use them to access all types of Internet resources, and not only hypertext.

In general, most URLs have one of two common formats:

```
scheme://hostname/description
scheme:description
```

We use the first format to describe resources that exist on one specific machine. We use the second to describe resources that are general Internet resources. Here are a couple of examples:

```
http://www.alan.com/alan
news:rec.humor
```

I will explain the details in a moment. For now, all I want you to notice is that the first example describes a particular web page on a particular computer. The second example describes a more general resource: a Usenet discussion group. (I discuss Usenet groups in Chapters 13 through 15. In this example, all I want you to know is **rec.humor** is the name of a Usenet group.)

Each URL begins with a SCHEME. This is a name or abbreviation, indicating a specific type of resource. In the first example, the scheme is **http**, which indicates a hypertext resource. (The name comes from the protocol used to send and receive such information: Hypertext Transport Protocol.)

In the second example, the scheme is **news**, which indicates a Usenet discussion group. (Usenet was first set up to distribute news; to this day, discussion groups are still referred to as "newsgroups".)

The most common schemes you will see are **http**, **ftp**, **gopher**, **mailto**, **news** and **telnet** (probably in that order). Later in the chapter, I will discuss each of these in turn. For reference, Figure 11-1 shows a list of all of the schemes that have been defined or proposed (remember, things change). However, this information is mostly for your interest; don't worry about the ones you don't recognize.

URLs and Host Names

As I mentioned in the previous section, there are two basic URL formats. Of the more common schemes, all of them except **news** and **mailto** specify a host name. (A "host name" is the name of a computer on the Internet. I discuss the idea of Internet hosts in Chapter 2.) Here are some examples of URLs that contain a host name:

```
http://www.wendy.com/~wendy
ftp://ftp.uu.net/usenet/news.answers/alt-sex/pointers.Z
gopher://gopher.loc.gov/11/congress
telnet://nightmare.winternet.com:1701/
```

Scheme	Meaning
afs	File accessed via Andrew File System
cid	Content identifier for a Mime body part
file	File
ftp	File accessed via ftp
gopher	Gopher resource
http	Hypertext resource
mailserver	Data accessed via a mail server
mailto	Mail a message to the specified address
mid	Identifier of a specific mail message
news	Usenet newsgroup
nfs	File accessed via Network File System
nntp	Usenet news for local NNTP access only
prospero	Resource accessed via a Prospero directory server
rlogin	Interactive rlogin session
telnet	Interactive telnet session
tn3270	Interactive 3270 telnet session
wais	Access to a Wais database
z39.50	Access to a database via a Z39.50-type query

Figure 11-1. *List of schemes used within URLs*

Here are two URLs that do not specify a host name:

```
news:rec.humor
mailto:president@whitehouse.gov
```

In the first set of examples the URLs point to resources that exist on a particular computer. In the second set of examples, the resources are general Internet resources. Since they do not reside on any particular computer, we do not use a host name.

In most cases, the host name specification consists of two **/** (slash) characters, followed by the Internet address of the computer that contains the resource, followed by a single **/** character. For example, here are the three host name specifications used in the examples above. (For a discussion of Internet addresses, see Chapter 6.)

```
//www.wendy.com/
//ftp.uu.net/
//gopher.loc.gov/
```

There is one important variation of the host name specification I want you to understand. In some cases, you will see a "port number" after the address of the computer.

I explain port numbers in Chapter 23, within the discussion of the telnet (remote login) facility. Basically, a port number identifies a request for a particular type of service. When a port number must be used, it is placed after the address, separated from the address by a **:** (colon) character. Here is an example, taken from one of the URLs above:

```
//nightmare.winternet.com:1701/
```

In general, you would never specify a port number unless you knew one was required. However, if it is required, you must use it.

URLs and Port Numbers

Each type of Internet service has its own specific port number. However, within a URL, you only have to specify a port number if it is not the default for that type of service.

For example, the default port number for telnet is **23**. If you request a telnet service without specifying a port number, it is assumed you want to use port number **23**. Thus, the following two URLs are equivalent:

```
telnet://locis.loc.gov/
telnet://locis.loc.gov:23/
```

When you use a telnet resource that does not use the standard port, you must specify a port number as part of the URL. For example:

```
telnet://nightmare.winternet.com:1701/
```

If you were to omit the port number in this URL, the telnet client would try to connect to the standard telnet port, **23**, which would not work properly. Something would happen, but it would not be what you wanted.

The **http** (hypertext) service, by default, uses port **80**. Similarly, the **gopher** service uses port **70**. In virtually all cases, such resources will use the standard ports, so they do not have to be specified. Still, you could do so if you wish.

For instance, the following two URLs are equivalent. They both point to the same hypertext resource, using port **80**, on the computer named **www.wendy.com**:

```
http://www.wendy.com/~wendy
http://www.wendy.com:80/~wendy
```

Similarly, the following two URLs both point to the same gopher resource, using port **70**, on the computer named **gopher.loc.gov**:

```
gopher://gopher.loc.gov/11/congress
gopher://gopher.loc.gov:70/11/congress
```

Pathnames

The most common type of URL you will see is one pointing to a hypertext resource. The scheme for this type of URL is **http** (which stands for Hypertext Transport Protocol). Here is a typical hypertext URL:

```
http://www.cathouse.org/cathouse/humor/sex/dates.from.hell
```

We can divide such URLs into three parts. The scheme (**http:**), the host name (in this case **//www.cathouse.org/**), and the pathname (in this case **cathouse/humor/sex/dates.from.hell**).

To analyze such a URL, all you need to do is look at each of the parts:

- The scheme (**http**) identifies this resource as being hypertext.
- The host name is the name of the computer.
- The pathname shows where on the host the hypertext resource is stored.

In our example, you could interpret the information as follows: The resource is hypertext, resides on the computer named **www.cathouse.org**, in a directory named **cathouse/humor/sex**, in a file named **dates.from.hell**. The scheme and the host name are straightforward. The pathname will take some explaining.

Many of the web servers on the Internet use an operating system called Unix. For this reason, the pathnames you will most often see in URLs are Unix pathnames. Such pathnames can get complicated, but you don't have to know it all. Here is a quick summary, the minimum you need to know to understand most URLs.

Within a computer system, information is stored in files. For our purposes, we can consider a FILE to be something with a name which holds data. To organize files, we use directories. Informally, a DIRECTORY is something with a name which can hold a collection of files or other directories.

For example, say you have four files containing information about your hobbies. The files are named **stamps**, **coins**, **quilting** and **diapers**. You might organize your files by keeping them in a directory named **hobbies**. (If you are a Macintosh or Windows person, you can consider directories to be the same as folders.)

Within Unix, we express the idea that a directory contains a specific file, by writing the name of the directory, followed by a **/** (slash) character, followed by the name of the file. For example, if we write **hobbies/stamps**, it means "the **hobbies** directory contains a file named **stamps**".

Now, directories can contain not only files, but other directories. For example, say you have three main activities in your life: family, school and your hobbies. You can organize your files so as to have one directory named **activities** to hold information about all three categories. Within **activities**, you have three other directories, **family**, **school** and **hobbies**. Thus, the four separate files relating to your hobbies would be stored within a directory named **hobbies**, which lies within another directory named **activities**. So a more precise name for the **stamps** file would be **activities/hobbies/stamps**.

In Unix terminology, a directory within another directory is called a SUBDIRECTORY; a specification showing a file name along with one or more directory names, is called a PATHNAME. So, in our example, the file **stamps** lies within **hobbies**, which is a subdirectory of **activities**. We can express this by writing the pathname **activities/hobbies/stamps**.

Using this terminology, we can define a typical hypertext URL as follows:

http://_host-name_**/**_pathname_

Notice how this pattern fits the URL from the beginning of this section:

http://www.cathouse.org/cathouse/humor/sex/dates.from.hell

Now it is easy to interpret this pathname.

One way to do so is to pretend you are an invisible being who can travel around the Internet. How would you find the hypertext resource in question? First you go to the computer named **www.cathouse.org**. On this computer, you would look for a directory named **cathouse**. Within this directory, you would look for a subdirectory named **humor**. Within this directory, you would look for another subdirectory named **sex**. And within this directory, you look for a file named **dates.from.hell**.

What's in a Name?

Pathname

In Unix, each file can be described by its name, and the names of the directories and subdirectories in which the file lies. For example:

`cathouse/humor/sex/dates.from.hell`

This specification is called a "pathname", because it tells you which path to follow, from one directory to another, to find the file you want.

One of the important characteristics of Unix is it is designed to support more than one user at the same time. Indeed, some Unix systems have literally thousands of registered users (although they won't all be using the computer at the same time). In order to keep all the files straight, each person is given a specific directory, called his HOME DIRECTORY, in which to store his personal files and subdirectories.

The most common way to specify the name of a person's home directory is to use a ~ (tilde) character, followed by the user name of that person. For example, if I had an account on a Unix system under the name **harley**, my home directory would be referred to as **~harley**. If a friend of mine has an account under the name **wendy**, her home directory would be **~wendy**.

Let's say that, under my home directory, I have a subdirectory named **fun**, which contains another subdirectory named **sports**, which contains a file named **surfing**. The full pathname of this file would be:

`~harley/fun/sports/surfing`

How might this pathname be used in a URL? Say that my Unix account is on an Internet computer named **nipper.ucsb.edu**, and within the **surfing** file, I keep a hypertext document showing pictures of me surfing. I can tell people to access this document by using the URL:

`http://nipper.ucsb.edu/harley/fun/sports/surfing`

Now you know why you see so many URLs whose pathnames begin with a ~ (tilde) character. It tells you the specified resource lies within someone's personal home directory on a Unix system.

HINT

If you want to learn more about Unix, check out my book *The Unix Companion*, published by Osborne McGraw-Hill. It is the best Unix book ever written.

Using Your Browser to Access Anonymous Ftp

From the beginning, the Web was designed to access a variety of Internet resources—not only hypertext, but gopher, ftp, Usenet, telnet and mail. All of these services are important in their own right, and I cover them elsewhere in the book in their own chapters. However, I do want to spend a little time showing you how to use these resources from within your browser. Indeed, many people use their browser for just about everything, rarely using other Internet client programs. (Before I start, you may want to take a quick look at Chapter 3, in which I summarize all of these services.)

There are two ways to use your browser to access a non-hypertext resource. First, within a hypertext document, a link may contain a URL that points to a non-hypertext resource. Just click on this link and you will be connected to the resource automatically.

For example, say you encounter a link that points to a gopher site. To connect to the gopher site, simply click on the link. Your browser will make the connection automatically. The same is true for an ftp site, a telnet session, a Usenet newsgroup or a mailing address. Indeed, sometimes the connection happens so fast and so smoothly, you don't even know what type of resource you are using (unless you look carefully at the URL).

HINT

All browsers can interact with Web servers, gopher servers and ftp servers. Thus, without any other software, you can use your browser to access hypertext, gophers and ftp.

The second way to access a non-hypertext resource is to enter the URL yourself. All browsers have a way for you to type a URL and then jump right to that link. For example, say that someone tells you about a great anonymous ftp site. He tells you there is a wonderful humor archive on the computer named `cathouse.org`. The path of the archive is:

`/pub/cathouse/humor`

If you were using a regular ftp client program (see Chapter 18), you would connect to `cathouse.org`, change to the `/pub/cathouse/humor` directory, and then start looking around. You can do the same thing using your browser by entering a URL equivalent to the specified host name and pathname. In this case, the URL would be:

`ftp://ftp.cathouse.org/pub/cathouse/humor`

Once you connect to this site, your browser will show you all the files and subdirectories in the specified directory. You can then move around by selecting items with your mouse. When you find an item you want to download, just click on it. Your browser will ask you where you want to put the file, and then start the downloading process.

Using Your Browser to Access a Gopher

You can use your browser to access a gopher in much the same way as you would with an anonymous ftp site. Either click on a link that points to a gopher or enter a gopher URL directly.

To enter a gopher URL, use a scheme of **gopher**, and specify the host name of the gopher server. (I discuss gopher in detail in Chapters 16 and 17.) For example, say you want to use the gopher at **gopher.loc.gov**. (This happens to be the U.S. Library of Congress gopher.) To access this site with your gopher, all you need to do is specify the appropriate URL. In this case, it would be:

`gopher://gopher.loc.gov/`

When you specify a URL for ftp, you can make the pathname as specific as possible. For instance, the following URL connects directly to a particular file:

`ftp://ftp.cathouse.org/pub/cathouse/humor/sex/dates.from.hell`

With a gopher site, you have to be more careful, because the names of the gopher menu items are usually not the same as the directory and file names. Here is an example.

The host name of the U.S. Library of Congress gopher is **gopher.loc.gov**. On that gopher system, you can find all kinds of information about the United States. In particular, you can access general information about California by making the following choices, starting from the main menu:

`Government Information`
`State and Local Government Information (U.S.)`
`California`
`California Government: General Resources`

Now, to access this information with your browser, you would have to know what URL to use. But what would you specify for the pathname? It happens that, in this case, the pathname to this information is **11/federal/state.local/ca/general**. If you knew this, you could use the following URL:

gopher://gopher.loc.gov/11/federal/state.local/ca/general

The thing is, in most cases, you don't know what pathname corresponds to a series of menu choices.

The solution is to use a URL that points to the gopher main menu. You can then use your browser to select menu items, one at a time, to find what you want. In this case, you would use the following URL:

gopher://gopher.loc.gov/

This URL will take you to the main menu, just as if you were using an ordinary gopher client. You can then navigate to the item you want by selecting menu items.

HINT

When you are accessing a gopher with your browser, and you find an item to which you would like to return, add the URL to your bookmark list (see Chapter 10). You will now be able to jump directly to the item whenever you want.

Using Your Browser to Read Usenet Articles

As I explained in the last few sections, you can use your browser to access not only hypertext, but anonymous ftp sites and gophers. In addition, most browsers will also allow you to read articles in Usenet discussion groups, send mail messages and initiate telnet sessions. However, before you can use these facilities, you will probably have to configure certain information within the browser. Let's discuss each facility in turn, and I will explain what you will need to do to get started.

Usenet is a vast collection of discussion groups—usually referred to as "newsgroups"—which is distributed across the entire Internet. The articles within these groups are not kept in one particular place. Rather, there are a large number of computers around the Net that act as "news servers".

To read articles from a Usenet newsgroup, you use a Usenet client called a newsreader. Your newsreader contacts your local news server to access whatever information you require. Thus, before you can use your browser to access Usenet, you must tell it the name of your news server. To do so, look for the menu item to set preferences or options or settings, and you should find a place to specify your news server. Normally, you would use the news server maintained by your Internet service provider. (Ask your provider for the name.)

HINT

Sometimes a news server is referred to as an NNTP server. The name stands for "Network News Transfer Protocol".

Aside from the name of your news server, there are other common newsreader settings you can specify. First, you may be able to specify the name and location of your "newsrc" file. This is the file that your newsreader uses to keep track of which newsgroups and articles you have read. (The term "newsrc" is traditional because, in Unix, this file is called the `.newsrc` file.)

A second common setting is to specify how many articles you want your newsreader to show at one time. If you ask for a large number, it will take longer to load the articles when you begin to read a particular newsgroup. However, once the articles are loaded, there will be more articles to read without reloading.

For more information on Usenet, see Chapters 13 through 15, where I provide a detailed discussion of newsgroups, articles and how the whole system works.

Using Your Browser to Send Mail Messages

As a convenience, most browsers allow you to send mail messages. To do so, you use the `mailto` scheme in a URL. The rest of the URL specifies the address to which the message should be sent. For example, say you want to send a message to the President of the United States. His address is `president@whitehouse.gov`. To do so, simply use the following URL:

```
mailto:president@whitehouse.gov
```

You will then be able to specify the standard parts of a message, such as the subject, the text of the message, whether or not you want to attach a file, and so on. The details will depend on the design of your particular browser, but they should be straightforward. One nice feature many browsers have is the capability of "quoting" the current web page within a mail message. This means, if you find something a friend would really like, you can send it to him by entering a `mailto` URL with his address and telling the browser to include the text of the current page.

As with other non-hypertext links, you will sometimes see `mailto` links embedded within a web page. One common convention is for people who design pages to put a link with their own address at the bottom of the page. For example, say you are reading a web page created by someone whose mailing address is `tln@nipper.com`. At the bottom of the page, you see a link that reads, "To send me mail, press here". If you examine the link, you will see it has a URL of `mailto:tln@nipper.com`.

To use the mail system from your browser, you will have to supply some configuration information. The most important item is the name of the computer that acts as your permanent post office, that is, your "mail server". This would normally be a computer maintained by your Internet service provider. (Ask them which name to use.)

HINT

Sometimes a mail server is referred to as a SMTP server. The name stands for "Simple Mail Transfer Protocol".

Aside from the name of your mail server, there may be other configuration settings you can modify, such as your full name, mail address and organization (for the message header), and the name of a signature file. I explain all of these ideas, and the mail system in general, in Chapter 7. Check there for more details.

Using Your Browser to Initiate a Telnet Session

The telnet service allows you to establish an interactive session with another computer on the Internet. Normally, you would expect to need an account (that is, a user name and password) to be able to use a remote computer directly. However, there are a number of computers around the Net set up specifically to provide public services. In such cases, you will be able to telnet to the computer and use it without a password. (For the details about telnet, see Chapter 23.)

You will occasionally find a link to a public telnet service within a hypertext document. For example, the U.S. Library of Congress operates a public telnet service. To access it, you would use a telnet client to connect to **locis.loc.gov**. (The name **locis** is an acronym for "Library of Congress Information System".) Thus, within a hypertext document, you might find a link that says "To access the Library of Congress system click here". If you examine the link, you will see it has a URL of **telnet://locis.loc.gov/**.

Alternatively, you can initiate a telnet session by entering a telnet URL of your own. For example, say you want to use telnet to connect to a computer named **nightmare.winternet.com** using port number **1701**. All you need to do is tell your browser to process the following URL:

```
telnet://nightmare.winternet.com:1701/
```

To initiate a telnet session, most browsers will call upon a separate client program. Thus, before you can use telnet, you must configure your browser so it knows the name and location of your telnet client. (If you don't already have a telnet client, you must find one and install it on your computer. Such clients are readily available on the Net.)

HINT

Standard telnet clients emulate a VT-100 terminal. (See Chapter 5 for a discussion of this topic.) If you need to connect to an IBM mainframe computer, you will probably need to use a "tn3270" client. This type of telnet client emulates an IBM 3270 terminal.

Hint for Using URLs

I have been using the Web for a long time and, during that time, I have encountered just about every common problem that exists. In this section, I would like to pass on some of the wisdom I have gained through the years.

- Don't change upper- and lowercase within URLs.

As a general rule, schemes should be lowercase, host names are case insensitive, and pathnames are case sensitive. Thus, the following URLs are equivalent:

```
ftp://ftp.uu.net/usenet/news.answers/alt-sex/pointers.Z
ftp://Ftp.Uu.Net/usenet/news.answers/alt-sex/pointers.Z
ftp://FTP.UU.NET/usenet/news.answers/alt-sex/pointers.Z
```

Some browsers allow you to use upper- or lowercase schemes (for example, **HTTP** or **http**). However, other browsers only accept lowercase, so play it safe and avoid uppercase.

Pathnames are almost always case sensitive. This is because many web servers reside on Unix computers and, in Unix, file and directory names are case sensitive. In our example, for instance, the last letter of the pathname must be an uppercase **Z**; if you use a lowercase **z** the URL will not work.

In general, my advice is to use lowercase schemes and host names, and to type pathnames exactly as written.

- Transcribe URLs carefully; use copy and paste when possible.

URLs can be long, complex and easy to mistype. For example, it is common to confuse a **1** (number one) with an **l** (lowercase letter **L**), or a **0** (zero) with an **O** (uppercase letter **O**). In addition, you must be careful not to change the case of any part of a pathname. Thus, I suggest you copy and paste URLs whenever possible. (You should be able to do this if you are using a GUI, such as with Windows, Macintosh, OS/2 or X Window.)

For example, if a friend mails you a message in which he mentions an interesting URL, use your GUI to copy the URL from the message, and paste it right into your browser.

- Recognize common host name patterns.

   Host names are usually chosen to indicate the type of service being offered. Thus, most web servers have host names beginning with **www** (remember, the old name for the Web was the World Wide Web); gopher servers often have names beginning with **gopher**; and anonymous ftp servers often have names starting with **ftp**. Here are several examples:

```
www.wendy.com
ftp.uu.net
gopher.loc.gov
```

- You can often guess which URL to use.

   Say you want to connect to the IBM web site, but you don't know the address. A reasonable guess would be to use a URL with a host name of **www.ibm.com**. In this case:

```
http://www.ibm.com/
```

(Indeed, this URL will work.) In general, if you want to see if the XYZ company has a web site, try:

```
http://www.xyz.com/
```

Similarly, if you are looking for the main web site at the University of Foobar, try:

```
http://www.foobar.edu/
```

You can also try this trick with **gopher** or **ftp** to look for a gopher or anonymous ftp site.

- If a URL doesn't work, try a shorter version of the pathname.

   Say someone gives you the following URL to try, but it doesn't work:

```
ftp://ftp.uu.net/usenet/news.answers/alt-sex/pointers.Z
```

   (In this case, the word **answer** should be **answers**, but you have no way of knowing that.)
   Try shortening the URL, one step at a time, until you get a pathname that works. You can then use your browser to select your way back out to what you are looking for. In this example, you could try:

```
ftp://ftp.uu.net/usenet/news.answers/alt-sex
```

If that doesn't work, try:

```
ftp://ftp.uu.net/usenet/news.answers
```

And then:

```
ftp://ftp.uu.net/usenet
```

Another alternative is to start with an empty pathname and work your way forward to what you want:

```
ftp://ftp.uu.net/
```

This technique is especially useful with a gopher, where the URL pathname will usually not be the same as the choices on the menus.

- You may be able to omit **http://** at the beginning of a URL.

  Some, but not all, browsers assume **http://** as a default. Thus, the following two URLs would be treated the same:

```
http://www.wendy.com/~wendy
www.wendy.com/~wendy
```

Remember, this will not work with all browsers. If it works with your browser, great, you can save some typing. But when you use a different browser, you may have to specify the entire URL.

Important: When you tell someone a URL—say, in a mail message, a posting to a Usenet newsgroup, or an advertisement—you must write the entire thing. Do not leave out the **http://** prefix.

- Files whose names end with **.html** or **.htm** contain hypertext.

  It is a general computer convention to use a suffix at the end of a file name to indicate what type of data the file contains. This suffix is called an "extension". Files containing hypertext are usually given names with an extension of **.html**, for example, **personal.html**.

  (The **.** [period] character is pronounced "dot". Thus, if you talk about the file **personal.html**, you would refer to it as "personal dot HTML".)

  On DOS-based systems--such as the old Windows 3.1--extensions cannot be longer than three letters. Thus, you will often see file names with an extension of **htm**, such as **personal.htm**.

  It is easy to make a typing mistake when copying such a file name. So if you see a URL with a file name ending in either **.html** or **.htm** and it won't work for you, try the other extension before you give up. For example, let's say you are reading a newspaper and you see a URL ending with **personal.htm**. You type the URL into your browser, but you get an error message saying the file was not found. Before you give up, try using **personal.html**; you might be dealing with a simple spelling mistake.

Why Hypertext Is Important

In Chapter 10, I explained that hypertext is information that contains links to other information. In the next few sections, I will show you some more details, to give you a better idea of what hypertext is, how it is stored, and what happens when you use your browser to look at a hypertext resource.

Hypertext, like all other types of data, is stored in files. When you select a link that points to a hypertext resource, your browser connects to the appropriate host computer and requests a copy of the file specified in the URL. When the copy arrives, your browser displays it for you on your screen. The contents of the file instruct your browser what to display and, in general terms, how to display it.

The key here is the phrase "in general terms". A hypertext file does not specify all the details about how it should be displayed. Rather, there are only general instructions; the details are left to the browser itself.

For example, a file of hypertext might contain a particular paragraph of text to be displayed. Within the hypertext, there will be an indication of the start and end of the paragraph. But there will be no explicit instructions as to how wide the lines should be, what specific size or typeface should be used, or which colors to employ. If there is a link within the text, the hypertext will contain the basic information about the link, but it will not specify how to highlight the link. Thus, many of the details of how information is displayed are left up to the browser.

Moreover, you can modify the optional settings of your browser whenever you want. By doing so, you have control over the typefaces, the colors, whether or not images are displayed automatically, and many other details. In addition, you can change the size of a window, which forces the browser to rewrite the text to fit within the new borders.

You might ask, are you telling me the same file of hypertext will look different for different people around the Net? Yes, that's exactly what I am telling you. After all, a large number of different browsers are in use, and each one has its own design philosophy. And even when people use the same browser, they can change the settings to suit their own preferences, so there is no guarantee what the final output will look like.

Certainly, there are some disadvantages here. When you design a web page, you really never know what it will look like to everyone else. Sometimes a page will look great with one browser, but not so good with another browser. However, the advantages of the system far outweigh the disadvantages. Here is why.

Say that you and I decide to develop a new type of resource to be used throughout the entire Net. Our basic design would have to take three fundamental requirements into account.

First, whatever we design will have to work on all types of computer equipment. In particular, we don't know what type of screen display each user will have; we don't know its size or quality, how many characters it can display, and so on. In addition, we don't know if the user will be using a PC, a Macintosh, a Unix computer or something else. And if the user has a PC, he might be using Windows 95, the old Windows, OS/2 or perhaps even DOS. We don't even know if the user will be using a mouse or another pointing device. Moreover, we must make our design so flexible as to work well with new computers that haven't even been invented.

Second, there are an enormous number of people using the Net, with more and more arriving all the time. Any system we offer must use as few communications resources as possible. If we bog down the Net, people will find our system too slow and move on to something else. Thus, we should try to keep to a minimum the amount of information passed from one computer to another.

Finally, we would certainly want our new system to take advantage of existing Internet resources. However, the basic design must be flexible enough to be able to utilize future Internet resources. In particular, we must make allowances for new ideas and services which have not as yet even been imagined.

The designers of hypertext respected all of these considerations and developed a system that is portable, efficient and extensible. These qualities are, in large part, what enabled the Web to grow so quickly and to become so useful.

Within a hypertext file are special instructions, embedded in the text. It is these instructions that are interpreted by the browser to create the hypertext experience. To appreciate how it all works, you need to understand the nature of these instructions, and HTML, the "language" in which such instructions are written.

Hypertext and HTML

The Web was designed so only textual information would have to be sent from one place to another (except, of course, for special material such as images, sounds or video). The great advantage of such a system is speed. Plain text requires much less storage than images, so loading a single page of plain text, for instance, would take much less time than loading the same material in the form of a picture.

Consider this example. Imagine you have two files on your computer. The first file contains all the characters on this particular page of this book. The second file contains an exact image of the page, dot by dot. You would find the first file to be a great deal smaller than the second file. Here is why.

To store a picture, we need to retain information about every single dot, its position and its color. To store text, we need only a short, simple code for each character. The details, as you can imagine, are technical, and not all that important right now. What is important is the idea that information stored as text takes up far less space than information stored as an image.

Now, suppose you were designing the Web. You anticipate that most of the information will be textual in nature. It only makes sense to create a system where, as much as possible, you are transferring textual data and not images. However, this means you cannot transfer an exact image of how the characters should be presented to the user at the other end. Instead, you must send instructions for displaying the text. In hypertext, these instructions are embedded in the text itself.

Here is an example: You want to design a simple home page. At the top is a heading in large letters which says:

WELCOME TO MY HOME PAGE

Below, in regular-sized letters, is a short paragraph which says:

My favorite thing in the whole world is leftover spaghetti for breakfast.

And below that is another short paragraph:

Here is more strangeness.

The word **strangeness** is a link which must be highlighted in some way. In addition, the link must be associated with the URL to which you want it to point (in this case it happens to be **http://bianca.com/shack**).

Now, you can't create an image of a home page just the way you want it. That would be a picture which would have to be downloaded in its entirety. Instead, you save the information as plain text and, within the text, embed instructions to tell the browser at the other end how you want the information to be presented.

The designers of the Web created a set of specifications for embedding instructions within regular text. These specifications are called HTML or HYPERTEXT MARKUP LANGUAGE. Thus, to make a web page, all you need to do is create a file of text with the appropriate HTML commands within the text. Whenever someone loads your page, their browser reads the HTML, follows the instructions, and presents the information according to what you have specified.

In other words, the principal responsibility of your browser is to connect to a web server, load a file of HTML, and then interpret that file in a manner appropriate to your particular computer system. This is what we mean when we say the job of your browser is to be a web client.

An Example of HTML

In the last section, I described the design of a sample web page. Here is the hypertext text necessary to create that page. We often refer to such text as hypertext SOURCE, to distinguish it from the final product.

```
<HTML>

<HEAD>
<TITLE>A GREAT HOME PAGE</TITLE>
</HEAD>

<BODY>
<H1>WELCOME TO MY HOME PAGE</H1>
My favorite thing in the whole world is leftover
spaghetti for breakfast.
<P>
Here is more <A HREF="http://bianca.com/shack">strangeness</A>.
</BODY>

</HTML>
```

Figure 11-2 contains a screen shot of what this short file looks like when interpreted by a browser. (Remember, the exact appearance may vary from one browser to another.)

This example is, of course, a simple one. Many web pages use much more complex HTML, and it is common to see hypertext source files which are long and involved. Learning how to use HTML well is a big topic which is beyond the scope of this book. (However, later in the chapter, I will give you an overview of what you need to create your own web page.) Before I move on, though, let me take a moment to explain our example, so the mysterious markings don't drive you crazy.

HTML uses TAGS to embed instructions within text. A tag starts with a < (less than) character and ends with a > (greater than) character. This means your browser

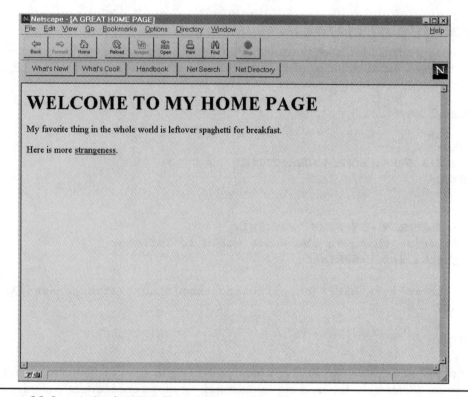

Figure 11-2. *A simple HTML file as interpreted by a browser*

can assume whatever is within **<** and **>** characters is an embedded HTML command. Everything else is regular text.

Most tags come in pairs. The second member in the pair will have a **/** character following the **<** character. In our example, there are six such pairs.

```
<HTML>      </HTML>
<HEAD>      </HEAD>
<TITLE>     </TITLE>
<BODY>      </BODY>
<H1>        </H1>
<A...>      </A>
```

Together, each pair of tags surrounds a particular section of the text. The first tag marks the beginning of the section; the second tag marks the end.

Some tags are complete in themselves and do not come in pairs. In our example, there is only one such tag:

```
<P>
```

Note: Within HTML tags, you can use either upper- or lowercase for the identifiers (for example, either **<HTML>** or **<html>** is acceptable). In this example, I like to use uppercase letters because it makes the tags stand out better.

Here is what the various tags in our example mean. To start, the **<HTML>** tag marks the beginning of the entire hypertext document; the **</HTML>** tag marks the end. Within these tags, there is a HEAD and a BODY. The head (contained within **<HEAD>** and **</HEAD>**) holds instructions relating to the document as a whole. The body (within **<BODY>** and **</BODY>**) holds the contents of the text to be displayed.

In our example, the head contains a single item, a TITLE (between **<TITLE>** and **</TITLE>**). A title is not part of the main text. Rather, it will be displayed by the browser above the text, in an appropriate location. For example, it may be placed within the title bar, above the window in which the text is displayed.

The body in our example contains four elements. First, there is a heading, contained within **<H1>** and **</H1>**. (The **1** indicates a type "1" heading; this is the largest heading. The next largest is **H2**, and so on, down to **H6**, the smallest.)

The next element is a sentence of text. Notice that, in our example, the text is broken onto two lines. However, browsers ignore line breaks as well as spaces between words. When the text is displayed, the actual breaks (if any), will depend on the typeface, the size of the window and other factors. In general, you cannot control how the text within a single paragraph will be formatted. The breaks will be put in by the browser.

The third element is a **<P>** tag. This tells the browser to start a new paragraph—that is, stop displaying text and insert a blank line.

Finally, we have the last line of text. Within this line lies a link, defined by the **<A...>** and **</A>** tags. These tags delimit what is called an ANCHOR, a description of a link. As such, it can point to any type of resource: another hypertext document, an image, a gopher site, an anonymous ftp resource, and so on. (Personally, I would have called such items "links", rather than "anchors", and used **<L>** and **</L>** as delimiters.)

The general format for an anchor is **<A...>** followed by the text that identifies the link, followed by **</A>**. In our example, we use **<A...>strangeness</A>**. This tells the browser that the word **strangeness** identifies the link and to highlight it suitably.

The information within the **<A...>** tag identifies the URL to which the link should point. In our example, we have:

```
<A HREF="http://bianca.com/shack">
```

Literally, we might read this tag as saying, "This is an anchor defining a hypertext reference (**HREF**) to the URL specified by **http://bianca.com/shack**".

So there you have it. A guided tour of a simple HTML document. Of course, there is a lot more to HTML than these few tags, but you do get the idea.

HINT

Most browsers will let you look at the hypertext source for the web page you are currently viewing. An interesting way to see how people use HTML is to display a web page, and then tell your browser to show you the source for that page. This will allow you to compare the raw text, with its embedded HTML tags, to the finished product as it is displayed on your screen.

INTERNET RESOURCE   *Look in the catalog under Internet Resources for*
HTML Tutorials

The Nature of HTML

The best way to think of HTML is as a collection of markings which, when embedded within text, describe how that text should be displayed. As such, HTML is properly called a markup language.

A MARKUP LANGUAGE is a formal set of specifications used to define information which can be added to the content of a document as an aid to processing it. HTML is a markup language derived from a system called SGML (Standard Generalized Markup Language). SGML is a highly complex blueprint for describing markup languages. In SGML terminology, a specific markup language based on SGML is called a DTD or Document Type Definition. (SGML, by the way, was derived from a product called GML—Generalized Markup Language—developed by IBM.)

So if you are ever at a party, and you want to impress a group of people who are talking about HTML, all you need to say is, "Ah, yes, HTML. If I recall correctly, isn't it simply an SGML DTD?" And when they ask you what in the world are you talking about, you can reply, "I should think it is obvious. HTML is a particular Document Type Definition based on the Standard Generalized Markup Language."

HINT

It's easy to make friends when you know what you are talking about.

The best way to think about HTML is to consider it a set of specifications (each with its own type of markup tag), which can be used to define the elements of a hypertext document. The purpose of the HTML is to specify how the text should be processed. The purpose of a browser is to act as a presentation engine, to interpret the HTML and to display the text in an appropriate manner.

The original version of HTML was developed in large part by Tim Berners-Lee, one of the creators of the World Wide Web. Since then, HTML has become a very big deal and has been enhanced through the efforts of many people around the world. Although basic HTML is well defined, the standards for newer versions are still evolving, and you may find different browsers support slightly different variations of the HTML specifications.

Making Your Own Home Page

Creating web pages can be an involved process. Although I can't go into all the details here (they could easily take an entire book), I will introduce you to the most important ideas, and explain what types of tools and resources you need to make a home page of your own.

In order to make your own web page, you will need four principal tools:

- an editing program to create and modify HTML files

- a knowledge of HTML and common web techniques

- a source of pictures and other images

- a graphics program to manipulate images

Let's take a look at each of these requirements, one at a time.

To start, you need to be able to create files of hypertext. To do so, you will use some type of editing program. Since hypertext source files are plain text, just about any editor will do, even a simple text editor (but read on).

If you use a text editor, you will have to type all the HTML tags yourself. This is okay for small jobs, but many people find it more convenient to use a special-purpose tool. There are several choices. First, some browsers have an HTML editor built right into the program. Second, there are separate HTML editing programs, designed specifically for creating and managing hypertext source files. (Figure 11-3 shows an HTML editor with a sample file.) Third, some word processors are capable of converting a regular document to HTML format (that is, to hypertext). This functionality may be part of the word processor or may require a special add-in program.

Your needs and your knowledge of HTML will determine which type of tool you should be using. If you like working with HTML directly, you may want to use a regular text editor and type all the technical information (tags and so on) for yourself. With a small file, this is often just fine.

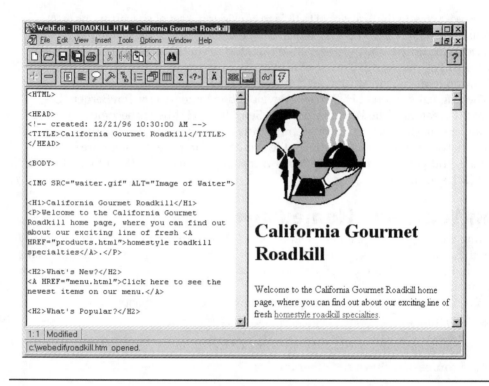

Figure 11-3.   *A hypertext file being edited with Kenn Nesbitt's WebEdit*

If you don't understand HTML (and you don't want to), you would certainly find it easier to create a document within your word processor, and let the program convert it to hypertext automatically.

HINT

Using a word processor to convert documents into HTML is a convenient way to make existing documents available in hypertext format. Some word processors can do the job directly; others require an add-in program.

For many people, using a text editor is too slow (after all, you do have to type all those confusing tags by hand), and using a word processor is just not powerful enough. The solution is to use a special-purpose HTML editor program. Such programs make it easy to create and manipulate hypertext. If you are at all serious about creating web pages, this is the type of tool you should be using.

A good hypertext editor should be able to show you what the source file will look like when it is displayed. Otherwise, you will have to switch to your browser program and load the current version of the file each time you want to see the effect of a new change.

There are two possibilities. First, you can use a hypertext editor that will use your browser (or a built-in browser). You create the hypertext, and the browser shows you what it looks like as a web page.

Second, you can use an editor that hides the HTML from you. You create the web page exactly how you want it to look and, behind the scenes, the program generates the necessary HTML. The term to describe this type of editor is WYSIWYG (pronounced "whizzy-whig"), which means "what you see is what you get".

HINT

In almost all cases, you should use an HTML editor with an integrated browser, not a WYSIWYG editor. The idea of a WYSIWYG hypertext editor sounds good, because you don't have to bother with the details of HTML. However, it won't be long before you are frustrated. There are just too many things you won't be able to do conveniently unless you bother with the HTML.

The next consideration has to do with graphics—that is, pictures, photos, drawings and so forth. Graphics are a big deal on the Web, and you will probably want some for your own home page. Although it is possible to create pages without graphics, most people use at least a few small images.

To use graphics within a page, you need to have each image stored in its own separate file. There are several ways to acquire such files. First, there are many free sources of images on the Net. Second, you can use a device called a SCANNER to convert a printed image to a computer file (say, a GIF or a JPEG file).

To work with images, it is handy to have a graphics program. Graphics programs allow you to perform all sorts of manipulations. You can change colors, cut out parts of an image, rotate the image, change its size and aspect ratio, add text, introduce distortions, and so on. You can also use the program to create brand new pictures or make a collage of existing ones.

HINT

When you find a web page with a particularly good design, use your browser to save the HTML source in a file. Later, you can take parts of the file to use with your own web pages. Here is a quick way to create a web page:

(1) Search the Net for a web page that is similar to what you want.
(2) Save the HTML source for that page in a file.
(3) Edit the file to customize the page for yourself.

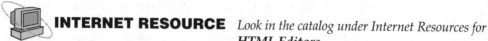

INTERNET RESOURCE *Look in the catalog under Internet Resources for*
HTML Editors
HTML Converters

Putting Your Home Page Onto the Net

To make your home page accessible to everyone on the Net, you need to store it on a computer with a web server. Once you do, anyone on the Net can access your page by using a URL with the name of the computer and the correct pathname.

If you work in an organization with Internet access—such as a company or a university—there will probably be a web server, or multiple web servers, available. Simply ask the system administrator where to put your particular hypertext files, and what URL to give out to people.

If you are using the Net via an Internet service provider, your provider will probably furnish you with some storage space on one of their computers. (This may cost extra.) To make your web pages available, all you need to do is use ftp to copy the files to your provider's computer and place them in the appropriate directory. (I explain ftp in Chapter 18.)

Alternatively, you can run a web server program on your own computer and do everything yourself. However, most people find it easier to use the web server on their provider's computer. For one thing, your provider is connected to the Net at high speed, 24 hours a day. Your personal computer will probably have a much slower, more intermittent connection, and if you keep your web pages on your own computer, they will only be available when your computer is connected to the Net. Moreover, since the connection is slower, people will have to wait longer for the pages to load.

Here is how a typical setup might work with an Internet service provider. Most likely, your provider will be using a Unix system on which they will furnish you with a home directory.

The name of this directory consists of a ~ (tilde) character, followed by your user name. For example, if your user name is **wendy**, your home directory is **~wendy**.

Within your home directory, you create a subdirectory to hold all your web files. Usually, you will be told to give this subdirectory a particular name. (The name **public_html** is commonly used.) Within the subdirectory, you will store your home page in a file called **index.html**. If you have any other files—hypertext pages, images, sounds, and so on—you can name them whatever you want and put them in this same directory. (Remember, though, all hypertext files should have an extension of **.html**; for example, **family.html**.) You can reference one of these files from within another page by specifying the appropriate URL. Thus, you can have any number of pages and images, linked together however you want.

HINT

If you have more than a handful of hypertext and image files, you should organize them into subdirectories within your **public_html** directory (or whatever it is called on your system). For example, you might keep all your images in a directory named **images**. Or you might choose to separate your hypertext (**.html**) files into subdirectories named **family**, **work** and **hobbies**.

That's all there is to it. As long as the file permissions are set properly (explained later in the chapter), anyone on the Net can now look at your web pages, starting with your home page. The details may differ with your particular Internet service provider, so be sure to ask where you should put your files and if there are any special considerations.

Default File and Directory Names

When a web server encounters a URL that does not specify a file name, it will automatically try to use a default name. For example, consider the URL:

```
http://www.wendy.com/~wendy
```

This URL works because the web server at that location will look in the **~wendy** directory for a subdirectory called **public_html** and, within that directory, for a hypertext file named **index.html**. Thus, using a pathname of **~wendy** is just fine.

Some servers do not even demand a directory name. They will look for a default directory if a pathname is not specified. For example:

```
http://www.ibm.com/
```

In this case, you can assume the web server knows which directory to use as a default.

The specific defaults depend on the web server and how it is configured. For example, some servers will automatically look for a file named **index.html** when they encounter a pathname that does not specify a file. Less commonly, you will find servers that look for default files with other names, such as **default.html**, **welcome.html** or **home.html**.

**HINT**

When you use a URL ending with **index.html**, you can often omit the file name. For example, either of the following URLs will work just fine.

```
http://bianca.com/shack
http://bianca.com/shack/index.html
```

Be careful though, not all servers are configured the same. This trick does not always work.

Unix File Permissions

Before we leave this chapter, I want to explain one important idea relating to Unix. All Unix files and directories have FILE PERMISSIONS to control access by outside users. For example, if you are using a **public_html** subdirectory, you must make sure you set the file permissions properly. Otherwise, other people will not be able to access the files. However, you must be careful not to use the wrong permissions, as you don't want other people to be able to change the files.

Unix uses three types of file permissions: read, write and execute. These permissions have slightly different meanings with files and directories.

With a file, read permission allows someone to read the file, write permission allows someone to change the file, and execute permission allows someone to execute the file (if it contains a program). Thus, you should set the permissions on your public web files to give people read permission, but not write or execute permission.

For a directory, read and write permissions are similar, but execute permission allows someone to access the directory. Thus, with your **public_html** directory and its sub-directories, you should give people read and execute permission, but not write permission.

In Unix, file permissions are usually expressed as a series of three numbers. Without going into details, I will tell you to set your public web files to **704**, and your public web directories to **705**. If you have any doubt about what to do on your particular system, ask your provider for guidance.

HINT

If you are storing your web pages on a Unix computer (and most Internet service providers use Unix computers), you will have to know something about the file system. Try my book *The Unix Companion*, published by Osborne McGraw-Hill. In it, I teach you everything you need to know about using Unix files and directories (as well as a lot of other things, most of which are much more cool than files).

Chapter Twelve

Using the Web from a Shell Account: `lynx`

If you are using a shell account to access the Web, your web client will be a program running on the remote host (which is probably a Unix system). In this chapter, I show you how to use **lynx**, a Unix-based web client for shell accounts.

As I discuss the various aspects of using **lynx**, I would like you to be familiar with the Web and the basic terminology (hypertext, link, URL, and so on). So, before you continue, please make sure you have already read Chapters 9 and 10, and have at least skimmed Chapter 11.

Why `lynx` Is So Cool

lynx is the program of choice for Unix users who use the Web via a shell account. As I explained in Chapter 5, a shell account allows you to use the Internet via a remote Unix host. On your computer, you run a communications program to emulate a VT-100 terminal and to connect to the remote computer. You run your Internet client programs on the remote host, not on your own computer.

The nature of such a connection is that you can use only text-based programs. This means you will see characters on your screen, but no images. At first, you might think this is a poor way to use the Web, as so many Web pages seem to be visually oriented. However, unless you have a particular need to look at the pictures, **lynx** is actually a *great* way to use the Web. Here is why.

Using the Web often means spending a lot of time waiting, for two reasons. First, images take a long time to load and, unfortunately, many people put spurious images on their web pages. The images make things look better, but they can really slow things down. Second, if you are using a telephone to access the Net, the connection between you and your Internet service provider is the slowest part of the link between you and everyone else. This means each time your browser loads a file, the data must travel from the remote host to your Internet service provider (which is fast), and then from your provider to you (which is slow).

When you use **lynx**, your web client runs on the remote Unix host. Thus, the client/server connection is between the Internet service provider and the web server. Your telephone line is not involved, which speeds things up considerably (most providers have a high-speed connection right into the Net).

HINT

As long as you don't need images, using **lynx** via a shell account is a lot faster than using a graphical browser with a PPP account.

If you ever get a chance to compare **lynx** to a graphical browser, you will be surprised how seldom you really need the images. It's nice to look at pictures, but when you are after information, **lynx** is the best game in town. Personally I prefer to use **lynx** when I am doing research, because it is so fast, and I don't have a lot of superfluous pictures cluttering up the screen.

Moreover, **lynx** has a straightforward interface that is easy to master, quick to use, and doesn't force you to use a mouse.

A Quick History of **lynx**

lynx was created at the University of Kansas. The original idea was for **lynx** to be the nucleus of a campus-wide information system. The **lynx** programmers created their own hypertext system and used gopher servers to hold the files. The first version of **lynx** was released in the late summer of 1992 (long before the Web became popular).

Eventually, use of the Web started to spread and, in 1993, the **lynx** designers added web functionality to the program. Since then, **lynx** has become the web browser of choice for people using Unix systems with a text-based interface. The original **lynx** designers were Lou Montulli, Charles Rezac and Michael Grobe. Since then, many other people have contributed to **lynx**, including users and programmers from around the world. However, the program is still maintained at the University of Kansas.

What's in a Name?

lynx

There are two theories as to the origin of the name **lynx**:

Theory #1: The name **lynx** is a pun on the word "links", because the program is a web browser, designed to read hypertext and follow the links.

Theory #2: The program was named after the University of Kansas mascot, the Jaybird.

Note: Very few people believe theory #2.

Starting

To start **lynx**, use the **lynx** command:

```
lynx
```

The program will start. If you have specified a home page (I will explain how to do so in a moment), **lynx** will load it automatically. On some systems, the system manager will define a default home page. So, if you do not specify your own, this is the home page you will see each time you start the program.

To begin with a particular web page, simply specify the URL as part of the command line. For example:

```
lynx http://www.cascade.net/dark.html
```

Alternatively, you can specify the name of an ordinary file. For instance:

```
lynx myfile
```

In such cases, **lynx** will read the file and display it for you, one screenful at a time. In other words, **lynx** can act like a regular paging program. (Strange but true.)

> ## HINT
>
> To define a home page for **lynx** to load each time it starts, set the value of the **WWW_HOME** environment variable. For example, say you want your home page to be **http://www.cascade.net/dark.html**. With the C-Shell, use the following command in your **.cshrc** file:
>
> ```
> setenv WWW_HOME http://www.cascade.net/dark.html
> ```
>
> With the Korn shell or the Bourne shell, use the following commands in your **.profile** file:
>
> ```
> WWW_HOME=http://www.cascade.net/dark.html
> export WWW_HOME
> ```
>
> If you use the Korn shell and you want to look as cool as a C-Shell person, you can do it all with a single command:
>
> ```
> export WWW_HOME=http://www.cascade.net/dark.html
> ```

Stopping

There are three ways to stop **lynx**. Normally, you would use the **q** (quit) command. Simply press **q**. **lynx** will ask you if you are sure you want to quit. Type **y** (yes) or press RETURN to quit. If you have made a mistake, type **n** (no) to return to the program.

Alternatively you can quit without being asked for confirmation. To do so, press either **Q** (uppercase **Q**), or **^D**.

(Note: In this chapter, I use the common Unix convention of indicating CTRL keys with a **^** (circumflex) character. For example, **^D** means CTRL-D.)

> ## HINT
>
> Be careful, the **lynx** quit commands work in almost all situations, and it is easy to stop the program by accident. It is a good habit to use **q**, not **Q** or **^D**. If you press **q** inadvertently, you will be asked to confirm that you really want to quit. With **Q** or **^D** the program will stop instantly.

Displaying Help

The first thing you should learn with any new program is how to display help information. With **lynx** you can display help whenever you want by pressing either **H** (uppercase **H**) or **?** (question mark).

When you ask for help, you are presented with a menu. However, the actual help information is not stored within the **lynx** program. Rather, each choice points to a hypertext document on a distant web server. (Most of links point to the University of Kansas.) To display help, use the UP and DOWN cursor keys to move to the topic you want and press RETURN. **lynx** will then contact the appropriate web server and load the document you requested.

If you want help about the **lynx** command itself, you can display the manual page from the online Unix manual. From the shell prompt, enter the command:

```
man lynx
```

Generally Useful Keys

lynx operates in what is called "cbreak mode". This is a Unix programming term which means you do not have to press RETURN whenever you type a command. For example, to display help, you need only press the **H** or **?** key, and **lynx** will perform the required action without waiting.

Aside from the help commands, there are a few more generally useful keys I want to mention.

First, from time to time you will need to type text: a URL, the name of a file, information for a form, and so on. As you type, there are several keys you can use to correct mistakes. To erase a single character, use BACKSPACE or DELETE (whichever works on your system). To erase the entire line, press **^U**. If you want to cancel the operation completely, press **^G**.

You can also use **^G** for another purpose: to interrupt a data transfer while it is in progress. For example, if you are loading a new web page or downloading a file, pressing **^G** will abort the process immediately. For convenience, you can also use **z** instead of **^G**.

If it ever happens that your screen display becomes garbled (say, because of a noisy phone line), you can tell **lynx** to redraw the screen, by pressing either **^L** or **^W**. An important variation of this is the **^R** (reload) command. Pressing **^R** causes **lynx** to reload the current web page and then redisplay the screen.

Finally, if you want to enter a Unix command without quitting **lynx**, press **!** (exclamation mark). **lynx** will pause itself and start a new shell (command processor). You can now enter as many Unix commands as you want. When you want to return to **lynx**, enter the **exit** command.

How `lynx` Displays a Page

When **lynx** starts, it will show you whichever home page was loaded automatically (if you have specified such a page). Otherwise, **lynx** will wait for you to tell it what to do. Regardless, eventually you will see a web page displayed on your screen. Figure 12-1 shows a typical web page, so you can see what it looks like.

First, at the bottom of the screen are two lines of help text. This serves as a constant reminder of the most important commands. Once you memorize these commands, you can get rid of the help text by setting an option (discussed later in the chapter).

Next, take a moment to look at the web page in Figure 12-1, because I want you to notice several things. In this example, you see the first part of a particular web page, which happens to be a guide to HTML. The guide is a long one and, in the right corner of the screen, there is an indication of the length of the text. Don't be confused by the actual message which says **(p1 of 54)**. This does not mean 54 web pages, it means 54 "screen pages". That is, the whole thing is one long web page, taking up 54 screenfuls of text.

```
                                      A Beginner's Guide to HTML (p1 of 54)

                    A BEGINNER'S GUIDE TO HTML



    This is a primer for producing documents in HTML, the markup language
    used by the World Wide Web.
      * Acronym Expansion
      * What This Primer Doesn't Cover
      * Creating HTML Documents
            + The Minimal HTML Document
            + Basic Markup Tags
                  o Titles
                  o Headings
                  o Paragraphs
            + Linking to Other Documents
                  o Relative Links Versus Absolute Pathnames
                  o Uniform Resource Locator
                  o Anchors to Specific Sections in Other Documents
                  o Anchors to Specific Sections Within Current Document
  --press space for next page --
   Arrow keys: Up and Down to move. Right to follow a link; Left to go back.
   H)elp O)ptions P)rint G)o M)ain screen Q)uit /=search [delete]=history list
```

Figure 12-1.   **Lynx:** *A typical screen*

Since the whole web page does not fit on the screen at once, **lynx** shows as much as it can, and then displays the message:

`-- press space for next page --`

This is just like a regular Unix paging program.

The next thing I want you to notice is how the links are displayed. All of the links, except one, are displayed in boldface. One of the links is highlighted in a special manner, often in reverse video. (The actual appearance depends on what software you are using, especially your terminal emulator.)

This link is called the SELECTED LINK. In our example, the selected link is **Acronym Expansion**. Since you don't use a mouse with **lynx**, you have to select a link by moving to it with the DOWN and UP cursor keys. Once a link is selected, you can follow it by pressing either RIGHT (the right cursor key) or RETURN. (I will go into the details in the next section.) The point is, at any time, the link you can follow—the selected link—is the one that is highlighted.

One last point: Since lynx is text-based, it cannot display pictures. Instead, it will show you where an image is located by displaying the word [IMAGE].

Now, there is a way for a web page designer to specify alternate text in case the user's browser cannot display an image. For example, if someone is designing a web page containing a picture of the Mona Lisa, he or she might specify the text **Picture of Mona Lisa** should be displayed if the user's browser cannot show the image. However, most web page designers don't bother, so as you explore the Web, you will see lots of **[IMAGE]** markers.

HINT

If you want to look at the HTML source of the current page, press \ (backslash). To switch back to regular viewing, press \ once again.

If you want to save the HTML source, press \ to display it, then use the **p** command (explained later in the chapter) to mail the page to yourself or to save it to a file.

Working with URLs

To load a specific web page, type **g** (go to) followed by the URL, then press RETURN. **lynx** will jump right to that page. For example, to jump to **http://bianca.com/shack**:

1. Type **g**
2. Type **http://bianca.com/shack**
3. Press RETURN

While you are typing, remember you can press BACKSPACE or DELETE to erase a single character, **^U** to erase the entire line, and **^G** to cancel the operation.

The next time you press **g**, **lynx** will display the last URL you used. This makes it easy to re-use a URL. For example, let's say someone told you about the URL in our last example, but you got the pathname wrong. So, without knowing any better, you typed **http://bianca.com/theshack** (which didn't work). Press **g** again. **lynx** will display the previous URL. Now press the BACKSPACE key 8 times. This will erase the pathname and leave you with **http://bianca.com/**. Although this URL is not exactly what you wanted, it will work. And once you load the page, you can look at the links and pick whichever one you want.

HINT

If you specify a URL that doesn't seem to work, press **g** to redisplay it, then erase part of the URL and try again. Repeat this process until you find a URL that loads successfully, and then work your way forward to what you want.

If you want to jump to a URL you have already visited, you can use the history list (explained later in the chapter). To jump to the very beginning—to the first web page you visited in the current session—there is a shortcut: press **m** (main screen).

To see the technical information about the current page—the page at which you are looking—press **=** (equals sign). This will display the URL of the page, as well as other information. However, if you want to be able to return to this page at a later date, you do not need to know the URL. All you need to do is place the page on your bookmark list (also explained later in the chapter).

If you really want to look at URLs, you can set an option called **User mode** (I will tell you how in a moment). If you set this option to **Advanced**, **lynx** will use the bottom line of the screen to display the URL of the selected link. This means, you can move from one link to another, and watch the URL change on the bottom line of the screen.

I will discuss options in general and how to set them later in the chapter. For now, here are the steps to set this particular option:

1. Press **o** to display the Options Menu.

2. Press **u** to select the **User mode** option.

3. Press the SPACE bar until the value of this option is set to **Advanced**.

4. Press RETURN to accept this value.

5. Press **>** (the greater-than character) to save this setting and leave the Options Menu.

Navigating

Navigating means moving around the current page, and jumping from one page to another. Navigating in **lynx** is easy: you can do just about everything you want by using the cursor keys and the SPACE bar.

First, if the web page is too large to fit on a single screen, **lynx** will display the first screenful. You can then display the rest of the web page, one screenful at a time, by pressing the SPACE bar, just as if you were using a paging program (such as **more**). If you page too far and you want to go back, press **b** (back up one screenful).

Another way to move around the current page is to move from one link to the next. As you do, the link you move to will become the selected link (and will be highlighted). To move forward to the next link in the document, press the DOWN key. To move backward to the previous, press the UP key.

To jump to a new page, all you have to do is press UP or DOWN to move to the link you want, and then press the RIGHT cursor key to follow that link. To move back to the page from which you came, press the LEFT key.

In other words, you use DOWN and UP to move from one link to another within a page, and RIGHT and LEFT to move from one page to another.

HINT

Here is an easy way to remember that RIGHT and LEFT move you from one page to another. Just think of what you do as you read a book. To read the next page, you move one page to the right. To revisit the previous page, you move one page to the left.

Finally, you can search the current web page for a particular pattern. To do so, press **/** (slash) followed by the pattern, then press RETURN. **lynx** will move to the next occurrence of that pattern.

For example, to search for the next occurrence of the word **hippopotamus**, do the following:

1. Press **/**
2. Type **hippopotamus**
3. Press RETURN

HINT

You can control whether searches are case insensitive (with no difference between upper- and lowercase letters) or case sensitive (matching upper- and lowercase letters exactly). To specify your preference, set the **Searching type** option to the type of search you want. (I explain how to set options later in the chapter.)

To search again for the same pattern, use the **n** (next) command. Thus, if the **/** command doesn't find what you want on the first try, you can press **n** repeatedly to repeat the search.

Searching works fine, but there are two limitations. First, **lynx** will only search forward. Second, if **lynx** gets to the bottom, it will not wrap around to the top of the web page.

HINT

lynx searches from the current position toward the bottom of the web page. To search the entire page, move to the top before you start.

As a convenience, there are some alternate keys you can use. These are summarized in Figure 12-2. Try the various keys and see which combinations you like best. Note: The HOME, END, PAGE UP and PAGE DOWN keys may not work on some systems. Try them and see if they work for you.

HOME	move to the beginning of the current page
END	move to the end of the current page
SPACE	move down one screenful
+	same as SPACE
PAGE DOWN	same as SPACE
b	(back) move up one screenful
-	same as b
PAGE UP	same as b
UP	move up one link on the current page
DOWN	move down one link on the current page
TAB	same as DOWN
LEFT	jump back to the previous web page
RIGHT	follow the selected link to a new web page
RETURN	same as RIGHT
/pattern	move to next occurrence of specified pattern

Figure 12-2.   Lynx: *Navigating keys*

Using Your Numeric Keypad to Navigate

If you have a PC-style keyboard, **lynx** will allow you to use the keys on your numeric keypad for navigation. The keys I am talking about are **1** through **9**, on the far right-hand side of the keyboard.

Look at the actual keys on your numeric keypad. You will see they can be used as follows:

1 —> END

2 —> DOWN

3 —> PAGEDOWN

4 —> LEFT

5 —> not used

6 —> RIGHT

7 —> HOME

8 —> UP

9 —> PAGEUP

lynx lets you use these keys in two different ways. By default, **lynx** will interpret the numbers from the keypad as if they were really special keys. For example, when you press **7** (on the keypad), **lynx** will pretend you pressed the HOME key and jump to the top of the current web page. When you press **1**, **lynx** will pretend you pressed the END key and jump to the end of the web page. This facility is useful if these special keys do not work on your system. Here is the complete list:

1 (END)   —> move to the bottom of current web page
7 (HOME)   —> move to the top of current web page

3 (PAGEDOWN)   —> move down one screenful
9 (PAGEUP)   —> move up one screenful

2 (DOWN)   —> move down one link on the current page
8 (UP)   —> move up one link on the current page

4 (LEFT)   —> jump back to the previous web page
6 (RIGHT)   —> follow the selected link to new web page

Using the numeric keys this way is convenient, as it allows you to zip around faster than a pickpocket at a bankers convention.

However, there is an alternative which, personally, I like much better. You can choose to use the keys on the numeric keypad as actual numbers. If you do, **lynx** will display an identification number beside each link. To follow a link, all you have to do is type the number and press RETURN.

As an example, take a look at Figure 12-3. It shows the same screen we looked at earlier, but with a number beside each link. This makes it easy to follow any particular link. For example, to jump to the page entitled **The Minimal HTML Document**, just type **4** and press RETURN.

```
                                   A Beginner's Guide to HTML (p1 of 54)

                   A BEGINNER'S GUIDE TO HTML


   This is a primer for producing documents in HTML, the markup language
   used by the World Wide Web.
      *  [1]Acronym Expansion
      *  [2]What This Primer Doesn't Cover
      *  [3]Creating HTML Documents
           +  [4]The Minimal HTML Document
           +  [5]Basic Markup Tags
                o  [6]Titles
                o  [7]Headings
                o  [8]Paragraphs
           +  [9]Linking to Other Documents
                o  [10]Relative Links Versus Absolute Pathnames
                o  [11]Uniform Resource Locator
                o  [12]Anchors to Specific Sections in Other Documents
                o  [13]Anchors to Specific Sections Within Current Document
-- press space for next page --
   Arrow keys: Up and Down to move. Right to follow a link; Left to go back.
 H)elp O)ptions P)rint G)o M)ain screen Q)uit /=search [delete]=history list
```

Figure 12-3. `lynx`: *A screen with link numbers turned on*

How does **lynx** know how you want to use the numeric keypad? You set an option to express your preference. I will discuss options in general and how to set them later in the chapter. For now, here are the steps to set this particular option:

1. Press **o** to display the Options Menu.
2. Press **k** to select the **Keypad** option.
3. Press the SPACE bar until the value of this option is set either to Numbers act as arrows or Links are numbered, whichever you prefer.
4. Press RETURN to accept this value.
5. Press **>** (the greater-than character) to save this setting and leave the Options Menu.

HINT

Before you can use the keypad to enter numbers, you must make sure to turn on the NUMLOCK light on your keyboard.

Special Keys for vi and emacs Users

If you are a **vi** or **emacs** user, you are no doubt used to moving the cursor by using special keys. For your convenience, **lynx** has options that allow you to use these same keys. The following table shows the keys you can use if you set these options:

	vi keys	emacs **keys**
LEFT	h	^B
DOWN	j	^N
UP	k	^P
RIGHT	l	^F

I discuss options and how to set them later in the chapter. For now, here are the steps to set these particular options:

1. Press **o** to display the Options Menu.
2. Press either **v** to select the **vi** option, or **m** to select the **emacs** option.
3. Press the SPACE bar until the value of this option is set to **On**.
4. Press RETURN to accept this value.
5. Press **>** (the greater-than character) to save this setting and leave the Options Menu.

If you want, you can turn both of these options on at the same time, and switch back and forth from one set of keys to another. This is especially helpful for people with a severed corpus callosum.

The History List

As I explained in Chapter 10, your browser maintains a history list of the web sites you have visited in the current session.

The `lynx` history list contains the links that trace your path from the first page you visited to the current page, with no branching. As you branch and retrace your steps, `lynx` changes the list.

At any time, you can display the history list and jump to one of the pages. This affords an easy way to return to a web page you have just visited.

To display your history list, press either the BACKSPACE or DELETE key (whichever is used with your system). `lynx` will display the list of places you have visited, from most recent to least recent. To revisit a web site from the past, all you have to do is select the link you want and jump to it.

Here is an example of a typical history list. (The original URL was **http://bianca.com./shack**.)

```
3.  -- You selected:  bianca's Sex Toys
2.  -- You selected:  bianca's Bedroom
1.  -- You selected:  Quick Reference Index
0.  -- You selected:  bianca's Smut Shack
```

To jump to one of these pages, simply select the link and press RETURN.

The Bookmark List

The history list is fine for recalling the places you visited recently, but to save a web location permanently, you need to add it to the bookmark list (see Chapter 10).

To add the current web page to your bookmark list, press **a** (add a bookmark). You will be asked if you want to save the "Document" or the "Link". If you choose "Document", `lynx` will save the URL of the web page you are reading. If you choose "Link", `lynx` will save the URL of whichever link is currently selected. Thus, you do not actually have to visit a web page to save its URL to your bookmark list. You can simply select (highlight) a link and save that link right to the list.

At any time, you can view your bookmarks by pressing **v** (view bookmarks). You can jump to one of the links by selecting it and pressing RIGHT or RETURN in the usual manner.

To delete an item from your bookmark list, select the item and then press **r** (remove item).

HINT

lynx keeps your bookmark list in a file named **lynx_bookmarks.html** in your home directory. You can change this by displaying the Option Menu and selecting the **Bookmark file** item.

You can use your bookmark file as your home page. This way, each time you start **lynx**, you will see all the links that are most useful to you.

Using Forms

Although forms do not look as nice with **lynx** as they do with a graphical browser, they are still easy to use. All you do is move to the form and type what you want. Then move to the link that submits the input and press RETURN.

Figure 12-4 shows an example taken from an automated confession service. The line with the word **Days:** is a form. To fill it in, move to the line and type your response. You can then move from one form to the next, filling in your response. (There are several more forms to fill in.) Near the bottom of the web page (although we can't see it in the example) is a link called **Transmit Confession**. When you are finished, you move to this link and press RETURN.

HINT

While you are typing in a form, you can press BACKSPACE or DELETE to erase a single character, and **^U** to erase the entire line.

The bottom part of Figure 12-4 shows a type of form called a RADIO BUTTON. Like the buttons on a car radio, only one of the choices may be selected at a time. (**lynx** calls this a "Checkbox Field".) To select a radio button, move to it and press RETURN. **lynx** will mark your choice with an * (asterisk) character. At the same time, if another radio button happens to be on, **lynx** will turn it off.

Saving, Mailing and Printing Files

If you want to preserve a web page, you have several choices. You can save the page to file on the Unix host; you can mail a copy of the page to yourself (or someone else); capture the file to a file on your local computer; or (maybe) print the page directly.

```
                              CONFESSION BOOTH

      Bringing the net to its knees since 1994



      Digital Priest: How long has it been since your last confession, my
      child?

      Days: _____



      And what is it you wish to confess?

      I committed the following sin:

      ( ( )Murder) ( ( )Adultery) ( ( )Sloth) ( ( )Lust) ( ( )Avarice)
      ( ( )Deception) ( ( )Gluttony) ( ( )Pride) ( ( )Anger)
      ( ( )Covetousness) ( ( )Misplaced Priorities) ( ( )Big-Time Kludgy Hack)
      ( ( )Fish in Microwave) ( ( )Didn't put printouts in bin)

     (Text entry field) Enter text. Use UP or DOWN arrows or tab to move off.
```

Figure 12-4. `lynx`: *An example using forms*

To start any of these operations, press **p** (print). **lynx** will show you a number of choices:

Save to a local file
Mail the file to yourself
Print to the screen
Use VT100 print sequence to print from your local terminal
Specify your own print command

Let's go through these choices, one at a time.

The first one will save the text of the web page to a file on the Unix host. This operation is straightforward; all you have to do is specify the name of the file. Note: If you are using the Unix computer via a phone line and you want the information to end up on your computer, you will have to download the file from the Unix machine to your machine. (Probably, you will use **zmodem**. See Chapter 21 for assistance.)

The second choice lets you mail a copy of the web page to someone. Although the screen says "mail the file to yourself", you can specify any address you want.

To understand the third choice, you need to know about the Unix custom of using the word "print" as a synonym for "display". In this case, the choice "Print to the screen" really means "Display the entire web page on your screen without stopping". (In the olden days, the first Unix terminals printed information on paper; hence, even today, "print" often means "display".)

This choice is handy if you are using a communications program and you want an easy way to get the entire web page into a file on your own computer. You can issue a command to your program to turn on the "capture buffer", tell **lynx** to display the entire file, and then turn off the capture buffer. This should save the information to a file on your own computer. Since each communications program has its own commands, I can't tell you the details for your particular program.

The fourth choice will print the file on your local computer if your VT-100 terminal is configured to do so. You will probably never get this to work, so don't bother. If you really want to print the file, get it to your computer first by using one of the other choices.

Finally, the last choice allows you to specify the name of your own print program. This is for printing on the remote Unix computer, which you probably won't want to do. However, if you are a Unix person, there is a trick you can use.

Select this choice but, instead of specifying a print program, use another program that can read from the standard input. You can even use a pipeline. For example, try this:

1. Load a web page containing a large amount of text.

2. Press **p**.

3. Select Specify your own print command.

4. Type: **cut -c10-20 | sort** (or some other fine series of commands).

This trick will not always work, so if you got this far, you are on your own.

(If you don't understand all the Unix talk, don't worry about it. However, if you want to learn about Unix, get my book *The Unix Companion*, published by Osborne McGraw-Hill.)

Accessing Anonymous Ftp and Gopher Sites

lynx, like all browsers, is able to handle non-hypertext resources. If you encounter a link to such a resource, **lynx** will know what to do. For example, it can handle URLs that specify a **gopher**, **ftp**, **telnet**, **news** or **mailto** resource. (See Chapter 11 for a discussion of such URLs.) You can even enter such a URL yourself, by using the **g** (go to) command. For example, to connect to the anonymous ftp site at **rtfm.mit.edu**, do the following:

1. Press **g**

2. Type **ftp://rtfm.mit.edu/**

3. Press RETURN

Using such URLs is straightforward, so I only have a few comments. When you are using anonymous ftp or gopher, and you encounter a file you want to download, just press **d** (download). **lynx** will give you the following choices:

```
Save to disk
Use Zmodem to download to the local terminal
```

(Remember, "download" means to copy a file from a remote computer to your computer.)

If you select the first choice, **lynx** will download the file to the Unix host computer. If you select the second choice, you may get **lynx** to download the file right to your own computer. For this to work, you need to configure your communications program to accept an automatic **zmodem** download and hope for the best. If you can get the **zmodem** transfer to work, fine. If not, download the file to the Unix host and transfer it from there.

If you are using ftp or a gopher and you select a file that **lynx** does not know how to display (such as a binary file), **lynx** will display the following message:

```
This file cannot be displayed on this terminal: D)ownload, or C)ancel
```

At this point, you can ask for a download or cancel the whole thing.

HINT

While a file is downloading, you can abort the process by pressing either **^G** or **z**.

Reading Usenet Newsgroups

You can use **lynx** to read Usenet newsgroups (discussion groups). Just specify a URL showing the **news** resource and the name of the newsgroup you want to read. (See Chapter 11 for information on such URLs.) For example:

news:rec.humor

Using lynx in this way provides a surprisingly good interface to Usenet. This is because Usenet articles have many natural links to other articles and to other newsgroups, and lynx makes it easy to follow the links.

In particular—while you are reading an article—**lynx** makes it easy to send a followup article to the newsgroup, or to mail a message to the person who posted the article. All you have to do is select the appropriate link and **lynx** will do the work.

(For a detailed discussion of Usenet, see Chapters 13 through 15.)

HINT

Try using **lynx** to read the news. I think you will like it.

Sending Mail

You can use `lynx` to send mail by selecting or specifying a URL with **mailto** (see Chapter 11). Such links are common on web pages, as they afford an easy way to allow a user to send mail (usually to the person who designed the page).

If you want to send a message to someone, you can enter a **mail** URL of your own whenever you want. For example, to send mail to the President of the United States, do the following:

1. Press **g**

2. Type **mailto:president@whitehouse.gov**

3. Press RETURN

4. Answer the questions appropriately

Once `lynx` sets up the message, you will be placed within your default editor (probably **pico**, **vi** or **emacs**).

HINT

When you send mail with `lynx`, it allows you to include the current web page within the message. This is a handy way to send part of a web page to someone. Include the page, and then use your editor to delete the parts you don't want and add your own comments.

When you mail a copy of a page using the **p** command, you don't get to edit the message before it is mailed.

Customizing `lynx`: Options

`lynx` has a number of options you can set to change your working environment. To set these options, press **o** (options) to display the Options Menu. Figure 12-5 shows this menu with the default settings. (Note: Your system may be set up with different defaults.)

To change a setting, press the letter of the option. For example, to change the **Editor** setting, press **E**. Once you select a setting, you can either type a new value or press any key to toggle from one value to another. (It will be obvious.) After you have made the change, press RETURN. You can now specify another option if you wish.

When you are finished, press **>** (greater than) to save the settings permanently and return to whatever you were doing. When you press **>**, `lynx` saves the settings to a file named **.lynxrc** in your home directory. If you want the changes to be temporary, press **r** (return) instead. `lynx` will make the changes, but will not save them to the **.lynxrc** file. Thus, the changes will be only for the current session.

Most of the settings are straightforward, and you can experiment with them when you get the time, so I will mention only a few details.

```
                        Options Menu

     E)ditor                     : /usr/local/bin/pico
     D)ISPLAY variable           : NONE
     B)ookmark file              : lynx_bookmarks.html
     F)TP sort criteria          : By Filename
     P)ersonal mail address      :
     S)earching type             : CASE INSENSITIVE
     C)haracter set              : ISO Latin 1
     V)I keys                    : OFF
     e(M)acs keys                : OFF
     K)eypad as arrows
            or Numbered links    : Numbers act as arrows
     l(I)st directory style      : Mixed style
     U)ser mode                  : Novice




  Select first letter of option line, '>' to save, or 'r' to return to Lynx.
  Command:
```

Figure 12-5. `lynx`: *The options menu*

First, the **DISPLAY Variable** is only for X Window users. If you don't use X Window, ignore this option.

Next, it is handy to fill in the **Personal Mail Address**. If you do so, **lynx** will use this address whenever you mail something. This saves you having to type the same information over and over (although you do have a chance to change it before the mail is sent out).

I mentioned the options for using **vi** or **emacs** keys earlier in the chapter. Setting either of these options allows you to use familiar commands to move around the screen.

I also discussed the **Keypad** option earlier in the chapter. Change this option if you have a PC-style keyboard, and you want to use the numeric keypad to navigate.

Finally, we come to the **User mode** option. This has three possible settings: **Novice**, **Intermediate** and **Advanced**. With **Novice**, **lynx** will display two lines of help at the bottom of the screen. With **Intermediate**, these lines will not be displayed. With **Advanced**, **lynx** will display the URL of the selected link on the bottom line of the screen. This allows you to move from one link to another and watch how the URL changes. My advice is to get yourself to the **Advanced** level as quickly as possible.

Chapter Thirteen

Introduction to Usenet

Usenet is a vast, worldwide system of discussion groups which allows you to partake in discussions with people from all over the world on virtually every conceivable topic.

In this chapter, I discuss the basics and lay the foundation for using Usenet. I start by answering the question, what is Usenet, and then move on to the basic terminology.

After this orientation, I discuss how Usenet information is transported from place to place and how it is organized. I will show you how Usenet works, and what you can expect to find.

In the following chapters, I will build on this foundation and show you the details of reading and participating in the Usenet system.

What Is Usenet?

USENET is a large collection of discussion groups involving millions of people from all over the world. Each discussion group is centered around a particular topic. Jokes, recipes, mathematics, philosophy, computers, biology, science fiction—just about any subject you can think of has its own group.

In total, Usenet has more than 13,000 different discussion groups. Many of these are of regional or local interest. For example, there is a discussion group for discussing restaurants in the San Francisco Bay Area. Nevertheless, over 4,700 groups are of general interest and are read by people throughout the world.

One of the first questions that people ask is: What does it cost to use Usenet?

The answer is Usenet is free. You may have to pay something for Internet access (as I discuss in Chapter 5), but there is no charge for Usenet per se. In fact, if you have access to the Internet at no cost, then everything, including Usenet, is free.

Just about every topic of interest to human beings has a place in some discussion group or another. When the need arises for a new group, there are well-established procedures to form one. Unlike the commercial services (such as America Online, Prodigy, and Compuserve), there is no central authority that controls Usenet. Thus, when the users decide that there should be a new discussion group, they form one.

This system has two important results: First, new groups can be created in a timely manner whenever the need arises. Second, there are a great many groups devoted to esoteric subjects.

HINT

No matter what your interests, there will be Usenet discussion groups for you.

Basic Terminology

The original Usenet network was conceived in order to display notices and news items. The idea was to create a computerized version of a bulletin board. Usenet soon outgrew its original blueprint, but the legacy of an electronic news network remains. Although Usenet is used primarily for discussion groups, I still talk about it using news-oriented terms.

For example, Usenet itself is often referred to as the NEWS or NETNEWS, even though there is little real news in the sense of a newspaper. For example, you might hear someone say, "I picked up a recipe for groat cakes while reading the news yesterday." What he means is that he found the recipe in one of the Usenet discussion groups.

Similarly, the Usenet discussion groups are usually referred to as NEWSGROUPS or, more simply, GROUPS. Within each newsgroup, the individual contributions are called ARTICLES or POSTINGS. When you submit an article to a newsgroup, we say that you POST the article. Thus, you can imagine the following conversation between two Usenet people in Fargo, North Dakota, both of whom happen to be named Mike:

Mike: These are great groatcakes. New recipe?

Mike: Yes, I saw an article in the vegetarian cooking group about how nutritious groats are, so I posted a request for recipes. The next day, someone from France had posted a reply with this wonderful recipe for groatcakes with truffles.

Mike: Well, they certainly taste good, Mike.

Mike: Thank you, Mike.

Newsreaders

To read Usenet articles, you use a program called a NEWSREADER. The newsreader acts as your interface: you tell it which newsgroups you want to read, and it presents the articles for you, one at a time. (Remember, although we call them newsgroups, they are really discussion groups.)

There are a large number of newsreader programs available. There are programs for PCs using Windows or OS/2, for the Macintosh, for Unix systems, and so on. If you are using a package of Internet software, it may contain a newsreader. If not, newsreader programs are readily available on the Net. Figure 13-1 shows a typical newsreader program.

 **INTERNET RESOURCE** *Look in the catalog under Internet Resources for* *Usenet: Newsreaders*

Alternatively, you can use a web browser to read the news (see Chapter 11). Many people prefer to use their browser, as it allows them to use one program for both the Web and Usenet (and gopher and anonymous ftp). However, if you find yourself

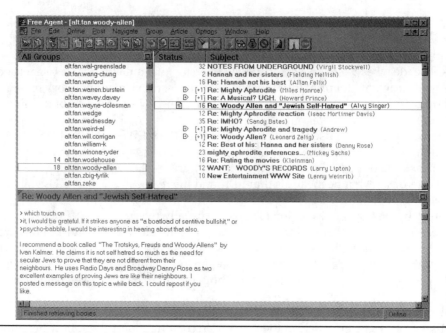

Figure 13-1. *A graphical newsreader client*

reading the news a lot, I suggest you try a dedicated newsreader. Such programs are designed only for news reading and are better suited for heavy duty Usenet action.

If you access the Net via a shell account (see Chapter 5), you will use a newsreader program on the remote Unix host. In Chapter 15, I discuss **tin**, the most popular such program. In addition, if your system has the **lynx** web browser, you can use it to access Usenet as well as the Web (see Chapter 12).

News Clients and Servers

One of the functions of a newsreader is to keep track of which newsgroups you want to read. At any time, you can add or delete newsgroups from your list. When you add a group to your personal list, we say that you SUBSCRIBE to that group. When you remove a group from your list, we say that you UNSUBSCRIBE.

Don't misinterpret these terms. There is no formal subscription process, nor is there any fee. Subscribing simply means that you tell your newsreader that you wish to read a newsgroup. Moreover, the system is private: no one keeps track of which groups you read.

As you select newsgroups and read articles, your newsreader maintains a file of information on your behalf. Your newsreader uses this file to keep track of which newsgroups are subscribed and which articles you have read. On Unix systems, this file is named **.newsrc** and is stored in your home directory. On other systems, the file is usually, but not always, named **newsrc** (without the **.** character). I discuss the **newsrc** file, including its strange name, in Chapter 14.

While you are reading an article, you can use your newsreader to perform many different actions. For example, you can move from one article to another, save an article to a file, mail a reply to the person who posted an article, compose an article of your own, and so on. If you were to watch someone reading the news, you would see him reading text on the screen and, from time to time, selecting a choice from a menu or typing a command.

In Chapter 2, I explain how Internet services are built upon a client/server relationship. The client is a program that requests a service; the server is a program that supplies this service. When you read the news, you are using such a system. The actual articles are stored and managed by a program called a NEWS SERVER. Your newsreader acts as a NEWS CLIENT. Each time you ask to read an article, your newsreader requests that article from the news server. (Sometimes a news server is called an NNTP SERVER. The name NNTP stands for "Network News Transfer Protocol".)

If you access the Net by using an Internet service provider, you will use a news server maintained by your provider for their customers. If you access the Internet via a local area network, one of the computers on the network will probably act as a news server. In either case, the server acts as a central news repository for all the users.

As a Usenet user, you can subscribe to any newsgroup you want, as long as it is available on your news server. Many providers do not carry every possible newsgroup, as it would take too much disk space. Still, there will be far more groups than you can possibly read regularly, so you will not want for variety.

When you use Usenet, your newsreader requests services from the central news server as the need arises. Normally, the whole thing works automatically. You tell your newsreader you want to read an article, and it just appears. However, if the news server should go down (stop working) for some reason, no one will be able to read the news until the person in charge fixes the problem.

In some large networks, such as a university, many people may want to read the news at the same time. If the news server is busy, you may experience a delay.

⚑ HINT

On some networks, you may not be able to read the news at peak periods. When you start your newsreader, it will display a message telling you that the work load on the news server is too high and suggesting that you try again later. For example:

```
Server hub.ucsb.edu responded with code 400, which
probably means the load on the server is too high.
Please try again later.
```

What Is the Difference Between Usenet and the Internet?

The names "Usenet" and "Internet" sound similar, and you may find it easy to confuse the two, so let's take a moment and get the differences straight in our minds.

The name "Usenet" was chosen as an abbreviation for "Users Network". However, the name is a misnomer. Usenet is not really a network in the sense that a network is a group of computers connected together. Usenet is a collection of discussion groups.

The Internet, conversely, really is a network. More precisely, the Internet is a collection of a large number of networks, worldwide.

In other words, the Internet is a general-purpose carrier of information, while Usenet is simply one type of service that makes use of this capability. (As you know, the Internet supports a number of other services, such as the Web, electronic mail, gophers, remote Telnet connection, file transfer and so on.)

Now, you might ask, is every Internet computer part of Usenet? The answer is no. Some Internet computers are used by people who do not have access to a news server. For example, they may work at a company that chooses to not participate in Usenet. To be a part of Usenet requires someone to act as an administrator. It also requires a computer with a large amount of disk space to hold news articles and programs. Some organizations do not want to spend the time and money it would take to maintain such a system.

You might also ask, are all Usenet sites part of the Internet? The answer again is no. The only requirements to being part of Usenet are (1) you must have access to a computer to act as a local repository for articles (a news server), (2) you must have someone to administer the system, and (3) you must find another Usenet site to which your computer can connect in order to swap articles back and forth.

There are a number of Usenet sites that are not part of the Internet; they use some other networking system. For example, there is an old Unix-based system called UUCP used by some computers. And there are many BBSs (bulletin board systems) which are not on the Internet, but which do provide Usenet (and mail) service to their users.

Who Runs Usenet?

The fascinating thing about Usenet is there is no central authority. Usenet is run by the people who use it.

Usenet was started in 1979 in North Carolina (USA) as an experiment. The idea was to create an electronic bulletin board to facilitate the posting and reading of news messages and notices. At first, there were only two sites: the University of North Carolina and Duke University.

Before long, other places joined and, with the explosion of networking in the 1980s and 1990s, Usenet expanded enormously. Today, there are hundreds of thousands of Usenet sites with more than eleven million participants.

Each Usenet site is run by a person called the NEWS ADMINISTRATOR. In some places, the news administrator is the same person who manages the system. However, this need not be the case. In large installations, such as a university, the news administrator may be a staff member, or even an ambitious volunteer, who reports to the system manager.

Each news administrator is responsible for his or her own site alone and nothing else. The arrangement works because the news administrators stay in contact with one another and cooperate. Indeed, there are Usenet newsgroups specifically set up for news administrators to have discussions.

This means that, in the global scheme of things, nobody can tell anybody else what to do. This lack of central authority is what gives Usenet its charm, and is what distinguishes it from other discussion group systems (such as Compuserve, Prodigy, and America Online) where there are Rules and People-In-Charge.

This is not to say that Usenet is total anarchy. There are a good number of conventions that have been developed over the years. As a responsible member of Usenet, you are expected to learn and follow these conventions. Still, when people misbehave—for example, by repeatedly sending silly or offensive messages to a newsgroup—more right-thinking people usually have to confine themselves to public criticism or to sending letters of complaint to the person's electronic mailbox.

Actually, as you will see, when there are no rules, most people choose to cooperate.

HINT

When everyone else is cooperating, acting like a jerk gets boring real fast.

How Is the News Transported?

If there is no central authority to coordinate everything, how are news articles transported all over the world? The answer is new articles are passed from one computer to another and, eventually, a copy of each article spreads throughout the entire Usenet system.

Let's discuss a typical example in which you read articles in one of the Usenet newsgroups devoted to mathematics. As you read, you decide to post an article of your own. Let's take a look at some of the details and follow your article as it travels around the world. These details may vary from one system to another, but the general idea is the same.

To begin, you connect to your Internet service provider and start your newsreader program. You start by telling the newsreader which newsgroup you want to read. As I mentioned earlier, your newsreader keeps a file in which it records the newsgroups you subscribe to and the articles you have read.

In this case, you specify a particular mathematics group, so the newsreader checks its records and then connects to the news server to request the next article from this particular newsgroup. The news server responds by sending the article, which your newsreader then displays on your screen. When you finish reading an article, your newsreader will request and display the next article.

As it happens, someone on the other side of the world has posted an article in which he asks if anybody has a *short* solution to Fermat's Last Theorem. You remember that you came up with just such a solution the other day, so you tell your newsreader that you wish to compose an article in response to the one you are currently reading. (This is called a "followup" article.)

Your newsreader presents you with a screen on which you can compose your article. (On some systems, the newsreader will start a separate text editor program.) In this case, you say you have a wonderfully short solution to the problem but, unfortunately, it is a bit too long to write down at this time.

After you finish writing, your newsreader sends a copy of your new article to your news server. At this point, your article can be read by anyone using the same server. However, the article still needs to be transported around the world.

Now, when one news server supplies Usenet articles to another server, we say the first server offers a NEWS FEED. In order to participate in Usenet, your news server must have a news feed from another Usenet site. From time to time, your news server will connect to the server at this site in order to get its feed.

Each time this happens, your server passes on any new articles which have not yet been received at the other location. In particular, the new article you just composed will be sent out. Later, when that news server connects to its own news feed, your article will be sent to another site. This is how Usenet works: your article is passed automatically from one news server to another, one connection at a time.

What makes the system fast is that some news servers act as way stations, providing news feeds for many other servers. Once your article hits one of these way stations, it will be sent to many news servers within a short amount of time.

So what about your mathematics article? By the next day, your article is available on many, many news servers and, within two or three days, it is available everywhere. By the end of the week, your great mathematical accomplishment is recognized worldwide and you are famous.

You might ask, if new articles are constantly being transported from one news server to another, don't they just pile up indefinitely? This is the same question that you might ask as you ride down an escalator: Why doesn't the basement fill up with steps?

With an escalator, the answer is, of course, the steps are recycled. With Usenet, the solution is to keep each article for a certain amount of time and then throw it away. Each news administrator decides how long articles should be kept. The news server regularly checks the articles and deletes those that are older than the specified time interval. When this happens, we say the articles have EXPIRED.

The news administrator at your location can specify different expiration dates for the various newsgroups. For example, he or she may decide that the newsgroup in which people discuss general Usenet questions should have a longer expiration period than the newsgroup in which people swap tasteless jokes. (Or, perhaps, the other way around.) If you want to know the exact expiration policy at your location, you will have to ask your local news administrator.

HINT

As a general rule, most newsgroup articles are kept from two days to two weeks.

How Big Is Usenet?

Since Usenet has no central administration, it is difficult to know exactly how big the system is. However, various people have implemented programs to estimate Usenet statistics.

At DEC Network Systems Laboratory, Brian Reid runs the Measurement Project, which regularly publishes such numbers. Reid uses a special program which many Usenet news administrators run on their systems. This program compiles data on how many people read Usenet, which newsgroups they read, and so on. (It is all anonymous so privacy is protected.) Reid then analyzes the results mathematically and estimates statistics for the entire Usenet system.

Here are the statistics that were current at the time I wrote this chapter. (Remember, these are estimates. The actual numbers are not important. All I want is for you to gain an appreciation of the size of Usenet.)

There were 330,000 different sites that carried Usenet. At these sites, there were 30,329,000 users of all types, of whom about 36% (11,033,000) participated in Usenet.

Another question to ask is, how much data is actually transported on Usenet? To answer this question, the Measurement Project looks at how much Usenet data is received at their own news server. This computer, named **decwrl**, receives most of the newsgroups and provides a news feed to other servers.

On average, **decwrl** received 127,446 new messages a day, containing a total of 586.4 megabytes (586.4 million characters) of data.

HINT

Usenet consists of about 11 million people, accessing 330,000 different news servers, who post 127,000 new articles every day.

If all the people who participate in Usenet were laid end to end, they would stretch from Newman's Grove, Nebraska, to Besalampy, Madagascar.

The Mainstream and Alternative Hierarchies

As I have explained, there are a vast number of Usenet newsgroups with new ones being added all the time. In order to make everything manageable, we use a system in which the newsgroups are collected into categories called HIERARCHIES. Each hierarchy has its own name and is devoted to a particular area of interest. Figure 13-2 shows the most important hierarchies.

The hierarchies in Figure 13-2 are distributed all over the world (although, as you will see in a moment, not all hierarchies are carried at every Usenet site). Each newsgroup is given a name that consists of two or more parts, separated by **.** (period) characters. The first part of the name is the hierarchy to which the newsgroup belongs.

For example, in the **news** hierarchy, there is a newsgroup for people who are learning how to use Usenet. In this newsgroup, you can ask any question you want about Usenet and some kind soul will answer you. The name of this newsgroup is **news.newusers.questions**.

HINT

When you talk about the name of a Usenet newsgroup, the **.** (period) character is pronounced as "dot". Thus, the name **news.newusers.questions** is pronounced "news dot new-users dot questions".

Name	Topics
`alt`	alternative newsgroups, many different topics
`bionet`	biology
`bit`	many topics: from Bitnet mailing lists
`biz`	business, marketing, advertisements
`comp`	computers
`humanities`	the arts and humanities
`k12`	kindergarten through high school
`misc`	anything that doesn't fit into another category
`news`	about Usenet itself
`rec`	recreation, hobbies, the arts
`sci`	science of all types
`soc`	social issues
`talk`	debate on controversial topics

Figure 13-2. *The most important Usenet newsgroup hierarchies*

Here are two more examples of newsgroup names. In the **rec** hierarchy, there are several newsgroups devoted to various aspects of Star Trek. For discussions about Star Trek conventions and memorabilia, there is **rec.arts.startrek.fandom**. For reviews of Star Trek episodes, movies and books, you can read **rec.arts.startrek.reviews**.

The two Star Trek examples each have a four-part name, with the first three parts the same. This is the system that is used to name newsgroups. The first part is the hierarchy, the other parts show categories and subcategories. For example, the newsgroup devoted to science fiction movies is **rec.arts.sf.movies**. The group for discussing boating is **rec.boats**.

The Usenet hierarchies are divided into two categories, MAINSTREAM and ALTERNATIVE. The mainstream hierarchies are carried on all Usenet news servers. The alternative hierarchies are considered optional. Many Usenet sites carry them, but other sites do not.

At each Usenet site, the news administrator decides which hierarchies and newsgroups to carry. At most places, you can expect to see all the mainstream hierarchies and at least some of the alternative hierarchies. However, bear in mind that even if your site carries a particular hierarchy, it may not have all the newsgroups in that hierarchy.

The principal difference between the two types of hierarchies has to do with the way new groups are formed. As I will explain later in the chapter, people must follow well-defined procedures to start a mainstream newsgroup. There must be a discussion and a vote, and enough people must express interest. The alternative hierarchy is more lax: any person who knows how to do so can start a newsgroup. Historically, the mainstream hierarchies were the original Usenet categories and were strictly controlled. The alternative hierarchies came later and were created as a less-restrictive facility.

As a whole, mainstream newsgroups tend to be more stable and are more readily accepted by news administrators. For example, an administrator who is short of disk space might decide that **news.newusers.questions** is more important than **alt.sex.bondage**. Even so, many of the alternative newsgroups are popular and are widely circulated. However, as you might imagine, you will often find ridiculous or spurious alternative newsgroups, especially within the **alt** hierarchy.

HINT

The distinction between mainstream and alternative newsgroups is made only for purposes of organization. When you read the articles, there is no real difference. The main consideration is that your news server may not carry all of the alternative newsgroups.

There are eight mainstream hierarchies and five major alternative hierarchies. They are shown in Figures 13-3 and 13-4.

Hierarchy	Number of Newsgroups
comp	794
humantities	3
misc	104
news	22
rec	533
sci	165
soc	182
talk	26
TOTAL	1829

Figure 13-3.   *The mainstream Usenet newsgroup hierarchies*

Hierarchy	Number of Newsgroups
`alt`	2563
`bionet`	89
`bit`	237
`biz`	41
`k12`	34
TOTAL	2964

Figure 13-4.   *The alternative Usenet newsgroup hierarchies*

The Cultural, Organizational and Regional Hierarchies

In Figures 13-3 and 13-4, I listed the mainstream and alternative hierarchies along with the number of newsgroups. In total, there are 1,829 mainstream groups and 2,964 alternative groups. (This was at the time I wrote this chapter. The numbers are always changing.) I said earlier that there are more than 13,000 different newsgroups. What about the others?

As you remember, the mainstream and alternative hierarchies are distributed worldwide (although most Usenet sites do not carry every single newsgroup). In addition, there are many other hierarchies that are more cultural, organizational or local in nature. These hierarchies are mainly circulated in their areas of interest.

Cultural hierarchies contain newsgroups devoted to a particular people. For example, four of the more well-known cultural hierarchies are **de** (German [Deutsch] newsgroups), **fj** (Japanese), **aus** (Australian) and **relcom** (Russian).

Although most Usenet articles are in English, the cultural hierarchies often have articles in their own language. For such articles, you may need special software to display the non-English characters. For example, some of the Japanese articles in the **fj** hierarchy use the Kanji alphabet.

The organizational hierarchies contain newsgroups devoted to a university, company or other organization. There are many such hierarchies. For instance, the University of California at Santa Barbara has its own hierarchy, named **ucsb**. Trinity College in Dublin, Ireland, has a **tcd** hierarchy. If you are part of a large organization, chances are it has its own hierarchy and its own newsgroups.

Within the **ucsb** hierarchy, for example, are newsgroups of interest to the university community. For instance, there is a group named **ucsb.general** for announcements and discussion of general interest. There is also a newsgroup, `ucsb.compsci.cs180`, just for one particular computer science class. As you might imagine, such newsgroups are created and removed as the need arises.

Aside from the cultural and organizational hierarchies, there are a large number of regional hierarchies. These contain newsgroups of interest to people who live in a particular area. For example, the **ba** hierarchy contains many newsgroups pertaining to the San Francisco Bay area, such as **ba.market.housing**.

A great many of the cultural, organizational and regional hierarchies are distributed throughout the world. For example, many Usenet sites carry the **fj** hierarchy. After all, there are Japanese people everywhere, not just in Japan. Similarly, someone who used to live in San Francisco may want to read a regional newsgroup to keep in touch. Moreover, if you are planning to move to a new area, you may want to post an article of your own to a regional newsgroup to ask for information, say, about housing.

How Many Different Newsgroups Are There?

Now that I have covered all the hierarchies, I am in a good position to answer the question: How many Usenet newsgroups are there?

The total number of newsgroups changes frequently, especially in the alternative hierarchies. At the time I wrote this chapter, there were 1,829 mainstream groups and 2,964 alternative groups. This makes a total of 4,793 newsgroups that are widely distributed throughout the world.

There were also an estimated 8,309 cultural, organizational and local groups. (I say "estimated" because many such groups never make it outside their local news server.) This gives us a grand total of 13,102 different newsgroups.

HINT

Even before I could finish writing this chapter, the number 13,102 was out of date. To give you a feeling for how Usenet grows, about a year before I wrote this chapter, there were 6,738 newsgroups. Thus, in the last twelve months, the number of newsgroups had grown by 6,364 (about 194 percent).

Newsgroup Naming Conventions

Newsgroup names are easy to understand. The first part of the name shows the hierarchy. For example, a group whose name begins with **comp**, such as **comp.unix.questions**, is in the computer hierarchy; the groups whose names that begin with **talk**, such as **talk.environment**, are debate oriented; and so on. You can expect to find the strangest (and most controversial) newsgroups in the **alt** hierarchy. For example, this is where you will find **alt.sex.bestiality** and **alt.fan.rush-limbaugh**.

Thus, when you are checking out a list of newsgroups and trying to decide what to read, start by looking at the first part of the name. To show you some examples, Figure 13-5 contains a list of newsgroups devoted to jokes, and Figure 13-6 shows some of the newsgroups related to sex. (As you might imagine, these newsgroups have some of the largest audiences on Usenet.)

 **INTERNET RESOURCE** *Look in the catalog under Internet Resources for*
Usenet: Humor Newsgroups
Usenet: Sex Newsgroups

After the hierarchy name, you will see categories and (possibly) subcategories. When two newsgroups are related, they will have similar names, differing only in the last part of the name. For example:

```
alt.binaries.pictures.erotica.blondes
alt.binaries.pictures.erotica.female
alt.binaries.pictures.erotica.male
```

Another point to notice is that some of the newsgroup names end in **.d**. This means that the group is for discussion of the contents of another group. For example, we have:

```
alt.sex.stories
alt.sex.stories.d
```

The first group contains stories about sex (check it out sometime) and only stories. The second group is for people who want to discuss the stories. If you post an article to **alt.sex.stories** that is not a story, someone may remind you that all discussion should take place in the **.d** group. This is so people who only want to read stories do not have to bother with anything else.

```
alt.jokes.limericks
alt.tasteless.jokes
rec.humor
rec.humor.funny  (moderated)
```

Figure 13-5. *Newsgroups devoted to jokes*

```
alt.binaries.pictures.erotica
alt.binaries.pictures.erotica.blondes
alt.binaries.pictures.erotica.d
alt.binaries.pictures.erotica.female
alt.binaries.pictures.erotica.male
alt.homosexual
alt.politics.homosexuality
alt.politics.sex
alt.sex
alt.sex.bestiality
alt.sex.bondage
alt.sex.escorts.ads
alt.sex.fetish.feet
alt.sex.magazines
alt.sex.masturbation
alt.sex.motss
alt.sex.movies
alt.sex.pictures
alt.sex.pictures.d
alt.sex.pictures.female
alt.sex.pictures.male
alt.sex.safe
alt.sex.sounds
alt.sex.stories
alt.sex.stories.d
alt.sex.wanted
alt.sex.wizards
alt.sexual.abuse.recovery
rec.arts.erotica (moderated)
soc.bi
soc.motss
```

Figure 13-6. *A selection of newsgroups related to sex*

There is another important example of this convention that you should know about. The newsgroup `rec.humor` is for people who want to post and read jokes. If you want to discuss jokes, you should post to `rec.humor.d`. This is also the place to send a request like, "Does anybody have the list of all the light bulb jokes?" (That is why I did not list `rec.humor.d` in Figure 13-5. It does not contain jokes. Rather, it is a group in which people talk *about* jokes.)

HINT

In the non-moderated joke newsgroups (`rec.humor` and `alt.tasteless.jokes`), the unofficial rule is that all postings must contain at least one joke. You will often see postings in which a person has given in to temptation and made some sort of non-joke comment. However, to be polite and to adhere to the convention, he or she has also included a joke. This is called an OBLIGATORY JOKE or OBJOKE.

You will sometimes see the same prefix, "ob", used in other groups to indicate the same convention: a person is respecting the purpose of the group by making sure to include a relevant item within an otherwise questionable posting.

Moderated Newsgroups

You will notice that some of the newsgroups listed in Figures 13-5 and 13-6 (jokes and sex) are MODERATED. This means that you cannot post articles directly to the group. You do submit articles in the regular way, but they are automatically rerouted and sent to one person, called the MODERATOR, who decides what will go in the group. The moderator—who is an unpaid volunteer—will not only pass judgment on what goes into a group, he or she will often edit and organize the articles.

The reason for moderators is to minimize the number of low-quality articles in a newsgroup. Perhaps the best examples are the humor groups. The groups `rec.humor` and `alt.tasteless.jokes` are not moderated. This means that anyone can post to these groups, with the result that there is usually a lot of silliness and repetition (not to mention old jokes).

The group `rec.humor.funny` is moderated. Only those jokes that are deemed funny by the moderator are posted. People from all over the world submit jokes, and the moderator picks the ones he thinks are best. As a result, `rec.humor.funny` is read by more people than `rec.humor` (although they are both popular).

Some moderated newsgroups offer a special type of posting called a DIGEST. The moderator creates a digest by collecting submissions, questions, answers and interesting bits of information. He or she will edit the information into a series of interesting items and post it as one large article, the digest. Two examples of such newsgroups are `comp.sys.ibm.pc.digest` and `comp.sys.mac.digest`.

A digest is much like an issue of an electronic magazine, with a volume and issue number, and a table of contents. Most newsreader programs have a special command to let you jump from one item to another as you read a digest.

Overall, the idea of moderated newsgroups provides a nice balance to Usenet. Many newsgroups carry a lot of low-quality articles and it can be nice to read a group where everything is interesting (at least by one person's standards).

Of course, moderated newsgroups are a form of censorship because one person controls everything that is posted to the group. However, Usenet has many groups, almost all non-moderated, so you need never feel deprived.

What Are the Most Popular Newsgroups?

One of the most interesting questions about Usenet is: What are the most popular newsgroups? There is more than one way to answer this question depending on what you mean by "popular".

At regular intervals, the Measurement Project (which I mentioned earlier in the chapter) sends estimates of readership statistics to several newsgroups. (If you want to read such postings, check out the group `news.lists`.)

One of the postings identifies the 40 most popular newsgroups based on the estimated number of total readers. The thing is, not all groups are carried at all Usenet sites. For example, many news administrators will not carry groups like `alt.sex` even though, as you can imagine, they are extremely popular.

Let's take a look at some of these statistics. One of the perennial favorites is `rec.humor.funny`. At the time I wrote this chapter, this newsgroup had an estimated audience of 332,008 people. The group `alt.sex.voyeurism` had only 219,798 readers. By this standard of measurement, the humor group is a lot more popular.

However, `rec.humor.funny` is carried at 80% of all Usenet sites. The group `alt.sex.voyeurism` is carried at only 36% of the sites. The real question is: How well would a particular newsgroup do if it were carried at all sites? In other words, instead of asking how many people read the group, we ask, how much do people like the group?

To come up with such numbers, we start with two of the statistics estimated by the Measurement Project: the total number of readers and the percentage of sites that carry each newsgroup. To compare readership equally, we divide the total readers by the percentage at that site. This gives us an estimate of how many total readers a newsgroup would have if it were carried at all sites.

For example, `rec.humor.funny` would have 332,008 divided by 0.80, or 415,010 readers. The `alt.sex.voyeurism` group would have 219,798 divided by 0.36, or 610,550 readers. Thus, the sex group is a lot more popular than the humor group.

To make these hypothetical readership numbers easier to understand, we can normalize them, setting the most popular one to the value 100. To do so, we divide each such number by the hypothetical readership of the most popular group, and multiply the result by 100. (The most popular newsgroup is `alt.sex.stories`. It has a hypothetical readership of 463,628 divided by 0.51, or 909,075.)

The result is a number between 0 and 100, which provides a picture of true popularity. I call this value the *Harley Index of Popularity* or *HIP*. For example, `rec.humor.funny` has an HIP value of 415,010 divided by 909,075 multiplied by 100, or approximately 46.

Figure 13-7 contains the relevant numbers with all the arithmetic done for the 25 most popular Usenet newsgroups at the time I wrote this chapter. Draw your own conclusions.

HINT

According to my research, the most popular newsgroup that could exist would be `alt.sex.jobs.offered.newusers`.

How Are New Newsgroups Started?

A new newsgroup is created by sending a special message, called a CONTROL MESSAGE, throughout Usenet. Various types of control messages are used by news administrators to govern the operation of Usenet. For example, there is one particular type of control message that is used to start a new group. (There is also another type of control message to remove an obsolete or spurious group.)

When a news administrator sends out such a message, it propagates from news server to news server, just like a regular article. Eventually, the message reaches all the news servers. Each administrator decides whether or not to create the new group on his or her system.

News administrators almost always honor an authorized request to start a new mainstream group. This is because such a message will not be issued until certain well-defined criteria are met (described below).

Conversely, a control message to start an alternative newsgroup can by issued be anyone who knows how to do it. As you might imagine, there are all sorts of requests to start bizarre alternative groups. For this reason, many news administrators will pick and choose which new alternative newsgroups they are willing to create on their systems.

Here is how a new mainstream group gets formed.

To start, somebody must have the idea for a new group. Perhaps an existing group should be split into two. Perhaps a whole new area of discussion has arisen. Most ideas are discussed in existing newsgroups or by mail for some time, as ideas are proposed, examined and modified.

Rank	Newsgroup	HIP Value	Readers	Sites
1	alt.sex.stories	100	463628	51%
2	alt.sex	98	510028	57%
3	alt.binaries.pictures.erotica	96	410019	47%
4	news.announce.newusers	75	623532	91%
5	alt.binaries.pictures.erotica.female	67	244939	40%
6	alt.sex.voyeurism	67	219798	36%
7	alt.sex.exhibitionism	63	210740	37%
8	alt.binaries.pictures.erotica.blondes	62	213328	38%
9	alt.binaries.pictures.erotica.orientals	56	177650	35%
10	alt.sex.breasts	55	145669	29%
11	alt.binaries.pictures.supermodels	51	193918	42%
12	rec.humor.funny	46	332008	80%
13	alt.sex.movies	43	196506	50%
14	alt.sex.stories.d	43	187817	48%
15	alt.sex.bondage	42	204085	54%
16	alt.tv.simpsons	42	215177	57%
17	alt.sex.pictures	40	145115	40%
18	rec.arts.erotica	40	233478	65%
19	alt.sex.wanted	37	158240	47%
20	alt.binaries.pictures.tasteless	37	43266	43%
21	alt.sex.wizards	35	154727	49%
22	alt.2600	35	157500	50%
23	misc.jobs.offered	32	229965	80%
24	news.answers	31	249191	88%
25	alt.music.alternative	31	152324	54%

Figure 13-7. *The 25 most popular Usenet newsgroups*

Once the idea for the new group is established, someone sends a message to the group **news.announce.newgroups** (which is moderated). At the same time, the message is cross-posted to any other relevant groups.

The moderator of **news.announce.newgroups** will post an article explaining the name and purpose of the proposed group. There is now a 30-day discussion. This discussion takes place in the newsgroup, in other related newsgroups, and by private mail correspondence.

At the end of 30 days, if there is clear agreement as to the name and purpose of the group, the moderator of **news.announce.newgroups** will post a general request for people to vote. Anyone who is interested can vote (once) by sending an appropriate mail message to a specified address. The period of voting is set in advance and is usually between 21 and 31 days.

At the end of the voting period, the totals are posted along with a full list of everyone who voted and how they voted. (No secrets on Usenet.) There is now a 5-day waiting period in which anyone can request a correction to a particular vote or to the voting procedure.

At the end of 5 days, the vote is finalized. The vote is successful if the new group was approved by at least two thirds of the voters, and if the yes votes were at least 100 more than the no votes. After a successful vote, the moderator of **news.announce.newgroups** sends out a control message to start the new group.

If the vote was unsuccessful, the same newsgroup cannot be brought up for discussion for at least six months.

⚑ HINT

If you want to start a new alternative group, do the following:

(1) Make sure that you have at least a few months of Usenet experience, so you understand how the system works.

(2) Suggest your idea by posting an article in one or more existing groups (choose appropriately), and see what other people think. The newsgroup **alt.config** is used for discussing proposals for new alternate groups. Remember, alternative groups can only be created successfully if other people cooperate.

(3) Read **news.announce.newgroups** for a while to see what types of issues arise during the formation of new groups.

(4) After a reasonable amount of time—and as a reader of this book I know you are reasonable—decide if you still want to start the group. If so, ask your local news administrator for help in sending the appropriate control message.

 **INTERNET RESOURCE** *Look in the catalog under Internet Resources for* ***Usenet: How to Start a Newsgroup***

Frequently Asked Question Lists (FAQs)

As you start to use Usenet, you have many questions. Moreover, each time you begin to read a new newsgroup, you will have specific questions relating to that group. Many of these questions will be the same ones everyone else asked when they first started to read that same newsgroup.

For example, the group **misc.consumers** is often used to discuss consumer credit. A common question is "What is the difference between Visa and Mastercard?" Here is another example. The newsgroup **rec.arts.disney** discusses general topics related to the world of Disney. A question often asked by newcomers is, "Is it true Walt Disney was frozen in cryogenic suspension after he died?"

You will find that the participants of most newsgroups have asked and answered questions like these many times. Although such questions are interesting to a beginner, you can imagine that experienced readers grow tired of seeing the same queries posted repeatedly.

The solution is the FREQUENTLY ASKED QUESTION LIST or FAQ. A FAQ is a document, maintained by a volunteer, that identifies and answers all the frequently asked questions for a particular newsgroup. Many newsgroups have a FAQ which is posted to the group regularly. It is considered good manners to refrain from asking questions in a newsgroup until you have read the FAQ. (Although, not all newsgroups have such lists.)

There are four ways to get a FAQ. First, you can read the newsgroup regularly and, if there is a FAQ, it will be posted eventually. (Typical intervals are every week, every two weeks or every month, depending on the group.)

Second, you can read the newsgroup named **news.answers** which consists of nothing but FAQs and related material. This is an interesting group to follow, as you will see lists of the best questions and answers on topics you would normally investigate.

The third way to get a FAQ is to use the Web or anonymous ftp to download the FAQ from one of the Usenet archive sites.

Finally, after trying the other methods, you can post a short article to the group asking if a FAQ list exists and, if so, can someone mail you a copy or tell you how to get it.

HINT

Learn how to use the Web or anonymous ftp and take a look at the FAQs in the Usenet archives. There are all kinds of interesting questions and answers.

 **INTERNET RESOURCE** *Look in the catalog under Internet Resources for FAQ (Frequently Asked Question List) Archives*

Chapter Fourteen

Reading and Posting Usenet Articles

In Chapter 13, I introduced Usenet, the worldwide collection of more than 13,000 different discussion groups. I explained how you can participate in Usenet by posting articles to the various groups and by using a program, called a newsreader, to read the articles.

In this chapter, I describe what you can expect to see when you read articles. I will show you what a typical article looks like and how to make sense of all the technical information. I will then discuss the Usenet conventions: the guidelines you should follow and the terminology you can expect to encounter.

After reading this chapter, you will be prepared to start reading the news and posting your own articles. In this chapter, I will discuss the general considerations and how it all works. If you use a Unix shell account, you will also want to read Chapter 15, in which I explain how to use the **tin** newsreader.

The Format of a News Article

A news article consists of three parts: a HEADER, followed by the BODY, followed by an optional SIGNATURE.

The header contains technical information about the article. There are twenty different types of lines that you might commonly see in the header, each of which contains a different type of information. I will discuss headers in detail in the next section.

The body of the article is the actual text: the main part of the article.

Finally, the signature consists of a few lines that come at the end of the article. These lines are composed by the person who sent the article and are automatically appended to the end of every article he or she posts. I will talk more about signatures later in the chapter.

Figure 14-1 contains a typical Usenet article. In this article, the header consists of the first 13 lines. The body of the article consists of the next 6 lines. In this case it happens to be a question about philosophy. Most articles are longer than our example and, in most cases, the body is larger than the header. Finally, the last 4 lines of our sample contain a signature. In our example, the signature identifies the person who posted the article, along with an address, phone number and a short quotation.

The Header

All Usenet articles have a header, consisting of special lines at the beginning of the article. As I mentioned in the last section, there are twenty different types of lines you might commonly see in a header. These are listed in Figure 14-2.

Not all articles will contain all twenty lines. For example, the article in Figure 14-1 contains only 13 header lines. These are the ones you will see most often. For reference, though, I will briefly describe all twenty types of header lines, so you will be able to understand them when you see them.

Before I do, you should understand that whether or not you even see the header at all depends on which newsreader program you are using and how it is configured. Some newsreaders show you all of the header lines by default. Other newsreaders will

```
Path: ucsbcs1!mustang.mst6.lanl.gov!nntp-server.caltech.edu!
  news.claremont.edu!uunet!news.univie.ac.at!email!mich
From: mich@music.tuwien.ac.at (Michael Schuster)
Newsgroups: rec.humor
Subject: The Secret of Life
Summary: Advice for understanding life.
Keywords: life, philosophy
Message-ID: <1995Sep15.073130.15261@email.tuwien.ac.at>
Date: 15 Sep 95 21:56:30 GMT
Distribution: world
Sender: news@email.tuwien.ac.at
Organization: Tech Univ Vienna, Dept of Realtime Systems, AUSTRIA
Lines: 12
Nntp-Posting-Host: idefix.music.tuwien.ac.at

Here is some great advice I just found:

"When you get serious about bullshit,
you are getting into serious bullshit."

By the way, does anyone know who first said it?


--
Michael Schuster          |"I love you for your beauty; love me
TU Vienna, Austria        | though I am ugly"
mich@music.tuwien.ac.at   | - Miguel Cervantes, Don Quixote
+43/1/12345
```

Figure 14-1.   *A typical Usenet article*

not show you any header lines unless you ask for them; you will see only the body and the signature. However, many newsreaders allow you to customize how articles should be displayed, and you will probably be able to display the full header if you really want to.

I will now discuss the various types of header lines you might see. Few articles contain all twenty of the standard header lines, but it is a good idea to know what they mean. The header lines in Figure 14-1 are the most common ones.

Please do not think you have to memorize what all these header lines mean. Just read through this section once. Then, whenever you see an article with a header line that puzzles you, you can look it up.

(From time to time, you will encounter other header lines I do not mention here. Almost always, these will be non-standard lines you can safely ignore.)

Header Line	Description
Approved:	identifies moderator who posted article
Control:	contains special administrative commands
Date:	time and date article was posted
Distribution:	recommendation for where to send article
Expires:	recommendation for when to remove article
Followup-To:	shows where followup articles will be sent
From:	userid and address that posted the article
Keywords:	one or more words to categorize the article
Lines:	size of the body + signature
Message-ID:	unique identifier for the article
Newsgroups:	newsgroups to which the article was posted
NNTP-Posting Host:	name of Internet host that posted article
Organization:	describes the person's organization
Path:	shows transit route of the article
References:	identifies article to which followup refers
Reply-To:	address to which to send personal replies
Sender:	address of computer that sent out article
Subject:	short description of contents of article
Summary:	one-line summary of article
Xref:	local cross-posting information

Figure 14-2.   *Header lines for Usenet articles*

Approved: In Chapter 13, I explained that some newsgroups are moderated. When you post an article to such a group, it is not sent to the group directly. Rather, it is sent to a person, called the moderator, who decides if an article should be sent to the group or discarded. Within moderated groups, the **Approved:** header contains the mail address of the moderator. This header line is also used with some types of **Control:** messages.

Control: This type of header line contains special commands used by news administrators to control the Usenet system. For example, there is a special control line used to start a new newsgroup. It is possible you will never see a **Control:** line, as it is not used in regular articles.

Date: This line shows the time and date the article was posted. The time will often be in Greenwich Mean Time [GMT], which is the standard Internet time. (Sometimes GMT is called Universal Time.) I discuss the Internet time conventions in Chapter 7.

Distribution: When you post an article you will be given a chance to specify where you would like the article to be sent. Some news posting programs will show you several choices and ask you to pick one. Typical choices include: your organization, your region, your country and worldwide. With other programs, you are not shown the choices, you just have to know what is available in your area. As an example, here are the choices you might see if you post an article at the University of California at San Diego.

local:	local to the site
ucsd:	local to the UCSD campus
uc:	all the University of California campuses
sdnet:	local to San Diego County
ca:	everywhere in California
usa:	everywhere in the USA
na:	everywhere in North America
world:	everywhere in the world

Here is another example, from one of the computers at the Technical University in Vienna, Austria.

inst182:	local to department #182 (Institut #182)
tuwien:	local to the university (Technische Universitaet Wien)
at:	everywhere in Austria
europe:	everywhere in Europe
world:	everywhere in the world

(Note: The international domain name for Austria is **at**.)

It is important to understand that a particular distribution does not guarantee where an article will be propagated. It is only a suggestion. Each news administrator decides which distributions he or she will accept. Some administrators will accept every newsgroup they can get. Thus, for example, I have had the experience of logging in to a computer in Palo Alto, California, and reading local news from Edmonton, Canada.

Expires: Each news administrator sets up time intervals specifying how long articles will be retained on his or her news server. The **Expires:** header is used when you want to recommend a different expiration date. For example, if an article is announcing an upcoming seminar, it makes sense to have the article expire the day after the seminar. Most articles do not use this header line. They expire according to whatever the local policy happens to be.

Remember though, it is the news administrator who has the last word about when articles expire. If you see an article with a particular expiration date, it's completely possible the article may disappear before then.

Followup-To: From time to time, you may wish to submit an article in which you respond to a previous article. In such cases, your posting is called a FOLLOWUP ARTICLE. All newsreader programs make it easy to compose and post such articles.

Normally, a followup article will be sent to the newsgroup (or newsgroups) in which the original article appeared. However, it is possible to control where the followup articles should go by using a **Followup-To:** header line.

For example, say you post a joke to the **rec.humor** newsgroup. It happens to be the type of joke that you know people will want to comment on. However, the **rec.humor** newsgroup is supposed to be for jokes only. Discussion of jokes should be in the group **rec.humor.d**. So, when you post the joke to **rec.humor**, you can use a **Followup-To:** header line that specifies **rec.humor.d**. This technique is handy when you post an article to more than one newsgroup, and you want to direct all subsequent discussion to a single group.

There is one special followup designation you should know about. If this header line specifies **poster**, it means followup articles cannot be sent to the newsgroup. Rather, you should continue the discussion with the person who posted the article by sending a message to his or her personal mail address. (Your newsreader program makes this easy to do.)

From: This header line is important, as it tells you who posted the article. You will always see the person's mail address. In most cases, you will also see their real name.

HINT

It is possible for people to control what "real name" is shown in the **From:** header line. So, if something looks suspicious, be suspicious.

Keywords: This line contains one or more words or terms that categorize the content of the article. Some people look at this line to decide if they want to read the article (although the **Subject:** line is usually more important).

Lines: This header line is straightforward. It shows the total number of lines in the article. The number of lines includes the body and the signature, but not the header.

Message-ID: This line contains a unique identifier which is automatically generated by the program that sent out the article. The last part of this name is the address of the computer from which the article was posted. This information is used only by news programs. You can ignore it.

Newsgroups: This is an important line. It shows the newsgroups to which the article has been posted. When you are using a newsreader program to look at an article, you know it has been posted to the newsgroup you are reading. However, if you are looking at an old article—which you have previously saved, or which someone has mailed to you, or which you have found in a Usenet archive—it is handy to know in what newsgroups the article originally appeared.

When you post an article, you will be asked to specify the group to which you want to send the article. If you so wish, you can specify more than one group. This is called CROSS-POSTING. When an article is cross-posted, you will see more than one newsgroup name in the **Newsgroups:** header line.

It is considered good etiquette to post each article to only one newsgroup (or at most, a small number of newsgroups). It is bad manners to send an article to many newsgroups, most of which have only a tenuous relationship to the topic under discussion. For example, if you have a Unix question, send it to the most appropriate of the many different Unix-oriented newsgroups. Do not send it to every Unix group.

HINT

When you cross-post an article, make sure to put a **Followup-To:** line in the header to direct subsequent discussion to one specific group. If appropriate, consider using **Followup-To: poster** to direct all subsequent discussion to your personal mailbox.

NNTP-Posting Host: In Chapter 2, I explained that TCP/IP is a large family of protocols. (A protocol is a set of technical rules.) In previous chapters, I have discussed TCP (Transmission Control Protocol) and IP (Internet Protocol), for transporting data packets, SMTP (Simple Mail Transfer Protocol) for sending mail messages, and HTTP (Hypertext Transfer Protocol) for transferring hypertext (web pages).

The protocol used to transport Usenet articles is called NNTP. The name stands for Network News Transfer Protocol. The **NNTP-Posting Host:** header line shows the name of the Internet computer from which the article was posted. The **Sender:** line, if present, shows the name of the computer—often the news server—that actually sent out the article over Usenet.

HINT

If you want to hunt for forgeries (which do turn up from time to time), look for articles in which the name of the computer in the **NNTP-Posting Host:** header line does not agree with the name of the computer in the **From:** line. It is easy to change the **From:** line but not so easy to modify the **NNTP-Posting Host:** line.

Organization: This header line contains a short phrase describing the organization to which the person who posted the article belongs, or the organization that owns the news server. The purpose of this header line is to help identify the person who posted the article. The **From:** line does contain an address, but sometimes such addresses can be difficult to understand.

Path: The information on this line consists of a number of computer names, separated by **!** (exclamation mark) characters. The names show the path the article took, from one computer to another, to reach your news server. (To understand the path, read it from right to left.)

Although this information is considered to be a single header line, it is often so long as to be broken onto more than one line on your screen. This is the case in Figure 14-1, where you can see the names of the computers the article passed through on its way from Vienna, Austria, to Santa Barbara, California.

You can safely ignore the information in this line.

References: You will see this header line only in followup articles. It will contain the identifier from the **Message-ID:** of the original article. The example in Figure 14-3 (later in this chapter) is a followup article and, as such, contains a **References:** header line.

This is another header line that you can ignore. It is used by newsreader programs to collect related articles. In this way, after you read an article, your newsreader can show the followup articles. A connected series of articles is called a THREAD. As you read the news, you will often want to FOLLOW a thread, reading one followup article after another.

Reply-To: This header line has the same format as the **From:** line. If a **Reply-to:** line is present, replies that should be sent to the person who posted the article will be mailed to the address in this line. This header line is handy when you want private mail replies to go to a different address than the one from which the article was posted.

Sender: The purpose of this header line is to show the name of the computer from which the article was posted. A **Sender:** line will be generated automatically whenever the information in the **From:** line might be misleading: for instance, if someone manually enters his own **From:** line rather than have the news posting program do it automatically.

For example, let's say that you are visiting a friend and you use her account to post an article. Normally, the news posting program will put in a **From:** header line with her name and address. Instead, you delete this line and put in a different **From:** line, showing your own name and address.

The news program will automatically generate a **Sender:** line containing the name of the computer that posted your article. Sometimes you will also see the name of the system userid that sends out news articles.

Yes, as you suspect, this feature makes it a little more difficult for bored undergraduates to get away with forging news articles.

Subject: This line is, by far, the most important header line. It contains a short description of what the article is about. You create this description when you compose an article.

Why is this header line so important? Most newsreader programs do not display the body of an article automatically. The user will see a list of **Subject:** lines, from which he will choose the articles he wants to read. In many cases, the contents of this line will be all someone sees before choosing whether or not to read your article.

HINT

When you post an article, it behooves you to take a moment to make your **Subject:** line interesting and accurate. Most people will not even look at an article unless the subject description takes their fancy.

Summary: A brief one-line summary of the article. This information is useful in followup articles. The **Summary:** header line is not used all that often, but you can put one in if you want.

Xref: When an article is cross-posted to more than one newsgroup, the **Xref:** header line (which stands for "cross reference") will show which newsgroups contain the article. It will also show the local article numbers that identify the article in each group. You can ignore this line. It is only there to be read by your newsreader program.

The Signature

A Usenet article has three parts: the header, the body and the signature. I have already talked about the header (the technical information) and the body (the actual text of the article). Let's take a moment now to discuss the signature.

The signature is an optional addendum that shows information about the person who sent the article. For example, here is the signature from our sample article:

```
Michael Schuster          |"I love you for your beauty; love me
TU Vienna, Austria        | though I am ugly"
mich@music.tuwien.ac.at   | - Miguel Cervantes, Don Quixote
+43/1/12345
```

If you want to use a signature, you must create one for yourself. Your newsreader program will have a menu item to allow you to specify a signature. Once you do, your program will automatically append the signature to each article you post, before it is sent out.

If you are using Unix with a shell account, you must use a text editor to create a file called **.signature** in your home directory. (The **.** character is part of the name.) Whenever you post an article, your news posting program will look to see if such a file exists. If it does, the program will append the contents of the file to the end of your article.

You might ask: What if I have a shell account, but I don't know how to use a text editor? This is one reason why, in Chapter 1, I suggested you learn some Unix. At the very least, you should know how to use a text editor so you can create things like a **.signature** file. You could, I suppose, ask someone else to help you create your **.signature** file. However, it wouldn't do you much good because if you can't use a text editor to create a signature, you wouldn't be able to compose a Usenet article in the first place.

(However, I don't want to be too dogmatic. Shell account users do not need a text editor for reading articles, only for creating articles to be posted or for composing replies.)

Most signatures contain the name of the person who posted the article, along with a mail address. You may also see the name of the organization to which the person belongs, a postal address and perhaps a telephone number. The signature in our example shows that the article was posted by Michael Schuster, at the Technical University of Vienna. We see his mail address and his phone number. To the right, we see an interesting quotation.

The wonderful thing about signatures is how imaginative and well-designed they can be. Michael Schuster, as you can see, includes a quotation. You will see many quotations, as well as witty sayings, drawings, jokes, and so on. Indeed, there are people who collect interesting signatures and post them, from time to time, as a unique bit of Usenet art (usually in the **rec.humor** newsgroup).

Once you start reading a lot of Usenet articles, you will find it annoying to have to read long signatures. For this reason, it is a well-established convention that signatures should be no more than four lines long. Some news posting programs will actually enforce this rule by removing any extra lines. Although this may seem restrictive, you will be amazed at how much a creative person can do with only four lines.

When it comes to creating a signature, anything goes. Aside from the four-line limit, there are no rules, so use your imagination.

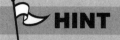

HINT

It is not considered imaginative to use your signature to publicize your religion.

INTERNET RESOURCE *Look in the catalog under Internet Resources for*
Usenet: Complaints About Signatures

Followup Articles

As I mentioned earlier, a followup article is one which is posted in response to a previous article. Creating a followup article is easy. All you have to do is select a menu item or enter a simple command.

Your newsreader will make everything as easy as possible by creating a skeleton for the new article (a header and part of the body). With Unix, your newsreader will automatically start your text editor. Once you finish and you quit the text editor, the newsreader will take over again and post the article for you automatically.

Take a look at the sample followup article in Figure 14-3. This article is a response to the one in Figure 14-1. Notice the body of the new article starts with two lines that identify the previous article and the person who posted it. These lines are followed by the original article with each line marked with a > character.

Most of this article was generated automatically by the newsreader program. All I had to do to create the followup was compose my response.

When you read an article, there are three ways to tell if it is a followup. First, the subject will be the same as the original article but will have the characters **Re:** in front of it. For example, in Figure 14-3, we see:

```
Subject: Re: The Secret of Life
```

This line is automatically inserted by the newsreader when it creates the header of a followup article. However, no more than one **Re:** will be used. Thus, a followup to a followup has only a single **Re:**.

The second thing to look for (if your newsreader is displaying the header for you) is a **References:** line. This contains the identifier of the original article. Although you can ignore this header line, it does serve as official notice that you are reading a followup article. If you are reading a followup to a followup, you may see more than one identifier in the **References:** line.

Finally, a followup article will often have all or part of the previous article embedded. As I mentioned, the lines from the previous article will be prefaced with a special character. Most of the time this will be > (a greater-than sign) as in our example. However, you will sometimes see other characters.

```
Path: ucsbcsl!nipper.ucsb.edu!harley
From: harley@nipper.ucsb.edu (Harley Hahn)
Newsgroups: rec.humor
Subject: Re: The Secret of Life·
Summary: Advice for understanding life.
Keywords: life, philosophy
Message-ID: <1995Sep16.060436.13827@nipper.ucsb.edu>
Date: 16 Sep 95 10:13:12 GMT
References: <1995Sep15.073130.15261@email.tuwien.ac.at>
Distribution: world
Lines: 22


In article <1995Sep15.073130.15261@email.tuwien.ac.at>
mich@music.tuwien.ac.at (Michael Schuster) writes:

> Here is some great advice I just found:
>
> "When you get serious about bullshit,
> you are getting into serious bullshit."
>
> By the way, does anyone know who first said it?

Yes, this advice was first offered by the
Canadian philosopher, Tim Rutledge.

Obligatory Joke...
Hahn's Maxim: If something is worth doing,
   it's worth doing to excess.


--
Harley Hahn
writer of Internet books
```

Figure 14-3. *Header lines for Usenet articles*

   In such cases, we say that the followup article is QUOTING those parts of the original article. In our example, the followup article quoted six lines from the original article.

Finally, if you see more than one **>** character at the beginning of a line, it means an article is quoting something that has already been quoted. Here is an example:

```
In article <1995Oct03.002440.8495@nipper.ucsb.edu>
harley@nipper.ucsb.edu (Harley Hahn) writes:

> In article <1995Oct02.222614.9344@unix1.tcd.ie>
> mepeirce@unix1.tcd.ie (Michael Peirce) writes:

>> Does anyone know the name of the computer that
>> contains the Usenet archives?

> Yes, it is pit-manager.mit.edu.

Actually, the name was changed to rtfm.mit.edu a long time ago.

--
Jonathan Kamens      Geer Zolot Associates       jik@GZA.COM
```

In this example, a reader named Michael Peirce had originally posted an article asking for the name of a particular computer. Another reader, Harley Hahn, sent a followup article answering the question. A third reader, Jonathan Kamens, then created a second followup article in which he corrected Hahn's answer.

HINT

It can be tiresome to read followup articles in which someone has quoted a long article and added only a small comment to the end. This is especially true when you are following a thread in which person after person has quoted the same long passages.

For this reason, when you create a followup article, it is considered good manners to delete as much superfluous material as possible. For example, if the original article was 100 lines long, but you are really responding to only 3 lines, you should delete all but those 3 lines.

Actually, some newsreader programs will refuse to post a followup article if the quoted material is longer than the reply.

HINT

From time to time, you will see people propagate a long series of silly followups, called a CASCADE. Sometime, when you have nothing to do, and you are in a capricious mood, check out the **alt.cascade** newsgroup (which is devoted to such creative endeavors).

Commonly Used Acronyms

What would a computer system be without acronyms? Those marvelous little abbreviations that make you feel important when you know what they mean and like a piece of cheese when you don't.

Not to fear. Figure 14-4 contains a list of acronyms commonly used on the Net, not every acronym you will ever encounter, but enough to get you through the night.

Study this table well. These acronyms are used in all manner of Internet discourse, not only within Usenet articles, but in mail messages and online conversation.

Usenet Slang

Aside from the acronyms and abbreviations I described in Figure 14-4, you will encounter a great number of slang terms and expressions. So to finish this chapter, let's take a few minutes and look at the world of Usenet slang.

To begin, let us recall the new terms I have already mentioned in this chapter and in Chapter 13.

Usenet is a vast system of discussion groups. We refer to Usenet as the NEWS, although there is little real news (in the sense of a newspaper). Thus, the discussion groups are often called NEWSGROUPS.

A computer that acts as the Usenet repository for an organization is called a NEWS SERVER. The person who manages the news server is the NEWS ADMINISTRATOR. Each news server gets its information from another news server on a regular basis. This arrangement is called a NEWS FEED.

The items you read in a Usenet discussion group are called ARTICLES or POSTINGS. A Usenet article is divided into three parts, the HEADER, the BODY and an optional SIGNATURE. When you send an article to Usenet, we say that you POST it. An article that is sent to more than one newsgroup is CROSSPOSTED. Usenet articles are kept for a predetermined time. When the time is up, the articles EXPIRE and are automatically deleted from the news server.

An article in which the author responds to a previous article is called a FOLLOWUP article. When a followup contains parts of the original article, we say it QUOTES the original. A series of followup articles is called a THREAD. When you read the articles in a thread, one after another, we say you are FOLLOWING the thread.

There are thousands of different newsgroups, organized into HIERARCHIES. MAINSTREAM HIERARCHIES are carried by all news servers. ALTERNATE HIERARCHIES are carried according to the wishes of the news administrator.

MODERATED NEWSGROUPS are managed by a person called a MODERATOR. The moderator decides which articles will be posted to the group. Such groups sometimes offer a collection of edited articles called a DIGEST.

To read Usenet articles, you use a program called a NEWSREADER. When you tell your newsreader to put the name of a particular group into the list of newsgroups you read, you SUBSCRIBE to that group. Similarly, when you tell your newsreader to remove a group from the list, you UNSUBSCRIBE.

Acronym	Meaning
AFAIK	as far as I know
BRB	be right back
BTW	by the way
CU	see you (good-bye)
CUL8R	see you later
F2F	face to face
FAQ	frequently asked question list
FOAF	friend of a friend
FRP	fantasy role-playing
FTL	faster then light
FWIW	for what it's worth
FYI	for your information
IMAO	in my arrogant opinion
IMHO	in my humble opinion
IMNSHO	in my not so humble opinion
IMO	in my opinion
MOTAS	member of the appropriate sex
MOTD	message of the day
MOTOS	member of the opposite sex
MOTSS	member of the same sex
Ob-	[as a prefix] obligatory
Objoke	obligatory joke
OS	operating system
OTOH	on the other hand
PMFJI	pardon me for jumping in
POV	point of view
ROTF	rolling on the floor
ROTFL	rolling on the floor laughing
RPG	role-playing games
RTFM	before you ask a question, read the manual
SO	significant other (spouse, boy/girlfriend...)
TTFN	ta-ta for now
TTYL	talk to you later
WRT	with respect to
YMMV	your mileage may vary

Figure 14-4. *Common acronyms used on the Net*

(I hope you have memorized all of that, because there will be a short quiz at the end of the class.)

Now here are some new terms. As I mentioned in Chapter 13, anyone can try to start a newsgroup in one of the alternate hierarchies if they know how to do it. As you might imagine, such latitude often leads to newsgroups that don't really exist. Someone might send out a control message to start a new group but, for one reason or another, the group never gets started.

Nevertheless, the name of such a newsgroup may find its way onto the master list on your news server. When your newsreader tries to read this group, it won't be there. Your newsreader will proudly inform you that it has found a BOGUS or empty newsgroup.

Another term you will encounter frequently is FLAME. This refers to a followup article (or a personal mail message) in which someone says something critical about someone else. The word "flame" is also used as a verb, as in "Scott posted an article without a joke to **rec.humor**, and he was flamed from all over the world."

All too frequently, a FLAME WAR will start, in which people send a large number of argumentative articles and mail messages excoriating one another. In such situations, it doesn't take long for other people to jump in and criticize the critics, which only fans the flames. Although flame wars can have their interesting moments, most such postings are the written equivalent of a person sticking his tongue out at someone else. Eventually, the thread will die out, more from boredom than anything else.

As you are reading an article, you can tell your newsreader to skip all the rest of the articles in the same thread. We say that you KILL or JUNK the thread. Some newsreaders will let you specify that all articles with certain subject descriptions or from a specific person should be killed automatically. Your newsreader will save such requests in a special KILL FILE.

HINT

If you read a newsgroup regularly, you may encounter someone who is a real jerk. Instead of complaining about his messages, simply put him in your kill file.

Some newsgroups discuss works of art such as movies or novels in which it would be reasonable to discuss the plot. Of course, if you have not yet seen the movie or read the book, you may not want to know about the plot ahead of time. For this reason, it is customary that, when an article gives away a plot, the **Subject:** header line should say that the article contains a SPOILER.

Well, that's it: about all the basic terminology you need to know to understand Usenet. However, to complete your basic education, there are five more terms that you need to know. They are so important, in fact, that I will discuss them in their own sections.

Foo, Bar and Foobar

There are three marvelous words you will see from time to time: FOO, BAR and FOOBAR. These words are used as generic identifiers throughout Usenet as well as within the world of Unix.

The idea is that whenever you want to refer to something without a name, you can use "foo" (or less often, "foobar"). When you want to refer to two things without a name, you use "foo" and "bar". Nobody knows how this tradition got started, but it is used a lot.

For example, say you are reading an article in the **comp.unix.questions** newsgroup. (This is the group to which you can send Unix questions for experienced people to answer.) Someone is asking about editing files. You read:

```
...Can anyone tell me how to move more than one file
at a time?  For example, say that I want to move two
files named foo and bar.  I tried using the command
'mv foo bar' but I got an error message...
```

Or you might read the following in **rec.arts.movies**:

```
...Can anyone remember the musical in which Frank Sinatra
played an old-time Chicago gangster?  The name is something
like "Foobar and the Seven Hoods"...
```

So where do these strange words come from? The word "foobar" derives from the World War II acronym FUBAR, which meant "fouled up beyond all recognition".

The word "foo", however, seems to have a more robust history. No doubt foo owes much of its popularity to foobar. Nevertheless, foo seems to have been used on its own even earlier. For example, in a 1938 cartoon, Daffy Duck holds up a sign that reads "Silence is Foo" (which is absolutely correct). Some authorities speculate that foo might have roots in the Yiddish "feh" and the English "phoo".

Rtfm

The term RTFM embodies the single, most important idea on the Internet. Rtfm means that, before you ask anyone else for help, you should try to solve your problem by checking with a book or some other reference.

This idea is not mean-spirited: after all, the Internet in general (and Usenet in particular) is filled with people who will be glad to help you with anything. However, it is usually faster, and a whole lot more satisfying, to find an answer for yourself. Moreover, all new users tend to ask the same questions, and it is understandable that many people feel that, before you post an article asking for help, you should at least check all the standard references.

This raises the question: What are the standard references? Books, of course, like this one, as well as technical manuals. There are also FAQs (see Chapter 13) which contain answers to frequently asked questions regarding a particular topic. In addition, if you are a Unix user, there is one standard reference you *must* know how to use.

Every Unix system has an *online manual*. This is a computerized facility which will display information about any Unix command. I won't go into all the details of using the online manual (for that you will have to read a Unix book). However, here is a brief summary:

To display information about a Unix command, use the **man** (manual) command. Enter **man** followed by the name of the command you want to learn about. For example, to learn about the Unix **cp** (copy files) command, enter:

```
man cp
```

Unix will display a technical description of the specified command, one screenful at a time. As you are reading, you can move to the next screenful by pressing the SPACE BAR (on some systems) or the RETURN key (on other systems). (Try both and see which one works for you.) If you want to quit reading, press the **q** key. To display information about the **man** command itself, enter:

```
man man
```

 **HINT**

Unix users: Before you post a question to Usenet asking about a Unix command, you must first use the **man** command to check the online manual. If, after checking the manual, you still don't have the answer you need, feel free to ask the Net.

If you do ask a question that is answered in a reference book or the Unix manual, you may be gently (or not so gently) reminded to rtfm. Now, where does this funny term come from? Originally, "rtfm" was an acronym that stood for:

Read The <expletive>* Manual

However, through the years, rtfm has taken on the more refined meaning of "Try to find the answer yourself before you ask someone." (Actually, you will be surprised how often you *can* find the answer yourself.) The term rtfm is also used as a verb as in:

```
...Does anyone know how to save previously read articles to a
file using the foo newsreader?  I rtfm'ed, but I couldn't find
the answer anywhere.
```

* *Deleted by Editor as a public service (to sell more books).*

By now it should make sense to you why the computer that contains the Usenet archives is named **rtfm.mit.edu**. This computer stores copies of the frequently asked question lists (FAQs), which you are supposed to check before you post a question to Usenet.

HINT

The longest word in the English language with no vowels is "rtfm".

Smileys

The last Usenet term I will discuss is both cute and useful. It is called a SMILEY, and it is used to indicate irony. Here is how it works:

When you talk with someone in person, you can use your body language and voice inflections to project all kinds of non-verbal messages. For example, you can jokingly insult someone and get away with it (at least sometimes), as long as they understand you are kidding.

In a Usenet article, this is not possible. Moreover, Usenet is used all over the world and not everybody will be able to appreciate the subtle nuances of another culture. For example, it is altogether possible that someone outside the U.S. would not understand why the term "Mother" is not always a term of endearment.

Enter the smiley.

A smiley is a small drawing, using only regular characters, that looks like a face. Here is the basic smiley:

```
:-)
```

To see the bright, smiling face, just tilt your head to the left.

We use smileys to keep someone from accidentally misinterpreting an ambiguous remark. Putting a smiley at the end of a sentence is like saying "just kidding".

For example, say you are participating in a flame war in **rec.food.cooking**. You might post a followup article with the sentence:

```
How do you expect people to use your recipe for
Consomme aux Pommes d'Amour when you don't even
know how to cook groat cakes :-)
```

HINT

Smileys are everywhere, not just within Usenet articles. For example, you can use them in private mail messages or when you are having an online conversation.

Throughout the years, people have developed many different smileys. Indeed, there are collections of smileys which are occasionally posted to **rec.humor**. Figure 14-5 shows a few such creations.

To conclude this section, here is one last smiley:

%-)

Turn your head to the left. This is the face of a writer of Internet books who has stayed up all night to finish a chapter.

INTERNET RESOURCE *Look in the catalog under Internet Resources for* ***Smileys***

Smiley as Typed	Smiley Sideways	Meaning
:-)		smiling
:-D		laughing
;-)		winking
:-(		frowning
:-I		indifferent
:-#		smiley with braces
:-{)		smiley with a mustache
{:-)		smiley with a toupee
:-X		my lips are sealed
=:-)		cool teenager
=:-(		real cool teenagers don't smile

Figure 14-5. *A selection of smileys*

How Does Your News Server Keep Track of All the Articles?

In order to keep track of the articles in each newsgroup, your news server assigns an identification number to each article. The numbers are assigned in the order in which the articles arrive, and each newsgroup has its own set of numbers.

The numbering for each newsgroup starts with **1**. Whenever a new article comes in, it is assigned the next number in the sequence. For instance, say a new article arrives for the **rec.humor** newsgroup, and it happens that the last such article was number **1055**. The new article will be assigned the number **1056**, the next article will be **1057**, and so on. Some newsreaders show you this number each time you read an article. Other newsreaders don't bother.

Once an article expires, its number is removed from the system. Thus, on any particular day, the **rec.humor** newsgroup might contain articles **1055** through **2110**, from which you can infer that articles **1** through **1054** have already expired. Eventually, the numbers will reach a particular maximum value, and the numbering will start again with **1**. Each newsgroup has its own separate set of numbers, so nothing gets mixed up.

⚑ HINT

Each system assigns its own numbers to articles as they arrive. Thus, the numbers on your system will be different from the numbers on another system. For

Your newsreader uses these numbers to keep track of which articles you have read for each newsgroup. To do so, it maintains a file which is usually given the name **newsrc**. (On Unix systems, the file is named **.newsrc** and is kept in your home directory.) This file contains the names of each newsgroup and, for each name, whether or not you are subscribed and which articles you have read.

You don't have to worry about what's in your **newsrc** file. The first time you read the news, your newsreader will create a **newsrc** file for you. From then on, your newsreader will maintain the file on your behalf, making changes whenever you read an article, and whenever you subscribe or unsubscribe to a newsgroup.

Some people like to use a text editor to make changes to their **newsrc** file directly. For this reason, I will describe the format of this file in the next section, along with some suggestions for making your own changes should you decide to do so.

What's in a Name?

.newsrc

It is common for programs to maintain a special file in which data can be saved from one work session to the next. For example, a newsreader will use such a file to keep track of the newsgroups to which you are subscribed and which articles you have read. This allows your newsreader to initialize itself properly whenever you start a new session.

In Unix, files containing initialization information are given names that end with the letters **rc**. This tradition comes from an old system called CTSS (Compatible Time Sharing System) which had a facility called "runcom" that would execute a list of commands stored in a file. Today, it is common to find initialization files with **rc**-style names on all types of systems.

The **.** character at the beginning of the name **.newsrc** is peculiar to Unix systems. It indicates a "hidden file": one whose name is not normally shown when you display a list of your files. When you pronounce names like this, the **.** character is called "dot". For example, someone might ask a friend, "What newsgroups are in your dot-news-r-c file?"

The Format of Your newsrc File

In the previous section, I explained that many newsreaders use a file named **newsrc** to keep track of which newsgroups you subscribe to and which articles you have read. For the most part, newsreaders keep such information in a standard format. In this section, I describe this format in case you want to edit your own **newsrc** file. If you don't care about such matters, you can safely skip this section.

To modify your **newsrc** file, you will have to use some type of text editor. If you don't have a text editor, it is possible to use a word processor, as long as you make sure to save the file as plain text (sometimes called ASCII text). If you are using Unix, your file will be called **.newsrc** and will be stored in your home directory. Otherwise, try looking for this file in the same directory or folder as your newsreader program.

There are two common reasons why you might want to edit your **newsrc** file. First, many newsreaders present the various newsgroups in whatever order they are found in your **newsrc** file. This is especially true for Unix newsreaders. By editing your **newsrc** file, you can put the names of the groups in whatever order you want. Some newsreaders will let you change the order of the newsgroups from within the program, but it is usually a lot easier to edit the **newsrc** file directly and do it yourself.

The second reason to edit your **newsrc** file is to make changes to your newsgroup subscriptions, that is, to specify which newsgroups you want to read. With some newsreaders, you will automatically start off by being subscribed to every newsgroup. Normally, you would want to unsubscribe to all but a few of these groups. Again, this is something you can do with your newsreader, but if you want to make a lot of changes, editing the **newsrc** file by hand is faster.

HINT

Before you edit your **newsrc** file, make a backup copy. If you ruin the original, you will be able to restore the file from your copy. In general, it is a good idea to make a copy before editing any important file.

The standard format for a **newsrc** uses one line for each newsgroup. This line contains:

- the name of the newsgroup
- a colon (:) or an exclamation mark (!)
- a space
- a list of numbers

If there is a colon after the newsgroup name, it means you are currently subscribed to that group. An exclamation mark means you are unsubscribed. The list of numbers indicates which articles you have already read. (You will remember that each article is given an identification number by your news server.) The list of numbers can contain single numbers or ranges of numbers separated by commas. To make this all clear, here are a few lines from a typical **newsrc** file:

```
alt.fan.wodehouse: 1-819
rec.humor.funny: 1-8192
rec.humor: 1-41234,41236,41239
comp.unix.questions! 1-6571
misc.books.technical!
```

The first three newsgroups are subscribed, and the last two are unsubscribed. Within each newsgroup, you can see which articles have been read. For example, in the **rec.humor** group, articles **1** through **41234**, as well as articles **41236** and **41239**, have been read.

If there are no numbers on a line, it means no articles have ever been read in that newsgroup. This is the case with **misc.books.technical**.

Finally, notice that although **comp.unix.questions** is unsubscribed, it was subscribed at one time. You can tell because articles **1** through **6571** have been read.

Posting Your Own Articles

Once you start using Usenet, you will want to post your own articles. You may wish to request some information, respond to a previous article, or offer a new idea for discussion. Each newsreader has its own menu items or commands to make posting articles simple and easy, but to make sure you get started properly, here are a few hints.

It is a good idea to begin by sending out one or two practice articles. To help you, there are special newsgroups set up for such tests. By convention, these groups have names ending with `.test`. At any time, you can send a posting to one of these groups just for practice.

If your location has a local hierarchy (see Chapter 13), you may find a local test newsgroup. If so, this is the best place to send a practice posting. Otherwise, you should use `misc.test` (to practice posting to a mainstream newsgroup) or `alt.test` (to send to an alternate group).

Gentle reminder: When you want to practice posting an article, please use the `.test` newsgroups. It is considered bad manners to send a test article to a non-test newsgroup.

To help you see if a test article was successful, there are a number of computers around the Net that are programmed to look for and respond to postings in the `.test` newsgroups. When you post such an article, each of these computers will automatically mail you a response. This is a good way to check if your articles are propagating around the Net. However, if you do not want responses, you can tell these computers to ignore your article by putting the word **ignore** in the **Subject:** line of the header.

HINT

If you want to check what a new signature looks like, send an article to one of the `.test` groups.

Flames and Good Behavior

Some people make a big deal about flaming. ("Oh no, I accidentally asked the wrong question, and I got flamed by people all over the world.") Well, let's not get excited here. A flame is just a complaint, so it's really nothing to worry about. If sticks and stones may break your bones, and if words will never hurt you, a few bad comments in your electronic mailbox or in a Usenet article won't hurt all that much.

People on Usenet feel relatively anonymous (even when they sign their own name), and it is common to find someone expressing him- or herself with a breezy candor unusual in face-to-face conversation. Don't let this hurt your feelings. Just because someone criticizes you in front of hundreds of thousands of people is no reason to get excited. My advice is to ignore anyone who says something you don't like. In general, fighting is dumb. On Usenet, it's a waste of time.

Although most flaming is pretty stupid, there are people who enjoy complaining just for fun. If you would like to join these people, there are newsgroups set up just for flames. Figure 14-6 lists the most interesting of these groups. So, the next time you are in a bad mood and you feel like complaining, check out one of these newsgroups and see how the pros do it.

 INTERNET RESOURCE *Look in the catalog under Internet Resources for* ***Usenet: Flame Newsgroups***

The Final Word

From the point of view of other Usenet users, reading the news is an invisible activity. You can read all day long, and nobody else will know or care. However, as soon as you start to post articles, people will expect you to respect the culture.

If you are a new user, there is a newsgroup set up especially for you: `news.newusers.questions`. This group is devoted to the needs of beginners, and is a good place to send a question that pertains to using Usenet.

Over the years, Usenet has developed many rules. Since the whole system runs on cooperation, it behooves you to follow the rules, at least in spirit. To help you, there

---

```
alt.flame  (general complaining)
alt.flame.abortion
alt.flame.airlines
alt.flame.landlord
alt.flame.parents
alt.flame.professor
alt.flame.right-wing-conservatives
alt.flame.roommate
alt.flame.rush-limbaugh
alt.flame.spelling
```

Figure 14-6. *Usenet newsgroups for complaints*

are several introductory articles posted regularly to **news.newusers.questions** as well as **news.answers**.

Unfortunately, as soon as you read these articles, you may be put off by how much other people are telling you what to do and what not to do. Much of the advice given to new users is "Don't do this, don't do this, don't do that..." Of course, people mean well. It's just that, at the beginning, you may not understand why we need to have so many rules.

Ironically, there is no real way for anyone to make anyone else do what he wants: there are no net.police to enforce the law. If a person does something *really* obnoxious, other people might complain to his system manager or Internet service provider who might throw the person off the system. However, this is rare.

Nevertheless, I do want you to be a good neighbor. One good way is to gain a little experience reading Usenet before you start posting your own articles. In particular:

- It is a good idea to read Usenet for at least two weeks before you post your first article. (Patience is a virtue.)

- Before you post to a particular newsgroup, read it for at least a week.

- Before you ask a question, check to see if the newsgroup has a FAQ (frequently asked question list). If so, read the FAQ first. Your question may already be answered.

I want you, as one of my readers, to be well-liked and happy, and I encourage you to learn and follow the Usenet traditions. In general, if you are pleasant and use common sense, you will do just fine, so to make life simple, I have summarized all of the rules for using Usenet into the following three guidelines:

1. Be considerate.
2. If you can't be considerate, at least don't be a jerk.
3. Don't let yourself be bothered by people who do not follow rules 1 and 2.

Chapter Fifteen

Using Usenet From a Shell Account: `tin`

If you are using a shell account to access the Net, you will be running text-based client programs on a Unix host. In this chapter, I explain how to use **tin**, the best and most popular text-based Unix newsreader. Before you start learning about **tin**, be sure to read Chapters 13 and 14, so you will understand how Usenet works, as well as the basic terminology.

A Quick History of `tin`

tin was created by Iain Lea and first released on August 23, 1991. At the time, there were several older, widely used newsreaders which had been designed when Usenet was a lot smaller. By 1991, Usenet had become huge, and the older newsreaders had trouble coping. Not only were there more articles than a single person could ever read, there were too many different newsgroups to manage using the older programs.

Lea designed **tin** to make it easy to scan a large list of newsgroups and choose the ones you want to read. Once you chose a group, **tin** would present you with a list of articles and let you choose which ones you wanted to read. Thus, you did not have to wade through a lot of material to find what you really wanted.

Although most of today's newsreaders follow this same design, in 1991, the idea was a new one, and **tin** soon received widespread acceptance around the Net. Today, **tin** is the most popular of the text-based Unix newsreaders. (It is also my personal favorite.)

What's in a Name?

`tin`

The **tin** newsreader was developed by Iain Lea who based it on an older newsreader named **tass**. Lea chose the name **tin** to stand for "Tass + Iain's Newsreader".

Overview of the `tin` Newsreader

The **tin** newsreader was designed to let you skim through a large number of newsgroups and a large number of articles. **tin** makes it easy to choose which newsgroups you want to look at and, within those groups, which threads of articles you want to read. **tin** is fast, easy to learn and powerful. However, it is a complex program with many options and commands, and offers far more functionality than you will ever need.

The best strategy is to learn the basics and practice for a while. Once you have some experience, you can look at the command summaries at the end of this chapter and experiment with whatever looks interesting. When you get really good, you can read the reference material on **tin** in the online Unix manual and find all kinds of cool stuff. (I'll show you the command to use later in the chapter.)

To introduce you to **tin**, I will start with an overview of how it works. Then, in the following sections, I'll go into the details.

You start the program by entering the **tin** command. The first thing **tin** does is read your **.newsrc** file (see Chapter 14) and compare it against the master list of active newsgroups. If there are new newsgroups, **tin** asks you whether or not you want to subscribe.

Once the check for new groups is finished, **tin** presents you with a newsgroup selection list. This is a list of newsgroups from which you can choose what you want to read.

After you select a newsgroup, **tin** shows you a thread selection list in which all the different threads for this newsgroup are shown. You can now choose a thread to read.

As you read, there are a number of actions you can take. You can save an article to a file, mail a copy of an article to somebody, kill all the articles with the same subject, and so on. You can also respond to an article, either by sending personal mail to the author or by posting a followup article of your own.

At all times, you are either in one of three situations: selecting a newsgroup, selecting a thread or reading articles. (Strictly speaking, **tin** has two other environments: spool directories and newsgroup indexing. However, these topics are not important to most people, and there is no need to discuss them.)

No matter what you are doing, there will be a large number of commands available. As a reference, I have summarized all of the important **tin** commands in four lists at the end of the chapter.

Figure 15-4 shows the commands you can use at any time. Figure 15-5 shows commands you can use while you are selecting a newsgroup. Figure 15-6 shows commands you can use while you are selecting a thread to read. And Figure 15-7 shows commands you can use as you are reading. You may want to take a minute now to glance at these summaries.

Within the summaries, I have followed the common Unix convention of indicating CTRL keys by using the ^ character. For example, when you see **^D**, it means CTRL-D. (That is, hold down the CTRL key and press **D**.)

In the following sections, I will discuss the details of using **tin**. As you read, and as you practice, there are three things I would like you to remember.

First, in almost all circumstances, you can press **h**, to display a help summary of all the commands that are currently available.

Second, for all single-letter commands, you do not have to press the RETURN or ENTER key. All you have to do is press a single key and **tin** will react immediately. For example, to display help information, you press the **h** key. (When a Unix program reads input in this way, we say the program is operating in "cbreak mode".)

Finally, there will be times when **tin** will ask you a question and present you with a list of possible answers. In such cases, **tin** will suggest one of the answers as being the most likely response. This is the default. If you would like to accept this suggestion, you can simply press RETURN.

For example, as you are reading an article, you can save a copy of the article to a file by using the **s** command. When you do, you will see the following:

```
Save a)rticle, t)hread, h)ot, p)attern, T)agged articles, q)uit: a
```

`tin` is offering you five choices. All you have to do is press the key that you want. Notice that after the colon, `tin` has put a default of **a**. Since this is the default, pressing RETURN is the same as pressing **a**.

> ## ⚑ HINT
>
> If your terminal or computer has cursor control keys—the keys with the arrows: UP, DOWN, LEFT and RIGHT—`tin` makes great use of them.
>
> In general, the UP and DOWN keys move up or down one line (or, where appropriate, one page).
>
> The LEFT and RIGHT keys move up or down a logical level. For example, when you are selecting a newsgroup, RIGHT moves you to the thread selection list. When you are selecting a thread, LEFT moves you back to the newsgroup selection list.
>
> Once you get a little practice, this will all make perfect sense. In the words of Iain Lea (Mr. `tin`), "You can drive `tin` all day long just by using these four keys."

Customizing Your Working Environment

`tin` has more ways to change settings and customize your environment than you would believe. Unfortunately, modifying most of these settings requires a degree of knowledge that is well beyond that of the beginning or casual user.

However, `tin` does make it easy for you to change some of the more basic settings. At any time, you can press the **M** (menu) key. (Try it.) This will bring up a list of a limited number of settings. Each of the settings will have a number. To change a setting, type the number, press RETURN and follow the instructions.

After you select a setting to change, you may see the following instruction:

```
<SPACE> toggles & <CR> sets.
```

This means that the setting you are modifying has a fixed number of choices. Pressing the SPACE bar will change from one choice to the next. When you are finished, and you want to set your final choice, press RETURN ("Carriage Return").

Starting and Stopping

To start `tin`, enter the `tin` command:

```
tin
```

If you have never used **tin** before, you will see a screen of introductory information. This screen only appears the first time you use **tin**. Read this over, but don't worry if you don't understand it all. Everything you need to know to get started is in this chapter.

When **tin** starts, it goes through a number of initialization procedures. You will see messages like:

```
Reading news active file...
Reading attributes file...
Reading newsgroups file...
```

When you see the last line, it means that **tin** is reading your **.newsrc** file and comparing it against the news server's master list of active **newsgroups**. If there are any new newsgroups, **tin** will add them to your **.newsrc** file and ask you if you want to subscribe.

If you have never read the news before, **tin** will create a **.newsrc** file for you (see Chapter 14). Initially, your **.newsrc** file will contain all of the active newsgroups with each newsgroup subscribed. You will probably want to unsubscribe to most of the groups. There are two ways to do this. First, you can do it within **tin** by using the **U** or **u** commands, although this will probably take a long time. The more practical method is to use a text editor, such as **vi** or **emacs**, and edit the **.newsrc** file for yourself.

To stop **tin**, you can use the **Q** (quit) command. Simply press the **Q** key. Notice that this is an uppercase (capital) letter. The **q** command is used to leave whatever part of the program you happen to be using and return to the previous level. The **Q** command will quit **tin** outright.

Most of the time, there is a better way to start **tin** than the simple command I mentioned above. You will remember I said the first thing **tin** does is to check to see if there are new newsgroups not listed in your **.newsrc** file. Although this is a good idea, it can be time consuming, perhaps taking several minutes each time.

Most people prefer to have **tin** skip this check. You can do so by using the command:

```
tin -q
```

The **-q** is called an "option" or a "switch". In this case, the **-q** option tells **tin** to perform a quick start. Using **-q** will start **tin** faster, but will not, of course, pick up any new newsgroups. For this reason, I recommend starting **tin**, say, once every week or two, without the **-q** option, just to see what is new.

There may be times when you are interested in reading just a single newsgroup. In that case, you can specify that group directly. For example, say you only want to read the **rec.humor** newsgroup. You can enter:

```
tin rec.humor
```

You can also specify more than one newsgroup on the same line:

```
tin rec.humor alt.tasteless.jokes
```

When you start **tin** in this way, it will show you only the newsgroups you specify.

tin has quite a few options, but most of the time you will not need any of them except **-q**. However, I will discuss a few of the more useful ones in case you do want to try them. For more information about options, you can read the entry for **tin** in the online manual by entering the Unix command:

```
man tin
```

If you would like to display a quick list of all the possible options, you can use the **-h** (help) option:

```
tin -h
```

Remember I said the first time you use **tin** it will display a screen of introductory information. If you would like to display this screen again sometime, you can do so by using the **-H** (help summary) option:

```
tin -H
```

Another option that you may want to use is **-w** (write). You use this when you want to start **tin** only for the purpose of posting a news article. I will discuss this later in the chapter.

The last option I will mention is **-z**:

```
tin -z
```

This tells **tin** to start only if there are articles you have not yet read. You can combine this option with the names of one or more newsgroups, which is handy when you want to check quickly if there is anything of interest to you.

For example, say that you follow the **rec.humor** newsgroup religiously. (That is, you start each day by covering your head and reading jokes.) The following command will start **tin** only if there are new articles in that newsgroup:

```
tin -z rec.humor
```

HINT

You can place a **tin -z** command in your initialization file, so each time you log in you will automatically start **tin** if there is news that you have not yet read. The name of your initialization file depends on which shell you are using. For the C-shell, the file is **.login**; for the Bourne or Korn shell, it is **.profile**.

The Newsgroup Selection List

To read the news, the first thing you must do is choose which newsgroup you want to look at. To help you make that choice, **tin** will display a list of newsgroups, one page at a time. Figure 15-1 shows a typical newsgroup selection list.

The top line tells us we are selecting newsgroups. The number in parentheses shows the number of subscribed newsgroups, in this case, 157. In the top right-hand corner, we see a reminder that we can display a help summary by pressing the **h** key.

Next follow as many newsgroups as will fit on one page. In our example, we see 16 newsgroups at a time. The entry for each newsgroup shows an identification number, the number of unread articles, the name of the newsgroup, and a short description. In our example, three of the newsgroups (**4**, **5** and **14**) have no unread articles.

The descriptions to the right are taken from a master file distributed regularly to news servers. You will find that not all descriptions are informative, and many of them are missing. If you decide you would rather not see the descriptions, you can tell **tin** to omit them by pressing the **d** (description) key. To bring back the descriptions, press **d** again. If you want to change this setting permanently, you can use the **M** (menu) command to modify the **Show description** setting.

```
                     Group Selection (157)                    h=help

     1     3    alt.1d                        One-dimensional imaging, and the thinki
     2     7    alt.3d                        Three-dimensional imaging
     3    27    alt.abortion.inequity         The inequity of abortion
     4          alt.abuse.offender.recovery   Helping offenders recover
     5          alt.abuse.recovery            Helping victims of abuse recover (Moder
     6    10    alt.activism                  Activities for activists
     7     3    alt.activism.d                A place to discuss issues in alt.activi
     8    27    alt.adoption                  For those involved with or contemplatin
     9     5    alt.aeffle.und.pferdle        German TV cartoon characters
    10    17    alt.agriculture.fruit         Fruit farming and agriculture
    11   143    alt.agriculture.misc          Agriculture and farming
    12    27    alt.aldus.freehand            Aldus Freehand software
    13    54    alt.aldus.misc                Other Aldus software products
    14          alt.aldus.pagemaker           All about Aldus PageMaker
    15    36    alt.alien.visitors            Space aliens on Earth! Abduction! Gov't
    16   131    alt.amateur-comp              The amateur computerist

      <n>=set current to n, TAB=next unread, /=search pattern, c)atchup,
   g)oto, j=line down, k=line up, h)elp, m)ove, q)uit, r=toggle all/unread,
    s)ubscribe, S)ub pattern, u)nsubscribe, U)nsub pattern, y)ank in/out
```

Figure 15-1. **tin**: *A typical group selection list*

The bottom part of the group selection list is a short summary to help you with the most important commands. After I discuss the commands (in the next section), this summary will make sense. If you decide you would like to get rid of this summary—and make more room for newsgroup names—press **H**. To bring back the summary, press **H** again.

You will notice our example shows a few newsgroups that have no unread articles. Quite possibly, you will not want to look at such newsgroups as there is nothing to read. If so, you can press the **r** key. This tells `tin` to display only those newsgroups that have unread articles. To change back, press **r** once again. If you want to change this setting permanently, you can use the **M** (menu) command to modify the **Show only unread** setting.

Selecting a Newsgroup

To start reading a newsgroup, all you have to do is move to the group you want and press RETURN. While you are working with the newsgroup selection list, there are many commands that you can use. As well as the general commands, there are commands for moving within the newsgroup list, and for telling `tin` to start reading when you have selected a newsgroup.

The general commands are summarized in Figure 15-4. The newsgroup selection commands are summarized in Figure 15-5. In this section, I will discuss the most basic of these commands. When you get some time, check out Figure 15-5 and try some of the others.

`tin` displays only as many newsgroup names as can fit on a single page (that is, one screenful). To display the next page, press PAGEDOWN. To move back one page, press PAGEUP. If your terminal or computer does not have these keys (or if you prefer not to use them), you can use SPACE (page down) and **b** (page up) instead.

At all times, one of the newsgroup names will be highlighted. To move down or up one line, use the DOWN and UP keys (the keys with the arrows). Again, if you do not have these keys (or you do not want to use them), there are alternatives. You can use **j** (down) and **k** (up) instead.

To jump directly to a particular newsgroup, you have two choices. First, you can enter its number. For example, to jump to newsgroup #4, press **4** and then press RETURN.

Second, you can press **g** (go to), type the name of the newsgroup, and press RETURN. When you use the **g** command, `tin` will suggest the last newsgroup you jumped to as a default choice. If you want to jump to this newsgroup again, just press RETURN. (It will make sense when you see it.)

Once you have chosen the newsgroup you want, you can enter it by pressing RIGHT (the right arrow key) or RETURN. Alternatively, you can press TAB to automatically enter the next group that has unread articles.

Finally, when you are finished reading the news, press **q**, **Q** or LEFT (the left arrow key) to quit `tin`.

The Thread Selection List

Once you have selected a newsgroup, **tin** shows you a list of threads. You examine this list and select the first thread you want to read. Figure 15-2 shows a typical thread selection list.

The top line tells us the name of the newsgroup, in this case **soc.culture.british**. Directly after the name, **tin** shows us the number of threads, the number of articles, the number of killed (junked) articles and the number of hot articles. (Hot articles are those that are selected automatically according to a predefined criteria. For more details, see the **tin** page in the online Unix manual.) In our example, there are 69 threads of 245 articles. None of these articles are killed or hot.

Next follow as many thread summaries as will fit on one page. In our example, we see 15 threads. The summary of each thread shows us an identification number, the number of followup articles, the subject and the author of the first article. For example, thread **12** contains the original article plus 63 followups. The thread was started by Galahad Threepwood, who has initiated a discussion as to whether or not the Ickenham System actually works. Thread **2** contains only a single article with no followups.

You will notice that, after the thread number, some of the summaries have a **+** (plus) character. This indicates that the thread has not yet been read. In our example, threads **2**, **6**, **7** and **15** have been read.

As you can see, the thread selector list shows both the subject and the author of the first article in the thread. If the subject descriptions are long, they will be truncated. To make more room, you can press **d** to tell **tin** to display only the subject. To change back and display both the subject and author, press **d** again. If you want to change this

```
             soc.culture.british (69T 245A 0K 0H)        h=help

  1   + 2  Empress of Blandings' silver medal   Clarence Emsworth
  2        A world full of loonies              Alaric Dunstable
  3   + 3  Making a proper marriage             Constance Keeble
  4   + 13 Five ways to call a pig              George Wellbeloved
  5   + 6  The best dog biscuits to use         Freddie Threepwood
  6     3  Choosing port                        Sebastian Beach
  7        Efficiency                           Rupert Baxter
  8   +    Things I don't understand            Veronica Wedge
  9   +    The Queen of Matchingham             Gregory Parsloe
 10   + 1  Poetry for Polly Pott                Ricky Gilpin
 11   +    My life with Sue Brown               Ronald Fish
 12   + 63 Does the Ickenham System work?       Galahad Threepwood
 13   +    On The Care Of The Pig               Augustus Whipple
 14   +    Housekeeping and etiquette           Mrs. Twemlow
 15     16 Canadian poetry                      Ralston McTodd
```

Figure 15-2. **tin**: *A typical thread selection list*

setting permanently, you can use the **M** (menu) command to modify the **Show author** setting.

Similarly, you can tell `tin` to display only the unread threads by pressing **r**. To change back and display both read and unread threads, press **r** again. If you want to change this setting permanently, you can use the **M** command to modify the **Show only unread** setting.

Selecting a Thread to Read

Once you have selected a newsgroup, `tin` shows you a list of threads. To read the articles, all you have to do is move to a thread and press RETURN.

While you are working with the thread selection list, there are many commands you can use. As well as the general commands, there are commands for moving within the thread list and for telling `tin` to start reading when you have selected a thread.

The general commands are summarized in Figure 15-4. The thread selection commands are summarized in Figure 15-6. In this section, I will discuss the most basic of these commands. When you get some time, check out Figure 15-6 and try some of the others.

`tin` displays only as many thread descriptions as can fit on a single page (that is, one screenful). To move throughout the list, you can use the same commands as with the newsgroup list.

To display the next page, press PAGEDOWN or SPACE. To move back one page, press PAGEUP or **b**. To move down one line, press **Down** or **j**. To move up one line, press UP or **k**.

To jump directly to a particular thread, type the number followed by RETURN. For example, to jump to thread #4, press **4** and then press RETURN.

To go to the next unread thread, press **N**; to go to the previous unread thread, press **P**. If you press **K** (kill), it will mark a thread as read and move to the next unread thread.

Once you have chosen the thread you want, you can start reading by pressing RIGHT or RETURN. Alternatively, you can press TAB to automatically start reading the next unread thread.

If you want to preserve a thread, you have three choices. You can press **m** to mail a copy to someone (including yourself), **o** to print it, or **s** to save it to a file.

Finally, when you are finished reading, you can return to the newsgroup selection list by pressing **q** or LEFT. To quit `tin` completely, press **Q**.

Reading Articles

Figure 15-3 shows a typical article as displayed by `tin`. Across the top three lines, we see descriptive information about the article. `tin` automatically extracts this information from the header.

The top line shows the time and date the article was posted, the name of the newsgroup and information about the thread. The second line shows the number of

```
Thu, 21 Dec 1995 10:30:00      soc.culture.british      Thread 12 of 69
Lines 16            Does the Ickenham System work?        63 Responses
gally@pelican.org                    Galahad Threepwood at the Pelican Club

Fred Ickenham tells me that his system is 100% successful --
in certain cases.

I believe that he advises that "The preliminary waggle is of
the essence."

Maybe so, but in my many years as a member of the Pelican Club,
I developed my own methods which, as Sue Brown and Ronnie Fish will
tell you, have been known to meet with some measure of success.

Does anyone else have any thoughts on this matter?


--
Hon. Galahad Threepwood                       Pelican Club, London
        The world will have to wait a hundred years before it
        hears the story of young Gregory Parsloe and the prawns.

<n>=set current to n, TAB=next unread, /=search pattern, ^K)ill/select,
    a)uthor search, B)ody search, c)atchup, f)ollowup, K=mark read,
    |=pipe, m)ail, o=print, q)uit, r)eply mail, s)ave, t)ag, w=post
```

Figure 15-3. `tin`: *A typical article*

lines, the subject and the number of responses (followups). The third line shows the author's mail address and description.

Next comes the body of the article, including, in this case, a signature.

Finally, the last three lines contain a short summary to help you with the most important commands. If you want to get rid of this summary—and make more room for the article—press **H**. To bring back the summary, press **H** again.

As you are reading an article, there are many commands you can use. As well as the general commands, there are commands for paging through the article, moving to a different article, preserving the article and responding to the article.

The general commands are summarized in Figure 15-4. The other commands are summarized in Figure 15-7. In this section, I will discuss the most basic of these commands. When you get some time, take a look at Figure 15-7 and experiment for yourself.

The most important commands are those that allow you to page through the article. To display the next page, press PAGEDOWN, **Down** or SPACE. To move back one page, press PAGEUP, UP or **b**. To go to the first page, press **g**. To go to the last page, press **G**.

To mark this article as read and go to the next article, press **k** (kill). To mark the entire thread as being read and go to the next thread, press **K**.

To redisplay the article showing the full header, press **^H**.

To jump to the next unread article, press RIGHT or TAB. To jump to the next thread, press RETURN.

If you want to preserve the article, you have three choices. You can press **m** to mail a copy to someone (including yourself), **o** to print it, or **s** to save it to a file.

To respond to an article, you can press **r** or **R** to send a private reply by mail to the author. The difference between these two commands is that **r** will include the text of the article in your reply, while **R** will not.

When you press **r** or **R**, `tin` will set up the header of your message and then start your text editor for you. When you are finished, quit the editor in the regular manner and `tin` will regain control. `tin` will now ask you what you want to do with your reply:

```
q)uit, e)dit, s)end: s
```

You can press whichever letter indicates your choice. As you can see, the **s** (send) choice is the default. So, if you want to send the message—which is usually the case—you need only press RETURN.

A second way to respond to an article is to post a followup article of your own. I will discuss this in the next section.

Finally, when you are finished reading, you can return to the thread selection list by pressing **q** or LEFT. To quit `tin` completely, press **Q**.

Posting an Article

There are three ways to use `tin` to post an article. First, as you are reading an article you can press **f** or **F** to post a followup. The difference between these two commands is that **f** will include the text of the article in your followup, while **F** will not.

When you press **f** or **F**, `tin` will set up the header of your followup and then start your text editor for you. When you are finished, quit the editor in the regular manner and `tin` will regain control. `tin` will now ask you what you want to do with your article:

```
q)uit, e)dit, i)spell, p)ost: p
```

You can press whichever letter indicates your choice. As you can see, the **p** (post) choice is the default. So, if you want to post the article—which is usually the case—you need only press RETURN.

The **i** choice will invoke an interactive spelling checker. However, it will only work if this feature is installed on your system.

The second way to post an article is to press **w** (write) at any time. This tells `tin` that you want to post a regular article (not a followup) to the current newsgroup. Thus, if you are reading the newsgroup selection list, you can post an article to any newsgroup you want by moving to it and pressing **w**.

After you press **w**, **tin** will ask you for the subject of your article. Type the subject and press RETURN. Everything will now proceed in the regular manner.

From time to time, you may wish to post an article when you are not reading the news (that is, when you are not using **tin**). To do so, you can invoke **tin** with the **-w** (write) option. **tin** will help you post an article and then quit automatically. You will probably also want to use the **-q** (quick start) option to bypass the automatic check for new newsgroups:

```
tin -q -w
```

In general, when you enter a Unix command, you can combine options using a single - character, so in this case you can also use:

```
tin -qw
```

When you start **tin** in this manner, it will ask you to enter the name of the newsgroup to which you want to post. After you type the name and press RETURN, everything will proceed in the regular manner. When you are finished posting your article, **tin** will quit automatically.

Commands That Are Always Available

Controlling the Program

q	return to previous level
Q	quit **tin**

Getting Help

h	display summary of commands [help]
H	off/on: show help menu at the bottom of the screen
v	show what version of **tin** you are using
M	display a menu of configurable options

Displaying Information

PAGEDOWN	display the next page
SPACE	same as PAGEDOWN
^D	same as PAGEDOWN [down]
^F	same as PAGEDOWN [forward]
PAGEUP	display the previous page
b	same as PAGEUP [back]
^U	same as PAGEUP [up]
^B	same as PAGEUP [back]

Posting an Article

w	post an article to the current newsgroup [write]
W	display a list of all the articles you have posted

Entering Unix Commands

!*command*	execute the specified Unix command
!	pause **tin** and start a new shell

Figure 15-4. `tin`: *Commands that are always available*

Commands to Use While Selecting a Newsgroup

Stopping

q	quit **tin**
LEFT	same as **q**

Displaying the Selection List

DOWN	move down one line
j	same as DOWN
UP	move up one line
k	same as UP
num RETURN	go to newsgroup number *num* (for example: **4** RETURN)
1 RETURN	go to the first newsgroup in the list
$	go to the last newsgroup in the list
N	go to the next group with unread news
g	go to specified newsgroup
/	search forward for specified newsgroup
?	search backward for specified newsgroup

Start Reading a Newsgroup

RIGHT	start reading the current group
RETURN	same as RIGHT
TAB	go to next group with unread news and start reading
n	same as TAB [next]

Controlling the Screen Display

d	toggle: show newsgroup names/ names+descriptions
r	toggle: show all newsgroups/ with unread articles only

Controlling Newsgroups

m	move newsgroup position within the list
s	subscribe to the current newsgroup
u	unsubscribe to the current newsgroup
S	subscribe to all groups that match specified pattern
U	unsubscribe to all groups that match specified pattern

Figure 15-5.   **tin**: *Commands to use while selecting a newsgroup*

Commands to Use While Selecting a Thread to Read

Stopping	
q	return to newsgroup selection list
LEFT	same as **q**
Moving From One Article to Another	
DOWN	move down one line
j	same as DOWN
UP	move up one line
k	same as UP
num RETURN	go to thread number *num* (for example: **4** RETURN)
1B RETURN	go to the first thread in the list
$	go to the last thread in the list
/	search forward for subject containing a pattern
?	search backward for subject containing a pattern
N	go to next unread thread
P	go to previous unread thread
K	mark thread as read then go to next unread thread
Start Reading an Article	
RIGHT	start reading the current thread
RETURN	same as RIGHT
TAB	start reading next unread thread
-	return to the last thread that you read
Controlling the Screen Display	
d	toggle: show subject/ subject+author
r	toggle: show all threads/ unread threads only
Changing Newsgroups	
n	go to next newsgroup
p	go to previous newsgroup
g	go to specified newsgroup
Preserving a Thread	
m	mail the thread to someone
o	print the thread
s	save the thread to a file

Figure 15-6. `tin`: *Commands to use while selecting a thread to read*

Commands to Use While Reading an Article

Stopping	
q	return to thread selection list
LEFT	same as **q**
Displaying the Article	
DOWN	display the next page
UP	display the previous page
g	go to the first page of the article
^R	same as **g** [redisplay]
G	go to the last page of the article
$	same as **G**
^H	redisplay article showing header
d	decode the current article using rot-13
/	search forward for specified pattern
?	search backward for specified pattern
Moving to a Different Article	
RIGHT	go to the next unread article
TAB	same as RIGHT
N	same as RIGHT
RETURN	go to the next thread
n	go to the next article
p	go to the previous article
P	go to the previous unread article
K	mark entire thread as read, go to next unread thread
k	mark article as read, go to next unread article
-	return to the last article that you read
Preserving the Article	
m	mail the article to someone
o	print the article
s	save the article to a file
Responding to the Current Article	
F	post a followup
f	same as **F**, include text of article
R	reply by mail to author
r	same as **R**, include text of article

Figure 15-7. `tin`: *Commands to use while reading an article*

Chapter Sixteen

Gopher, Veronica and Jughead

The gopher is a menu-driven system which is particularly easy to use. With a few simple keypresses or mouse clicks, you can access a large variety of information on thousands of different servers around the world.

In this chapter, I will explain this most useful resource and show you how to use it. In addition, I will describe two special tools—veronica and jughead—which will help you search the gopher system for the information you want.

What Is the Gopher?

The GOPHER system is a powerful tool that allows you to access many of the resources of the Internet in a simple, consistent manner. All you have to do is select items from a series of menus, and the system does all the work.

Like other Internet tools, the gopher system uses clients and servers (see Chapter 2). To access the system, you run a program called a GOPHER CLIENT. Your gopher client displays the menus and carries out your requests. Each time you make a selection from a menu, your gopher client contacts a GOPHER SERVER to request the information on your behalf. If it becomes necessary to use another type of service—say to set up a telnet session or to download a file—your client will take care of that as well.

Using a gopher client is easy: All you need to do is make one selection after another from a series of menus. Within a menu, the individual items can refer to specific information or services, or to a completely different menu. When you make a selection, your client does whatever is necessary to carry out your request.

For example, if you select a menu item that represents a text file, your client will get that file—wherever it happens to be on the Internet—and display the information on your screen. If the menu item points to a different menu, your client will fetch it, display it, and wait for you to make another selection.

The gopher system is based on a hierarchy of menus and sub-menus, and all you have to do is choose what you want. Moreover, a menu from one gopher server can contain links to a menu on another gopher server, anywhere on the Internet. As a gopher user, you can navigate around the Net, quickly and easily, by selecting one menu item after another.

There are thousands of gopher servers around the Net, and they store all manner of information. You will find gopher servers in many universities, companies, government departments and other organizations. Indeed, within a large organization, you will often find that many departments have their own gopher server.

Because it is so easy to move from one menu to another, it is convenient to think of all the gopher servers in the world as being part of one large, interconnected system. We refer to this massive information resource as GOPHERSPACE. Thus, you can imagine your gopher client as a space ship, which transports you from one part of gopherspace to another. Perhaps a more accurate analogy would be to think of your client as a magic window. To look at any part of gopherspace, all you have to do is choose a menu item, and your client will connect to the gopher server at that particular location.

A Quick History of the Gopher

The gopher system was developed at the University of Minnesota in April of 1991 by a team consisting of Bob Alberti, Farhad Anklesaria, Paul Lindler, Mark McCahill and Daniel Torrey. The work was done within the Department of Computer and Information Systems in order to provide a cheap and easy way for various campus departments to make information available to the campus at large. The idea was—and still is—that each interested organization can maintain their own gopher server and put whatever they want on it. Thus, every organization has control over its own information, which it shares with anyone who has a gopher client.

Within a short time of its development, the gopher system became popular all over the world. Thousands of gopher servers were established, and many people believed this system would become the general Internet interface for everyone. However, it was not to be. What happened was the Web.

The Web was a lot more powerful than the gopher system. Within a short time, the Web had taken over almost completely. (Remember this when it comes to predicting how long the Web itself will last.) As a result, active gopher development has diminished significantly.

Does this mean the gopher system is useless? Not at all. There are still many, many gopher servers with all kinds of useful and important information. For example, at the time I wrote this chapter, the University of Minnesota had over 110 different gopher servers.

Gopher clients are easy to use, and accessing a gopher is often a lot faster than using the Web. As long as there are gopher servers, you will find it worthwhile to understand the system and how to access it.

What's in a Name?

Gopher

As I am sure you already know, the state of Minnesota is nicknamed the "Gopher State". For example, at the campus of the University of Minnesota where the gopher system was developed, the sports teams are named the "Golden Gophers".

The name "gopher" has two connotations. First, it reminds us that Minnesota is the Gopher State. Second, you can imagine a cute little computerized animal tunneling through the Internet to fetch information on your behalf.

Moreover, there is a serendipitous association between the name "Gopher" and the American slang expression "gofer". This epithet describes a person whose position in life is to run errands for someone else, someone who can be told to go for this or go for that.

In the charming argot of the American Midwest, "go for" becomes "gofer" which becomes "gopher". Indeed, this is probably why many tourists who visit Minnesota are astonished to find the natives so cooperative about running errands for other people.

Which Gopher Client Should You Use?

To discuss which gopher client you might use, we need to consider two different situations. First, if you connect to the Internet via PPP or a direct network connection, you will use a graphical client running on your own computer. In this case, you have two main choices: You can use your browser, or you can use a separate gopher client program.

As I discuss in Chapter 11, you can use your browsers to access more than the Web. You can also use a browser as a gopher client, an ftp client, a Usenet client, and so on. Using a browser in this way has several advantages:

- You only have to learn how to use one program. Your browser will do almost everything you need to access the Internet.

- The gopher is integrated into your mainstream Internet activities.

- Your bookmark list (of items you want to recall) can hold both web and gopher items.

If you prefer, there are separate graphical gopher clients you can use instead of your browser.

 **INTERNET RESOURCE**   *Look in the catalog under Internet Resources for*
Gopher Clients Programs

These clients are designed specifically for using the gopher and have some differences. The most important is how they handle menus. With a browser, each time you select an item, your browser fetches it and displays it within your current window. If you want to return to a previous item, you can do so by moving backward. (See Chapter 10 for a discussion on navigating with a browser.)

Most graphical gopher clients work differently. Each time you select a new item, your program will open a brand new window. Thus, if you have selected six items, you will get six new windows, one on top of another. Personally, I find this unwieldy and I usually look for an option to turn off this feature. However, if you get into serious gophering, you may like the multiple windows. My advice is to download a gopher client, try it, and see what you think. To help you compare, Figure 16-1 shows a browser accessing the gopher menu, while Figure 16-2 shows a gopher client displaying the same menu.

If you use a shell account to access the Internet, you will not use a client program on your own computer. Rather, you will use a Unix text-based client, named **gopher**, which runs on the Unix host computer. (For a discussion of shell accounts and Unix systems, see Chapter 5.) The gopher system was originally designed for just this environment, and the **gopher** program works smoothly and quickly.

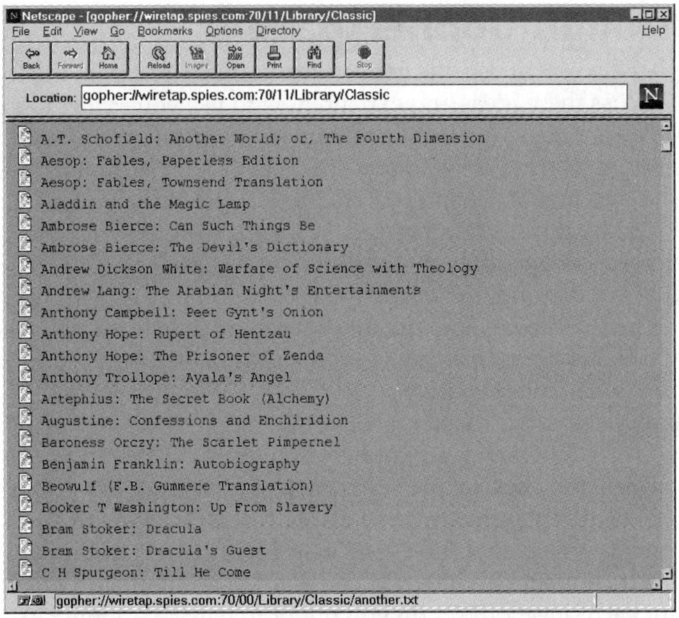

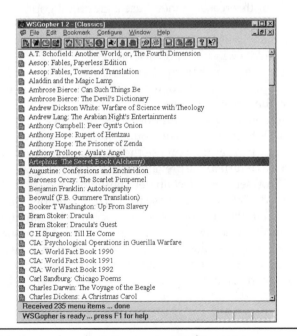

Figure 16-1. *Using a browser to access a gopher menu*

Figure 16-2. *Using a gopher client to access a gopher menu*

Traveling Through Gopherspace

Whichever gopher client you use, the general ideas are the same. In the following sections, I will discuss these ideas and explain how to use your client to explore gopherspace. If you are using the Unix **gopher** program, you must also learn the various commands, which are covered separately in the next chapter. Thus, if you are a Unix person, be sure to read Chapter 17 after you finish this chapter.

Using a gopher client is straightforward. You are presented with a menu of choices, you select one choice after another, and your gopher client does whatever is necessary to carry out your requests. How you select a choice depends upon your client. Usually there is a choice. You can either select an item by double-clicking it with your mouse, or you can move to an item and press the ENTER key. Try both to see what works for you and what you prefer.

Navigating gopherspace is easy: just select one menu item after another. As you do, there are two ways in which your gopher client might display a new item. If you use a browser or the Unix **gopher** program, each new menu replaces the old one. The graphical gopher clients are different: they display each new item in its own window.

This dichotomy is important. The question is, as you travel through gopherspace, choosing one menu item after another, do you want to accumulate a whole lot of windows, one for each selection? Or do you prefer to have everything in one main window?

Personally, I do not like many windows. I find they clutter up the screen and muddy my thinking. For this reason, when I use a graphical gopher program, I look for an option that will let me turn off the one-window-per-item feature. There is an advantage to having many windows: If you want to return to a previous gopher item, all you need to do is find its window and click on it.

As you explore gopherspace, there are two basic skills: selecting an item, and moving backward to a previous item. So, when you start to use a new program, take a moment and see how these features work.

With a browser you would use your mouse to select items, and then click on the "forward" or "backward" buttons to move around, just as you do with hypertext.

With the Unix **gopher** program, you use the RIGHT arrow key to make a selection and the LEFT arrow key to return to the previous selection (more details in Chapter 17).

With a graphical browser, you select an item with your mouse, but there are two ways to move backward. First, you can close the current window. Doing so will automatically place you in the previous window. Second, you can find and select the previous window directly. As a convenience, your program will probably allow you to close the current window by pressing the ESCAPE key (which may be labeled ESC on your keyboard). Thus, you will find that pressing ESCAPE repeatedly is a good way to retrace your path, one step at a time.

Gopher servers were designed to make it easy to change the menus. For this reason, it is common to find that a server has been reorganized. If one of your favorite menu items seems to have disappeared, it may have been moved to another menu on the same server.

If you can't find the item you want by looking around, there are search tools you can use. The two most common are veronica and jughead (discussed later in the chapter). If the site you are visiting has a jughead facility, try it first.

Gopher Addresses

There are several ways you can jump from one gopher item to another. The easiest way is to choose an item from a menu. When you do, your gopher client will contact the appropriate gopher server in order to carry out your request. You do not have to specify an address, because your gopher client already knows the address of each item on the menu.

Normally, your gopher client will display only menu titles and not the addresses associated with those titles. However, if you do want to see an address for a particular item, all you have to do is move to that item and then tell your client to display the technical information. (All gopher clients have a command to perform this function.)

If you have a particular address to which you want to connect, you can do so directly. Your gopher clients will have a command to allow you to enter an address of your own. If you are using a browser, the address must be in the form of a URL (uniform resource locator). If you are using a graphical gopher client or the Unix **gopher** program, just specify a regular Internet address.

Here is an example. You want to use the gopher server for the U.S. Library of Congress (the address is **gopher.loc.gov**). If you are using a graphical client or the **gopher** program, issue the command to jump to a new address and type:

```
gopher.loc.gov
```

If you are using a browser, you must use a URL:

```
gopher://gopher.loc.gov/
```

(For more information on how to use URLs and gophers, see Chapter 11.)

If there is one gopher server you use a lot, you may want to connect to it each time you start your gopher client. To do so, your client will let you define a HOME GOPHER SERVER. All you need to do is tell your client which address you want to use. Once you do, your client will connect to this address automatically each time you start the program.

> ## ⚐ HINT
>
> It is customary for gopher servers to be given addresses beginning with the word **gopher**. For instance, the U.S. Library of Congress uses **gopher.loc.gov** for their server.
>
> If you would like to find a gopher server for a particular company or organization, you can often check by guessing at the name. For example, computers at the University of California at Berkeley use names ending with **berkeley.edu**. If you were looking for a U.C. Berkeley gopher, you could try **gopher.berkeley.edu**.

History Lists and Bookmark Lists

Gopherspace is large, and you will frequently encounter menu items that you want to remember. There are two ways to do so.

First, most (but not all) gopher clients maintain a HISTORY LIST. This is a list of all the menu items you have selected since you started the program. At any time, you can display your history list and choose an item. This allows you to revisit any item from the current work session.

Note: Not all programs call this facility a "history list". You may have to look for a list of "recent" items, or something similar. If you are using a browser, it will have its own type of history list. (See Chapter 12 for the details.)

The history list is fine for items from the current work session, but you will often want to remember an item permanently. To do so, you tell your client program to save the address of a specific item or menu. Each item or menu you save is called a BOOKMARK, and the collection of such items is called your BOOKMARK LIST. In order to maintain your bookmarks permanently, your program will save the bookmark list in a file (called your BOOKMARK FILE) on your computer. Thus, your bookmark list is available from one session to the next.

At any time, you can tell your client to display your bookmarks. You can then select an item and jump to it directly. As the need arises, you can also delete items from the list, in order to keep things manageable.

> ## ⚐ HINT
>
> Whenever you find an item which is particularly useful or interesting, take a moment to save it to your bookmark list. Over time, you will build up a customized menu of all your favorite gopher sites.
>
> Since your bookmark list is stored as a regular file, you can share it with a friend simply by giving him or her a copy of the file. (This will work best if your friend uses the same gopher client.)

Different Types of Resources

As you explore gopherspace, you will see various types of items on gopher menus. In this section, I will survey the different types of items and explain what you should know about the most important ones.

To start, the most common items are those representing menus and text files. When you select a menu item, you get another menu. When you select a text file item, your gopher client will fetch the file and display it for you. Thus, most of the time, you are either selecting items from one menu or another, or reading a text file.

However, sometimes you will encounter several other types of items. First, there are items that represent non-textual data, such as pictures, sounds or binary files. Second, there are items that represent Internet services, such as telnet sessions. Third, there are databases which you can search for various types of information.

If your gopher client is configured properly, you will be able to access all of these items. To ensure this is the case, find the configuration facility for your program—look for something named "configuration" or "options" or "setup"—and make sure your gopher client has the information it needs to process each type of data.

For example, in order to display a picture, your gopher client needs to know the name of the program on your computer that should be used to display a picture file. Such programs are called "viewers", and I discuss them in Chapter 10 in the context of the Web. (They work the same way with a gopher client.)

Listening to sounds is similar. When you select a menu item that represents a sound, your gopher client will request a copy of the sound file from the gopher server, and then use your audio program to play the sound. Of course, before this can happen, you must configure your client so it knows the name of the audio program on your computer.

Here is another example. The telnet facility allows you to connect to a remote computer anywhere on the Internet (see Chapter 23 for the details). Normally, of course, you would need a user name and password to log in to another computer. However, there are a number of Internet sites that provide a public service via telnet. (Many of these sites are libraries which offer telnet sessions to let you perform catalog searches.)

In order to use telnet with your gopher, you must first configure your gopher client so it knows the name of your telnet client. Then, whenever you select a telnet item from a gopher menu, your gopher client will use your telnet client to connect to the remote computer. When you are finished with the telnet session just quit, and you will be returned to your gopher client automatically.

Finally, I will conclude this section by discussing two other types of gopher menu items, both of which allow you to search for data.

The first type of item is a CSO NAMESERVER. This facility is used by organizations to allow people to search local databases. CSO nameservers are usually set up to contain information about the people in the organization. For example, many universities maintain such databases to provide phone numbers and addresses for the staff, faculty and (sometimes) students.

Using a CSO nameserver is easy. When you select the item, your gopher client will present you with a form to fill in. Just type whatever information is appropriate and submit the form. Your client will send it to the nameserver and wait for a reply.

📖 What's in a Name?

CSO nameserver, `qi`, `ph`

The CSO nameserver facility gets its name from the Computing Services Office at the University of Illinois, Urbana, where the software was developed.

When you read about CSO nameservers, you may also see two other names. The name of the server program is `qi` (it stands for "query interpreter"), and the name of the client program is `ph` (which stands for "phone book"). For this reason, you will sometimes see CSO nameservers referred to as `ph` directories or `ph` servers.

The last resource I want to mention is WAIS: a system developed to search very large amounts of data at lightning speed. Wais databases contain information in the form of articles. All you have to do is specify one or more keywords that describe the types of articles you want. Wais will quickly search the database and send back a list of articles, ranked according to relevancy. The articles that best match your search criteria will be at the top of the list. You can then select whichever articles you want to read, and wais will send you the entire text.

At one time, there were a good number of wais databases available. Nowadays, wais is not used as much, but you will still encounter a wais resource from time to time. When you do, searching is straightforward. Simply specify the word or words that best describe the type of information for which you are looking. Your client will send the request to the wais server, and then display the reply.

📖 What's in a Name?

WAIS

The name "wais" is pronounced "wayz", and stands for "Wide Area Information Service".

The wais database system grew out of a project started by three companies: Apple, Thinking Machines and Dow Jones. The original idea was to spawn a large number of databases, many of which could be used by people all over the Internet who would pay money to search for data. Like many new ideas on the Internet, this one did not flourish (especially the part about paying money for data).

Saving, Printing, Mailing and Downloading

Once you find an item, there are several ways to preserve it. The easiest way is to save the item to a file on your computer. (Just look for a "Save" or "Save As" function on one of the pull-down menus.) With some gopher clients, you can also print text items or mail them to someone. I find the mail facility especially useful: Whenever I see something I think a friend might enjoy, I can just send him a copy. Unfortunately, not all gopher clients can send mail. You will have to check with your particular program to see which options are available.

If you are using a browser, you will have all the facilities of the browser available to you (just like when you use the Web). All browsers make it easy to save, print or mail items.

With a Unix shell account, it is possible to save a file, but it will be stored on the Unix host. Instead, you can use an alternate command to download the file directly to your own computer. In Chapter 17, I discuss the details of how to do this using the **gopher** program.

What Is Veronica?

VERONICA is a gopher-based resource that allows you to search gopherspace for menu items that contain specified words. For example, say you are interested in math jokes. You know that somewhere out in gopherspace, there must be some menu items that contain math jokes. But where are they? Veronica can find out.

The first version of veronica was developed in November 1992. The work was done by Steven Foster and Fred Barrie of the University of Nevada at Reno, System Computing Department. Foster and Barrie were gopher users who realized that the potential of the gopher system could never be reached unless there was an easy way to find items in gopherspace. They saw how frustrating and unproductive it was to hunt for specific items when they did not know where to look.

For inspiration, Foster and Barrie turned to archie, an Internet resource that provides a searchable database for anonymous ftp archives (see Chapter 18). They developed what they called a VERONICA SERVER to provide a similar function for the gopher system. Here is how veronica works.

On a regular basis (say, every one to two weeks) a special program will contact every known gopher server and ask for a copy of all the menus. These menus are stored in a database. At any time, you can search for items in the database by sending a request to a veronica server. The server will check the database, and then send back a list of menu items that satisfy your request. You can then investigate whichever items look promising.

There are a number of veronica servers around the Internet, which are set up and maintained by various organizations as a public service. Although all veronica servers are similar, they do not always yield the same results. Thus, if one server does not find what you need, you should try another one.

Veronica is an extremely useful tool: Without it, gopherspace would be all but unnavigable. However, veronica is not perfect. It is too easy to come up with a lot of irrelevant items or even no items at all. Some of this has to do with how veronica works, and some of it reflects the nature of gopherspace itself. After all, each gopher server is maintained locally, and there are no global standards as to how menu items should be named or organized. Nor should there be.

The strength of the Internet lies in the fact that no one person or organization is in charge. This makes for a fertile environment in which tools such as the gopher system, anonymous ftp and the Web can develop. Of course, it also makes for a certain amount of disorganization and chaos. In this sense, the Internet is a lot like life (only more fun).

What's in a Name?

Veronica

Before veronica, there was an older system named archie, which was designed to search anonymous ftp servers. (The name "archie" stands for "archive server".) When it came time to name the gopher search tool, Steven Foster and Fred Barrie (the developers) wanted a name like "archie".

Now, the name "archie" reminded Foster and Barrie of Archie Andrews: the perennial teenager who is the mainstay of a series of American comic books. In those books, Archie's girlfriend is Veronica Lodge, so Foster and Barrie decided to name their new search tool after her.

Some people believe that the name "veronica" stands for "Very Easy Rodent-Oriented Netwide Index to Computerized Archives". This is not true. The name was chosen from the Archie comics, and the acronym was invented afterwards.

Using Veronica

Veronica is easy to use. All you have to do is find a veronica resource on a menu somewhere and select that item. You will then be presented with a window into which you can type a search pattern. Veronica will check its database, find all the items that contain the search pattern, and send them to you in the form of a menu.

Thus, the result of a veronica search is a menu of regular gopher items, each of which contains the search pattern you specified. Once veronica presents you with this menu, you can select any item you want in the regular manner. For example, if you see an item that looks promising, just select it, and your gopher client will fetch it for you. If an item turns out to be especially interesting, you can save it to your bookmark list. This will allow you to access the item directly without having to search for it.

To use veronica, you will have to find it somewhere on a gopher server. You will often find veronica under the same heading as a list of gopher servers. For example, a good place to look would be within an item like:

Other Gopher and Information Servers

The veronica item will usually look something like this:

Search titles in Gopherspace using veronica

Once you find such an item, select it and you will be shown a menu of veronica-related resources. Here is a typical example:

```
How to Compose veronica Queries
Frequently-Asked Questions (FAQ) about veronica
Simplified veronica: Find Gopher MENUS only <?>
Simplified veronica: find ALL gopher types <?>
Find GOPHER DIRECTORIES by Title word(s) (via U. of Bergen) <?>
Find GOPHER DIRECTORIES by Title word(s) (via NYSERNet) <?>
Find GOPHER DIRECTORIES by Title word(s) (via PSINet) <?>
Search GopherSpace by Title word(s) (via U. of Bergen) <?>
Search GopherSpace by Title word(s) (via NYSERNet) <?>
Search GopherSpace by Title word(s) (via PSINet) <?>
```

In this example, the first menu item will display information about using veronica; the second item will display information about veronica itself; the other items are used to perform searches.

HINT

You only need to find a veronica menu once. Once you do, save it to your bookmark list. You can now use veronica whenever you want simply by selecting it from your bookmark list.

Let's take a look at the previous example. There are several different ways to start a veronica search. You can search for either items or menus, and you can choose a particular veronica server, or use a "simplified" search. With a simplified search, the system will pick a server for you.

The most common veronica search is one in which you look for menu items that contain certain words. In our example, the following item will perform such a search by using the veronica server at the University of Bergen:

Search GopherSpace by Title word(s) (via U. of Bergen) <?>

If you want to let the system choose the server for you, you could use:

```
Simplified veronica: find ALL gopher types <?>
```

The second type of veronica search looks for menu titles rather than individual items. Such a search will often yield the best results. In our example, the following selection would perform a menu search using the University of Bergen server:

```
Find GOPHER DIRECTORIES by Title word(s) (via U. of Bergen) <?>
```

(Don't let the description fool you. "GOPHER DIRECTORIES" are the same as menu titles.) To perform a simplified search for menu titles—that is, to let the system choose a server for you—you could use:

```
Simplified veronica: Find Gopher MENUS only <?>
```

HINT

Veronica servers are often busy. If you select a particular server, you may have to try repeatedly to get a response. In such cases, a simplified search may work faster, as the system will do its best to find a server that is not busy.

Specifying Words for a Veronica Search

Here is an example in which I will demonstrate some of the techniques you can use with veronica searches. As a test, I decided to use veronica to search for math jokes. To start, I specified a simple search pattern:

```
math
```

(Note: When veronica performs a search, it does not distinguish between upper- and lowercase letters. Thus, you would get the same results searching for **math**, **Math** or **MATH**.)

The first time I searched, I received only one response. Clearly this was wrong, as the entirety of gopherspace should contain many items with the word **math**. So, I selected a different veronica server and tried again. This time I got 102 items, which was overwhelming. To refine the search I used a more complex pattern:

```
math joke
```

This time I found only one item:

```
Math Joke Collection
```

This was just what I wanted, so I selected it and read the jokes.

Quick break: In case you are wondering what math jokes look like, here is a representative example. However, I will warn you in advance, this joke will not mean much to you unless you have studied complex analysis. If this is not the case, you will have to take my word for it that the joke really is funny.

> Question: What is the contour integral around Western Europe?
> Answer: Zero, because all the Poles are in Eastern Europe.

(You see, in the complex plane, when you integrate around a closed curve, everything cancels out except the residues at the singularities, which happen to be poles. And, if the curve around which you are integrating does not contain any poles, the total value of the integral around the curve will be zero.... Oh never mind, let's push on.)

In the last example, I used veronica to search for items containing two words, **math** and **jokes**. To form more complex expressions, veronica allows you to use certain qualifiers: **and**, **or**, and **not**. You can also place expressions within parentheses to indicate groupings.

When you use **and**, it tells veronica to search for items that contain more than one word. By default, veronica assumes you are using **and** whenever you specify more than one word. For example, the following two search patterns are equivalent:

```
math jokes
math and jokes
```

You can use **or** to tell veronica to search for items that contain any of the specified words. For example, to find all the items that contain either the word **jokes** or the word **humor** (or both), search for:

```
jokes or humor
```

You can use parentheses to indicate that a particular combination should be treated as a single word. For example, to find all the items that contain the word **math** and at least one of the words **jokes** or **humor**, search for:

```
math and (jokes or humor)
```

As I mentioned, veronica will assume that you are using **and** by default. Thus, the last search is equivalent to:

```
math (jokes or humor)
```

Finally, you can use **not** to indicate the item must not contain a specific word. For example, to find all the items that contain the words **math** and **jokes**, but not the word **wanted**, you would search for:

```
math jokes not wanted
```

There will be times when you want to search for (or not search for) words that are similar to one another. For example, you may want to search for items that contain **mathematics** as well as **math**, or **joke** as well as **jokes**. To do so, you can use an * (asterisk) character at the end of a word to represent any number of extra characters. For example, to find all the items that contain any word that begins with **math** and any word that begins with **joke**, you would search for:

```
math* joke*
```

To find all the items that contain these same words but do not contain any word that begins with either **want** or **need**, search for:

```
math* joke* not (want* or need*)
```

HINT

You may find that a veronica search will come up with nothing when you know there must be something. For example, if you search for **math*** and veronica cannot find anything, you should be suspicious.

There are several reasons why this may happen. The most common reason is you have specified a bad search pattern. Ask veronica to search again and, this time, recheck your spelling and your logic.

The second most common reason is the remote veronica host may not be working. If you suspect this is the case, try using a different veronica server or try again later.

Using Jughead to Search Gopherspace

As I explained in the previous sections, veronica is a tool that allows you to search gopherspace. Using veronica, you can find menu titles and individual items that match a particular search pattern. JUGHEAD is a similar tool, except it searches only a confined area of gopherspace.

Jughead is important as there will be times when you will want to search only one small part of gopherspace. For example, if you are interested in information at a particular university, you might want to confine your search to the gopher servers at that university.

When a system manager decides that his users would benefit from some type of limited gopherspace search, he sets up a JUGHEAD SERVER. The role of a jughead server is to maintain a database of all the menu items within the part of gopherspace specified by the system manager.

For example, let's say you are interested in books and libraries at the University of Utah. You might consider using veronica to search for menu items containing the following pattern:

```
book* librar*
```

However, there are three problems with this approach.

First, veronica will find menu items throughout gopherspace, which would be too much. Second, veronica has a built-in limit as to how many items it will find on a single search, and this limit may be exceeded before anything is found at the University of Utah. Third, it may take a long time for veronica to perform such a general search.

However, if you use jughead, it will confine the search to only those gopher servers at the University of Utah. The search will be faster than a veronica search and will yield more complete results. The only requirement is that someone must have already set up a jughead server for that part of gopherspace.

So how do you access jughead? The same way you access veronica: by selecting an item from a gopher menu. The difference is that, where there are relatively few veronica servers in the world, there are many jughead servers, each of which can search a limited part of gopherspace.

To use jughead, you will have to find it on a gopher server. Look for an item similar to the following:

```
Search menu titles using jughead
```

When you select such an item, you may see a jughead-related menu. For example:

```
Search University of Utah menus using jughead
About jughead
All Known jughead Servers
Search other institutions using jughead
jughead source
```

In this case, you would choose the first item to use jughead to perform a search.

Sometimes you will find just a single jughead item and not a whole menu. If so, this item will place you directly into a jughead search.

HINT

Some jughead servers are hidden behind misleading menu items. Here is an example:

```
Keyword Search Gopher Documents <?>
```

Although this item is ambiguous, it actually does refer to a jughead search.

Searching with jughead is a lot like searching with veronica. You enter one or more words, and jughead looks for them. The results are returned to you as gopher menu items, so you can select them in the regular manner. When you compose a jughead search, you can use the special words **and**, **or** and **not**. (For more information and some examples, see the previous discussion about veronica.)

If you want to display help, all you need to do is use jughead to search for **?** (question mark). You will then see an item for jughead help, which you can display.

What's in a Name?

Jughead

As I mentioned earlier, the developers of veronica chose a name that reminded them of Veronica Lodge, the girlfriend of the comic book character Archie Andrews. An earlier search tool (used for anonymous ftp servers) was named "archie", so it seemed natural to name a similar tool after Archie's girlfriend.

Jughead was developed by Rhett (Jonzy) Jones at the University of Utah Computer Center and was first released on March 25, 1993. At the time, Jones decided to carry on the tradition and used the name of Archie's best friend, Jughead Jones.

Later, Jones created the expression "Jonzy's Universal Gopher Hierarchy Excavation And Display" to be a longer name for jughead. However, as with veronica, the name was chosen first, and the acronym was invented afterwards.

(If you are at all inclined towards metaphysical speculation, think about this: In the comic books, Jughead's last name is Jones. On the Internet, the jughead program was developed by Rhett Jones. Is that cosmic or what?)

Chapter Seventeen

Using Gopher from a Shell Account: gopher

In Chapter 16, I cover the gopher system, a menu-driven Internet resource which allows you to access data from gopher servers around the Internet using a simple, consistent interface. If you use the Internet with a shell account, your gopher client will be a Unix program running on the Unix host.

This chapter shows you how to use the Unix gopher program. Before you read the chapter, however, be sure to look at Chapter 16. That is where I discuss the basic ideas of the gopher system and how it works.

Starting the gopher Program

The text-based Unix gopher client is called **gopher**. To start the program, enter the **gopher** command:

```
gopher
```

If you enter the command without options or parameters, **gopher** will start by displaying a home gopher server (if one was defined by your system administrator). As an alternative, you can start the program using a particular gopher server by specifying the name of the server as a parameter. Here is an example:

```
gopher wiretap.spies.com
```

This command will start the **gopher** program and automatically connect to the server whose address is **wiretap.spies.com**.

A small number of gopher servers require you to type a "port number" after the address of the computer. I explain port numbers in Chapter 23, within the discussion of the telnet (remote login) facility. Basically, a port number identifies a request for a particular type of service.

If the gopher server to which you are connecting requires a port number, just type the number after the address. For example:

```
gopher gopher.vt.edu 10010
```

Many people prefer to start work with their own personal bookmark list. If you use a bookmark list, you can have it loaded automatically instead of connecting to a server. To do so, start the program with the **-b** (bookmark) option:

```
gopher -b
```

HINT

Take the time to create a bookmark list of your favorite items. Then, whenever you enter the **gopher** with the **-b** option, you will be starting with your own personal gopher menu.

If you would like to read the official documentation for the **gopher** program, you can use the **man** command to display the **gopher** page from the online Unix manual:

```
man gopher
```

This documentation is handy as it contains a quick reference of the various **gopher** commands.

Stopping, Displaying Help, Shell Commands, Redrawing the Screen

Before I go into the details of using the **gopher** program, I would like to cover a few preliminary ideas and commands. When I describe commands in this chapter, I will use the Unix convention of indicating a CTRL key by using a ^ (circumflex) character. For example, **^L** indicates CTRL-L.

There are two ways to stop the **gopher** program. The usual way is to press **q** (quit). As a safeguard, you will be asked if you really want to quit, to which you can answer either **y** (yes) or **n** (no).

To quit immediately, without being asked for confirmation, you can press **Q** (uppercase "Q").

The **gopher** program works in what is called CBREAK MODE. This means that when you type commands consisting of a single character, you do not use the RETURN key. Pressing the command key is enough. For example, to stop the program, you need only press the **q** key. Do not press RETURN.

As with all programs, the most important commands are the ones that display help information. With the **gopher** program, there are two such commands.

Most of the time, you press the **?** (question mark) key for help. This will display a command summary. However, when you are typing information for a search, you use a different help key. Instead of **?**, you use the **^-** (CTRL minus sign) key. (If the **?** character were the help key, you would not be able to type it as part of a search pattern.)

If you want to enter a regular Unix command, you do not have to stop the **gopher** program. Press either **!** (exclamation mark) or **$** (dollar sign). This will pause the program and start a new shell. You can now enter as many Unix commands as you want. When you are finished, type **exit** to return to the **gopher** program.

Finally, if your screen display ever becomes garbled, you can redraw it by pressing either **^L** (the usual Unix key for this function), **^R** (redraw) or **^W** (wipe the screen). They all do the same thing; use whichever one is easiest for you to remember.

Understanding a gopher Menu

To help you get a feeling for using the **gopher** program, I would like to start with Figure 17-1, which contains a typical gopher menu.

```
┌─────────────────────────────────────────────────────────────────┐
│                                                                   │
│           Internet Gopher Information Client v2.0.16              │
│                                                                   │
│      University of Foobar, Unix Studies Department Gopher Server  │
│                                                                   │
│   -->   1.    About the Unix Studies Department                   │
│         2.    Where to buy the book "A Student's Guide to Unix"   │
│         3.    Search the Online Unix Manual <?>                   │
│         4.    The Internet Studies Department Gopher/             │
│         5.    Gopher Servers at the University of Foobar/         │
│         6.    Other Gopher Servers Around the World/              │
│         7.    University of Foobar Directory <CSO>               │
│         8.    The Unix Daemon <Picture>                           │
│         9.    University of Foobar Library Catalog <TEL>         │
│        10.    The Sound of Unix <)                                │
│        11.    Fun and Games/                                      │
│                                                                   │
│   Press ? for Help, q to Quit, u to go up a menu      Page: 1/1   │
│                                                                   │
└─────────────────────────────────────────────────────────────────┘
```

Figure 17-1.   gopher: *A typical gopher menu*

At all times, a pointer, shown as **-->**, will be displayed at the left of the current menu item. In Figure 17-1, the pointer is beside item number **1**. The idea is to move the pointer to the item you want and then select it.

Notice that some menu items have a symbol at the end of the line. This symbol tells you what type of resource is represented by that item.

The most common symbol is a **/** (slash) character. This indicates the item represents another menu. For example, look at item number **4**.

4.   The Internet Studies Department Gopher/

If you choose this item, you will get another menu (the main menu for the Internet Studies gopher server).

If you have ever worked with files and directories, the design of the gopher's menu system may seem familiar to you. This is because gopher menus are stored as directories and subdirectories, and the user interface is based upon this model. For this reason, you will sometimes see gopher menus referred to as directories. For example, while you are waiting for a menu to be fetched from a remote server, you will see the message:

Retrieving Directory...

HINT

From time to time, you may end up waiting for something. For example, you might be waiting for your gopher client to connect to a server. Or you may initiate a database search that seems to go on and on.

Unfortunately, there is no easy way to tell the **gopher** program to abort the operation. In such cases, you have two choices. You can wait, or you can press ^C (the Unix interrupt key). (If ^C doesn't work, try the DELETE key.)

If you press ^C, be careful. This is a signal to the **gopher** program to abort. You will see the following message:

```
Really quit (y/n) ?
```

Respond by pressing **y** (for yes). The program will quit, and the operation for which you were waiting will be aborted.

Aside from the **/** character, the next most common item type is one without a symbol. Such items represent text files: something to read. In our example, item number **1** represents a text file that contains information about the Unix Studies Department:

```
1.   About the Unix Studies Department
```

When you select such an item, the **gopher** program will fetch it and display it for you, one page at a time.

HINT

You can control which paging program is used by setting the **PAGER** environment variable. For example, if you use the C-Shell and you like the less paging program, you could place the following command in your **.login** initialization file:

```
setenv PAGER less
```

If you use the Korn shell or Bourne shell, you could place the following two commands in your **.profile** initialization file:

```
PAGER=less
export PAGER
```

These commands will define the **PAGER** environment variable automatically each time you log in. Moreover, the **PAGER** variable is used by a number of programs (such as your mail program), not just your gopher client.

A discussion of environment variables and initialization files is beyond the scope of this book. For more information, see my Unix book *The Unix Companion*, published by Osborne McGraw-Hill.

To continue, the **<TEL>** symbol indicates a completely different type of resource: a telnet session. In our example, we see:

9.   University of Foobar Library Catalog <TEL>

If we select this item, our gopher will initiate a telnet connection to a remote host. In this case, it is a host that offers access to the University of Foobar Library catalog. Just before the connection is made, you will see a warning telling you that, in order to make the connection, you are going to have to go outside the gopher system:

```
+----------University of Foobar Library Catalog------------+
|                                                          |
|    Warning!!!!!, you are about to leave the Internet      |
|    Gopher program and connect to another host. If        |
|    you get stuck press the control key and the ] key,     |
|    and then type quit                                     |
|                                                          |
|                          [Cancel - ^G] [OK - Enter]      |
|                                                          |
+----------------------------------------------------------+
```

When you see such a message, you are about to embark on a telnet session. To continue, press RETURN. To forget the whole thing, press CTRL-G.

Once you finish with the telnet session, you will be returned to your gopher client. However, during the session, whatever you type will be under the auspices of telnet. In particular, you can use the telnet escape key **^]**. For more details on how telnet works, see Chapters 23 and 24.

The next gopher symbol is **<CSO>**. This indicates a CSO nameserver. Such servers usually contain information about the people at a particular organization (see Chapter 16). In our example, we see:

7.   University of Foobar Directory <CSO>

In this case, you could select this item to search for information about a person at the University of Foobar. For example, you might want to find someone's electronic mail address.

If you select a **<CSO>** item, you will see a screen asking you what to search for. The following example shows one such screen. If you use a number of CSO nameservers, you will encounter variations, but, in principle, they all work the same way.

```
+---------------University of Foobar Directory---------------+
|                                                            |
| name          _____               |
| email         _____               |
| department    _____               |
|                                                            |
|   [Switch Fields - TAB]         [Cancel ^G] [Accept - Enter] |
|                                                            |
+------------------------------------------------------------+
```

All you have to do is fill in whatever information you know and press RETURN. The CSO nameserver will check its database and send back whatever it finds. As you are typing, you can move from one field to another by pressing the TAB key. If you decide to forget about searching, simply press **^G** to return to the last gopher menu.

The next symbol to discuss is **<?>**. This indicates a database which you can search by entering one or more keywords. For example, this might be a wais database or a jughead server (see Chapter 16). In our example, we have:

3. Search the Online Unix Manual <?>

When you select such an item, you will see a screen which asks you to specify what you want to search for. For example:

```
+----------------Search the Online Unix Manual----------------+
|                                                             |
| Words to search for  _____             |
|                                                             |
|                         [Cancel ^G] [Accept - Enter]        |
|                                                             |
+-------------------------------------------------------------+
```

Fill in one or more keywords and then press RETURN. Your gopher client will initiate the search. When the results come back, the **gopher** program will display them in the form of a menu, and you can select whatever looks good.

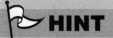
HINT

You can use the **=** command to display technical information about a **<?>** menu item. This will sometimes give you a hint as to the type of database. For example, if you display the technical information, you may see the word "wais".

If you are pleased with the results of a search, you can save it to use again. To do so, wait until the search is finished, and then use the **A** command. This will save the search (not its results) to your bookmark list. Whenever you want, you can display your bookmark list and select this exact search.

For example, say you find a gopher item that allows you to search news articles in a database. You can create a specific search that checks the news for your favorite topic, and then save the search to your bookmark list. Then, each day when you start work, you can call up your bookmark list and use your preconfigured search to look for new articles.

The last two menu symbols I will discuss are **<Picture>** and **<)**. The **<Picture>** symbol indicates a binary file containing a picture. The **<)** symbol indicates a binary file containing a sound. (The **<)** is supposed to look like a stereo speaker.) Here are two examples showing these symbols:

```
 8.   The Unix Daemon <Picture>
10.   The Sound of Unix <)
```

HINT

If you are connecting to the Unix host by using a PC or Macintosh, you can use the **D** command (described later) to download picture and sound files to your own computer.

Aside from the menu symbols I have covered, there are others you may encounter once in a while. For reference, Figure 17-2 contains a full list of these symbols.

Using Menus

There are a variety of commands you can use to move around a menu and to select items. However, as you will see, almost all the time, all you need are six keys: the four cursor control keys (with the arrows) RIGHT, LEFT, DOWN and UP; the SPACE key; and the **b** key.

As I explained earlier, your current position within a menu will be marked by a pointer. There are several ways to move this pointer. The easiest way is to use the UP and DOWN keys. If your keyboard does not have these keys, or if you prefer not to use them, you can use **k** or **^P** to move up, and **j** or **^N** to move down. Although these choices may seem odd, they are used within the **vi** and **emacs** text editors and are second nature to a great many Unix users.

To select the current item, you can press either RIGHT or RETURN. To go back to the previous menu, press LEFT or **u** (for up). As a shortcut, you can select a particular item directly by entering its number. For example, to select item number 10, type **10** and press RETURN.

(none)	text file
/	menu
`<TEL>`	telnet connection
`<3270>`	3270 (IBM mainframe) telnet connection
`<CSO>`	CSO nameserver
`<?>`	searchable database
`<Picture>`	image file
`<)`	sound file
`<Movie>`	movie file
`<Bin>`	binary file
`<PC Bin>`	DOS binary file
`<HQX>`	BinHexed Macintosh file
`<HTML>`	HTML file
`<MIME>`	Mime-encoded file
`<??>`	ASK form

Figure 17-2.   `gopher:`   *Menu item symbols*

Some menus are so long, they cannot be displayed all at once. In such cases, the message at the right-hand side of the bottom line will tell you the length of the menu. For example, the following line indicates we are looking at page (screen) 1 of 7.

```
Press ? for Help, q to Quit, u to go up a menu        Page: 1/7
```

To move to the next page, press SPACE. To move to the previous page, press **b** (back). Again, there are alternative keys you can use. To move to the next page, you can press PAGEDOWN, **>** (greater than) or **+** (plus). To move to the previous page, you can press PAGEUP, **<** (less than) or **–** (minus).

HINT

You can jump to an item, even if it is not on the current page. For example, say that you are looking at page 7 of a long menu. You can select item number 1 directly. Simply type **1** and press RETURN.

Another way to jump to an item is to search the current menu for an item containing a particular pattern. To do so, type a **/** (slash) character, followed by the pattern, and then press RETURN. (Note: Such searches do not distinguish between upper- and lowercase letters.)

Here is an example. Say you are looking at a very long list of gopher servers, and you would like to jump directly to the item for the University of Foobar. Enter:

```
/foobar
```

If the item found by the search is not the one you wanted, you can repeat the same search by pressing the **n** (next) key.

As you know, many of the items you select will themselves be menus. When you select such an item, your gopher client will request the menu and then display it for you. Thus, traveling through gopherspace entails moving back and forth through a tree of menus.

Now you can see the beauty of the **gopher** program. You can spend all day traveling through gopherspace with only six basic commands: UP and DOWN (to move within a menu); RIGHT and LEFT (to move from one menu to another); and SPACE and **b** (to page forward and backward through long menus).

To conclude this section, here is one final command: At any time, you can press **m** to jump to the main menu (the one you started with). The **m** command is handy when you are at the end of a long chain of menus, and you want to jump back to the beginning quickly.

Advanced Menu Commands

There are several commands you can use to display information about menus and items, and to jump directly to particular menus. In this section, I will explain these commands and give you some hints how to use them effectively.

To display information about menus and items, you can use the **=** (equals sign) and **^** (circumflex) commands. The **=** command displays technical information about the current menu item (the one marked by the pointer). The **^** command displays technical information about the menu itself.

Here is an example. Take a look at the menu in Figure 17-1. The pointer is set at item number 1:

```
-->  1.  About the Unix Studies Department
```

If you were to press **=**, you would see technical information about this particular item. Here is a reasonable facsimile:

```
Type=1+
Name=About the Unix Studies Department
Path=1/about
```

```
Host=gopher.unix.foobar.edu
Port=70
Admin=U of Foobar Unix Gopher Team <gopher@unix.foobar.edu>
ModDate=Mon Sep 18 23:42:10 1995 <19950918234210>
URL: gopher://gopher.unix.foobar.edu:70/1/about
```

This information is useful if you want to know where the item resides in gopherspace. (Remember, though, you don't need to know the location of an item in order to use it.)

If you press ^, you get the same sort of information about the menu as a whole. In the example in Figure 17-1, the name of the menu is:

University of Foobar, Unix Studies Department Gopher Server

If you were to press ^, you would see information like this:

```
Type=1
Name=University of Foobar, Unix Studies Department Gopher Server
Path=
Host=gopher.unix.foobar.edu
Port=70
URL: gopher://gopher.unix.foobar.edu:70/1
```

HINT

Harley Hahn's Sixth Law of Unix: Whenever you use an unusual special command to display information, it is safe to ignore whatever you don't understand.

In the last section, I discussed a number of navigation commands. Aside from these, there are three more that pertain specifically to menus.

First, the **m** (main menu) command will jump to the very first menu of your work session, that is, the main menu of your home gopher server. If you started with your bookmark list (by using the **gopher -b** command) rather than a gopher server, pressing **m** will display the bookmark list.

The next two commands will jump to a different main menu. The **R** (root) command will jump to the main menu for the gopher server on which the current menu resides. The **r** (lowercase **R**) command will jump to the main menu for the server on which the current item resides. Here is an example to show you how these commands work.

You are working with the gopher server at the University of Foobar's Unix Studies Department (**gopher.unix.foobar.edu**). As you explore this server, you find a submenu entitled **Unix Jokes and Humor**. This menu contains a number of items relating to Unix humor (such as a picture, entitled "Why do you think they call it Unix?" showing a beautiful woman waiting patiently for a Unix nerd to finish work).

In our example, on the **Unix Jokes and Humor** menu, the pointer is at item number 1:

```
-->  1.  Collected Jokes from A Student's Guide to Unix
```

You use the ^ and = commands, and see that the menu itself lies on the Unix Studies Department gopher server (the one you are exploring). But the current item is on a completely different machine, **gopher.nipper.com**.

So here is the situation: You are looking at a menu on the machine **gopher.unix.foobar.edu**, while the current item points to a resource on the machine **gopher.nipper.com**. If you press **R**, you will jump to the main menu for **gopher.unix.foobar.edu** (where the menu lives). If you press **r**, you will jump to the main menu for **gopher.nipper.com** (where the item lives).

HINT

The **r** command is useful when you are exploring a gopher server, and you encounter an item that looks as if it would be worth investigating. Pressing **r** will take you directly to the main menu for that server.

Bookmarks

As I discuss in Chapter 16, you can save the location of any item or menu by creating a bookmark, which is placed in a bookmark list. At any time, you can display this list and select one of the bookmarks. The **gopher** program will then connect to the original item.

To save an item to your bookmark list, use the **a** (add) command. This will save the current item, whether you are pointing to it or displaying it. If you want to save an entire menu, use the **A** (uppercase **A**) command instead.

To display your bookmark list (which is itself a menu), use the **v** (view) command. Once you do, you can select an item in the regular manner. If you change your mind, you can return the previous menu by pressing LEFT or **u**.

To delete an item from your bookmark list, display the list, point to the item you want to delete, and then press **d** (delete).

The **gopher** program saves your bookmark list in a file named **.gopherrc** in your home directory. It is possible to edit this file directly, but be careful: there is some information at the beginning of the file, before the bookmarks, which you should be careful to preserve. In addition, the individual bookmarks have a certain format which you should not change.

The **.gopherrc** file was not designed to be edited by hand, so, before you start, make a copy. For example, you might use the command:

```
cp .gopherrc .gopherrc-backup
```

This way, if you mess up the file, you can restore it from your copy.

HINT

The art of using the gopher system well is to build up a useful bookmark list. Many people forget to use this facility and end up retracing their steps time and again.

It is all too easy to forget where in gopherspace you found a particular item. If you do not save interesting items to your bookmark list, you may never see them again.

Saving, Mailing and Downloading

Many of the items you will find in gopherspace are text files. When you select such an item, the **gopher** program will download the file and display it for you, one screenful at a time.

While you are reading, there are several things you can do with the text. To save it as a file on the Unix computer, press **s** (save); to mail the text to someone (including yourself), press **m** (mail); and to download a copy of the file to your own computer, press **D** (download). (Notice this is an uppercase **D**.)

Be sure you understand the difference between **s** and **D**. The **s** command saves the file on the Unix computer; the **D** command downloads the file to your own computer. When you use the **D** command, you will get a menu of choices:

```
+-------------------------------------------+
|                                           |
|   -->     1. Zmodem                       |
|           2. Ymodem                       |
|           3. Xmodem-1K                     |
|           4. Xmodem-CRC                    |
|           5. Kermit                       |
|           6. Text                         |
|                                           |
|   Choose a download method (1-6):         |
|   [Help: ?]   [Cancel: ^G]                |
+-------------------------------------------+
```

I discuss downloading in Chapter 21. Basically, the **gopher** program will use whichever file transfer protocol (download method) you choose. Depending on how you set up the communication program on your computer, the file transfer may start automatically, or you may see a message telling you to start your download. If you are not sure what to do, see Chapter 21 and check with the documentation for your communication program.

HINT

Most of the time, the best file transfer protocol to use is zmodem. However, if you want to save text to a capture buffer on your computer, you can do so by using the "text" protocol. (A capture buffer is a file in which text is saved as it is displayed on the screen. The details lie with your communication program.)

As a shortcut, you can save or download a file without having to select it first. Just move the pointer to the item and press either **s** or **D**. This is useful when you have a binary file (such as a picture or sound) which you cannot process within the **gopher** program. You can point to the item, use **D** to download the file, and then use it on your own computer.

Note: Although the **s** and **D** commands will work when you are pointing to an item, you cannot use the **m** command in this way. In other words, you cannot mail a file until you have already selected and displayed it.

Summary of gopher Commands

Basic Commands		
	Q	quit gopher immediately
	q	quit gopher, but ask for confirmation
	?	display a help summary
	^-	display a help summary while typing a search pattern
	o	connect to a new gopher server (open)
	!	start a shell in order to enter Unix commands
	$	same as **!**
	^L	redraw the screen
	^R	same as **^L** (redraw)
	^W	same as **^L** (wipe)
	^G	cancel entering a search pattern
	O	examine and change gopher options

Figure 17-3. gopher: *Summary of commands* (continued on next page)

Moving Around a Menu

UP	move pointer up one item
k	same as UP
^P	same as UP (previous)
DOWN	move pointer down one item
j	same as DOWN
^N	same as DOWN (next)
/*pattern*	jump to the next menu item containing pattern
n	repeat previous **/** command (next)

Selecting Items

RIGHT	select the current item
RETURN	same as RIGHT
*number*RETURN	jump to and select the specified item
LEFT	back up one level to the previous menu
u	back up one level to the previous menu (up)

Paging Through a Menu

SPACE	display next page of the menu
PAGEDOWN	same as SPACE
>	same as SPACE
+	same as SPACE
b	display previous page of the menu (back)
PAGEUP	same as **b**
<	same as **b**
−	same as **b**

Figure 17-3. gopher: *Summary of commands* (continued)

Reading a Text File

SPACE	display next page of text
DOWN	same as SPACE
PAGEDOWN	same as SPACE
b	display previous page of text (back)
UP	same as **b**
PAGEUP	same as **b**
/*pattern*	jump to next page containing pattern
n	repeat previous **/** command (next)
LEFT	return to the previous menu
u	same as LEFT (up)
^G	same as LEFT

Advanced Menu Commands

=	display technical information about current item
^	display technical information about current menu
m	(main menu) jump to first menu of the work session
R	(root) jump to main menu of server: current menu
r	(root) jump to main menu of server: current item

Using Bookmarks

a	add current item to the bookmark list
A	add current menu or search to the bookmark list
v	display the bookmark list (view)
d	delete a bookmark

Saving Information

s	save current item to a file on the Unix computer
S	save menu (titles only) to a file on the Unix computer
m	mail current item
D	download current item to a file on your computer

Figure 17-3.   gopher: *Summary of commands* (continued from previous page)

Chapter Eighteen

Anonymous Ftp

A nonymous ftp is one of the most important and most widely used services on the Internet. Using anonymous ftp, you can copy files from thousands of different computers all over the Net. These files contain virtually every kind of information that can be stored on a computer.

Would you like a program for your PC or Macintosh? Would you like an issue of an electronic magazine? How about a frequently asked questions list from a Usenet discussion group? Just about any type of information or computer software is waiting for you on the Internet, and it is all free.

In this chapter, I will explain what anonymous ftp is, what type of client program you need, and how the system works. If you use a shell account, you should also read Chapter 19 in which I explain how to use the Unix text-based ftp client.

What Is Ftp?

The name "ftp" is an acronym for "File Transfer Protocol". Ftp is the Internet service that allows you to transfer files from one computer to another. Like all Internet services, ftp uses a client/server system (see Chapter 2). You run a client program on your computer which connects to a server program on a remote computer. You tell your client what to do, and it carries out your orders by sending commands to the server.

When you copy a file from a remote computer to your own computer, we say that you are DOWNLOADING the file. When you copy a file from your computer to the remote one, you are UPLOADING the file.

HINT

If you have trouble remembering the difference between uploading and downloading (and I always do), just imagine the remote computer floating above you in the sky. Up is away from you, down is toward you.

In ftp terminology, your computer is called the LOCAL HOST. The other computer is called the REMOTE HOST. Thus, we can say that ftp allows you to upload and download files to and from a remote host.

Sometimes we use the word "ftp" as a verb. For example, imagine the following conversation between two friends who happen to meet on the sidewalk outside the local Unix store:

Friend 1:
What ho, Friend 2. Fancy meeting you here.

Friend 2:
What ho, what ho, Friend 1. I ordered a special copy of a frequently asked questions list, and I was just checking to see if it arrived yet.

Friend 1:
But Friend 2, don't you know you can get a copy of any frequently asked questions list by ftp-ing to **rtfm.mit.edu**?

Friend 2:
I tried, but it was busy.

Friend 1:
So why didn't you ftp somewhere else?

Friend 2:
Oh, I couldn't be bothered, so I thought I would just order a copy from the Unix store. I also wanted to pick up a copy of the C-Shell man page for my mother's birthday.

Friend 1:
Oh. Well, it certainly was nice to see you again, Friend 2. Better luck next time you ftp to somewhere.

Friend 2:
Thank you, Friend 1. See you again sometime.

Anonymous Ftp

The ftp service lets you transfer files from one Internet computer to another. However, there is one basic restriction: you cannot access a computer unless you can log in to it. In other words, you cannot copy files to or from a remote computer unless you have a user name and a password.

ANONYMOUS FTP is a facility that lets you connect to certain remote hosts and download files without having to be registered as a user. To do so, you log in using a special user name: **anonymous**. With this user name, you do not need a regular password. Instead, you type your mail address.

For example, say your mail address is **tln@nipper.com**. When you connect to an anonymous ftp server (don't worry about the details for now), you would log in as **anonymous** and use a password of **tln@nipper.com**. The beauty of this system is it allows anyone on the Internet to log in to a remote host and download public files without having an account on that system.

It is important to understand that the **anonymous** user name will only work with computers that have been set up to act as anonymous ftp servers: that is, with those computers that are set up as repositories of publicly-available files. Moreover, the **anonymous** user name is only for ftp access. You cannot, for example, use a telnet connection (see Chapter 23) and expect to log in as **anonymous**.

As you might imagine, allowing people all over the Internet to access your computer is not something you do frivolously. There are a number of security considerations which must be addressed. Anonymous ftp hosts are set up to be secure so that outsiders cannot cause trouble, even inadvertently. For example, the system manager can control exactly which files on the computer are available for anonymous ftp access. The rest of the files are off limits and cannot be accessed except by people with valid user accounts.

As an extra security measure, many anonymous ftp hosts will not allow you to upload files. In other words, you can copy all the files you want from the remote host to your computer, but you cannot copy files from your computer to the host.

Some anonymous ftp hosts do allow anyone to upload files, which will then be made available for public downloading. However, such systems usually require you to upload the files to a special, designated directory which is not accessible for downloading. Later, after the system manager has had a chance to check out the new files, he or she will move them to one of the public download areas. In this way, remote users are protected against people who might upload troublesome files, such as programs with viruses.

HINT

Most system managers do not have time to be eternally vigilant, so when you download programs, it is a good idea to take normal precautions. For example, before you run a new program, it behooves you to check it with a virus scanning program.

The Importance of Anonymous Ftp

At first, anonymous ftp sounds useful but not really all that special. Okay, so anyone on the Internet can access files on an anonymous ftp host. What's the big deal?

The big deal is that the public anonymous ftp archives are so vast as to be well beyond human understanding. The Internet has thousands of anonymous ftp hosts offering all kinds of files for free. Virtually every type of information and every type of computer program is available somewhere on the Internet, because many people and many organizations have generously donated disk space and computing facilities to make these files available. Why? Because, as I explained in Chapter 1, the tradition on the Internet is one of sharing. Nobody gets paid for providing an anonymous ftp service, but countless people set up and maintain anonymous ftp hosts as a public service available to anyone.

Until you start to use anonymous ftp this may not sound like much. Nevertheless, I can solemnly assure you that anonymous ftp is one of the most significant inventions in the history of mankind. If you are new to the Internet, I don't blame you one bit for thinking that such a statement is the rankest hyperbole. Still, what I say is absolutely true, for three important reasons.

First, anonymous ftp allows you to download virtually any type of information. Until you are an experienced Internet user it is difficult to appreciate how important this is, but, put simply, anonymous ftp provides access to the largest library of information ever accumulated. Moreover, it is an ever-growing library that never closes, covers every conceivable topic and, best of all, is free.

Second, anonymous ftp is the principal way in which software is distributed on the Internet. Indeed, the reason the Internet can exist at all is that we all use standardized programs. Most of these programs are distributed via anonymous ftp and, hence, are available to anyone who wants to use the Internet or to set up an Internet host.

For example, in order to provide access to the Usenet discussion groups (Chapter 13), your Internet service provider must have installed the Usenet software on their computer. Where does the system manager acquire this software? Anonymous ftp.

Here is another example. In order to use the Internet with a PC or Macintosh, you need client programs to run on your computer. Where do you get such clients? You could buy them, or get them for free from your Internet service provider, but many people download their clients for free by using anonymous ftp. This is especially important when a new version of a client is released. You can download it the same day from one of the anonymous ftp sites. Indeed, if you were to write a new Internet client—such as a new web browser—the only realistic way to gain widespread exposure for your product would be to make it available to the public via anonymous ftp (and this is exactly what people do).

The final reason anonymous ftp is so important is it is used to archive and disseminate the technical information that defines the Internet itself. As I explained in Chapter 2, the Internet is based on a large number of protocols and conventions. Each such protocol is explained in a technical publication called a REQUEST FOR COMMENT or RFC. (Don't take the name too literally. An RFC is usually a detailed technical explanation of how something is supposed to work, not an invitation for people to send in comments.)

Each RFC is given a number and is made freely available to anyone who wants to read it. In this manner, the technical information that supports the Internet is distributed around the world in an organized, reliable manner. Programmers and engineers who must design products to work with the Internet protocols can download the RFCs via anonymous ftp and use them as reference material. This ensures that everyone is using the same specifications and that all Internet programs are designed to follow the same set of standards. Thus, without anonymous ftp, there would be no modern-day Internet. (Indeed, until anonymous ftp was invented, the development of the Internet was slow and limited.)

HINT

The economy of the world depends, in no small way, upon anonymous ftp.

Using a Browser for Anonymous Ftp

There are two different types of **ftp** clients. First, there are programs that can serve as ftp clients, but which were really designed for some other primary purpose. For example, web browsers are designed to serve as web clients, but can also act as ftp clients (and gopher and Usenet clients for that matter; see Chapter 11).

Alternatively, there are programs designed specifically to be ftp clients and nothing else.

If you spend most of your time using the Web and your anonymous ftp needs are small, a browser will work just fine. However, if you use anonymous ftp a lot, you will be better off with an actual ftp client program.

HINT

Using a browser for anonymous ftp is fast and easy for limited amounts of downloading, but an actual ftp program will have more features and allow you better control over what you are doing. Moreover, if an error occurs, an ftp program will often give you a better error message. For these reasons, I recommend that you find an ftp client and become familiar with how to use it.

There are two ways to access an anonymous ftp resource using a browser. From time to time, you will encounter an ftp resource as a link on a web page. When you click on that link, your browser will automatically contact the ftp site, log in as **anonymous**, send your mailing address as a password, and request the file. Depending on how your browser has been configured, you may have to specify where you want to put the file before the actual data transfer takes place.

For example, say you are reading a web page having to do with stupid things and you encounter a link that says **The Stupid FAQ**. (A FAQ is a frequently asked question list; see Chapter 13.) When you move your mouse pointer to this link, you see the following URL:

```
ftp://ftp.sunet.se/pub/usenet/news.answers/stupidity/FAQ
```

(All of these ideas are explained in Chapter 11.)

This URL points to a particular anonymous ftp resource on the computer named **ftp.sunet.se**, in a directory named **/pub/usenet/news.answers/stupidity**. Within that directory is the information in question, stored in a file named **FAQ**.

When you click on this link, your browser will act like an ftp client and contact the specified computer in order to download the file on your behalf. It will all be automatic (although, as I mentioned, you may have to specify where you want to store the file on your own computer).

As an alternative to finding an anonymous ftp resource on a web page, all browsers have a way for you to enter a URL directly. This means you can jump directly to an ftp site by just entering the appropriate URL. Here is an example that shows how this works. (For more details, see Chapter 11.)

Let's say you read about a file containing bread recipes. The file is available via anonymous ftp from the computer named **ftp.spies.com**. On that computer, in a directory named **/Library/Article/Food**, the recipes are contained in a file named **bread.rcp**. To construct the appropriate URL, use the following format:

ftp://_computer_**/**_pathname_

(The pathname is the directory + file name.) In this case, the URL to use would be:

ftp://ftp.spies.com/Library/Article/Food/bread.rcp

Just tell your browser that you wish to enter a URL and type this URL. The browser will connect to the remote ftp host and download the recipe file for you. (I will discuss directories and files in more detail later in the chapter.)

HINT

If you access the Internet via a shell account (see Chapter 5), you will likely use **lynx** (see Chapter 12) as your web browser. If so, you can access anonymous ftp resources either by selecting them from a web page or by specifying them directly using the **g** (goto) command. To use this command press **g**, then type the URL, then press RETURN.

Using an Ftp Client for Anonymous Ftp

An ftp client is a program designed for one purpose: to use the ftp service to copy files from one Internet computer to another. As I mentioned in the previous section, it is possible to access anonymous ftp resources with a browser, but an ftp client will provide more features and afford more control over the process.

In this section, I describe how to use an ftp client for anonymous ftp. Within the discussion, I will refer to files and directories. In the next section, I will discuss these ideas in more detail. For now, if you are not familiar with how directories are used, you only need to understand three things:

- On a Macintosh or a Windows computer, directories are called "folders".
- Directories are used to organize files.
- Directories can contain either files or other directories, or both.

If you access the Internet via PPP or a direct network connection (see Chapter 5), you will use a graphical ftp client that runs on your own computer. If you access the Internet via a shell account, you will use a text-based ftp client that runs on the host computer. The most common text-based client is called **ftp** and runs under Unix. I describe how to use this program in Chapter 19.

HINT

If you use a system that allows you to get to a command prompt, you may have a text-based ftp client installed as part of your overall TCP/IP facility. If you are using Windows or Windows 95, go to a DOS prompt and type **ftp**. (If you use OS/2, go to an OS/2 prompt.)

If the **ftp** program starts, you have a text-based client which will work almost exactly like the one I describe in Chapter 19. Many people prefer to use a text-based client, so you may want to read Chapter 19 as well as this chapter.

(Note: To exit the **ftp** program, type **quit**.)

 **INTERNET RESOURCE**   *Look in the catalog under Internet Resources for*
Ftp Clients Programs

All graphical clients work more or less the same way. Typically, your window will be divided into two sections, one on the right and one on the left. The right section will show you information about the remote host. The left section will show you information about the local host (your computer).

Figure 18-1 shows an ftp client. The right section shows the names of the directories and files on the remote computer. The directory names are in the top part; the file names are in the bottom part. On the left, you can see similar information about the local computer.

All ftp clients have their own nuances, of course, but the general process of accessing an anonymous ftp resource generally involves the following steps:

1. Establish a connection to the remote host.

To establish a connection, you will have to specify the name of the remote computer. You may also have to enter a user name and password. (Use a user name of **anonymous** and your mail address for a password.) Some ftp programs let you select "anonymous ftp" as an option, in which case you will not need to specify a user name and password: the program will know what to use.

Once the connection is established, your ftp client will request a listing of the contents of the top level directory. When it arrives, the information will be displayed

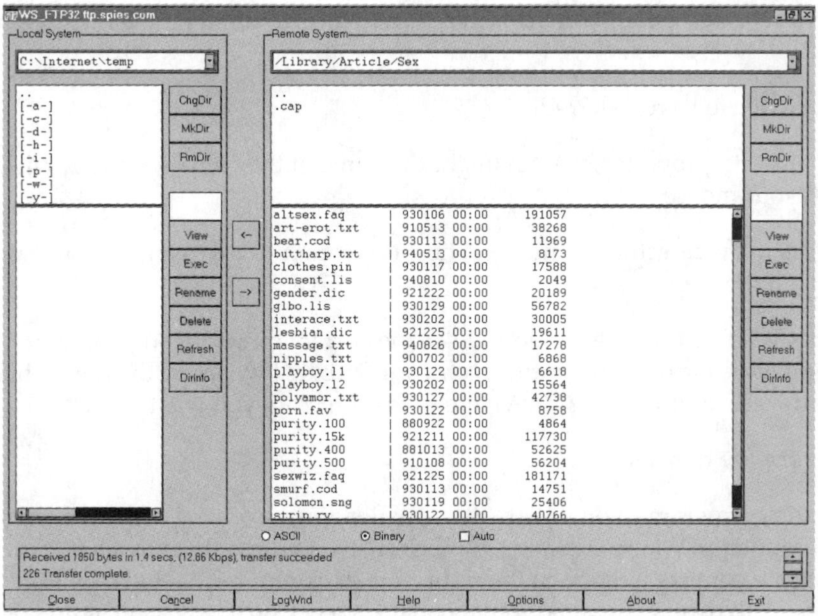

Figure 18-1. *An ftp client program*

on the right with the directory names on top and the file names on the bottom. (Remember, the exact details may vary with your particular program.)

2. Navigate to the directory on the remote host that contains the file you want.

To navigate on the remote computer, you select directory names from the list on the right, one name after another, until you get to where you want. Each time you select a directory name, you will have to wait for your ftp client to request a listing of the new directory from the remote computer. When this listing arrives, it will be displayed, directories on top, files on the bottom. Eventually, you will reach the directory that contains the file you want. At that point, you should see the name of your file in the list.

3. Set the options you want for the transfer.

There are various options you can set to specify what type of file transfer you want. In particular, you can use either an "ASCII" transfer for text files, or a "binary" transfer for binary files. (If you are downloading software, be sure to use "binary".)

Your program may also have special options or settings pertaining to your type of computer. For example, a Macintosh ftp client might have a setting to decode binhex files automatically. (Binhex is a file type used to transport Macintosh files.) For information about the common file formats you will encounter on the Internet, see Chapter 21.

4. Select the file to be transferred.

With most ftp programs, you highlight the name of the file you want by clicking on it with your mouse.

5. Navigate to the directory on the local host (your computer) to which you want to download the file.

Check the left side of the window to see the current directory on your own computer. This is the directory into which your ftp client will copy the file. If this is not where you want to copy the file, navigate to the directory you want.

6. Initiate the file transfer.

With some programs, you initiate the downloading—copying of the file from the remote computer to your computer—by clicking on a button that has a left arrow. The idea is you are copying a file from the right (remote computer) to the left (local computer). With other programs, you may have to click on a "transfer" button or something similar.

Basically, that is all there is to downloading a file via anonymous ftp. Your ftp client will have its own special features, but the general idea is the same with all ftp programs.

There are two features that are especially useful which I want you to look for in your ftp program. The first feature is a "view" function. This allows you to select a file and then view it without actually copying it to your local directory. The file is copied to your computer, but it is not stored permanently. Instead your ftp client stores the data in a temporary file and then calls upon an editor program to display the file for you. This feature is handy when you want to take a quick look at a file but you don't want to keep a copy of it (such as a **README** file).

The second feature to look for in your ftp client is the capability of storing various configurations. This allows you to save the names of your favorite anonymous ftp sites, so you can connect to them easily whenever you want. Indeed, most client programs include configurations for well-known, useful anonymous ftp sites. For example, if your program has a list of configurations, you will probably see well-known software archives for Windows, DOS and Macintosh systems, as such sites are useful to just about everyone.

Files

Once you start using anonymous ftp, you will find you need to know something about files and directories. And since most of the anonymous ftp hosts are Unix computers, you will need to know something about the Unix file system.

You may remember that, in Chapter 1, I told you that it is a good idea to learn some Unix. I pointed out that, even if you do not use Unix yourself, many of the computers you will access are Unix computers. This is especially true when you are using anonymous ftp, so let's take a few moments to discuss some basic ideas.

HINT

In this section, I will give you the short, 75-cent tour of the Unix file system. If you want more information, the best idea is to consult a good Unix book. The one I recommend is *The Unix Companion*, written by me and published by Osborne McGraw-Hill.

Within Unix, the definition of a file is a highly generalized one. A file is considered to be any source of input or any target of output. For our purposes, this definition is too technical so let us be a bit more informal: a FILE is a collection of data.

Files can hold any type of information that can be stored on a computer: programs, documents, pictures, sounds, and so on. Files are kept on some type of storage device: a hard disk, a floppy disk, a CD or a tape. When you use anonymous ftp, you are almost always accessing files stored on a hard disk.

Every file has a name. Whenever you want to do something with a file, you must refer to it by its name. For example, if you want to download a file using anonymous ftp, you must be able to tell your ftp client the name of the file you want. Unix file names can consist of letters, numbers and certain punctuation characters. Here, for example, are two typical Unix file names: `rfc1325.txt` and `rfc-index.txt`.

Unix distinguishes between uppercase (capital) letters and lowercase (small) letters. For this reason, you must be careful to use the exact letters when you type a file name. For example, it would be wrong to refer to the file above as `Rfc1325.txt`. To Unix, the letters `R` and `r` are completely different, so `rfc1325.txt` and `Rfc1325.txt` are two completely different names.

For the most part, Unix file names consist of all lowercase letters. However, there will be times when you encounter a file name that has uppercase letters. When you do, be sure to type the name exactly.

HINT

Many anonymous ftp sites have a file named **README**, which contains special information about that site. The name **README** is spelled in uppercase letters in order to draw attention to the file.

Directories

Within Unix, files are organized into collections called DIRECTORIES. When you connect to an anonymous ftp site, you will find a number of directories. In order to download a file, you must be able to specify the exact name of the directory in which the file lies, as well as the name of the file itself. Here is an example.

In Chapter 13, I explain that many Usenet discussion groups have lists of questions and answers that cover the basic topics discussed in that group. These lists are called FAQs (frequently asked question lists). For instance, the discussion group that discusses urban legends is named **alt.folklore.urban**. This group has a FAQ which is stored in a file named **folklore-faq**.

Around the Net, various computers act as Usenet archive sites by making copies of the FAQs available via anonymous ftp. For example, all of these sites will have the file **folklore-faq**. One well-known Usenet archive is the computer **rtfm.mit.edu**. On this computer, the file **folklore-faq** is kept in the directory named **/pub/usenet/news.answers**.

How can we make sense of that name? To do so, all we need to understand how Unix organizes directories.

Being able to collect files into directories is important. However, many Unix systems have thousands of files and merely collecting them into directories is not enough: we need more levels of organization. The solution is to collect the directories themselves into other directories, to form a hierarchy.

For example, on the **rtfm.mit.edu** computer, all the public directories are kept in a directory named **pub**. Within **pub**, all the directories containing Usenet information are kept in a directory named **usenet**. Within the **usenet** directory, there are files and directories that contain information relating to the various discussion groups.

Now, it happens that there is a special group named **news.answers** whose purpose is to act as a repository for all the FAQs that are posted to the various other groups (see Chapter 13). Thus, on the **rtfm.mit.edu** host, the **usenet** directory contains a directory named **news.answers** which is used to hold all the FAQs. That is why the file named **folklore-faq** is found within the directory named **/pub/usenet/news.answers**.

When a directory contains another directory, the first directory is called the PARENT DIRECTORY, and the second directory is called a SUBDIRECTORY. In our example, **usenet** is a subdirectory of **pub**, while **pub** is the parent directory of **usenet**. Similarly, **news.answers** is a subdirectory of **usenet**, while **usenet** is the parent directory of **news.answers**.

Each Unix computer has one main directory which is the overall parent for all the subdirectories and files on the system. This main directory is called the ROOT DIRECTORY. Within the root directory are subdirectories; within these subdirectories are other subdirectories; and so on. If you were to draw a diagram of such a system, it would look like a tree with branches and sub-branches growing from one main trunk: hence the name "root directory" for the main trunk.

When we write the full name of a subdirectory, we start at the root directory and show each directory we must pass through in order to reach the ultimate branch. In our example, we start at the root directory, pass through the **pub** subdirectory, the **usenet** subdirectory, and finally, we reach the **news.answers** subdirectory. To write this down, we use the following two rules.

First, we use a single **/** (slash) character to indicate the root directory; we do not actually spell the name "root". Second, we use **/** characters to divide one subdirectory name from another, hence, the name **/pub/usenet/news.answers**. Literally, it means, "Start from the root directory, then go to the **pub** subdirectory, then go to the **usenet** subdirectory, and finally, go to the **news.answers** subdirectory."

When you are connected to a Unix computer, you can think of yourself as sitting somewhere in the directory tree. Whichever directory you are in is called your CURRENT DIRECTORY or WORKING DIRECTORY. By using the appropriate commands, you can move from one directory to another. (Imagine moving from one branch of a tree to another.) Each time you move, your current directory changes.

For convenience, we often describe the location of a file by tacking its name onto the end of a sequence of directories. For example, if you want to tell a friend where to find the urban folklore FAQ list, all you have to do is tell him to ftp to **rtfm.mit.edu** and copy the file **/pub/usenet/news.answers/folklore-faq**. Using this name is the same as saying, "The file is **folkore-faq**, and it is found in the directory named **news.answers**, which is in the directory named **usenet**, which is in the directory named **pub**, which is in the root directory."

A description like this—in which the names are separated by **/** characters—is called a PATHNAME or a PATH. Thus, in order to ftp a file, anywhere on the Internet, all you need to know is (1) the name of an anonymous ftp host that has the file, and (2) the pathname of that file. If you take a look at a catalog of Internet resources (such as my book *The Internet Yellow Pages* or the catalog in the back of this book), you will see that ftp resources are described in just this way.

HINT

The trick to making sense out of a pathname is to recognize that the **/** (slash) character is used in two different ways. The **/** at the beginning of a pathname stands for the root directory. The other **/** characters are used as delimiters, to separate one name from another.

As a convenience, there are two special names used as abbreviations within the Unix file system. First, the name **.** (a single period) refers to the current directory. The name **..** (two periods) refers to the parent of the current directory. When you talk about these abbreviations, the **.** character is referred to as "dot".

For example, say you are connected to the **rtfm.mit.edu** computer, and your current directory is **/pub/usenet**. The **.** (dot) directory is **/pub/usenet**. The **..** (dot-dot) directory is **/pub**.

You won't use these abbreviations a lot, but you should know what they mean when you see them. In particular, you should know that selecting the item named **..** from a list of directories will move you one level higher in the tree. For example, if your current directory is **/pub/usenet** and you select the **..** directory, you will move to **/pub**.

Finding Your Way Around a New Computer

When you ftp to a computer for the first time, it may take a while for you to find your way around. To orient yourself, start by looking for certain files and directories.

First, look for a directory called **pub**. Most anonymous ftp hosts contain such a directory to hold all the public files and subdirectories.

Next, in each directory you use, look for one or both of the following files:

```
README
index
```

If either of these files exist, take a look at them before you download other files. The **README** file will contain general information; the **index** file will have a description of what is available.

HINT

The first time you use a new anonymous ftp host, look for a file named **README** in the root directory.

Requesting Anonymous Ftp Services by Mail

If you do not have access to an **ftp** program, there is a way you can request anonymous ftp services by mail. You use a program called ftpmail (which was written by Paul Vixie, who was then working at the DEC Network Systems Lab).

Even if you regularly use the **ftp** program, you may occasionally find it convenient to make ftp requests by mail, for instance, when you need a long directory listing. (See the last example in this section.) You may also find it is sometimes easier to send a request by mail than to use the **ftp** program and do all the work yourself.

To use ftpmail, you mail a message to an ftpmail server. There are several ftpmail servers on the Internet, the principal one being a host computer with the name **ftpmail.decwrl.dec.com**. In this section, I will discuss how to use this particular ftpmail server. At the end of the section, I will show you a list of the other ftpmail servers that you might use.

To use ftpmail, you mail a message to **ftpmail@decwrl.dec.com**. Within the message, you enclose commands, one per line. The commands are instructions for conducting an anonymous ftp session. The ftpmail server will receive the message and carry out the commands on your behalf. The results of the session will be mailed to you automatically. In addition, ftpmail will mail you a note when it receives your request and another note reporting on the actual anonymous ftp session.

When you mail a message to ftpmail, it ignores anything in the **Subject:** line. However, if you do specify a subject, ftpmail will use it as part of the **Subject:** line when it mails you back a note. Thus, if you are mailing more than one request to ftpmail, it is handy to use different subjects to help you identify the replies. To get instructions on how to use ftpmail, send a message to **ftpmail@decwrl.dec.com**. In the body of the message, put the single word **help**.

Before you use ftpmail, it is a good idea to read all the instructions. For reference, Figure 18-2 contains a summary of the most important ftpmail commands. In order for these commands to make sense, you must understand the general principles of anonymous ftp that I explained earlier in the chapter. If you are a Unix person, note that the ftpmail command to change directories is **chdir**, not **cd**.

Using ftpmail is straightforward. To make things easy, use the ftpmail commands in the order they are listed in Figure 18-2, leaving out the commands you don't need. For example, to retrieve a text file, you would normally use the following commands (in this order): **reply**, **connect**, **ascii**, **chdir**, **get**, **quit**.

The following example shows a sample mail message in which we send commands to connect to the anonymous ftp host **cathouse.org**, change to the **/pub/cathouse/humor/british.humour/monty.python/flying.circus** directory, and request the text file named **argument.clinic**.

```
To: ftpmail@decwrl.dec.com
Subject: Example of how to request a text file
reply harley@fuzzball.ucsb.edu
connect cathouse.org
ascii
chdir /pub/cathouse/humor/british.humour/monty.python/flying.circus
get argument.clinic
quit
```

If the file you are retrieving is large (more than 64,000 characters), ftpmail will automatically split it into pieces and mail each piece separately. It is up to you to take the separate messages and put them back together to re-create the original file. (Don't worry, they will be numbered.)

Remember, the results of your request will be sent to you by mail. And, as I explain in Chapter 7, only text files can be sent by regular mail. Thus, if you request a binary file, it must first be converted to a text file. When it arrives, you will have to decode the text in order to re-create the original binary file.

Specifying Your Mail Address

    reply *address*   mail responses to specified address

Connecting to the Host

    connect *host*   connect to specified anonymous ftp host

Setting Options

    ascii   files to be mailed are text files

    binary   files to be mailed are binary files

    uuencode   convert binary files to text using **uuencode**

    compress   compress binary files

Specifying the Directory

    chdir *directory*   change to the specified directory

Requesting Files

    get *file*   send a copy of the specified file

Requesting Information

    help   send a description of how to use ftpmail

    dir [*directory*]   send a long directory listing

    ls [*directory*]   send a short directory listing (names only)

    index *pattern*   search for specified pattern in ftp server's index

Ending the Session

    quit   terminate session, ignore rest of message

Figure 18-2.   *Summary of important ftpmail commands*

In the Unix world, the most common system for encoding binary files as text uses two programs: **uuencode** (to encode binary as text) and **uudecode** (to decode the text back to binary). I discuss these programs and how to use them in Chapter 21. For now, all I will say is that if you ask for a binary file, you will have to tell ftpmail that you want it encoded by using the **uuencode** command. A good place to do this is right after the **binary** command (which tells ftpmail that you are requesting a binary file). If you request a binary file and do not specify what type of encoding you want, ftpmail will, by default, use another less common program named **btoa** (which is probably not what you want).

Thus, to request a binary file, you would normally use the following commands (in this order): **reply**, **connect**, **binary**, **uuencode**, **chdir**, **get**, **quit**. The next example shows a mail message in which we send commands to connect to the anonymous ftp host **ftp.uu.net**, change to the **/doc/literary/obi/DEC/humor** directory, and request the text file named **Lawyer.jokes.Z**. (After we receive this file, we will have to use the **uudecode** program to recover the original binary file, and the **uncompress** program to uncompress the file. This is all explained in Chapter 21.)

```
To: ftpmail@decwrl.dec.com
Subject: Example of how to request a binary file
reply harley@fuzzball.ucsb.edu
connect ftp.uu.net
binary
uuencode
chdir /doc/literary/obi/DEC/humor
get Lawyer.jokes.Z
quit
```

Our last example requests a directory listing by mail. Requests such as this are handy even when you have access to the **ftp** program. In this example, we will request a large list of humor files. Since we will receive this list as a mail message, it is easy to save it for further reference or even forward a copy to a friend.

The anonymous ftp host **cathouse.org** contains a wonderful repository of humor called the Cathouse Archives, compiled by Jason R. Heimbaugh. In the following example, we send ftpmail commands to connect to **cathouse.org**, change to the **/pub/cathouse/humor** directory, and request a long listing of all the subdirectories. (The command **dir *** specifies that we want to look into all the subdirectories.) Once we receive this directory listing, we can scan it for interesting files to request.

```
To: ftpmail@decwrl.dec.com
Subject: Example of requesting a directory listing
reply harley@fuzzball.ucsb.edu
connect cathouse.org
ascii
chdir /pub/cathouse/humor
dir *
quit
```

As I mentioned earlier, there are several other ftpmail servers on the Internet. Figure 18-3 shows their addresses. In spirit, they work the same way I have described in this section, although the details and some of the commands are different.

Before you use one of these ftpmail servers for the first time, send a message asking for instructions. Simply mail a message that contains only one line with the word **help**.

Location	Internet Address
Australia:	`ftpmail@cs.uow.edu.au`
England:	`ftpmail@doc.ic.ac.uk`
France:	`ftpmail@grasp.insa-lyon.fr`
Germany:	`ftpmail@ftp.uni-stuttgart.de`
Ireland:	`ftpmail@ieunet.ie`
Russia:	`ftpmail@kiae.su`
Sweden:	`ftpmail@ftp.luth.se`
USA: California	`ftpmail@decwrl.dec.com`
USA: New Hampshire	`ftpmail@ftp.dartmouth.edu`
USA: New Jersey	`bitftp@pucc.princeton.edu`
USA: North Carolina	`ftpmail@sunsite.unc.edu`

Figure 18-3. *Ftpmail servers*

HINT

The ftpmail server **decwrl.dec.com** is often overloaded. You can usually get a faster response by using one of the other servers. For best results, use the server closest to you.

Chapter Nineteen

Using Anonymous Ftp from a Shell Account: `ftp`

In Chapter 18, I explain how to use anonymous ftp, a system which provides Internet users around the world with free access to many thousands of files. To use anonymous ftp, you run an ftp client program to act as your interface. If you access the Internet via a shell account (Chapter 5), your ftp client will be a program, named **ftp**, running on the Unix host computer. In this chapter, I will show you how to use the **ftp** program. Before you continue, please make sure you have read Chapter 18.

HINT

If you are using Windows or OS/2, you may have a text-based ftp client much like the Unix client. Go to a DOS prompt and type **ftp**. (For OS/2, go to an OS/2 prompt.) If the **ftp** program starts, you have a text-based client, and you should read this chapter.

HINT

If you are using a Unix shell account, it is possible your system manager has installed a program called **ncftp**, a replacement for the standard **ftp** program. **ncftp** has important advantages over **ftp**, which make **ncftp** easier and more convenient to use. If **ncftp** is available on your system, you can display the documentation from the online Unix manual by using the command:

```
man ncftp
```

Starting the ftp Program

To download or upload files from a remote host, you use the **ftp** program. This program acts as a client and connects to the ftp server on a remote host. Once the connection is made, you will be asked to specify a userid and password. You can then enter whatever **ftp** commands you want.

There are two ways to start the **ftp** program. In this section, I will show you how it is done most of the time. In the next section, I will show you an alternate method.

To start **ftp**, enter the name of the command followed by the address of the remote host to which you want to connect. For example, say you want to download files from the computer named **rtfm.mit.edu**. Enter the command:

```
ftp rtfm.mit.edu
```

HINT

As I explained in Chapter 6, all Internet hosts have an official address known as an IP address. This address consists of several numbers separated by periods. For example, the official IP address of **rtfm.mit.edu** is **18.181.0.24**.

Some systems have trouble dealing with certain standard addresses. If you encounter such a problem with **ftp**, try using the IP address. For example, either of the following commands will connect to the same host:

```
ftp rtfm.mit.edu
ftp 18.181.0.24
```

When the **ftp** program starts, it will initiate a connection to the remote host you specified. Once the connection is made—which might take a few moments if the host is far away—you will see a message like the following:

```
Connected to BLOOM-PICAYUNE.MIT.EDU.
220 rtfm ftpd (wu-2.4(26)); bugs to ftp-bugs@rtfm.mit.edu
Name (rtfm.mit.edu:harley):
```

The first line of this message shows us that we have made the connection. Notice that the name of the computer we have connected to is really **bloom-picayune.mit.edu**. This is because the name **rtfm.mit.edu** is actually an alias for **bloom-picayune.mit.edu**.

Such aliasing is fairly common in the world of anonymous ftp because it allows us to use easily remembered names. It also gives system managers the flexibility to change computers whenever they want without confusing people. For example, if it should become necessary for the **rtfm** system manager to use a different computer for anonymous ftp, he does not have to inform everybody of the change. All he has to do is ensure that the address **rtfm.mit.edu** is aliased to the new computer. (Indeed, this did happen: When I wrote the first edition of this book, **rtfm.mit.edu** was aliased to a different computer, **charon.mit.edu**.)

It is especially common to see names that begin with **ftp**. For example, the Electronic Frontier Foundation has an anonymous ftp host named **ftp.eff.org**. (The EFF is a public-service organization dedicated to "the pursuit of policies and activities that will advance freedom and openness in computer-based communications". As part of its work, the EFF maintains an anonymous ftp host that contains a wealth of interesting information, including electronic magazines.)

The public name of the EFF's anonymous ftp host is **ftp.eff.org**. However, when you ftp to this address, you will see that it is actually aliased to another computer. At the time I wrote this chapter, the real computer happened to be **krager.eff.org**.

Now, to return to our example, the second line we saw was:

```
220 rtfm ftpd (wu-2.4(26)); bugs to ftp-bugs@rtfm.mit.edu
```

This tells us the name of the ftp server and the version of the ftp software being used, and where to send mail if you find a bug.

HINT

Notice that the message starts with the number **220**. All messages from the ftp server start with such numbers, and there is no way to get rid of them. However, the numbers are not important and you can ignore them.

One nice thing about the numbers is that they show you exactly which messages are coming from the remote server. Lines that do not begin with a number are from the **ftp** client program.

Finally, let us look at the last line of the message:

```
Name (rtfm.mit.edu:harley):
```

This is a request from our **ftp** client program, asking us what userid we want to use to log in to the computer named **rtfm.mit.edu**. As it happens, we are currently logged in to the local host as **harley**. The **ftp** program knows this and suggests that we may want to use the same userid on the remote system. That is why you see the name **harley** in parentheses.

If you press RETURN, the **ftp** program will use this userid as a default and send it to the remote host. However, in this case (and most of the time), you will want to log in as **anonymous**. Simply type this name and press RETURN:

```
anonymous
```

You will now see:

```
331 Guest login ok, send e-mail address as password.
Password:
```

The ftp server has approved the userid **anonymous**. You are now being asked to enter your mail address as a password. Out of courtesy, it is a good idea to honor this request. Indeed, some ftp servers will not let you log in if your password does not look like a valid address.

HINT

Some ftp servers will examine your password and decide if it looks like your real mail address. If not, you may be denied access.

HINT

Here are two tips to making logging in to an anonymous ftp server faster and easier:

- Use **ftp** as a user name instead of **anonymous**. Most servers will accept either name, but **ftp** is easier to type.

- Instead of using your full mail address as a password, type only your user name and the **@** character. Most servers will accept this abbreviated address and fill in the computer name for themselves.

For example, if your mail address is **harley@fuzzball.ucsb.edu**, you could log in as **ftp** and type **harley@** as a password.

Once you have entered an approved userid and password, you will see a message like the following:

```
230 Guest login ok, access restrictions apply.
ftp>
```

This means that you are officially logged in and can use the anonymous ftp facility.

The second line, **ftp>**, is a prompt from your **ftp** client program. Whenever you see this prompt, you can enter one of the **ftp** commands. I will discuss the various commands later in the chapter and, at that time, I will show you a full anonymous ftp session in which we download a file.

For now, I just want to mention two commands. To display a list of all the **ftp** commands, enter the **?** command. To end the ftp session, use the **quit** command.

The last point I want to cover is what to expect if your ftp client is unable to connect to the remote host. There are three ways in which this might happen. First, the ftp service may be temporarily unavailable. In such cases, you will see:

```
ftp: connect: Connection refused
```

Second, the network connection to the remote host may be inoperative. This might be a problem with the network to which the host is connected, or it might be that the host computer itself is not working. In such cases, you will see a message like:

```
ftp: connect: Host is unreachable
```

The best thing to do is try again later.

Finally, there may be a problem with the address you specified. For example, say that you want to download files from **rtfm.mit.edu**, but you accidentally enter the wrong address:

```
ftp rtff.mit.edu
```

You will see a message like the following:

```
rtff.mit.edu: unknown host
ftp>
```

At this point, you can enter the name of another host. (I will explain how to do this in the next section.) Otherwise, you can use the **quit** command to stop the program.

HINT

The **ftp** message "unknown host" can be misleading. There are many reasons why your ftp client might not be able to make a remote connection. The two most common are:

- You spelled the address of the computer wrong.
- You specified the name of a computer that is not on the Internet.

A Second Way to Start the `ftp` Program

In the previous section, I mentioned there are two ways to start the ftp client program. The first way is to enter the **ftp** command along with the address of the remote host. For example:

```
ftp rtfm.mit.edu
```

The second way is to start **ftp** without specifying a host. Simply enter:

`ftp`

The program will start, but will not make a connection. Instead, you will see:

`ftp>`

This is the **ftp** prompt. It means that the program is waiting for you to enter a command. To connect to a remote host, type **open**, followed by the address of the host. For example:

`open rtfm.mit.edu`

The connection will be made just as if you had specified the address when you entered the **ftp** command.

At the end of the previous section, I gave an example in which an **ftp** command had a bad address. In the example, the remote host was named **rtfm.mit.edu**, but we mistakenly entered:

`ftp rtff.mit.edu`

What happens in such a case is that the **ftp** program tries to make the connection. When it can't, it gives up and displays its prompt, waiting for you to enter a command. In this case, you would see:

```
rtff.mit.edu: unknown host
ftp>
```

You can now enter:

`open rtfm.mit.edu`

If this address doesn't work, you can try another one. If you decide to give up, enter:

`quit`

This will stop the **ftp** program.

Summary of Starting and Stopping the `ftp` Program

There are two ways to start the **ftp** program. Either enter the command with the address of a remote host:

```
ftp rtfm.mit.edu
```

or enter the command by itself:

```
ftp
```

and then, at the **ftp>** prompt, enter an **open** command:

```
open rtfm.mit.edu
```

To stop **ftp**, wait for the **ftp>** prompt and enter the **quit** command:

```
quit
```

An Overview of the `ftp` Commands

Once you have entered the **ftp** command and established a connection with a remote host, you will see the prompt:

```
ftp>
```

At this point, you can enter an **ftp** command (of which there are many). The ftp client program will send whatever command you enter to the ftp server, which will carry out your request. The idea is to enter one command after another until you have achieved your goal (say, to download a file). Then enter the **quit** command to terminate the ftp session.

At any time, you can display a list of all the **ftp** commands by entering **?** or **help** (either will do). Figure 19-1 contains a typical response from such a command. (Do not worry if your **ftp** client does not have all these commands. It will have the most important ones.)

If you want to see a one-line summary of a particular command, enter **?** (or **help**) followed by the name of the command. For example, if you enter:

```
? quit
```

you will see:

```
quit    terminate ftp session and exit
```

Notice how many commands there are in Figure 19-1. The number of commands you see will vary, depending on what version of the ftp software you are using.

You might wonder, do you have to learn all these commands? The answer is no. For normal anonymous ftp sessions, all you need to know are the commands summarized in Figure 19-2. I will discuss these commands in the following section.

HINT

To stop an **ftp** command as it is executing, press CTRL-C. (On some systems, you may have to press DELETE.)

The Basic ftp Commands

We can divide the **ftp** commands into several groups. First, there are the basic commands. I have already discussed **quit**, **?** and **help** (which is the same as **?**).

The other basic command is **!** (exclamation mark). This command is used to send a regular Unix command to your local computer. Simply type the command after the **!**

At the **ftp>** prompt, you can enter **?** or **help** to display a summary of all the possible commands that are recognized by the ftp server. Here is such a summary:
Commands may be abbreviated. Commands are:

!	cr	macdef	proxy	send
$	delete	mdelete	sendport	status
account	debug	mdir	put	struct
append	dir	mget	pwd	sunique
ascii	disconnect	mkdir	quit	tenex
bell	form	mls	quote	trace
binary	get	mode	recv	type
bye	glob	mput	remotehelp	user
case	hash	nmap	rename	verbose
cd	help	ntrans	reset	?
cdup	lcd	open	rmdir	
close	ls	prompt	runique	

Figure 19-1.   *A list of all the ftp commands*

Basic Commands

`quit`	close connection to remote host, stop **ftp** program
`?`	display a list of all the **ftp** commands
`? `*command*	display one-line summary of the specified command
`help`	display a list of all the **ftp** commands
`help `*command*	display one-line summary of the specified command
`!`	local: pause **ftp** and start a shell
`! `*command*	local: execute specified shell command

Connecting

`open `[*host*]	establish connection to specified computer
`close`	close the connection to remote host, stay in **ftp**
`user `[*name* [*password*]]	set user name

Directories

`cd `[*directory*]	remote: change to specified directory
`cdup`	remote: change to parent directory
`dir `[*directory* [*local-file*]]	remote: display a long directory listing
`lcd `[*directory*]	local: change directory
`ls `[*directory* [*local-file*]]	remote: display a short directory listing
`pwd`	remote: display name of current directory

Transferring Files

`get `[*remote-file* [*local-file*]]	download one file
`mget `[*remote-file...*]	download multiple files

Setting Options

`ascii`	(default) set file type to ASCII text file

Figure 19-2. *Summary of the most useful* **ftp** *commands*

character and then press RETURN. The **ftp** program will put itself on hold and send the command to your Unix shell to be executed. Once the command is finished, the **ftp** program will regain control and redisplay its prompt.

Here is an example. We want to use the Unix **date** command to display the time and date on your local system. At the **ftp>** prompt, we enter **!date**. After the **date** command displays its output, we are returned to an **ftp>** prompt:

```
ftp> !date
Thu Dec 21 19:20:42 PDT 1995
ftp>
```

If you would like to enter more than one Unix command, you can use the ! character by itself:

```
ftp> !
```

The **ftp** program will put itself on hold and start a new shell. You can now enter as many Unix commands as you want. When you are finished, terminate the shell and the **ftp** program will regain control. With most shells, you would press CTRL-D to terminate the shell. If this does not work, try the **exit** command.

The Connection ftp Commands

The next category of **ftp** commands are those that control the connection to the remote host: **open**, **close** and **user**. I have already discussed the **open** command, which you can use to establish an ftp connection.

The **close** command will terminate an ftp connection without quitting the **ftp** program. You can use **close** when you want to close one connection and then open another one.

If you connect to a remote host successfully, but there is something wrong with your user name or password, you may or may not lose your connection. (This depends on the ftp server.) However, if you do not lose the connection, you will not be able to do anything until you specify a valid userid and password. To do so, you can use the **user** command. Simply enter:

```
user
```

The **ftp** program will ask you to enter a userid and then a password. If you want, you can specify the information directly:

```
user anonymous harley@fuzzball.ucsb.edu
```

In this case, we are specifying a userid of **anonymous** and a password of **harley@fuzzball.ucsb.edu**.

The Directory ftp Commands

The third group of **ftp** commands are those which move from one directory to another and display the contents of a directory. Whichever directory you are in is called your working directory (or current directory). Once you establish an ftp connection, you have two working directories to keep track of: one on the remote host and one on your local computer.

With most anonymous ftp hosts, you are automatically placed in the root (top-level) directory to start. To move to another directory, use the **cd** (change directory) command. Type the command name, followed by the name of the directory you want to move to, and then press RETURN. For example, if you want to move to the directory named **/pub/usenet/news.answers**, enter:

```
cd /pub/usenet/news.answers
```

If you understand the Unix file system, you can move one directory at a time by using separate **cd** commands. For example:

```
cd pub
cd usenet
cd news.answers
```

Unfortunately, the techniques you need to use the **cd** command in this way are beyond the scope of the book. Please refer to a Unix book for more details. (I recommend my book *The Unix Companion*, published by Osborne McGraw-Hill.)

At any time, you can display the name of your remote working directory by using the **pwd** (print working directory) command. For example, if you enter:

```
pwd
```

you will see a message similar to the following one:

```
257 "/pub/usenet/news.answers" is current directory.
```

(Remember, messages from the ftp server start with a number.)

At times, you may see a directory name that is different from what you expect. For example, on the **rtfm.mit.edu** system, if you move to the directory named **/pub/usenet/news.answers** and then enter a **pwd** command, you will actually see:

```
257 "/pub/usenet-by-group/news.answers" is current directory.
```

Do not be confused. All that this means is that the system manager has given the second level directory two different names: **usenet** and **usenet-by-group**. (In Unix, files and directories can have more than one name.) In such cases, you can use whichever name you want. The name **usenet-by-group** is more informative, but the name **usenet** is a lot easier to type.

In Unix, the word "print" is often used to mean "display". Thus, the job of the **pwd** (print working directory) command is to display the name of your working directory. This tradition dates back to the earliest days of Unix when terminals actually printed their output on paper.

The working directory on your local computer will be whatever directory you happened to be in when you entered the **ftp** command. When you download files, this is the directory into which they will be placed. If you want your files to be placed into a different directory, you can use the **lcd** (local change directory) command to move to a different directory before you start the downloading. For example:

```
lcd faq-files
```

This command changes your local working directory to **faq-files**. Again, it will help you to read a Unix book for more information. In particular, you should learn how to make your own directories and how to move from one directory to another.

There is no **ftp** command to display the name of your local working directory. However, it is possible to do this by using the **!** command to send a **pwd** command to your local computer:

```
!pwd
```

Before you start an anonymous ftp session, decide which directory on your local computer you want to use to store the downloaded files. Use the Unix **cd** command to move to that directory *before* you enter the **ftp** command. That way, you will not have to use a **lcd** command to ensure that your downloaded files are placed in the proper directory.

To display the contents of a directory on the remote host you can use two different commands. The **ls** (list) command will display the names of all the files in the

directory. Here is some typical output. It shows the names of some of the files in the
news.answers directory I discussed above:

```
esperanto-faq
feminism
finding-addresses
finding-sources
fleas-ticks
folklore-faq
fonts-faq
```

The **dir** command will display a longer listing. Along with the file name, you will
also see extra information. Here is some typical output:

```
-rw-rw-r--   8 root    3    27120 Jun  2 01:24 esperanto-faq
drwxrwxr-x   2 root    3      512 Jun 12 00:07 feminism
-rw-rw-r--  14 root    3    28880 Jun 12 03:37 finding-addresses
-rw-rw-r--  12 root    3    41939 Jun 16 04:04 finding-sources
-rw-rw-r--  10 root    3    41533 Jun 16 03:30 fleas-ticks
-rw-rw-r--   8 root    3    84701 Jun 15 03:33 folklore-faq
drwxrwxr-x   2 root    3      512 Jun 18 01:46 fonts-faq
```

If you have some experience with the Unix file commands, you will recognize this
output as being from the **ls -l** command. Otherwise, don't worry about it. You only
need to understand four things.

First, the character at the far left tells you if the line describes a directory or a file. A
d character indicates a directory while a - (hyphen) character indicates a file. In this
example, we have two directories and five files.

At the far right of each line, we see the name of the file or directory.

To the left of the name, the time and date show you when the file or directory was
updated.

Finally, the number to the left of the time and date shows the size of the file in
bytes (characters). This number is not meaningful for directories.

Thus, we can see that **folklore-faq** is a file, it was last updated on June 15 at
3:33 AM, and is 84,701 characters long. You can ignore the rest of the information.

You will find that it is often convenient to download a copy of a long directory
listing to a file on your local computer. To do so, simply specify the name of the
directory followed by the name of a file. For example:

```
ls /pub/usenet/news.answers ls.list
dir /pub/usenet/news.answers dir.list
```

Each of these commands generates a directory listing of the specified directory. The
first command downloads its output to a file on your local computer named **ls.list**.

The second command sends its output to a local file named **dir.list**. (Of course, you can choose whatever names you want.)

When you use this form of the **ls** and **dir** commands, you must always specify a directory name and a local file name. If you want to download a listing of the working directory, you can use a directory name of **.** (a single period character). In Unix, a single **.** character stands for your working directory. For example:

```
ls . ls.list
dir . dir.list
```

The File Transfer `ftp` Commands

There are two commands you can use to download files (that is, to copy files from the remote host to your computer). These commands are **get** and **mget**.

The **get** command allows you to download one file at a time. The **mget** (multiple get) command allows you to download more than one file at a time.

To use **get**, specify the name of the remote file followed by the name that you want to give the file on your local computer. For example, say that you have established an anonymous ftp session with the **rtfm.mit.edu** computer I mentioned earlier. You would like to download the **folklore-faq** file. You want the file to be named **urban-legends** on your computer. First, move to the directory that contains the file:

```
cd /pub/usenet/news.answers
```

Now, enter the **get** command to download the file:

```
get folklore-faq urban-legends
```

You will see the following messages:

```
200 PORT command successful.
150 Opening ASCII mode data connection for folklore-faq (84701 bytes).
```

At this point, the file is being copied to your computer. Once the copy is complete, you will see:

```
226 Transfer complete.
local: urban-legends remote: folklore-faq
86113 bytes received in 17 seconds (4.9 Kbytes/s)
ftp>
```

You can now enter another command. (By the way, don't worry about the fact that the file is 84,701 bytes long but we received 86,113 bytes. The extra bytes have to do with how certain characters are encoded when you copy a text file. Rest assured that the actual downloaded file will be exactly the right size.)

If you use the **get** command with only a single file name, the **ftp** program will use this name for the new file on your local computer. For example, if you enter:

```
get folklore-faq
```

HINT

If you already have a file with the same name on your local computer, the existing file will be replaced. Once a file is replaced, there is no way to get it back, so be careful.

the downloaded file will automatically be named **folklore-faq**.

If you are using a Unix system, there is a way to send the remote file as input to a Unix command on your local computer, rather than to a local file. Instead of a second file name, you type a | (vertical bar, called the pipe symbol), followed by the name of the command.

For example, suppose that you want to read a remote file named **README**. One way is to download it to a local file, stop or pause the ftp session, read the file, delete the file, and then resume the ftp session. Alternatively, you can read the remote file by sending it directly to a paging program (such as **more**) on your local computer:

```
get README |more
```

Notice that you cannot put a space after the | character (like you can with a regular Unix command). This is because **get** expects only two words: the remote file name (in this case, **README**) and the name of the local target (in this case, **|more**).

The **mget** (multiple get) command is used when you want to download more than one file at the same time. Type the command, followed by the names of the files you want to download. For example:

```
mget finding-addresses finding-sources folklore-faq
```

When you use **mget**, you cannot specify alternate names, so the files will be given the same names when they are copied to your local computer.

The **mget** command will transfer one file at a time. Before transferring a file, **mget** will display the file name and ask you for confirmation. For example:

```
mget finding-addresses?
```

At this point you can type either **y** (yes) or **n** (no) and press RETURN.

HINT

You can interrupt any **ftp** command, including **get** and **mget**, by pressing CTRL-C. (On some systems, you have to use DELETE.)

Here is what I like about **mget**: You can specify the name of a directory and **mget** will process each file in the directory. Similarly, if you know how to use the Unix wildcard characters, you can download all the files whose name matches a particular pattern.

If you do not know about wildcard characters, I will mention briefly that an ***** (asterisk) character matches zero or more characters, and a **?** (question mark) character matches any single character. For example, to download all the files in the remote working directory whose names begin with the letters **fi**, you can use:

```
mget fi*
```

For more information on using such patterns, consult a Unix book. (Or experiment using the **ls** command; for example, try **ls fi*** to list the names of all the files that begin with **fi**.)

HINT

In this chapter, I have concentrated on downloading because that is what you usually do with anonymous ftp. However, the **ftp** program also has commands to upload. They are **put** (to upload a single file) and **mput** (to upload more than one file at a time). These commands use the same format as **get** and **mget**.

For more information, see the documentation for your local **ftp** program. If you are using a Unix computer, you can display the **ftp** entry in the online manual by entering the command **man ftp**.

Setting ftp **Options**

Within the **ftp** program, there are several commands you can use to control the downloading operation. The ones I will talk about are **binary**, **ascii**, **hash**, **prompt** and **status**.

In Chapter 7, I explain the difference between text files and binary files. If you are not sure, you might want to take a quick look now. Briefly, a text file (also called an ASCII file) holds ordinary characters: letters, numbers, punctuation, and so on. The files I used as examples in this chapter are all text files.

A binary file contains information that is not textual. For example, if you want to download files that contain pictures, you will be dealing with binary files.

By default, the **ftp** program assumes that it is working with text files. If you want to download binary files, you should tell the program before you enter the **get** or **mget** command.

The **binary** command tells the **ftp** program that you will be downloading binary files. If you want to switch back, the **ascii** command indicates that you will be downloading text files. When you use one of these commands, we say that you are setting the REPRESENTATION TYPE.

For example, say that you are about to download some files that contain pictures. Before you do, you enter the command:

binary

When you enter this command, you will see the following message:

200 Type set to I.

The **I** stands for "image". (Don't worry about it.)

If you use the **binary** command and then download a text file, it will work just fine (although it may be a bit slower). It's only when you are copying binary files that you should be exact. With some remote hosts, a binary file will not be copied properly unless you have set the representation type to **binary**.

HINT

You will often encounter files whose names end in **.Z** or **.tar**. These files use special formats that I discuss in Chapter 21. (A **.Z** file is compressed; a **.tar** file contains a collection of files called an archive.) Such files are always binary files.

Files whose names end in **.txt** are always text files.

If you are not sure what type of file you are downloading, set **binary** just to be safe.

The next option I want to mention is **hash**. This tells the **ftp** program to display a **#** character (sometimes called a hash mark) after each data block is transferred. This allows you to watch the progress when you are downloading a large file. The size of a data block depends on the nature of your ftp connection, but you will be told what it is before the downloading starts.

To turn on the **hash** option, just enter:

```
hash
```

To turn it off, enter the same command again.

The last option I want to mention is **prompt**. As I explained in the previous section, the ftp client will query you about each file whenever you use **mget**. If you set the **prompt** option off, **mget** will automatically transfer each file without asking your permission. To turn off the **prompt** option, just enter:

```
prompt
```

To turn it back on, enter the same command again.

Finally, if you want to display the current setting of all the options, you can use the **status** command:

```
status
```

When you do, you will see many options, most of which you can safely ignore.

A Typical Anonymous Ftp Session

Figure 19-3 contains the full listing of a typical anonymous ftp session. The commands you would type are printed in boldface.

In this example, we connect to **rtfm.mit.edu**. We use a userid of **anonymous** and a password of our mail address. (As with all such systems, the password is not echoed as we type it.)

We then change to the **/pub/usenet/news.answers** directory and set the **hash** option on. Next, we use **get** to download the file named **folklore-faq**.

Once the downloading is complete, we enter the **quit** command to close the connection to **rtfm.mit.edu** and end the session.

```
% ftp rtfm.mit.edu
Connected to BLOOM-PICAYUNE.MIT.EDU.
220 rtfm ftpd (wu-2.4(26)); bugs to ftp-bugs@rtfm.mit.edu

Name (rtfm.mit.edu:harley): anonymous
331 Guest login ok, send e-mail address as password.
Password:
230 Guest login ok, access restrictions apply.

ftp> cd /pub/usenet/news.answers
250 CWD command successful.

ftp> hash
Hash mark printing on (8192 bytes/hash mark).

ftp> get folklore-faq
200 PORT command successful.
150 Opening ASCII mode data connection for folklore-faq (84701 bytes).
##########
226 Transfer complete.
local: folklore-faq remote: folklore-faq
86113 bytes received in 17 seconds (4.9 Kbytes/s)

ftp> quit
221 Goodbye.
```

Figure 19-3. *A sample anonymous ftp session*

Chapter Twenty

Archie

In Chapter 18, I discuss anonymous ftp and how it provides us with one of the largest collections of public information ever amassed by human beings. Best of all, the anonymous ftp archives are available for free to anyone on the Internet. Indeed, as I discussed at the end of Chapter 18, even people who only have access to Internet mail can request anonymous ftp files.

In order to download a file via anonymous ftp, you need to know where that file is located. In particular, you need to know the address of an anonymous ftp host and the name of the directory that contains the file. This is not a lot to ask but, in the enormous world of anonymous ftp, how do you know where to look?

The answer is you use archie: the card catalog for the largest library in the history of the world.

What Is Archie?

In the vast reaches of the Internet, there are tens of thousands of anonymous ftp servers. However, there is no central directory in which you can look up a particular file. The ARCHIE service, however, does help fill this gap. If you know the name of a file, or even part of the name, archie can help you find it. Here is how the system works.

Throughout the Internet, there are a number of computers, called ARCHIE SERVERS, that provide a very important service: they help you find the names of anonymous ftp servers that contain a particular file or directory. The name archie was chosen because it sounds like the word "archive". Because of its name, we tend to talk about archie as if it were a person, or at least an intelligent robot.

When you need to find an anonymous ftp file or directory, all you have to do is tell archie what you are looking for. Archie will search its database and display the names of each anonymous ftp server that has the file or directory. Archie will also show you the exact directory path. Thus, once you have the information from archie, all you need to do is ftp to the server and download your file.

There are three ways to use an archie server, all of which I will cover in this chapter.

First, you can use an archie client to contact an archie server on your behalf. You tell the archie client what you are looking for. It connects to the server, asks it to perform the search, waits for the output, and then displays the results for you.

 **INTERNET RESOURCE** *Look in the catalog under Internet Resources for*
Archie Clients Programs

The second way to use archie is to telnet to an archie server and log in with a userid of **archie**. (The telnet service allows you to connect to a remote computer, log in, and work with it directly; see Chapter 23.) Once you log in to an archie server, a special program will start automatically. You can now enter commands, one at a time, and work with the archie server interactively. You tell the program what you want. It will search the database as you wait and then display the results. If you are not sure exactly what file you want, archie offers another facility—called a "whatis" service—that has descriptions of thousands of different programs, data files and documents.

Finally, if you are not in a hurry or you don't have direct access to the Internet, you can mail a request to any archie server. The server will carry out your request and mail back the results.

 **INTERNET RESOURCE** *Look in the catalog under Internet Resources for* ***Archie Search Facilities on the Web***

How Does Archie Work?

Conceptually, the workings of archie are surprisingly simple. At regular intervals, special programs connect to every known anonymous ftp host and download a full directory listing of all the public files. These lists are stored in what is called the "Internet Archives Database". When you ask archie to look for a file, all it needs to do is check the database.

The various archie server sites around the world each keep track of the anonymous ftp hosts in a certain portion of the Internet. For example, the Australian archie host keeps track of all the Australian anonymous ftp hosts. This information is shared so that all archie servers are kept up to date as much as possible. On the average, anonymous ftp hosts are checked about once a week.

Of course, there are a lot of details to take care of, so we should be grateful that someone else is providing this service. Archie servers keep track of several million files on thousands of different anonymous ftp hosts.

Archie was originally developed as a project by students and volunteer staff at the McGill University School of Computer Science in Montreal, Canada. The software was written by Alan Emtage and Bill Heelan with help from Peter Deutsch.

HINT

As you read about archie, you may see references to Prospero. This is a tool that allows you to access information spread around the Internet. Using Prospero, you can organize and use files that are stored on remote computers as easily as if they were on your own local computer.

The distributed file system that Prospero creates is based on an idea called the Virtual System Model, and is widely used throughout the Internet. Anyone can use Prospero by installing a Prospero client on their computer. Archie clients and servers use the Prospero technology to implement their client/server relationship, although the details are hidden from view.

Prospero was developed by Cliff Neuman of the Information Sciences Institute, a part of the University of Southern California.

Using an Archie Client

In general, archie clients are easy to use. After all, the real work is done by the server. All you need to do is tell your client the name of the file for which you are looking. It will contact an archie server on your behalf, issue your request, wait for the output, and then display it on your screen. And, as you will see in the next section, you don't even have to know the complete file name. If you know part of the name, you can tell archie to look for files whose names match a particular pattern.

If you connect to the Net using either PPP or a direct network connection, you will use a graphical archie client. If you connect via a shell account, you will use a text-based archie client which runs on the remote Unix computer. (I discuss the various types of Internet connections in Chapter 5.) In this section, I will discuss how to use a graphical archie client. Later in the chapter, I will show you how to use the text-based Unix client. If you use Unix, read this section anyway, as it contains several important ideas I want you to understand.

Using archie can be astonishingly fast; I have often received a response in just a few seconds. (Of course, when the server gets busy, your response time can slow down considerably.)

Graphical archie clients are especially easy to use. All you have to do is specify the file name (or pattern) for which you want to search. Tell your client to submit the request and then wait for the results. Figure 20-1 shows a screen shot of a typical graphical archie client.

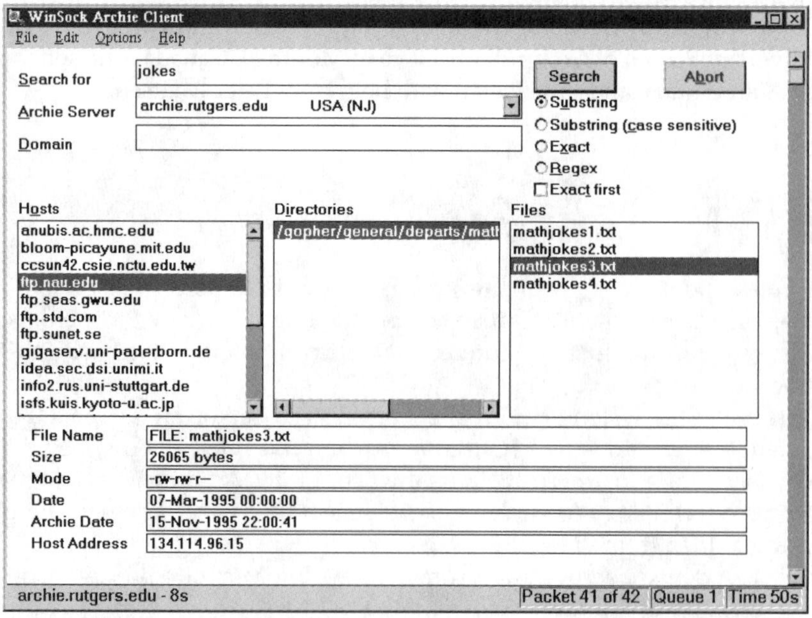

Figure 20-1. *A graphical archie client*

Most archie clients have options to give you some control over the search process. The three most important options are specifying a search pattern, choosing which archie server you want to use, and limiting the results of the search.

Specifying a search pattern can be a bit complex, so I will discuss it as a separate topic in the next section.

Choosing an archie server is straightforward. Your archie client will have a list of possible archie servers. You can use whichever one you want, or let the program choose one for you. Why would you want to choose the archie server yourself? If you find yourself waiting too long, you might try a different server to see if you can get a faster response. For reference, Figure 20-4, later in the chapter, has a list of public archie servers.

HINT

To choose an archie server, start with the one which is geographically closest to you. If the response time is too slow, try the next-closest server. Keep going until you find a server you like.

The third important option allows you to limit the results of the search by domain name. Remember, the results of a search consist of a list of anonymous ftp servers that contain the file you want. If there are many such servers, there is no point listing them all. The most useful thing to do is to list the ftp servers that are close to you. The way to do so is to specify an appropriate domain restriction.

For example, if you are in England, you could tell your archie client to limit the search to ftp servers with a top-level domain of **uk**. This tells the archie server you are interested only in ftp servers whose address ends with **uk**.

HINT

If you want to confine an archie search to the United States, use a domain restriction of **usa**. Archie will know what to do.

In this context, the name **usa** is a "pseudo-domain". Here is a list of the most useful pseudo-domains:

```
america, northamerica, centralamerica, southamerica, usa
europe, westeurope, easteurope, scandinavia
asia, mideast
africa
```

Once you find an anonymous ftp server that has what you want, the next step is to download the actual file. Most graphical clients make it easy to do an archie search and then download the file without having to copy the address of an ftp server from one program to another.

Some programs combine the functionality of both archie and ftp in a single program. If you have such a client, it will search for what you want and then download it with a minimum of fuss.

Other programs can act only as archie clients. However, there will usually be some way to make downloading easy after an archie search. For example, your archie client may have a way for you to specify the name of your ftp program. If so, whenever an archie search finishes, your archie client can launch the ftp program for you and tell it the name of the file and ftp host to use in order to download what you want.

Specifying a Search Pattern

The main function that an archie server performs is to search its database for the name of a file or directory. If you know the exact name, the search is straightforward. Archie will look for it and send you the results. However, there will be many times when you know only part of a name. In such cases, you can specify a pattern, and archie will search for names in the database that match the pattern.

For example, say you are looking for anonymous ftp sites that have free games. You might tell archie to search for all the names in its database that begin with the characters **game**. This would find such names as **games**, **game-archive**, **games-PC**, and so on. To help you find just what you want, archie recognizes three different types of searching: exact, substring, and regular expression.

An exact search tells archie to look for names that match the search pattern exactly. For example, an exact search for **harley** would only match names consisting of exactly those characters.

A substring search tells archie to look for any names that contain the search pattern. For example, a substring search for **harley** would match, not only the exact name **harley**, but any name that contains the pattern, such as **harley1**, **harley.exe**, **charley**, **new-harley-file.zip**, and so on.

A regular expression search allows you to be more sophisticated. The idea of a REGULAR EXPRESSION is taken from Unix, where it is used as a compact way of defining a pattern in which a number of variations are possible.

For example, by using a regular expression, you could tell archie to search for all the names that contain the characters **harley** followed by a single digit, from **0** to **9**. In this case, the regular expression to use would be:

```
harley[0-9]
```

Here is a more complex example. Say you wanted archie to look for all the names beginning with **harley**, followed by one or more numbers, followed by zero or more characters of any type, and ending with **.zip**. The regular expression to use would be:

```
^harley[0-9][0-9]*.*\.zip$
```

HINT

When you want to match the beginning or end of a name, you must use the beginning (^) and end ($) characters explicitly. Otherwise, archie will automatically surround the regular expression with .* (which will match any number of characters).

As you can see, regular expressions can be complex. I won't go into all the details here; for that, you should consult a good Unix book. (Any one of mine will do; regular expressions are a basic part of Unix.) For reference, I have summarized all the important archie regular expressions for you in Figure 20-2. If you want more information about how archie uses regular expressions, you can telnet to an archie server (explained later in the chapter) and use the command:

```
help regex
```

HINT

Unlike standard Unix regular expressions, archie regular expressions that are not anchored with ^ or $ characters are assumed to have .* (match zero or more characters of any type) at the beginning and end of the search pattern.

For example, the regular expression **harley** is the same as .*harley.*; that is, it will match any name containing zero or more characters, followed by **harley**, followed by zero or more characters.

In other words, a regular expression search with no special characters is the same as a substring search.

Symbol	Meaning
.	match any single character
*	match zero or more occurrences of the preceding character
.*	match zero or more occurrences of any character
^	the beginning of a name
$	the end of a name
[ ]	match any one of the enclosed characters
[^]	match any character that is not one of the enclosed characters
x-y	a range of characters, from x to y
\x	treat character x literally (ignore special meaning)

Figure 20-2. *Important symbols used in archie regular expressions*

All archie clients allow you to use variations of the three main types of searches (exact, substring and regular expression). For example, you may be able to specify whether or not a search should be case sensitive. (That is, whether or not archie should distinguish between upper- and lowercase letters.)

The fastest type of archie search is an exact search, because it is the simplest. Your archie client may offer you an option to start with an exact search, and proceed with another type of search only if the exact search was unsuccessful. If so, this combination is often faster than a plain substring search.

HINT

Take some time to get to know the search options provided by your archie client. Whenever possible, start with an exact search.

Using an Archie Client From a Shell Account: `archie`

If you access the Internet via a shell account (see Chapter 5), you use text-based Unix client programs that run on the remote computer. The name of the text-based Unix archie client is **archie**. To use this program, it must be installed on your system. To find out if this is the case, try performing a search by entering the **archie** command followed by something to search for. For example:

```
archie rfc1325.txt
```

If you do not have the **archie** program on your system, you will see a message like the following:

```
archie: Command not found.
```

If this is the case, the only ways for you to access archie are to telnet to an archie server or to send a request by mail (both of which are explained later in the chapter). Since using an archie client is so much more convenient, you may want to politely ask your system manager if he or she could install **archie** on your system. The program is available by **anonymous ftp**. (Just telnet to a public archie server and search for **archie**.)

If you do have the **archie** program on your system, you can read the official documentation from the online manual by using the **man** command:

```
man archie
```

The easiest way to use **archie** is to specify the name of a file or directory you want to find. For example:

```
archie rfc1325.txt
```

The archie client will connect to an archie server, have it perform a search, and return the results to you.

One nice thing about using an archie client is you can manipulate the output using the standard Unix tools. For example, the following command performs the same archie search and saves the output in a file named **rfc**:

```
archie rfc1325.txt > rfc
```

If a file named **rfc** does not already exist, Unix will create it for you. If the file does exist, it will be replaced and the original contents will be lost, so be careful.

HINT

In Unix, you can use a **>** (greater than) character followed by a file name at the end of any command to send output to the specified file. This is called "redirecting the standard output to a file". To find out more about such matters, I refer you to any good Unix book. (The best one is my book *The Unix Companion*, published by Osborne McGraw-Hill.)

As with many Unix commands, **archie** has a number of ways for you to change the behavior of the command. To do so, you include what are called OPTIONS or SWITCHES directly after the command name. For example, the **-t** option tells archie to sort the output by the time and date that the file was last modified, from newest to oldest:

```
archie -t rfc1325.txt
```

For reference, Figure 20-3 contains a summary of the most important **archie** options.

To perform a substring search, use the **-s** option:

```
archie -s rfc1325
```

The **-e** option performs an **exact** search, which is the default. Thus, the following two commands are equivalent:

```
archie rfc1325.txt
archie -e rfc1325.txt
```

You can combine the **-e** option with another search type to indicate a combined search. That is, start with an exact search (which is fast) and, if nothing is found, try another type of search. For example:

```
archie -e -s rfc1325
```

Option	Description
-c	search for substrings, case sensitive
-e	search for an exact match [default]
-r	search using a regular expression
-s	search for substrings
-o*filename*	send the output to the specified file
-1	list one item per line
-t	sort the output by time and date
-m*number*	set the maximum number of items to find
-h*address*	send archie server requests to the specified host
-L	show a list of archie servers known to the program
-v	(verbose) make comments during a long search

Figure 20-3.   *Summary of important options for the Unix* **archie** *client*

This command tells archie to start with an exact search, then if that doesn't work, to try a substring search.

You can control the formatting of the output by using the **-t** and **-1** options. The **-t** option sorts by time. The **-1** option formats the output so that it is suitable to send to another Unix program for further processing. For example:

```
archie -l rfc1325.txt
```

Here is some sample output from the previous command. Notice that archie has formatted the output so that each item is on a single line:

```
199205150000000Z   91885 esel.cosy.sbg.ac.at /pub/mirror/rfc/rfc1325.txt
199205150000000Z   91885 swdsrv.edvz.univie.ac.at /doc/rfc/rfc1325.txt
199205140000000Z   91884 plaza.aarnet.edu.au /rfc/rfc1325.txt
199206010000000Z   91884 sunb.ocs.mq.edu.au /Documents/RFC/rfc1325.txt
199208170000000Z   91885 sifon.cc.mcgill.ca /pub/ftp_inc/doc/rfc/rfc1325.txt
```

If you know how to use Unix, you can send this type of output to another program. For instance, the following series of commands displays all the items that are stored on Australian computers (those whose addresses end in **.au**):

```
archie -l rfc1325.txt | grep '.au '
```

For the details of how the **grep** command works, check with a good Unix book. (Guess which one I recommend?)

The **-m** option specifies the maximum number of items you want to see. For example, to ask for a maximum of 10 items, use a command like the following:

```
archie -m10 rfc1325.txt
```

HINT

To speed up an archie search, use the **-m** option to limit the amount of output. (I recommend **-m10**.) If you do not find what you want, re-enter the command with a larger value.

As I explained above, you can use the Unix redirection facility to send the output of an archie search to a file. Alternatively, you can do the same thing with the **-o** option. Thus, the following two commands are equivalent:

```
archie rfc1325.txt -orfc
archie rfc1325.txt > rfc
```

When you use the **archie** program, it connects to the archie server whose name was specified by your system manager when he or she installed the program. If you want to see the name of this server, enter:

```
archie -L
```

This command will also display a list of other archie servers. If you would like to send a request to a specific archie server, you can use the **-h** (host) command and specify the server you want. For example, the following command sends a request to the archie server whose address is **archie.au**:

```
archie -harchie.au rfc1325.txt
```

Finally, the last option I will discuss is useful when you are requesting a time consuming search. By using **-v** (verbose), you tell your archie client to make comments every now and then:

```
archie -v rfc1325.txt
```

Whenever the search seems to be taking a long time, you will see a suitable message. For example:

```
Searching...
```

In this way, you are reassured that something is happening, and your anxiety remains at a comfortable level.

Using an Archie Server Interactively

Archie servers are unique (compared to other Internet servers) in that you can use them directly. To do so, you connect to an archie server using telnet (see Chapter 23) and then enter commands. I feel it is important for you to learn how to use an archie server in this way. Much of the time, an archie client program will be all you will need. However, there will be situations in which you want to do one search after another and, at such times, being able to use an archie server directly is a big help. Moreover, if you use a shell account and your system does not have the **archie** client program, using telnet to connect to an archie server is the only reasonable alternative.

In order to log in to an archie server, you will have to enter a user name. Use the name **archie**. No password is necessary. (If you are asked for a password, simply press RETURN.)

Figure 20-4 contains a list of the public archie servers available to Internet users. For example, the following Unix **telnet** command will connect to the archie server at Rutgers University:

```
telnet archie.rutgers.edu
```

If you are using a PPP connection (see Chapter 5), start a telnet client and specify the address of the archie server you want to use. You can use any archie server you want, but you will probably find it faster to use one that is relatively close to you.

HINT

Archie servers generally have a limit on how many people can telnet to them at the same time. If the closest archie server is busy, use the next closest one, or wait for a while and try again.

Once you log in as **archie**, you will see some welcoming messages. You will then see the following prompt:

```
archie>
```

Archie is now ready for your commands. To stop archie, enter the command **quit**. To display help information, use the **help** command. (I will talk more about **help** later, because there are some nuances.)

Using archie is a three-part process. First, you set things up the way you want, according to your preferences. Then you do the actual work. Then you quit. (Just like life.)

Location	Internet Address
Australia	archie.au
Austria	archie.univie.ac.at
Canada	archie.bunyip.com
Canada	archie.cs.mcgill.ca
Finland	archie.funet.fi
France	archie.univ-rennes1.fr
Germany	archie.th-darmstadt.de
Israel	archie.ac.il
Italy	archie.unipi.it
Japan	archie.wide.ad.jp
Korea	archie.kornet.nm.kr
Korea	archie.sogang.ac.kr
New Zealand	archie.nz
Norway	archie.uninett.no
Poland	archie.icm.edu.pl
Spain	archie.rediris.es
Sweden	archie.luth.se
Switzerland	archie.switch.ch
Taiwan	archie.ncu.edu.tw
England	archie.doc.ic.ac.uk
USA: (Maryland)	archie.sura.net
USA: (Nebraska)	archie.unl.edu
USA: (New Jersey)	archie.internic.net
USA: (New Jersey)	archie.rutgers.edu
USA: (New York)	archie.ans.net

Figure 20-4.   *Public archie servers*

Setting Variables With an Archie Server

As you are working with an archie server, you can control your working environment by changing the value of quantities called VARIABLES. Each variable has a name and a value. You can tell archie how you want something to work by changing the value of a particular variable. For example, you can specify how you want to sort the output of a search by setting the **sortby** variable. To examine the current value of all the variables, use the **show** command:

```
show
```

If you only want to display the setting of a single variable, you can specify that variable. For example:

```
show sortby
```

Figure 20-5 shows typical output from a **show** command. For now, don't worry about what all the variables mean; I will explain the important ones in a moment.

The best way to begin an archie session is to start with a **show** command. Take a moment to examine the important variables and see if they are set up to your liking. If not, change them by using the **set** command (described in a moment). Once you have everything just the way you want it, you can enter the commands to tell archie to search for what you want.

HINT

Before you start an archie search, make sure that the most important variables are set the way you want. These variables (discussed below) are **maxhits**, **output_format**, **pager**, **search**, **sortby** and **status**. Pay particular attention to the **search** variable. In addition, if you plan on asking archie to mail you the results of a search, set the **mailto** variable.

```
# 'autologout' (type numeric) has the value '60'.
# 'compress' (type string) has the value 'none'.
# 'encode' (type string) has the value 'none'.
# 'language' (type string) has the value 'english'.
# 'mailto' (type string) is not set.
# 'match_domain' (type string) is not set.
# 'match_path' (type string) is not set.
# 'max_split_size' (type numeric) has the value '51200'.
# 'maxhits' (type numeric) has the value '100'.
# 'maxhitspm' (type numeric) has the value '100'.
# 'maxmatch' (type numeric) has the value '100'.
# 'output_format' (type string) has the value 'verbose'.
# 'pager' (type boolean) is not set.
# 'search' (type string) has the value 'sub'.
# 'server' (type string) has the value 'localhost'.
# 'sortby' (type string) has the value 'none'.
# 'status' (type boolean) is set.
# 'tmpdir' (type string) has the value '/tmp'.
# 'term' (type string) has the value 'vt100 24 80'.
```

Figure 20-5. *Archie Servers: Typical output from a **show** command*

As you can see from Figure 20-5, there are three types of variables: boolean, numeric and string.

A BOOLEAN VARIABLE is one that acts as an on/off toggle switch. (The word "boolean" is a programming term named after the nineteenth century English mathematician George Boole.) To turn on a boolean variable, use the **set** command. To turn off a boolean variable, use the **unset** command.

Archie has only two boolean variables: **pager** and **status**. The **pager** variable determines how archie will display its output. When **pager** is set, the results of a search will be sent to a special program, called a paging program, that will display the output one screenful at a time. When **pager** is unset, all the output will be displayed on your screen without stopping. Most of the time, this would cause all but the last part of the information to scroll off the top of your screen so, normally, you will want to make sure that **pager** is set. If it is not already set, you can do so yourself by using the command:

```
set pager
```

There are three common paging programs used in Unix: **more**, **pg** and **less**. Archie servers display their output using **less**, so that is the paging program you will have to learn. Like many Unix programs, **less** has enough commands to choke a horsefly. Fortunately, you can usually get by with knowing only two commands: press <Space> to display the next screen of information, and press **q** (quit) to return to archie. For reference, I have included a quick summary of the most useful **less** commands later in the chapter.

What's in a Name?

less

The **more** program gets its name from the fact that, at the bottom of each screen of output, the program displays the word "more". The **less** program is newer and was written to replace **more**. The name **less** was chosen as a wry comment, because the **less** program actually offers more functionality than the **more** program. In other words, "**less** is more".

The other boolean variable, **status**, is a lot simpler. As archie performs a search, it can display a status line at the bottom of the screen. When **status** is set, archie will display this line. When **status** is unset, archie will not display the line. Normally, you want **status** to be set. If it is not already set, use:

```
set status
```

The second type of variable is a NUMERIC VARIABLE. As the name implies, you use the **set** command to give these variables a numeric value. There are only two numeric variables that you need to understand: **autologout** and **maxhits**.

The **autologout** variable controls how long archie will wait for you to enter a command without logging you out. In our example, **autologout** has a value of 60. This means that if you do not enter a command for 60 minutes, archie will log you out and terminate your connection. To set **autologout** to another value, use a command like:

```
set autologout 75
```

The permissible range is from 1 to 300 minutes.

When you use archie to search for a file, you will often find there are many anonymous ftp servers (perhaps hundreds) that contain the file. To speed things up, you can set **maxhits** to tell archie the maximum number of items that you want to find. When archie reaches this number, it will stop searching. For example:

```
set maxhits 10
```

Setting **maxhits** is something you will probably want to do because most archie servers default to a large number (such as 1000) and you really only need one good host name.

HINT

To save time, start searching with **maxhits** set to 10. If the results of your search are not adequate, set **maxhits** higher and try again.

The third type of variable is a STRING VARIABLE. As the name indicates, these variables store values consisting of a string of characters. The only string variables you need to know about are **mailto**, **output_format**, **search** and **sortby**. The most important of these is **search**.

The **mailto** variable is used to store a mailing address. As I will explain later, you can use the **mail** command to tell archie to mail you the results of a search. If you set the **mailto** variable before you issue the **mail** command, archie will know where to send the output. Otherwise, you will have to specify your address each time you use the **mail** command.

To set the **mailto** variable, use the **set** command and specify your address. For example:

```
set mailto harley@fuzzball.ucsb.edu
```

The **output_format** variable tells archie in what format you would like the output. You have three choices: **verbose**, **terse** and **machine**. To make a choice, use the **set** command with the name of the variable, followed by your choice. Be sure to include the _ (underscore) character in the variable name:

```
set output_format verbose
set output_format terse
set output_format machine
```

Normally, you would use either the **verbose** or **terse** formats (which I will show you in a moment). Just experiment and pick the one you like. The **machine** format is designed to be used when you will be mailing the result of a search to yourself, and then using a Unix program to manipulate the raw output. You will see an example of this later in the chapter.

Here is a sample of one item of output in each of the three formats. I generated this example by using archie to search for a file named **shoo-fly-pie**. The **verbose** output looked like this:

```
Host mthvax.cs.miami.edu    (129.171.32.5)
Last updated 09:32 17 Jun 1993

    Location: /recipes/ovo
       FILE    -rw-r--r-- 1095 bytes 01:00  4 Dec 1991  shoo-fly-pie
```

Here is the **terse** output:

```
mthvax.cs.miami.edu  01:00  4 Dec 1991 1095 bytes /recipes/ovo/shoo-fly-pie
```

Finally, the **machine** output:

```
19920103010000Z mthvax.cs.miami.edu 1095 bytes -rw-r--r-- /recipes/lacto/shoo-fly-pie
```

The next variable, **search**, is used to tell archie how you want it to compare patterns as it searches. I will discuss this variable on its own in the next section.

The **sortby** variable indicates in what order you want archie to display the results of a search. There are several choices:

set sortby none	do not sort
set sortby filename	alphabetical by file name
set sortby hostname	alphabetical by host name
set sortby size	largest to smallest
set sortby time	newest to oldest

You can tell archie to sort in reverse order by placing an **r** in front of the variable setting:

set sortby rfilename	reverse alphabetical by file name
set sortby rhostname	reverse alphabetical by host name
set sortby rsize	smallest to largest
set sortby rtime	oldest to newest

For example, each file and directory has a time and date that marks when it was last modified. To tell archie to display its output sorted by time, with the most recently modified items first, enter:

```
set sortby time
```

Setting the `search` Variable

To tell an archie server to start a search, you use the **find** or **prog** commands (discussed later in the chapter). Before you start the search, you can set the **search** variable to control how archie looks for a match.

There are seven possible settings: **exact**, **sub**, **subcase**, **regex**, **exact_sub**, **exact_subcase** and **exact_regex**. To set the **search** variable, use the **set** command, followed by **search**, followed by your choice. For example:

```
set search exact
```

The **exact** setting performs a basic, straightforward search. It tells archie to look for names that are exactly like the one you specified, including upper- and lowercase. For example, if you asked archie to search for the pattern **IBM-PC**, it would match **IBM-PC** but not **IBM-pc** or **ibm-pc**. When you know exactly what you want, these types of searches are the fastest and yield the best results.

The **sub** setting tells archie to search for patterns that contain your specification as a substring. For example, if you asked archie to search for **PC**, it would match **IBM-PC**, **PC** or **PC-dos**. This setting does not distinguish between upper- and lowercase, so **PC** will also match **IBM-pc**, **pc** and **pc-dos**.

The **subcase** setting is the same as **sub** except that upper- and lowercase letters are considered to be different. With this setting, **PC** would match **IBM-PC** but not **IBM-pc**.

The **regex** setting allows you to use a regular expression (which I explained earlier in the chapter). Regular expressions are used within Unix as a compact way to specify general patterns. For example, if you tell archie to search for the regular expression **PC$**, it means to find all names that end with the letters **PC**.

Regular expressions can be complex and I won't go into all the details here. If you want more information, use the command **help regex**. (I explain the **help** command later in the chapter.)

The last three settings are **exact_sub**, **exact_subcase** and **exact_regex**. They tell archie to first try an **exact** search. Then, if no matches are found, to try again using the second setting. Here is an example:

```
set search exact_sub
```

This tells archie to start by searching for the specified pattern exactly. If that fails, then archie will search for the pattern as a substring.

Performing a Search

To prepare for an archie search, use the **show** command, check the settings and change the ones you don't like. If you are not sure what to set, use the following:

```
set mailto your-mail-address
set maxhits 10
set output_format verbose
set pager
set search exact_sub
set sortby time
set status
```

To perform the search, use the **find** command. Enter **find** followed by the pattern you want archie to locate. Here are some examples:

```
find shoo-fly-pie
find rfc1325.txt
find recipes.tar.Z
```

Another command that you may need to know about is **prog**, which is a synonym for **find**. When archie was first invented, its database was used primarily to hold information about computer programs. For this reason, the command to start a search was named **prog**.

Today, archie's database contains information about all kinds of anonymous ftp resources: not only programs, but documents, electronic magazines, Usenet archives—just about every type of information that you can imagine. Thus, the search command has been renamed from **prog** to **find**.

HINT

To stop an archie search before it finishes, you can press **CTRL-C**.

Mailing the Results of an Archie Search

Once archie has completed a search, you may find it useful to mail the results to yourself (or to someone else). To do so, all you have to do is enter the **mail** command:

```
mail
```

If you have set the **mailto** variable, archie will already know where to send the mail. Otherwise, you will have to specify the address as part of the **mail** command:

```
mail harley@fuzzball.ucsb.edu
```

HINT

If you plan on mailing the results of more than one archie search, it is a lot easier to set the **mailto** variable once, before you start, than to specify your address each time you use the **mail** command.

Commands to Use While Reading Archie Server Output

I explained earlier that setting the **pager** variable tells the archie server to display its output by using a paging program called **less**. When **less** displays output, it shows you one screenful at a time. After each screenful, **less** pauses and waits for a command.

At this point, you can press SPACE to display more data, or **q** to quit **less** and return to archie. For reference, Figure 20-6 summarizes the important commands you can use as you are viewing archie's output. For most of the commands, you just press a single key; do not press RETURN. However, for the **/** and **?** commands, you do have to press RETURN.

Command	Description
SPACE	go forward one screenful
q	quit the program
RETURN	go forward one line
*n*RETURN	go forward *n* lines
b	go backward one screenful
y	go backward one line
*n***y**	go backward *n* lines
d	go forward (down) a half screenful
u	go backward (up) a half screenful
g	go to the first line
*n***g**	go to line *n*
G	go to the last line
*n***p**	go to the line that is *n*% through the output
/*pattern*	search forward for the specified pattern
?*pattern*	search backward for the specified pattern
n	repeat the previous search command

Figure 20-6. *Commands to use when viewing output with* **less**

Using the whatis **Database**

If you know the name of a file or directory (or part of the name), you can use the **find** command to have the archie server search its database. However, what if you know what you want, but you don't know the name?

To help in such cases, archie maintains a second collection of information called the "software description database". This database contains short descriptions of thousands of the programs, documents and data files that are found in the anonymous ftp archives (a lot more than software, actually).

To search this database, you use the **whatis** command. Type the command followed by any word you want. Archie will search the software description database and display all the entries it finds that contain the word you specified. Each entry will show you a description and a file name. If the description looks like what you want, you will know exactly which file to search for.

Where do the entries come from? Whenever someone makes a file available via anonymous ftp, he or she can send a short description to the people who maintain archie, who will place the description in the software description database.

Thus, there is a built-in restriction that limits the effectiveness of the **whatis** command. If the person who created the file you are looking for did not submit a description—which is the case for most files—you will not find it in the software description database. Moreover, unlike the main anonymous ftp database, this one is not updated regularly. Thus, you may find the description of a file that does not exist anymore.

Still, when it can find what you want, the **whatis** command can be a great tool, saving you from long searches in the dark. (The name, by the way, comes from the Unix **whatis** command, which performs a similar function for the online Unix manual.)

Here is an example using **whatis**. You would like to find something interesting that has to do with telephones. Enter:

```
whatis phone
```

Here is part of the output:

```
dialup      Maintain a database of phone services and use cu(1)
            to call them
phone       Multi-user real-time "talk" program
phone_kl    Phone another user, typing screen to screen
phoneme     Translate English words into their phonetic spellings
ringback    Implements a ring-back system that allows a phone
            line that is normally used as a voice line and a
            dial-out data line to be used as a limited dial-in
            data and voice line
sys5-phone  VAX-like Phone Utility for SysV
telewords   Telephone number to word conversion
telno       A telephone number permutation program
```

You decide to try the **telewords** program. All you have to do is enter the command **find telewords** to display its anonymous ftp location.

There are several things I would like to point out about this example. First, notice that **whatis** does a straight character by character search, ignoring the difference between upper- and lowercase letters. Second, you will often find items that have nothing to do with what you are looking for. For example, the **phoneme** program (although it does look interesting).

Finally, remember that **whatis** does not perform an exhaustive search of the full anonymous ftp database. It only knows about the items listed in the software description database. For example, several anonymous ftp hosts have directories named **telephone** that contain useful information, but **whatis** cannot find these directories because they are not in its database.

Displaying Help Information

There are several ways to have an archie server display help information. First, you can use the **help** command to display information about any command you want. All you need to do is enter **help** followed by the name of the command. For example:

```
help find
help set
```

To display a list of all the commands, enter:

```
help ?
```

If the **pager** variable is set, archie will use the **less** paging program to display the information, so when you are finished you will have to press **q**. Once you quit **less**, you will see a new prompt:

```
help>
```

At this point, you can enter the name of one command after another and receive more help. When you do not need any more help, simply press RETURN, and you will return to the regular prompt:

```
archie>
```

You can now enter a regular archie command. If you want help for setting a variable, type **help set** followed by the name of the variable. For example:

```
help set search
help set pager
```

Again, the information will be displayed using **less**. However, this time, when you quit you will see the prompt:

```
help set>
```

You can now enter the name of one variable after another and receive more help. When you press RETURN, you will see the **help>** prompt. Pressing RETURN once again, will return you to the regular **archie>** prompt.

HINT

Within the help facility, each time you press RETURN by itself, you move back out a single level. For example, if you are at the **help set>** prompt, you would have to press RETURN twice to get back to the **archie>** prompt.

As a convenience, you can return directly to the **archie>** prompt from any of the help prompts by using the command **done**.

Another way to learn about archie is to read the official documentation. Here is how the archie documentation is organized:

All Unix systems come with an online manual that contains entries for each command. At any time, you can read the documentation for a particular command by using the **man** command. It is customary to refer to each particular entry in the online manual as a "page" (even though many entries are much longer than a single page). It is common for people who create new software to write a manual page explaining how the software works.

Archie itself has such documentation that explains how to use an archie server. This documentation, of course, is not available on your local computer. Rather, you can enter the **manpage** command while you are using the archie server:

```
manpage
```

Archie will now display its manual page for you.

HINT

After you use a **help** or **manpage** command, you can mail the output to yourself by using the **mail** command. This is a good way to get your own copy of the official archie server documentation.

To finish this section, I will mention three more information commands. Whenever you log in to an archie server, you will see a welcoming message. Indeed, many public Internet hosts, such as anonymous ftp hosts, display general information when you log in. The custom is to call such information the MESSAGE OF THE DAY. With an archie server, you can redisplay this information at any time by entering the **motd** command.

If you would like to find out about other archie servers, you can display a list by entering the **servers** command.

And finally, you can use the **version** command to display the version of archie software that your server is using.

A Summary of Archie Server Commands

For reference, here is a summary of all the important archie server commands.

Stopping the Archie Session

quit	stop the archie session and disconnect

Performing a Search

find *pattern*	search the anonymous ftp database
prog *pattern*	same as **find**
whatis *pattern*	search the software description database

Displaying Information

help ?	display a list of commands
help *command*	display help for the specified command
help set *variable*	display help for the specified variable
RETURN	(from within help) back out one level
done	(from within help) back out all the way
domains	display a list of pseudo-domains
manpage	display the archie manual page
motd	re-display the message of the day
servers	display a list of archie servers
version	show what version of archie is being used

Mailing Information

set mailto *address*	specify a mail address
path *address*	same as **set mailto**
mail [*address*]	mail output

Figure 20-7.   *Archie Servers: Summary of important commands*
(continued on next page)

Displaying Variable Settings

`show`	display the value of all the variables
`show variable`	display the value of the specified variable

Setting General Variables

`set autologout minutes`	set maximum idle time before auto logout
`set maxhits number`	set the maximum number of items to find
`set pager`	display output by using paging program
`unset pager`	do not display output with paging program
`set status`	display a status line during search
`unset status`	do not display status line during search

Setting Output Preferences

`set output_format verbose`	display output using long format
`set output_format terse`	display output using short format
`set output_format machine`	display output using machine format
`set sortby none`	do not sort output
`set sortby filename`	sort alphabetically by file name
`set sortby hostname`	sort alphabetically by host name
`set sortby size`	sort by size, largest to smallest
`set sortby time`	sort by time and date, newest to oldest
`set sortby rfilename`	sort reverse alphabetically by file name
`set sortby rhostname`	sort reverse alphabetically by host name
`set sortby rsize`	sort by size, smallest to largest
`set sortby rtime`	sort by time and date, oldest to newest

Setting Search Preferences

`set search exact`	search for an exact pattern
`set search sub`	search for anything that contains pattern
`set search subcase`	same as sub, but case sensitive
`set search regex`	search for a regular expression
`set search exact_sub`	try exact, then **sub**
`set search exact_subcase`	try exact, then **subcase**
`set search exact_regex`	try exact, then **regex**

Figure 20-7. *Archie Servers: Summary of important commands* (continued from previous page)

A Typical Session With Archie

It was a dark and stormy night.

Outside, the harsh, driving rain beat a monotonous tattoo against the windowpane. I sat at my desk, hat brim pulled down over my face, grabbing a few quick winks between cases. Things had looked tight for a while in Tangier, but once I had put the screws to the dwarf he had come through. They all do.

I lay back, the old number twelves resting on a desk covered with a month's worth of paperwork, a half empty bottle of Scotch, and a tarnished .45 that was still smoking. In the corner, the screen of my computer glowed silently.

I didn't hear when she entered, but my nostrils flared at the fragrance of her perfume. "Go away," I said, "we're closed for repairs."

"Well then," said a sultry Barbara Stanwyck voice, "you'll just have to open early today. I need help and I'm willing to pay for it."

I looked up and blinked twice at a vision of innocence: five foot three, periwinkle blue eyes, and long blond curls winding over her shoulders like water cascading down a mountain creek. She was dressed in a skintight outfit that showed more curves than a politician with the bends, and as she gazed at me with those baby blues, I could feel the hair on the back of my neck stand up and salute.

She looked innocent. Too innocent. Something was fishy here, and I didn't mean her perfume.

"Listen," she said, "I need help, and you're the only one who can help me. I'm in an awful jam."

"So what else is new?"

"I've only got seven more hours, or else..."

"Or else what? I already told you, kid, that I wasn't going to pull your chestnuts out of the fire any longer. What is it this time? Blackmail? Murder? Or did you have another misunderstanding with Sergeant Rogers?"

She looked at me with large, round innocent eyes.

"Calculus," she said.

I closed my eyes and sighed.

"Okay, kid, spill it."

Well, I listened to her tale and it wasn't a pretty one. The old, old story. A young, guileless girl from a small country town, still wet behind the ears, full of hope and dreams of tinsel, comes to the big city to make her fortune. But then she falls in with the wrong crowd and gets into trouble.

It starts innocently enough. First, someone takes her to a party where, unknown to her, people in the back room are solving differential equations. Next, she gets invited to a small, private gathering where a few street-wise punks introduce her to basic algebra. At first, the thrill is intoxicating, and she goes along with it just for the kicks. Soon, she's into simultaneous equations, conic sections and fractional exponents. She tells herself she can take it or leave it, that she can stop whenever she wants, until one day she finds herself breaking into a pawn shop to steal a protractor and a trigonometry book.

And now, Calculus.

"You have to help me," she pleaded. "You're my last hope. My first Calculus class starts tomorrow and I'm not ready. And you know what The Doctor does to people who are unprepared."

I sighed again.

"Okay," I said, "I'll help you, but it will cost you a hundred bucks. In advance."

"How about a trade," she said. "I know where I can get my hands on a used copy of a complex analysis text."

"That's all I need around here, with the cops breathing down my neck. A hundred bucks, in advance. Think on your feet."

"All right," she pouted and, reaching into the hidden recesses of her outfit, extracted two fifty-dollar bills that had definitely seen better days.

"That's more like it," I said. "Now come over here and sit down."

I pulled her over to the computer, which was already logged in to the Internet.

"Do you have your own PC at home?"

She nodded.

"Good. We'll get archie to find a program to help you."

Telneting to a handy archie server, it was the work of a moment to set the variables and start a search for anything named "calculus". I hit paydirt on the first try: an anonymous ftp server at Washington University, in St. Louis, Missouri. (The session is shown in Figure 20-8.) I quit archie, ftp-ed to the anonymous ftp server, changed to the **calculus** directory, and displayed a directory listing. I then changed to a subdirectory.

"There it is," I said. "This is what you want. A file named **rurc1.zip** in the **rurc1** subdirectory. Do you know how to uncompress a zip file?"

She looked at me with scorn. "Does your grandmother know how to suck eggs?"

"Okay then, all you have to do is unzip this file and you will find a program called *Are You Ready For Calculus?*, written by David Lovelock at the University of Arizona. It will help you figure out what you need to review before you start Calculus."

She stared at me.

"How is it you know all about this?" she asked suspiciously.

I stared back.

"That's what you're paying me for, kid."

"Okay. I guess I know better than to ask questions."

I downloaded the program to my computer and copied it onto a floppy disk. She took the disk, slipped it into her blouse and walked to the door.

She turned and looked at me with those large, blue innocent eyes.

"I like your style," she said. "Maybe you'd like to come up to my place and uncompress a file sometime."

She paused.

"You do know how to uncompress, don't you? You just put your fingers on the keyboard—and unzip."

And she was gone, like a wisp of steam on a double-sided razor blade ready to do its work.

I looked outside. It was still a dark and stormy night.

```
% telnet archie.rutgers.edu
Trying 128.6.21.13 ...
Connected to archie.rutgers.edu.
Escape character is '^]'.

Solaris 2 (dogbert.rutgers.edu) (pts/1)
login: archie

          Welcome to the Rutgers University Archie Server!

...message of the day deleted...

archie> show
# 'autologout' (type numeric) has the value '60'.
# 'compress' (type string) has the value 'none'.
# 'encode' (type string) has the value 'none'.
# 'language' (type string) has the value 'english'.
# 'mailto' (type string) is not set.
# 'match_domain' (type string) is not set.
# 'match_path' (type string) is not set.
# 'max_split_size' (type numeric) has the value '51200'.
# 'maxhits' (type numeric) has the value '100'.
# 'maxhitspm' (type numeric) has the value '100'.
# 'maxmatch' (type numeric) has the value '100'.
# 'output_format' (type string) has the value 'verbose'.
# 'pager' (type boolean) is not set.
# 'search' (type string) has the value 'sub'.
# 'server' (type string) has the value 'localhost'.
# 'sortby' (type string) has the value 'none'.
# 'status' (type boolean) is set.
# 'term' (type string) has the value 'vt100 24 80'.

archie> set maxhits 10
archie> set pager
archie> set search exact_sub
archie> set sortby time
archie> find calculus

...some responses deleted...

Host wuarchive.wustl.edu (128.252.135.4)
Last updated 05:12 18 Sep 1995

    Location: /edu/math/software/msdos/calculus
      DIRECTORY    drwxr-xr-x    512 bytes  15:00 20 Nov 1994   calculus

archie> quit
# Bye.
Connection closed by foreign host.

% ftp wuarchive.wustl.edu
```

Figure 20-8. *A typical session with archie and anonymous ftp*
(continued on next page)

```
Connected to wuarchive.wustl.edu.
220 wuarchive.wustl.edu FTP server (Version wu-2.4(3)
    Tue Oct 17 13:24:04 CDT 1995) ready.

Name (wuarchive.wustl.edu:harley): anonymous
331 Guest login ok, send your complete e-mail address as password.
Password:

...message of the day deleted...

230 Guest login ok, access restrictions apply.

ftp> cd /edu/math/software/msdos/calculus
250 CWD command successful.

ftp> dir
200 PORT command successful.
150 Opening ASCII mode data connection for /bin/ls.

...some lines deleted...

drwxr-xr-x 2 root   archive  512 Oct 14 22:26 rurc1
drwxr-xr-x 2 root   archive  512 Oct 14 22:26 rurc2
drwxr-xr-x 2 root   archive  512 Oct 14 22:26 rurc3

ftp> cd rurc1
250 CWD command successful.

ftp> dir
200 PORT command successful.
150 Opening ASCII mode data connection for /bin/ls.
total 185
-rw-r-r-- 1 root   wheel   1664 Jul 22 1994 rurc1.abstract
-rw-r-r-- 1 root   wheel   6982 Jul 22 1994 rurc1.readme
-rw-r-r-- 1 root   wheel  171950 Jul 22 1994 rurc1.zip
226 Transfer complete.
214 bytes received in 0.28 seconds (0 Kbytes/s)

ftp> binary
200 Type set to I.

ftp> get rurc1.zip
200 PORT command successful.
150 Opening BINARY mode data connection for rurc1.zip (171950 bytes).
226 Transfer complete.
local: rurc1.zip remote: rurc1.zip
171950 bytes received in 17.37 seconds (9 Kbytes/s)

ftp> quit
221 Goodbye.
```

Figure 20-8. *A typical session with archie and anonymous ftp*
(continued from previous page)

Using Archie by Mail

I have already discussed two ways to use archie. Most of the time, the best way is to use an archie client program to send requests to an archie server on your behalf. If this is not possible, you can telnet to an archie server, log in as **archie**, and enter commands for yourself. In this section, I will describe the third way to access an archie server: by sending it commands in a mail message.

Using an archie server by mail is handy if you do not have access to a client and, for some reason, you cannot telnet directly to an archie server. It is also convenient when you do not need your answer in a hurry, or when you need to make multiple searches. You can mail your request and pick up the results later in your mailbox.

To use archie by mail, send a message to the userid **archie** at the address of one of the archie servers (which are listed in Figure 20-4). When you compose the message, you can leave the subject blank. Within the body of the message, use as many archie commands as you want, each one on its own line.

Archie will carry out your commands and mail a response back to you. For the most part, the commands that you can use are the same ones that I described earlier (see the summary in Figure 20-7). The only exception is you cannot use commands that do not make sense in a mail request (for example, **set pager**).

The first command you should always use is **set mailto**. This will ensure that archie has your correct return address. If you leave out this command, archie will look for your address in the header of your message. Most of the time this will work, but it is better to specify the address explicitly, so you know there will not be any ranygazoo. For convenience, you can also use the older version of this command, which is **path**. Thus, the following two commands are equivalent:

```
set mailto harley@fuzzball.ucsb.edu
path harley@fuzzball.ucsb.edu
```

The last command should always be **quit**. This tells archie you are finished and to ignore any lines that follow. It is important to include the **quit** command if you have a signature that is appended automatically to all your messages (see Chapter 7). By using **quit**, you ensure that archie will ignore any extra lines at the end of the message.

Before you use a particular archie server by mail for the first time, you should send it a message asking for help information. This will show you exactly what commands that particular server will recognize. Here is a sample message in which we send such a request to the archie server named **archie.rutgers.edu**:

```
To: archie@archie.rutgers.edu
Subject:
set mailto harley@fuzzball.ucsb.edu
help
quit
```

When you get your response, take a moment to read it carefully.

Here is a sample message in which we ask archie to search for the file named **rfc1325.txt**:

```
To: archie@archie.rutgers.edu
Subject:
set mailto harley@fuzzball.ucsb.edu
set maxhits 25
set output_format verbose
set search exact
set sortby time
find rfc1325.txt
quit
```

Once you receive your response from archie, you can send a message to an anonymous ftp mail server to retrieve the actual file. (See Chapter 18.)

## Chapter Twenty-One

File Types Used on the Internet; Downloading Software

There are a large variety of file types used on the Internet. However, you do not
need to understand them all. In this chapter, I discuss the most important types
and show you what you *do* need to understand. I explain where on the Net you
are likely to encounter the various types of files, and what tools you need to
understand to use these files properly. I will then show you how to download and
install software from the Net to use on your own computer.

The Five Important Ideas Regarding File Types

There are many different types of files used on the Internet. To make sense out of them
all, however, you only need to understand five basic ideas. They are:

- Different file types are used to hold different kinds of data.

- A few of these file types are plain ASCII text, the rest are binary.

- You can compress a file so it will take up less space.

- To make a group of files easier to handle, you can collect the files into one
  single large file called an "archive".

- When you send a message by electronic mail or post an article to Usenet, you
  can use only plain ASCII text, not binary files.

The Harley Guarantee: You have my personal guarantee that once you understand
these five ideas, you will be able to understand everything important having to do
with Internet file types. To help you, I will discuss these ideas, one at a time, in the
following sections.

File Types

I want you to think about the idea that there are a great many types of data in the
world. There are textual documents, pictures, sounds, video, and so on. Each different
kind of data is stored in its own type of file. For example, a file containing a word
processing document uses a different format than a file containing a picture or a sound.

It is important to understand that, on your computer, all files are manipulated in
the same way: they all have a name, they all take up space on the disk, they can all be
moved from one directory to another, and so on. The essential difference between two
different types of files is that, inside the file, the actual data is arranged differently.

Here is an example. To view a picture you need a picture viewing program. Its job
is to read a file containing picture data and then display that data on your screen in the
form of a picture. To listen to a sound, you need a sound playing program. Its job is to
read a file containing audio data and then play that sound for you using the speakers
on your computer.

If you could compare the contents of a picture file with the contents of a sound file,
you would find that the data is stored in two completely different formats. That is, if
we looked inside the file, we would see that picture data is different from sound data.

Of course, from our point of view, we don't really need to worry about how the data is stored. Our programs read the files on our behalf. We just have to make sure we have the right type of programs. For instance, to look at a picture, we need a program that knows how to understand picture data.

Because there are so many different types of data, we use a system in which the name of the file can tell us what type of data the file contains. To do so, the file name is given an EXTENSION. This is a short suffix, added to the main part of the name. The extension is separated from the main part of the name by a **.** (period) character.

There are a number of standard extensions, and once you learn to recognize them, you will be able to tell what type of file you have. For example, I can tell, just by looking, that a file named **harley.exe** is a program that runs on a PC. A file named **harley.gif**, however, would contain a picture, while **harley.au** would hold a sound.

There are hundreds of different file types (and file extensions) and well over 100 in general use in the online world. However, to help you, I have created a master list of the most common file types used on the Internet along with the corresponding extensions (see Figure 21-1). You don't have to memorize all these extensions. Just read the list over once and, whenever you run into an extension you don't recognize, refer back to Figure 21-1. Eventually, you will remember the ones that are important to you.

File Extensions for Common File Types

Before I move on, I would like to spend a few moments acquainting you with the most common file extensions. An extension is a suffix used as part of a file name. By looking at an extension, you can often identify a file type.

For example, if you see a file named **cat.gif**, you know it contains a picture stored in the GIF format (probably a picture of a cat). On the other hand, if you see a file named **cat.au**, you would know it contains a sound.

To help you identify files, Figure 21-2 shows the most common extensions for several categories: pictures, sound, video, text and documents, and DOS/Windows executable files.

Notice that the extensions which are longer than three characters have a corresponding three-character extension. For example **html** and **htm** are both used to indicate a file of hypertext. The shorter extension is used for DOS, which allows a maximum of three characters for an extension. Thus, if you copy a file named **harley.html** from a Unix computer to a DOS computer, you would have to rename the file **harley.htm**.

 **INTERNET RESOURCE** *Look in the catalog under Internet Resources for File Types: Reference List*

Using a Sound, Picture or Video File

To use a sound, picture or video file, you need a program that knows how to process that type of data. There are two ways to use such a program. First, graphical web

File Extension	Description
aif	sound (Macintosh)
arj	compressed file/archive (DOS)
au	sound
avi	video
bat	executable batch file (DOS)
bin	MacBinary file (Macintosh)
bmp	picture (Windows, OS/2)
com	executable file (DOS)
cpt	compressed file (Macintosh)
doc	plain ASCII text or word processing document
exe	executable file (DOS)
gif	picture
gz	compressed file/archive (Unix)
hqx	compressed file/archive (Macintosh: Binhex)
html	hypertext web document
htm	same as html
jpeg	picture
jpg	same as jpeg
lha	compressed file (Amiga)
mid	music: MIDI
mov	video (Macintosh)
mpeg	video
mpg	same as mpeg
ps	postscript file
qt	video (Macintosh)
sea	self-extracting archive (Macintosh)
sit	compressed file/archive (Macintosh)
tar	archive (Unix: tarfile)
tar.gz	compressed tarfile (Unix)
tar.Z	compressed tarfile (Unix)
tgz	compressed tarfile
tiff	picture
tif	same as tiff
txt	plain ASCII text
wav	sound (Microsoft)
xbm	picture (X Window: Unix)
z	compressed file (Unix)
zip	compressed file/archive (DOS: zipfile)

Figure 21-1. *Master list of common file types*

Pictures

`bmp`	picture
`gif`	picture
`jpeg`	picture
`jpg`	same as jpeg
`tiff`	picture
`tif`	same as tiff
`xbm`	picture

Sounds

`aif`	sound
`au`	sound
`mid`	music: MIDI
`ra`	real-time sound (RealAudio)
`ram`	real-time sound (RealAudio)
`wav`	sound
`xdma`	real-time sound/video (StreamWorks)
`xdm`	same as xdma

Video

`qt`	video
`mov`	video
`avi`	video
`mpeg`	video
`mpg`	same as mpeg
`xdma`	real-time sound/video (StreamWorks)
`xdm`	same as xdma

Text and Documents

`doc`	plain ASCII text or word processing document
`html`	hypertext web document
`htm`	same as html
`ps`	postscript file
`txt`	plain ASCII text

DOS/Windows Executable Files

`bat`	executable batch file (DOS)
`com`	executable file (DOS)
`exe`	executable file (DOS)

Figure 21-2. *Common file extensions, organized by category*

browsers are able to handle the most common types of files. All you need to do is select a file, and your browser will display it for you. (I explain how this works in Chapter 10.)

Second, you can download a program designed to handle a particular type of data. You can then use the program to view or listen to a file of that type. You can use such programs by themselves, or you can configure your browser so it calls upon the program as necessary.

Here is an example. You want to listen to real-time audio using the RealAudio format. Such files are identified by an extension of **ra** (for example, **harley.ra**). If your browser knows how to play RealAudio files, fine. If not, you will have to download the appropriate audio program, and install it on your computer.

Once you have the audio program installed, you can configure your browser by setting the preferences or options. By doing so, you tell your browser to call upon the RealAudio program, whenever you select a file with an extension of **ra**. From now on, whenever you select a RealAudio file, your browser will download the file and start the audio program automatically. (For a discussion of configuring a web browser, see Chapter 10.)

Some programs can process more than one type of data. For example, most viewing programs can display a variety of picture types (**gif**, **jpg**, **bmp**, **tif**, and so on). However, some data formats are highly specialized or proprietary and require a specific program. For example, if you want to listen to more than one type of real-time audio, you may need to use a different audio program for each type.

 **INTERNET RESOURCE**   *Look in the catalog under Internet Resources for*
Viewer Utilities
Audio Utilities

Using a Document or Postscript File

To read a document, you may need a special program. If the document is plain ASCII text, you can use any text editor or word processor. However, if the document is in the format of a particular word processor, you will need a word processor to read the document. For example, to read a Microsoft Word document, you need Microsoft Word (or at least another program that knows how to read Microsoft Word documents).

Postscript is more complicated. Postscript is a "page description language", developed by the Adobe Company. A postscript file is actually a set of instructions describing what the output is supposed to look like. The output device reads and interprets these instructions in order to generate the output.

Printing a postscript file is easy, but you *must* have a postscript printer. Just print the file in the usual manner; your postscript printer will interpret the instructions in the file and print the specified output.

Displaying a postscript file on your screen requires two separate programs. First, you need a program named Ghostscript to act as a postscript interpreter. Second, you need a postscript viewer named GSview, to act as the graphical interface for Ghostscript. You can download both of these programs using anonymous ftp. (If you need help finding them, use archie; see Chapter 20.)

HINT

Postscript is stored in text files. Thus, when you use anonymous ftp to download a postscript file, be sure to specify that the transfer should be ASCII text, not binary.

 **INTERNET RESOURCE** *Look in the catalog under Internet Resources for* ***Postscript Utilities***

Text Files and Binary Files

Broadly speaking, all files can be classified as either text files or binary files. A TEXT FILE is one that contains only regular characters like the ones you can type on your keyboard: letters, numbers, punctuation, and so on.

The data in a text file is stored using the ASCII CODE: a system in which each character is represented by a certain pattern of bits. I won't go into the details, and you don't really need to know them. All I want you to remember is that a text file contains regular characters and not much else. There are no pictures, sounds, drawings or special formatting. You will often see text files referred to as ASCII FILES. (The name ASCII stands for "American Standard Code for Information Interchange.)

All other types of files are BINARY FILES. In this context, the term "binary" has a highly technical meaning that I don't want you to worry about. Just remember, if a file contains anything but plain text, it's a binary file.

The reason we distinguish between text files and binary files is that, in certain contexts, they must be handled differently. In such cases, it is up to you to know which class of file you are dealing with so you can make sure it is processed correctly.

For example, when you download a file via anonymous ftp (see Chapter 18), you should tell your ftp client whether the file is text or binary. This is because the details of downloading a file depend on its internal structure. If you download a binary file as an ASCII text file, it will be corrupted and, when it gets to you, it won't work. For example, if you download a program as a text file, you won't be able to run it; or if you download a picture as a text file, you won't be able to look at it.

Here is another example. The mail system can only deal with text files. Thus, before you can mail a binary file, you must convert it to a special text format. At the other end, the person who receives the file must convert it from the special text format back into its original binary format. Normally, this is done for you automatically by a service called Mime (see Chapter 7). The details don't matter, but I do want you to understand the basic idea: Sometimes it matters if a file is text or binary.

HINT

You can often tell if a file is text or binary by looking at its name. For example, plain text, hypertext and postscript are all text. Thus, files with an extension of `txt`, `html`, `htm` or `ps` will be text files (for example, `harley.txt`, `harley.html`, `harley.htm` and `harley.ps`). In addition, when you are using anonymous ftp, files whose names contain **README**, **index** or **faq** are almost always text.

Otherwise, unless you specifically recognize a file as being text, assume it is a binary file. In particular, programs, pictures, sounds and video are all stored in binary files.

Compressed Files and Archives

Many of the files you will encounter on the Net are COMPRESSED. This means they are converted to another format that takes up less space than the original file. You cannot use a compressed file directly; you must first UNCOMPRESS it. (This is done by a program, so you don't need to care about the details.)

The important thing is, since compressed files require significantly less space, they do not take up as much room on a disk. For this reason, people who maintain large anonymous ftp sites will usually store files in a compressed format, as it saves a huge amount of disk space. In addition, compressed files take significantly less time to download than uncompressed files. This means that, when you download a file, you may have to uncompress it before you can use it.

HINT

Virtually all programs on the Net are stored in a compressed format, so if you want free software, you will have to understand compression and uncompression.

From our point of view, the most important benefit of compression is that smaller files are faster to download than larger, uncompressed files. For example, a large uncompressed file might take five minutes to download to your computer. If the file were compressed, it might take only two minutes. Of course, you will have to uncompress the file at your end, but uncompressing a file is very fast compared to downloading.

You will find that most programs consist of more than just a single file. For example, one of the web browsers I use is actually a set of 12 different files, and some programs have tens of files. It would be highly inconvenient to have to transfer each of these files separately just to download one program.

The solution is to collect a group of related files into a single large file called an ARCHIVE. To get the entire set of files, all you need to do is download a single archive file. Once you have the archive on your computer, you use a special program to extract the separate files.

As you might imagine, an archive can itself be compressed, and most of the programs you will find on the Net are in the form of a compressed archive. In general, you need to go through the following steps to use a free program:

1. Find the program somewhere on the Net. (Use the Web or archie.)

2. Download the compressed archive. (Use the Web or anonymous ftp.)

3. Uncompress the archive and extract the separate files.

4. Install the program.

With a PC using DOS or Windows, or with a Macintosh, uncompressing and extracting are done at the same time by a single program. (In fact, on a Macintosh, everything can be done automatically.) With Unix, you must use two separate programs: one to uncompress and one to extract. I will discuss the details for each type of system later in the chapter.

📖 What's in a Name?

Archive

The word "archive" has two meanings, so don't be confused. First, an archive is a group of files which are gathered into a single large file (and often compressed). Thus, when you download a program from the Internet, it will likely be a compressed archive, which you will need to process in order to extract the original files.

Second, the word "archive" is also used in a more conventional sense, like an archive of historical documents or an archive of old manuscripts. On the Net, there are many large collections of files which are made available to the general public. We refer to these collections as "archives". For example, an anonymous ftp site which contains a great many computer programs would be called a "software archive".

Thus, you might download a program in the form of an archive (the first meaning) from an anonymous ftp software archive (the second meaning).

Using Mime to Encode Binary Files for Mailing

If you use a text editor program to look inside an ASCII text file, you would see regular characters. If you look inside a binary file, you would see gobbledegook. This is because text files contain normal characters (letters, numbers, punctuation, and so on), while binary files contain data that must be interpreted by a program. For example, a binary file might contain data that represents a picture or a sound. As I explained earlier in the chapter, you will find many different types of files on the Internet, most of which will be binary files.

The distinction between text and binary files becomes important when you want to mail a file to someone, or when you want to send a file to a Usenet discussion group. This is because both the mail system and Usenet are designed to handle only regular characters and, hence, can work only with text files. In other words, you can't mail a binary file to someone, and you can't post a binary file to a Usenet group.

Thus, in order to mail or post a binary file, you must first convert it to regular ASCII text. And in order to use the file later, the person who receives it must convert it from text back into binary.

There are a number of systems used to perform such conversions. For mail, the most popular system is called Mime. The name stands for "Multipurpose Internet Mail Extensions". When you use Mime, you can "attach" a binary file (or any file for that matter) to a regular message. At the other end, the recipient uses Mime to "detach" the file and save it on his own computer. In order to do this, both you and the other person must use a mail program that supports Mime. (Although you don't have to use the same program.)

To use Mime, you don't have to worry about any of the details, because your mail program does all the work. However, I do want you to understand the main idea: When you use Mime to attach a binary file to a message, the file is encoded using plain ASCII text. At the other end, the text file is decoded back into its original binary format. (For more information about Mime and attachments, see Chapter 7.)

HINT

In the Macintosh world, another system, called Binhex, is frequently used instead of Mime. Macintosh files have special characteristics which Mime will not preserve. For this reason, if you are sending a Macintosh file to another Macintosh user, you should use Binhex and not Mime. (I will discuss this in more detail later in the chapter.)

Using Uuencode to Encode Binary Files for Usenet

Like the mail system, Usenet can use only ASCII text, not binary data. Most of the time, text is all you will need. After all, Usenet articles consist of regular characters that you type at your keyboard. However, there are times when you will want to share a binary file with the rest of the world. For example, many people like to share pictures or sounds on Usenet, and there are a number of discussion groups set up purely for this purpose.

In order to post such files (remember, pictures and sounds are stored in binary files), they must first be encoded as plain ASCII text. The text can then be posted to

Usenet in the form of a regular article. When you see such an article, it will look like gibberish. But once you download the file and convert it back to binary, it will have its original format.

The system that is used on Usenet is called UUENCODING. The name comes from a Unix program, named **uuencode**, which is used to encode binary data to ASCII text. The program which is used to decode the text back to its original format is called **uudecode**. Sometimes we use these names as verbs. For example, you might hear someone say, "I uuencoded a picture of my cat and posted it to Usenet." Or, if you were to ask me how you can view a picture from a Usenet group, I would say, "You must download the file, and then uudecode it."

Some uuencoded files are so long, they must be divided into several parts before they can be posted. (Usenet has limits as to how large an article can be.) Since images require large files, you will often see pictures posted just this way, as a series of articles. For example, in one of the picture groups, you might see four articles in a row with the following subject:

```
cat.gif 1 of 4
cat.gif 2 of 4
cat.gif 3 of 4
cat.gif 4 of 4
```

In this case, someone has posted a picture of his cat. The name of the file is **cat.gif**, and it is so large that it had to be broken into four parts. (Some cats are big.) If you want to view this file, you will have to download all four parts, put them together, and uudecode them to produce the original binary file.

HINT

To read Usenet articles, you use a program called a "newsreader". Most newsreaders will automatically put together a series of uuencoded articles and perform the uudecoding for you. Thus, with the right newsreader, it is not a lot of trouble to download and process a multi-part picture or sound file, because your newsreader will do most of the work for you.

If you want to post a picture or sound to Usenet, you will first have to uuencode the file. If you are using a Unix system, you will already have a **uuencode** program. (For instructions, you can display the documentation from the online Unix manual by using the command **man uuencode**.)

If you are using a PC or a Macintosh, there are versions of **uuencode** for Windows, DOS, OS/2 and Macintosh available for free on the Net. To find the program you need, you can use either a web search engine (see Chapter 10) or archie (see Chapter 20).

INTERNET RESOURCE   *Look in the catalog under Internet Resources for*
Uuencode/Uudecode

Downloading Software for Windows and DOS

On the Internet, PC programs are generally stored as ZIPFILES. A zipfile is a compressed archive with a file extension of **zip**: for example, **harley.zip**. The most popular program used to create zipfiles is **pkzip** (named after its original developer, Phil Katz).

When you find a PC program on the Net, it will likely be stored as a single zipfile. To use the program, you must first download and then process the zipfile. The procedure, which involves uncompressing the file, is called UNZIPPING. (Creating a zip file is called ZIPPING.) There are a number of programs available to unzip files, the most popular being **pkunzip**.

Both pkzip and pkunzip are products of the Pkware Company and are shareware (which means you can try the programs for free and, if you like them, you are asked to send a small registration fee to the company). You don't have to use the Pkware programs, as there are a number of other DOS and Windows programs available that can work with **zipfiles**. I like to use **pkzip** and **pkunzip** from the DOS command line, but you may prefer to use a Windows program.

The unzipping process involves uncompressing the file and extracting it from the archive. However, your unzip program will do this all automatically, so you don't have to worry about the details.

For reference, here is a description of all the steps you need to follow in order to download and install PC software from the Net:

1. Find the software you need.

I have several favorite web pages that contain collections of software. For convenience, I keep these pages on my bookmark list (see Chapter 10), and they are always the first places I look when I want an Internet-related program (such as an Internet client or a picture viewer). If I can't find the program I want on one of these pages, I use a web search engine (also Chapter 10) or archie (Chapter 20).

2. Create a temporary directory on your PC.

It is a good idea to download and process all new programs in a temporary directory. This helps you isolate the files in a well-known place. Moreover, if you don't like the program, it is easy to delete all the files. Once the program is installed successfully in its own directory, you can remove the temporary directory.

3. Download the program (a single zipfile) into your temporary directory.

You can use either your web browser (Chapter 10) or your ftp client (Chapter 18) to download the program.

4. Unzip the zipfile.

If you are using **pkunzip** from a DOS prompt, simply specify the name of the zipfile. For example, if you have downloaded a file named **harley.zip** into your temporary directory, you can unzip it by using the command:

```
pkunzip -d harley.zip
```

The **-d** option tells the program to create any subdirectories that are necessary. (I assume, of course, that you already have **pkunzip**. If not, I will tell you how to get it, later in this section.)

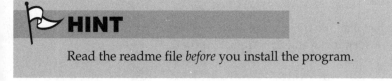

HINT

Zipfiles, when unzipped, often contain a collection of files. In addition, some programs also use a number of subdirectories. This means the unzip program must create these subdirectories during the unzipping process. If you suspect the zipfile you are processing contains subdirectories, you must use the **-d** option with the **pkunzip** command. For example:

```
pkunzip -d harley.zip
```

Without **-d**, **pkunzip** will not create the proper subdirectories. (Note: Using the **-d** option when you do not need it will not cause any harm.)

5. Look for a readme file.

A README FILE contains information you should read before you install a program. The readme file will be named **readme** or **readme.1st** or something similar. Be sure to read this file *before* you proceed. There may be instructions you should understand about the installation.

HINT

Read the readme file *before* you install the program.

6. Install the program.

The installation instructions will be in the readme file. With simple programs, there is really nothing to do. Unzipping the zipfile creates an executable program that is ready to go. If so, create a subdirectory for your program, and copy the file or files to this subdirectory.

With more complex software, there will be an installation program. For Windows, it will be named **setup.exe**. Just run this program. (You may have to use the "Run" function from within Windows. See the example below.) For DOS, the installation program is often named **install.exe**.

HINT

Read the readme file *before* you install the program.

7. Check the program for viruses.

Use a virus checking program to see if the files you unzipped contain any known viruses. Do this *before* you run the program for the first time. If you don't have a virus program, you can get one for free on the Net.

If you are downloading software from a secure site—for example, if you are downloading the latest web browser from the browser company's anonymous ftp site—you probably don't need to check for viruses. Still, to coin a phrase, it is better to be safe than sorry.

HINT

If you catch a sexually transmitted disease, it can be a minor annoyance, but if you download a virus to your PC, you can cause real damage to your hard disk.

8. Run the program.

Run the program and see if it looks okay. The first time you use the program, it is a good idea to spend a few minutes looking at the help information to orient yourself.

9. Clean up the temporary directory.

Once you have successfully installed the program in its own directory, you can delete the files in the temporary directory, including the original zipfile.

HINT

I use **C:\TEMP** as my temporary directory, and I do not delete it after installing a program; I just delete the files. In this way, I always have a directory available into which I can download files.

So far, I have discussed zipfiles and how to process them. To summarize, you download the file and then unzip it. However, how do you get the unzip program in the first place? If it were stored as a zipfile, there would be no way for you to unzip it. Instead, the unzip program (and many other programs) are stored as SELF-EXTRACTING ARCHIVES.

A self-extracting archive is an executable program that, when run, automatically unzips itself into as many files and subdirectories as necessary. Such programs are easy to use. All you need to do is download the file to your temporary directory, and then execute the program. At the time I wrote this chapter, the current version of **pkzip** and **pkunzip** was available in many places around the Net under the name **pkz204g.exe**.

If you download a program in the form of a self-extracting archive, you process it as I have described above with one change: Instead of using **pkunzip** to unzip the file (step 4), all you need to do is execute the downloaded file.

For example, say you download the file **pkz204g.exe** to your temporary directory. From DOS, you unzip it by moving to that directory and entering the command:

```
pkz204g
```

Within Windows 95, open the "Start" menu and select "Run". Then use "Browse" to navigate to the directory where the file is stored. Select the file and run it. If you are using the old version of Windows, you can do the same thing by pulling down the "File" menu and selecting "Run".

HINT

Program names that have numbers in them usually refer to the version of the program. For example, **pkz204g.exe** contains version 2.04g of **pkzip**. When you have a choice, always download the file with the highest numbers.

If you see a file name that contains word **beta**, it means the program is a pre-release version. Use it at your own risk.

 **INTERNET RESOURCE** *Look in the catalog under Internet Resources for File Compression*

Important File Types for Windows and DOS Users

For reference, Figure 21-3 contains a summary of the most important file extensions for Windows and DOS users. If you become familiar with the extensions on this list, they will be all you need most of the time.

Background Information About Macintosh Files

Note: In this section I am going to get into some technical details regarding Macintosh files. If you don't like reading about details, the whole thing can be summarized as follows:

- On the Net, most Macintosh files are stored in Binhex format.

- When you attach a Macintosh file to a message and mail it to another Macintosh user, you must use Binhex.

File Extension	Description
au	sound
avi	video
bat	executable batch file
bmp	picture
com	executable file
doc	word processing document
exe	executable file; self-extracting archive
gif	picture
html	hypertext web document
htm	same as html
jpg	picture
mpg	video
ps	postscript file
txt	plain ASCII text
wav	sound
zip	compressed file/archive

Figure 21-3. *The most important file types for Windows and DOS users*

On the Internet, Macintosh programs are stored using special formats which are different from those used with DOS, Windows or Unix. Here is why.

Macintosh files have a special characteristic which is unique. Although you don't notice it from minute to minute, all Macintosh files actually have two parts: a DATA FORK and a RESOURCE FORK. The details are technical, and you don't really need to worry about them. The important point is that, when you transfer a Macintosh file to someone else, you have to make sure you transfer both parts.

HINT

What are the data fork and resource fork?

If you are a programmer, you can think of the data fork as being data, and the resource fork as being code. More precisely, the data fork is usually text and is the only part of the file which would be meaningful on a different computer system. For example, if you have a file of data on a Macintosh and you want to send the data to a friend who uses a PC, you would send only the data fork.

The resource fork contains a collection of arbitrary attribute/value pairs. These pairs include program segments, icon bitmaps and parametric values. The resource fork is where all the special Mac stuff is hidden.

Although a great deal of Macintosh software is available for free on the Net, very little of it is actually stored on Macintosh computers. Most of the anonymous ftp sites in the world are Unix computers (and, to a lesser extent, PCs). The important thing is that these computer systems do not support the idea of data and resource forks and, as such, are fundamentally incompatible with Macintosh files. (In Macintosh terms, Unix and DOS files only have a "data fork".)

Thus, before a Macintosh file can be stored on a non-Macintosh anonymous ftp site, the file must be converted to a special format. There are three such formats in common use. They are BINHEX, CPT and MACBINARY. Each of these formats can encode a two-part Macintosh file as a standard one-part Unix or DOS file.

Binhex files are given an extension of **hqx**; CPT files have an extension of **cpt**; and MacBinary files have an extension of **bin**. (The name "Binhex" refers to "binary" and "hexadecimal", two technical computer terms describing how data is stored. "CPT" refers to "Compact Pro", the name of the program that creates CPT files.)

Here is an example. Consider the following three files: **huey.hqx**, **dewey.cpt** and **louie.bin**. The first file is a Binhex file, the second file is a CPT file, and the third file is a MacBinary file.

Both Binhex and CPT files are ASCII text. MacBinary files (as the name implies) are binary files. In practice, most Macintosh files on the Net are encoded as Binhex; however, you will see some CPT files. MacBinary is not used much.

HINT

In order to mail a binary file to someone (even as an attachment), the file must first be converted to ASCII text. On the Net, the two most common systems are Mime and Binhex. However, Mime will only convert the data fork of a Macintosh file; the resource fork will be lost. Binhex will convert both forks and preserve them in a single ASCII text package.

Thus, if you are attaching a file to a message and mailing it to a friend who uses a PC, you should use Mime. The resource fork will be lost but, on a PC, only the data fork part of a Macintosh file will be useful anyway.

However, if you are mailing a file to another Macintosh user, you should *always* use Binhex. This guarantees that, at the other end, the file will emerge intact as a complete Macintosh file.

This is why Macintosh people use Binhex, and everyone else uses Mime.

Downloading Software for a Macintosh

Most Macintosh programs are stored as compressed archives which have been converted to Binhex format. In other words, when you find a Macintosh program on the Net, it will probably be a single Binhex file. (To a lesser extent, you will also find programs stored as CPT files.)

In order to use a program, you must download it, convert it to Macintosh format, uncompress it, extract the individual files from the archive, and then install the program. Fortunately, you are using a Macintosh, and just about everything will be done for you automatically.

The most common compression and archiving program is called Stuffit. Files that have been created by Stuffit are given an extension of **sit**, for example, **harley.sit**. When someone prepares a program for distribution, he will collect the files into an archive, compress the archive into a single **sit** file, and then use Binhex to convert the **sit** file to ASCII text. Thus, the final result will have a double extension **sit.hqx**, for example, **harley.sit.hqx**. If CPT is used instead of Binhex, the double extension will be **sit.cpt**, for example, **harley.sit.cpt**.

This means most of the Macintosh programs you will find on the Net will have names like **something.sit.hqx** or **something.sit.cpt**.

For reference, here is a description of all the steps you need to follow in order to download and install Macintosh software from the Net:

1. Find the software you need.

I have several favorite web pages that contain collections of software. For convenience, I keep these pages on my bookmark list (see Chapter 10), and they are always the first places I look when I want an Internet-related program (such as an Internet client or a picture viewer). If I can't find the program I want on one of these pages, I use a web search engine (also Chapter 10) or archie (Chapter 20).

2. Create a temporary folder on your Macintosh.

It is a good idea to download and process all new programs in a temporary folder. This helps you isolate the files in a well-known place. Moreover, if you don't like the program, it is easy to drag the whole thing to the trash can.

3. Download the program (a single **sit.hqx** or **sit.cpt** file) into your temporary folder, and then process the file.

You can use either your web browser (Chapter 10) or your ftp client (Chapter 18) to download the program. Once the file is downloaded, you still need to convert it to a Macintosh file, uncompress it, and extract the original files from the archive. All of this can be done by a single file processing program, the most common one being Stuffit Expander.
(This assumes, of course, that you already have Stuffit Expander. If not, I will tell you how to get it, later in this section.)

⌫HINT

Configure your web browser and your ftp client to launch Stuffit Expander automatically whenever you download a **sit**, **hqx** or **cpt** file. Now, whenever you download a program (in either **sit.hqx** or **sit.cpt** format), everything will be done for you automatically.

4. Install the program.

With simple programs, there is really nothing more to do. There will be a single program ready to run. If so, all you have to do is move the program to whichever folder you want to keep the program in permanently. With more complex software, you will need to run an installation program. Look for an icon with a name containing the word "Install". Double-click on this icon and the installation program will run automatically. When it is finished, you will probably be left with a folder containing all the program files. You can then move this folder to a permanent location.

5. Look for a readme file.

A README FILE contains information you should read before you install a program. The readme file will have a name containing the word "Readme". Be sure to read this file *before* you use the program for the first time. There may be important instructions you should understand.

HINT

Read the readme file *before* you run the program for the first time.

6. Check the program for viruses.

Use a virus checking program to see if the files you downloaded contain any known viruses. Do this *before* you run the program for the first time. If you don't have a virus program, you can get one for free on the Net.

If you are downloading software from a secure site—for example, if you are downloading the latest web browser from the browser company's anonymous ftp site—you probably don't need to check for viruses. Still, to coin a phrase, it is better to be safe than sorry.

HINT

If you catch a sexually transmitted disease, it can be a minor annoyance, but if you download a virus to your Macintosh, you can cause real damage to your hard disk.

7. Run the program.

Run the program and see if it looks okay. The first time you use the program, it is a good idea to spend a few minutes looking at the help information to orient yourself.

8. Clean up the temporary folder.

Once you have successfully installed the program, and moved it to another folder, you can delete the files in the temporary folder. For example, if you download and install a program named **harley.sit.hqx**, you will be left with this file, plus a file named **harley.sit**, both of which should be removed.

HINT

I have a folder named "Temp" that I use for downloading files. After I install a program, I drag the extra files to the trash can, but I do not delete my Temp folder. In this way, I always have a folder available to receive incoming files.

HINT

You can configure Stuffit Expander so it will automatically delete the original **hqx** file, as well as any intermediate files. If you do this, you won't have to clean up your temporary folder by hand.

So far, I have discussed how to get programs from the Net. To summarize, you download the file and then use Stuffit Expander to process it. However, how do you get Stuffit Expander in the first place? If it were stored as a compressed Binhex file, there would be no way for you to process it. Instead, the Stuffit Expander program (and many other programs) are stored as SELF-EXTRACTING ARCHIVES.

A self-extracting archive is an executable program that, when run, automatically converts itself into as many files and subdirectories (folders) as necessary. Self-extracting archives are given names with an extension of **sea**, for example, **harley.sea**.

Such programs are easy to use. All you need to do is download the file to your temporary folder, and then execute the program (by double-clicking on it). At the time I wrote this chapter, the current version of Stuffit Expander was available in many places around the Net under the name **stuffitexpander3.52.sea**. Stuffit Expander is freeware (which means you can use it for free and share it with anyone you want).

HINT

Program names that have numbers in them usually refer to the version of the program. For example, **stuffitexpander3.52.sea** contains version 3.52 of Stuffit Expander. When you have a choice, always download the file with the highest numbers.

 **INTERNET RESOURCE** *Look in the catalog under Internet Resources for File Compression*

Important File Types for Macintosh Users

For reference, Figure 21-4 contains a summary of the most important file extensions for Macintosh users. If you become familiar with the extensions on this list, they will be all you need most of the time.

File Extension	Description
aif	sound
au	sound
avi	video
bin	binary file (MacBinary)
cpt	ASCII text version of Macintosh file (Compact Pro)
gif	picture
html	hypertext web document
htm	same as **html**
hqx	ASCII text version of Macintosh file (BinHex)
jpeg	picture
jpg	same as **jpeg**
mov	video
mpeg	video
mpg	same as **mpeg**
ps	postscript file
qt	video
sea	self-extracting archive
sit	compressed file/archive (Stuffit)

Figure 21-4.   *The most important file types for Macintosh users*

Working With Unix Compressed Files (z and gz)

Even if you don't use Unix directly, as an Internet user, you depend on Unix computers a great deal. This is because many of the servers on the Net use Unix. For example, when you download a file via anonymous ftp, or contact a web server or a gopher server, chances are the computer at the other end is running Unix. And, of course, if you are accessing the Internet via a shell account, you are using a Unix computer to run your Internet client programs (see Chapter 5). For these reasons, it is important for you to learn to recognize a few of the important file types used with Unix.

Actually, there are only three main types of files you need to understand: two types of compressed files and one type of archive. In this section, I will discuss compressed files. In the next section, I will discuss archives.

In the Unix world, there are two systems used for compressing files. The old system uses two programs: **compress** and **uncompress**. You use **compress** to compress a file, and **uncompress** to uncompress. The new system uses **gzip** and **gunzip**. You use **gzip** to compress a file, and **gunzip** to uncompress.

compress produces a compressed version with an extension of **Z** (uppercase "Z"). **gzip** produces a compressed file with an extension of **gz**. For example, if you see two files named **recipe.Z** and **game.gz**, you can tell that **recipe** was compressed by the **compress** program, while **game** was compressed by **gzip**.

⚑ HINT

The **compress** and **uncompress** programs are part of traditional Unix and, as such, are available on all Unix systems. The **gzip** and **gunzip** programs were written by Jean-loup Gailly and are distributed by the Free Software Foundation (an organization dedicated to the creation of free, high-quality software). These programs are not included with all Unix systems. However, most system managers install **gzip**, **gunzip** and related programs, so they should be available to you.

To uncompress a **Z** file, use the **uncompress** program along with the name of the compressed file. For example:

```
uncompress recipe.Z
```

To uncompress a **gz** file, use the **gunzip** program along with the name of the compressed file. For example:

```
gunzip game.gz
```

Both **uncompress** and **gunzip** expect the compressed file to have the appropriate extension, so you do not have to actually type it. For example, the following two commands are equivalent:

```
uncompress recipe
uncompress recipe.Z
```

Similarly, these two commands are also equivalent:

```
gunzip game
gunzip game.gz
```

HINT

The **gunzip** program can actually uncompress both **Z** and **gz** files. Thus, you can use **gunzip** exclusively. For example, both of these commands will work just fine:

```
gunzip recipe.Z
gunzip game.gz
```

Both **uncompress** and **gunzip** delete the compressed file and replace it with the uncompressed file. For example, say you uncompress a file named **game.gz** by entering the command:

```
gunzip game.gz
```

As part of the uncompression process, **gunzip** will erase the file **game.gz**. You will be left with only one file, in this case, **game**.

To find out more about **compress**/**uncompress** or **gzip**/**gunzip**, use the **man** command to display the appropriate pages in the online Unix manual. The commands to use are:

```
man compress
man gzip
```

HINT

If you use a PC or a Macintosh, you will often find **Z** and **gz** files you will want to download and uncompress. With a PC, there are a number of utility programs you can use—for both DOS and Windows—to process such files. Just use the Web or archie to find such a program and install it on your computer.

With a Macintosh, life is simpler. The Stuffit Expander program (described earlier in the chapter) knows how to uncompress **Z** and **gz** files, so you don't have to do anything special.

 **INTERNET RESOURCE**   *Look in the catalog under Internet Resources for File Compression*

Working With Unix Archives (Tarfiles)

An archive is a set of files collected together into one large file. The Unix program used to create an archive is named **tar**. The same program (with different options) is used to reverse the process: that is, to unpack an archive by extracting the individual files. Archives created by **tar** are called TARFILES and are given an extension of **tar**, for example, **game.tar**.

What's in a Name?

tar

The name **tar** stands for "tape archive", because the original use for this program was to create archives to be stored on magnetic tape. Today, **tar** can be

There are two situations in which you might want to process a tarfile. First, you might want to unpack the archive on a Unix computer. Second, if you are using a shell account, you might want to download the tarfile to your PC or Macintosh and then do the unpacking. In this section, I will show you how to process a tarfile using Unix. Later in the chapter, I will show you how to download a file from a Unix computer to your PC or Macintosh.

HINT

To unpack a tarfile on a PC or Macintosh, you will need a **tar** program that runs on your system. You can find such programs (for DOS, Windows and the Macintosh) by using a web search engine (Chapter 10) or archie (Chapter 20). Such programs work pretty much the same as the Unix **tar** command (but do read the documentation).

To unpack a tarfile, you use the **tar** command with the **-xvf** options. Simply type the name of the command, followed by these options, followed by the name of the tarfile. For example:

```
tar -xvf game.tar
```

The **x** option tells **tar** you want to extract files; the **v** (verbose) option tells **tar** to display extra information about each file as it is processed; the **f** option tells **tar** that the name of the tarfile follows directly.

Tarfiles will often contain not only files, but subdirectories as well. When you unpack the archive, **tar** will automatically create these subdirectories in the current directory. Thus, before you unpack a tarfile, it behooves you to create an empty directory to use for the unpacking operation. This ensures that all the unpacked files and directories will be segregated from your other files.

In this section, I can't go into all the details of creating directories and moving files. For that, you will have to consult a Unix book. (If you don't already have one, I suggest my book *The Unix Companion*, published by Osborne McGraw-Hill.) However, I will show you an example of how it all works.

Suppose you have downloaded a game via anonymous ftp (see Chapters 18 and 19). The game consists of a number of program and documentation files contained in a single tarfile named **game.tar**. Here is what to do, once you have downloaded the file.

Start by creating a new directory for the game:

```
mkdir game
```

Next, move the tarfile to this directory:

```
mv game.tar game
```

Now, change your working directory to be the new directory:

```
cd game
```

Finally, unpack the tarfile:

```
tar -xvf game.tar
```

HINT

In Unix, you can enter more than one command at a time by separating them with semicolons. For example:

```
mkdir game;  mv game.tar game;  cd game;  tar -xvf game.tar
```

At any time, you can display the name of your working directory by using the **pwd** (print working directory) command.

After you unpack an archive, it is a good idea to list the new files and directories. To do so, use the **ls** (file list) command with the **-l** (long listing) option:

```
ls -l
```

The final consideration is that **tar** will not remove the original tarfile. You will have to do this yourself, by using the **rm** command:

```
rm game.tar
```

To summarize, the following series of commands will process an archive named **game.tar**. The commands create a new directory, move the tarfile to that directory, change to the directory, unpack the archive, list all the new files, and then remove the original tarfile:

```
mkdir game
mv game.tar game
cd game
tar -xvf game.tar
ls -l
rm game.tar
```

If you would like to see what is inside a tarfile without actually unpacking it, you can use the **t** (table of contents) option instead of the **x** (extract) option:

```
tar -tvf game.tar
```

HINT

The **tar** command is unusual in that the options do not need to be preceded by a **-** (hyphen) character, as is the case with most Unix commands. Thus, the following two commands are equivalent:

```
tar -xvf game.tar
tar xvf game.tar
```

You will often see **tar** commands written this way, so don't be confused.

I believe that it is better to get in the habit of using the **-** character to precede options, because that is the convention that you must follow with virtually all other Unix commands.

To create an archive of your own, use the **tar** command with the **-cvf** options (**c** for create). Type **tar -cvf**, followed by the name you want for the archive, followed by the names of the files you want to include in the **archive.** For example, let's say that you want to collect three files named **groatcakes**, **chicken-soup** and **brownies** into an archive named **cookbook.tar**. Use the command:

```
tar -cvf cookbook.tar groatcakes chicken-soup brownies
```

If you would like more information about using **tar**, you can use the **man** command to display the **tar** entry from the online Unix manual:

```
man tar
```

Compressed Tarfiles

As you rummage through the Internet's anonymous ftp sites, you will find many tarfiles that have been compressed (to save space and to make downloading faster). Such files will have one of several extensions.

If the tarfile was compressed with **compress**, the extension will be **tar.Z**, for example, **book.tar.Z**.

If the tarfile was compressed with **gzip**, the extension will be **tar.gz**, for example, **document.tar.gz**. Sometimes, this particular double extension is replaced by **tgz**. For example, the following file names both indicate a tarfile named **document.tar** which has been compressed using **gzip**:

```
document.tar.gz
document.tgz
```

To use such files, all you need to do is follow the steps I have already outlined for uncompressing and unpacking. Just remember to uncompress first.

HINT

The **gunzip** program will uncompress both **gz** and **Z** files.

Here is an example. You download a copy of a book via anonymous ftp. The various chapters of the book have been collected into a tarfile named **book.tar**. This tarfile has been compressed into a file named **book.tar.Z**, which is the file you downloaded. To process this file, you need to do the following:

1. Create a new directory for the book.

2. Move the compressed tarfile to this directory.

3. Change your working directory to be this directory.

4. Uncompress the compressed tarfile.

5. Unpack the tarfile.

6. List the new files.

7. If it looks okay, remove the tarfile.

Here are some sample commands that do the job:

```
mkdir book
mv book.tar.Z book
cd book
uncompress book.tar.Z
tar -xvf book.tar
ls -l
rm book.tar
```

If the file had been compressed with **gzip** (that is, if it had been a **tar.gz** file), we would have used **gunzip** instead of **uncompress**.

> **HINT**
>
> The **uncompress** and **gunzip** programs will remove the compressed file, but **tar -xvf** will not remove the tarfile.

For reference, Figure 21-5 contains a summary of the file extensions used with Unix compressed files and archives.

Uploading and Downloading Files with a Shell Account

The second most frequent question I am asked by people who use shell accounts is: How do I download files from the Unix host to my PC or Macintosh? (The most frequent question is: Where can I find erotic pictures to download?)

Remember, when you use a shell account, you do all of your work on the Unix host. On your computer, you run a communications program that emulates a terminal and connects to the remote host (see Chapter 5). If you want to copy Internet files to your own PC or Macintosh, you must first download those files to the Unix computer and, from there, download them to your computer.

If you have the right software, downloading and uploading files between your personal computer and your Unix host is easy. If you don't have the right software—or if it doesn't work properly—downloading and uploading will drive you crazy.

> **HINT**
>
> Quick review: Downloading refers to copying files from the remote host to your computer. Uploading refers to copying files from your computer to the remote host. To remember, think of the other computer as floating above you in the sky.

File Extension	Description
z	compressed file (**compress**)
gz	compressed file (**gzip**)
tar	archive [tarfile]
tar.Z	compressed tarfile (**compress**)
tar.gz	compressed tarfile (**gzip**)
tgz	same as tar.gz

Figure 21-5.   *File extensions used with Unix compressed files and archives*

To download files from the Unix host to your PC or Macintosh, you use what is called a FILE TRANSFER PROTOCOL. The most common protocol is called Zmodem. Thus, in order to download and upload files, you need Zmodem software on both your computer and the remote Unix host. All modern PC and Macintosh communication programs come with Zmodem functionality. What you need to ensure is that such a program exists on your host.

On Unix systems, the most common Zmodem program is named **sz** (the name means "send a file from the Unix computer to another computer using **Zmodem**"). If your system has **sz**, there will be a companion program named **rz** ("receive using Zmodem"). You should be able to display the documentation for both these programs by using the command:

```
man sz
```

If your Unix system does not have a Zmodem program, you may find another file transfer protocol called **Kermit**. The program will probably be named **kermit**. I will not talk about Kermit here, except to say it is very slow, and you should use it only if you can't use Zmodem.

To download a file from the remote host to your PC or Macintosh, type **sz**, followed by either **-a** or **-b** (I will explain in a moment), followed by the name of the file. For example:

```
sz -a document
sz -b picture.gif
```

If you are downloading an ASCII text file, use **-a**. If you are downloading a binary file, use **-b**. If you are not sure what type of file you have, use **-b**.

HINT

Never download a binary file without using **-b**. The **sz** program may look like it is working okay, but when the file gets to your PC, the data inside the file will be damaged. This is the most common answer to the question: Why can't I unzip the zipfile I downloaded to my PC?

As soon as you enter the **sz** command, one of two things will happen. Your communication program may detect that a Zmodem transfer has been initiated and start transferring the file automatically. (Some communication programs can be configured to do this.) Otherwise, you will see a message similar to:

Sending in Batch Mode

If you see such a message, you will have to tell your communication program to start a Zmodem download. How you do this varies from program to program, so you will have to read the documentation that came with your program. As an example, if you use Telix (a PC shareware communications program), you would press the PAGEDOWN key and then select "Zmodem" from a menu.

To upload a file from your PC or Macintosh to the remote host, start by entering one of the following commands (on the host):

```
rz   -a
rz   -b
```

(Remember to use **-b** if you are uploading a binary file.) After you enter this command, you will see a message similar to:

rz waiting to receive.

You must now tell your communications program to begin a Zmodem upload. Again, how you do this depends on your program. For example, with Telix you would press the PAGEUP key, select "Zmodem" from a menu, and then enter the name of the file you want to upload.

As I said before, when it all works, it's simple. When it doesn't work, it will make you tear your hair out and wonder if man is really Nature's last word.

HINT

There are no publicly accessible ftp or web sites with erotic pictures. From time to time, some enterprising individual will try to start such a service, but within a few days, the network traffic to that site will become overwhelming, and the person will be forced to close it down.

The only dependable source of erotic pictures on the Net is Usenet.

Chapter Twenty-Two

Mailing Lists

In this chapter, I will show you how to access a huge network of discussion groups that are carried out entirely by mail. To participate in these discussions, you do not need Usenet or any other Internet services. In this chapter, I will explain how mailing lists work, how to find them, and what you need to get started.

There are thousands of discussions going on right now on every topic imaginable, and to participate, all you need is an electronic mail address.

What Is a Mailing List?

Like all successful Internet services, mailing lists are based on a simple idea. When you mail a message to someone, you specify an address. If you want to mail a message to more than one person, you can set up a special name, called an ALIAS, that represents a group of people.

For example, let's say you set up an alias called **executives** to represent the addresses of three people named Curly, Larry and Moe. Whenever you mail a message to **executives**, the mail program will automatically send it to each of these three users.

Imagine how these three people could use this alias to have a discussion group. Say that Curly gets an idea that he wants to share with the others. All he has to do is mail a message to **executives** and everybody gets a copy. Now let's say that Moe wants to comment on something in Curly's message. He sends his own message to **executives**. Again, the message is automatically sent to everybody on the list.

Now, think about the same sort of thing on a larger scale. Imagine an alias that contains the mail addresses of dozens or even hundreds of users, scattered all around the Internet. Any message sent to the alias will be sent automatically to everyone in the group. People can talk, argue, help one another, discuss problems, share information, and so on. Everything that anyone says goes to all the people in the group.

This is a MAILING LIST. As an Internet user, you have access to thousands of such lists, each of which is devoted to a specific topic.

How Are Mailing Lists Different From Usenet Newsgroups?

In Chapters 13 and 14, I discussed Usenet: the worldwide collection of newsgroups. (We refer to Usenet discussion groups as "newsgroups" even though they do not contain actual news.) I mentioned there are over 13,000 different Usenet newsgroups.

Many of these newsgroups are of local or regional interest, and even large computer systems will usually carry no more than a couple of thousand groups. Still, that is a huge variety. Since Usenet offers such a large variety of discussion topics, it is natural to ask how Usenet newsgroups differ from mailing lists.

The first big difference is that you have to learn a lot more to participate in Usenet. In particular, you have to learn how to use a program to read the articles, and it may take a while for you to feel at home with Usenet. With a mailing list, all you need to know is how to send and read mail, something which you should probably learn anyway. This means that people who do not have access to Usenet—or don't want to learn how to use it—can still participate in discussion groups.

The next difference is that the discussions in a mailing list come to you in the form of messages sent to your personal mailbox. Some lists have only a few messages a day. However, it is not uncommon for a busy list to generate tens of messages a day. Since all these messages show up in your mailbox, you have to do something with them. Usenet articles, on the other hand, are stored in a central location and are administered by a system manager. When you participate in mailing lists, it is not uncommon to return from a two-week vacation and find hundreds of messages in your mailbox. (However, as I will explain later in the chapter, it is usually possible to tell a mailing list to stop sending you messages temporarily.)

HINT

Mailing lists can generate a lot of messages. Although you can subscribe to as many mailing lists as you want, it is best to confine yourself to no more than five. Otherwise, you are guaranteed to find your mailbox constantly filled with unread messages.

One of the nice things about mailing lists is that you can choose a few that interest you and count on getting the messages automatically. There is nothing for you to do but read your mail. With Usenet, you have to start your newsreader program and check your favorite newsgroups every time you want to see what has arrived. Moreover, most system managers automatically delete Usenet articles after they have been around for a fixed period (anywhere from 1-2 days to several weeks).

However, Usenet is more convenient in other ways. As a Usenet user, you only need to participate when you want. This means that you can drop in and out of discussions as the mood strikes you. Moreover, it is easy to sample a variety of newsgroups quickly. With a mailing list (as you will see), you have to send a special mail message to be put on the list and another message to be taken off.

HINT

To use a mailing list, there are two main ideas you need to understand. First, you should understand the basic concepts behind the Internet mail system and how to use a mail program. Second, you need to know how to read and understand Internet addresses.

If you feel like you need a quick review, you might want to take a few moments to skim Chapters 6 and 7 where I discuss these topics. If you have a shell account and use the **pine** Unix mail program, you can also read Chapter 8.

Moderated and Unmoderated Mailing Lists

Each mailing list has an administrator in charge of the list. In most cases, this is one person, variously referred to as the list manager, administrator or coordinator. Most mailing lists are run by a program, so there is not a lot for the administrator to do. The program keeps track of who is on the list, and automatically handles the request to add or remove a name.

Every mailing list has an official address. When you send a message to this address, the message is automatically mailed to everyone on the list. In other words, anyone can contribute to a mailing list just by sending a message to the appropriate address.

When you receive a message from a mailing list, it will be sent from the same address. Thus, if you reply to a mailing list article, your reply will automatically be sent to everyone on the list.

HINT

Before you reply to any message, always ask yourself if it would be better to send a private response to the person who sent the message. (The person's name and address will be in the message.) In many cases, it is more appropriate to send a private response than a message that will be sent to everyone in the group.

Some mailing lists are MODERATED. This means that all the messages go to one person, called the MODERATOR (which may or may not be the same person as the administrator). The moderator decides which articles should be sent out to the members of the list. Most moderators also perform some basic editing and organization on the raw material.

Some moderators organize messages into a collection called a DIGEST. A digest is like an issue of an electronic magazine: a whole set of messages and articles in one easy to read package. Some moderators will include a table of contents with each digest so it is easy to find the messages that interest you.

The advantage of a moderated mailing list is you see only the best messages (in someone's opinion, anyway). Many unmoderated mailing lists have a lot of boring and redundant messages that you will have to wade through to find the jewels.

The main disadvantage of a moderated list is that maintaining it is a lot of work. Moreover, the only compensation that moderators receive is that warm feeling that comes to those who help their fellows. (Thus, most mailing lists are not moderated.)

How Mailing Lists Are Administered

The most important part of administering a mailing list is keeping track of the people on the list. When you request to be put on a mailing list, we say that you SUBSCRIBE to that list. When you ask to be taken off the list, you UNSUBSCRIBE. (Remember, though, even though we talk about "subscribing" there is no charge for this service; mailing lists are free.)

There are two basic ways in which mailing lists are administered. Most lists are maintained by a program. To subscribe, you send a message to a special address. All mail to this address is automatically processed by the list administration program. Since the message will be read by a program, you must use a particular format (which I explain later).

A few lists are maintained by a person. With these lists, you send a message that is read by the administrator who manually adds or deletes people from the list. Although most lists are public, there are some private lists you cannot join without the permission of the administrator.

The three most common mailing list programs are Listserv, Listproc and Majordomo. I will discuss how to use these systems later in the chapter. In general, all three programs are easy to use. You send one message to subscribe to a list and another message to unsubscribe. Before I talk about the details, however, I want to take a few moments to discuss some important background topics. I will start with Bitnet, a network that has been associated with mailing lists for a long time.

Bitnet

BITNET is a worldwide network—separate from the Internet—that connects well over a thousand academic and research institutions in more than 40 countries. Many of the Bitnet sites are IBM mainframe computers running the VM operating system and supporting hundreds of users. Thus, Bitnet serves a very large number of people. In this section, I will explain a little about Bitnet because, as you will see, it is the source of many of the mailing lists to which you have access.

Bitnet began in 1981 as a small network of IBM mainframe computers at the City University of New York (CUNY). The name "Bitnet" was chosen to stand for the "Because It's Time Network". (No doubt, this name would make sense to you if you were using an IBM mainframe computer in New York in 1981.)

Outside of the U.S., Bitnet is known by different names. In Canada, it is called Netnorth. In Europe, it is the European Academic Research Network (EARN). In Latin America and Asia, you will find other names.

In Chapter 2, I discussed protocols (technical specifications) and explained how the Internet is based on a family of protocols called TCP/IP. Bitnet is based on a family of IBM protocols called RSCS (Remote Spooling Communications Subsystem) and NJE (Network Job Entry).

Historically, Bitnet developed within a technology that did not allow for systems like Usenet. Thus, an elaborate mailing list system, based on the Listserv system, was developed. Today, many Bitnet computers are also on the Internet. This means that, as an Internet user, you have access to all of the Bitnet mailing lists, many of which have been in existence for years.

When you subscribe to Bitnet mailing lists, you will see that Bitnet people use a number of common abbreviations in the names of their computers and mailing lists. Here are a few such abbreviations:

- **-1**: Many Bitnet mailing lists have names that end with **-1** (lowercase "L"), for example, **film-1**. The **-1** suffix stands for "list", and is an old, unnecessary tradition.

- **vm**: The name of an IBM mainframe operating system. You will often see **vm** in the name of a Bitnet computer, for example, **cunyvm.cuny.edu**.

- **cuny**: City University of New York, where Bitnet was developed.

- **bitnic**: Bitnet Network Information Center, a main site of Bitnet in the U.S.

- **earn**: European Academic and Research Network, the European part of Bitnet.

You will also find that Bitnet people tend to use acronyms and commands that are all uppercase letters, like "BITNET" and "LISTSERV". This is part of the IBM mainframe culture. Compare this to our more genteel Internet traditions, which encourage the use of terminology that is almost exclusively lowercase.

HINT

You can learn a lot about a culture by observing how it uses upper- and lowercase letters.

Bitnet Mailing Lists and Usenet

To participate in a mailing list, you subscribe to it. Once you do, all the messages that are posted to the list will be sent to you via electronic mail. When you send a message to the official address of the list, the message will automatically be sent to all the subscribers. However, with many of the Bitnet mailing lists, there is another way to participate.

Many (but not all) of the Bitnet lists are available on Usenet as well as through the mail. Each such mailing list has a corresponding Usenet discussion group. All the messages sent to the list are automatically posted to the discussion group. Thus, you can read the messages either by subscribing to the list or by reading the corresponding Usenet group. (I explain Usenet in Chapters 13 and 14.) All the Bitnet-related discussion groups are in the **bit** hierarchy and have names that start with **bit.listserv**.

For example, there is a Bitnet mailing list named **film-1** which is devoted to film and the cinema. Messages to this list can also be read as Usenet articles in the newsgroup **bit.listserv.film-1**. Moreover, when you send an article to the

Usenet group, it will be forwarded to the list itself and from there to all the subscribers (although this doesn't always work properly).

The actual work of sending messages between Usenet and Bitnet is done by a computer called a BITNET/USENET GATEWAY. There are a number of such computers that act as gateways for the various lists.

INTERNET RESOURCE   *Look in the catalog under Internert Resources for*
Bitnet Oriented Usenet Groups

Sending Mail to Bitnet

To subscribe to a mailing list all you have to do is find the list and send a message asking to subscribe. I will explain how to do this later in the chapter. First, though, I need to take a moment to discuss how to mail a message to Bitnet, because many of the mailing lists you will encounter are Bitnet lists. To subscribe or unsubscribe to such a list, you will need to send a message to a Listserv server residing on a Bitnet computer.

Virtually all Bitnet computers are on the Internet and have regular Internet addresses. However, you will sometimes find mailing list information that specifies only a Bitnet address, and not an Internet address. In such cases, it is possible to send mail to Bitnet by using a special addressing format.

Here is an example. You hear about an interesting mailing list on a Bitnet computer named **templevm**. To subscribe to this list, you have to send a message to the user name **listserv** on the **templevm** computer. (I will explain the details later in the chapter.) However, you do not happen to have an Internet address for the **templevm** computer.

To send the message, you can use an address that looks like an Internet address, but uses a top-level domain of **bitnet**. In this case, you would use:

```
listserv@templevm.bitnet
```

The suffix **bitnet** is called a "pseudo domain". The computer that handles your outgoing mail will recognize the **bitnet** pseudo domain and route your mail to Bitnet.

**HINT**

The **bitnet** pseudo domain is not an official Internet domain, and some mail servers do not recognize it. If this is the case with your system, your mail will be returned to you marked "Host unknown" (like in the Elvis Presley song). If so, you will have to send mail to Bitnet through a "Bitnet/Internet gateway". I explain how to do so in Chapter 6.

Finding Mailing Lists

There are a vast number of mailing lists on the Internet and on Bitnet. Within these lists, you will find a discussion on just about any topic you can imagine. Moreover, there are new lists being formed all the time, and (less often) old lists being canceled.

If you want to find out what is available, there are a number of sources from which you can obtain a summary of mailing lists. Such a summary is often referred to as a LIST-OF-LISTS. In this section, I will show you where to obtain various lists-of-lists. I will also show you related resources that can help you search for a specific list.

Each of these resources is maintained by different people (usually volunteers) and covers the territory in its own way. Thus, it is a good idea to try them all when you are looking for something in particular.

HINT

The lists-of-lists are large and take up a lot of disk space. If you copy such a list to your computer, you may want to delete the file when you are finished looking at it. There is no real reason to save a list-of-lists: it would just go out of date and you can get a newer version for free whenever you want.

Publicly Accessible Mailing Lists (PAML)

This is a huge list-of-lists used to keep track of publicly available Internet mailing lists. This list is updated regularly and posted to the Usenet newsgroup **news.lists**. The list is so large that it is posted in over 20 parts.

 **INTERNET RESOURCE**   *Look in the catalog under Internet Resources for*
Mailing Lists: Publicly Accessible Mailing Lists

The Internet List-of-Lists

Another large mailing list reference is the Internet List-of-Lists. Its purpose is to offer a description of every public mailing list—both Internet and Bitnet—along with instructions on how to subscribe.

This list is a useful, albeit very long reference. Unfortunately, the explanations are confusing. However, to subscribe to a mailing list, all you need to do is find the basic information (name, address and type of list) and then follow the instructions later in this chapter.

INTERNET RESOURCE   *Look in the catalog under Internet Resources for*
Mailing Lists: Internet List-of-Lists

Listserv Mailing Lists

You can get a summary of all the Listserv mailing lists on Bitnet by mailing a message to any Listserv server. In the body of the message, put the command **lists global**. The server will mail you back a list in which each mailing list is summarized on a single line.

If you are interested in a particular subject, use the command **lists global/***subject*, specifying whatever subject you want. For example, if you want a summary of all the lists that have something to do with poetry, use **lists global/poetry**.

You can send such a message to any Bitnet computer that has an Internet address. The best computers to use are the ones that act as Bitnet/Internet gateways (see Chapter 6). For reference, here are several such addresses that will work:

Bitnet/Internet Gateways
brownvm.brown.edu
cunyvm.cuny.edu
pucc.princeton.edu
uga.cc.uga.edu
vm1.nodak.edu

Here is an example of a message that requests the overall list. Notice that when you send commands to a Listserv server you do not need to specify a **Subject:** line. (Remember, you can send such a request to any Bitnet/Internet gateway.)

To: listserv@cunyvm.cuny.edu
Subject:
lists global

Because the list is so large, it may be broken into separate pieces by your mail program.

Mailing List Search Engine

If you use the Web, there is a special search engine you can utilize to search a large mailing list database. The database contains the name and a one-line description for each list. You specify keywords and the search engine will find each mailing list whose name or description contains the words.

The results of the search are returned as links containing the subscription addresses. In this way, if you find what you want, it is easy to send the appropriate message to subscribe to the list.

 **INTERNET RESOURCE** *Look in the catalog under Internet Resources for* *Mailing Lists: Search Engine*

New Bitnet Mailing Lists

There is a Bitnet mailing list named **new-list** that people use to announce new mailing lists. You can subscribe to this list in order to keep up on what is new and exciting. This list is also available as the Usenet newsgroup **bit.listserv.new-list**.

 **INTERNET RESOURCE** *Look in the catalog under Internet Resources for* *New Bitnet Mailing Lists*

Listserv, Listproc and Majordomo

Almost all mailing lists are managed by a computer program. Although every list has a person who acts as an administrator, he or she does not handle the housekeeping details by hand. The program does it all.

There are three common mailing list management programs: Listserv, Listproc and Majordomo. The Listserv program was originally developed to run on IBM mainframe computers. There were a good number of such computers connected together into the Bitnet network, but the system did not lend itself to the creation of Usenet-like discussion groups. Instead, people started to hold discussions via electronic mail. The Listserv program was developed to manage the mailing lists. The name "Listserv" stands for "List Server".

When the Internet became popular, it did have Usenet. Still, many people enjoyed participating in discussions by mail. Although Internet users could participate in Bitnet discussion groups via the Bitnet/Internet gateways, many people wanted to start their own lists, and the Listserv software worked only on IBM mainframe computers. To fill the void, various versions of Listserv were developed to run under Unix. (Most Internet servers use Unix.) One such version was named "Listserv". However, a more popular Listserv-like program was developed by the Corporation for Research and Educational Networking (CREN). This program was called "Listproc". The name stands for "List Processor".

Finally, a completely different mailing list system was developed by Brent Chapman. He chose the name "Majordomo", because a major-domo is traditionally the name given to the highest official in a large household (for example, a butler). The Majordomo program—like Listserv and Listproc—acts like an automatic butler, handling all the requests from the users of the mailing list.

The Two Types of Mailing List Addresses

To subscribe to a mailing list, all you have to do is mail a simple message to the computer program that administers the list. (If the list is administered by a person, you send a message to that person.) However, each mailing list has two different addresses, and you must take care to use the right one. Here are several examples to show you how it works.

There are three important items of information about each mailing list: the name of the list, the name of the computer, and the type of mailing list program. For example, say you are reading my book *The Internet Yellow Pages*, and you see the following mailing lists:

Buckminster Fuller: Listserv mailing list
List Name: **geodesic**
Subscription Address: **listserv@ubvm.cc.buffalo.edu**

Ancient Philosophy: Listproc mailing list
List Name: **sophia**
Subscription Address: **listproc@liverpool.ac.uk**

Michael Tucker: Majordomo mailing list
List Name: **explosive-cargo**
Subscription Address: **majordomo@world.std.com**

In the first example, the name of the list is **geodesic**, the name of the computer is **ubvm.cc.buffalo.edu**, and the mailing list program is Listserv; in the second example, the list is **sophia**, the computer is **liverpool.ac.uk**, and the mailing list program is Listproc; and in the final example, the list is **explosive-cargo**, the computer is **world.std.com**, and the mailing list program is Majordomo.

Each mailing list has two addresses. First, there is an administrative address which you use to communicate with the mailing list program. The second address is the one which you use to send messages to the list itself.

The administrative address uses the name of the program and the name of the computer. For example, here are the administrative addresses for the examples above:

listserv@ubvm.cc.buffalo.edu
listproc@liverpool.ac.uk
majordomo@world.std.com

These are the addresses to which you would send a message to subscribe, unsubscribe, or perform any other administrative function.

The address to which you would send messages to the list uses the name of the list and the name of the computer. For example, here are the list addresses for our examples:

geodesic@ubvm.cc.buffalo.edu
sophia@liverpool.ac.uk
explosive-cargo@world.std.com

It is important to understand the difference between these two types of addresses. If you send a message to **listserv@ubvm.cc.buffalo.edu** to subscribe to the **geodesic** mailing list, everything will work just fine. But if you send the same message to **geodesic@ubvm.cc.buffalo.edu**, it will be sent to everyone on the list. Not only will you not be subscribed, you will probably receive a lot of mail from irate subscribers telling you to use the administrative address. (Although they may not be so polite.)

> ## HINT
>
> If you send a message to a moderated mailing list, the message will go to the moderator, not to everyone on the list.

Listserv: Subscribing and Unsubscribing

To subscribe to a Listserv mailing list, you mail a short message to the administrative address of the list. The format of this message is simple. You use a single line containing:

- the word **subscribe**
- the name of the list
- your first and last names

You do not have to specify anything on the **Subject:** line.

Here is an example. Your name is Chuck Wagon, and you want to subscribe to the Listserv list named **geodesic** on the computer named **ubvm.cc.buffalo.edu**. Use the following message:

```
To: listserv@ubvm.cc.buffalo.edu
Subject:
subscribe geodesic Chuck Wagon
```

This message asks the Listserv program at **ubvm.cc.buffalo.edu** to add the person named Chuck Wagon to the **geodesic** mailing list. Notice that you do not have to specify your mailing address: the Listserv program will figure it out from the header of your message.

> ## HINT
>
> What do you do if you accidentally spelled your name wrong when you subscribed to a Listserv mailing list? Not to worry. Simply send in another **subscribe** message with your name spelled correctly. You do not need to unsubscribe just to change your name.

With some Listserv mailing lists, you will be asked to confirm your intention to subscribe. The Listserv program will send a message to your address asking if you really mean to subscribe. You must reply to this message with the single word **ok**. Once your reply is received, your subscription will be approved. This procedure is to prevent someone from forging your mail address and subscribing you to all kinds of mailing lists as a prank. (Although I don't explain how to forge mail in this book, it is a relatively simple process if you are a nerd.)

To unsubscribe to a Listserv mailing list, send a message to the administrative address of the list. In the body of the message, put a single line that contains:

- the word **unsubscribe**
- the name of the mailing list

For example, to unsubscribe from the list in the previous example, you would use:

```
To: listserv@ubvm.cc.buffalo.edu
Subject:
unsubscribe geodesic
```

As I explained earlier in the chapter, many Listserv mailing lists are maintained on IBM mainframe computers within the Bitnet network. When you send an administrative message to such a computer, you will always be sent a confirmation message. At the bottom of the message will be some useless mainframe information (which you can ignore). Here is an example:

```
Message 5/19  From L-Soft list server at UBVM
   Dec 21, 95 05:47:33 pm -0500


(message addressed to Chuck Wagon)


Date:          Thu, 21 Dec 1995 17:47:33 -0500
Subject:       Output of your job "chuck"


> ok
Confirming:
> SUBSCRIBE GEODESIC Chuck Wagon
You have been added to the GEODESIC list.


Summary of resource utilization
-------------------------------
  CPU time:       0.753 sec      Device I/O:     133
  Overhead CPU:   0.108 sec      Paging I/O:       3
  CPU model:         3090        DASD model:    3380
```

Aside from **subscribe** and **unsubscribe**, there are many other commands you can send to a Listserv program. I won't go into the details here. For more information, send the **help** command to any Listserv program. The program will send you an information document. For reference, Figure 22-1 summarizes the most important Listserv commands.

Listproc: Subscribing and Unsubscribing

To subscribe to a Listproc mailing list, you mail a short message to the administrative address of the list. The format of this message is simple. You use a single line containing:

- the word **subscribe**
- the name of the list
- your first and last names

You do not have to specify anything on the **Subject:** line.

Here is an example. Your name is Chuck Wagon, and you want to subscribe to the Listproc list named **sophia** on the computer named **liverpool.ac.uk**. Use the following message:

```
To: listproc@liverpool.ac.uk
Subject:
subscribe sophia Chuck Wagon
```

Subscribing and Unsubscribing

> **subscribe** *list firstname lastname*
>
> **unsubscribe** *list*

List Information

lists global	send summary of all known lists
lists global/*keyword*	send summary of lists matching *keyword*
review *list*	send information about specified list

Help Information

help	send summary of basic commands
info ?	send list of information topics
info *topic*	send information about specified topic

Figure 22-1. *Summary of important Listserv commands*

This message asks the Listproc program at **listproc@liverpool.ac.uk** to add the person named Chuck Wagon to the **sophia** mailing list. Notice that you do not have to specify your mailing address: the Listproc program will figure it out from the header of your message.

To unsubscribe to a Listproc mailing list, send a message to the administrative address of the list. In the body of the message, put a single line that contains:

- the word **unsubscribe**
- the name of the mailing list

For example, to unsubscribe from the list in the previous example, you would use:

```
To: listproc@liverpool.ac.uk
Subject:
unsubscribe sophia
```

Aside from **subscribe** and **unsubscribe**, there are many other commands you can send to a Listproc program. I won't go into the details here. For more information, send the **help** command to any Listproc program. The program will send you an information document. For reference, Figure 22-2 summarizes the most important Listproc commands.

Subscribing and Unsubscribing

    subscribe *list firstname lastname*

    unsubscribe *list*

List Information

lists global	send summary of all known lists
lists global/*keywords*	send summary of lists matching *keywords*
information *list*	send information about specified list

Help Information

help	send summary of basic commands
help me	send list of information topics
help *topic*	send information about specified topic

Figure 22-2. *Summary of important Listproc commands*

Majordomo: Subscribing and Unsubscribing

To subscribe to a Majordomo mailing list, you mail a short message to the administrative address of the list. The format of this message is simple. You use a single line containing:

- the word **subscribe**
- the name of the list

You do not have to specify anything on the **Subject:** line.

Here is an example. You want to subscribe to the Majordomo list named **explosive-cargo** on the computer named **world.std.com.** Use the following message:

```
To: majordomo@world.std.com
Subject:
subscribe explosive-cargo
```

This message asks the Majordomo program at **world.std.com** to subscribe you to the **explosive-cargo** mailing list. Notice that you do not have to specify your mailing address: the Majordomo program will figure it out from the header of your message.

To unsubscribe to a Majordomo mailing list, send a message to the administrative address of the list. In the body of the message, put a single line that contains:

- the word **unsubscribe**
- the name of the mailing list

For example, to unsubscribe from the list in the previous example, you would use:

```
To: majordomo@world.std.com
Subject:
unsubscribe explosive-cargo
```

Aside from **subscribe** and **unsubscribe**, there are several commands you can send to a Majordomo program. I won't go into the details here. For more information, send the **help** command to any Majordomo program. The program will send you an information document. For reference, Figure 22-3 summarizes the most important Majordomo commands.

Manually Administered Mailing Lists

Most mailing lists are managed by a computer program (usually Listserv, Listproc or Majordomo). However, there are still some lists which are completely administered by

Subscribing and Unsubscribing

`subscribe` *list*	subscribe to specified mailing list
`unsubscribe` *list*	unsubscribe to specified mailing list

List Information

`lists`	send summary of lists on this server
`info` *list*	send information about specified list

Help Information

`help`	send summary of commands

Figure 22-3.   *Summary of important Majordomo commands*

a person. In such cases, you will have to send a message to that person in order to subscribe or unsubscribe to the list. The main thing you need to know is where to send your request.

By convention, all manually administered lists have a special user name to which you can send requests: the name of the list followed by **-request**.

For example, say you are reading about a mailing list and you decide to subscribe. The address of the list is given as **foobar@muffin.com**. In other words, the name of the mailing list is **foobar**, and the list is maintained on the computer named **muffin.com**. It happens that this list is managed by hand so, in order to subscribe, you have to send a personal message to the administrator.

Do not send your request to **foobar@muffin.com**. Anything sent to this address will go to all the members of the list (who will not be happy with you). Instead, send your request to:

foobar-request@muffin.com

In this way, the message will go to the list manager.

Make sure you understand how this convention works. If the mailing list were named **nipper**, you would send the message to **nipper-request**; if the list were named **important-stuff**, you would send the message to **important-stuff-request**; and so on.

When you subscribe to a manually administered mailing list, remember that your message will be read by a human, not a program. Thus, be sure to be polite. Use a subject that says what you want, and include your full name and mailing address in the body of the message. Here is an example of how you might ask to subscribe to the **foobar** mailing list:

```
To: foobar@muffin.com
Subject: subscription request
Please subscribe me to the foobar mailing list.
Thank you.
Chuck Wagon    chuck@nipper.com
```

Here is an example of how you might ask to unsubscribe:

```
To: foobar@muffin.com
Subject: unsubscription request
Please unsubscribe me to the foobar mailing list.
Thank you.
Chuck Wagon    chuck@nipper.com
```

Chapter Twenty-Three

Telnet: Logging In to a Remote Computer

One of the wonderful things about the Internet is that it is as easy to use a computer on the other side of the world as it is to use a computer across the hall. In this chapter, I will explain how to log in to a remote computer by using the telnet service. When you use telnet, it is as if your keyboard and screen are connected to the remote computer.

For example, say you have a shell account on a computer in Holland. You are visiting a friend in California who has an Internet connection. Using telnet from his computer, you can connect to your computer in Holland, log in, and work as if you were there in person.

Telnet is important for two reasons. First, you can use it to access a remote computer on which you have an account. Second, the Internet has many public resources which you access via telnet. For example, this is how you would access a MUD (interactive virtual environment; see Chapter 28).

Using telnet is so transparent, it is easy to forget you are separated from the remote computer. The main limitation you will find is that, when Internet traffic is high, the response from a faraway computer may slow down. Still, it is common for experienced users to log in to several different Internet computers at the same time, moving from one to another smoothly and easily. I do it all the time.

What Is Telnet?

TELNET is the Internet service that allows you to log in to a remote Internet computer. To utilize this service, you run a telnet client program on your computer. This program uses the Internet to connect to the remote computer. Once the connection is made, your telnet client acts as an intermediary between you and the other computer. Everything you type on your keyboard is passed on to the other computer. Everything the other computer displays is sent to your computer, where it appears on your screen. As a result, your keyboard and screen seem to be connected directly to the remote computer.

Telnet is actually the oldest of the various Internet services. I would like to take a moment to explain the background as, to this day, the historical roots still affect telnet and how we use it.

The Internet is the descendent of the Arpanet, a network created in the late 1960s by the U.S. Department of Defense (see Chapter 1). At that time, there were no personal computers. There were only large, expensive mainframe computers and smaller, expensive "minicomputers". To work a computer interactively, you used a terminal: a device with a screen, a keyboard, some electronics, and not much more.

The first service provided on the Arpanet was "remote login", that is, telnet. This service—which was a remarkable achievement—allowed researchers to work on remote computers from a distance. To do so, they used the Arpanet to connect their terminal to a computer that was part of the Arpanet. Once the connection was made, a researcher could log in (by typing a user name and password) and use the keyboard and screen on his terminal, just as if it were connected directly to the remote computer.

In those days, terminals could only display characters—letters, numbers, punctuation, and so on—there were no graphics or windows or pictures. However, compared to other methods of using a computer (such as punch cards) terminals were extremely convenient. For this reason, when the Unix operating system was developed, it was designed to work with terminals. And, within a few years, Unix became an important part of the Arpanet.

Although Unix was designed to work with many types of terminals, one specific terminal became a de facto standard. This was the VT-100 terminal, manufactured by the Digital Equipment Corporation. The VT-100 standard became so accepted that, whenever someone wrote a program which needed to provide the functionality of a terminal, he would design the program to act like a VT-100. In technical terms, we would say that the program would "emulate" a VT-100.

Why am I telling you all this? Because today we have a global network—the Internet—connecting millions of computers all over the world. Tens of millions of people connect to this network using personal computers that are many times more powerful than the old mainframes. However, the main computers on the Internet run Unix and, to this day, the way to access Unix on a remote computer is to use a program that acts like a terminal. This program is telnet. And the terminal that telnet emulates is the old, primitive standby, the VT-100: a character-based device that has been obsolete for years.

So this is what telnet really is: a service that (1) connects to a remote Internet computer and (2) emulates a VT-100 terminal. Since the VT-100 is a character-based terminal, you cannot use graphics (pictures, icons, windows, and so on) when you use telnet.

HINT

Some telnet client programs offer more than VT-100 emulation. You may also choose VT-102 or VT-220. These are variations of the standard VT-100 and, in almost all cases, you can simply use VT-100 and ignore the differences.

HINT

To access the Net via a shell account (see Chapter 5), you use a communications program on your PC or Macintosh to dial the phone and connect to your Internet service provider. Once the connection is made, your communications program emulates a VT-100. In other words, when you use a shell account, you are using the same VT-100 terminal as the telnet service.

Thus, here is another way to describe telnet: Telnet is a service that allows you to log in to a remote Internet computer as if you were accessing it with a dial-up connection and a shell account.

Basic Concepts

In telnet terminology, your computer is called the LOCAL computer. The other computer, the one to which your telnet client connects, is called the REMOTE computer. We use these terms no matter how far away the other computer actually is: whether it is across the world or in the same room. On the Internet, we sometimes refer to Internet computers as "hosts". Using this terminology, we can say the job of your telnet client is to connect your local computer to a remote Internet host.

In general, there are two ways to use telnet. First, you can connect to any computer on the Internet for which you have a shell account. When you do, you will see the standard **login:** and **Password**: prompts. You can now log in and use the computer in the usual manner.

Second, there are many public resources which you can access via telnet. Some of these do not require a password. As soon as your telnet client makes the connection, you can start working with the remote computer. For example, a number of public library catalogs are set up in this manner.

Other public services (such as MUDs) do require passwords. The first time you connect to one of these systems, you will be asked to choose a user name and password. From then on, you would log in using whatever name and password you have chosen.

⚑ HINT

You can use the word "telnet" as a verb. For example, say you are visiting a friend in a distant city. You might ask him, "Can I use your computer for a minute? I want to telnet to my shell account to read my mail." (Or, "I want to telnet to my favorite MUD to see what is happening.")

Using Your Telnet Client

To use telnet, you run a telnet client program. This program connects you to a remote Internet host and then emulates a VT-100 terminal. If you access the Internet using a shell account, your telnet client will be the Unix **telnet** program. Otherwise, you use telnet by running a client program on your own computer. If you have a PC, you will run a Windows (or OS/2) client. If you have a Macintosh, you will run a Macintosh client program. (I discuss these ideas in Chapter 5.) In this chapter, I will discuss how to use a telnet program on a PC or Macintosh. In Chapter 24, I will show you how to use the Unix **telnet** program with a shell account.

Both Windows 95 and OS/2 come with their own telnet clients. You can use the built-in client, or you can find another one. If you use a Macintosh, you will have to find your own telnet client. Telnet clients for both PCs and Macintoshes are readily available on the Net.

 INTERNET RESOURCE *Look in the catalog under Internet Resources for* ***Telnet Clients***

With Windows 95, you can start the telnet program in the regular manner (by double-clicking on an icon or by putting it in your Start menu), or you can go to a DOS prompt and enter the `telnet` command. Regardless of how you start the program, it works the same.

With OS/2 there is more choice. The system comes with two different programs: `telnetpm` and `telnet`. The `telnetpm` program is the graphical telnet client. (The "pm" stands for "Presentation Manager".) The `telnet` program is a character-based program virtually identical to the Unix `telnet` program. You can choose whichever telnet client you want. Moreover, you can start either program graphically (by double-clicking on an icon) or from the OS/2 command line (by entering the `telnetpm` or `telnet` command). If you decide to use the OS/2 `telnet` program, it will work like the Unix program, which I explain later in the chapter.

Using a telnet client is easy. All you have to do is start the program, and tell it the name of the remote host to which you want to connect. Once the connection to the host is established, you will see whatever message that computer displays as part of the starting procedure. Figure 23-1 shows a telnet program connected to a public library catalog.

If you connect to a Unix computer which expects you to log in, it will start by displaying the line:

```
login:
```

Type the appropriate user name and press ENTER. You will then see the line:

```
Password:
```

Type the password and press ENTER. You will now be logged in.

Once your telnet client starts, there is generally nothing special to do. Just log in to the remote computer and start work. However, there are certain facets of the telnet program you can control by using the pull-down menus. Each program operates differently, so be sure to read the help information for your particular program.

HINT

Some telnet clients allow you to create a LOG FILE. This is a facility that will save the output from your session to a file on your computer. Using the log file is handy when you want to retain some information permanently. For example, say you are using a remote system that has a help command that you can type to display a large amount of help information. If you turn the log file on just before you type the command, you can save all the help information to a file on your computer. That way, you can view it whenever you want (say, in a separate window).

Connecting to a Specific Port Number

Within the Internet, numerous hosts offer telnet access to public services. Many of these hosts require that you specify a particular PORT NUMBER when you make the connection. The port number identifies the type of service that you are requesting. Here is an example.

There is a well-known MUD named Nightmare which you can use by telnetting to a computer named **nightmare.winternet.com**. (I discuss MUDs in Chapter 28.)

```
Telnet - melvyl.ucop.edu
Connect  Edit  Terminal  Help
                    Welcome to the University of California's

                        MELVYL× LIBRARY SYSTEM

   -  Catalog of books for UC and California State Library
   -  Catalog of periodicals titles for UC and academic libraries of California
   -  Journal article information, abstracts, and text in major subject areas
   -  Internet access to databases and systems across the world

   ------------------------ =>> SYSTEM NEWS <<= -----------------------
     Images of IEEE journals available in Experimental mode; type SHOW EXP 67
       New USE UCD GOPHER command connects to Davis; type EXPLAIN UCD GOPHER.
       National Library of Medicine special announcement; type SHOW MED NEWS.
             ESTC now available via USE EUREKA; type SHOW DLA 4.

   -------------------------------------------------------------------------

(c)1984. ×Registered trademark of The Regents of the University of California.
=========================================================================
   To select a database for searching:      press RETURN
   For help getting started:                type HELP and press RETURN

-> _
```

Figure 23-1.   *A telnet client program*

When you connect to this computer to use Nightmare, you must specify a port number of **1701**. This tells the system that you want to use the MUD.

With most graphical telnet clients, there will be a place to specify a port number when you type the name of the computer. If you are using the **telnet** program from the command line (with Unix, Windows 95 or OS/2), type the port number after the computer name. For example:

```
telnet nightmare.winternet.com 1701
```

(Be sure to leave a space between the computer name and the port number.)

When you connect to a remote host that uses a port number, the program that you want will usually start automatically, and you will not have to log in. When you end the program, the connection will be broken and **telnet** will stop by itself.

More About Port Numbers

In computer terminology, the term PORT refers to a connection between two devices or systems. For example, you might attach a printer to a port on the back of your computer. On a Unix system, we say that each terminal is connected to its own port on the host computer.

This same idea is used in Internet terminology. On the Internet, a protocol named TCP (Transmission Control Protocol) is used to transfer data from one host to another (see Chapter 2). Whenever TCP connects one Internet host to another, a port number is used to identify the type of connection. In fact, there is an Internet organization—called the Internet Assigned Number Authority—that maintains the official list of port numbers (of which there are many), and makes sure that unique numbers are allotted when necessary.

By default, ordinary telnet connections are made using port number **23**. In other words, when you do not specify a port number, the **telnet** program automatically connects using port **23**. Thus, the following two commands will make the same type of connection:

```
telnet fuzzball.ucsb.edu
telnet fuzzball.ucsb.edu 23
```

In order for you to connect to a remote host, it must be running a program that is prepared to communicate over the port that you use. When such a program is waiting for a connection, we say that it is LISTENING on that port.

Thus, we can say that, for a host to support regular telnet connections, it must have a program listening on port **23**. Another way to put it is that, when you use **telnet** to make a regular connection to a remote host, it contacts that host and checks to see if there is a program listening on port **23**.

It is only when you want to use a telnet connection over a different port that you need to specify an actual port number. Many Internet systems use different port numbers to offer some type of special service.

In the previous section, I showed you an example of using telnet to connect to a computer named **nightmare.winternet.com** using port number **1701**. By specifying a port number, it tells the remote computer to connect you to a special-purpose program (in this case, a MUD). In order for this connection to work, the MUD program must be running on this computer and it must be listening on port number **1701**. In most cases, a host can support more than one connection to a specific port at the same time. This particular MUD, for example, will support tens of users at the same time.

HINT

If you connect to a telnet resource that requires a special port number, you must specify that number. If you do not, your telnet client will use port **23** by default. At the other end, the remote computer will assume you want to log in using a shell account and display the standard **login:** prompt. If this happens, disconnect and re-establish the connection using the proper port number.

Chapter Twenty-Four

Using Telnet from a Shell Account: `telnet`

In Chapter 23, I discuss the telnet service and how you can use it to log in to a remote computer anywhere on the Net. In this chapter, I show you how to use the **telnet** program, the client you use with a Unix shell account. Before you read this chapter, make sure you have read Chapter 23 in which I explain the basic concepts.

OS/2 users: There is a program named **telnet**, which you can run from the OS/2 command line. This program works the same as the Unix version, and so this chapter pertains to you as well. In addition to **telnet**, there is also a graphical client named **telnetpm**; you can use whichever program you prefer. (Personally, I like the **telnet** program, but then I am also a Unix person, and I would rather memorize twenty commands than use my mouse.)

Starting the `telnet` Program

There are two ways to start the **telnet** program. In this section, I will show you how it is done most of the time. In the next section, I will discuss an alternate method.

To start **telnet**, enter the name of the command followed by the address of the remote host to which you want to connect. For example, say that you want to connect to a computer named **fuzzball**, whose full address is **fuzzball.ucsb.edu**. Enter:

```
telnet fuzzball.ucsb.edu
```

If you are connecting to a computer on your local network, you can usually get by with just the name of the computer, instead of the full address. For example:

```
telnet fuzzball
```

HINT

All Internet hosts have an official address known as an IP address (see Chapter 6). This address consists of several numbers separated by periods. For example, **128.54.16.1** is the official IP address of the computer whose regular address is **ucsd.edu**.

Some systems have trouble dealing with certain standard addresses. If you encounter such a problem with **telnet**, try using the IP address. For example, either of the following commands will connect to the same host:

```
telnet ucsd.edu
telnet 128.54.16.1
```

For more information about IP addresses and Internet addresses in general, see Chapter 6.

When the **telnet** program starts, it will initiate a connection to the remote host that you specified. As **telnet** is waiting for a response, you will see:

Trying...

or a similar message. Once the connection is made—which might take a few moments if the host is far away—you will see a message like the following:

```
Connected to fuzzball.ucsb.edu.
Escape character is '^]'.
```

(I will explain the reference to an "Escape character" later.)

If, for some reason, **telnet** is unable to make the connection, you will see a message telling you that the host is unknown. For example, say that you want to connect to the remote host **nipper.com**. However, you mistakenly enter:

```
telnet nippet.com
```

You will see:

```
nippet.com: unknown host
telnet>
```

At this point you can either specify another host name or quit the program. I will explain how to do this in the next section.

HINT

The **telnet** message "unknown host" can be misleading. There are many reasons why **telnet** might not be able to make a remote connection. The three most common are:

- You spelled the address of the computer wrong.
- The remote computer is temporarily unavailable.
- You specified the name of a computer that is not on the Internet.

Another problem that may arise is that your local network may, for some reason, not be able to make connections to certain parts of the Internet. One reason is that a particular host may be off-limits for security reasons. Another reason is that some locations just do not have a way to connect to other locations.

For example, one of my friends in Ireland complains that he is sometimes unable to connect to computers in Australia. In such cases, **telnet** will display a message like:

Host is unreachable

If this happens to you, double-check that you are entering your **telnet** command correctly. You can also ask your system manager if there is some trick that you don't understand about making such a connection. However, if the remote host is really unreachable from where you are, there is not much you can do about it. (The best advice I could give to my Irish friend is that many people never connect to Australian computers and still live full, rich lives.)

Once **telnet** makes a connection, you will be interacting with the remote host. At this point, most hosts display some type of informative message, usually identifying the computer. If you are expected to log in, you will see the standard prompt. For example, if you have connected to a remote Unix computer, you will see:

login:

You can now log in in the regular manner. Type your userid and press RETURN. You will then see:

Password:

Now enter your password and press RETURN again. (Note: When you type your password, it will not be displayed. This prevents someone else from finding out your password by watching you log in.)

When you are finished working with the remote computer, all you need to do is log out in the regular manner. The connection will break and **telnet** will stop automatically.

A Second Way to Start `telnet`

In the previous section, I mentioned that there are two ways to start the **telnet** program. The first way is to enter the **telnet** command along with the address of the remote host. For example:

telnet fuzzball.ucsb.edu

The second way is to start **telnet** without specifying a host. Simply enter:

telnet

The program will start but will not make a connection. You will see:

`telnet>`

This is the **`telnet`** prompt. It means that the program has started and is waiting for you to enter a command. To make a connection to a remote host, type **open**, followed by the address of the host. For example:

`open fuzzball.ucsb.edu`

The connection will be made just as if you had specified it when you entered the **`telnet`** command. If you need to specify a port number, simply type it after the computer name. Be sure to leave a space before the number. For example:

`open nightmare.winternet.com 1701`

In the previous section, I gave an example in which a **`telnet`** command had a bad address. In the example, the remote host was named **`nipper.com`**, but we mistakenly entered:

`telnet nippet.com`

What happens in such a case is that **`telnet`** tries to make the connection. When it can't, it gives up and displays its prompt, waiting for you to enter a command. In this case, you would see:

`nippet.com: unknown host`
`telnet>`

You can now enter an **open** command with the correct address:

`open nipper.com`

If this address doesn't work, you can try another one. If you decide to give up, enter:

`quit`

This will stop the **`telnet`** program.

Summary of Starting and Stopping `telnet`

There are two ways to start **telnet**. Either enter the command with the address of a remote host:

```
telnet fuzzball.ucsb.edu
```

or enter the command by itself:

```
telnet
```

and then, at the **telnet>** prompt, enter an **open** command:

```
open fuzzball.ucsb.edu
```

There are two ways to stop **telnet**. If you are connected to a remote host, log out in the regular manner and **telnet** will stop automatically. Otherwise, at the **telnet>** prompt, enter the **quit** command:

```
quit
```

The `telnet` Escape Character: CTRL-]

As you interact with a remote host, there is a way to put your work on hold and enter commands directly to **telnet**. For example, if you are having problems with the remote host, you can pause your work session, return to **telnet**, and enter the **quit** command. To do so, you press the special key combination CTRL-]. That is, you hold down the CTRL key and press **]** (the right square bracket). When you press this key, it sends a signal to **telnet** to pause the remote connection and display the prompt:

```
telnet>
```

You can now enter any **telnet** command that you want. (I will discuss the most important ones in a moment.) With some commands, **telnet** will automatically resume the connection after carrying out the command. Otherwise, you can resume the connection at any time by pressing RETURN at the **telnet>** prompt.

The technical term for a key like CTRL is an ESCAPE CHARACTER. Many programs allow you to use an escape character to request a special service or to indicate that what follows is to be interpreted differently. In the world of Unix, there is a convention that CTRL keys are often indicated by using the ^ (circumflex) character. For example, CTRL-C would be written as **^C**.

Now we can make sense out of the message that appears whenever **telnet** makes a remote connection:

Escape character is '^]'.

You are being reminded that the telnet escape character is CTRL. It is possible to change this to another character but there is usually no reason to do so.

Using telnet **Commands**

Any time you are at the **telnet>** prompt, there are a number of different commands that you can use. In this section, I will go over the most important ones. Before I do, I will remind you that if instead of entering a command you just press RETURN, **telnet** will resume the remote connection.

To display a summary of the various **telnet** commands, you can enter the **?** character:

?

Here is a typical summary:

```
Commands may be abbreviated.  Commands are:

close    close current connection
display  display operating parameters
mode     try to enter line-by-line or character-at-a-time mode
open     connect to a site
quit     exit telnet
send     transmit special characters ('send ?' for more)
set      set operating parameters ('set ?' for more)
status   print status information
toggle   toggle operating parameters ('toggle ?' for more)
z        suspend telnet
?        print help information
```

Out of all these commands, the most important ones are **?**, **open**, **close**, **quit** and **z**.

The **open** command tells **telnet** to make a connection to a remote computer. Enter **open** followed by the address of the computer. For example:

open fuzzball.ucsb.edu

This will leave the **telnet>** prompt and connect you to the remote computer.

The **close** command terminates a remote connection without stopping the **telnet** program. Here is how this might come in handy.

Let's say you are working with a remote host and something goes wrong. For some reason, the host seems to be ignoring your commands. No matter what you type, nothing happens and you can't even log out. One solution is to press CTRL, wait for the **telnet>** prompt, and then enter the **close** command. You can now re-establish a connection to the same host. You can, of course, also connect to a different host.

The **quit** command stops **telnet**. If a remote connection is active, **telnet** will terminate it.

HINT

Before you close a connection or quit **telnet**, remember to log out from the remote host. Most hosts will log you out automatically when the connection drops, but it is better to do so for yourself. This way you can ensure whatever program you were using is terminated properly and all your data was saved.

All the other commands (except **z**, which I will discuss in the next section) are less important and you will probably never need to use them. For the most part, they control various technical aspects of the communication session that you can almost always ignore. If you want to display a summary of the **send**, **set** or **toggle** commands, enter the command followed by a **?** character. For example:

send ?

HINT

If you want more technical information about **telnet**, see the documentation for your particular system. If you are using a Unix computer, you can display the **telnet** entry in the online manual by using the command:

man telnet

Job Control

Unix systems support a facility, called JOB CONTROL, that allows you to pause a program, work with another program, and then return to the first one. I won't go into all the Unix details here, but I will explain how, if your system has job control, **telnet** will cooperate.

At the **telnet** prompt, you can enter the **z** command. (I will explain the name in a moment.) This tells **telnet** to pause itself and return you to the shell (the program that reads and processes your commands). This allows you to enter regular commands on your local computer in the middle of a remote session.

The **z** command will only work if your shell supports job control. If you are using a modern shell, such as the C-Shell or the Korn shell, this will be the case. If you are using the older Bourne shell, there will be no job control and the **z** command will not work. In fact, **telnet** itself may freeze.

The program with which you are currently working is said to be in the FOREGROUND. When you put a program on hold, we say that it is in the BACKGROUND.

When you enter the **z** command, **telnet** will put itself in the background and return you to your local shell. You can now enter as many regular Unix commands as you want. For example, you can check your mail, display the time and date, or whatever. When you want to resume your remote connection, enter the command:

fg

This tells Unix to reactivate (move to the foreground) the last program that was put on hold. You can now resume your remote connection.

You might wonder, why is the **telnet** job control command named **z**? The answer is that, on Unix systems that support job control, you can move your current program into the background by pressing the **susp** (suspend) key. Usually, this key is CTRL-Z. Thus, the **telnet** command is named after the Unix **susp** key.

HINT

If you are using the OS/2 **telnet** program, there is no **z** command. Instead, use the **!** command. This will pause **telnet** and start a new command processor. When you are finished entering OS/2 commands, use the **exit** command (instead of **fg**) to stop the command processor and return to **telnet**.

HINT

Many hosts will automatically log you out if nothing happens for a specified period of time. For example, a system might log you out if you have not typed anything for 15 minutes. Remember this when you use the **z** command to put a **telnet** session on hold. If you do not resume the session before it times out, you may be disconnected automatically.

```
nipper% telnet fuzzball.ucsb.edu

Trying...
Connected to fuzzball.ucsb.edu
Escape character is '^]'.

SunOS Release 4.1.3
Welcome to the Fuzzball System.

login: harley
Password:

Last login: Thu Dec 21 08:20:54 from nipper.com
fuzzball% date
Thu Dec 21 10:30:00 PST 1995
fuzzball% <Ctrl-]>
telnet> z
Stopped

nipper% from
nipper% fg
telnet fuzzball.ucsb.edu

fuzzball% logout
Connection closed by foreign host.

nipper%
```

Figure 24-1.   *Using job control with* `telnet`

Figure 24-1 shows an example of how this all works. The commands that we entered are printed in boldface.

At the beginning of the example, we are logged in to a computer named **nipper**. You can see the shell prompt:

nipper%

At this prompt, we enter a **telnet** command to connect to the remote computer whose address is **fuzzball.ucsb.edu**:

telnet fuzzball.ucsb.edu

Once the connection is made, **fuzzball** displays the standard Unix login prompt and we log in with a userid of **harley**. Notice that, for security reasons, the password is not displayed as we type it. After the login is complete, the remote host displays some information followed by a shell prompt:

fuzzball%

We now enter the **date** command to display the time and date.

At this point, we decide to return to **nipper** temporarily and check our mail. First, we press CTRL-]. This puts the remote connection on hold and returns us to **telnet**. You can see the prompt:

telnet>

Next, we enter the **z** command. This places the **telnet** program in the background. We now see the **nipper** shell prompt. We use the **from** command to check our mail. In this case, there are no messages.

We then enter the **fg** command. The shell responds by displaying the last command that was placed in the background (in this case, it was the **telnet** command). The shell then brings this program back into the foreground, which automatically resumes the remote connection. Once again, we see the **fuzzball** shell prompt.

Finally, we enter the **logout** command to log out from **fuzzball**. The remote connection is closed automatically and **telnet** stops. We are left where we started, at the **nipper** shell prompt.

HINT

On Unix systems, the shell is the program that reads and processes your commands. There are several Unix shells and you may be able to choose the one you want.

When a shell is ready to accept a command, it displays a prompt. If you have an account on more than one computer, it is a good idea to customize your prompts so that they contain the name of the computer. (I won't go into the details here.) In this way, your shell prompt is always a handy reminder of which system you are using.

Traditionally, the last character of a prompt is used to show the type of shell you are using. The **%** character (as in our example) indicates the C-Shell. The **$** character indicates the Korn shell or Bourne shell.

Chapter Twenty-Five

Talk Facilities

Imagine a group of children in a classroom, working quietly under the supervision of a gimlet-eyed schoolteacher. What do they do when the teacher turns her back? They whisper furtively to one another and pass notes, hoping the teacher won't see.

Skip ahead twenty years and the same kids are now sitting in a conference room, listening to the Vice President of Marketing go on and on about the sales projections for the winter quarter. Look closely, and you will see one person quietly slip a piece of paper to his neighbor. She opens the paper to read: "He sure is boring, isn't he? He reminds me of my Uncle Arthur."

Like the child of twenty years ago, the man in the meeting is perfectly willing to do whatever is necessary to make personal contact with another person. When he shares his feelings and ideas he feels better. Moreover, he may be interested in establishing a more personal relationship with the woman sitting next to him.

Put human beings together anywhere and, in a short time, they will have figured out a way to talk to one another. So, as you might expect, as an Internet user, there are many ways for you to talk to someone else.

In this chapter, I discuss the ideas involved in talking over the Internet and describe some of the more common services. Two of the services are so important that I have given them chapters of their own: Internet Relay Chat (Chapter 27) and Muds (Chapter 28). In addition, in Chapter 26, I explain how to use `talk`, a Unix program for shell account users. However, before you read any of these chapters, do start with this one, so I can make sure you understand the basic concepts.

Overview of Talk Facilities

When we use the word TALK on the Net, we mean any type of communication in which you can send messages back and forth with someone in real time (that is, while you wait). The "talking" may involve text messages or actual voice transmission. For example, you might tell someone, "Last night I was talking to a friend in Australia," even if you and your friend were typing back and forth with no voice. On the Net, anytime you make contact with another person, you are talking.

(You will sometimes see people use the word CHAT. Usually this refers to talking to more than one person at a time, although there is no strict definition.)

The Internet has many different talk facilities available for free. The most basic service lets you type messages back and forth with another person. Whatever you type shows up on the other person's display, and whatever he or she types shows up on your display.

A typical setup will use a window divided into two areas. Your typing is displayed in one part; the other person's typing is displayed in the other part. As you talk, you can see both sides of the conversation at once. Since there are two display areas (one for each of you), you can both type at the same time without getting mixed up. An example of this is shown in Figure 25-1.

Many such systems allow you to talk to more than one person at the same time. When you do, your program will divide the window into as many talk areas as necessary. You can see this in Figure 25-2 which shows Bill Gates talking to four people at the same time.

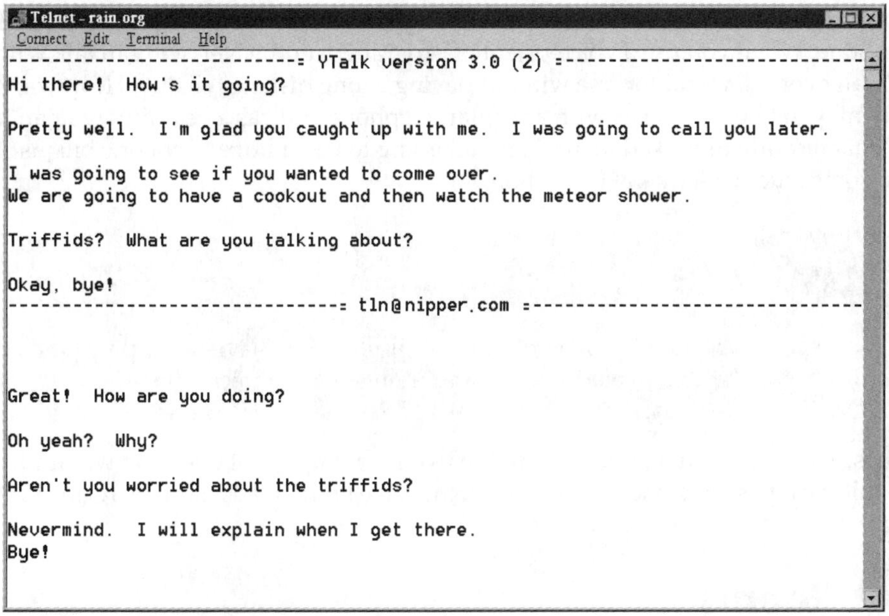

```
  Telnet - rain.org                                      _ □ ×
 Connect  Edit  Terminal  Help
---------------------------: YTalk version 3.0 (2) =----------------------------
Hi there!  How's it going?

Pretty well.  I'm glad you caught up with me.  I was going to call you later.

I was going to see if you wanted to come over.
We are going to have a cookout and then watch the meteor shower.

Triffids?  What are you talking about?

Okay, bye!
-----------------------------: tln@nipper.com =---------------------------------



Great!  How are you doing?

Oh yeah?  Why?

Aren't you worried about the triffids?

Nevermind.  I will explain when I get there.
Bye!
```

Figure 25-1.   *A text-oriented talk program*

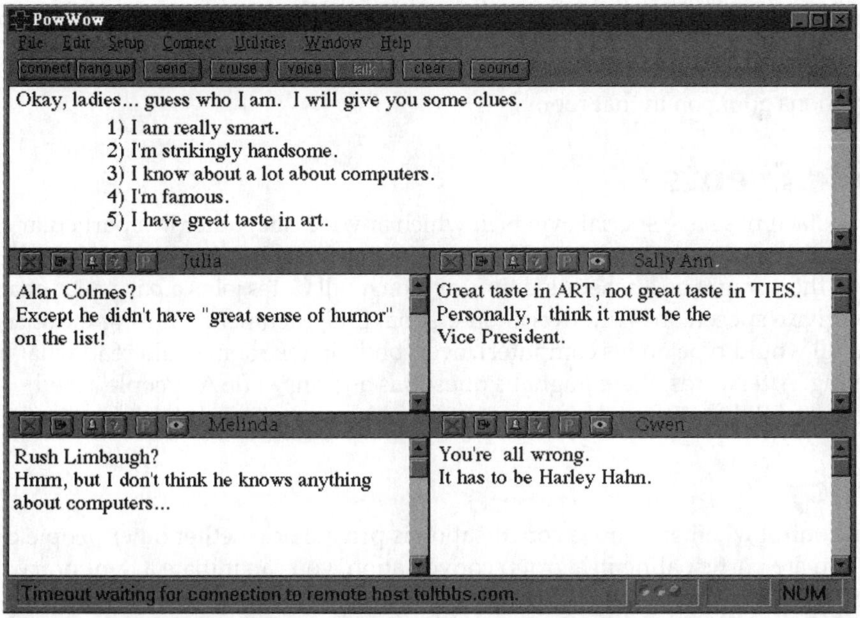

Figure 25-2.   *A talk program with a multiple-person conversation*

A more complex talk facility will let you send and receive actual voice sounds, like a telephone. When you use a voice-oriented program over the Net, you can talk with people all over the world for free without paying a long distance charge. However, the quality may not be as good as with a regular telephone. Still, as a beautiful woman in California recently remarked to me, "I'm not going to pay a huge telephone bill just to talk to some stud in Germany for an hour."

🏴 HINT

To use a voice-oriented talk facility, your computer must have the appropriate hardware. It must be able to play sounds, and it must have a microphone.

These services—text and voice—are the two most important ones you will find. Some talk facilities have one or the other, some have both. In addition, there are a number of other features you may find.

Chat Rooms

A CHAT ROOM is a facility that allows more than one person to talk at the same time. Chat rooms simulate an environment in which people gather together to talk. Although chat rooms are imaginary, it is common to talk about them as if they really exist. When someone joins the conversation, we might say he or she "enters" the room. Similarly, a talk facility may have several chat rooms, each with different names. So you might, for example, enter the "Zen room". Once you do, you can see all the conversations going on in that room.

Public Events

Some talk facilities have special events in which anyone can gather in a particular chat room and listen to a guest speaker. (That room might be called the "Auditorium".) For example, there might be a scheduled time at which Bill Gates joins a particular chat room to give a speech on "Windows and Personal Enlightenment". During the speech (which Bill would type on his computer), everybody in the room could read what he was saying. Afterwards, there might be questions and answers. As people asked questions and Bill answered them, everyone could see what was happening.

Privacy

You can control whether or not a conversation is private or whether other people can join. If you are participating in a group conversation, you can initiate a temporary, private connection with one of the people (and tell secrets about everyone else). Generally speaking, if you are in a chat room, your conversation is not private.

White Pages Directory

Some talk systems keep a public directory in which you can look up someone's name (like a telephone book without the phone numbers). Once you find a name, you can send a request to that person to see if he or she wants to talk to you. Aside from the name, you may also see an email address, a link to the person's home page and other information.

A Personal Address Book

Most talk programs allow you to create your own personal address book. You can save the names and addresses of your friends on the Net, making changes whenever you want. To initiate a talk connection, all you have to do is display your address book and select the person to whom you want to talk.

Embedded HTML

HTML (Hypertext Markup Language) is the descriptive language used to build web pages (see Chapter 11). Some web-based talk facilities let you type HTML instructions. When these instructions are "read" by someone's browser, they will be interpreted as valid HTML. For example, as you are talking, you can send a link to your home page (or any web page), display buttons, make words blink, and so on. Of course, to do this, you have to know a little HTML. (It won't be long, though, until HTML is taught in schools as a second language.)

Sounds

You can send a sound effect to the person to whom you are talking. For example, you might send a laugh, a sigh, applause, and so on. Aside from pre-installed sounds, you can use sounds of your own. The other day, I was talking to someone in Sweden and he played a sound of a California surfer dude saying, "Okay, so I'll see ya later, huh?" I liked what I heard, so my Swedish friend used the file transfer facility to send me the actual sound file. I then registered the sound with my own talk program, so I could use it myself.

Pictures

You can use a picture to identify yourself. When people talk to you, they will see the picture. Some people use a photo of themselves, although this is not necessary: the picture can be any GIF or JPEG file. Some talk facilities have a library of pictures for you to choose from, if you don't have one of your own.

Video

There is a system called CU-SeeMe that allows you to send video images to another person on the Net. The video shows motion, although it is not of high quality like a television.

File Transfer

You can send a file to someone while you are talking without having to stop talking or without using a separate file transfer or mail program.

Answering Machine

If you are busy and do not wish to be disturbed, you can have your talk program send a specific message to people when they try to talk to you. When you want to start talking again, you can turn off the answering machine and take the calls yourself.

Remote Control

While you are talking to someone, you can control a program that is running on his or her computer. This will work for more than one person. For example, you could take control of someone's web browser and show them specific web pages. Or one person might take a group of people on a guided tour of the Web.

How Does It All Work?

Like all Internet services, talking on the Internet is based on a client/server system. There are two ways in which such systems are organized.

One design uses a central talk server, somewhere on the Net. Each person who uses the service runs a talk client on his own computer. The individual clients communicate by sending messages to and from the server.

For example, say you are using a centralized system to talk to a friend named Norman Sweetcream. Each time you type a line of text, your client program sends it to the server. The server relays the text to Norman's client program, which displays your message on his screen. When Norman types a line of text, his client sends it to the central server, which then sends the text to your client to display. In other words, everything you and Norman type goes through the server.

The other basic design connects people directly without using a central server. When you talk with Norman, everything you type goes right to his computer. When he responds, his messages go directly to your computer. With such systems, the program you run on your computer must be more than a talk client: It must act as both a client *and* a server.

There are advantages and disadvantages with both systems. The most obvious advantage of a decentralized system is there are no middlemen to slow down the talking. When everything has to go through a central server, things bog down and there is often a noticeable delay in the conversation.

In addition, with a decentralized system, no one has to maintain a central server. After all, why should someone (or some organization) have to pay for the hardware, software and administration time to support a talk server, just so people on the Internet can talk for free? Moreover, when someone *does* offer such a service to the Net, you must play by his or her rules or you are out.

Finally, a decentralized system is more dependable. When a central server goes down, everything stops. Such servers are attractive targets for hackers: talented programmers, who love to see how much mischief they can cause. From time to time, you will see a notice that the administrator has removed the "such and such feature" from a central server, because hackers were using it to cause trouble.

Centralized systems do have two big advantages, however. First, because the talk server is centralized, it can be more elaborate and offer more services than a server program you would run on your own computer. For example, a centralized server might create an imaginary environment (such as a mud) which the users can explore as they talk.

Second, a centralized system can provide a place for people to gather and to find one another. When you use IRC (Internet Relay Chat), for example, you will find many groups of people talking about different topics. Similarly, many people like to use muds because it allows them to meet new people and to hang out with their friends. When you use a decentralized system, there is no easy way to join a group of people or to just hang out.

What Do You Need to Use a Talk Facility?

To use an Internet talk facility, you need several things. First, your Internet connection should be either PPP or a direct network connection. If you use a shell account you will not be able to access some of the talk facilities. You will be able to use the Unix **talk** program (see Chapter 26), IRC (Chapter 27) and Muds (Chapter 28), but not much else. (For more information about Internet connections, see Chapter 5.)

Second, your Internet connection should be as fast as possible, especially if you want to use a voice facility. Thus, do not buy a modem that is slower than 28,800 bits per second. ISDN is even better. (See Chapter 4.)

Third, your computer should be capable of playing sounds. With a Macintosh, this capability is built in. With a PC, you must have a sound card or the equivalent. In addition, if you want to talk using voice, your computer must have a microphone.

Finally, you need the appropriate software. For all the talk systems I describe in this book, the software is available for free on the Net.

Types of Internet Talk Facilities

In this section, I will take you on a tour of some of the talk facilities you will encounter on the Internet. All of these are fun and useful. When you get a chance, experiment and see which talk facilities you like best.

The Unix `talk` Program

The oldest of the Internet talk facilities is a program named **talk** that runs under Unix. The **talk** program provides a basic, text-based talk facility. You can type messages back and forth to another person, and all the conversations are private.

The **talk** program allows you to talk with anyone else on the Internet, as long as they have a **talk** program. Virtually every Unix computer on the Internet has a **talk** program, so if you have a shell account, you can use **talk**. If you do not have a shell account (that is, if you use PPP or a direct network connection), you need to find a client for your own computer that is compatible with Unix **talk**.

When you use **talk** with a shell account, both the client and server run on the Unix computer. Thus, when you use a compatible program on your PC or Macintosh, the program must act as both a client and a server. Such programs are available for free on the Net.

The **talk** program is an important Internet service, and I discuss it in detail in Chapter 26.

 **INTERNET RESOURCE**   *Look in the catalog under Internet Resources for Talking: **talk** Clients*

Internet Relay Chat (IRC)

IRC is a huge Internet-wide system which supports a large number of group conversations. It is text-based and uses a number of central talk servers around the Net to coordinate the flow of data. IRC is a lot of fun and is a great place to meet people. To use IRC you need an IRC client for your computer. There are clients for all types of computers, including Unix, so you can use IRC with a shell account.

I discuss IRC in detail in Chapter 27.

 **INTERNET RESOURCE**   *Look in the catalog under Internet Resources for Talking: IRC Clients*

Muds

A mud is an imaginary environment in which you can talk to people and meet new friends. Moreover, some muds are set up as fantasy worlds, where you travel around and have adventures while assuming the role of an imaginary character. Many such muds are complex and require a long time to master.

You can access a mud by using a plain telnet client (see Chapter 23). However, there are specialized mud clients available as well. If you get into serious mudding, get yourself a serious mud client.

Muds can be a lot of fun and I encourage you to try a few. Many people tend to think of the Internet as being mostly the Web, but that is not true at all. If you haven't experienced a mud, you are missing out on one of life's most interesting experiences.

I discuss muds in detail in Chapter 28.

 INTERNET RESOURCE *Look in the catalog under Internet Resources for*
Mud Clients
Telnet Clients

Web-Based Chat Rooms

The Web is huge, and there are a lot of talk facilities that make use of its size and popularity. To use these facilities you do not need a special talk client. All you need to do is connect to a centralized talk server, and your web browser will act as your talk client.

There are a lot of chat rooms on the Web, and they are worth checking out. However, there are some special considerations you should understand, which I discuss in detail in the next section.

 INTERNET RESOURCE *Look in the catalog under Internet Resources for*
Talking: Web-based Talk

Bulletin Board Systems (BBSs)

Before the Internet became popular, there were a large number of Bulletin Board Systems (BBSs) that offered dial-up online services. Today, some of these BBSs, along with many new ones, have moved to the Internet. Many BBSs are run by an individual, although some are large enough to require a group of administrators. In general, the person who runs a BBS is called the SYSOP, and the personality of an individual BBS very much depends on the sysop.

Most BBSs allow you to send messages to people who are logged in. This is a good way to talk with people and meet new friends. There are usually ongoing discussion groups to which you can post messages as well as read the messages left by others. In addition, all BBSs have archives from which you can download files or to which you can contribute files of your own.

There are general-purpose BBSs, as well as BBSs devoted to just about any topic you can imagine: meeting people, religion, hobbies, corporate and government information, X-rated talk and resources, and so on.

To access a BBS over the Internet, you use telnet (see Chapter 23). Before you can use most BBSs, you will have to register and ask for an account. Many BBSs are free, although some of them do charge a membership fee (especially the ones with the X-rated resources).

 **INTERNET RESOURCE** *Look in the catalog under Internet Resources for Talking: Bulletin Board Systems (BBSs)*

Talkers

A TALKER is a multiuser talk facility that is easy to use and is devoted primarily to conversation. You connect to a talker by using telnet (see Chapter 23). Once you do, you can talk to anyone else who happens to be connected at the same time. The word "talker" is a descriptive term. For example, some talkers are muds, while others are BBSs; there is no strict definition. If it's easy to use, and you connect in order to talk to other people, it is a talker.

 **INTERNET RESOURCE** *Look in the catalog under Internet Resources for Talking: Talkers*

Direct Talk Connections

Aside from the system based on the Unix **talk** program, there are other facilities that connect two people with a direct connection. Since such systems do not depend on a central server, the communication is fast and private. Some programs allow you to make connections between more than one person at a time to have a group conversation. The other people can be in the next room or on the other side of the world.

One program I particularly like is named Powwow. It not only supports text but, if you have the right hardware, voice as well. I use Powwow to send messages to my chief researcher, even though she often works in a room just down the hall. Such systems are great when you are participating in a telephone conference call. You can type secret messages back and forth to one of the people on the call without everyone else seeing what you are saying.

The Powwow system has a nice feature that is common to other talk facilities. There is a white pages server to which you can connect to find lists of people who use the same program. You can then choose someone on the list and see if they want to talk with you. In addition, while you are talking, one person can take control of the other people's web browsers (with permission, of course) and guide the other people on a tour of the Web.

 **INTERNET RESOURCE** *Look in the catalog under Internet Resources for Talking: Direct Connections*

Telephone-Like Systems

There are a number of voice-only talk facilities that are designed to work like a telephone. In order to use the system, you must have a PPP or a direct network connection (not a shell account). You run a special program on your computer, which acts as both a client and server. Using this program, you can talk to anyone else on the Net who is running the same program. (Of course, your computer needs a microphone and sound capabilities.)

How do you find someone to talk to? There are two ways. First, you can specify the exact address of someone's computer. If the computer name in the mail address doesn't work, you can always use a numeric IP address (see Chapter 6). However, you must know this address in advance, and you must be sure the person to whom you want to talk has his telephone program running, waiting for a connection.

Second, some systems have a number of special servers on the Net (maintained by the company that sells the telephone program). You can connect to a server and tell it you are ready to talk. At the same time, you can see all the other people who are ready to talk. To talk with someone, you simply select their name from the list on the server. The server will send a signal to that person. If he agrees to talk with you, a direct connection will be made between your computer and his. From that point on, you are not using the server (and everything you say is private).

Of course, since all of this happens on the Net, you do not have to pay long distance phone charges. So why doesn't everyone use the Net instead of a telephone? There are two reasons. First, the voice quality is not as good as a real telephone. Second, you can't call someone unless he has an Internet connection, a computer with a microphone and sound capability, and the same telephone program.

However, if you like talking to people for fun, try one of these systems. In most cases, you can use the software for free in a limited way. (For example, your conversations may be limited to one minute.) If you have someone to whom you would like to talk regularly for a long time, you can pay a small fee to the company and upgrade your program, so it allows you to talk as long as you want.

 **INTERNET RESOURCE** *Look in the catalog under Internet Resources for Talking: Telephone-like Systems*

Video Conferencing

A video conferencing system allows you to send live video and sound over the Internet. The most important such system is called CU-SeeMe. (The name is a pun. The "CU" stands for Cornell University where the original program development was done. However, when you say the name out loud, it sounds like "see you, see me".)

CU-SeeMe will run on either a Macintosh or a PC using Windows as long as you have a PPP or direct network connection (not a shell account). To watch video, all you need is the software, which is available for free on the Net. To broadcast, you need a video camera, a digitizing board and the appropriate video software.

When you watch, you will see actual video. (See Figure 25-3.) However, the quality is not all that good. (It looks like the video broadcasts from the space shuttle.) Still, it is exciting to watch people from all over the world. Although you need special equipment to send video, it is not that expensive, and there are a surprising number of people broadcasting over the Net.

By itself, the CU-SeeMe software will enable you to establish a video link between any two computers. However, by connecting to a "reflector" you can watch or broadcast to more than one site at a time.

One word of warning: A lot of schools use CU-SeeMe to let the kids talk to one another. Please remember, though, there is no censorship on the Internet. While I was working on this chapter, I saw more than one site broadcasting naked people performing quasi-sexual acts. Depending on your outlook, this could be either erotic or immoral. What I want you to appreciate is that the Internet is an open forum, and the only effective way to censor something is to control what comes into your own computer.

Web-Based Talk Facilities

The Web was not designed to allow individual users to communicate, so the talk facilities had to be fitted into the existing web client/server system. Because of this, you will often find web-based talking to be less smooth than other systems. When you

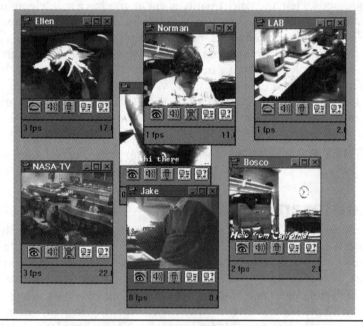

Figure 25-3.   *Live video over the net, using CU-SeeMe*

talk with someone, you would like to see the words as the person is typing. With a web-based talk facility, this is not possible. Here is why.

Within the Web, you use a talk facility by connecting to a specific web page that represents a chat room. Whenever you load that page, you will see whatever messages people have typed in the last few minutes. An example of this system is shown in Figure 25-4.

How do you send a message of your own? On the Web, there is only one way to type information and send it to a server. The server must send you a web page that contains a special input area called a "form" (see Chapter 10). You type information into the form and then submit it, either by pressing the ENTER key or by clicking on a button. (Notice the input form in Figure 25-4.)

This means the information you type is not sent to the server until you submit the form. At that time, everything you typed into the form is sent all at once. The talk server receives your input in chunks.

Similarly, there is no way for a web server to send you information one character or one word at a time. All the server can do is wait for you to reload a web page and then send you updated information.

When you put this all together, it explains why talking on the Web is not a smooth process. Say you are talking to a friend. You must type your message into a form, and nothing will be sent to the server until you submit the form. At the other end, your

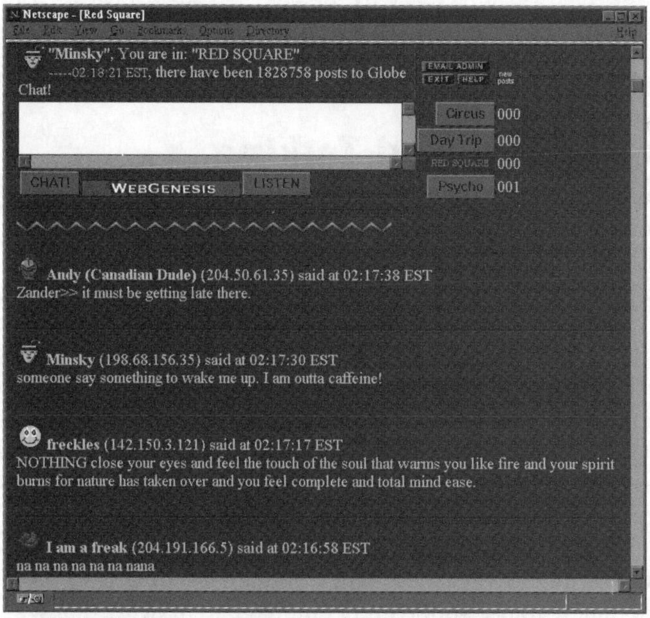

Figure 25-4. *A typical web-based chat room*

friend will not see anything until he or she reloads the web page. It is only at then that the server will be able to send any new information.

(Some talk systems mitigate this problem by using server push [see Chapter 10]. This allows the web server to update your web page automatically at regular intervals. With such systems, you can sometimes specify the interval, so you can control the time between updates.)

Thus, web-based talking is not smooth for several reasons. First, all messages must pass through a central server. Second, a message is sent to the server as one large chunk, not one character at a time. Third, you will not see any new messages until you reload the chat room web page. Finally, everyone in the room can talk at the same time. Thus, each time you reload your web page, you will see *all* the messages that have been sent by everyone in the room, since the last time you reloaded the page. As you might imagine, this can be a tad confusing.

Still, after a while, you will get used to web-based talking. It is only a matter of waiting for certain cells in your brain to change appropriately. Moreover, many of the servers are quite elaborate, offering an interesting variety of talk-related resources such as specialized chat rooms, public events, and so on. So, in spite of all the limitations, web-based talk facilities are worth investigating.

HINT

Most web-based chat systems place the newer messages at the top of the web page. Thus, to look at the messages in chronological order, you must read from the bottom up.

Guidelines for Text-based Talking

Having a text-based conversation on the Internet combines the immediacy of a face-to-face encounter with the verbosity of written language. For this reason, you will notice two significant differences between talking by computer and talking by mouth.

First, talking by computer is a lot slower, because almost everybody can speak faster than they can type (not that this is always an advantage). Second, because you are not looking at the other person, the customary nuances and inflections that comprise so much of the non-verbal aspects of communication are missing.

We make up for these limitations in two ways. First, there are a number of abbreviations that are commonly used to speed things up. Some of these are shown in Figure 25-5. These abbreviations are the spiritual descendants of the Morse-code conventions used by ham radio operators since the 1920s.

The second important convention recognizes that it is easy to offend someone (or at least have your words misconstrued) when you are not talking in person. Over the computer, we are unable to use subtle body language to indicate that what we just said was debonair and ironic, and not really as dumb and insensitive as it looks.

Abbreviation	Meaning
BBL	be back later
BCNU	be seeing you
BRB	be right back
BTW	by the way
BYE	goodbye (I am ready to stop talking)
BYE?	goodbye? (are you ready to stop talking?)
CU	see you (goodbye)
CUL	see you later
CUL8R	see you later
F2F	face to face
FWIW	for what it's worth
IMHO	in my humble opinion
JAM	just a minute
L8R	later
LOL	laugh out loud
OBTW	oh, by the way
R U THERE?	are you there?
ROTF	rolling on the floor
ROTFL	rolling on the floor laughing
SEC...	wait a second
TTFN	ta-ta for now
TTYL	talk to you later
WRT	with respect to

Figure 25-5. *Common communication abbreviations*

Thus, when there is any doubt as to whether or not the other person might be offended, it is a good idea to use a smiley to show that you are just kidding. A smiley is a little face that we draw with punctuation characters. Here is the basic smiley:

`:-)`

(To see the face, tilt your head to the left.) You can use a smiley whenever you say something that might bother the other person, for example:

```
I'd feel the same way as you, if I had a
head that looked like a ripe eggplant :-)
```

If you want to see a few more smileys, look at Figure 14-5 in Chapter 14.

It is also important to become aware of what is private and what is not. With some talk systems, it is possible for people to sit quietly and watch what other people are saying. Such people are called LURKERS. Just because you see only one person talking does not mean that no one else is watching.

HINT

When in doubt, assume your conversation is not private.

Some talk programs have a way for you to talk with a group, but break off temporarily to have a private conversation with just one person. If you have never used this facility, be sure to test it. It is a good idea to be completely sure that you understand how the privacy option works before you say anything you will regret.

A further consideration has to do with how the words you type are sent to the other person. With some systems, what you type is not sent until you press the ENTER key or click on a button. In such cases, you can backspace to make corrections before you send the text. On other systems, the message is sent, one character at a time, as you type it. (This is the case with the Unix **talk** program.) Thus, if you accidentally say something insulting, by the time you backspace and change it, the other person will already have seen it.

If the network or the talk server slows down, you may notice replies are delayed and become unsynchronized, leading to various amusing and incoherent situations. In such cases, we refer to the delay as LAG. Thus, you might see someone say, "There was so much lag, I thought you had forgotten all about me."

HINT

For possibly the first time in your life, spelling does not count.

Because typing is so much slower than talking, it is perfectly acceptable to type as fast as you can and not worry about spelling mistakes. Nothing is worse than watching someone laboriously backspacing and correcting each word. Just go ahead and type and don't worry. Almost evrWything is underftandabll with kust a few worng lettrs and. no doubt,m the other pweosn will get the g9ist of thwta you are syaing.

Chapter Twenty-Six

Using Talk from a Shell Account:
`talk, ytalk`

In Chapter 25, I discussed talk facilities on the Internet. In this chapter, I will show you how to use the Unix **talk** program, the oldest such program on the Net. If you have a shell account, **talk** will probably be available on your system. If you use a PC or Macintosh, there are **talk**-compatible programs available for free on the Net.

Once you learn how to use **talk**, you will be able to talk with anyone else who uses a compatible program. The **talk** command will connect your computer to the other person's computer and allow you to type messages back and forth. He will see what you type, and you will see what he types.

The **talk** program is a handy and convenient communication tool... when it works. For those times when it doesn't work, I will show what might be wrong and give you hints on what to do.

Finally, I will tell you about **ytalk**, a replacement for **talk**, a much more powerful program that allows several people to have a group conversation, sort of like an Internet conference call.

Before you read this chapter, take a moment to skim Chapter 25. In particular, read the sections that describe guidelines for talking.

Introducing the `talk` Program

The **talk** program allows you to connect your computer to someone else's computer, and then type messages back and forth. (Of course, both computers must be on the Internet.) The great thing about the **talk** program is that you can talk with people all over the world for free. For example, as I worked on this book in California, I often had conversations with a well-known computer expert in Austria.

Like all Internet services, the **talk** program uses a client/server system. The client—the program you use—is **talk**. The server is a program called a TALK DAEMON. Both programs run on the Unix host computer.

What's in a Name?

DAEMON

In Unix, there are a number of programs, named DAEMONS, that execute in the background in order to provide services of general interest. Some daemons are started automatically when the system is initialized and are always available. Other daemons sleep most of the time, waking up at predefined intervals or in response to some event.

Daemons perform all kinds of functions to keep the system running smoothly: managing memory, overseeing print jobs, executing commands at specific times, and so on. Daemons also provide many of the services on the Internet. For example, webservers are actually daemons, as are ftp servers, gopher servers, and the programs that send and receive mail.

Although the name is pronounced "dee-mon", it is correctly spelled "daemon". Nobody knows if the name used to be an acronym or why we use the British variation of the spelling. (In Celtic mythology, a daemon is usually good or neutral, merely a spirit or inspiration. A demon, however, is always an evil entity.)

You may occasionally read that the name stands for "Disk and Executing Monitor", a term from the old DEC 10 and 20 computers. However, this explanation was made up after the fact.

The name "daemon" was first used by MIT programmers who worked on CTSS (the Compatible Time-Sharing System), developed in 1963. They coined the name to refer to what were called "dragons" by other programmers who worked on ITS (the Incompatible Time-sharing System). Both CTSS and ITS were ancestors of Unix.

To start a conversation, type **talk**, followed by the address of the person to whom you would like to talk. For example, say that your userid is **harley** and you are logged in to the computer named **fuzzball.ucsb.edu**. You want to talk to a friend whose userid is **wendy** and who is logged in to the computer named **muffin.com**. Enter:

```
talk wendy@muffin.com
```

The program will send a message to your friend's computer and tell her you wish to talk. Out of nowhere she will see the following message on her screen and hear a beep:

```
Message from Talk_Daemon@muffin at 13:56 ...
talk: connection requested by harley@fuzzball.ucsb.edu.
talk: respond with:  talk harley@fuzzball.ucsb.edu
```

At this point, all she has to do is follow the instructions. In this case, she would enter the command:

```
talk harley@fuzzball.ucsb.edu
```

Once she does, the connection is complete and you can start talking.

If the person you are trying to reach is logged in but is not responding, the **talk** daemon will keep sending him a message, about every 10 seconds. As it does, you will see:

```
[Ringing your party again]
```

If you decide to give up, just press CTRL-C to stop the **talk** program.

Of course, you yourself may receive a **talk** request unexpectedly. If you do, just remember to enter the **talk** command exactly as you are requested in order to make the connection.

When you are finished with your conversation, either person can quit by pressing CTRL-C. (If you are not using a Unix system, just press whatever key is used with your computer to stop a program, or close the window.)

If you want to talk to someone who is logged in to the same computer as you, you need specify only a userid and not the full address. For example, say that you want to talk to someone on your computer whose userid is **mike**. You can use the command:

```
talk mike
```

The `talk` Screen

Once your **talk** client has made the connection with another person's **talk** daemon, you will see the message:

```
[Connection established]
```

and hear a beep.

The **talk** program will draw a horizontal line in the middle of your screen, dividing it into an upper half and a lower half. Whatever you type will be displayed in the upper half; whatever the other person types will be displayed in the lower half. Figure 26-1 shows a typical **talk** screen.

HINT

If you notice that the output is displayed in a garbled fashion, it may be that you have not initialized your terminal type: that is, you have not told Unix what type of terminal you are using. Typically, you will see a line of characters going down the left-hand side of the screen.

If you are not sure how to initialize your terminal, ask someone for help or check with a good Unix book. (If you have my book *The Unix Companion*, look in Chapter 6.)

Both people can type at the same time. Whatever you type will be displayed immediately on your screen and the other person's screen. As you type, you can press BACKSPACE to correct the previous character. You can also use CTRL-W to erase an entire word and CTRL-U to erase an entire line. At any time, you can tell **talk** to redisplay the entire screen by pressing CTRL-L. The CTRL-L command is handy when an unexpected message—like someone else trying to talk with you—appears on your screen.

(You may have to experiment a little. With some computers, you have to use DELETE instead of BACKSPACE to erase a single character. Similarly, you may have to use CTRL-X instead of CTRL-U to erase an entire line.)

HINT

Because the other person can see each character as you type it, he will also see you backspace when you make corrections. Thus, do not type something offensive thinking that you can change it. The other person will see exactly what you type, as you type it.

HINT

One of the biggest mistakes that people make is pressing BACKSPACE repeatedly to correct a few words or the entire line. It is much faster to use CTRL-W and CTRL-U (or CTRL-X).

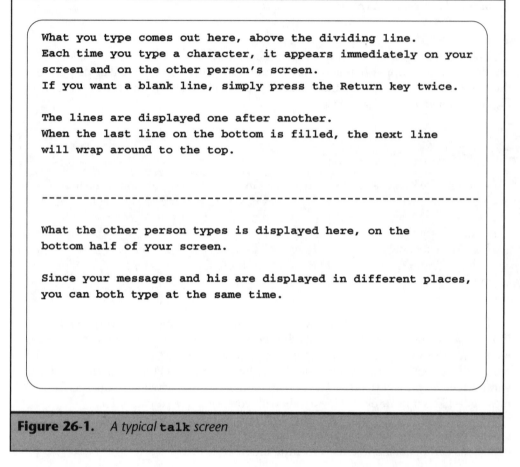

```
What you type comes out here, above the dividing line.
Each time you type a character, it appears immediately on your
screen and on the other person's screen.
If you want a blank line, simply press the Return key twice.

The lines are displayed one after another.
When the last line on the bottom is filled, the next line
will wrap around to the top.



------------------------------------------------------------

What the other person types is displayed here, on the
bottom half of your screen.

Since your messages and his are displayed in different places,
you can both type at the same time.
```

Figure 26-1.   *A typical* `talk` *screen*

Once you have a connection, you can talk as long as you like. When you are finished, either person can sever the connection by pressing CTRL-C. It is considered good manners to say goodbye and to wait for an acknowledgment before ending a conversation.

When the **talk** program is finished, you will see:

`[Connection closing. Exiting]`

You will then be returned to the shell prompt.

Problems with Addresses and What to Do

There are several problems that might keep you from establishing a **talk** connection. First, the person you want to talk to may not be logged in. If this is the case, you may see a message like:

`[Your party is not logged on]`

The solution, of course, is to try again later. You may also want to mail the person a message, asking him to talk to you when he logs in.

Second, it may be that the computer you are trying to reach is not on the Internet. Remember, there are some computers that can exchange mail with the Internet but are not on the Internet itself. If you specify the address of a computer that is not on the Internet, you will see a message similar to:

`elmer.com is an unknown host`

You may also see either of these messages if you make a typing mistake when you enter the **talk** command. For example, say that you want to talk to a friend whose userid is **wendy** on the computer named **muffin.com**. However, by mistake, you type:

`talk wendi@muffin.com`

You will see the message:

`[Your party is not logged on]`

Do not misinterpret this message. It does not imply that the userid you typed was valid, but the person was not logged in. All it means is that no one with that userid is currently logged in. Thus, when you get this message, be sure to check your spelling and, if necessary, retype the command. Similarly, if you enter:

`talk wendy@mufiin.com`

you will see:

`mufiin.com is an unknown host`

At least this time, the message is more informative and your spelling mistake is obvious.

The next reason your connection might not work is that you may be using a mail address that is an alias and not the person's actual address. Some organizations allow their users to use a simplified mailing address. For example, say that you have a friend named Eugene who has userid **wx1523** on the computer named **sdcc99.ucsd.edu**. For convenience, his organization allows him to receive mail at the address **eugene@ucsd.edu**. When a message arrives, the local mail program looks up the name in a master list and sends the mail to the correct local address.

However, if you want to talk to your friend, you cannot use **eugene@ucsd.edu**, as this is only a mail alias. You must use the exact address of **wx1523@sdcc99.ucsd.edu**. If you are not sure of the correct address, you can always mail your friend a message and ask.

The "Checking for Invitation" Problem and What to Do

So far, I have discussed problems that stem from an incorrect address, or from a person not being logged in. However, there is a problem that commonly arises even when you have the correct address and the person is logged in. The problem is that not all Internet computers can use **talk** to connect to one another.

There may be a time when you enter a **talk** command and see the following message:

```
[Checking for invitation on caller's machine]
```

This looks like a nice, benign message. It seems to imply that the other person has been notified that you want to talk, and you are just waiting for him or her to enter the appropriate **talk** command.

In reality, this message is highly misleading. What it usually means is that your **talk** program and the other **talk** program are incompatible. (More precisely, your daemons are incompatible.) The reason is a little technical, but here it is.

As you may know, computer data is stored in bytes, each byte holding a single character. Inside the computer, the bytes are collected into words. There may be 2 bytes per word, 4 bytes per word, or whatever. The question is, within each word, what order are the bytes stored in?

For example, say that you have a word that contains 2 bytes—call them **A** and **B**. Some computers store the bytes as **AB**, while other computers store the bytes as **BA**. Normally, the hardware takes care of all the details, so you don't have to worry about it. The trouble comes when one **talk** program tries to communicate with another one.

If you are using the original version of **talk**, communication can only be established between two computers that store bytes in the same order. Unfortunately, many Internet computers still use this version of **talk** and when two incompatible computers try to connect, you get stuck with the "checking for invitation" message. In this situation, the only thing you can do is press CTRL-C and abort the command. (But see below for some more ideas.)

⚑ HINT

The two schemes that I described above are called BIG-ENDIAN ("big end first") and LITTLE-ENDIAN ("little end first"). Sun computers and Macintoshes are big-endian. VAX computers and PCs are little-endian.

This incompatibility is sometimes referred to as the "NUXI problem", because if you switch the order of each pair of letters in "UNIX", you get the word "NUXI".

This means that if you are using the original version of **talk**, you can only talk to people who are using compatible computers. To solve this problem, another version of talk, called **ntalk** (new talk), was developed. The **ntalk** program can talk to any other **ntalk** program, regardless of what computer it is running on. (In case you are interested, **ntalk** communicates via a facility called "sockets", which bypasses the byte order problem by making it easy for the program to convert data from one representation to another.)

Many system managers have installed **ntalk** on their machines, so if you are having trouble with **talk**, try entering the same command again using **ntalk**. For example:

```
ntalk wendy@muffin.com
```

Still, there can be a problem. Some system managers install **ntalk** under that name. When you want the new version, you use **ntalk**; when you want the old version, you use **talk**. Other system managers install **ntalk** under the name **talk** (to make it more convenient!) and rename the original version to **otalk** (old talk). On those systems, you use **talk** to get the new version and **otalk** to get the old version.

Don't be confused. If you have problems using **talk** to connect to a particular computer, just experiment with **ntalk**, **talk** and **otalk** until you find the combination that works.

The real solution to all of this silliness is to use a much better program called **ytalk**, that I will discuss later in the chapter. Not only will **ytalk** work with any other computer—whether it is running **talk**, **ntalk** or **ytalk**—it allows more than one person to talk at the same time. The **ytalk** program is readily available via anonymous ftp and, if you are having **talk** problems, you might prevail upon your system manager to install **ytalk**.

HINT

What can you do if you and your friend do not have two compatible versions of **talk**? You will have to find another way to get together.

For example, you could agree to meet on IRC, which I discuss in Chapter 27. You could also use a mud (Chapter 28) or one of the Internet-accessible bulletin board systems (Chapter 25). And, of course, you can always send messages by mail.

Refusing to Talk

There may be times when it is inconvenient to receive an invitation to talk. For example, you may be editing an important file, and you do not want your screen cluttered up with messages from the **talk** daemon. Or you may be a private person who simply does not want to talk to anyone else.

By using the **mesg** (message) command, you can tell your system to refuse **talk** requests on your behalf. To refuse all such invitations, type **mesg** followed by **n** (no):

```
mesg n
```

To ask your talk daemon to show you such invitations, use **mesg** followed by **y** (yes):

```
mesg y
```

Normally, **mesg** is set to **y**, so you do not have to worry about it unless you want to cut yourself off from the outside world. To check your status, just enter the command by itself:

```
mesg
```

and **mesg** will display the current setting. If you try to talk to a person who has set **mesg** to **n**, you will see a message like:

```
[Your party is refusing messages]
```

In such cases, about all you can do is mail a message.

One way to check if a person is accepting messages is to use the **finger** command. This command can display information about users on any Unix system (as long as the finger server on that system has not been disabled for security reasons). Some finger servers will tell you whether or not a userid is accepting messages. Other servers will not; you will just have to try. (If you do not know how to use **finger**, ask someone for help or check in a Unix book.)

Here is an example. You have a friend whose address is `tln@nipper.com` and who has set **mesg** to **n**. You enter:

```
finger tln@nipper.com
```

As part of the output, you see the line:

```
Login name: tln (messages off) In real life: The Little Nipper
```

This shows you that this person is not accepting **talk** requests. You can also finger the `nipper.com` computer to show a summary of all the users who are currently logged in:

```
finger @nipper.com
```

When you do, one of the lines of output is:

```
tln      The Little Nipper    *p4  7 Tue 21:48
```

I won't go into all the details of reading such output. What I want you to notice is the
* character. This tells you that the person is not accepting **talk** requests.

> ## HINT
>
> Before you try to talk to someone, you may want to finger his userid. Aside
> from checking if the person is rejecting **talk** requests, you may also see if he is
> logged in.
> If the person is logged in, but you see he has been idle for a long time (some
> finger servers tell you this), it is unlikely that he will respond to your talk request.

The ytalk Program

The **ytalk** program was written by Britt Yenne as a replacement for the standard
Unix **talk** programs. The name **ytalk** stands variously for either "Yenne **talk**" or
"Why talk?", depending on your state of mind.

The nice thing about **ytalk** is it will work with both the old and the new versions
of **talk** I discussed earlier in the chapter. If you use **ytalk**, you never have to worry
about what type of **talk** your friends are using. Moreover, if you know other people
who have **ytalk**, you can use it to hold a group conversation. If the **ytalk** program
is not already installed on your computer, you can find it for free on the Net.

In its most basic form, the **ytalk** command is the same as the **talk** command.
Enter the command, followed by the address of the person you want to talk to:

```
ytalk wendy@muffin.com
```

When you talk to a single person, the screen divides into two parts, just like with
talk. One important difference is that **ytalk** will show you the userid of the person
to whom you are talking. Figure 26-2 shows such a screen. What you type is displayed
on the top half. What the other person types is displayed in the bottom half. The top
line of our example tells us we are using **ytalk** version 3.0, patchlevel 2.

If you want to talk with more than one person, all you have to do is specify more
than one address as part of the command. For example, here is a command that sets
up a five-way conversation:

```
ytalk  wendy@muffin.com  mike  ron@sigmastar.com  tln@nipper.com
```

In such cases, **ytalk** will divide the screen into as many partitions as necessary. In this
example, the screen would look like Figure 26-3.

```
------------------= YTalk version 3.0 (2) =------------------

What you type is displayed here.

Just as with the regular talk command,
one can type at the same time as
the other person.




--------------------------= wendy =--------------------------
What the other person types is displayed here.

He can type at the same time as you and
both parts of the screen will be updated
simultaneously.
```

Figure 26-2. *A* `ytalk` *screen with a two-way conversation*

At any time, you can change the participants by calling up a special menu. To do so, press the ESC (Escape) key. You will see:

```
= YTalk version 3.0 (2)   =
#         Main Menu        #
#                          #
# a: add a user            #
# d: delete a user         #
# o: options               #
# s: shell                 #
# u: user list             #
# w: output user to file   #
# q: quit                  #
###########################
```

```
----------------= YTalk version 3.0 (2) =-------------------
What you type is displayed here.



------------------------= wendy =------------------------
What Wendy types is displayed here.



-----------------------= mike =------------------------
What Mike types is displayed here.



------------------------= ron =------------------------
What Ron types is displayed here.



------------------------= tln =------------------------
What The Little Nipper types is displayed here.
```

Figure 26-3.   *A* ytalk *screen with a five-way conversation*

You can now press either **a**, **d**, **o**, **s**, **u**, **w** or **q**. If you change your mind, and you don't want to make a selection, press either RETURN or ESCAPE. This will remove the menu and return you to the main talk screen.

If you press **a**, you will be asked to enter the address of the person you want to add. Once you enter this address, **ytalk** will send him a message. When he responds, he will be incorporated into the conversation.

If you press **d**, you will be asked to enter the userid of the person you want to delete. In this case, you need only enter the userid and not the full address. Once you do, the person will be removed from the conversation.

If you press **o**, you will see another menu of options. These options control several aspects of the program. I won't go into them in detail, however, I do suggest that you experiment to find the settings you like best.

If you press **s**, the **ytalk** program will place you at a shell prompt. However, you will still be within **ytalk**. You can now enter any command you want, and the output will be displayed in your part of the screen. This means that the other people to whom you are talking can also see the output of your commands. For example, you can demonstrate how to use a Unix command.

When you are finished with the temporary shell, you can quit the shell by entering the **exit** command. You will see the following message:

```
##############################
#        Ytalk Error         #
#                            #
# command shell terminated   #
#    (no system error)       #
##############################
```

The top line of the message is misleading in that it does not signal an error. This message is simply a notice that the temporary shell has terminated. To remove the message, press any key.

To return to our discussion of the menu: If you press **u**, you will see information about all the users who are connected. To return to the main talk screen, press any key.

If you press **w**, you will be asked to select the name of a userid and then the name of a file. From then on, everything that is typed by that person will not only be displayed on your screen, but will be copied to the file as well. This option is useful when you want to save what someone is typing.

Finally, if you press **q**, it will quit the **ytalk** program. Be careful not to press **q** by mistake, as you will lose all your connections.

In order to have a group conversation, all the people need to be using **ytalk**. However, if you have **ytalk**, you can still talk to people who are using the regular **talk** program. It's just that they will only be able to talk to one person at a time.

For example, say you have **ytalk** and you want to talk with two friends who only have **talk**. If you connect to both of them, you will see a three-person conversation. Each of them, however, will only see the standard two-person **talk** screen. They will be able to talk with you but not with each other.

What happens if you are in the middle of a conversation and a new person tries to talk to you? You will see a message like the following:

```
#############################################################
# Talk with mschuster@schnitzel.com?                        #
#############################################################
```

You can now press **y** (yes) to add the person to the conversation, or **n** (no) to turn him down like a bedspread. If you press **y**, **ytalk** will redraw your screen to add another partition. When this happens, each person who is using **ytalk** will be asked if he wants to add the new person to his screen. He will see a message like:

```
#############################################################
# Import mschuster@schnitzel.com?                           #
#############################################################
```

He can now answer **y** or **n** as he wishes.

As you can see, **ytalk** is an especially handy program. However, it is not a standard part of Unix, so there is a good chance it may not be on your system. (Indeed, it will only be on your system if someone has deliberately installed it.) If **ytalk** is not on your system, you can ask your system manager to install **ytalk** for you. Alternatively, if you know how to install programs, you can download **ytalk** for free from the Net and install it yourself.

For more information about **ytalk** and how it works, use the **man** command to display the **ytalk** documentation from the online Unix manual. The command to use is:

```
man ytalk
```

INTERNET RESOURCE   *Look in the catalog under Internet Resources for*
Talking: **ytalk**

Chapter Twenty-Seven

IRC (Internet Relay Chat)

Y ou are at a large party with thousands of people. You are standing with a small group who are having several conversations at the same time. Whatever you say can be heard by everyone else in your group. You can also eavesdrop on other people's conversations. If you like, you can walk from one group to another, joining in one of their conversations or just listening. You can also invite someone, or several people, into a corner for a more private talk. And, if the need arises, you can whisper a completely private message in somebody's ear.

At first, everything is confusing because so many people are talking at the same time. But soon you get used to the rhythm, and it all makes sense. Within a short time, you are carrying on several conversations at the same time, saying hello to your old friends, welcoming newcomers, all the while talking about anything and everything.

Soon you find it harder and harder to leave the party. You drag yourself away reluctantly, returning every chance you get. After a while the party begins to take on a life of its own. You spend all your spare time there, leaving only when you must work or sleep. And whenever you return—day or night—there are always thousands of people: talking, talking, talking...

Welcome to IRC.

What Is IRC?

HINT

Before you read about IRC, take a look at Chapter 25 (Talk Facilities). In particular, read the section called "Guidelines for Text-based Talking" at the end of the chapter.

IRC—INTERNET RELAY CHAT—is an Internet-wide talk facility developed in 1988 by Jarkko Oikarinen in Finland. Since its inception, IRC has become one of the most popular Internet resources and is frequented by people in many different countries. Here is how it works. (Of course, everything you read about here is free.)

You use a client program to act as your interface. Your client connects to an IRC server. You can then enter IRC commands, of which there are many.

Using IRC commands, you can join a group of people and, whenever you want, move from one group to another. Once you have joined a group, whatever you type is sent to all the people in the group. Similarly, you can see all the messages that everyone else types. (There is a special way to enter IRC commands so they don't get mixed into the conversation.) A sample IRC group conversation is shown later in the chapter in Figure 27-3. Notice that each message is preceded by the nickname of a person. Notice also how more than one conversation is going on at the same time.

IRC is so powerful because servers can connect to other servers to form an IRC network. Once you connect to a server, you can talk to anybody using any server in the network. To you, the whole thing looks like one large system. On the larger IRC networks, there are often several thousand people. At any time, twenty-four hours a day, you can connect to a server and talk to people all over the world.

There are tens of different IRC networks. To use a particular network, all you need to do is connect to a server on that network. The two most well-known networks are EFNet and Undernet. EFNet is the "main" IRC network, a descendent of the first large IRC network. Undernet was started as an alternate network and is growing in popularity.

Here are some interesting numbers. As I was working on this chapter, I connected to an EFNet server and found a total of 6537 users on 108 servers. A little while later, I connected to an Undernet server and found 3420 users on 32 servers.

HINT

If you feel having like a conversation, there is always someone to talk to on the Net.

What's in a Name?
EFNet, Undernet

The history of IRC is filled with agreements, disagreements, alliances, break-ups and intrigue (sort of like *Lord of the Rings* on speed). In 1990 the people who programmed and administered the various IRC servers had fundamental disagreements over how to expand the network. One group wanted to use a central IRC server named `eris.berkeley.edu` to which all the IRC servers in the U.S. would connect. They also proposed similar central servers for Europe and other parts of the world. A second group of people wanted to use a non-centralized "backbone" of servers.

The differences proved to be irreconcilable and the server `eris.berkeley.edu` was banished from the network. (In IRC terms, the server was "q-lined"; the "q" stands for "quarantine".) The people who were pushing for the centralized system rallied behind `eris.berkeley.edu` and formed their own smaller network named A-net (Anarchy network). Other servers were moved to A-net, effectively splitting the global IRC network into two parts.

Within a short time, the remainder of the original network came to be known as the "Eris-Free Network" or EFNet. Thus, the name EFNet actually means "the network that is free from the `eris.berkeley.edu` server".

In the next few years, the EFNet expanded rapidly while the A-net died. Today, there are many IRC networks, but EFNet is still the largest. The next largest is Undernet, developed as an alternate network. The name Undernet was originally chosen to refer to an "underworld net", hidden from the main IRC network.

Ironically, Undernet is considered to be a conservative, well-managed network compared to today's EFNet, which still retains some of the anarchy of early IRC.

INTERNET RESOURCE *Look in the catalog under Internet Resources for*
IRC: List of IRC Networks

IRC Clients

To use IRC you need an IRC client program to connect to a server. Once you are
connected, your client acts as your interface into IRC.

If you use the Net via PPP or a direct network connection, you will run a client
program on your own computer. If you use a shell account, you will run a Unix client
on the remote host. (I discuss the various types of connections in Chapter 5.)

There are a number of PC and Macintosh IRC clients available on the Net. All of
these clients provide the basic functionality. Some are more sophisticated, offering
enough features to supply the entire Peruvian army. Figure 27-1 shows one of my
favorite IRC clients, a program named mIRC. Notice there are two conversations, each
in its own window. In addition, one window contains general status information,
while another contains a list of all the conversations (channels) available at the time.

If you are new to IRC, it doesn't really matter which IRC client you use. The
advanced features won't matter. The most important thing is to get a program running
and get yourself connected. After a few weeks, when you have some experience with

```
mIRC32 mwahahahah                                                    _ □ ×
File  Misc  Tools  DCC  Window  Help

Status: Minsky [+] on us.undernet.org                      _ □ ×    Channels List  _ □ ×
#Callahans Callahan's Place for Drinks, Puns and Friendship         AA            5
-                                                                   abril         2
#Callahans Minsky @ree Drizzle @hilary @Polar @Bangmo @gherk        accura        1
          @Faith gizmo @Sid @Admire @YP @Claude Bear Signin         acro          14
#Callahans End of /NAMES list.                                      acrua         1
-                                                                   ad&d          1
                                                                    adagio        2
                                                                    adb           2
                                                                    adelaide      1
 #cafebleu [+tn]  Lags-R-Us :(                              _ □ ×    adsf          2
× Grimstone breathes a sigh of relief that her platypus waasn't  @Wooke  Adult    1
  hurt                                                      @Xi     adult_pics    1
<barb> Grimstone: hehe                                     alikatin adultpics    11
<barb> Gimp: what havent you done before?                  barb    Adventist    1
<tree> hello                                               Bluefire advice        3
<barb> Gimp Gimster Gimpwhimpster dimpster                 Bud     AEGEE          1
× Grimstone tosses barb a bag....                          Columbia aerosmith    3
<Gimp> wake up late throw on some clean clothes and a hat and get  Grimstone afd  1
   to class.                                                tree    AIDS/HIV+     4
                                                                   ainhoa         1
                                                                   ajax           2
 #Callahans [+n]  Callahan's Place for Drinks, Puns and Friendship  _ □ ×  akeran  2
<Admire> Hi                                                @Bangmo Aladdin        1
<gizmo> heh                                                @hilary ALASKA         1
<gizmo> neat.                                              @ree    alone          3
<Lizard> 6 SECS LAG!!!!! Yikes!!!                          @Faith  alternative    1
<hilary> icky!                                             @gherk  amen           1
<Bangmo> back                                              @gizmo  amergoth       1
<Bangmo> Carrrrrr!!!!                                      @Admire america         2
×gizmo confesses to having interpreted bobdylan as bobdy LAN @Polar americaonline 2
  instead of bob dylan                                     @Sid    amigal         1
                                                                   amigacafe      8
                                                                   amistad       12
                                                                   amsterdam      1
                                                                   Andrew         1
                                                                   AndysWORLD     3
                                                                   Angeltown      1
                                                                   animaniacs     1
                                                                   anime          3
                                                                   ANIMEsp        2
```

Figure 27-1. *An IRC client (mIRC)*

IRC, you can take time to evaluate the different clients for your particular system and pick the one you like best.

INTERNET RESOURCE *Look in the catalog under Internet Resources for*
IRC: Client Programs

IRC Clients for a Shell Account

With a shell account, you access IRC by running a client program on your remote Unix host. The most common Unix client is a program named **irc**. Figure 27-2 shows this program running from a shell account. The **irc** program is sometimes called IrcII (IRC client, second edition), so don't be confused. The names **irc** and IrcII refer to the same program.

If **irc** is installed on your Unix host, you should be able to connect to IRC by entering **irc** followed by the nickname you want to use. You can use any nickname you want, up to nine characters. If you are not sure what to use, just type your first name. (I will explain nicknames later in the chapter.) For example:

irc Harley

```
 Telnet                                                              _ □ ×
 Connect  Edit  Terminal  Help
  times--it works with me...heh...heh...
 <wild>crazy:That is exactly what I am doing but I am waiting until 3:30.
 ××× araja has left channel #friends
 <Dina> Ancient: I'm sure
 <italian> nope
 ××× parano has left channel #friends
 <Dina> Boasty...thanks for the support...=)
 <tach> ano ba itong napasukan ko?
 <meekr> italian nope???
 <crazy> wild: What's going on at 3:30?
 <Beele> Thanx Kigor
 <Beele> :)
 <Kigor> crazy:  sorry I don't know anyhting about that
 <crazy> wild: I have a doctor's appt. at 3:15, and I have a late class
  today at 4:20pm
 <italian> meekr nope just everything else that comes with it
 <Beele> With what?
 ××× Tuff has left channel #friends
 <Boasty> Dina but for real.. she sucks..
 ××× tach has left channel #friends
 <meekr> italian cool beans
 ××× Palpatrea (lefte@imadoctor.com) has joined channel #friends
 [1] 11:35 Nipper on #friends (+lnt 30) × type /help for help
```

Figure 27-2. *An IRC client from a shell account (***irc***)*

To display technical information about the **irc** program, you can read the documentation in the online Unix manual. The command to use is:

man irc

(Be sure to enter this command at the Unix shell prompt, not from within IRC.)

If an IRC client is not installed on your Unix host, the **irc** command will not work, and you will see an error message. For example:

irc: Command not found.

In such cases, you have three choices.

First, you can ask your system manager to install an IRC client. (Ask nicely; some system managers feel IRC is a waste of time.)

Second, you can download the client program via anonymous ftp. (I discuss anonymous ftp in Chapter 18.) If you download a client program, you will have to install it yourself. If you have trouble, you may need to ask for help from your system administrator or a friendly computer nerd.

HINT

If you decide to download an IRC client, make sure you get the program for the client, not for the server.

Some universities and companies do not allow people to use IRC on their computers. Indeed, this may be the reason there is no IRC client on your system. If so, the People In Charge will not want you to install your own IRC client. If they find one, they may remove it unilaterally.

However, there is a solution: Use a public IRC client. To do this, you telnet to a remote computer and use the IRC client at that location. (I explain telnet in Chapters 23 and 24.) When you enter the **telnet** command, be sure to include the appropriate port number.

As you might imagine, public IRC clients are an important resource for people who otherwise would not be able to access IRC. So please, do not abuse the service. There are only a small number of public clients, and such services tend to disappear when people use them to cause trouble.

HINT

The least preferred way to use IRC is by telneting to a public client. Such systems limit the number of users they will accept, and they are often busy. If you are at all serious about IRC, you will find it much more convenient to use a client program on your own computer.

INTERNET RESOURCE *Look in the catalog under Internet Resources for*
IRC: Client Programs
IRC: Public IRC Clients

Channels

To bring order to what otherwise would be conversational chaos, IRC maintains separate conversation groups called CHANNELS. When you first connect to IRC, you choose a channel to join. Once you do, you can talk to all the other people on the same channel. When you feel like switching, you can join another one. You can join as many channels as you want at the same time (although, it's hard to participate in more than four or five conversations at the same time).

At any particular time, you will find many different channels. For example, I recently found 2904 channels on EFNet and 1277 channels on Undernet. As you move from one channel to another, you will find people from all over the world. Most of the conversations will be in English, but many are in other languages.

To keep things from being too confused, IRC uses two conventions. First, every channel has its own name. Most channel names begin with a **#** character, for example, **#hottub**.

Some channels are for discussing specific topics. Others are just for talking about whatever comes up. There are public channels, private channels, and secret "invisible" channels.

How does a channel get created? Very simply. Whenever you enter the command to join a channel, IRC checks to see if that channel already exists. If so, you will join it. Otherwise, IRC will create a new channel using whatever name you specified. At first, of course, you will be the only one on the channel, but you can wait for other people to join you. When the last person leaves a channel, IRC removes it automatically.

HINT

IRC channels are *not* permanent. They are created and deleted as necessary. However, some channels seem permanent because there is always someone on them, so they never get deleted.

When a channel is started, the person who starts it can set a topic. This topic is displayed whenever someone uses the **/list** command (explained later in the chapter) and can be changed at any time. People on IRC tend to talk about whatever they want, so don't be surprised when the conversation on a channel drifts a long way from the designated topic.

The first person who joins (and thus, creates) a channel is given the status of CHANNEL OPERATOR, usually referred simply as the OP. The op has control over various aspects of the channel. For example, he or she can make the channel private, so that only people who are invited are allowed to join. An op can also pass the operator status for that channel to another person and set the topic for discussion.

Thus, IRC is more than people talking on public channels. You can set up your own channels whenever you want. For example, the President of the United States might send you a mail message and ask, "Would you like to join Hillary and me on channel **#whitewater** tonight at 8:30 PM, Eastern time?"

HINT

If you would like to mail a message to the President, asking him to join you on IRC, his address is **president@whitehouse.gov**. If he can't make it, Rush Limbaugh's address is **70277.2502@compuserve.com**.

Nicknames

Every IRC participant has a NICKNAME or NICK. Each time you connect to an IRC server, you specify a nickname, which you can also change at any time. Nicknames can be up to nine characters. There is only one limitation: You cannot choose a nickname that is currently in use anywhere on the IRC network. There is no way to register a nickname permanently, so if someone is using your favorite name, you will have to choose another.

As your IRC client displays messages, it will preface each one with the nickname of the person who typed it. Here is an example from Figure 27-3, which we will look at in a moment:

```
<Nipper> Actually, I was hoping for tuna fish.
```

This line was typed by someone who is using the nickname **Nipper**.

HINT

Experienced IRC people usually refer to nicknames as "nicks". For example, "What is your favorite nick?"

As you might imagine, the world of IRC is filled with all manner of imaginative nicknames. However, nicknames offer more than a chance to project whimsy (such as **kewl-d00d**) or a particular image (such as **StudMUFIN**). Nicknames are important as they allow people to participate freely and openly while still retaining their anonymity.

Watching a Conversation

At all times, your IRC client maintains a window, showing what everyone is saying. If you are using a graphical client, it will show each channel in its own window. With a text-based client, you may see all the channels mixed in together. (Of course, you will only see the channels you have joined.)

Figure 27-3 shows a sample IRC conversation. The lines you type are prefaced by a single **>** (greater than) character. Other people's messages are prefaced with their nicknames.

The bottom line of the window is where you type your input. In Figure 27-3, I have typed:

Here is where you type, on the bottom line...

What you type is shown on this line, but is not actually transmitted until you press the ENTER key. This allows you to backspace and make corrections before the message is actually sent.

The second line from the bottom is a status line. In our example, it is:

[1] 23:06 Harley (+i) on #hottub (+nt) * type /help for help

In this case, I am using the nickname **Harley** and have joined the **#hottub** channel. We can see the time (23:06, which is 11:06 PM) and some technical information.

The rest of the screen is given over to the actual conversation. As you watch the screen, you will see what is being typed by all the people in the channel. Line after line will appear at the bottom of the display area. As new lines appear, the old ones scroll up. Thus, an IRC experience is one of watching many messages, one after the other.

It is common to encounter times when the network or one of the servers slows down, causing lag. At such times, there may be a significant delay in passing messages from one person to another, and the conversation will become even more fragmented.

```
<Peter> So of course I told her to go ahead
<Eric-J> So then what happened?
<KennN> How can you say that, Sharkface?
<Peter> How about you, Harley?
> I have had never had that exact same experience
<Peter> How do you know?
*** Nipper (tln@nipper.com) has joined channel #hottub
> Well, I'm not exactly sure
*** Gwen (gwen@fuzzball.ucsb.edu) has joined channel #hottub
<Nipper> Hi everyone
<tms> Hello Nipper
<Gwen> Hi Nipper, how are you?
<Eric-J> Peter, you never told us what happened
<Nipper> Gwen, I am doing just fine, just ate dinner.
<Nipper> It was fresh turkey liver.
<Nipper> Actually, I was hoping for tuna fish.
<tms> Does anyone have a good math joke?
*** KennN has left channel #hottub
*** Kitty (whoami@arkansas.com) has joined channel #hottub
[1] 23:06 Harley (+i) on #hottub (+nt)
Here is where you type, on the bottom line...
```

Figure 27-3. *A typical conversation with IRC*

However, this is not necessarily bad. If there is enough lag—and you have just the right type of brain—you will be able to carry on even more conversations than usual. (Consider, for example, how many balloons you could keep in the air at the same time if gravity were to decrease.)

Another problem may occur when one of the network connections between servers is dropped temporarily. Eventually the connection will be reestablished, but until it does, some people will seem to disappear from the channel. This phenomenon is called NETSPLIT.

In our example, you can see several people talking at once. Each line is prefaced by the nickname of the person who typed the message. For example:

```
<Nipper> Actually, I was hoping for tuna fish.
```

This line was typed by someone whose nickname is **Nipper**. The lines that you type do not have a nickname when they are displayed on your screen. Rather, they have a single **>** character. For example, I typed the line:

```
> Well, I'm not exactly sure
```

On everyone else's screen, that same line appeared with my nickname:

```
<Harley> Well, I'm not exactly sure
```

Lines that begin with ******* show informative system messages. For example:

```
*** Nipper (tln@nipper.com) has joined channel #hottub
```

You will often see people carrying on more than one discussion at the same time and, when things get busy, the conversation can be somewhat disorienting. Still, you will find that in a short time, you will synchronize with the IRC rhythm and it will all make sense. So much so that, unless you develop some self-discipline, you will find yourself spending more and more time chatting and less and less time participating in regular life (paying your bills, studying, washing dishes, buying computer books, and so on). Thus, before you get started, let me warn you:

HINT

IRC is addictive.

IRC Commands

As you use your IRC client, whatever you type is displayed on the bottom line of your window. However, nothing is processed until you press the ENTER key. This means you can make corrections as you type.

Any line that begins with a **/** (slash) character is interpreted as a command to your IRC client. For example, you can use the **/join** command (explained later in the chapter) to join a particular channel, and you can use the **/leave** command to leave a channel.

When you type an IRC command, the **/** character must be the first character of the line. Otherwise, your client will consider the line to be a message and will display it for everyone on the channel. For example, consider the following command:

```
/leave *
```

It tells your client to leave the current channel. But suppose you forget the **/** character:

leave *

Since this line does not begin with a **/** character, your client assumes you typed a regular message and sends it to your channel for everyone to read (which makes you look like a dweeb).

In general, the basic IRC commands are the same from one client to another. However, many of the more esoteric and advanced commands are not available with every client. Each client will have the commands that make sense in its particular environment. For instance, the Unix **irc** client offers many commands that are not necessary when you are using a graphical client under Windows. Here is an example.

Within IRC, it is possible to join more than one channel at the same time. Some graphical clients will start a new window for each channel. This allows you to keep each conversation isolated.

However, when you use the Unix **irc** client (from a shell account) there is only one window in which to display everything. As you might imagine, having more than one channel in a single window can be confusing. For this reason, by default, the **irc** client only lets you join one channel at a time. To change this, you must enter a special command (**set novice off**).

Here is another example. Some commands can generate a lot of output. For instance, the command **/list** (discussed later in the chapter) will list information about all the current channels (and there may be several thousand). With a graphical client, the output can be placed in a separate window. It might take a long time to display all the information in that window, but it doesn't matter to you. You can simply move to another window, and do something else while you are waiting. For example, you can move to another window and talk on a channel while you are waiting for the **/list** command to finish. When **/list** finally finishes, you can use the scroll bar to move up and down through the window to view the entire output.

With the **irc** client, there is only one window. If you enter the **/list** command, it can tie up the window for a long time, and you won't be able to do anything until all the output is displayed. For this reason, the **irc** client has special commands to help you manage the flow of output. One command tells the client to display information one screenful at a time (**set hold_mode on**); another command tells the client to flush all remaining output from the current command (**/flush**). These commands are generally not used with a graphical client, because they are not necessary.

In this chapter, I describe the most important IRC commands, which I will summarize at the end of the chapter. These commands will work with most IRC clients. However, for more details, you will have to check the help information for your particular client. When you get a spare moment, take some time to investigate the more advanced commands offered by your client and experiment to see how they work.

HINT

If you type a command that your client cannot recognize, you may or may not see an error message. Some clients will display a message, other will not. So if you enter a command and nothing happens, check your spelling.

IRC does not distinguish between upper- and lowercase letters for command names, nicknames or channel names. Thus, you can use any mixture of upper- and lowercase letters. Here is an example.

You can send a private message to someone by using the **/msg** command (explained later in the chapter). For instance:

```
/msg nipper Do you want to hear some gossip?
```

The following commands will all have the same effect:

```
/MSG NIPPER Do you want to hear some gossip?
/Msg Nipper Do you want to hear some gossip?
/msG niPpeR Do you want to hear some gossip?
```

Of course, it is usually easiest to use all lowercase letters.

HINT

You will often see people using nicknames that mix upper- and lowercase letters, for example, **StudMUFIN**. When you enter a command that uses such a nickname, you can type all lowercase letters, for example, **studmufin**, to save time.

Basic Commands

In this section, I will explain the basic IRC commands, the ones you should understand before you use IRC for the first time. The first such command is the one you use to quit:

```
/quit
```

This command will disconnect you from the IRC server. With the **irc** client program (for shell accounts), **/quit** will also stop the program itself.

The next command is used only with the **irc** program. This command is:

```
/set hold_mode on
```

This command tells **irc** to display large amounts of output one screenful at a time. If you do not set **hold_mode** to **on**, and you enter a command that generates a lot of output, **irc** will display the output all at once. Most of the output will scroll off the screen so quickly, you will only be able to read the last few lines.

When you use the **irc** program, the **/set** command allows you to control many different settings. If you want to see all the settings with their current values, enter the command:

```
/set
```

With graphical IRC clients, you do not need a **/set** command, because you can control all the settings by using pull-down menus.

HINT

With the **irc** client, you can use the **/save** command to save the current value of your settings to a file on the Unix computer. (The file will be **.ircrc** in your home directory.) The next time you run the **irc** program, it will read this file and automatically establish the settings according to your preferences.

If you save the settings in this way, you won't have to reset the **hold_mode** setting to **on** each time you start; it will be done for you automatically.

When you first connect to an IRC server, you will not be in any particular channel. Anything you type, except an IRC command, will be discarded. The first thing you will want to do is decide which channel to join. To display a list of all the channels, enter:

```
/list
```

For each channel, you will see the name, the number of users, and the topic (if one is set).

HINT

Commands such as **/list** can display a long list of information that seems to go on and on. For example, it is not unusual to connect to an EFNet server and find more than 3000 different channels.

Some clients will have a "flush" command to allow you to stop such output. With the **irc** program, this command is:

```
/flush
```

When you use a flush command, have patience. With some clients, the command does not always take effect right away. The best thing is to avoid using commands that produce so much output.

To make the channel list more manageable, you can ask to see only those channels that have a minimum number of participants, by using **-min** followed by a number. For example, to list only those channels that have at least 15 people, use:

```
/list -min 15
```

You can also use **-max** to display channels that have no more than a specified number of participants:

```
/list -max 5
```

To display information about a particular channel, you can specify its name. For example:

```
/list #hottub
```

Once you find a channel that looks good, you can join by using **/join** followed by the name of the channel. Remember, channel names start with a **#** character, for instance, **#hottub**. Thus, to join this channel, you would enter:

```
/join #hottub
```

Once you join a channel, everything you type (except commands) will be sent to that channel. If you are composing a long message, it is not necessary to keep pressing ENTER. IRC will allow you to type up to 256 characters in a single message.

HINT

If you are not sure which channel to join, **#hottub** is a good place to start. Think of it as a large group of people, sitting around in a hot tub, talking about anything that enters their mind. (You will need to supply your own water.)

To leave a channel, type **/leave** followed by the name of the channel. For example:

```
/leave #hottub
```

As a shortcut, you can leave the current channel by typing:

```
/leave *
```

HINT

With the **irc** program, you will automatically be removed from the current channel when you join a new one. Once you get more experienced, you can issue the command:

```
/set novice off
```

This changes several things about your IRC session. In particular, it allows you to join more than one channel at the same time.

Note: An older name for the **/leave** command is **/part** (as in "depart from this channel"). If you ever see a reference to the **/part** command, just remember it is a synonym for **/leave**.

From time to time, you will see a message, called an ACTION, that says that someone has done something. For example, you might see:

```
* Nipper waves hello and pats you on the head.
```

Actions are used to imply feelings and ideas where regular messages would be inadequate. To display an action, you use the **/me** command. Type **/me** followed by your action. Everyone on the channel will see your nickname, followed by the action. For example, if your nickname is **Nipper** and you enter:

```
/me breaks the glass.
```

Everyone (including you) will see:

```
* Nipper breaks the glass.
```

When you use **/me**, the action you describe will be sent to everyone in the channel. If you want to display an action privately for one person, you can use the **/desc** (describe) command. Type the command, followed by a nickname, followed by the action. For example, the following command displays a private action for the person using the nickname **Wendy**:

```
/desc wendy gives you a big kiss
```

At the other end, your nickname will be displayed along with the action. For example, if your nickname is **Harley** and you type the **/desc** command above, the person named **Wendy** would see:

```
*> Harley gives you a big kiss
```

Notice that the action begins with the characters ***>**. This shows that it was sent privately, with the **/desc** command. A regular (public) action, sent with the **/me** command, will begin with a single ***** character.

HINT

The **/desc** command does not work with all clients. You will have to try it and see if it works for you.

Help Information

The command to display help information is **/help**. For general information, enter **/help** by itself:

```
/help
```

What you see depends on which client you are using. In general, your client will show you the online help that comes with the program.

If you are using the **irc** client with a shell account, the **/help** command will only work if the system manager has installed the help files along with the **irc** program. Unfortunately, many system managers do not install these files and you are left without help. However, the same information is available elsewhere on the Net.

INTERNET RESOURCE   *Look in the catalog under Internet Resources for*
IRC: Help for irc *Client Program*

If you use **irc** and **/help** is available, you can display information about a specific command by typing **/help** followed by the name of that command. For example:

```
/help join
```

For new users, there is a special **/help** command:

```
/help newuser
```

This will display information of interest to beginners.

Learning More About IRC

The best way to learn about IRC is to use it. Whenever you get a chance, use the **/help** command (or whatever documentation comes with your program) and teach yourself a new command. However, for those long winter nights when you feel like curling up to a warm computer and reading something light, there are a number of important documents you can find on the Net.

One of the best documents for beginners is the IRC primer. Alternatively, you can start with the IRC FAQ (frequently asked question list). And if you have access to the Web, there are also large collections of IRC-related documents.

INTERNET RESOURCE   *Look in the catalog under Internet Resources for*
IRC: Primer
IRC: FAQ (Frequently Asked Question List)
IRC: Document Collections

Using a Nickname

When you first connect to IRC, you specify a nickname (which can be up to nine characters). At any time, you can change your nickname by typing **/nick**, followed by the new nickname. For example, if your nickname is **Irishboy** and you want to change it to **MikeP**, use:

```
/nick MikeP
```

When you do, IRC will notify everybody in your channel. You will all see a message like:

`*** Irishboy is now known as MikeP`

When you specify a nickname, you can type upper- or lowercase letters, and IRC will remember what you use. Whenever IRC displays your nickname, it will be just as you specified it. However, when you type a nickname as part of a command, you can use all lowercase letters, which is a lot easier to type.

Whenever you use **/nick** to ask for a new nickname, IRC checks it against all the nicknames currently in use in the IRC network (ignoring any differences due to upper- and lowercase). If someone is already using the same name, you will be asked to select another one.

To display your current nickname (in case you get hit on the head and develop amnesia during your IRC session), enter the **/nick** command by itself:

`/nick`

If you would like to see the last person who used your current nickname, enter:

`/whowas`

To find out who the last person was to use a particular nickname, use **/whowas** followed by that name. For example:

`/whowas MikeP`

Note: With some clients, the **/nick** and **/whowas** commands will not work unless you specify a name.

Commands for Talking to Specific People

To send a private message to someone, use **/msg**, followed by the person's nickname, followed by the message. For example:

`/msg Kenn What's up guy?`

The message will be seen only on that person's screen.

When you send private messages, you do not have to be on the same channel as the recipient. Wherever the person is, he will get the message, as long as he is connected to the same IRC network. (That is one reason why no two people are allowed to use the same nickname at the same time.)

As you look at your screen, normal messages are prefaced by the nickname of the originator, enclosed in **< >** characters. For example:

```
<Kenn> Hi Harley, how are you?
```

When someone sends you a private message, the nickname will be marked with *****
characters instead. For example:

```
*Kenn* What are you working on?
```

When you send a private message to someone, it will show up on your screen with
their nickname preceded by the characters **->**. For example, if you send a message to
the person whose nickname is **Kenn**, what you see on your screen looks like this:

```
-> *Kenn* I am working on Chapter 27.
```

HINT

Because the world of IRC is so open and public, it is necessary to maintain a
protective aura of anonymity. At any time, there may be thousands of people talking
to one another, but each particular person is known only by a nickname. For this
reason, many people consider it good manners to refer to a person only by his or her
nickname, even if you know the person's real name.

When you use **/msg**, there are two shortcuts available. First, if you use a **,**
(comma) character instead of a nickname, the message will go to the last person who
sent you a private message. For example, if the last person who sent you a private
message was **Nipper**, the following two commands would be equivalent:

```
/msg nipper What's up guy?
/msg , What's up guy?
```

Alternatively, if you use a **.** (period) character instead of a nickname, the message will
go to the last person to whom you sent a private message. For example:

```
/msg . Did you get my last message?
```

If you want to send a private message to more than one person, you can specify more
than one nickname. However, you must separate the names with a comma and not
put in any spaces:

```
/msg nipper,harley  Hello you two.
```

In this example, the exact same message would be sent to both nipper and harley.

Remember, any line that starts with a **/** (slash) character is considered to be a command, and is not sent to the channel. Similarly, any line that does not begin with a **/** is considered to be part of the general conversation and is sent to the channel.

Thus, if you type a **/msg** command, but accidentally put a space in front of the **/** character (or omit the **/** character), the line would be broadcast for everyone to see.

HINT

To make new friends, join a channel with a lot of people and then type the following line. Be sure to put a space in front of the **/** character.

```
/msg . sounds great!  Shall I bring my whip with me too?
```

If you find yourself sending more than a few **/msg** lines to the same person, you can simplify things by using the **/query** command followed by one or more nicknames. As with **/msg**, you must separate the nicknames with a comma and not put in extra spaces.

This command tells IRC that, until further notice, everything you type (except commands, of course) should be sent to the specified people. Here are two examples:

```
/query harley
/query harley,nipper
```

The first command says all of your messages should go only to **harley**. The second command sends messages to both **harley** and **nipper**.

When you are finished with your private conversation, you can turn it off by using the command without a nickname:

```
/query
```

Now, all of your messages will go to your channel.

If you are noticing a significant delay when you talk with a particular person, you can use the **/ping** command to see exactly how long the lag really is. Type **/ping** followed by the person's nickname. For example:

```
/ping harley
```

The IRC server will respond by showing you how long it takes a message to travel from you to that person and back again. For example, you might see:

```
*** CTCP PING reply from harley: 3 seconds
```

In this case, it takes 3 seconds for a message to get from you to **harley** and back again. (The word **CTCP** stands for "Client To Client Protocol", the protocol used to support parts of IRC.)

HINT

Even though you may be sending private messages with **/msg** or **/query**, your screen will still show all the other messages that are being sent to your channel, which can be distracting. If you want a quiet conversation with someone, ask the person to join you on another channel. For example, you might type:

```
/msg harley Let's talk more quietly. Join me on '#foobar'.
```

If you specify a channel name that is unused, you will have your own private channel. After you are both on the channel, you can keep it private by entering the command:

```
/mode * +pi
```

For more information about the **/mode** command, use **/help mode** or see the online help for your client program.

Displaying Information About People

There are several commands you can use to display information about people. First, to display information about a particular person, use **/whois** followed by the nickname, for example:

```
/whois nipper
```

You also can display information about a person by using the **/who** command:

```
/who nipper
```

However, **/whois** is better as it shows you more information.

Where **/who** comes in handy is in showing you information about all the people in a particular channel. For example, to find out who has joined channel **#hottub**, use:

```
/who #hottub
```

If you want to see a list of everybody who has joined your current channel, you can enter:

`/who *`

HINT

If you have not joined a channel, some IRC clients will interpret the command **/who *** as meaning that you want a list of everybody who is using IRC. Similarly, if you type **/whois ***, IRC will display information about everybody who is connected.

If you are using the **irc** client, do not enter either of these commands unless you are in a channel. Otherwise, the list will go on forever (or until you die, whichever comes first). If you do find yourself in this situation, remember you can use **/flush** to stop the rest of the output (eventually).

Using Direct Connections with DCC

In general, all information passes through an IRC server on its way to other people. For example, every time you type a remark, your client sends it to the server. The server then sends the remark to all the people on your channel.

There will be times, however, when you want to talk in complete and utter privacy. In addition, you may want to transfer a file to a particular person. To do so, you can use a system called DCC that connects two IRC clients directly without going through a central server. (The name DCC stands for "Direct Client to Client connection".)

To use DCC, all you have to do is enter a DCC command. When you do, your client will automatically contact the other person's client and initiate the appropriate activity. Here, then, are the DCC commands.

To talk to someone directly, use the command **/dcc chat** followed by the nickname of the person to whom you want to talk. For example:

`/dcc chat harley`

The person will receive a request, saying that you want to initiate a direct connection.

When someone sends you such a request, your client will display the request and wait for you to respond. For example, a graphical client will display a dialog box showing the person's nickname and asking if you want to establish a direct connection. You can select either "yes" or "no".

The **irc** client will display the request on a single line. For example:

```
-nipper- Initiating DCC Chat
```

This tells you that **nipper** is trying to initiate a DCC connection. To respond you can enter a **/dcc chat** command of your own. In this case, the command would be:

```
/dcc chat nipper
```

The DCC connection will now be established.

Some graphical clients will place the newly established DCC connection in its own window. To talk to the other person, all you need to do is move to that window and type. However, the **irc** client displays everything in a single window, so you need a special command to send messages over a DCC connection. This command is **/dmsg**. Type the command, followed by the nickname of the person with whom you have already established a DCC connection, followed by the message. For example:

```
/dmsg nipper  Hi Nipper.  Would you like tuna for dinner?
```

The message will then be sent privately over the DCC connection.

To shut down a DCC connection with a graphical client, simply close the window or select the appropriate item from a menu.

With the **irc** program, use the command **/dcc close chat**. Type the command followed by the nickname of the person to whom you are talking. For example:

```
/dcc close chat nipper
```

The DCC connection will now be closed.

You can also use DCC to send a file to someone. To do so, type the command **/dcc send** followed by the nickname of the person to whom you want to send the file and the name of the file. For example, to send the file named **secret.doc** to the person using the nickname **harley**, you would use the following command:

```
/dcc send harley secret.doc
```

The person will then receive a request, saying that you want to transfer a file.

When someone sends you such a request, it will be displayed by your client. With a graphical client, you will see a dialog box to which you can respond.

With the **irc** client, you will see a message similar to the following:

```
*** DCC SEND (secret.doc 12367) request received from harley
```

This shows the name of the file, **secret.doc**, and its size, 12367 bytes. To respond to such a request and accept the file, use the **/dcc get** command. Type the command followed by the nickname of the person who is sending the file. For example:

```
/dcc get harley
```

The file transfer will now start. When it is finished, you will see an appropriate message.

Bots

A BOT is a program or a script that is designed to interact with the IRC system. A bot can be programmed to read input, generate output and respond to particular events. A good programmer can design a bot that acts like a person, so when something strange happens, you can't always tell if it was caused by a bot or by a real human.

Bots can provide useful functions. However, there is a long history of people using bots to cause trouble and abuse the IRC system. For this reason, some IRC networks have banned bots completely. Using a bot on such networks will get you thrown out and perhaps even banned permanently.

If you are interested in bots, there are resources on the Net that can provide general information. There are also archives of bot programs and scripts. However, if you cause trouble, you will find IRC administrators have zero tolerance.

 **INTERNET RESOURCE**   *Look in the catalog under Internet Resources for*
IRC: Bots

What's in a Name?

Bot

The name "bot" comes from the word "robot". However, bots are actually computer programs, not real robots.

The name "robot", by the way, was coined in 1920 by the Czech writer Karel Čapek, in a play entitled *R.U.R.* In the play, an Englishman named Rossum creates artificial human beings in large quantities. Čapek called these creations "robots", which is the Czech word for "forced workers" or "slaves". The name of the play, *R.U.R.*, stood for "Rossum's Universal Robots".

Some people create bots simply to cause trouble, but you can't always tell they are bots. Similarly, some people are fond of telling beginners to do things that could cause you a lot of trouble (such as erase all of your files). To be safe, you should always follow these simple guidelines.

Harley Hahn's Rules for Safe IRC

1.) No matter what anyone says, never type your password.

2.) No matter what anyone says, never enter a command unless you are absolutely sure you know what it does.

3.) Never give out your phone number, home address, credit card number or (if you are American) your Social Security number.

Summary of Important IRC Commands

For reference, Figures 27-4 through 27-8 contain a summary of the IRC commands I have covered in this chapter. These commands are enough to get you started. However, there are a lot more commands to learn and a lot of surprises waiting for you.

Remember, IRC commands are processed by your client program, so the list of commands available to you depends on which client you are using.

Command	Description
/flush	throw away remaining output for current command
/help	display online help, or a list of all the IRC commands
/help *command*	display help regarding the specified command
/help newuser	display information for new users
/nick	display your current nickname
/nick *nickname*	change your nickname to specified name
/ping *nickname*	see how long it takes to get to specified person and back
/set hold_mode on	**irc** client: display output one screenful at a time
/set novice off	**irc** client: allow certain actions (like joining multiple channels)
/save	**irc** client: save current settings in your initialization file
/quit	quit IRC

Figure 27-4. *IRC: Basic commands*

Command	Description
/join *#channel*	join the specified channel
/leave *#channel*	leave the specified channel
/leave *	leave the current channel
/list	display information about all channels
/list *#channel*	display information about the specified channel
/list –min *n*	display channels that have at least *n* people
/list –max *n*	display channels that have no more than *n* people
/mode * +pi	make the current channel completely private
/part	same as **/leave**

Figure 27-5.   *IRC: Commands for working with channels*

Command	Description
/desc *nickname action*	display the specified action to one person only
/me *action*	display the specified action to everyone in the channel
/msg *nicknames text*	send a private message to specified people
/msg , *text*	send a message to last person who sent you a message
/msg . *text*	send a message to last person you sent a message to
/query *nicknames*	until cancelled, send all messages to specified people
/query	cancel the sending of private messages

Figure 27-6.   *IRC: Commands for sending messages*

Command	Description
/who *nickname*	show information about the specified person
/who *	show who is joined to the current channel
/whois *nickname*	show all information about the specified person
/whois *	show all information about everybody

Figure 27-7. *IRC: Commands for displaying information about people*

Command	Description
/dcc chat *nickname*	start or accept a direct talk connection
/dcc close chat *nickname*	close a direct talk connection
/dcc send *nickname file*	send a file to another person
/dcc get *nickname*	accept a file from another person
/dmsg *nickname message*	irc client: send message to specified person

Figure 27-8. *IRC: DCC commands*

Chapter Twenty-Eight

Muds

In many ways, muds are the epitome of what you can do with a large, worldwide computer network. When you connect to a mud, you enter a world that exists only in the minds of other people. There are many different kinds of muds, but what they all have in common is a degree of sophistication, creativity and imagination that exists nowhere else on the Net.

Muds provide environments that are unlike anything ever created in the history of mankind. All around the world, right now, there are thousands of people sitting at their computers, typing commands and messages, and looking at nothing more than words on a computer screen. These people are participating in a world that exists in the minds of other people—people whom they may never see in "real life", but whom they know as intimately as anyone they will ever meet. Moreover, it is a world that cannot exist on its own. It requires not only the participation of people, but the services of a complex computer program to create and support the imaginary infrastructure.

Using a mud requires you to develop and refine skills that other people cannot even imagine. To learn how to use a mud competently can take weeks or months. To master a mud may take years. At first a mud may seem like nothing more than a complex computer program. But it won't take you long to realize that thriving on a mud requires you to grow socially and culturally more than it requires mastering technical details.

In Chapter 27, I mentioned that IRC (a large talk-oriented system) can be addictive. Muds too can be seductive, but in a completely different way. IRC is addictive in the same way that a cup of coffee every morning will soon become habit forming. Muds are more complex, much more difficult to understand, and ultimately, a lot more satisfying.

Using IRC is like jolting yourself regularly with caffeine. Participating in a mud is like cultivating a long-term appreciation of fine art or classical music.

What Is a Mud?

A MUD is an elaborate computer-mediated, imaginary environment. To use a mud, you connect over the Internet to a special computer program. Once you connect, you log in by typing a user name and password. You then assume the role of a particular character.

As a character, you participate in whatever activities are available on the mud. These may include talking to other people, playing games, solving puzzles, exploring, fighting, having adventures, and so on. From time to time, you may even take part in a group event, such as a wedding.

Each time you return to a mud, you will be the same character. Although it is possible to change, many people will develop a character and maintain it for months or even years. If you join more than one mud, you can use similar characters—perhaps with the same name—or you can adopt a completely different persona for each mud.

The interface to a mud is text-based, which means that most everything is done with words. In essence, your experience will be one of typing and reading. You participate in a mud by typing commands and messages. At the same time, you read words typed by another person (greetings, messages, and so on) or generated by the mud program itself (descriptions of places or events).

All muds have a geography: a planned layout that describes an imaginary environment. One mud might have different rooms to explore; another mud might look like a village with roads, houses, stores, and so on. Some muds are modeled after real places. For example, there is a mud that looks like part of London, England; another mud looks like Harvard University; other muds are modeled after well-known imaginary places, such as King Arthur's Camelot or the world of Alice in Wonderland.

Although all muds include lots of talking with other people, some are designed primarily for talk while others are designed for action. Most muds are designed around a general theme, for example, fantasy, medieval, sci-fi, cyperpunk, gothic or post-apocalypse. Some muds have a specific theme. For instance, there are muds based on Pern, Star Trek, Star Wars, Snow Crash and other well-known settings.

As a character in a mud, you use commands to travel from one place to another. The mud program interprets your commands and keeps track of your current location. When you move, the program will tell you where you are and describe your surroundings. You can travel through a mud by yourself or with other people. All muds—even those designed primarily for talking—have some type of geography. You are always somewhere, and there is always somewhere to go.

Muds are enduring because people log in regularly. The people in the mud form a large extended family, who over a period of time, come to know each other well. It is common for people to spend a lot of time on their favorite mud, returning every day, sometimes for years. (For example, a college student who is a regular mud user would probably talk to his mud friends more often than he phones his mother.) Figure 28-1 shows an actual message sent from one mud person to another. Don't worry if you can't understand what they are talking about. By the time you finish this chapter, it will all make sense.

```
I tried a diku tonite named Aesir. Have you heard of it?

It's a really friendly mud. PK is optional. They have 11 races.
(I've never been on a mud with so many races.)

I haven't figured out the clan thing, but they have 4.
(I don't know if that is typical or not.)

But the thing that strikes me the most is 1) diku seems quite
complicated compared to an LP, and 2) Aesir is sooooooo friendly.
Truly amazing.

Embarrassing, but lucky thing: I got killed in their mud school,
so I ended up meeting this guy who gave me a ton of gold and all
the equipment I could possibly hold. :-) (yay!)
```

Figure 28-1. *A typical message sent from one mud person to another*

Aside from meeting your friends, there is another reason to return to the same mud repeatedly. You can explore the environment and learn more about that particular mud. On some muds, as you get better and better, you achieve a higher status and are given more privileges.

As I mentioned, your time on a mud is spent as a character, not as yourself. This is true even on a mud devoted to talking. For example, you would never refer to someone by his or her real name, even if you knew the person in real life.

On a mud devoted to action and adventure, your character becomes an avatar: a surrogate whom you control as you travel around, talking with others and interacting with the environment. For example, you may need to fight a giant or avoid a monster who hides in a cave. When you do, you use your skill as best you can, so your character is not killed. On such muds, who and what you are is of prime importance. At all times, the mud program, as well as the other people, will recognize your identity, description, skills, possessions and experience, and will react accordingly. For instance, if you are an evil female elf warrior, your life will be different than if you are a male human magician who uses his powers for good.

It is important to understand that muds are *not* based on organized role playing in the traditional Dungeons and Dragons sense. There is no one person who rolls the dice, or asks people to make decisions, or invents a story within the bounds of a make-believe universe. Some muds, however, do have people who work actively behind the scenes, expanding the mud and creating new theme areas.

In addition, all muds have one or more administrators. After all, somebody has to set up the computer and the mud itself, and somebody has to see to all the administrative tasks. However, within the mud, everyone is a character. Although some characters may be more experienced and have significantly more privileges, no one leads you on a day-by-day basis. You are free to explore and talk to people in your own way. Muds do have rules and customs that you are expected to follow, but on a well-run mud, there are no insecure authority figures who will tell you what to do whenever they feel like it, as you might find at school, on the job, in your family or on America Online.

⚑ HINT

To learn how to mud well, you have to be smart. However, you do not have to know a lot about computers.

What's in a Name?

Mud

The first mud was developed by Richard Bartle and Roy Trubshaw in 1978. At the time, the name "MUD" was chosen to stand for "Multi-User Dungeons" (as in Dungeons and Dragons). Within a few years, muds had evolved to the point where the original name was too confining, and people started to say that "MUD" stood for the more generic "Multi-User Dimension" or "Multi-User Domain".

Today, muds are well established with a highly developed culture of their own. The name "mud" is meaningful in its own right and is no longer an acronym (which is why I write "mud" in lowercase letters).

You will find all kinds of muds on the Internet, and there are many different names used to describe the variations. Some of these names begin with the letter "M" and look like acronyms, for example, MUCK, MUSH, MUSE, MAGE, MUG, MOO, and so on. All of these things are muds, but you don't really need to know the technical details. The best way to think of such terms is to consider them as specialized words, not acronyms.

From time to time you may see an explanation as to what one of these words "means". For instance, you may read that MUSH stands for "Multi-User Shared Hallucination". My advice is to forget the acronyms. Consider all of these strange things to be types of muds and leave it at that.

The word "mud" is also used as a verb. For example, you might hear someone say, "I like to mud more than I like to sleep," or "I am a bit tired, as I was up all night mudding, so maybe you better go to class without me."

 INTERNET RESOURCE *Look in the catalog under Internet Resources for*
Muds: FAQs (Frequently Asked Questions)
Muds: History
Muds: Timeline
Muds: Usenet Discussion Groups

Mud Clients

As with all Internet services, muds are based on a client/server system. You use a client program to contact a server (the mud). If you access the Net using PPP or a direct network connection, you will run a client program on your own computer. If you access the net using a shell account, you will run a client program on the remote Unix host. (I explain these ideas in Chapter 5.) Regardless of what client you run, the basic mud experience is the same.

To connect to a mud, you use telnet (see Chapter 23). Thus, it is possible to use a regular telnet client. However, there are specialized mud clients that have features to make mudding easy, convenient and more enjoyable. Since such clients are available on the Net, I suggest you find one for yourself and install it before you start to mud.

Figure 28-2 shows a mud client. Notice the separate typing area at the bottom of the window. As you type, the characters are displayed in this typing area, and nothing is sent until you press ENTER. The output from the mud is displayed separately in the larger area. With a regular telnet client, things can be confusing, because the characters you type are mixed in with the output from the mud.

INTERNET RESOURCE *Look in the catalog under Internet Resources for*
Muds: Client Programs

Figure 28-2. *A mud client program*

If you do use a telnet client, I have a few hints for you. Some telnet clients have trouble with muds unless you change how the client is configured. In particular, you must ensure that your telnet client is in "line mode". This means that, rather than send each character as you type it, the client will wait until you press ENTER and then send the entire line at once. If you try to use a mud and you can't seem to sustain a connection, configuring your client to line mode may solve the problem.

In addition, you may have to change the setting that controls the local echo and the setting that determines which characters are sent at the end of each line (carriage return, linefeed or both).

Mud Clients for Shell Accounts

If you have a shell account, you can use the **telnet** program on the remote Unix computer. However, many Internet service providers have Unix mud clients and, if one is available, you should use it instead of telnet. There are several popular Unix mud clients. Try each of them and see if they exist on your system. They are **tf** (TinyFugue), **vt** (VaporTalk) and **tt++** (Tintin). To see if one of these programs is installed, simply enter its name as a command. For example:

```
tf
```

If the program is not there, you will see a message like:

```
tf: Command not found.
```

If the program is found, you can display the documentation in the online Unix manual by using the **man** command. For example:

```
man tf
```

If you are using a Unix system that does not have a mud client, you should ask your system manager to install one. (Ask nicely; many system managers think that mudding is a waste of time.) However, since muds are so popular, many Internet service providers have installed one or more mud clients for the benefit of their users.

Social Muds and Adventure Muds

In a few moments, I will tell you how to go about choosing a mud. Before I do, however, I want to explain the various types of muds and how you should think about them.

Broadly speaking, there are two types of muds: SOCIAL MUDS and ADVENTURE MUDS. Social muds are for talking. Adventure muds are for talking as well as game playing. (By the way, I am using these names informally; they are not strict technical terms.)

The main purpose of a social mud is to provide a place for people to meet and talk. Although you participate as a character of some type, you spend most of your time walking around, meeting other people. Many social muds are organized around a particular theme or area of interest. Some involve role playing, others are less concerned with staying in character. Over time, social muds attract a core of regulars who develop their own culture and traditions. Although you will sometimes find quests and puzzles, social muds are primarily for people who want to socialize.

Some social muds are devoted to utilitarian pursuits. For example, there are a number of educational muds (without role playing) where people gather to learn, teach or have serious technical discussions.

You will sometimes see social muds referred to as "talkers" or "chat lines" (although not all talkers and chat lines are real muds).

HINT

You may be familiar with the American television program "Cheers." The setting was a bar in which a group of regular customers would gather to talk, philosophize and discuss the issues of the day (including personal problems). If you ever thought it would be nice to be a regular in such a place—where everybody knows your name and they're always glad you came—a social mud is for you.

Adventure muds offer more than socializing. There will be some type of overall activity in which you participate actively (in the role of your character). Adventure muds are complex environments, usually designed around a single main theme, where you will find many places to visit and things to do. As you travel throughout the mud, you will talk, interact, plot, fight, kill, explore, gather materials, meet people, go on quests, encounter obstacles, form alliances, and so on. On a typical adventure mud, you will get equipment and weapons. As you travel around, you will find monsters (and sometimes other people) to kill.

One of the appealing features of an adventure mud is that you can return again and again, playing with more and more skill as you gain experience. With most adventure muds, you can move from one level to another as you achieve certain goals. Moving to a higher level will increase your privileges and improve your status.

There are a large variety of adventure muds with no clear-cut groupings. However, it is possible to loosely categorize adventure muds into three main types. First, some muds involve a lot of strategy and are based on a complex set of rules and interactions. These muds—which are often DikuMuds (see the next section)—are heavy on thinking and planning. If you like Advanced Dungeons and Dragons, you will like this type of mud.

Other muds have more action and are less obsessed with elaborate scenarios and characterizations. These muds are sometimes referred to as HACK-N-SLASH muds (although the term is somewhat derogatory). Hack-n-slash muds are satisfying because they have a nice mixture of culture, planning, learning, achievement and killing.

Finally, PLAYER KILLING MUDS are devoted to killing other players. On other muds, you devote the bulk of your aggressive instincts to killing monsters. On a player killing mud, you spend all of your time trying to kill everyone else. When you die, you are automatically reincarnated, at which time you go back for more. ("Please sir, may I have another?")

HINT

The main activity on all muds is talking. Even on adventure muds, you will spend more time talking than any other single activity.

LPMuds, DikuMuds and TinyMuds

Most muds are based on one of three principal technologies. You certainly don't have to know the details of how they work, but I do want you to recognize the names, as you will see them a lot. The names of the three main mud-building technologies are LPMuds, DikuMuds and TinyMuds.

LPMUDS are based on a computer language called LPC. LPC is designed to be easy to use by someone who understands programming, and LPMuds are readily customized. In fact, it is possible to add new features to an LPMud while it is running. For these reasons, it is common to find LPMuds that are constantly being enhanced.

With some LPMuds, there are two well-defined groups of people involved in a symbiotic relationship. One group spends time using the mud, while another group (who are not players) works on enlarging and modifying the mud. On an LPMud, anyone with permission can add new features to the mud. Indeed, in one sense, an LPMud can be thought of as an ongoing software project. On a well-run LPMud, the head administrator will coordinate the efforts of the individual creators to make sure that new features are in harmony with the overall mud environment.

The original LPC language was designed to create hack-n-slash muds. If you heard that a particular mud was an LPMud, you could guess what type of mud it was. In recent years, though, LPC has been redesigned into a general-purpose mud-creation language and, nowadays, virtually any type of mud might be an LPMud.

DIKUMUDS are adventure muds that involve a great deal of strategy and elaborate characterization (like you might find with Advanced Dungeons and Dragons). DikuMuds are usually written in the C programming language, not LPC, and, as such, are more difficult to customize. With many DikuMuds, you play the same game each time you log in. The idea, of course, is to master the game and all its intricacies.

TINYMUDS are social muds. Although they offer an imaginary environment and make-believe characters, TinyMuds are almost always oriented toward talking and socializing. New TinyMuds are not programmed in a computer language. Rather, they are generated from a database system. The mud designer configures the database according to his or her preferences, and then uses a special program to read the specifications and generate the mud.

There are many different types of LPMuds, DikuMuds and TinyMuds, all with strange names. In most cases, the names don't tell you much. However, many types of TinyMuds have names that are short words beginning with the letter "M". So if a mud is described as a MUCK, MUSH, MUSE, MAGE, MUG or MOO, you can guess it is a TinyMud, oriented toward socializing rather than action.

As a general rule (which does have exceptions):

- LPMuds can be any type of mud and are often expandable.
- DikuMuds are elaborate adventure muds that tend to stay the same.
- TinyMuds are social muds.

📖 What's in a Name?

LPMud, DikuMud, TinyMud

LPMuds are named after Lars Pensjö, who created the original LPMud in 1989.

DikuMuds are named after the Datalogisk Institut Københavns Universitet (Department of Computer Science, University of Copenhagen), where the original DikuMud was created in 1990 by Katja Nyboe, Tom Madsen, Hans Henrik Staerfeldt, Michael Seifert and Sebastian Hammer.

TinyMuds were named by Jim Aspnes, who wrote the first such mud in 1989. He chose the name "Tiny" because his program was smaller and more manageable than other mud programs.

How to Choose a Mud

To choose a mud successfully, all you need to do is follow my simple three-step plan:

1.) Decide if you want to spend your time on a social mud or an adventure mud.

2.) Ask your friends for recommendations. If you don't have the right type of friends, look at a list of muds and guess.

3.) Try three muds for a short time and choose the one you like best.

HINT

If you like a lot of action, choose an adventure mud, so you can talk and kill things at the same time.

INTERNET RESOURCE *Look in the catalog under Internet Resources for*
Muds: List of Muds
Muds: Educational Muds

As you evaluate a mud, there are a number of questions to consider. First, do you enjoy the theme? When you come right down to it, walking around an imaginary environment pretending you are an imaginary character is a bit silly, and there is no point spending your time being silly within a theme you don't like. If there is a particular part of the popular culture about which you are obsessive, there are probably other people who feel the same way, and you may be able to find a mud that follows your favorite theme.

The second question to consider is, does the mud look as if it is well-managed? The person who manages the mud is called the MUD ADMIN. Large muds will usually have more than one admin, as will most adventure muds. If a mud has more than one admin, there will be one person in charge who guides the others. Within the mud, admins are referred to in various ways. The customs differ depending on the type of mud. Common names for an admin are a GOD, an ARCH, a WIZARD or an IMP (short for implementer).

A poorly administered adventure mud can be miserable, and even social muds are more pleasant when they are managed well. One way to tell if a mud is well-managed is to look at the documentation. Are the general rules for the mud listed clearly? Is the help information easy to understand and well-organized? Does it look complete? You can tell a lot about how a mud is managed by how the basic facilities are organized.

Finally, as you try a new mud, ask yourself the question, do you like the people? As the late football coach Vince Lombardi once put it, "On a mud, talking is not the most important thing; it's the only thing." So when you choose a mud, make sure you like the people you meet, and that you enjoy talking to them.

HINT

It's nice to be important, but it's important to be nice.

Getting Started on a Mud

Getting started on a new mud is a multi-step process. There is no standard routine, but there are general procedures followed by most muds. In the next few sections, I will take you through the process of connecting to a mud and show you what you are likely to encounter.

1) Getting started.

When you connect to a mud, the first thing you will see is a welcome screen. You will then be asked to enter the name of your character and a password. The first time you use a mud, you will need to create a name and password. There are several ways in which this might happen.

On some muds, you can create a character immediately. This involves choosing a name and a password, and entering other information which I will discuss in a moment.

On other muds, you will have to apply for permission to use the mud. Typically, you will have to send a message to the mud admin, specifying your email address and the name you want to use for your character. With muds that are heavily into role playing, you may also have to send a character description as part of your application. Within a few days, you should receive a message confirming your new character and giving you a temporary password (which you can change at any time). You can then start to use the mud. Until then, you will have to be patient.

Finally, some muds allow you to log in as a guest by using the name **guest**. If a password is requested, it will probably also be **guest**. For example, with many TinyMuds, you log in by typing **connect** followed by your name and password. (There will be instructions on the welcome screen.) To log in as a guest, you would enter:

```
connect guest guest
```

2) Choosing a name.

When you choose a name, you can use anything you want, although you will probably not be allowed to use anything obscene. Do not use your real name, but do select a name you will like and enjoy. My advice is to choose something that is easy to type. For example, the name **Mxyzptlk** may seem cool at first, but you and your friends will soon get tired of trying to remember how to spell it.

Some muds discourage name changing because it requires the assistance of a mud admin (who is probably busy). Other muds will let you change your name whenever you want.

HINT

When you join an adventure mud, do not choose a name that sounds like the name of a monster or other non-player character such as **demon**, **vampire**, **beggar** or **guard**. Someone who is careless or in a hurry might attack you without thinking. By the time you figure out what happened, you will be dead (which is inconvenient).

3) Choosing a password.

Whatever you do, do *not* use your regular password (the one you use to log in for Internet access). Make up a special password just for the mud. Most muds take care to protect passwords, but there is no sense taking unnecessary chances.

Choose your password with care. Do not pick a word in any language, or a name of any type. Use something meaningless that contains letters, numbers and punctuation, for example, **t1n99!C**. If someone guesses your mud password, he will have access to your character and can cause a lot of trouble. For example, he can go around being rude to people or breaking the rules, and you will get blamed for everything he does. In addition, he can steal your equipment and possessions for his own character.

HINT

Some muds let you enter a brand new name and password as soon as you connect. If you happen to pick a name that is already in use, the mud will assume you are an existing user and ask you for a password.

So if you enter a name and password, and you get a message saying that the password is wrong, it means the name you have chosen is already in use. Start again and choose a different name.

4) Registering as a new user.

Some muds allow you to pick a name and password right away. On such muds, you will often have to register by entering information about yourself. Typically, you will be asked for your real name and your email address. This information is for the mud admins, who want to make sure you are a serious player and not a troublemaker. Some muds will let you choose a name and password the first time you connect, but will not let you play until your registration has been processed by the mud admin and you have been sent confirmation. In such cases, you will just have to be patient.

HINT

On many muds, you can specify that your email address should not be made public. (Real names, however, are never disclosed.)

5) Creating your character.

The main purpose of social muds (such as TinyMuds) is to talk and socialize. Your character becomes your persona, and what you are to other people is based on your ability to socialize within the role you have chosen. On some social muds, people emphasize the role playing aspects of their characters. On other muds, the characters are less important, as people just want to talk. Regardless, you will not need to develop your character beyond giving it a name and writing a description.

On adventure muds (such as DikuMuds and many LPMuds), developing your character is an important part of the game. To develop a character, you specify various attributes. These attributes are of prime importance, as they will significantly affect how you interact with the mud and with the other players. For example, on a DikuMud, life is different for a dwarf than for a giant.

To build your character, you choose characteristics in a variety of areas. In each area, you will have a number of possible selections. On a DikuMud, for example, you will usually have to choose a race, a class, a gender and an alignment. On other muds, the choices will be different, but the main idea is the same (see Figure 28-3 for some examples).

If you have never used a mud before, it will be difficult to know which choices to make. On a well-designed mud, there will be help commands to assist you in creating your character. However, there is nothing wrong with guessing and picking what seems reasonable.

A lot of your character development will occur later as you use the mud. So make selections that seem reasonable, but don't worry about getting too detailed at the beginning. While you are creating a character, you may be offered a chance to customize the character. Say no. If you say yes, you will get a whole bunch of choices you won't understand, and if you try to guess what to do, you will just make a mess. My advice is to refrain from customizing your character until you have used the mud for a while.

HINT

Playing on an adventure mud is like going to a costume party where the costume evolves over time.

Each adventure mud has its own choice of attributes for building a character. For example, a typical DikuMud might have the following choices:

Race: dwarf, elf, giant, gnome, hobbit, human
Class: cleric, mage, thief (rogue), warrior (fighter)
Gender: male, female, neuter
Alignment: good, evil, neutral

Virtually all adventure muds require you to choose a race for your character. There is a large variety of races, although you may only see a few on any particular mud. Here is a list that I have compiled from some of the muds I have visited.

Artrell	Elf	Halfling	Orc
Cartoon	Fairy	High Elf	Pixie
Darkling	Feline	Human	Satyr
Deep Gnome	Gargoyle	Imp	Snotling
Demon	Giant	Kender	Sprite
Dragon	Gnome	Lizard Man	Troglodyte
DragonKin	Goblin	Merman	Troll
Drow Elf	Half Elf	Minotaur	Vampire
Duergar	Half Giant	Mutant	Wolf
Dwarf	Half Orc	Ogre	Xenomorph

Some races—such as human, dwarf, elf and giant—are so common as to be found on most muds. However, there is no official list and mud admins can add races as they see fit. Moreover, a race on one mud may not be exactly the same as the same race on another mud.

Figure 28-3. *Selecting attributes for a new character*

6) Teaching yourself the basic facts about the mud.

Once you have logged in, registered and (if appropriate) built a character, you will be eager to start using the mud. Before you do, take just a few minutes to do four more things. You don't have to read pages and pages of documentation. Just do these four things:

- Read the rules that explain how to behave on that particular mud.

- Figure out how to display a list of all the possible commands. If you are not sure what to do, enter the command **help** and see what happens.

- Figure out how to display help for a specific command. On a well-maintained mud, every command will have its own help file.

- Read the FAQ (frequently asked question list) for the mud. If you are not sure how to display the FAQ, try the command **faq**. In addition, many of the large muds have their own web page which is always worth checking out. Such pages often have extensive documentation.

HINT

If you get lost, try the following commands until you find one that works:

```
help
help newbie
info
news
commands
faq
```

7. Meeting the other players.

The best way to orient yourself to your new environment is to talk to other people. Mudding is primarily a multiuser experience. Although there will be help files explaining how the mud is designed to work, talking to other people will show you how the mud really works from day to day.

On some adventure muds, certain things may be left undocumented on purpose. To find out how they work, you will have to talk to other people and sift the rumors to see what makes sense to you. On adventure muds, you must depend on the help of your fellow players. The mud admins are not allowed to help you with the game. They can only help you if there is a technical problem, such as a bug in the program.

HINT

As in real life, you will learn more from other people than from trying to figure out everything by yourself. However, it is expected that you will spend some time learning on your own, especially when it comes to the basics. As long as you put in an honest effort, most people will be glad to take the time to help you when you really need assistance.

Talking

There are several ways to talk on a mud. You can talk to someone privately, or you can talk with a group of people. Moreover, you can follow multiple conversations at the same time.

There are a variety of commands you can use to talk. In this section, I will discuss some typical talk commands, so you can get a feeling for how they work. The actual commands may vary slightly from one mud to another, but the general ideas will be the same. For more information, check with the help system on your particular mud.

There are separate commands for talking in different ways. You can talk to a specific person, to everyone in the room (your current location), to everyone in the surrounding area, or to everyone on the mud. DikuMuds and LPMuds tend to share the same set of talk commands. These are shown in Figure 28-4. TinyMuds (which are almost always social muds) have their own commands, which are shown in Figure 28-5.

Here are a few quick examples to show you how it all works. Let's say your characters name is **Harley** and you want to say something to everyone in the room. Use a command such as this:

say Hi everyone.

All the people in the room will see your message:

Harley says: Hi everyone.

---

say *message*	send a message to everyone in the same room
" *message*	same as **say**
' *message*	same as **say**
tell *name message*	send message to the specified person only
whisper *name message*	whisper a message to someone in the same room
yell *message*	broadcast a message to your room and adjoining rooms
shout *message*	broadcast a message to the entire mud
emote *action*	express an action or emotion
: *action*	same as **emote**

The **"** (double quote) and **'** (single quote) commands will not work on some muds. The **say** command will always work.

Figure 28-4.   *Talk commands for DikuMuds and LPMuds*

say *message*	send a message to everyone in the same room
" *message*	same as **say**
page *name* = *message*	send a message to the specified person only
whisper *name* = *message*	whisper a message to a person in the same room
w *name* = *message*	same as **whisper**
pose *action*	express an action or emotion
: *action*	same as **pose**

Figure 28-5. *Talk commands for TinyMuds*

For convenience, you could use:

```
"Hi everyone.
```

To say something to one person only, you can use the **tell** command (DikuMuds or LPMuds) or the **page** command (TinyMuds). For example, on an LPMud, you might type:

```
tell Wendy Hi, I missed you.
```

On a TinyMud, you would type:

```
page Wendy = Hi, I missed you.
```

(Notice the use of the **=** sign.)

Only the person you specified will see the message. For example:

```
Harley tells you: Hi, I missed you.
```

Aside from talking, you can also whisper, yell or shout (see Figures 28-4 and 28-5). Whispering is considered genteel, while yelling and shouting are frowned upon unless you have a good reason. If you shout too much, you may find yourself gagged.

You can also express emotions and actions. Use **emote** on DikuMuds and LPMuds, and **pose** on TinyMuds. For convenience, you can use a **:** (colon) command as an abbreviation. Here are some examples:

```
emote does a dance of joy.
pose does a dance of joy.
: does a dance of joy.
```

Such expressions will be shown to everyone in the room. For example, if your character name is **Harley**, the previous commands would produce a message like the following:

```
Harley does a dance of joy.
```

Learning to use **emote** and **pose** imaginatively will add spice to your conversation.

DikuMuds and LPMuds also have "feelings" commands, also called "socials". These are special commands you can use to express a particular feeling or emotion without having to type a specific **emote** command. For example, you might enter:

```
smile
```

Everyone in the room will see a message like:

```
Harley smiles happily.
```

For information o the feelings commands, you can use **help**:

```
help feelings
help socials
```

If you are a particularly emotional person, using the feelings commands can save a lot of typing.

All muds have some way to have group conversations. In fact, you can have several such conversations going on at the same time. On social muds, you generally have a group conversation by hanging out in a room and talking to everyone in that room. When you get tired of the conversation, you can go to another room.

On adventure muds, you can sit in a room and have a group conversation, but it is more common to spend your time traveling around the mud having adventures. Thus, adventure muds have ways to hold group conversations with people who are not in your immediate vicinity.

For example, there will be a variety of permanent CHAT LINES which are used by different groups of people. There will be a general chat line for everyone in the mud, as well as special chat lines for specific types of people. For instance, there may be a chat line for new people, for administrators, for general announcements, and so on. It is also common to have chat lines that are restricted to members of a particular class or guild.

In addition, you can set up a temporary group conversation, called a PARTY LINE or a GROUP LINE. This facility will serve as a chat line, but only for people who have been invited to participate. The group of people on a particular party line is referred to as a PARTY or GROUP. A common reason to form such a party would be to fight monsters together. When the party is disbanded, the party line will vanish automatically.

HINT

On a mud, all the conversations are mixed with the descriptions and actions on your screen display. At first, it is easy to be overwhelmed. To reduce the clutter, you can turn off one or more of your chat lines until you become more comfortable. Eventually, you will be able to watch everything at the same time, and what started out as a confusing babble will become perfectly understandable.

HINT

Mudding on a regular basis is a great way to increase your typing speed. People who mud well are usually fast typists. If you mud frequently, I guarantee your typing will improve significantly.

Illusion and Reality

In one sense, muds are not real. After all, they are just programs running on some computer on the Internet. Moreover, the characters that people choose are also imaginary, as are the settings, the rules and the interactions.

However, you must remember that, even if it all looks like make-believe, the people who use the mud are real, with real feelings and real needs. Human beings have an amazing capacity for using their imaginations, and once you mud for a while, you can't help but identify with your character and your particular mud.

It may seem strange to a beginner, but on a mud, a person's character is an important part of his life and must be treated with the same respect you would show for the person himself. The character a person chooses to build for himself is, to a large extent, a manifestation of his personality and his unconscious desires. People who use a mud regularly come to look upon it as a real place, and they expect you to be as respectful on the mud as you would be if you were visiting them in their home.

The people you meet on a mud are well aware of the difference between the mud reality and the outside world. However, for many of them, the mud is an expression of how they would like the world to be, and it behooves you to respect that.

HINT

When you visit a mud, treat the people as courteously as you treat everyone else in your life.

Getting Along with People

You get along with people on a mud the same way you do in the outside world. If you are polite, fun to be with and easy-going, you will have no trouble making friends. Still, my experience is that, since a mud is far removed from the stresses of day-to-day life, you will find it easy to mellow out and to be cooperative.

Remember, the characters you see on a mud are not the same as the people behind the scenes. Of course, you don't expect an elf to be an elf in real life. However, it is altogether possible that the seductive young maiden you have been flirting with all evening is actually a balding, middle-aged male accountant from Fargo, North Dakota.

Once you get to know someone, you will be able to look behind the character and get a feeling for the real person. As time goes by, you may be in for a surprise or two. Although it may look as if the other people on the mud are hiding behind masks, you will come to find that most of the masks are actually mirrors.

Moving Around

All muds have a definite geography, and you can move from one place to another by issuing certain commands. There are many such commands, but they fall into patterns. On an adventure mud, the basic commands are directional: **north**, **south**, **east** and **west**. For convenience, you can abbreviate these commands as **n**, **s**, **e** and **w**. You can also use combinations—**northwest** (**nw**), **northeast** (**ne**), **southwest** (**sw**) and **southeast** (**se**)—as well as **up** and **down**.

Social muds tend to use more keywords, such as **out**, **upstairs**, **hallway**, **basement**, and so on.

On a social mud, you can wander with impunity. Eventually you will find your way around, but there is no hurry. On an adventure mud, however, you must be more careful. If you are being chased by monsters in an unfamiliar area and you get lost, you might be killed.

If you use an adventure mud, I suggest you take some time to make a map for yourself. A good map will go a long way toward keeping you out of trouble. In addition, having a map is a good way to keep track of your favorite places and to remember where to find hidden treasures.

Player Killing

On an adventure mud, you spend a lot of time looking for things to kill (and trying to avoid being killed yourself). Most of the time, you will be killing monsters that are part of the mud itself. However, it is possible to kill another player.

PLAYER KILLING, or PK, is the general term used to refer to the killing of one player by another. When a player is killed, what happens depends on how the mud is organized and on the experience level of the player. As a general rule, being killed is bad and will lead to the loss of accumulated points, skills and possessions.

The policy on player killing varies from one mud to another. Some muds prohibit the practice absolutely. Other muds allow player killing, but only for a good reason, or only in specific areas of the mud.

A number of muds have a pk setting which you can control. If the setting is on, you can kill other players and they can kill you. Otherwise, you cannot be killed by another player. (You can, of course, be killed by a monster.)

Finally, some muds are devoted to player killing. On such muds, killing is considered to be an art form and you will spend all of your time either creating art or avoiding it.

HINT

Whenever you join a new adventure mud, take a moment to find out the policy on player killing.

INTERNET RESOURCE *Look in the catalog under Internet Resources for Muds: Player Killing Muds*

On a social mud, it is possible to kill someone, but the consequences are benign. In most cases, killing a person will send him out of the room and back to his "home". Thus, killing is usually reserved for those times when someone is irritating you beyond what you can tolerate, and you want to get rid of him temporarily.

Mud Sex

MUD SEX refers to the acting out of erotic feelings by two people while typing a series of sexually explicit messages. (Mud sex is also referred to as NET SEX or—on a TinyMud—TINYSEX.) Typical mud sex takes place between two consenting people in a private place, although, as in the outside world, there are significant and intriguing exceptions.

The goal of mud sex is the same as the goal of regular sex (without the babies): to bond temporarily in a way that is physically and emotionally satisfying. To do so, two people will exchange messages so as to lead one another into a high level of sexual arousal, culminating in a well-defined resolution. To be blunt, most mud sex is also accompanied by the people sexually gratifying themselves in real life at the same time. There is nothing wrong with this, but if you get involved, I want you to understand the implications of what you are doing.

Is mud sex common? Personally, I am too busy writing books to spend much time on recreational activities, but many of the people who frequent muds have at least tried mud sex at one time or another.

I won't go into a lot of dos and don'ts, because, with some thoughtful practice, I'm sure you can figure them out for yourself. However, I do want to mention three important points that might take you a while to figure out on your own.

First, do not confuse mud sex with real-life sex. If you ever meet a mud sex partner in real life, you must appreciate that there is no correlation between what you have done on the mud and what you might do in person. Any personal expectations during such a meeting are probably unrealistic and will most likely lead to disappointment.

Second, it is possible to use your mud client program to record a transcript of your mud session. (This is called a LOG.) There have been a number of cases in which someone has logged a session in which he has induced another person to have mud sex. Later, the first person has shown the log to other people, sometimes even posting it to a Usenet discussion group. For this reason, some people will not have net sex with anyone they do not know well.

Finally, don't forget that the characters on a mud will not correspond exactly to the people in real life. In particular, what looks like a woman may really be a man.

⚑ HINT

If you are a guy, and you go up to a female character on a mud and say, "Hi, wanna have sex?", and she says yes right away, chances are she is another guy playing a female role.

Appendix A

List of Top-Level Internet Domains

I n Chapter 6, I explain that Internet addresses have the form:

userid@domain

Here are two examples:

harley@nipper.ucsb.edu
michael@music.tuwien.ac.at

The domain consists of a number of sub-domains, separated by **.** characters. The rightmost sub-domain is called the top-level domain. Top-level domains are standardized across the Internet.

There are two types of top-level domains: organizational and geographical. For reference, this appendix shows the top-level domains that were current at the time I last revised this book. As new countries connect to the Internet, new domains will be created using the standard international country codes. For more information about Internet addressing, see Chapter 6.

If you are a student of current events and world politics, you will be interested to know that, since the last time I updated this list, two top-level domains were actually dropped. They are **cs** (Czechoslovakia) and **yu** (Yugoslavia).

The only country that uses more than one international domain is Great Britain. They use **uk** (United Kingdom) as well as **gb**. (Of course, they also speak English with an accent.)

Old-Style Top-Level Domains

com	commercial organization or miscellaneous
edu	educational institution
gov	government
int	international organization
mil	military
net	networking organization
org	non-commercial organization

International Top-Level Domains

am	Armenia
aq	Antarctica
ar	Argentina
at	Austria

International Top-Level Domains (continued)

au	Australia
az	Azerbaijan
be	Belgium
bg	Bulgaria
bm	Bermuda
br	Brazil
by	Belarus
ca	Canada
ch	Switzerland ("Confoederatio Helvetica")
cl	Chile
cm	Cameroon
cn	China
co	Colombia
cr	Costa Rica
cy	Cyprus
cz	Czech Republic
de	Germany ("Deutschland")
dk	Denmark
dz	Algeria
ec	Ecuador
ee	Estonia
eg	Egypt
es	Spain ("España")
fi	Finland
fj	Fiji
fo	Faroe Islands
fr	France
gb	Great Britain
gl	Greenland
gn	Guinea
gr	Greece
gu	Guam (US)
hk	Hong Kong

International Top-Level Domains (continued)

hr	Croatia
hu	Hungary
id	Indonesia
ie	Ireland
il	Israel
in	India
ir	Iran
is	Iceland
it	Italy
jm	Jamaica
jp	Japan
kr	Korea (South)
kw	Kuwait
kz	Kazachstan
lb	Lebanon
li	Liechtenstein
lk	Sri Lanka
lt	Lithuania
lu	Luxembourg
lv	Latvia
ma	Morocco
md	Moldavia
mo	Macao
mx	Mexico
my	Malaysia
ni	Nicaragua
nl	Netherlands
no	Norway
nz	New Zealand
pa	Panama
pe	Peru
ph	Philippines
pl	Poland

International Top-Level Domains (continued)

pr	Puerto Rico
pt	Portugal
re	Reunion (French)
ro	Romania
ru	Russian Federation
sa	Saudi Arabia
se	Sweden
sg	Singapore
si	Slovenia
sj	Svalbard and Jan Mayen Islands
sk	Slovakia (Slovak Rep)
su	Soviet Union
th	Thailand
tn	Tunisia
tr	Turkey
tw	Taiwan
ua	Ukraine
uk	United Kingdom (England, Scotland, Wales, Northern Ireland)
us	United States
uy	Uruguay
ve	Venezuela
za	South Africa
zm	Zambia
zw	Zimbabwe

Glossary

action: On IRC, a message indicating that a person is pretending to perform a particular action. (27)

address: A formal description of the user name and address used by someone on the Internet. (6)

address book: A collection of names and mail addresses, maintained by a mail program. (7)

adventure mud: A mud oriented toward game playing as well as talking. (28)

alias: In the mail system, a name that represents a list of addresses. When you send a message to the alias, the message is automatically sent to each address on the list. (22)

alternate: Within Usenet, describes a hierarchy of newsgroups, not all of which are carried on all news servers. Compare to **mainstream** hierarchy. (13)

analog: Describes data that is represented by quantities which vary continuously; compare to **digital**. (4)

anchor: Within a hypertext document, a description of a link. As such, an anchor can point to any type of resource: another hypertext document, an image, a gopher site, an anonymous ftp resource, and so on. (11)

anonymous ftp: A facility that lets you connect to certain remote hosts and download files without having to be registered as a user. (18)

applet: On the Web, a program that is loaded and executed dynamically, whenever you select a link to the web page with which the program is associated. Same as a **distributed application**. (10)

arch: Synonym for **mud admin**. (28)

archie: An Internet service that helps you find the names of anonymous ftp sites that have a particular file. (20)

archie server: A server that provides an archie facility. (20)

Arpanet: The ancestor of the Internet, a networking project sponsored by the United States Department of Defense in which the basic Internet technology was developed. (1)

article: Within Usenet, a message that has been posted to a newsgroup. (13)

ASCII: Abbreviation for "American Standard Code for Information".

Chapter references are indicated by the numbers in parentheses.

ASCII code: A standardized system in which character data is represented by a distinct pattern of 8 bits (1 byte). (7, 21)

ASCII file: A file that contains characters and can be displayed or printed. Same as **text file**. Compare to **binary file**. (7, 21)

attach: To join a file to a mail message so that the file is delivered along with the message. (7)

attachment: A file that is joined to a mail message so that the file is delivered along with the message. (7)

B channel: Within ISDN, a "bearer" channel, used to carry the bulk of the data; compare to **D channel**. (4)

backbone: A high-speed link used to connect local area networks. (2)

background: In Unix, describes a program that has been paused in order to allow you to work with another program. (24)

bandwidth: A measure of the capacity to transmit information. (4)

bang: The ! (exclamation mark) character. (6)

bar: A meaningless word used to represent an unnamed item during a discussion or exposition. The word "bar" is usually used along with "foo" to refer to two unnamed items. The convention is to use "foo" for the first item and "bar" for the second item. See also **foo** and **foobar**.(14)

basic rate interface: Same as **BRI**. (4)

baud: An older, obsolete term for **bps**. (4)

binary file: A file that contains data that is not plain text and must be interpreted by a program to make sense. Compare to **text file**. (7, 21).

binary system: A mathematical number system based entirely on the digits 0 and 1. (4)

big-endian: Describes computers in which two consecutive bytes that represent a binary value are stored with the most significant byte first. Compare to **little-endian**. Sun computers and Macintoshes are big-endian. VAX computers and PCs are little-endian. (26)

bit: The smallest unit of computer memory, a tiny entity that can be thought of as being either off or on, or represented by either a 0 or a 1. The name is an abbreviation for "binary digit." (4)

Chapter references are indicated by the numbers in parentheses.

Bitnet: A worldwide network—separate from the Internet—that connects well over a thousand academic and research institutions in many countries, and supports a large number of mailing lists. (22)

Bitnet/Internet Gateway: A computer that acts as a mail gateway, passing messages between Bitnet and the Internet. (6)

Bitnet/Usenet Gateway: A computer that acts as a connection between Bitnet and Usenet, facilitating the posting of mailing list messages as Usenet articles. (22)

body: 1. Within a mail message, the main part of a message, the text. (7) 2. Within a hypertext document, the contents of the text to be displayed. (11) 3. Within a Usenet article, the main part of the article, the text. (14)

bookmark: Within the gopher system, a menu item that has been retained for further reference. (16)

bookmark list: 1. With a web browser, a permanent list of links, chosen by you, which are maintained from one work session to the next. (10) 2. With a gopher client, a permanent list of gopher items, chosen by you, which are maintained from one work session to the next. (16)

bookmark file: Within the gopher system, the file in which a bookmark list is saved. (16)

boolean search: A search in which the search pattern you specify can combine "and" and "or" operations. (10)

boolean variable: With archie, a variable that acts as an on/off toggle switch. (20)

bot: On IRC, a program or script that is designed to interact with the IRC system. A bot can be programmed to read input, generate output and respond to particular events. A good programmer can design a bot that acts like a person, so when something strange happens, you can't always tell if it was caused by a bot or by a real human. (27)

bounce: To send to another person an identical copy of a mail message that you have received. (7)

bps: Abbreviation for "bits per second"; units in which the data transmission speed of a modem is measured. (4)

BRI: A small-scale ISDN connection suitable for a home or small business; an acronym for "Basic Rate Interface". (4)

browser: A client program used to access the Web and other Internet resources. (9)

Chapter references are indicated by the numbers in parentheses.

cache: A storage area used to hold recently accessed data, especially with a web browser. (10)

cascade: In Usenet, a series of silly followup articles. (14)

case insensitive: Describes a program, system, or operation that does not distinguish between upper- and lowercase letters. (6)

case sensitive: Describes a program, system, or operation that distinguishes between upper- and lowercase letters. (6)

cbreak mode: In Unix, describes a program that reads each character as it is typed. Such programs will interpret single-character commands as soon as the character is typed. (17)

CGI script: On the Web, a list of instructions used by a web server to process data that was received via a form. CGI stands for "Common Gateway Interface". (10)

channel: 1. Within ISDN, a discrete communication element that provides a specified amount of bandwidth. (4) 2. On IRC, a facility that allows a single group conversation. (27)

channel operator: On IRC, the person who, at the present time, controls various aspects of a channel. (27)

chat: On the Internet, to talk to more than one person at a time. (25)

chat line: On a mud, a permanent facility used by people to hold a group conversation. (28)

chat room: A facility that allows more than one person to talk at the same time. (25)

client: A program that you use to access a resource provided by a server. (2)

client pull: On the Web, a facility that allows a browser to request data from a web server automatically. (10)

clipboard: A storage area, maintained by an operating system, used for data that is being copied and pasted from one window to another. (7)

Common Gateway Interface: On the Web, a system set up to allow web servers to process data that was received via a form. See **CGI script**. (10)

configure: To prepare a program for use by furnishing it with specific information needed by the program to perform its job. (5)

Chapter references are indicated by the numbers in parentheses.

control message: Within Usenet, a special type of article used to send administrative commands and messages throughout the system. (13)

cross-posting: Within Usenet, posting an article to more than one newsgroup. (14)

CSO name server: A program that searches for names and addresses associated with a particular institution. The name "CSO" refers to the Computing Services Office at the University of Illinois, Urbana, where the first CSO name server was developed. (16)

current message: In the `pine` mail program, the highlighted message in the index. (8)

cyberspace: A vague term, used by people who do not know what they are talking about, to refer to the Internet and other network-based information systems. Do not use this word. (10)

D channel: Within ISDN, a "data" channel, used to carry the signals that control the system; compare to **B channel**. (4)

daemon: In Unix, a program that executes in the background, usually to provide a service of general interest. Some daemons are started automatically when the system is initialized and are always available. Other daemons sleep most of the time, waking up at predefined intervals or in response to some event. Although the name is pronounced "dee-mon", it is correctly spelled "daemon". (7, 26)

data: Any type of information that might be stored or processed by a computer. (7)

demodulate: A process that converts data from an analog format to a digital format. (4)

digest: 1. In Usenet, a collection of articles posted as a single long article. (13) 2. With a mailing list, a collection of articles mailed to a subscriber on the list as a single large message. (22)

digital: Describes data that is represented by discrete numbers; compare to **analog**. (4)

digital modem: Within ISDN, a poorly defined term describing devices that, in a single small box or adaptor card, combine the functionality of various ISDN devices, such as an NT-1, a terminal adaptor, or a power supply.

directory: A collection of files and other directories. (11, 18)

display: Within the X Window system, the keyboard, screen and pointing device associated with a particular computer.

Chapter references are indicated by the numbers in parentheses.

display server: Same as X server. (2)

distributed application: On the Web, a program that is loaded and executed dynamically, whenever you select a link to the web page with which the program is associated. Sometimes referred to as an **applet**. (10)

DNS: Abbreviation for Domain Name System. (6)

DNS server: A server that converts domain names into IP addresses. (5)

Document Type Definition: Same as DTD. (11)

domain: The part of a standard Internet address that indicates the name of the computer. For example, in the address `harley@nipper.ucsb.edu`, the domain is `nipper.ucsb.edu`. (6)

domain name: A standard Internet address, consisting of two or more names (domains) separated by `.` characters. (5)

domain name system: A service, part of TCP/IP that can translate an address from a domain name to an IP address and vice versa. (6)

dotfile: In Unix, a file whose name begins with a `.` (period) character. When listing file names with the `ls` command, dotfiles are not listed unless requested specifically. Also called a hidden file. (7)

download: To transfer data from a remote computer to your computer. (18)

DTD: A specific markup language based on SGML, for example, HTML. DTD stands for "Document Type Definition". (11)

dynamic IP address: With a TCP/IP connection, a non-permanent IP address, assigned each time you log in. (5)

emulate: To use a program to simulate the workings of a hardware device. (5)

escape character: A special character that, when read by a program, tells the program that the data that follows is to be treated in a special way. (24)

expire: Describes a Usenet article that is deleted because its posting date is older than a specific threshold. Most system managers set up their news servers so that articles expire automatically within one to three weeks. (13)

extension: Part of a file name, a short suffix, separated from the main part of the name by a `.` (period) character. (21)

Chapter references are indicated by the numbers in parentheses.

external image: On the Web, a picture that is a web page in its own right and which must be loaded separately. (10)

FAQ: A list of basic questions and answers regarding a particular topic. FAQ stands for "frequently asked question list". (13)

file: An object, stored on a computer and having a name, which contains data. (11, 18)

file permissions: In Unix, specific values associated with each file that describe how the file is allowed to be accessed. (11)

file transfer protocol: A system used to transfer files from one computer to another. (21)

flame: 1. Within Usenet, an angry or abusive response to a previous article. A flame may be sent as a followup article to the newsgroup in which the original article appeared, or it may be sent as a private communication via mail to the author of the original article. (14) 2. To send a flame via mail or to post a flame to a Usenet newsgroup. (14)

flame war: Within Usenet, a situation in which people post many flames on a specific topic. (14)

flush: To clear a cache of all its data, especially with a web browser. (10)

folder: 1. Within a mail program, a file containing messages. (7) 2. Within an operating system, a collection of files; a synonym for **subdirectory**. (7)

follow: On the Web, to access a resource referenced on a web page by selecting the link that represents the resource. (10)

followup: Within Usenet, describes an article in which the author responds to a previous article. (14)

foo: A meaningless word used to represent an unnamed item during a discussion or exposition. When a second unnamed item must be discussed, it is often referred to as "bar". See also **bar** and **foobar**. (14)

foobar: A meaningless word used to represent an unnamed item during a discussion or exposition. See also **foo** and **bar**. (14)

foreground: In Unix, describes a program with which you are currently working. Compare to **background**. (24)

form: On the Web, a facility that allows you to enter information to be sent to the remote web site for processing. (10)

Chapter references are indicated by the numbers in parentheses.

forward: To mail an edited copy of a mail message to another person. (7)

freenet: An organization that provides free Internet access to members of the community. (5)

frequently asked question list: Same as **FAQ**.

gateway: A computer that acts as a link between programs running on two different networks. (6)

geographical domains: A two-letter top-level domain based on an abbreviation for a particular country. (6)

god: Synonym for **mud admin**. (28)

gopher: An Internet service that allows you to use a simple, consistent menu to access a wide variety of distributed information and services. (16)

gopher client: A program you use to access the gopher system. (16)

gopher server: A server that provides access to gopher information. (16)

gopherspace: Describes all the information and services that, potentially, are accessible via the gopher. (16)

graphical interface: Describes the capabilities of a program that can display graphical elements (such as rectangles, lines, circles, drawings, images, and so on) as well as characters. (5)

graphical user interface: A computer interface that takes advantage of the graphics capabilities of a computer to display windows, scroll bars, dialog boxes, icons, pictures, and related elements. (2)

group: 1. Within Usenet, a discussion group. Same as **newsgroup**. (13) 2. On a mud, a group of people, often with a common goal, who share a common party line. Same as **party**. (28)

group line: On a mud, a temporary facility used by people to hold a group conversation. Same as **party line**. (28)

GUI: Abbreviation for **graphical user interface**; pronounced "goo-ey". (2)

hack-n-slash mud: An adventure mud which is oriented toward action rather than elaborate scenarios and characterizations. (28)

head: Within a hypertext document, information containing instructions relating to a document as a whole. (11)

Chapter references are indicated by the numbers in parentheses.

header: 1. In a mail message, a number of lines at the beginning of the message that contain technical information. (7) 2. In a Usenet article, a number of lines at the beginning of the message that contain technical information. (14)

helper application: On the Web, a program that provides a function which your browser cannot perform, such as processing pictures, sound, video or other types of data, or initiating a telnet session. (10)

hierarchy: Within Usenet, a standard category containing a large collection of related newsgroups. (13)

highlighted: On the Web, describes data on a web page that is displayed in a special manner to indicate a link to another resource. (9)

history list: 1. With a web browser, a list of the links you have visited in the current work session. (10) 2. With a gopher client, a list of gopher items you have visited in the current work session. (16)

home directory: In Unix, a specific directory assigned to a particular person in which the person can store his own files and directories. (11)

home gopher server: The gopher server to which your gopher client connects automatically each time you start the program. (16)

home page: 1. On the Web, the main page of a particular web site. (10) 2. On the Web, the page to which your browser connects automatically upon starting. (10)

host: 1. A computer connected to the Internet. (2) 2. A computer system capable of supporting more than one user. (2)

HTML: A set of specifications for embedding instructions within regular text in order to create a web page. The name HTML is an abbreviation for "Hypertext Markup Language". (11)

http: On the Web, a designation within a URL that indicates a hypertext resource. (10)

hypertext: On the Web, information that contains links to other information or services. (9)

hypertext markup language: Same as **HTML**. (11)

Hypertext Transfer Protocol: A protocol used on the Web to transfer hypertext. (10)

image map: On the Web, a type of line consisting of a picture (typically a photo or a drawing) in which the various parts of the image act as separate links. (10)

Chapter references are indicated by the numbers in parentheses.

IMP: A special-purpose communication computer that was used within the Arpanet project to act as an interface between a regular computer and the Arpanet network. IMP stands for "Interface Message Processor". (1)

imp: Synonym for **mud admin**. Abbreviation for "implementer". (28)

index: In the **pine** mail program, a summary of the messages in your incoming mailbox. (8)

infobahn: A vague term, used by people who do not know what they are talking about, to refer to the Internet and other network-based information systems. Do not use this word; it is even more stupid than "information superhighway". (10)

information superhighway: A vague term, used by people who do not know what they are talking about, to refer to the Internet and other network-based information systems. Do not use this phrase. (10)

inline image: On a web page, a picture that is part of the page. (10)

Internet: A vast, worldwide system consisting of people, information, and computers; often referred to as the Net. (1)

Internet Protocol: Same as IP. (2)

Internet Relay Chat: Same as IRC. (27)

Internet service provider: An organization or business offering public access to the Internet, usually using a telephone dial-up connection. (5)

IP: One of the TCP/IP protocols, the basic Internet protocol used to move packets of raw data from one computer to another; an acronym for **Internet Protocol**. (2)

IP address: A standard Internet address, using numbers, rather than names (domains). (5, 6)

IRC: An Internet-wide talk facility connecting a number of servers into one large network, allowing many people to participate at the same time, talking with one another in separate conversation areas called channels. (27)

ISDN: A type of telephone facility that uses digital technology to provide high-speed connections to another computer as well as voice service; an acronym for "Integrated Services Digital Network". (4)

job control: In Unix, a facility implemented by the shell (the command processor) that allows you to suspend and restart programs. (24)

Chapter references are indicated by the numbers in parentheses.

jughead: An Internet service that allows you to search a specific area of gopherspace. (16)

jughead server: A server that provides the service of searching a jughead database. (16)

junk: Within Usenet, to discard all the unread articles with the same subject. That is, to discard the rest of the thread. Synonym for **kill**. (14)

kill: Within Usenet, to discard all the unread articles with the same subject. That is, to discard the rest of the thread. Synonym for **junk**. (14)

kill file: In Usenet, a special file, maintained by your newsreader program, in which information is kept regarding articles you do not want to read which should be killed automatically. (14)

lag: On a talk facility, a condition that occurs when the network or the talk server slows down, and replies become delayed and unsynchronized, possibly leading to amusing or incoherent situations. (25)

LAN: Abbreviation for **Local Area Network**. (2)

link: On the Web, a logical connection from a position on a web page to another resource. (9)

list-of-lists: With respect to mailing lists, a large organized summary of available lists. (22)

listen: With respect to a program that provides a service when another program makes a connection using a specific port, to wait for such a connection to occur. (23)

little-endian: Describes computers in which two consecutive bytes that represent a binary value are stored with the least significant byte first. Compare to **big-endian**. Sun computers and Macintoshes are big-endian. VAX computers and PCs are little-endian. (26)

load: On the Web, with respect to a browser, to receive a copy of a web page from a web server. (10)

Local Area Network: A network in which the computers are connected directly, usually by some type of cable. (2)

local host: With respect to Internet services, refers to your computer. Compare to **remote host**. (18, 23)

log: On a mud, a transcript of your mud session as created by your mud client program. (28)

Chapter references are indicated by the numbers in parentheses.

log file: A file in which the output of a session is saved. Sometimes called a "log". (23)

log in: To initiate a work session with a remote computer. (5)

log out: To terminate a work session with a remote computer. (5)

lowercase: Describes small letters, "a" to "z". (6)

lurker: On a talk facility, someone who reads what other people are saying without saying anything himself. (25)

mail client: A program, running on your computer, that provides an interface for the mail system. (7)

mail server: A program, running on a host computer, that acts as a way station for electronic mail. (7)

mailbox: A file in which incoming mail is stored for a particular user. (7)

mailing list: An organized system in which messages are sent to a collection of addresses in order to support discussion by mail of a particular topic. (22)

mainstream: Within Usenet, describes a hierarchy of newsgroups, all of which are carried on all news servers. Compare to **alternate** hierarchy. (13)

markup language: A formal set of specifications used to define information which can be added to the content of a document as an aid to processing. (11)

message of the day: A welcoming message, displayed when you connect to a remote computer. (20)

Mime: An abbreviation for "Multipurpose Internet mail extensions".

modem: A device that acts as the interface between a computer and a telephone line; the name is a contraction of "modulator/demodulator". (4)

moderated: 1. Within Usenet, describes a newsgroup whose postings are controlled by a person called a moderator. All articles are sent to the moderator who then decides which ones should be posted to the newsgroup. (13) 2. With respect to a mailing list, describes a list controlled by a person called a moderator. All messages are sent to the moderator who then decides which ones should be mailed to the people on the list. (22)

moderator: 1. In Usenet, the person who controls which articles are posted to a moderated newsgroup. (13) 2. With respect to a mailing list, a person who controls which articles are posted to the list. (22)

Chapter references are indicated by the numbers in parentheses.

modulate: A process that converts data from a digital format to an analog format. (4)

mud: An elaborate computer-mediated, imaginary environment. (28)

mud admin: A person who manages all or part of a mud. (28)

mud sex: On a mud, the acting out of erotic feelings by two people while typing a series of sexually explicit messages. Also called "net sex". On a TinyMud, also called "tinysex".

multimedia: Describes a computer system that is suitable for displaying pictures and working with sounds, as well as running regular computer programs. (4)

Net, the: A synonym for the **Internet**, a vast, worldwide system consisting of people, information, and computers. (1)

Netnews: A synonym for **Usenet**. (13)

net sex: The acting out of erotic feelings by two people while typing a series of sexually explicit messages. On a mud, the same as **mud sex**. On a TinyMud, the same as **tinysex**. (28)

netsplit: On IRC, a situation that may occur when one of the network connections between servers is dropped temporarily. Eventually the connection will be reestablished, but until it is, some people will seem to disappear from the channel. (27)

network: Two or more computers connected together. (1, 2)

news administrator: The person who manages the Usenet service for a particular computer system. (13)

news client: A client program used to read Usenet articles. Same as a **newsreader**. (13)

news feed: The service of providing a news server with a link to Usenet. (13)

news server: A computer that provides users on a network with access to the Usenet news. (13)

newsgroup: Within Usenet, a discussion group. (13)

newsreader: A client program used to read Usenet articles. (13)

nick: On IRC, a synonym for **nickname**. (27)

nickname: On IRC, the name you use to identify yourself. (27)

Chapter references are indicated by the numbers in parentheses.

NNTP: The protocol used to transfer Usenet articles from one server to another. NNTP stands for "Network News Transfer Protocol". (13)

NNTP server: Same as a **news server**. (NNTP is the protocol used to transfer Usenet articles from one server to another.) (13)

node: A term used by nerds to refer to an Internet **host** (a computer connected to the Internet). (2)

NT-1: Within ISDN, a device that acts as the interface between your equipment and the outside ISDN line; the name stands for "Network Terminator for layer 1". (4)

numeric variable: With archie, a variable that stores a numeric value. (20)

objoke: Synonym for obligatory joke. (13)

obligatory joke: Within a humor newsgroup on Usenet, a joke that, by convention, must be included with an otherwise non-humorous posting. Also known as objoke. (13)

online manual: In Unix, information available at all times that contains documentation about Unix commands and important system facilities. The online manual is divided into sections. Each section contains many entries (called pages), each of which documents a single topic. To access the online manual, use the **man** command. Unix users are encouraged to check the online manual before asking for help about a Unix command. (See **rtfm**.) (14)

op: On IRC, a synonym for **channel operator**. (27)

operating system: The master control program that runs a computer. (4, 5)

organizational domains: A three-letter top-level domain based on type of organization (**com, edu, gov, int, mil, net** and **org**). (6)

packet: A small package of data sent from one Internet host to another using the TCP/IP protocols. (2)

page: On the Web, a file of hypertext. Same as **web page**. (10)

parent directory: A directory that contains another directory. (18)

party: On a mud, a group of people, often with a common goal, who share a common party line. Same as **group**. (28)

party line: On a mud, a temporary facility used by people to hold a group conversation. Same as **group line**. (28)

Chapter references are indicated by the numbers in parentheses.

path: Same as **pathname**. (18)

pathname: A specification, consisting of a sequence of subdirectories and a file name, that describes the location of a file within the file system. (11, 18)

PK: On a mud, player killing. See **player killing mud**. (28)

player killing mud: An adventure mud which is oriented toward killing other players.

point: On the Web, to reference a resource. For example, a URL points to a resource on the Net. (10)

point of presence: A particular location in which an Internet service provider has local access. (5)

point-to-point protocol: Same as **PPP**. (5)

POP: 1. An abbreviation for **point of presence**. (5) 2. A protocol used by a mail client program and a mail server program to communicate with one another; stands for "Post Office Protocol". (7)

POP server: A mail server that supports POP (Post Office Protocol). (7)

port: 1. With respect to computer hardware, a connection between two devices or systems. 2. With respect to a computer program, to modify or rewrite the program so that it runs on a new system. 3. A logical connection to a remote computer, in order to provide a particular service identified by a port number. (23)

port number: When connecting to a remote Internet host, a number that describes the type of service you are requesting. Telnet, for example, uses port number 23. (23)

post: Within Usenet, to send an article to a newsgroup. (13)

Post Office Protocol: Same as POP. (7)

posting: Within Usenet, a message that has been posted to a newsgroup. (13)

PPP: A protocol, used to support a TCP/IP connection over a phone line. The name stands for "Point-to-Point Protocol".

PRI: A large-scale ISDN connection suitable for connecting many devices; an acronym for "Primary Rate Interface". (4)

primary rate interface: Same as PRI. (4)

Chapter references are indicated by the numbers in parentheses.

protocol: A set of rules describing, in technical terms, how something should be done. (2)

quote: In Usenet, when writing a followup article, to put in the part of the article to which you are responding. (14)

radio button: On a web page, one of a set of choices set up in such a way that only one choice at a time can be selected. (12)

readme file: A file containing information you should read before you install a program. (21)

real-time sound: On the Web, a facility in which a sound being loaded from a web server is played continuously as the data arrives, without waiting for all the data to arrive. (10)

redirect: To send to another person an identical copy of a mail message that you have received. Same as **bounce**. (7)

regular expression: A compact way of specifying a pattern of characters in which a number of variations are possible. (20)

remote host: With respect to Internet services, the computer to which you connect. Compare to **local host**. (18, 23)

reply: To mail a response to a message. (7)

representation type: When using the Unix **ftp** program, indicates the type of file you will be transferring, either binary or ASCII text. (19)

router: A special-purpose computer used to link one network to another. (2)

request for comment: Same as RFC. (18)

RFC: A technical publication documenting a topic relating to the Internet. The name RFC stands for "Request for Comment". (18)

root directory: In Unix, the main directory of the file system. The root directory is, directly or indirectly, the parent directory of all other directories. (18)

rtfm: 1. An exhortation to someone to try and answer a question for himself before asking for help. Interesting fact: rtfm is the longest word in the English language without a vowel. (14) 2. To search for information for yourself before asking for help. (14)

scanner: A device used to process a printed image and create a computer file that contains a picture of the image. (11)

Chapter references are indicated by the numbers in parentheses.

scheme: In URL, a name or abbreviation indicating a specific type of resource. (11)

script: With SLIP, a set of instructions followed as part of the connection and login procedure. (5)

search engine: On the Web, a program that provides a directory service. (10)

selected link: In the `lynx` browser, a link that is highlighted in a special manner. (12)

self-extracting archive: A zipfile in the form of an executable program that, when run, automatically unzips itself into as many files and subdirectories as necessary. (21)

serial line IP: Same as SLIP. (5)

server: A program that provides a resource of some type. (2)

server push: On the Web, a facility that allows a web server to send data to a browser without waiting for the browser to make a request. (10)

SGML: A complex system used to describe markup languages. SGML stands for "Standard Generalized Markup Language". (11)

shareware: A program that you can try for free, usually for a limited time period, and pay for only if you want to use it permanently. (5)

shell: In Unix, a program that provides the primary interface by acting as a command processor and by interpreting scripts of commands. (6)

signature: 1. In a mail message, a short, predefined set of lines that is appended automatically to each message you send. (7) 2. Within Usenet, a short, predefined message that is appended automatically to each article you post. A signature should contain your name and address and should not be more than four lines. (14)

Simple Mail Transfer Protocol: Same as SMTP. (7)

SLIP: An obsolete protocol, used to support a TCP/IP connection over a phone line or over a serial connection. The name stands for "Serial Line IP". (5)

smiley: Several consecutive characters that, when viewed sideways, look like a small face. The basic smiley is `:-)` (Tilt your head sideways to the left to see the face.) A smiley is used in electronic communication to indicate a sense of irony or frivolity. In other words, a smiley replaces the charming smile you would use in person to avoid the wrath of someone to whom you have just said something obnoxious or argumentative. (7, 14)

Chapter references are indicated by the numbers in parentheses.

SMTP: A member of the TCP/IP family of protocols, describes how mail is to be delivered from one Internet computer to another. The name stands for "Simple Mail Transfer Protocol". (7)

snail mail: Regular postal system mail. (7)

social mud: A mud primarily oriented toward talking. (28)

socket: A facility used by programs to communicate with one another while they are running. (5)

source: The hypertext description corresponding to a particular web page. (11)

spoiler: In a Usenet article, a remark that gives away the ending to a movie or book. (14)

stack: The software that provides TCP/IP functionality on a particular computer. (5)

Standard Generalized Markup Language: Same as SGML. (11)

static IP address: With a TCP/IP connection, a permanent IP address which you use each time you log in. (5)

string variable: With archie, a variable that stores values consisting of a string of characters. (20)

subdirectory: A directory that lies within another directory. (11, 18)

subdomain: In a standard Internet address, one part of the domain. For example, in the address **harley@nipper.ucsb.edu** there are three subdomains, **nipper**, **ucsb** and **edu**. (6)

subscribe: 1. In Usenet, when using a newsreader, to indicate that you want to read the articles in a particular newsgroup. (13) 2. With a mailing list, to register with a list manager (which will probably be a program) in order to have your address placed on the list. (22)

surf: A term, used by people who do not know what they are talking about, to refer to using the Internet; often used to denote playing on the Net or exploring just for fun. Don't use this word. (10)

sysop: The person who manages a BBS (Bulletin Board System). (25)

tag: Within a hypertext document, an embedded instruction. A hypertext tag starts with a < (less than) character and ends with a > (greater than) character. (11)

Chapter references are indicated by the numbers in parentheses.

talk: On the Internet, any type of communication that allows you to send messages back and forth with someone in real time (that is, while you wait). The talking may involve text messages or actual voice transmission. (25)

talk daemon: A daemon that facilitates connections using the Unix **talk** program (or a compatible program). (26)

talker: A multiuser talk facility that is easy to use and is devoted primarily to conversation. (25)

tarfile: An archive created by the Unix **tar** program. (21)

TCP: One of the TCP/IP protocols, used to coordinate the moving of packets of data from one computer to another by managing the flow and ensuring that data arrives intact; the name is an acronym for **Transmission Control Protocol**. (2)

TCP/IP: A family of more than 100 protocols used to connect computers and networks, in particular, computers on the Internet; the name, an acronym for **Transmission Control Protocol** and **Internet Protocol**, is pronounced as five separate letters without the slash: "T C P I P". (2)

telnet: An Internet service that allows you to log in to a remote Internet computer. (23)

terminal: Within a multiuser computer system such as Unix, the hardware used by a single person to access the system; that is, the keyboard, screen, and possibly a mouse or other pointing device. (2)

terminal adaptor: Within ISDN, a device that converts data from devices such as computers, telephones, and fax machines into ISDN data. (4)

text: Data that consists of ASCII characters: letters, numbers, punctuation, and so on. (7)

text-based interface: Describes the capabilities of a program that can display only characters—letters, numbers, punctuation, and so on—but not graphics or pictures. (5)

text file: A file that contains characters and can be displayed or printed. Same as **ASCII file**. Compare to **binary file**. (7, 21)

thread: Within Usenet, a set of related articles in the same newsgroup. (14)

timesharing system: A multiuser computer system in which more than one person can access a host computer, each person using his or her own terminal. (2)

tinysex: The term for **mud sex** on a TinyMud. (28)

Chapter references are indicated by the numbers in parentheses.

title: Within a hypertext document, an element that is displayed above the main text. (11)

top-level domain: In a standard Internet address, the most general subdomain. The top-level domain is the last subdomain in the address. For example, in the address `harley@nipper.ucsb.edu` the top-level domain is `edu`. (6)

Transmission Control Protocol: Same as **TCP**. (2)

transport agent: A mail program that functions behind the scenes to ensure that messages are transported in an orderly fashion according to the SMTP protocol. (7)

Uniform Resource Locator: Same as **URL**. (10)

Unix: 1. A family of operating systems and tools. (1) 2. A worldwide culture with its own technical terms, conventions, traditions and a wide variety of computer-oriented facilities. (1)

unsubscribe: 1. In Usenet, when using a newsreader program, to indicate that you do not want to read articles from a particular newsgroup. (13) 2. With a mailing list, to tell the list manager (which may be a program) that you want your address removed from the list. (22)

unzip: To run a program that uncompresses files stored in a zipfile. (21)

upload: To transfer data from your computer to a remote computer. (18)

uppercase: Describes the capital letters, "A" to "Z". (6)

URL: On the Web, a technical description of the location of a particular Internet resource; a URL points to a resource on the Net. URL stands for "Uniform Resource Locater". (10)

user agent: On a Unix system, a program that acts as the interface between a user and the mail system. (7)

Usenet: A vast, decentralized system of discussion groups. (13)

userid: A user name, registered with a computer system, that identifies a particular account; pronounced "user-eye-dee". (5, 6)

UUCP: A Unix-based networking system that allows any Unix computer to exchange files with any other Unix computer. (6)

UUCP Mapping Project: A group that regularly publishes updated connection maps for the UUCP network. (6)

Chapter references are indicated by the numbers in parentheses.

uuencode: In Unix, a system used to encode binary data as ASCII text. (21)

variable: With archie, a quantity with a name and a value, used to control the operation of an archie search. (20)

veronica: An Internet service that allows you to search gopherspace for specific items. (16)

veronica server: A server that provides the service of searching a veronica database. (16)

viewer: On the Web, a program used to display a picture stored in a particular file format. More generally, a program used to process a picture, sound, video or other type of data that the web browser cannot process itself. (10)

VT-100: The de facto standard for terminal emulation, at one time an actual terminal manufactured by the Digital Equipment Corporation. (5)

wais: An Internet service that finds information for you by quickly searching one or more databases that may be stored anywhere on the Internet. The name "wais" stands for "wide area information service". (16)

WAN: Abbreviation for **Wide Area Network**. (2)

Web, the: A client/server system used to access all types of information (hypertext, graphics, sounds, gopher information, Usenet newsgroups, Wais databases, and so on), and to allow users to send their own information to a program to be processed. (9)

web page: On the Web, a file of hypertext. Often referred to as a **page**. (10)

Wide Area Network: A network in which more than one local area network are connected together. (2)

Winsock: The standard Windows sockets interface. (5)

wizard: Synonym for **mud admin**. (28)

workstation: A powerful single-user computer, often a Unix computer. (2)

World Wide Web: (obsolete) The old name for **the Web**. (9)

WWW: Abbreviation for **World Wide Web**. (9)

Chapter references are indicated by the numbers in parentheses.

WYSIWYG: Describes systems in which the image of information displayed on the screen strongly resembles the output which would be generated from that information. WYSIWYG stands for "What You See Is What You Get" and is pronounced "whizzy-whig". (11)

X: Same as **X Window**. (2)

X client: Within the X Window system, a program that calls upon an X server to act as its interface. (2)

X server: Within the X Window system, a program that takes care of the details of interacting with a graphical user interface on behalf of other programs. (2)

X Window: A system, used mostly with Unix workstations, that supports a graphical user interface and a client/server system. (2)

zip: To run a program that creates a zipfile out of one or more files. (21)

zipfile: A compressed archive with a file extension of **zip**, created by **pkzip** or a compatible program. (21)

Chapter references are indicated by the numbers in parentheses.

Harley Hahn's

Catalog of
Internet
Resources

Y**ou** will enjoy this catalog. I have spent a long time time exploring the Internet and tracking down hundreds of interesting and useful resources. Moreover, the items in this catalog are only starting places. Almost all of them will lead you to something else: There are many hours of enjoyment and fascination ahead of you on the Net.

Throughout this book, I have mentioned a lot of resources to help you find the software and information you need to use the Internet. All these items are included in the Internet Resources category in this catalog. In addition, I have included more than 150 other categories with a variety of interesting and useful resources.

Within the catalog, you will see a number of ways to access information: the Web, gopher, anonymous ftp, Usenet, and so on. If you are not completely familiar with any of these services, you can use the table below to consult the appropriate chapter for more information. For a quick guided tour of the Internet, see Chapter 3.

If you would like an even larger catalog, you will enjoy my book, *Harley Hahn's Internet & Web Yellow Pages*, published by Osborne McGraw-Hill. It has over 5,000 items in more than 180 categories, as well as enough jokes to amuse you and your loved ones through the turn of the century.

Chapter	Topic
7, 8	Mail
9, 10, 11, 12	The Web
13, 14, 15	Usenet
16, 17	Gopher
18, 19	Anonymous Ftp
20	Archie
22	Mailing Lists
23, 24	Telnet
25, 26	Talk Facilities
27	IRC (Internet Relay Chat)
28	Muds

Harley Hahn's Catalog of Internet Resources

Table of Contents

AGRICULTURE

Agricultural Mailing List

Grassland husbandry, crop science, ecological simulation, crop production, tropical forestry, plant physiology, water management, irrigation, and anything else to do with agriculture.

Listserv Mailing List:
List Name: **agric-l**
Subscribe to: **listserv@uga.cc.uga.edu**

Agriculture Links

Farming doesn't have to be lonely business. Being out in the boonies won't keep you isolated if you can reach this great load of agricultural resources. This is just about all the information you will need if you are interested in any aspects of agriculture: Usenet groups, web resources, archives, mailing lists and other cool stuff is available.

Web:
http://ipm_www.ncsu.edu/cernag/cern.html
http://www.gennis.com/aglinks.html

ANARCHY

Anarchist Resources

After going through a three-hour corporate meeting, it's refreshing to look at a nice web site that can help you fantasize about throwing off the political ties that bind you. This site has lots of interesting resources that are related to anarchy and anarchists. It includes lists of newsgroups, archive sites, web pages, newsletters, mailing lists, publications, and more.

Web:
http://www.duke.edu/~eagle/anarchy

Anarchy Talk and General Discussion

To some people, anarchy is society without government. To others, anarchy is life without television. Still, whether you are an armchair social critic or a couch potato with a plan to reform the world, you won't want to miss the discussion. Talk may be cheap, but good plans to reform the world the hard way are in short supply.

Usenet:
alt.anarchism
alt.society.anarchy

Spunk Press

Spunk Press collects and distributes electronic literature with an emphasis on anarchism and related issues. Their home page offers a manifesto, a large catalog of anarchy articles as well as a list of anarchist resources.

Web:
http://www.cwi.nl/cwi/people/Jack.Jansen/spunk/Spunk_Home.html

ANIMALS AND PETS

Animal Information Database

Created by Sea World and Busch Gardens, this web page is loaded with information, not only about aquatic animals, but also on a variety of terrestrial critters. Learn about manatee bodysurfing, hippos that sweat pink oil, and other interesting animal facts that will make you the life of any party.

Web:
http://www.bev.net/education/SeaWorld/infobook.html

Animal Talk and General Discussion

Animals are for more than eating or making into pets. Some are pretty or lovable, and some are to be admired for their skill in stalking and devouring small prey or unsuspecting pizza-delivery boys. On the Net there are several places you can go to participate in discussions of your favorite animal.

Usenet:
alt.animals.badgers
alt.animals.bears
alt.animals.dolphins
alt.animals.foxes
alt.animals.giraffes
alt.animals.lampreys
alt.animals.pandas
alt.animals.raccoons
alt.animals.whales

Electronic Zoo

If you love animals, this is the place to spend your spare time. Enjoy a compilation of animal-related resources: mailing lists, web sites, Usenet newsgroups, archives, databases, and much more. The next time you have an extra ten minutes, start here and explore. I bet you'll find something to distract you from your work.

Web:
> http://netvet.wustl.edu/e-zoo.htm

Pet Cemetery

Finally, here is the perfect venue for you to publish "Ode to Wilhelmena, Marsupial Companion of my Youth". The Virtual Pet Cemetery is just the place to send an honorable epitaph for that favorite pet who, after handing in his dinner pail, has passed on to his final reward, beloved by all and sundry.

Web:
> http://www.lavamind.com/pet.html

ARCHEOLOGY

Archnet

I have a friend, Virginia (Ginny) Hatfield, who is an archeologist. She spends a lot of time running around the country digging up small pieces of whatnot and making esoteric discoveries. Myself, I prefer to stay at home with my cat and cruise the University of Connecticut's Archnet site. That way I can spend hours poring over all kinds of archeological resources without getting my hands dirty. Ginny may have more fun, but I'm a lot closer to the fridge.

Web:
> http://www.lib.uconn.edu/ArchNet/ArchNet.html

Egyptian Artifacts

You can be Indiana Jones without having to worry about sharp spikes being driven through your head or giant rolling rocks crushing you to death. Take a look at beautiful Egyptian artifacts at the Institute of Egyptian Art and Archaeology.

Web:
> http://www.memphis.edu/egypt/artifact.html

National Archeological Database

Throughout most of recorded history, people have had to dig around for official archeological data. Now, however, the National Archeological Database puts hard-to-find information at your virtual fingertips. Never again need you spend hours looking for documents such as the Notice of Inventory Completion for Native American Human Remains from Lake Winnepesauke, New Hampshire.

Web:
> http://www.cast.uark.edu/products/NADB/

ARCHITECTURE

Architecture Talk and General Discussion

In my opinion, architects are some of the most talented, visionary, imaginative people in the world. Join the general architecture discussion group for all manner of architecture-oriented topics: building design, construction, architecture schools, materials, and so on. If they can build it, you can talk about it.

Usenet:
> alt.architecture

Interior Design

It's a hard choice to make—should you be traditional with your home design or should you be quaintly archaic and put an outhouse in the backyard? Don't let these architectural dilemmas keep you up at night. Get together with other people who are interested in interior design as it relates to architecture.

Usenet:
> alt.architecture.int-design

ART

Grotesque in Art

This is an exhibit of visual images that explores violence, horror, and the grotesque in art. Send the kids out of the room, don't eat before viewing, and don't meditate on these just before bedtime because they can be very graphic.

Web:
> http://www.ugcs.caltech.edu/~werdna/grotesque/grotesque.html

Surrealism Server

If you don't understand it, I can't explain it. Let your mind dance on the edge of radical thought. (Fish.) Take a look at paintings of famed Surrealists or participate in some fun Surrealism games like The Infinite Story or The Exquisite Cadaver. Don't be afraid. The only thing it can hurt is your brain.

Web:
> http://pharmdec.wustl.edu/juju/surr/surrealism.html

ART GALLERIES AND EXHIBITS

Leonardo da Vinci Museum

See the work of the master who put the word "Renaissance" in "Renaissance Man". Painter, inventor, architect, writer, musician, and all-around genius, Leonardo is a household name in the world of art. This site displays his oil paintings, futuristic designs, drawings and sketches, and biographical information on the man who made Mona Lisa smile.

Web:
> http://www.leonardo.net/museum/

Louvre Museum

Here's your chance to visit Paris free of charge. Get a ticket to the virtual Louvre, which is conducting tours around the city. You will see the Eiffel Tower and the Champs Elysees, among other sights. At the Louvre itself, they offer tours of a collection of famous paintings and a demonstration of French Medieval art. You have to bring your own pastries.

Web:
> http://www.louvre.fr/

World Wide Art Resources

There are a large number of art museums and galleries in the world, many of which have informaton and exhibits on the Net. This site offers a comprehensive collection of information and is definitely the place to start when you are looking for a museum or gallery anywhere in the world. I like visiting this site for two reasons. First, when I have a few minutes, it's a great place to browse. I can always find a new online exhibit to explore. Second, before I travel anywhere, I check out all the museums and galleries in the area to see what looks good.

Web:
> http://wwar.com/galleries.html
> http://wwar.com/museums.html

ASTRONOMY

Astronomical Museum

Instruments used by Bolognese astronomers from the early 18th to mid-19th century are on display here in the same rooms of the ancient tower originally devoted to observations. A history of the museum and astronomy in Bologna, Italy, and a guided tour of the Meridian, Globe, and Turret Rooms are available here. There are gif images of the early scientific equipment, along with lengthy descriptions.

Web:
> http://boas3.bo.astro.it/dip/Museum/MuseumHome.html

Astronomy Talk and General Discussion

Would you like to talk with people who really do understand black holes? Join the astronomers on Usenet and discuss all aspects of astronomy and astrophysics: stars, planets, telescopes, cosmology, space exploration, and so on. The **sci.astro.amateur** group is specifically for amateur astronomers.

Usenet:
> sci.astro
> sci.astro.amateur

Observatories and Telescopes

One of the things I like best about the Net is that it provides a place for information that literally did not exist before there was an international computer network. For example, say that you want to look for a particular observatory or telescope. Before the Net existed, where could you even look for an up-to-date master list? Now it's easy to find what you want. Just check these sites and find links to hundreds of observatories and telescopes all over the globe.

Web:
> http://webhead.com/WWWVL/Astronomy/astroweb/yp_telescope.html
> http://webhead.com/WWWVL/Astronomy/observatories-optical.html

AVIATION

Aviation Enthusiast Corner

This site has lots of information and links related to aviation as a hobby. It offers an aircraft reference, air events guide, a large list of aviation museums and displays, and links to other aviation and aerospace sites.

Web:
http://aeroweb.brooklyn.cuny.edu/air.html

Aviation Talk and General Discussion

You'll go into a flat spin when you see all the information you can find in this group. If you don't know how to choose one of the specific aviation groups, this is a great place to start. There are often cross-postings from other groups to **.misc**, so you'll see a wide variety of topics, including comparisons of different types of planes, what to do about engine fires, pros and cons of leasing, and what happens when an instrument malfunctions. There's something for everyone.

Web:
http://www.aero.com/news/news.htm

Usenet:
rec.aviation
rec.aviation.misc
rec.aviation.questions

Landings Aviation Server

Landings is a large collection of aviation information, including aeronautical research servers, flight planning software, newsgroups, FAQs, piloting tips, federal aviation regulations, weather information, and much more. When you are not busy, up in the air, this is a good place to land.

Web:
http://www.landings.com/

BBSS (BULLETIN BOARD SYSTEMS)

ISCA BBS

The largest and most popular BBS on the Internet (and the largest nonprofit BBS in the world). There are discussion groups to fit all tastes, especially some of a more esoteric nature that seem to be lacking from Usenet. ISCA is often full, with users from all over the globe busily rambling away.

Telnet:
> Address: **bbs.isca.uiowa.edu**
> Login: **guest**
> Address: **whip.isca.uiowa.edu**
> Login: **guest**

List of BBSs on the Internet

BBS junkies can celebrate over these comprehensive lists of BBSs on the Net. These resources give an overview of Internet BBSs, connect information, as well as links web pages.

Web:
> http://aug3.augsburg.edu/~schwartz/ebbs.html
> http://dkeep.com/sbi.html

Sunspot BBS

A widely varied BBS, with a wide spread of discussion boards, public files, chat and talk facilities. Friendly people are always ready to chat, day or night, through the numerous online communication programs.

Telnet:
> Address: **bbs.augsburg.edu**
> Login: **bbs**

BIOLOGY

Biology Resources

A great collection of the favorite web pages of anyone involved with biology. If you like biology, you simply must check this out.

Web:
> http://pillo.unipv.it/~marcora/surf.htm

Virtual Genome Center

Find out what's hot and what's not in the genome world. Software and applications are available as well as documentation and images of some very unusual yeast sequences.

Web:
http://alces.med.umn.edu/VGC.html

BIZARRE

Bizarre Talk and General Discussion

The unusual, curious, and often stupid: here is Usenet's newsgroup for canonical strangeness. Just don't make the mistake of sending in an article that is not bizarre enough.

Usenet:
talk.bizarre

Dark Side of the Net

When the history of the twentieth century is written, the section on gothic culture will have one simple entry: see Carrie Carolin. Carrie is a wonderfully resourceful and talented bundle of energy who maintains The Dark Side of the Web, the pre-eminent Internet site for things gothic. Here you will find a fabulous list of resources regarding gothic, horror, vampires (and vampyres), occult, magick, zines, magazines and much more. Root around a little, and you will find links to Carrie's other, equally fascinating enterprises. Not recommended for normal people or Republicans.

Web:
http://www.gothic.net/darkside/

Geeks and Nerds

Remember, if it weren't for geeks and nerds, there wouldn't be an Internet (and you wouldn't be able to read this totally cool Internet book). Pay tribute to these unsung heroes of the Star Trek generation. Join Usenet's own mutual admiration society: take a nerd to lunch today.

Usenet:
alt.geek

Zombie Hangman

Add a little danger to the classic game of Hangman. Solve the word as best you can, but for every letter you miss, the zombie loses a body part. This is definitely no Wheel of Fortune.

Web:
> http://www.dtd.com/rip/

BOATING AND SAILING

Boating Talk and General Discussion

When I was a kid at camp, I earned my Master Canoeist award. To this day, I can still recall all the esoteric canoeing strokes I had to be able to demonstrate, equally well on both sides. Truly, moving on water invokes deep feelings in all of us. If you care about things that float, join the Internet boating discussion groups: **rec.boats** for general boating topics; **rec.boats.paddle** for discussion of canoes, rowboats, and related craft.

Usenet:
> rec.boats
> rec.boats.paddle

Kayaking and Canoeing

When I was an undergraduate student at the University of Waterloo in Canada, I spent a little time with the Whitewater Canoe Club. However, I never got close to the action: my participation was limited to paddling a kayak around the swimming pool. Later, after I moved to California, I once went kayaking in the ocean, and I found it a lot more fun than the pool in Waterloo. If you want to keep afloat of the happenings in the world of the paddle, check out this web site for links to kayak and canoe organizations around the world.

Web:
> http://www.gfi.uib.no/~svenn/padling/norway/world.html

BOOKS

Bibliomania

Curl up by the fireplace and cozy down with Data Text Processing's fiction collection, which includes author biographies and HTMLized book texts. Authors include such notables as Joyce, Hardy, Dickens, Alcott, Defoe, Wilde, Stevenson, Kipling and Lawrence.

Web:
> http://www.bibliomania.com/

Book Authors

Books are good for those times when the computer is down and you can't connect to the Net. If there is a particular kind of book that catches your fancy, check in Usenet to see if there is a group relating to your favorite author.

Usenet:

      alt.books.anne-rice
      alt.books.arthur-clarke
      alt.books.brian-lumley
      alt.books.bukowski
      alt.books.clive-barker
      alt.books.crichton
      alt.books.cs-lewis
      alt.books.dean-koontz
      alt.books.deryni
      alt.books.george-orwell
      alt.books.h-g-wells
      alt.books.isaac-asimov
      alt.books.julian-may
      alt.books.kurt-vonnegut
      alt.books.larry-niven
      alt.books.m-lackey
      alt.books.phil-k-dick
      alt.books.poppy-z-brite
      alt.books.pratchett
      alt.books.raymond-feist
      alt.books.robert-rankin
      alt.books.sf.melanie-rawn
      alt.books.stephen-king
      alt.books.terry-brooks
      alt.books.toffler
      alt.books.tom-clancy
      rec.arts.books.tolkien
      rec.arts.sf.written.robert-jordan

BookWeb

Part of the American Booksellers Association, this web page offers you news about books and bookstores, author interviews and gossip about new bookstores opening up.

Web:
      http://www.ambook.org/

BOTANY

Botany Databases

Botany lovers will have a great time with the Smithsonian's botany resources on the Net. One of the many interesting resources is a massive database of hundreds of thousands of records in the United States National Herbarium.

Web:
> http://nmnhwww.si.edu/departments/botany.html

Botany Talk and General Discussion

How does your garden grow? Discover the myth and mystery of plant growth and reproduction. Discussion of all aspects of plant biology is encouraged. You'll never have a guilt-free salad again.

Usenet:
> bionet.plants

Botany Web Sites

Students, teachers, scientists or plain old plant lovers must immediately make their way to this web page. There are a huge amount of resources for botanists around the Net, and you will find most of them here: links to databases, mailing lists, archive sites, software, organizations and much more.

Web:
> http://www.biol.uregina.ca/liu/bio/botany.shtml

BUYING AND SELLING

Catalog Mart

Don't have enough junk mail? I have a way for you to get even more. This site offers hundreds of subjects of interest from which you can select. Choose all the ones you like, fill in your name and address and before long, your mailman will be bringing catalogs straight to your mailbox.

Web:
> http://catalog.savvy.com/

Classified Ads

Shopping, shopping, shopping. Do you like to shop, but don't like to get dressed to leave the house? Shop at home, by checking out the great classified ads on the Net.

Web:
> http://ep.com/
> http://www.funcity.com/ads

Computers

Buying a computer? For buying and selling particular machines, see these specialized groups. Here's my hint for the day: it is difficult to buy too much speed, too much memory, or too much video resolution.

Usenet:
> biz.marketplace.computers.discussion
> biz.marketplace.computers.mac
> biz.marketplace.computers.other
> biz.marketplace.computers.pc-clone
> biz.marketplace.computers.workstation
> biz.marketplace.services.computers
> comp.os.os2.marketplace
> comp.sys.amiga.marketplace
> comp.sys.apple2.marketplace
> comp.sys.ibm.pc.games.marketplace
> comp.sys.mac.games.marketplace
> comp.sys.next.marketplace
> misc.forsale.computers.workstation

CANADA

Canadian History

Here is a little-known fragment of Canadian history: When my sister, Melissa, was two years old and I was baby-sitting her, she fell off my parents' bed and hit her head on the floor. (Come to Toronto with me some time, and I will show you the exact spot.) Of course, not all Canadian history is that interesting, but still, there are jewels if you only take the time to look.

Web:
> http://www.msstate.edu/Archives/History/Canada/canada.html

Canadian Talk and General Discussion

What do you at 9:30 PM on Saturday night, when you are just dying to talk to a Canadian and William Shatner's line is busy? Hop over to IRC, where nimble-fingered Canadians are cutting fast, loose and easy. Need a French-Canadian fix? Try the **#quebec** channel ("ici, on parle Français"). Who says Saturday night has to be dull?

IRC:
> #calgary
> #canada
> #edmonton
> #montreal
> #ontario
> #quebec
> #toronto
> #vancouver
> #winnipeg

Canadian Web Sites

Wanna fast way to get your finger on the pulse of the Canadian Net? Here is the master link that points to everything worth pointing to in Canada. ("Be there *and* be square.")

Web:
> http://www.netlinks.net/netlinks/canada.html

CARS AND TRUCKS

Antique Cars

Wash it, buff it, tuck your baby in at night. Antique automobiles hold a special place in everyone's heart. Care and feeding of all older automobiles is covered in **alt.autos.antique**. Automobiles over 25 years old are parked in **rec.autos.antique**.

Web:
> http://www.tgis.co.uk/home/caargb/

Usenet:
> alt.autos.antique
> rec.autos.antique

Car Place

Here's someone who knows his cars. Here's someone who knows other people's cars. Here's someone who spends his time driving cars and lives to tell about it. Check out the reviews of all types of cars, new and old. Here's someone worth listening to.

Web:
> http://www.cftnet.com/members/rcbowden/

Car Talk and General Discussion

When you're not driving, you can talk about driving and, on the Net, there is no end to the discussion: automobile design, construction, service, tires, competitions, driving, manufacturers, and on and on and on.

Usenet:
> alt.auto.mercedes
> alt.autos
> alt.autos.bmw
> alt.autos.camaro.firebird
> alt.autos.classic-trucks
> alt.autos.corvette
> alt.autos.dodge.trucks
> alt.autos.ferrari
> alt.autos.ford
> alt.autos.isuzu
> alt.autos.karting
> alt.autos.microcars
> alt.autos.mini
> alt.autos.toyota
> rec.autos
> rec.autos.misc

CHEMISTRY

Chemistry Talk and General Discussion

Let's talk chemistry. Let's talk about substances and how they react when they are combined. Let's talk about mixing diatomaceous earth into sulphuric acid in order to make it sticky. Let's talk about everything under and inside of the sun. Let's talk about cleaning up the mess.

Usenet:
> sci.chem

Chemist's Art Gallery

Spectacular visualization and animations in chemistry. Among the offerings are animations of small molecules, visualization of chromosomes and viruses based on electron microscopy tomography, visualization of micelles, and much more. There are also links to other chemistry visualization and animation sites.

Web:
http://www.csc.fi/lul/chem/graphics.html

Periodic Table in Hypertext Format

A hypertext version of the Periodic Table that allows you to click on any individual element to obtain details of that element. The details include standard state, color, discoverer, date discovered, name meaning, radii, valency, electronegativities, effective nuclear charge, bond enthalpies, temperatures, enthalpies, ionization enthalpies, isotopic abundances, and more.

Web:
http://www.cchem.berkeley.edu/Table/

COLLECTING

Antique Talk and General Discussion

Capture the past by collecting antiques and vintage items. Learn to restore your old Victrola, music box, or clock. Find out where you can get issues of the Charlie Chaplin comics. Buy, sell, and trade.

Usenet:
rec.antiques

Collecting Talk and General Discussion

Is there anyone who doesn't collect anything? (I, for example, collect Internet books.) Collecting seems to be part of our nature as human beings. Thus, if you are human, there is a place in this discussion for you. Use your imagination: anything that can be quantified or categorized is fair game. The **.cards** newsgroup is for those who collect trading cards, both sport and non-sport.

Usenet:
rec.collecting
rec.collecting.cards.discuss
rec.collecting.cards.non-sports

Stamp Collecting

If you like to collect stamps, these stamp collecting resources could be just the ticket for you! Check out the mailing lists to horse trade for stamps or just chat with other collectors and hobbyists.

Web:
> http://www.execpc.com/~joeluft/resource.html

Usenet:
> rec.collecting.postal-history
> rec.collecting.stamps

Listserv Mailing List:
> List Name: **stamps**
> Subscribe to: **listserv@psuvm.psu.edu**

COMICS

AAA Aardvark Comics Index

A gargantuan, well-organized hotlist of comics-oriented links. Lots of web sites, zines, images, comics archives, mailing lists, and more and more and more (and more).

Web:
> http://comics.redweb.com/

Comic Cafe

Get the latest in hot comic book gossip at the Comic Cafe. Read this tabloid full of the latest news, new releases, collectible information and reader-submitted electronic whispers. And if you know a secret, be sure to tell the rest of the world while you are here.

Web:
> http://www.hype.com/comics/cafe/comicafe.htm

Daily Comics

This is one of my favorite sites on the whole Internet. Lots of daily comic strips to look at for free. Along with the comics, you will find background information on the cartoonists and on the strips themselves. Just between you and me, this site eliminated the only reason I ever had to buy a newspaper.

Web:
> http://www.unitedmedia.com/comics/

COMPUTERS: CULTURE

Computer History and Folklore

One day, while you are driving, you see an old bearded man wearing a Grateful Dead T-shirt, standing beside the road, and holding a sign that says "Will set up a Usenet news server for food." This is not your average homeless person. This is a man who used to be *someone* in the early days of the Net. There was life—lots of life—before the Web, and you can read all about it in the archive of Internet-oriented history and folklore.

Web:
> http://yoyo.cc.monash.edu.au/~mist/Folklore/

Geek Code

Are you a geek? Do you want to be? Check out the Geek code and see how you rate. Then put your own personal geek code in your email signature for the whole world to see. If you are a geek, walk tall.

Web:
> http://krypton.mankato.msus.edu/~hayden/geek.html

Geek Site of the Day

If you are a geek, you should be proud of it. And what better way to show your appreciation than to visit the Geek Site of the Day every day of your life. Get a daily treat, your recommended daily allowance of something truly geeky like a calculus problem, recipes for snack food that you can eat on those 24-hour mudding binges, or links to technoid gidgets and gadgets that only a geek would love.

Web:
> http://www.owlnet.rice.edu/~indigo/gsotd/

CONSUMER INFORMATION

Consumer Fraud

You know you have to be careful when someone is trying to offer you a deal that sounds too good to be true. Chances are, it probably *is* too good to be true. The U.S. Postal Service has a fantastic selection of information on consumer fraud that everyone should read. Some of the schemes they cover are chain letters, free prizes and vacations, 900-numbers, foreign lotteries, personal finance-related schemes, multilevel marketing, work-at-home schemes, telephone solicitations and many more. This is an excellent site for consumer information.

Web:
> http://www.usps.gov/websites/depart/inspect/consmenu.htm

Consumer Talk and General Discussion

Here is Usenet's general consumer forum. And, since we are all consumers, there is something for everyone. Send in your questions, share your answers, read the reviews, opinions, and general bad-mouthing of the bad guys. Before you spend your next dime, check with the world at large.

Usenet:
> misc.consumers

Free Offers

There is free stuff out there in the world, just waiting for you to ask for it. You can get all kinds of cool things for free—phone calls, food, clothes, recipes, tickets and endless samples of miscellany—just for asking. All the information is here, so clean out the garage in order to make room for more stuff.

Web:
> http://home.earthlink.net/~boughter
> http://www.fabfreebies.com/
> http://www.winternet.com/~julie/ntn1.html

Usenet:
> alt.consumers.free-stuff

IRC:
> #FreeStuff

CONTESTS

Contest Web Resources

Is your working area covered in a flurry of sticky notes and random scraps of paper, in a vain attempt to keep track of all the contests on the Net? Here's a better idea. These web sites keep track of many of the contests, drawings, raffles, sweepstakes and promotions that are happening on the Web. My advice is to check in every day, just in case the contest of your dreams has materialized while you were asleep.

Web:
>   http://www.4cyte.com/ThreadTreader/
>   http://www.contestguide.com/

Riddler Game

Right now, as you read this, you could be out making money on the Web just by using your brain along with some clever mouse-button clicking. The Riddler Game gives you the opportunity to answer trivia questions and solve puzzles for cash prizes. The game is free, but you have to register to play.

Web:
>   http://www.riddler.com/

Sweepstakes Information

Here is information on lots of sweepstakes and contests: dates, rules, and information on how to enter. You will also find links to sweepstakes and contests you can enter without even leaving the Web. How much more convenient can modern life get? In the Usenet group, people send in information about new contests all the time.

Web:
>   http://www.sweepstakesonline.com/

Usenet:
>   alt.consumers.sweepstakes

Cookie Recipes

Everybody has their own favorite type of cookie. Mine are made from organic seaweed, brewer's yeast, whey and (for fiber) biodegradable sawdust. However, if you happen to be one of those people who is not a health food junkie, your taste in cookies may be a tad more mainstream. If so, check out this web site for more cookie recipes than you could use in a month of Sunday bake sales.

Web:
> http://www.cs.cmu.edu/~mjw/recipes/cookies/cookie.html
> http://www.universaltech.net/patw/cookies.htm
> http://www.wester.net/Momz/cookies.html

Cooking Talk and General Discussion

If you like messing around the kitchen and trying out new recipes, there are lots of people on the Net who will love to talk to you. Join one or all of the cooking discussion groups, and talk about cooking techniques, equipment, recipes, vegetarianism, and so on. This is a great place to trade tips and techniques, and to ask questions about things culinary.

Usenet:
> alt.cooking-chat
> alt.creative-cook
> rec.food.cooking
> rec.food.recipes

Insect Recipes

If you are having a party, this page offers the perfect recipes for little appetizers. Insects are not only freely found in the environment, but they make perfect finger food. Try some dry-roasted leafhoppers or Army worms. For dipping, use the rootworm beetle dip or for dessert try my personal favorite: the chocolate chirpie chip cookies.

Web:
> http://www.ent.iastate.edu/Misc/InsectsAsFood.html
> http://www.uky.edu/Agriculture/Entomology/ythfacts/bugfood2.htm

Recipe Archives

I promise you: As long as you have the Net, you will never ever run out of recipes. How about a new a idea for dinner tonight? Or perhaps you'd like to cook up a special something for that special someone. Here are some great archives with more recipes than you can shake a wooden spoon at.

Web:
> http://english-www.hss.cmu.edu/Recipes/
> http://mel.lib.mi.us/reference/REF-food.html
> http://soar.berkeley.edu/recipes/
> http://www.cs.cmu.edu/~mjw/recipes/
> http://www.ichef.com/ichef-recipes/

Virtual Kitchen

Here's a snazzy kitchen space offered by Time Warner. Get recipes, tips and general cooking information from these beautiful cookbooks. Spend time browsing or search by keywords for exactly what you want. Even if you have trouble boiling water, this site is worth a look.

Web:
> http://pathfinder.com/twep/kitchen/

CRAFTS

Clay Art

It's so much fun to play in the mud. The problem is you can't do it and use the computer at the same time. But when you get clean and dry, take some time to subscribe to this mailing list to partake in the discussion of ceramic arts, clay, kilns, glazes and other hot clay art topics. The web site has some nifty stuff you can read when you aren't out getting your hands dirty.

Web:
> http://www.vicnet.net.au/~claynet/clayhome.htm

Usenet:
> bit.listserv.clayart

Listserv Mailing List:
> List Name: **clayart**
> Subscribe to: **listserv@lsv.uky.edu**

Craft Resources

A web page with links to many craft-related resources on the Internet. Here you will find links to general craft sites, craft suppliers, craft associations, information about fairs and events and even fun craft links for kids.

Web:
   http://www.wyomingcompanion.com/janacraft/links.htm

CRYPTOGRAPHY

Cryptography Archive

Here is a well-organized, compact collection of cryptography resources from around the Net. If you are at all serious about cryptography, you will want to put this site on your bookmark list. If you are not serious about cryptography, put this site on your list anyway. It's bound to impress your friends.

Web:
   http://www.austinlinks.com/Crypto/

PGP Encryption/Decryption Program

Where to get and how to use the ubiquitous PGP (Pretty Good Privacy) encryption package. Use it to send secret messages to your friends.

Web:
   http://bs.mit.edu:8001/pgp-form.html

Usenet:
   alt.security.pgp

CYBERPUNK

Cyberpunk FAQ

You can't be totally cool, hip or rad until you know just what cyberpunk is. And you can't just fake it. You have to know the real stuff, like the difference between the literary movement and the culture. Read this FAQ which will answer all your questions about cyberpunk and never again will you have to worry about not being in with the In Crowd.

Web:
   http://www.knarf.demon.co.uk/alt-cp.htm

Cyberpunk Literature

People who are immersed in the cyberpunk culture understand what it is, but they have a lot of trouble explaining it to anyone else. My advice is to start with the idea that technology touches virtually every aspect of our life. From there, you can enter the cyberpunk world by reading, and here is a good place to start: a collection of cyberlit (cyberpunk literature) resources on the Net.

Web:
> http://omni.cc.purdue.edu/~stein/stein.htm

 DANCE

Ballet and Modern Dance

The only thing that is not cool about ballet and modern dance is that you can't do it on the Internet. The closest thing you will find is a place where people talk about their experiences in the dance scene and share information on upcoming dance tours as well as dance opportunities. Strap yourself into some shoes and sashay on over to where the dance action is happening.

Usenet:
> alt.arts.ballet

Dance Resources

After six hours of school, I've had enough of a day, I grab the radio dial, and turn it up all the way, I've got to dance, right on the spot, the beat's really hot, dance, dance, dance, dance... (And when I'm not dancing, I'm on the Net, looking at dance resources and talking on Usenet.)

Web:
> http://emporium.turnpike.net/~dpd/
> http://www.cyberspace.com/vandehey/dance.html
> http://zeus.ncsa.uiuc.edu:8080/~hneeman/dance_hotlist.html

Usenet:
> rec.arts.dance

Dancescape

Ballroom dancing is not for sissies. For those of you with more cutthroat tendencies, this site has loads of information about competitive ballroom dancing. Check the calendar of events to see what's happening in your area. Get information on publications about competitive dancing, organizations dedicated to the sport of dancing and personal ads for people who love to dance. You will also find a list of places where competitive dancing events are held, including Asia, Europe and North America. This is not your mother's ballroom dancing.

Web:
> http://wchat.on.ca/dance/pages/dscape1.htm

DIET AND NUTRITION

Dieting FAQ

When you are suffering from too much information, get some help sorting it all out with the FAQ from **alt.support.diet**. This list of frequently asked questions covers issues such as general diet and nutrition, weight loss, liquid diets and fasts, weight loss organizations and diet books, motivation, exercise, diet aids and more.

Web:
> http://www.cis.ohio-state.edu/hypertext/faq/usenet/dieting-faq
> http://www.lib.ox.ac.uk/internet/news/faq/alt.support.diet.html

Dieting Talk and General Discussion

Does your diet work? Or like the other 99.9 percent of humanity, do you have to suffer to lose excess weight? Join ultra-nutrition-conscious people around the world who will thank you for sharing. Trade stories, scientific trivia, and leftover Weight Watchers' menus. Are you just about ready for your own zip code? Lonely no more.

Usenet:
> alt.support.diet

Healthy Diet Guidelines

When the doctor says it's time to get off the Pepsi and cheeseburger express, get help from your friend the Net. This resource contains everything you need to eat well except willpower and a credit card.

Web:
> http://www.uiuc.edu/departments/mckinley/health-info/nutrit/hlthdiet/hlthdiet.html

DISABILITIES

Computers for the Handicapped

CHIPS is the Computers for the Handicapped Independence Program. Get information about software and hardware for the visually impaired, quadriplegics, mobility impairments, speech and language impairments, and for the hearing impaired.

Web:
> http://www.wolfe.net/~dr_bill/

Disability Information

Information about many disability-related resources. There is an enormous amount of such material on the Net, and these sites are a good place to start.

Web:
> http://www.eskimo.com/~dempt/disability.html
> http://www.eskimo.com/~jlubin/disabled.html
> http://www.indie.ca/

Handicap Talk and General Discussion

If you have a handicap, you will find something helpful from these groups. Useful information and personal support covers topics such as problems facing amputees, medical issues for the disabled, handicap access concerns, politics and personal interest stories such as biographies of famous people.

Usenet:
> misc.handicap

Playbill Online

Who needs the newspaper when you can get access to this snazzy online magazine that offers news and information listings for Broadway, off-Broadway and national theater tours? Have fun browsing around or use Playbill's search mechanism for speedier results.

Web:
 http://piano.symgrp.com/playbill/

Theater Resources

As long as you have Internet access, you will never have to be without a good dose of theater. This list of resources covers just about every theater topic imaginable. Now, when you are left home on Saturday night because your BMW broke down and you can't get to the theater, you can amuse yourself with a virtual experience that has a compelling drama all its own.

Web:
 http://www.monmouth.com/user_pages/snaef/theatre2.html
 http://www.theatre-central.com/dir/res/

D

DRUGS

Drug Culture

There is an entire group of people who choose not to hang out in reality some of the time. Instead of going to Disneyland, they like to spend lots of money on chemicals that are illegal and bad for their health. Commune with members of the drug culture as they talk about various drugs, music to trip to, and becoming one with nature and getting in touch with themselves and on special occasions with each other.

Usenet:
 alt.drugs.culture

Drug Pix

Who says art is only for cultured people? Here are some drug-related photos that are bound to enlighten and amuse you. See what street drugs and drug paraphernalia look like, and enjoy pictures of rare curiosities. For example, the last time I visited, I saw a photo of Cary Grant taking a hit of LSD, as well a piece of drug paraphernalia signed by U.S. comedian Oliver North. My only hint is, if you see an invitation to lick the screen, don't do it. (I am serious.)

Web:
> http://www.links.net/drugz/pix.html
> http://www.sppd.ci.st-pete.fl.us/drugs/drugs.htm

Street Drug Slang

Brush up on your street drug lingo the next time you are in desperate need for a decongestant and all the drug stores are closed. Learn how seemingly innocent words can have other, more sinister meanings.

Web:
> http://www.addictions.com/slang.htm
> http://www.drugs.indiana.edu/slang

ECONOMICS

Economic Resources

Let's face it, no one really understands the economy any more than anyone really understands, say, why beer comes in six-packs when people only have two hands. Still, that is no reason to feel left out in the financial cold. There are lots of economics resources out there, just waiting for you to explore, and here are some good places to start. After all, when we are living in a world when an American basketball player can sign a $120,000,000 contract and Internet authors have trouble making that much money in a *good* year, you know that things are getting out of control.

Web:
> http://econwpa.wustl.edu/
> http://www.helsinki.fi/WebEc/

Economics of the Internet

These days, information is a premium commodity and everyone is trying to cash in. Get a gander at these links that will inform you about the economics of the Internet, information goods and services, network economics, intellectual property and related information.

Web:
http://www.sims.berkeley.edu/resources/infoecon/

Economists on the Web

A large list of economists on the Internet, with pointers to their web pages. If there is a better way to impress a hot date quickly with why the Internet is so important, I have yet to find it.

Web:
http://eclab.ch.pdx.edu/ecwww

EDUCATION

Adult Education

These forums offer interesting discussions on ways to educate adults. People talk about all sorts of subjects, such as textbooks, education using interactive computer environments (like Muds and IRC), and audio tapes. There is also lots of discussion about teaching in conventional classroom settings.

Usenet:
misc.education.adult

Listproc Mailing List:
List Name: **adult-ed**
Subscribe to: **listproc@lists.fsu.edu**

Education Conferences

Here's a great web page for those of you (you know who you are) who are just itching to go to an education conference. Check out this updated list of exhibitions, seminars and conferences for educators. You will never have to spend another dull weekend hanging around the house.

Web:
http://teams.lacoe.edu/documentation/news/conferences.html

Netschool

Netschool is a cooperative effort by students, families, teachers and schools. The goal is to create a group of schools that will work together even though they are remote from one another. Well, the Net is certainly the right place to try something like this. If you like the idea of cooperating over long distances, give this site a look.

Web:
> http://www.netschool.com/

EDUCATION: COLLEGES AND UNIVERSITIES

College Net

Here is a search tool for college admissions information, including graduate programs. Search, browse by geography, or look at featured schools. Search for financial aid and scholarships.

Web:
> http://www.collegenet.com/

Graduate Students

After years of school, it begins to look like you might never graduate into the real world. That's why there is the Association for Support of Graduate Students. They provide information about theses, dissertation news and a professional consultant directory. Read the free articles at their web site.

Web:
> http://www.asgs.org/

Student Governments

Today's student body will be tomorrow's civic and political leaders. If that scares you, at least you can take comfort in the fact that they can organize themselves on the Internet. This universal home page leads to many student government organizations at colleges and universities across the United States.

Web:
> http://www.umr.edu/~ihsg/

EDUCATION: K-12

High School Newspapers on the Net

In the old days, high school newspapers would be circulated on paper to a relatively small number of people. Thus, anonymous gossip about the principal and the head of the science department had only a limited audience. Today, we have the Net and many, many high school newspapers are online and accessible to the world. Take a look.

Web:
> http://www.nvnet.k12.nj.us/newsweb/

Kidlink

Kidlink is an organization that helps children aged 10-15 from all over the world talk to one another using the Net. Kidlink supports not only English, but other languages as well. To participate in Kidlink children register by answering several questions about themselves. They can then participate—either on their own or with their class at school—in any of the Kidlink activities: mailing lists, entering art contests, IRC, and so on. The most important resources are the Kidcafe mailing lists, which children can use to talk to one another. For information on Kidlink and how to participate, see the web page. Teachers and parents: This is a good way for your kids to talk to other kids around the world, and to show them how important the Net is to human culture.

Web:
> http://www.kidlink.org/

School Projects by Kids

There are lots and lots of kids on the Net who love to share their work. Here are links to projects, reports and writing, all done by kids. Now that we have the Net, growing up will never be the same.

Web:
> http://sln.fi.edu/tfi/hotlists/kids.html

E

EDUCATION: TEACHING

Academic Magazines

Here is a list of pointers to a great many magazines and journals relating to schools, education and universities. Just the place to look for something to read in your copious spare time.

Web:
http://www.enews.com/monster/education/

Explorer

A remarkable collection of ideas, lesson plans, and general information for educators and students that is easy to work with and simple to understand. Outlines for math and science lessons, newsletters, and resource keyword searching capabilities.

Web:
http://explorer.scrtec.org/

Teachers Resources

A plethora of resources for teachers (and other related fauna): there are various guides, resources categorized by subject, instructional materials and a list of educational supply vendors. Also, a nice list of links to other related Internet resources.

Web:
http://www.westnet.com/~rickd/Teachers.html

ELECTRONICS

Electronics Repair

What a feeling of power to wield your mighty soldering iron knowing that you can fix anything. Share the thrill of wiring up the world with other electronics pros and enthusiasts and hear adventure stories about sparking microwave ovens, glowing Halloween gadgets, and televisions that generate X-rays. The talk is technical in detail, but these electronics gurus have a sense of humor (and the joy buzzers to prove it).

Usenet:
sci.electronics.repair

EMERGENCY AND DISASTER

Disaster Situation and Status Reports

Information and reports about natural disasters and events from agencies like the U.S. Weather Service and the U.S. Geological Survey. Information includes earthquake reports, weather reports, and hurricane forecasts. The **nat-dsr** mailing list is for situation reports from various humanitarian emergency response organizations and covers natural disasters only. The **sitreps** list is for situation reports about natural disasters as well as complex disasters (events that are socially or politically initiated). The **fireline** list is for the dissemination of information about wild land fires in North America.

Web:
> http://www.vita.org/disaster/disaster.html

Listproc Mailing List:
> List Name: **fireline**
> Subscribe to: **listproc@vita.org**

Listproc Mailing List:
> List Name: **nat-dsr**
> Subscribe to: **listproc@vita.org**

Listproc Mailing List:
> List Name: **sitreps**
> Subscribe to: **listproc@vita.org**

Emergency Medical Services for Children

911, along with the iron lung and the electric sewer rooter, is an awesome invention that we all hope we never have to use. It's nice to know that in the event of a personal disaster, an emergency medical team will come racing to help you. In an effort to continually update information and to improve services, EMS providers discuss emergency medical services and general emergency medical care for children.

Listproc Mailing List:
> List Name: **ems-c**
> Subscribe to: **listproc@lists.colorado.edu**

ENERGY

Alternative Energy

Tired of the same old energy? Try an alternative energy lifestyle. This site has information on alternative-fueled vehicles, the American Hydrogen Association, alternative fuel newsgroups, mailing lists and archives that relate to alternative forms of energy.

Web:
> http://solstice.crest.org/online/aeguide/

Renewable Energy

Right now, as you read this there are clever people around the world thinking about ways to use renewable energy. They are coming up with new designs for batteries, generators, pumps and chargers to use wind, water and sun for fuel. Read about the neat gadgets they have modified or invented or just check out the ideas and philosophy behind using renewable energy.

Web:
> http://www.nrel.gov/

Usenet:
> alt.energy.renewable

World Energy Statistics

Numbers, numbers, numbers. What do you do when you need to find out how much natural gas the world is going to use in the year 2010? Well, you could just wait until 2010, but that would take a long time. Wouldn't it be faster to check with the Net?

Web:
> http://equus.dur.ac.uk/15.html
> http://www.eia.doe.gov/emeu/mer/contents.html

ENGINEERING

Build a Flying Saucer

This one is a few years old, but I am leaving it in the book anyway. Or let me put it another way: this was the best Internet resource I could find discussing how to build a flying saucer. "...A set of superconducting magnets can be charged by metal sheet circuits, within limits, to whatever frequency is needed and will continue to transmit that magnetic field frequency almost indefinitely..." (And some people think the Information Superhighway is a waste of money.)

Web:
    http://wiretap.spies.com/Gopher/Library/Fringe/Ufo/build.ufo

Electronics Engineering

Electronics engineers: Now you have your own cool hangout on the Net. Check out this web page with links to FAQs on electronics, discussion groups, archives and other web pages relating to electronics.

Web:
    http://engr-www.unl.edu/ee/eeshop/netsites.html

Engineering Index

Engineering covers so wide a range of activities as to almost defy definition. Still, such trifles never stopped me, so here goes: Engineering is the profession in which a knowledge of science and mathematics is used to control the materials and forces of nature. If you have any interest in any type of engineering, paste this web site in your hat. Here you will find links to just about any type of engineering you can imagine (and several you can't imagine).

Web:
    http://www.englib.cornell.edu/ice/ice-index.html

Robotics

Robotics is the study and creation of machines guided by automatic controls (robots). Although it is fashionable to think of robots as being humanoid, outside of science fiction, robots look a lot more like your toaster than like your Uncle Henry.

Web:
    http://piglet.cs.umass.edu:4321/robotics.html

Usenet:
    comp.robotics.misc
    comp.robotics.research

E

ENVIRONMENT

Conservation OnLine

Conservation OnLine (CoOL) is a full text database of conservation information. This database covers a wide spectrum of topics of interest to anyone involved with the conservation of libraries, archives and museum materials.

Web:
http://palimpsest.stanford.edu/

Ecoweb

Do your part for Mother Earth by checking in at the Ecoweb, a network for the environmentally conscious. Ecoweb has audio clips, movies, and Ecochat—a place where you can chat with other green people. Connect to a large number of mailing lists sponsored by the Student Environmental Action Coalition. Explore other environment-related resources on the Net through links that offer everything from simple text to the whole multimedia shebang.

Web:
http://ecosys.drdr.virginia.edu/EcoWeb.html

Environmental Protection Agency

The EPA has collected a massive amount of information on the environment with regard to legislation, regulations, job vacancies, grants, newsletters and journals, press releases, announcements and consumer information.

Web:
http://www.epa.gov/

EXERCISE

Balance Magazine

An online monthly fitness magazine with information on diet, exercise, health and other necessary information to stay in balance.

Web:
http://www.hyperlink.com/balance/

Fitness

This site provides exercise and fitness guidelines, programs and resources as well as what to do in case of injury. Find overall fitness information to assist you with maintaining a healthy and well-rounded body composition.

Web:
> ftp://ftp.cray.com/pub/misc.fitness/misc.fitness.faq.html
> http://k2.kirtland.cc.mi.us/~balbachl/fitness.htm
> http://www.cdc.net/~primus/fpc/fpchome.html

Stretching and Flexibility

This document attempts to compile a wealth of information in order to answer some frequently asked questions about stretching and flexibility. It is organized into chapters covering the physiology of stretching, flexibility, types of stretching and how to stretch. Look out Gumby!

Web:
> http://www.cis.ohio-state.edu/hypertext/faq/usenet/stretching/top.html

F

Training and Nutrition

The last thing that anyone wants to do is give up their favorite treats. Learn about how exercise affects body metabolism and check out a safe fast food list. There's also a training and nutrition FAQ as well as mailing list archives about how to eat right while exercising and body building.

Web:
> http://www2.dgsys.com/~trnutr/

FAMILIES AND PARENTING

Child Safety on the Internet

If you are worried about your kids wandering around the Internet by themselves, have a look at these tips that will give you a better idea of how to protect young minds from inappropriate material.

Web:
> http://www.missingkids.org/childsafety.html

Children

Kids say the darnedest things. Impart your information and experience regarding children from the cradle onward. Anecdotes, advice on doctors, behavior, activities, discipline, and schooling legislation are just a few of the topics covered. The web site has information on the various issues that arise when rearing children.

Web:
> http://www.familyweb.com/faqs/

Usenet:
> misc.kids

Family Resources

The family that webs together stays together. This web page covers family topics like adolescence, pre-school, infants, children and marriage. Links on these topics will result in a list of related articles that will lead you to even more links for hours of interesting reading.

Web:
> http://www.einet.net/galaxy/Community/Family.html

Parents and Teens

What works? What doesn't? Share your experiences with other parents, give advice, ask questions.

Usenet:
> alt.parents-teens

FAQS (FREQUENTLY ASKED QUESTION LISTS)

FAQ Talk and General Discussion

The reason for frequently asked question lists is that newcomers to a Usenet discussion group often seem to ask the same questions. Veterans don't mind answering new questions, but nobody wants to explain, over and over and over, what "Unix" means. Through the years, many groups have developed a frequently asked question list (FAQ) that contains all the common questions that have been answered repeatedly in that group. Some FAQs are so large as to be divided into several parts. Whenever you start reading a new group, look for a FAQ to orient yourself. More important, before you post a question to the group, check the FAQ to see if your question has already been answered. The people who maintain FAQs post them regularly, not only to their own group, but to special groups that have been created just to hold FAQs and related material. The **news.answers** group contains FAQs from every possible source. The other **.answers** groups contain FAQs for their respective hierarchies. For example, **comp.answers** contains computer FAQs. When you have a spare moment, check out these groups, especially **alt.answers**. You will see a lot of interesting and strange stuff that you might never encounter otherwise. These groups contain not only FAQs, but important summaries of information not tied to specific Usenet groups.

Usenet:
> alt.answers
> comp.answers
> misc.answers
> news.answers
> rec.answers
> sci.answers
> soc.answers
> talk.answers

F

Periodic Informational Postings List

On Usenet, there are a great many articles that are sent to various discussion groups on a regular basis. For example, there are a lot of FAQs. There are also other types of regularly posted articles, such as lists of various things. You might ask, does anyone collect the names of all the articles that are posted regularly to Usenet? The answer is yes, and this list—called the Periodic Informational Postings List—is itself posted regularly to Usenet. (Imagine the philosophical implications.) This list is a long one, so here is a web site that makes it easy to find what you want.

Web:
> http://www.cis.ohio-state.edu/hypertext/faq/usenet/periodic-postings/top.html
> http://www.lib.ox.ac.uk/internet/news/faq/by_category.periodic-postings.html

Usenet FAQ Archives

It's the middle of the night. An emergency arises that requires you to read one of the Usenet frequently asked question lists. So you fire up your favorite newsreader program only to find that the article you want has expired. Never you mind. Many of the Usenet FAQs are available on the Web.

Web:
> http://www.cis.ohio-state.edu/hypertext/faq/usenet/top.html
> http://www.cs.ruu.nl/cgi-bin/faqwais
> http://www.lib.ox.ac.uk/internet/news/faq/by_group.index.html

FASHION AND CLOTHING

Fashion Talk and General Discussion

It's a nice feeling when you're dressed in a spiffy new outfit with all the right accessories and people turn to look as you walk down the street. Impress your friends, family, and total strangers with your fashion sense and the clothing tips you've learned while hanging out on the Internet. Clothing pros, trendsetters, and the hopelessly unfashionable find their way to these newsgroups to share ideas or get answers to questions.

Usenet:
> alt.fashion

Hair Care

Do you look good? Do you want to? Consult this web site if you want to be in style, look good, and be the envy of everyone on the Net.

Web:
> http://www.hairnet.com/

FOLKLORE, MYTHS AND LEGENDS

Encyclopedia of Myths and Legends

High in content and easily searchable, these sites offer a wealth of information about mythology, legends, and folkore. Read about all sorts of creatures, gods, goddesses, and their origins and history.

Web:
> http://www.clubi.ie/lestat/godsmen.html
> http://www.pantheon.org/myth/

F

Mythical Animals

As cute as they are, little groundhogs and frolicking squirrels can get tiresome after a while. Imagine a world in which all sorts of bizarre creatures were alive and roaming your neighborhood. What fun it would be to have to worry about gorgons and harpies hastening your demise, mischievous satyrs, graceful unicorns, and beautiful mermaids who nip at your toes as you tread water. Read about all forms of mythical creatures and their origins.

Usenet:
> alt.mythology.mythic-animals

Myths and Legends

The perfect place for storytime, this site has a large archive of myths and legends from a variety of cultures: Norse, Teutonic, Greek, Roman, Native American, Spanish, Gothic Horror, Medieval and Renaissance.

Web:
> http://pubpages.unh.edu/~cbsiren/myth.html

FOOD AND DRINK

Fat-Free Food

Remember, just because it has no taste doesn't mean it's good for you. Immerse yourself in the world of fat-free fanatics and lower your cholesterol, blood pressure, and enjoyment quotient.

Usenet:
>   alt.food.fat-free

Food Labeling Information

Rulings on labeling requirements for ingredients, serving sizes, terms, fat and cancer, fruits and vegetables, nutritional claims, and other related topics.

Web:
>   http://vm.cfsan.fda.gov/label.html

A mailing list for the exchange of recipes, discussion of cooking procedures, nutrition, cookbooks, spices, cookware and any other fun things you can do in a kitchen. The **vnr-cul** list is for culinary professionals.

Listserv Mailing List:
>   List Name: **eat-l**
>   Subscribe to: **listserv@listserv.vt.edu**

Majordomo Mailing List:
>   List Name: **vnr-cul**
>   Subscribe to: **majordomo@freud.thomson.com**

Foodplex

Don't feel guilty about your food. Enjoy yourself with the help of this guilt-free web page dedicated to the pleasure of fine food. Information about food, recipes, food humor and a column which will answer readers' food questions.

Web:
>   http://www.gigaplex.com/food/index.htm

Internet Bar

Bartenders, entertainers and party animals will love this site, which offers a variety of interesting mixed drink information. Browse the recipe archives, look at the drink of the week or ask a bartender a question. There is lots of great information here.

Web:
>   http://www.epact.se/acats/

FREEDOM

ACLU

The ACLU is the American Civil Liberties Union. Their charter is to protect American constitutional rights even when everyone else is asleep at the political switch. You may not always agree with the ACLU, but I guarantee that you will always have an opinion. Their web site contains speeches, publications, reports, legislative alerts, Supreme Court filings, and other information from the land of the generally free and occasionally brave.

Web:
>   http://www.aclu.org/

Banned Books

The only thing worse than a banned book is two banned books. Unfortunately, banning books did not die out with Hitler and the Nazis. Today, even in the U.S., there are still people who are trying to ban books that challenge their particular political and social agendas. Find out more about it on the Net. You will be surprised how many books have been banned over the years. Moreover, since you are on the Net where everything can be linked to something else, you can not only learn about the banned books, you can, in many cases, read them on your own screen, in the privacy of your own home.

Web:
>   http://www.cs.cmu.edu/Web/People/spok/banned-books.html

F

Free Speech Mailing List

A forum for discussing free speech issues. Topics here include current and historical issues in freedom of expression, reviews of recent books and articles related to free speech, constitutional interpretation, research opportunities, privacy, censorship, and other areas relating to freedom of expression in the United States and elsewhere.

Listserv Mailing List:
List Name: **amend1-l**
Subscribe to: **listserv@uafsysb.uark.edu**

Medical Privacy

A compilation of companies who do some form of human quality tests that violate your rights to privacy. Who wants urine? Who wants blood? Who wants to crack open your skull and look inside? Helpful hint: Whatever happens, you can always say that you didn't inhale.

Web:
http://www.eff.org/pub/Privacy/Medical

FUN

Chat

Are you bored? Here are a some great places to chew the virtual fat with other Internet folks. Once you are on the Net, there will always be someone (or many someones) to whom you can talk, day and night, night and day.

IRC:
#chat
#hello
#talk

Electronic Postcards

Send greetings to friends so they will think you are thoughtful and considerate. Pick from a selection of graphics, fill out the form with your message and send it on its way. You can preview the card before you send it in case you made any really embarrassing mistakes.

Web:
http://home.stlnet.com/~binnie/cybrcard.htm
http://www.maxracks.com/
http://www.webcircle.com/users/ladydi/index5a.htm

Madlibs

If your Web browser has forms, you will have loads of fun filling in nouns, adjectives, and other words out of which the computer will weave a story. This is just like the paper Madlibs, only you don't need a group of friends to play it.

Web:
> http://www.mit.edu:8001/madlib/

GAMES AND PUZZLES

Crossword Puzzles

Do you like crossword puzzles? There are many, many puzzles on the Net that you can access for free whenever you want. There are also dictionaries, word lists, guides, computer programs, helpful tips, and a great deal of other crossword-related material, including a FAQ (frequently asked question list). Now, if someone would only tell me the three-letter word for an Australian bird, and the two-letter name for the sun god, my life would be complete.

Web:
> http://www.dareware.com/cross.htm
> http://www.lib.ox.ac.uk/internet/news/faq/archive/crossword-faq.part1.html
> http://www.primate.wisc.edu/people/hamel/cp.html
> http://www.zia.com/life/web-games/crossword-puzzles/

Games Domain

The Games Domain is a large, well-organized collection of games, games and more games. No matter what you enjoy, I guarantee there will be something here for you. Aside from links to actual games, you will find information, articles, FAQs, patches, tips and hints, and more.

Web:
> http://www.gamesdomain.co.uk/
> http://www.gamesdomain.com/

Interactive Web Games

Here's a fun web page with several interactive games, including Java games. Just the ticket when work gets slow.

Web:
> http://www.bu.edu/Games/games.html

G

GARDENING

Garden Encyclopedia

Flip through this easy-to-use encyclopedia of gardening and get information on soils, plants, tools, trimming, digging, mulching, and more. Never again will you have to wonder how much osmunda fiber to use for your epiphitic orchids or what the difference is between a bush hook and a sickle.

Web:
http://www.btw.com/garden_archive/

Garden Gate

It's possible to spend hours reading about gardening instead of actually doing any real gardening. When you can't be participating in the real thing, try the virtual thing at the Garden Gate. Find FAQs, plant lists, a reading room, information on houseplants, reviews of gardening software and tours of botanical gardens and greenhouses around the world.

Web:
http://www.prairienet.org/ag/garden/

Virtual Garden

Time-Life has created a beautifully designed web site containing an interactive plant encyclopedia, directory of house plants, and gardening articles from major magazines.

Web:
http://pathfinder.com/vg/

GAY, LESBIAN, BISEXUAL

Collected Queer Information

A large collection of gay, lesbian and bisexual resources, including articles, a list of gay, lesbian, bisexual and supportive businesses, film lists, news, a bisexual resource list, advice, a link to the Queer National Homeland in Webworld, and links to other related resources.

Web:
http://www.cs.cmu.edu/Web/People/mjw/Queer/MainPage.html

Domestic Partners

It's amazing that problems can be caused by not having a little piece of paper. Even if you have signed on to your relationship for life, it doesn't legally count without the certificate. This site has information about domestic partnerships, same-sex marriages, legal status, policies at various universities, and related issues.

Web:
> http://www.cs.cmu.edu/afs/cs.cmu.edu/user/scotts/domestic-partners/mainpage. html

Gay, Lesbian and Bisexual Resources

There are lots of gay-related resources on the Net. Here is a good place to start when you are searching for something in particular or simply browsing for something new and interesting.

Web:
> http://www.suba.com/~outlines/hotlist.html

Queer Zines

Looking for something good to read? Have a look at this list of zines that relate to gays, lesbians and bisexuals. This informative list covers print zines that are not accessible on the Net, but it gives all the details on how to subscribe or find the publications in question.

Web:
> http://www.qrd.org/qrd/media/magazines/

GENEALOGY

Genealogy Software

Once you get started with genealogy, you will find that using a computer makes things a *lot* easier. For example, the program I use is able to print nice charts of various parts of the family tree. I then send these charts to relatives and ask them for changes and additions, which has worked out nicely. Here are some places to help you find the software you need to do the best possible job.

Web:
> http://www.coast.net/SimTel/msdos/genealgy.html
> http://www.oz.net/~cyndihow/software.htm
> http://www.toltbbs.com/~kbasile/software.html

Genealogy Talk and General Discussion

The Internet is a global community—a great place from which to track down family members from way-back-when. Usenet offers a convenient forum not only to discuss ways of researching, what kinds of software and resources are available, or to compare anecdotes of your quests, but you can also ask for information on family names. Plenty of sharing goes on here. Find that long-lost second-half-cousin-twice-removed who broke all your crayons when you were seven and remind him you want all 64 colors, plus the built-in sharpener.

Usenet:
>   alt.genealogy
>   soc.genealogy.misc

Special Genealogy Resources

Here are some Internet sites that will point you in the right direction for finding genealogy resources. Lots of useful information whenever you need it, as well as some great places to browse.

Web:
>   http://genealogy.emcee.com/
>   http://www.genhomepage.com/

GEOGRAPHY

CIA World Factbook

Detailed information about every country and territory in the world. Includes geographic, climate, economic, and political information. This is a fantastic resource with which you should become familiar; you never know what you will find. For example, I just found out that 97 percent of Canadians over 15 years old can read and write. (The others, presumably, use a graphical user interface.)

Web:
>   http://www.odci.gov/cia/publications/nsolo/wfb-all.htm

Earth Rise

Images of the Earth by region, movies of the Earth rotating, images of the Earth from space and the moon, Earth icons, details of the Xearth globe picture creation program, and more.

Web:
   http://earthrise.sdsc.edu/

Geography-Related Web Sites

Here are lots of sources of geographical information on the Net. Maps, data, products—a good selection of resources for the geographically inclined.

Web:
   http://www.geog.le.ac.uk/cti/geosub.html

GEOLOGY

Earthquakes

People talk a lot about earthquakes, but few people actually know much about them. Moreover, most people don't realize that earthquakes are not unusual. Every week, there are a number of earthquakes around the world, some of them large. This site contains a variety of information designed to allow anyone to keep up on how Mother Earth is shaking. Tune in at any time and you may be surprised what happened in the last week.

Web:
   http://www.seismo-watch.com/

Smithsonian Gem and Mineral Collection

A collection of images and descriptions of different types of gems and minerals. This page presents you with a thumbnail picture of the images available, then you can select these to view the gem or mineral in more detail in a full-size image.

Web:
   http://galaxy.einet.net/images/gems/gems-icons.html

G

U.S. Geological Survey

The U. S. Geological Survey (USGS), a part of the United States Department of the Interior, is America's largest agency devoted to earth science. The USGS creates and provides (for free) an enormous amount of information relating to geology (rocks and soil), topography (lay of the land), and hydrology (water). There are lots of maps and databases, as well as many research analyses of natural resources.

Web:
> http://info.er.usgs.gov/

GOVERNMENT: INTERNATIONAL

Embassies in Washington, D.C.

When it's late at night and you are in the mood for a little political intrigue, take a look at these embassy-related links. You'll get the goods on the staff and resources of the Washington, D.C., embassy community, embassy web sites, press releases, commerce and trade information, as well as travel and tourism reports. Remember, when you're in Washington, D.C., you can't be too careful. Today's attaché to the assistant secretary for international trade regulations could be tomorrow's industrial spy.

Web:
> http://www.embassy.org/

United Nations

On January 1, 1942, during World War II, representatives of 26 countries signed the "Declaration by United Nations", in which they promised to continue fighting together against the Axis (the bad guys). The name "United Nations" was coined by U.S. President Franklin Roosevelt. On June 26, 1945, the United Nations as we know it was established with the signing of the "United Nations Charter". In 1945, the U.N. had 51 member countries. Today, there are 185. The United Nations oversees a great many international organizations such as the Security Council, the General Assembly, the International Court of Justice, the United Nations Children's Fund (UNICEF), the World Health Organization, the World Bank, and so on. Overall, the U.N. has 54,000 employees—about the same as Disney World + Disneyland.

Web:
> http://www.un.org/
> http://www.unsystem.org/

Usenet:
> alt.politics.org.un

U.S. International Aid

USAID (United States Agency for International Development) is an independent government agency that provides foreign assistance and humanitarian aid to "advance the political and economic interests of the United States". Read about their goals and studies: regional information, population and health information, economic growth studies, and global environmental issues. I'm trying to get a government grant to send me on an all-expense paid trip to the south of France. The only problem is showing how such a trip would be in the economic interests of the United States.

Web:
  http://www.info.usaid.gov/

World Government

Do you think that we would be better off with one large world government, rather than a whole bunch of countries continually arguing with one another (not to mention clogging up the Olympics and the United Nations)? Here are some resources that you can use to explore and learn about the idea of world government. In the old Superman comics, Superman came from the planet Krypton, which was much more advanced than the Earth. In particular, the Kryptonians had one large world government. (And look where they are today.)

Web:
  http://www.bath.ac.uk/~adsjrc/eu/eu-main.html
  http://www.webcom.com/~worldgov/

G

GOVERNMENT: UNITED STATES

Executive Branch

Never again will you have to hotfoot it around the Net looking for information about the President and his minions. The Library of Congress has compiled a web page that covers resources pertaining to the executive branch of the federal government and its various departments, as well as independent executive agencies.

Web:
  http://lcweb.loc.gov/global/executive/fed.html

FedWorld

An enormous resource for scientific, technical, and other information provided by the federal government. FedWorld is taxpayer-supported through the National Technical Information Service (NTIS). It is an easy-to-use system that offers information on a wide variety of subjects.

Web:
> http://www.fedworld.gov/

Justices of the Supreme Court

The Supreme Court is the highest federal court in the United States and has jurisdiction over all the other courts in the nation. The Supreme Court consists of judges—a chief justice and eight associate justices—all of whom are nominated by the President and confirmed by the Senate. The Supreme Court has two main duties: to interpret acts of Congress, and to determine whether federal and state statutes conform to the United States Constitution. If you want the scoop on those people currently serving on the Supreme Court, check out this web site. It has a list of the justices, along with biographical data and their pictures (in case you run into one of them in the supermarket). You will also find a lengthy and fascinating collection of each judge's opinions for the court: important majority opinions, important concurring opinions, and selected dissenting opinions.

Web:
> http://www.law.cornell.edu/supct/justices/fullcourt.html

Legislative Branch

Keep up with what's going on in the U.S. legislative branch of the government. The Library of Congress has put together a nice selection of resources pertaining to Congress, including links to web pages of various members of Congress and notations on the members' voting records.

Web:
> http://lcweb.loc.gov/global/legislative/congress.html

HEALTH

Good Health Web

The Good Health Web is a collection of links to health-related Internet resources. Here you will find information about organizations, news, discussions, FAQs, mailing lists, and a library of health topics.

Web:
> http://www.social.com/health/

Nutrition

Should you eat the Twinkie or opt for another seaweed sandwich? Join the conversation and talk about all aspects of diet and eating. Vitamins, carbohydrates, proteins, fats, minerals, fiber—the usual gang of suspects is waiting for you here.

Web:
> http://web.bu.edu/COHIS/nutrtion/nutri.htm

Usenet:
> sci.med.nutrition

Smoking Addiction

The phrase "the only way to break a bad habit is to drop it" was invented by someone who never had to quit smoking. It's a habit that is hard to break whether you quit altogether or try to taper off. Find support from other people recovering from their addiction to cigarettes or from people who have already recovered.

Usenet:
> alt.support.non-smokers
> alt.support.stop-smoking

H

HERBS

Herb Talk and General Discussion

Things that grow and things that don't, plants that heal and plants that won't, little herbs that stink and flower, have their merit and their power. Here's the place where people go, to talk about the herbs to grow, for cooking, eating, dying blue, to give as gifts, for healing, too.

Usenet:
    alt.folklore.herbs

Herbs and Spices

When you are looking for the real dirt on herbs and spices, have a look at this web page, which offers a lengthy index of various herbs for cooking and medicinal purposes. Learn how to cook with herbs, read historical and geographical information, see pictures and recipes, or get tips on how to grow your own herbs.

Web:
    http://www.teleport.com/~ronl/herbs/herbs.html

Medicinal Herbs

The Medicinal Herb Garden is located on the campus of the University of Washington in Seattle. It provides a great resource for anyone interested in herbs, and is a pleasant place to visit. This Internet site has lots of information about the many herbs that grow in the garden, as well as a photo tour. Just the thing to share with that special someone in your life.

Web:
    http://www.nnlm.nlm.nih.gov/pnr/uwmhg/

Pictures of Herbs

Herbs are sometimes hard to identify, and if you are putting them in your mouth, it's not a good idea to make a mistake. This archive can help. It has a collection of pictures of herbs in various stages of growth.

Web:
    http://www.rt66.com/hrbmoore/HOMEPAGE/

HISTORICAL DOCUMENTS

American Historical Documents

Many people have heard about the important American historical documents. But few people have had the opportunity to look at the actual texts. Here is your chance. Take a look at the Unites States Constitution, Amendments to the Constitution, Annapolis Convention, Articles of Confederation, Bill of Rights, Charlottetown Resolves, Continental Congress Resolves, Japanese and German surrenders, M. L. King's "I Have a Dream" speech, inaugural addresses, the Monroe Doctrine, Rights of Man, treaties, and more.

Web:

http://history.cc.ukans.edu/carrie/docs/docs_us.html
http://www.rci.rutgers.edu/~snash/amhist.html

Emancipation Proclamation

In the United States, the expression "Lincoln freed the slaves" is commonly used as an all-purpose rejoinder in certain sticky social situations, such as when your boss tells you to work overtime without extra pay, or when your mother forces you to clean up your room. But just how did Lincoln free the slaves? At the time of the Civil War, Lincoln was president of the Union (the northern states), leading them against the Confederacy (the southern states). On September 17, 1862—possibly the bloodiest day of the Civil War—the Battle of Antietam in western Maryland ended with combined losses of over 23,000 men. Lincoln used the occasion to issue the Emancipation Proclamation, which declared free all slaves in states still in rebellion against the Union. The slaves were not actually freed until April 9, 1865, when the Union won its final victory against the Confederacy. If any of this interests you, take a few minutes to look at the actual proclamation (and at the fine print contained therein).

Web:

http://www.nps.gov/ncro/anti/emancipation.html

Historical Document Archive

An archive of historical documents, including the Magna Carta, the U.S. Bill of Rights, Lincoln's Second Inaugural Address, the Monroe Doctrine, the Mayflower Compact, the Emancipation Proclamation, and many others.

Web:

http://grid.let.rug.nl/~welling/usa/othertexts.html

H

HISTORY

American Memory Collection

The Library of Congress has put together these "scrapbooks" of American history and culture. Flip through and look at Civil War photographs, portraits of literary figures, artists and celebrities, photos of rural America, and hear sound recordings of speeches that were delivered around the World War I era.

Web:
> http://lcweb2.loc.gov/ammem/

Feudal Terms

Feudalism was a form of social organization common in Western Europe from the fall of Charlemagne's empire (9th century) to the rise of the absolute French, Spanish and English monarchies (14th century and later). An exact definition of feudalism is hard to give, but you won't go far wrong if you think of it as a system with three main characteristics: strict social classes, law based on local customs, and land holding dependent upon a fee. If you want to read or talk about things feudal, you will need the proper vocabulary, so here is an online glossary with a large number of feudal words, from "abbey" to "witen".

Web:
> http://history.cc.ukans.edu/history/subject_tree/e3/gen/feudal-terms/
> http://www.arts.cuhk.hk/LocalFile/feudalterm.html

This Day in History

Fill your mind with some trivial thoughts by finding out who was born and who died on this day in history. You never know when an important event or holiday is coming up for which you need to dress appropriately. Don't be caught unaware.

Web:
> http://www.eb.com/cgi-bin/bio.pl
> http://www.historychannel.com/historychannel/thisday/

HOBBIES

Origami

In the 6th century, the secret of paper was carried by Buddhist monks from China to Japan. The Japanese soon integrated paper into their culture. Traditional designs were passed down orally, from one generation to the next. Creative paper folding with non-traditional designs was popularized by Akira Yoshizawa, starting in the 1930s. Modern origami (from the Japanese words for "fold paper") is a pastime enjoyed all over the world. Origami is a wonderful hobby to explore, and the Net is the place to start learning. Read about all facets of origami including bibliographies, folding techniques, display ideas and materials.

Web:
   http://www.datt.co.jp/Origami/

Usenet:
   alt.arts.origami

Listserv Mailing List:
   List Name: **origami-l**
   Subscribe to: **listserv@nstn.ca**

Puzzles

What's a six-letter word for the best place to participate in a discussion over the Net? Drive your friends wild with an endless supply of puzzles, quizzes, and problems. Open yourself up for a little brain teasing, or be merciless and create a puzzle that hardly anyone can solve. (!tenesU :rewsnA)

Web:
   http://www.scit.wlv.ac.uk/university/scit/maths/puzzle.htm

Usenet:
   rec.puzzles
   rec.puzzles.crosswords

Treasure Hunting

Treasure is good. Imagine a great fantasy scenario in which you are walking along the beach and stumble across a barnacle-encrusted chest. You break it open and out tumble thousands of gold coins. Then a thousand federal agents come racing toward you waving paper and red tape. Wait, strike that last part. This is a fantasy. If you like treasure hunting, this is a great place to start.

Web:
   http://onlinether.com/

H

HOLIDAYS AND CELEBRATIONS

Party Talk and General Discussion

On the Internet, it's party time all the time. At least in Usenet. Thousands of people around the world crash **alt.party** to see the latest business in the party scene. Talk about upcoming parties, ideas and plans for parties, or wild party experiences. And you don't have to worry about regretting anything in the morning.

Usenet:
    alt.party

HOME MAINTENANCE

Books That Work

If you are too proud to ask for advice or help around the house, you can safely gain assistance without anyone ever knowing. Utilize these Books That Work. You'll find lots of interesting articles and hints about problems with home repair, landscaping, gardening, automotive and real estate.

Web:
    http://www.btw.com/

Controlling Pests

Information about how to be inhospitable to those tiny pests who just love to make themselves at home in your home. If it moves, it's on the Net.

Web:
    http://www.nj.com/yucky/getrid/
    http://www.orkin.com/

HUMANITIES AND SOCIAL SCIENCES

Coombspapers Social Sciences Server

A large repository of social science and humanities papers, offprints, departmental publications, bibliographies, directories, abstracts of theses, and other material.

Web:
    http://coombs.anu.edu.au/

Humanities Hub

A fabulous collection of links relating to anthropology, theology, cultural studies, dictionaries, architecture, women's resources, sociology, European studies, film and media, gender studies, philosophy, languages and many other humanities resources.

Web:
> http://www.gu.edu.au/gwis/hub/hub.home.html

Sociology Resources

The difference between a sociologist and a voyeur is that a sociologist gets paid to watch people. There are lots of sociology resources on the Net and one nice collection is at the Virtual Library. This list of links will take you to institutions, specialized resources and related fields.

Web:
> http://www.w3.org/hypertext/DataSources/bySubject/Sociology/Overview.html

HUMOR AND JOKES

Best of Usenet

Don't spend hours searching through thousands of newsgroups looking for the funny stuff. Someone has already done the dirty work for you. If you are in the market for humor, you can find lots of laughs with one-stop shopping by checking out the group that claims to have the best of what Usenet has to offer. The **alt.humor.best-of-usenet** group has the funny stuff and **alt.humor.best-of-usenet.d** is where you can talk about the funny stuff.

Usenet:
> alt.humor.best-of-usenet
> alt.humor.best-of-usenet.d

Canonical Lists

Need that joke for a special occasion? Check out the **rec.humor** archives where you can find not only canonical lists of jokes, but the canonical list of canonical lists. Blonde jokes, answering machine messages, lawyer jokes, things that are politically incorrect, and a list of people in need of a good, hard caning. The archives go on and on.

Web:
> http://www.yotta.com/rechumor/

H

Humor Archives

Where do you go when you need a good laugh, and you can't find your old high school yearbook? To the Net, of course. Here are some Internet resources that will lead you to enough jokes, humor and overall silliness to supply the entire Peruvian army.

Web:
> http://www.intermarket.net/laughweb/
> http://www.visi.com/~nathan/humor/

INTERNET

Domain Name Registration

Within any type of Internet address, the name of the computer is called the domain name or, more simply, the domain. For example, in the address **president@ whitehouse.gov**, the domain is **whitehouse.gov**. In **http://canada.gc.ca/**, the domain is **canada.gc.ca**. Have you ever wondered how these names are assigned? There are two systems. Outside the United States, all addresses end with a two-letter country code. In our second example, for instance, the two-letter country code is **ca**, indicating that this is a Canadian domain. The United States uses a different system. There is a country code (**us**), but it's not used much. Instead, most people use an older system that was devised before the Internet became international. The last part of the domain—called the top-level domain—is a three-letter code. The most common of these top-level domains are **com** (commercial), **edu** (educational), **gov** (government), **org** (non-profit organizations) and **net** (network providers). If you have used the Net much, you will have noticed that the **com** top-level domain is also used for miscellaneous addresses that don't fit into another category. So how do you register a domain? You can either have your Internet service provider (ISP) do it for you, or you can do it yourself. In the U.S., most of the registration is done by the InterNIC Registration Services. For assistance, connect to their web page and read the help information. If you are outside the U.S., I have included a second web site (also maintained by the InterNIC) that contains links to other registration organizations.

Web:
> http://rs.internic.net/help/other-reg.html
> http://rs.internic.net/rs-internic.html

Internet News

The Internet changes so fast that literally no one can keep up on what's happening. However, if you would like to keep in touch, here are some places that can help. You can check every week, every day, or even every hour, and you will find lots and lot of news articles. In particular, you will find coverage of all the companies that are doing business related to the Net.

Web:
> http://www.cnet.com/
> http://www.iworld.com/

Internet Service Providers

An Internet service provider (ISP) is a company or organization that provides access to the Internet. For example, if you have a computer at home, you access the Net by having your computer connect to an ISP. The web page contains a list of public Internet service providers. If you need to find an ISP for a particular area, this is a good place to look. (If you do not already have access, ask a friend to help you by looking at the list to find out what providers serve your area.) For discussion about Internet access, you can read the Usenet groups.

Web:
> http://thelist.iworld.com/

Usenet:
> alt.internet.access.wanted
> alt.internet.services

Web Talk and General Discussion

Would you like to talk about the Web? Goodness knows there is a lot to say. The Usenet groups are for ongoing discussions about various aspects of the Web. The **advocacy** group is for opinion. The **announce** group is for announcements. This is a good place to let people know about a new web site. The **misc** group is for everything else related to the Web. For talking in real time, try the IRC channel.

Usenet:
> comp.infosystems.www.advocacy
> comp.infosystems.www.announce
> comp.infosystems.www.misc

IRC:
> #www

INTERNET RESOURCES

Archie Client Programs

Archie clients for Windows and Macintosh.

Web:

http://cws.iworld.com/16ftp.html
http://cws.iworld.com/32ftp.html
http://tucows.iwebstudio.com/archie95.html
http://tucows.iwebstudio.com/mac/archie.html
http://tucows.iwebstudio.com/softarc.html
http://www.jumbo.com/pages/utilities/mac/comm3/

Archie Search Facilities on the Web

Forms-based methods of archie searching via the Web. Simply enter the keywords for which you want to search.

Web:

http://hoohoo.ncsa.uiuc.edu/archie.html
http://www-ns.rutgers.edu/htbin/archie
http://www.lerc.nasa.gov/archieplex/

Audio Utilities

Software used for listening to sound files you download to your computer from the Internet.

Web:

http://cws.iworld.com/16audio.html
http://cws.iworld.com/32audio.html
http://tucows.iwebstudio.com/mac/audio.html
http://tucows.iwebstudio.com/softsoun.html
http://tucows.iwebstudio.com/sound95.html
http://wwwhost.ots.utexas.edu/mac/pub-mac-sound.html

Bitnet-Oriented Usenet Groups

A list of Bitnet mailing lists that also have their own equivalent Usenet newsgroups. This list has a brief description of what each group is about.

Web:

http://tile.net/news/bit.html

Bulletin Board Systems (BBSs)

BBSs are a fun place to spend your spare time. Try the ISCA BBS or browse the BBS list to find another BBS that suits you.

Web:
> http://dkeep.com/sbi.html

Telnet:
> Address: **bbs.isca.uiowa.edu**
> Login: **guest**

Computer Names (Strange and Interesting)

Take a look at this list containing some of the strange, interesting and funny names people have used for their computers and domains.

Web:
> http://homepage.seas.upenn.edu/~mengwong/coolhosts.html

Domain Name Registration

No matter where you are on planet Earth, you can find directions on how to register your domain name. Pick the file that relates to your geographic locality and follow the directions from there.

Web:
> http://www.yahoo.com/Computers_and_Internet/Internet/Domain_Registration/

FAQ (Frequently Asked Question List) Archives

Most questions you have can be answered by FAQs. This list of archives has FAQs from many, many Usenet groups.

Web:
> http://www.cis.ohio-state.edu/hypertext/faq/usenet/FAQ-List.html
> http://www.cs.ruu.nl/cgi-bin/faqwais
> http://www.lib.ox.ac.uk/internet/news/faq/by_group.index.html

File Compression: Macintosh

Macintosh software for archiving and compressing files.

Web:
> http://wwwhost.ots.utexas.edu/mac/pub-mac-compression.html

I

File Compression: OS/2

OS/2 software for archiving and compressing files.

Web:
> http://www.columbia.edu/~chs11/hvm/HVMindex.hobbes.os2.util.archiver.html

File Compression: Windows

Windows software for archiving and compressing files.

Web:
> http://cws.iworld.com/16comp.html
> http://cws.iworld.com/32comp.html
> http://tucows.iwebstudio.com/comp.html
> http://tucows.iwebstudio.com/comp95.html
> http://www.cdrom.com/pub/infozip/Info-Zip.html

File Types: Reference List

An explanation of various file types found on the Internet.

Web:
> http://www.matisse.net/files/formats.html
> http://www.personal.psu.edu/users/e/m/emb121/xplat/xplat.html

Ftp Client Programs

Ftp clients for Windows and Macintosh.

Web:
> http://cws.iworld.com/16ftp.html
> http://cws.iworld.com/32ftp.html
> http://mirror.apple.com/ftp-clients.html
> http://tucows.iwebstudio.com/ftp95.html
> http://tucows.iwebstudio.com/softftp.html

Gopher Client Programs

A selection of gopher clients for a variety of operating systems.

Web:
> http://cws.iworld.com/16gopher.html
> http://cws.iworld.com/32gopher.html
> http://tucows.iwebstudio.com/mac/gopher.html

HTML Converters

HTML converters make it easy to turn ordinary documents into HTML suitable for web pages. Don't do everything by hand. Pick out powerful tools to do the work for you.

Web:
> http://union.ncsa.uiuc.edu/HyperNews/get/www/html/converters.html

HTML Editors

Making web pages goes easier and faster if you use an HTML editor. Download this free software and make it do all the hard work of putting in the appropriate HTML tags and anchors.

Web:
> http://union.ncsa.uiuc.edu/HyperNews/get/www/html/editors.html

HTML Tutorials

Learn to make beautiful and interesting home pages. Take a look at these tutorials which offer documentation on HTML, how to build a page and helpful hints about style and design.

Web:
> http://www.ncsa.uiuc.edu/General/Internet/WWW/HTMLPrimer.html
> http://www.netusa1.net/~jbornema/html.html

Internet Service Providers

There are quite a few listings of service providers on the Net. Check all of them to get a more complete look of the available service providers in your area. These lists offer pricing and contact information. Some will even rate the listed providers.

Web:
> http://thelist.iworld.com/
> http://www.herbison.com/herbison/iap_meta_list.html
> http://www.netalert.com/

Internet Timeline

A timeline of the Internet, beginning in 1956. This document shows the growth of the Internet in relation to significant landmarks in history.

Web:
> http://info.isoc.org/guest/zakon/Internet/History/HIT.html

I

IRC: Bots

Bot programs, scripts and documentation.

Web:
>   http://www.indy.net/~trekkie/botfq1.html
>   http://www.valuserve.com/~robey/eggdrop/

Usenet:
>   alt.irc.bots

IRC: Client Programs

IRC clients for a variety of operating systems.

Web:
>   http://www.neosoft.com/~biscuits/

IRC: Client Programs for Macintosh

Join in the IRC fun using this IRC client for the Mac.

Web:
>   http://www.xs4all.nl/~ircle/

IRC: Client Programs for Windows

Browse these collections of IRC clients for Windows and pick the one you like. Or try them all out and decide which is best for you.

Web:
>   http://cws.iworld.com/16irc.html
>   http://cws.iworld.com/32irc.html
>   http://tucows.iwebstudio.com/room95.html

IRC: Document Collections

Collections of informative writings, documents, FAQs and technical abstracts relating to IRC.

Web:
>   http://urth.acsu.buffalo.edu/irc/WWW/ircdocs.html
>   http://www2.undernet.org:8080/~cs93jtl/IRC.html

IRC: FAQ (Frequently Asked Question List)

Frequently asked questions and answers about Internet Relay Chat.

Web:

http://www.kei.com/irc.html

IRC: Help for the `irc` Client Program

Help documentation for the **irc** client program. This is a list of useful commands along with explanations.

Web:

http://www.kei.com/irc.html

IRC: List of IRC Networks

A list of various IRC networks accompanied by descriptions of each.

Web:

http://www2.undernet.org:8080/~cs93jtl/IRCNets.html

IRC: Primer

An IRC primer that offers information on the history of IRC, basic tips on how to start, explanations of various commands and hints on where to get IRC clients.

Web:

http://cbl.leeds.ac.uk/nikos/tex2html/examples/IRCprimer1.1/IRCprimer1.1.html

IRC: Public IRC Clients

If you want to use IRC with a shell account, but there is no IRC client on your system and you can't get the system administrator to install one, you can telnet to one of these public Undernet IRC clients.

Web:

http://murc.undernet.org/undernet/telnet.html
http://www2.undernet.org:8080/~cs93jtl/Undernet.html

ISDN

A directory of various resources around the Net, including user guides, local information, a directory of ISDN service providers, user groups, vendors and sellers, and technical information about ISDN.

Web:
http://www.alumni.caltech.edu/~dank/isdn/

Macintosh Internet Client Programs

Macintosh users, don't feel left out of the free software gold rush on the Internet. Here is a list of clients you can download to your computer. In no time you will be set up and ready to go.

Web:
http://www.tfs.net/business/tbutler/PPP/main.html

Mail Client Programs

Mail clients are great if you want to store your mail on your own computer. Check out these two powerful mail clients: Eudora and Pegasus.

Web:
http://mirkwood.ucc.uconn.edu/pmail/pmail.html
http://www.eudora.com/

Mail to Other Networks

Having trouble sending mail to your friend on an obscure network? The **nova** site has an easy-to-use form you can fill out which will translate addresses for you so you will know how to send from one network to another. You can also find documents on sending email, as well as information about various networks.

Web:
http://www.nova.edu/Inter-Links/cgi-bin/inmgq.pl

Mailing Lists: Internet List-of-Lists

A large, searchable collection of mailing lists along with brief descriptions of what each list is about.

Web:
http://catalog.com/vivian/interest-group-search.html

Mailing Lists: New Bitnet Mailing Lists

When you are looking for a new mailing list to spice up your mail box, try this mailing list which announces new mailing lists as they are made available.

Usenet:
bit.listserv.new-list

Listserv Mailing List:
List Name: **new-list**
Subscribe to: **listserv@vm1.nodak.edu**

Mailing Lists: Publicly Accessible Mailing Lists

A huge list of publicly accessible mailing lists. These lists cover a variety of topics. Browse through them; you are bound to find something you like.

Web:
http://www.neosoft.com/internet/paml

Usenet:
news.lists

Mailing Lists: Search Engine

Enter keywords into this handy web form and get back a list of mailing list descriptions that contain your keyword. This is a fast way to find a mailing list pertaining to specific topics.

Web:
http://www.liszt.com/

Muds: Client Programs

Make mudding even more fun and adventurous with the help of a mud client. This site has clients for a variety of operating systems.

Web:
http://www.mudconnect.com/mud_links.html#clients

I

Muds: Educational Muds

A list of educational muds which act not only as learning environments, but also as gathering places for educators. Among the topics covered at these muds are foreign languages, history, geography and science.

Web:
>http://www.pitt.edu/~jrgst7/MOOcentral.html

Muds: FAQs (Frequently Asked Question Lists)

Frequently asked questions and answers about DikuMuds, LPMuds and the TinyMud family.

Web:
>http://www.cis.ohio-state.edu/hypertext/faq/usenet/games/mud-faq/top.html

Muds: History

A collection of writings, Usenet postings and letters relating to the history of muds.

Web:
>http://www.apocalypse.org/pub/u/lpb/muddex/

Muds: Lists of Muds

There are several lists of muds which offer the addresses of all types of muds, both adventure and social.

Web:
>http://www.cm.cf.ac.uk/User/Andrew.Wilson/MUDlist/
>http://www.gulf.net/~kverge/
>http://www.mudconnect.com/

Muds: Player Killing Muds

Muds that are specifically centered around players killing each other.

Telnet:
>Address: **genocide.shsu.edu**
>Port: **2222**
>Address: **mud.stanford.edu**
>Port: **2010**
>Address: **stickmud.jyu.fi**
>Port: **7680**

Muds: Timeline

A timeline that relates important events in the culture and history of muds.

Web:
> http://www.apocalypse.org/pub/u/lpb/muddex/

Muds: Usenet Discussion Groups

Discussion groups relating to various mud topics such as types of muds, particular muds, programming and general mud discussion.

Usenet:
> alt.fan.furry.muck
> alt.flame.mud
> alt.mud
> alt.mud.bsx
> alt.mud.chupchups
> alt.mud.german
> alt.mud.lp
> alt.mud.moo
> alt.mud.programming
> alt.mud.tiny
> alt.mudders.anonymous
> rec.games.mud.admin
> rec.games.mud.announce
> rec.games.mud.diku
> rec.games.mud.lp
> rec.games.mud.misc
> rec.games.mud.moo
> rec.games.mud.tiny

OS/2 Internet Client Programs

Those of you who are sticking with OS/2 through the frantic development of the various Windows operating systems have no reason to worry. Yes, you can find OS/2 clients on the Net.

Web:
> http://www.phoenix.net/~vccubed/os2apps.html
> http://www.state.ky.us/software/os2.html

Personal Home Pages

A collection of personal home pages: huge lists of people around the world who have made web pages for themselves.

Web:
> http://www.peoplepage.com/

Postscript Utilities

Documentation and utilities for viewing and printing postscript files.

Web:
> http://www.jumbo.com/pages/utilities/dos/postscript/
> http://yoyo.cc.monash.edu.au/~wigs/postscript/

PPP Software

Get connected to the Internet with PPP software. These sites offer a variety of PPP software to suit your needs regardless of your computing platform.

Web:
> http://theory.cs.uni-bonn.de/ppp/part5.html
> http://www.grfn.org/admin/pppsoft.html

Smileys

Tired of using the same old smiley? Find one that is just right for you or use these files to decipher a strange smiley you have seen on the Net.

Web:
> http://members.aol.com/bearpage/smileys.htm
> http://www.io.com/internet/eegtti/eeg_286.html

Talking: `talk`-Compatible Client for Macintosh

A great Macintosh **talk**-compatible client that will allow you to talk one-on-one with other Internet users.

Web:
> http://www.umich.edu/~archive/mac/util/comm/talk1.11.sit.hqx

Talking: `ytalk`

The **ytalk** program is a fantastic talk program. Download it for free and spend all night talking to a friend.

Web:
> ftp://ftp.digital.com/pub/usenet/comp.sources.unix/volume27/ytalk-3.0/

Talking: Direct Connections

There are a variety of ways to talk to other people on the Internet. These sites offer software for making direct connections from your computer to someone else's computer.

Web:
> ftp://ftp.deltanet.com/pub/macintosh_files/talk-111.hqx
> http://www.elf.com/elf/wintalk/wintalk.html
> http://www.tribal.com/powwow/

Talking: Talk Clients for Windows

This page offers a selection of talk clients for Windows users, including **talk**-compatible clients.

Web:
> http://tucows.iwebstudio.com/direct.html
> http://tucows.iwebstudio.com/direct95.html
> http://www.ccs.org/winsock/talk.html
> http://www.tridel.com.ph/oasis/chat.htm

Talking: Talkers

These sites have lists of talkers, social environments where you can meet and chat with people from around the world.

Web:
> http://proffa.cc.tut.fi/~k113973/talkers/
> http://ulibnet.mtsu.edu/~msimms/lists/talkers/

Talking: Telephone-like Systems

If you've been looking for a way to spend less money on long-distance bills, try talking over the computer. With this software and the proper equipment, you can talk for hours to people all over the world and not have to pay long-distance charges.

Web:
>   http://cws.iworld.com/16phone.html
>   http://cws.iworld.com/32phone.html
>   http://tucows.iwebstudio.com/direct.html
>   http://tucows.iwebstudio.com/direct95.html

Talking: Web-based Talk

You don't have to have a talk client to talk over the Internet. Use your browser to chat with people around the world at some of these colorful servers.

Web:
>   http://wbs.net/
>   http://www.mojoski.com/chat/
>   http://www.theglobe.com/
>   http://www2.infi.net/talker/

TCP/IP Software

Windows users can find TCP/IP software on the Net for free. There are several types available. Browse around and take your pick of the software you like the best.

Web:
>   http://www.winsock.com/wsdir/

Telnet: Client Programs for Macintosh

Telnet clients for the Macintosh operating system.

Web:
>   http://www.x-net.net/x-net/software.htm#telnet

Telnet: Client Programs for Windows

Telnet clients for the Windows operating system.

Web:
>   http://tucows.iwebstudio.com/softterm.html
>   http://tucows.iwebstudio.com/term95.html

Top-Level Internet Domains

This is an updated list of top-level Internet domains and their corresponding countries.

Web:
> http://www.ics.uci.edu/WebSoft/wwwstat/country-codes.txt

Usenet: Complaints About Signatures

This newsgroup is dedicated to the pastime of complaining about and making fun of signatures people use on their Usenet posts. The group is full of wit and interesting to read.

Usenet:
> alt.fan.warlord

Usenet: Flame Newsgroups

Usenet groups entirely devoted to ranting, raving and complaining about various aspects of life.

Usenet:
> alt.flame
> alt.flame.abortion
> alt.flame.airlines
> alt.flame.landlord
> alt.flame.mud
> alt.flame.net-cops
> alt.flame.parents
> alt.flame.pascal
> alt.flame.pizza.greasy
> alt.flame.professor
> alt.flame.right-wing-conservatives
> alt.flame.roommate
> alt.flame.rush-limbaugh
> alt.flame.spelling

Usenet: How to Start a Newsgroup

Here's all the information you need to know about starting your own **alt** group or mainstream hierarchy group. Each of these files is a FAQ compiled and regularly posted to Usenet.

Web:
> http://www.math.psu.edu/barr/alt-creation-guide.html

Usenet: Humor Newsgroups

There are lots of humor-related newsgroups on Usenet. This list offers a variety of different types of humor to pass the time.

Usenet:
> alt.atheism.satire
> alt.humor
> alt.humor.best-of-usenet
> alt.humor.best-of-usenet.d
> alt.humor.puns
> rec.humor
> rec.humor.d
> rec.humor.funny
> rec.humor.oracle
> rec.humor.oracle.d

Usenet: Newsreaders

A selection of newsreader clients enabling you to read Usenet newsgroups. This site has newsreaders for Windows, Macintosh and Unix.

Web:
> http://www.teleport.com/support/news/

Usenet: Sex Newsgroups

Usenet newsgroups related to discussion of sex and sexuality. Some are for fun, some are utilitarian.

Usenet:
> alt.homosexual
> alt.homosexual.lesbian
> alt.journalism.gay-press
> alt.motss.bisexual-l
> alt.pantyhose
> alt.personals.bi
> alt.personals.transgendered
> alt.seduction.fast
> alt.sex
> alt.sex.asphyx
> alt.sex.bestiality
> alt.sex.bondage
> alt.sex.cu-seeme
> alt.sex.erotica

alt.sex.erotica.market.place
alt.sex.erotica.marketplace
alt.sex.exhibitionism
alt.sex.fat
alt.sex.femdom
alt.sex.fetish.boyfeet
alt.sex.fetish.diapers
alt.sex.fetish.drew-barrymore
alt.sex.fetish.fashion
alt.sex.fetish.feet
alt.sex.fetish.orientals
alt.sex.fetish.sailor-moon
alt.sex.fetish.smoking
alt.sex.fetish.tickling
alt.sex.fetish.wrestling
alt.sex.first-time
alt.sex.girl.watchers
alt.sex.girls
alt.sex.graphics
alt.sex.homosexual
alt.sex.incest
alt.sex.menstruation
alt.sex.motss
alt.sex.movies
alt.sex.oral
alt.sex.orgy
alt.sex.pictures
alt.sex.pictures.female
alt.sex.pictures.male
alt.sex.prostitution
alt.sex.prostitution.tijuana
alt.sex.services
alt.sex.spanking
alt.sex.stories
alt.sex.stories.d
alt.sex.stories.gay
alt.sex.stories.incest
alt.sex.stories.tg
alt.sex.strip-clubs
alt.sex.swingers
alt.sex.teens
alt.sex.telephone
alt.sex.trans

alt.sex.video-swap
alt.sex.voyeurism
alt.sex.wanted
alt.sex.watersports
alt.sex.weight-gain
alt.sex.wizards
alt.sex.young
alt.support.disabled.sexuality
alt.transgendered

Uuencode/Uudecode

Uuencode and uudecode for the DOS and Windows operating systems.

Web:
  http://www.snd.uc.edu/download/msdos/dos.html

Viewer Utilities

Software used for viewing the pictures and graphics you download from the Internet.

Web:
  http://cws.iworld.com/16image.html
  http://cws.iworld.com/32image.html
  http://tucows.iwebstudio.com/grap95.html
  http://tucows.iwebstudio.com/softgrap.html
  http://wwwhost.ots.utexas.edu/mac/pub-mac-graphics.html

Web: Browsers

A collection of graphical web browsers. This site offers browsers for a variety of operating systems.

Web:
  http://browserwatch.iworld.com/browsers.html

Web: CGI (Common Gateway Interface)

An introduction, documentation and examples for CGI (Common Gateway Interface). This site also offers an archive of various CGI programs.

Web:
  http://hoohoo.ncsa.uiuc.edu/cgi/

Web: Helper Applications

To fully enjoy the Web, you need to have the appropriate helper applications. At this site you can download a variety of software such, as sound players, image viewers and more.

Web:
>   http://www.mcom.com/assist/helper_apps/

Web: Image Map Tutorial

Learn to make image maps for your web page. This tutorial explains how image maps work, answers frequently asked questions, and offers information on image map clients.

Web:
>   http://www.ihip.com/

Web: Search Engines

With a handful of search engines, you can find anything on the Web. Try all of these to find the one you like best. Read the documentation on how to make your web searches more effective. These are powerful tools to have at your disposal.

Web:
>   http://altavista.digital.com
>   http://index.opentext.net/
>   http://www.albany.net/allinone/
>   http://www.excite.com/
>   http://www.hotbot.com/
>   http://www.infoseek.com/
>   http://www.lycos.com/

Windows 3.1 Internet Client Programs

There is no shortage of Windows software on the Net. Take your pick of all these free clients and find the one you like best. Read reviews and see how the clients are rated.

Web:
>   http://cws.iworld.com/
>   http://www.tucows.com/

Windows 95 Internet Client Programs

Windows 95 users, treat yourself to vast amounts of free software. Here is a great repository for Windows 95 clients along with reviews, ratings and download information.

Web:
> http://cws.iworld.com/
> http://www.tucows.com/

X Window Software

A great place to begin your search for X Window software. Find games, HTML editors, utilities, scripts, viewers and much more.

Web:
> http://www.ee.ryerson.ca:8080/~elf/xapps/Q-I.html

INTERNET: HELP

IRC Questions

Once you immerse yourself in IRC, you are going to have a great many questions about all the commands you can use. FAQs (frequently asked question lists) are available, but it's nice to know that there is a more interactive option. Post your questions on this Usenet group and, not only may you get the answer, but you will meet some interesting people in the process.

Usenet:
> alt.irc.questions

Web Tutorial for Beginners

If you are new to the Net, here is an easy-to-follow guide to help you learn about the Internet and the Web. (If you are a woman, pretend that I am sitting beside you, holding your hand. If you are a man, pretend that your mother is holding your hand.)

Web:
> http://www.gactr.uga.edu/exploring/toc.html

INTRIGUE

Cloak and Dagger

Find out what is going on in the world's intelligence services. This site includes information about special operations forces and counterterrorist units.

Web:
> http://www.abdn.ac.uk/~u01ded/candd/cd2.html

Conspiracies

The world (or so they say) is full of many amazing conspiracies of all kinds: AIDS being a government plot, Russia's operational Star Wars system, secret wars, what really happened at Waco, the final analysis of the JFK assassination, and much more.

Web:
> http://www.paranoia.com/~fraterk/conspire.html
> http://www.webcom.com/~conspire/

Spies

Wouldn't it be fun to be a spy? You could pretend to be any kind of person you want and cleverly infiltrate other governments and risk your life for people who don't even know or care one bit about what you are doing. If this idea appeals to you, check out this page on spies. Explore links to security resources, security services, Usenet groups, industrial and military intelligence, spy publications and U.S. intelligence agencies.

Web:
> http://www.dreamscape.com/frankvad/covert.html

J

JOBS AND THE WORKPLACE

Career Mosaic

Career Mosaic is an online employment guide with information about employers, companies and job opportunities. Through a colorful interface, it presents information about where employers are, what they specialize in, and what's important to them.

Web:
> http://www.careermosaic.com/

Jobs for College Students and Graduates

There are so many career resources around the Net that you might never even have to leave the house to go to the employment agency. These sites have loads of links for college graduates and students. Look for a job and read useful information about resumés, interviewing, negotiating and more.

Web:
> http://www.att.com/college/jobs.html
> http://www.collegegrad.com/

Jobs Offered

Nothing to do all day? Perhaps you might like a job. Here are two general announcement forums for all types of employment.

Usenet:
> biz.jobs.offered
> misc.jobs.offered

JOURNALISM AND MEDIA

Computer-Assisted Reporting and Research

How can you use computers to help you research and report the news? Here are some mailing lists devoted to that very subject. Subscribe to these lists and you will be able to hang out with working journalists, journalism teachers, news librarians, researchers, as well as various nattering nabobs of negativism. The **carr-l** list is for the discussion of general computer-assisted reporting and research. The **nicar-l** list is for the discussion of the activities of the National Institute for Computer-Assisted Reporting and for general computer-assisted reporting topics.

Listproc Mailing List:
> List Name: **nicar-l**
> Subscribe to: **listproc@lists.missouri.edu**

Listserv Mailing List:
> List Name: **carr-l**
> Subscribe to: **listserv@ulkyvm.louisville.edu**

Email the Media

Do you like to sound off? Have you ever thought about writing a letter to the editor? If so, you'll love this site. First, choose a publication from among a large list of magazines, newspapers and periodicals. Next, use the handy web-based interface to create your own personal letter. Then, with a click of the mouse button, your letter will be emailed to the appropriate address. (And, since you are one of my readers, your letter will, no doubt, be published quickly, with the full respect it deserves.) In order to test the service, I sent a letter to Time magazine. The letter began as follows: "Dear Editor: I never thought I would be writing one of these letters to a magazine such as yours. I am, by trade, a writer and, to tell you the truth, I always believed that the first-hand personal accounts I read in your magazine were invented by your editors. However, the experience I had last week showed that such experiences can happen to people like me, and I felt that I just had to share the details with your readers. It all started when the young widow next door asked me if I would help her carry in her groceries. She was wearing a low-cut blouse, a tight, very short miniskirt, and black high-heeled pumps. As I deposited the groceries on the kitchen table, she asked if I would like to visit and have a drink while she changed into something more comfortable..." (So, anyway, that's the beginning of what I sent as a test of this web site. I don't have room for the whole thing here, so if you would like to find out how the story ends, you will have to find the back issue of Time magazine in which the letter was published.)

Web:
> http://www.mrsmith.com/

Gonzo Journalism

In the tradition of Hunter S. Thompson, gonzo journalism is the method of reporting in which the journalist is a participant in the series of events or story being reported on. Follow the discussion about Thompson and the concepts of gonzo journalism.

Usenet:
> alt.journalism.gonzo

J

Journalism Resources

Journalists spend their time collecting and publishing information, so it makes a lot of sense that the Net would be a wonderful tool for a working reporter or researcher. Here are some collections, where you can find many, many resources. When you get a spare moment, I suggest that you explore, looking for those places that can help you. As you know, one of the most valuable possessions a journalist can have is a list of reliable sources. The time you spend creating such a list of Internet resources for yourself will be repaid many times over.

Web:
> http://www.it-kompetens.se/journ.html
> http://www.online-journalist.com/

KEYS AND LOCKS

Guide to Lock Picking

This page is Ted the Tool's Guide to Lock Picking. Start out by learning how a key opens a lock, and then build on your knowledge to learn about pin columns, scrubbing, and analytic thinking about lock-picking.

Web:
> http://www.lysator.liu.se/mit-guide/mit-guide.html

History of Locks

Take a historical tour of locks through the ages. There are lots of cool pictures of old locks and the different uses to which locks were put in ancient times. Read interesting factual tidbits such as Catherine the Great collected locks, and Marie Antoinette's husband—King what's-his-name XIV—was a locksmith. If you like locks, you will enjoy these brief, interesting historical articles.

Web:
> http://www.schlagelock.com/halllock.html

Lock Talk and General Discussion

Do you need the name of a book that will show you how to get into a locked, keyless automobile? How about a reference on safe-cracking? Or an electronic copy of The MIT Guide to Lockpicking, by Ted the Tool? Or are you an amateur locksmith with a picky problem? Check with the lock and key set for all your needs. Just don't tell anyone where you found out about it.

Usenet:
   alt.locksmithing

KIDS

Best Sites for Children

Here is a supermarket of children's Internet sites. The list covers all the basics and is arranged by subject. Find links to animals, art, the environment, astronomy, history, fun, safety, stories and much more.

Web:
   http://db.cochran.com/db_HTML:theopage.db

Cyberkids Magazine

This is an online magazine made by kids for kids. Visit the reading room and the art gallery. Listen to music compositions by other children. Read messages from kids around the world. There is lots to do at this web site.

Web:
   http://www.cyberkids.com/

Kids Talk and General Discussion

Clubhouses and playhouses are always fun because they are great places to hang out and be yourself with no parents allowed. There is a place like that on Usenet, where you can talk about anything you want and it's just for you—so, parents, no peeking.

Usenet:
   alt.kids-talk

K

White House Tour for Kids

Would you like to take a kids tour of the White House? Learn about this famous building (the home of the U.S. President and his family). Read about its history, the President, children of various Presidents, White House pets, and so on. You can also send a letter to the President and tell him your ideas. Note: Enjoy yourself writing the President if you want, but please understand that nobody really reads the letters. In fact, nobody even reads the letters that are sent to the President's regular email address. (Actually, I think you would be better off writing a letter to Santa Claus and leaving it where your parents can see it accidentally.)

Web:
  http://www.whitehouse.gov/WH/kids/html/

LANGUAGE

Foreign Language Dictionaries

Dictionaries to translate words from one language to another. For example, if you speak English, there are dictionaries to translate words to and from Spanish, French, Russian, Swedish, Chinese, Japanese and many more.

Web:
  http://math-www.uni-paderborn.de/HTML/Dictionaries.html

Language IRC Channels

Here are a few IRC channels where you can meet new friends and talk in different languages. Whether you are a native speaker or a student of a second language, IRC is the place to be.

IRC:
  #espanol
  #francais
  #france
  #italia
  #russian
  #turkey

Languages of the World

Here are some collections of information about the various languages spoken by humans and other animals. If you are interested in any particular language or country, I guarantee you can find information that will astonish you. For example, did you know that in the United States, there are 191 languages, 164 of which are living, 26 of which are extinct, and one that is a second language only with no mother tongue speakers?

Web:
> http://www.hardlink.com/~chambers/HLP/
> http://www.sil.org/ethnologue/ethnologue.html

Law Resources

This is a useful collection of law resources divided into sections: commercial law, defense funds, human rights, institutes, intellectual property, international trade, law firms, legal agencies, libraries, newsletters, Supreme Court, and more.

Web:
> http://www.io.org/~jgcom/librlaw.htm

Supreme Court Rulings

With Project Hermes, the United States Supreme Court makes its opinions and rulings available in electronic format within minutes of their release.

Web:
> http://www.law.cornell.edu/supct/

Virtual Law Library

When you are looking for law information on the Net, here is a great place to start. The Virtual Law Library contains a long list of links to online legal information. This resource offers topical and alphabetical listings of organizations, including a list of United States government law resources.

Web:
> http://www.law.indiana.edu/law/v-lib/lawindex.html

L

LIBRARIES

Hytelnet

Hytelnet is a program that presents library resources on an easy-to-use menu interface. When you choose a resource, Hytelnet will show you how to access the resource, or even connect you to it automatically. Executables for various machines, as well as source code, are available.

Web:
> http://library.usask.ca/hytelnet/

Librarian's Resources

Put together as only librarians and library students know how, here are some lists of library-related sites. There is lots of information here for librarians and other information experts.

Web:
> http://www.ex.ac.uk/~ijtilsed/lib/wwwlibs.html
> http://www.library.nwu.edu/resources/library/

Library and Information Science

If there is anything in the world that you want to know, ask a librarian. Library and information science turns ordinary mortals into oracles of facts. Even if they don't know it off the tops of their heads, librarians will know where to find what you are looking for. See discussion on librarianship from a technical and a philosophical point of view.

Listserv Mailing List:
> List Name: **libres**
> Subscribe to: **listserv@listserv.kent.edu**

LITERATURE

Classics

If you are looking for something old to go with your something new, borrowed and blue, you can easily find something on the Net. Here are some databases, information on classical antiquity, Roman law, Latin language, links to museums, college classics departments, classical organizations and journals. The mailing list is for discussions about classics, classical literature, and Latin in general.

Web:
> http://www.dla.utexas.edu/depts/classics/links.html

Listserv Mailing List:
> List Name: **latin-l**
> Subscribe to: **listserv@lists.psu.edu**

Literary Calendar

If you have ever wondered what happened in the world of literature on a particular day, this web site can tell you. Select any day of the year, and you will find out all the interesting literary events that occurred on that day. Of course, the first thing you have to do is put in your birthday. I did and I found out that the most interesting thing that happened on my birthday was that, in 1940, F. Scott Fitzgerald died of a heart attack in Los Angeles at the age of 44. (By the way, my birthday is December 21, and money is always in good taste.)

Web:
> http://www.yasuda-u.ac.jp/LitCalendar.html

Literature Mailing Lists

The Internet has many mailing lists devoted to literature and its relatives, writing and books. Here is a long list of such mailing lists, in an easy to understand form. If you want to talk about literature, I guarantee that you will find something here to interest you.

Web:
> http://tile.net/listserv/literature.html

L

LITERATURE: AUTHORS

Dickens, Charles

Charles Dickens (1812-1870) is perhaps the most famous English novelist of all time. Blessed with an extraordinary gift of satirical humor, melded with the ability to bring his readers both to laughter and to tears, Dickens managed to arouse the conscience of his audience while capturing the popular imagination of his time. More so than any other English novelist, Dickens had the ability to tell a story. Within his many novels (Oliver Twist, Great Expectations, A Christmas Carol, and so on), Dickens created the most marvelous gallery of characters in English fiction. When I was an undergraduate, I had a friend named Ralph who liked to read Dickens to relax. Now, you don't know Ralph, but believe me, the fact that Dickens could write stories that, a hundred years later, could interest a guy like Ralph, really says something.

Web:
> http://humwww.ucsc.edu/dickens/index.html
> http://lang.nagoya-u.ac.jp/~matsuoka/Dickens.html

Listserv Mailing List:
> List Name: **dickns-l**
> Subscribe to: **listserv@ucsbvm.ucsb.edu**

Faulkner, William

William Faulkner (1897-1962) was an American novelist from Mississippi. His greatest writing was based on the legends and history of the Southern United States, as well as the characteristics of his own family. His most famous works (such as the novel "The Sound and the Fury") are set in the town of Jefferson in the mythical county of Yoknapatawpha (pronounced just as it looks). In 1949, Faulkner was awarded the Nobel Prize for literature.

Web:
> http://www.mcsr.olemiss.edu/~egjbp/faulkner/faulkner.html

Shakespeare, William

William Shakespeare (1564-1616) was an English playwright and poet, considered to be the greatest dramatist of all time. Shakespeare wrote a large variety of plays: histories, tragedies, romances and comedies, and his skillfulness and insight were developed to such a high degree as to almost defy description and analysis. That, of course, never stopped anyone, and today, in just about every high school and university in the world, there is an active Shakespeare industry, carefully discussing, memorizing, studying and generally taking apart just about everything that Shakespeare ever wrote. Although Shakespeare never wrote a made-for-TV movie or a vampire book, his plays are still performed frequently all over the world (even though he is dead and is, therefore, not entitled to any of the royalties).

Web:
> http://ipl.sils.umich.edu/reading/shakespeare/shakespeare.html
> http://library.utoronto.ca/www/utel/rp/authors/shakespe.html
> http://the-tech.mit.edu/Shakespeare/works.html
> http://www.gh.cs.usyd.edu.au/~matty/Shakespeare/

Wodehouse, P.G.

Pelham Grenville Wodehouse (1881-1975) was an English writer of novels, short stories, plays, and song lyrics. Wodehouse (pronounced "Woodhouse") is the creator of a great many enduring characters, including Bertie Wooster and his valet Jeeves, Mr. Mulliner, Lord Emsworth and the Empress of Blandings, and Stanley Featherstonehaugh ("Fanshaw") Ukridge. Wodehouse is unique in that, over a long and successful career, he consistently demonstrated a level of skill that would be difficult to overpraise. He is, by far, my favorite author and, if you have never read any of his books, my advice to you is go out and buy one right now. If you happen to be reading this in a bookstore, it should be the work of a moment for you to pick up a Wodehouse book on the way out. Everything he created was uniformly pleasant and well-written: the best human nature has to offer. If you have not met Wodehouse, you have not led a full life.

Web:
> http://mech.math.msu.su/~gmk/pgw.htm
> http://www.serv.net/~camel/wodehouse/
> http://www.smart.net/~tak/wodehouse.html

Usenet:
> alt.fan.wodehouse

L

LITERATURE: COLLECTIONS

Electronic Books

There are many, many books available to read for free on the Net. Although it is not always as comfortable to read books on your computer screen as it is on paper, there are some advantages to using an electronic version. For example, it is easy to search the entire text for a particular word or phrase. And, once you have the text, you can manipulate it with a regular editing program or word processor. When you have some time, take a look at some of the literature available on the Net. I bet you will find something enjoyable.

Web:
> http://masala.colorado.edu/internet/library.html
> http://wcarchive.cdrom.com/pub/obi/
> http://www.cs.cmu.edu/Web/books.html
> http://www.lib.ncsu.edu/staff/morgan/alex/alex-index.html

English Server

A web site dedicated to the sharing of texts in English and other languages. Titles include autobiographies, plays, essays, hypertexts, jokes, novels, poems, speeches, short stories, and other items of interest.

Web:
> http://eng.hss.cmu.edu/

Fairy Tales

A fairy tale is a legendary story involving imaginative characters and unusual adventures. Use the Net to enter the wonderful world of childhood magic. There are lots of fairy tales for you to read to children and enjoy on your own.

Web:
> http://itpubs.ucdavis.edu/richard/tales/
> http://wcarchive.cdrom.com/pub/obi/Fairy.Tales/
> http://www.stud.ntnu.no/~rikardb/folktales.html
> http://www.ualberta.ca/~mshane/text.htm

Secular Web

The Secular Web—which contains a literature archive—is maintained by a group called the Internet Infidels. The Infidels promote the philosophy of secularism: the belief that morality and education should not be based on religion. If you are religious, I understand that this philosophy may be in direct contradistinction to everything you believe (or have been taught). However, the books and articles at this site all resonate around the idea that people can actually think for themselves and should be able to choose to accept or reject important ideas on their own merit. Take a look and see what you think.

Web:

http://www.infidels.org/

LITERATURE: TITLES

Alice's Adventures in Wonderland

What people commonly refer to as the story of Alice in Wonderland is actually two different books: "Alice's Adventures in Wonderland" and the sequel "Through the Looking Glass". These stories are clever tales written by Lewis Carroll about a young girl named Alice who has strange adventures in a surrealistic place. In the first story, Alice enters Wonderland by following a rabbit down a hole. In the second story, she begins her journey by climbing through a looking glass (mirror). If you have children—or if you ever were a child at one time—I suggest that you set aside a few hours and read these stories to someone smaller than yourself. (Even though it's possible that you may enjoy the stories even more than the children.)

Web:

http://www.cstone.net/library/alice/aliceinwonderland.html
http://www.cstone.net/library/glass/alice-lg.html
http://www.literature.org/Works/Lewis-Carroll/alice-in-wonderland/
http://www.literature.org/Works/Lewis-Carroll/through-the-looking-glass/index.html

L

Canterbury Tales

Geoffrey Chaucer (c. 1340-1400) was an English poet who wrote the Canterbury Tales, a 17,000-line poem about a group of pilgrims traveling to see the shrine of St. Thomas à Becket at Canterbury. The Tales are fascinating because Chaucer is a master storyteller who creates characters that are full of life. The Canterbury Tales is an unfinished work, but shows a delightful slice of 14th-century English life.

Web:
> http://etext.virginia.edu/CT.html

Peter Pan

James Matthew Barrie (1860-1937) was a British playwright and novelist. In 1904, he wrote the popular tale about Peter Pan, the boy who would never grow up. The story of Peter Pan is popular today in cartoons and film. Enjoy this story about Peter, Wendy, Captain Hook, the Lost Boys and their adventures in Never Never Land.

Web:
> http://www.teachersoft.com/Library/lit/barrie/contents.htm

MAGAZINES

Entertainment Magazines

Something new is always going on in the world of entertainment and *you* need to keep up. There's only one good way. Connect to the Net and read some online entertainment magazines. After all, we are all part of the popular culture and, as such, we have a civic obligation to make sure we know what's happening in the world of television, film and music. Start here: Comedy, Details, Entertainment Weekly, Premiere and Vibe.

Web:
> http://pathfinder.com/ew/
> http://www.earthchannel.com/comedymg/
> http://www.premieremag.com/hfm/
> http://www.swoon.com/j_mag_rack/01_details/details.html
> http://www.vibe.com/

Gossip Magazines

Not only is talk cheap, talking about other people is essential to your health. That's why medical scientists consider gossip magazines an integral part of a well-balanced intellectual diet. Tell me the truth—when I mention Diana, Wills, Lisa Marie, Liz, Madonna, Roseanne, Barbra, Fergie and Keanu, do you know who I mean? Of course you do. So don't waste any more time. Connect right now to this online version of the grandmother and grandfather of gossip—National Enquirer and People magazine—and see what the rich and famous are doing while you and I are busy working and paying taxes.

Web:
> http://pathfinder.com/people/
> http://www.nationalenquirer.com/

Magazine Talk and General Discussion

This is better than going to the newsstand, because you don't have to take off your fuzzy slippers and leave the house. Check out zines, newsletters and magazines from your computer. Read contents and summaries of electronic and printed publications and find out how to get them.

Usenet:
> rec.mag

MATHEMATICS

Algebra Assistance

It's a total bummer when you are working on an equation at three o'clock in the morning and you have nobody to ask for help. Never again will you be left mathematically stranded. With this Usenet group, you will always have a place to turn. Too bad you can't take the computer in with you when you have a test.

Usenet:
> alt.algebra.help

Calculus Graphics

This is a collection of graphical demonstrations for first year calculus. It includes sections on derivatives and differentials, computing the volume of water in a tipped glass, Archimedes' calculation of pi, and a bouncing ball.

Web:
> http://www.math.psu.edu/dna/graphics.html

M

Chance Server

What exactly is a snowball's chance in hell? Check in at the Chance Server and you might find out. Get the Chance News, a bi-weekly report with popular news items that can be used in classroom settings to make teaching statistics and probability fun. (Not that it isn't normally fun, of course.) Teaching aids are also available.

Web:
http://www.geom.umn.edu/docs/snell/chance/

History of Mathematics

Get the real story of mathematics, the one your teachers never told you. Read these well-researched essays on various topics in the history of math as well as the biographies of several hundred mathematicians. Contemplate those yet-unsolved questions about prime numbers and whether Konigsberg burned his bridges behind him.

Web:
http://www-groups.dcs.st-and.ac.uk/~history/

MEDICINE

Anatomy Teaching Modules

Some days there are just not enough cadavers to go around. Not to worry. Learn anatomy online with these teaching modules. They come complete with information text as well as images.

Web:
http://www.rad.washington.edu/AnatomyModuleList.html

Virtual Library of Medicine

The Virtual Library of Medicine is an ambitious project to make massive amounts of useful medical information available over the Net. Here you will find various types of medical information and resources: plain text, multimedia textbooks, patient simulations, practice guidelines, journals, and on and on—organized in several different ways to make it easy to find what you want.

Web:
http://vh.radiology.uiowa.edu/Providers/Providers.html

MEDICINE: ALTERNATIVE

Alternative Medicine Resources

Tired of legal drugs and poor bedside manner? Drop in to the alternative medicine forum where alternative-oriented people share alternative medical tips, alternative home remedies, and alternative approaches to healing. (If you can't make it, send an alternate.)

Web:
> http://www.pitt.edu/~cbw/altm.html
> http://www.talamasca.org/avatar/alt-healing.html

Usenet:
> misc.health.alternative

Complementary Medicine

A list of alternative forms of medicine that some people choose to use in addition to regular medicine. Find a huge list of topics such as acupuncture, diet and nutritional therapy, biofeedback, rolfing, aromatherapy, cryogenic medicine, shiatsu and many more.

Web:
> http://galen.med.virginia.edu/~pjb3s/ComplementaryHomePage.html

Holistic Healing

Going to the doctor is no fun. Everyone is wearing a uniform, it's all sterile and rigid, and various people take turns poking you with sharp instruments. Experience a gentler alternative to medicine in the form of holistic concepts and methods of living, which are reported to be a more natural way of dealing with the hairpin turns on the road of life. A variety of holistic topics are discussed, such as states of consciousness, meditation, healthy diet, herbs, vitamins, rolfing, and massage.

Web:
> http://www.holistic.com/~holistic/

Listserv Mailing List:
> List Name: **holistic**
> Subscribe to: **listserv@siu.edu**

M

MEN

Fathers

Whether you are a single father or a father in a traditional family, there are resources on the Net that will interest you. These sites have lots of information on parenting, rights of fathers, at-home dads, things to do with the kids and lots more. Join the mailing list and talk to other online dads.

Web:
    http://aipnet.com/workshop/
    http://www.cyfc.umn.edu/FatherNet.htp
    http://www.fathermag.com/contents.html
    http://www.parentsplace.com/readroom/frc/
    http://www.pitt.edu/~jsims/singlefa.html

Listserv Mailing List:
    List Name: **father-l**
    Subscribe to: **listserv@tc.umn.edu**

Men's Issues

Check out this great collection of men's issues resources. These pages cover topics such as attitudes toward men, domestic violence, employment, fatherhood, health, history of men's movements, romance and relationships, the justice system and much more. You will also find reviews of books and links to information about various men's organizations.

Web:
    http://www.contact.org/usmen.htm
    http://www.msn.fullfeed.com/~rschenk/hotspots.html

Men's Voices

This magazine was created to offer information, support and advocacy for men. Various nationally recognized authors have written stories and articles dealing with conflicts with children, grief, love, child abuse recovery, divorce and other related men's issues. While you are here, check out the calendar of events to see if there are any conferences you would like to attend.

Web:
    http://www.vix.com/menmag/

Armed Forces of the World

These web sites are great sources of information about various military organizations around the world. You can find links to defense forces, journals, documents, maps, military bases, military reserves, research centers and intelligence organizations. For example, I was able to learn how the Israeli military forces follow a doctrine of "speed, initiative and audacity". You can also find a lot of interesting information (such as the fact that Cyprus has four aircraft and eight helicopters even though they don't have an air force or a navy). Hint: If you are a student looking for a topic on which to write an essay, here are some wonderful sources of information.

Web:
>   http://members.aol.com/rhrongstad/private/milinksr.htm
>   http://www.cfcsc.dnd.ca/links/milorg/
>   http://www.iaw.on.ca/~awoolley/lwformil.html

Disarmament Talk and General Discussion

Discussion and monthly digests of military and political strategy, technology, sociology, and peace activism involved in accelerating disarmament of nuclear, conventional, and chemical weapons. **disarm-d** provides monthly digests of selected mail discussions that are posted to **disarm-l**. It also includes essays, papers, reviews, and excerpts from important publications.

Listserv Mailing List:
>   List Name: **disarm-d**
>   Subscribe to: **listserv@cnsibm.albany.edu**

Listserv Mailing List:
>   List Name: **disarm-l**
>   Subscribe to: **listserv@cnsibm.albany.edu**

M

United States Armed Forces

These are the official web sites of the main branches of the United States armed forces: the Air Force, Army, Coast Guard, Navy and Marine Corps. Each of these sites is independent, and the information varies from one page to the next. In general, though, you can find out a lot about each of the services, including what they do and how to join. I find visiting these sites interesting, as they show how the various branches of the U.S. armed services have distinct personalities and ways of looking at the world. If you need any information at all about part of the U.S. military, one of these web sites is a good place to start. You can read about what each service does, its history, recruiting policies (including various careers), retirement information, alumni organizations, news and press releases, upcoming public events, and much more.

Web:
> http://www.af.mil/
> http://www.army.mil/
> http://www.dot.gov/dotinfo/uscg/
> http://www.navy.mil/
> http://www.usmc.mil/

War

Let's face it, war has been given a bum rap. Okay, so lots of people die, and many more suffer in horrible ways. Yes, families are broken, and people are changed for the worse permanently. And, I guess, it is true that all kinds of property is damaged and destroyed, and huge amounts of money and resources are funneled away from social productive uses and into a military machine. But, don't fall into the trap of assuming these are all *negative* things. Listen to some of the war discussion in Usenet and make up your own mind.

Usenet:
> soc.history.war.misc

MISCHIEF

April Fools

The Ides of March is the least of the Internet's worries. The first day of April is the time when tricksters all over the world unleash their clever plots of lighthearted deceit. April Fools' pranks have been developed into an art form and are brought together in the form of archives which you can view from the safety of your own home.

Web:
> http://www.2meta.com/april-fools/
> http://www.cse.psu.edu/~skovrins/fools.html
> http://www.zia.com/holiday1/april-fools-day/

Canonical List of Pranks

Never again will you have to worry about running out of tricks to play on people. Get the canonical list of pranks and drive everyone around you crazy.

Web:
> http://k2.scl.cwru.edu/~mcw6/fool/pranks.htm
> http://www.cs.indiana.edu/hyplan/ameiss/humor/pranks.html
> http://www.lehigh.edu/~sjb3/pranks3

Practical Jokes

For serious enjoyment, what could be more good clean fun than embarrassing your friends and neighbors by making them look foolish? The dribble glass and plastic vomit are child's play. On the Net, you can read about lots and lots of ideas, techniques, and experiences with practical jokes. Make your loved ones say "uncle", and make your uncle say, "bork, bork, bork".

Web:
> http://humor.ncy.com/type/practical_joke/
> http://www.lysator.liu.se:7500/jokes/practical.html

M

MONEY: BUSINESS AND FINANCE

Entrepreneur Talk and General Discussion

Tired of being manacled to that creaking metal desk with the file drawer that always sticks? Take charge of your life: own your own business. See the pitfalls and glories that await you, the entrepreneur.

Usenet:
> misc.entrepreneurs

Marketing Discussion

There are lots of different facets of marketing and, on the Net, there are lots of mailing lists—discussion lists, that is—which you can join to talk to people. Each list is devoted to its own particular slice of the economic pie. Here is a resource to help you choose which mailing list is best for you.

Web:
> http://www.wolfbayne.com/lists/

Mutual Funds

If I were smarter, I would probably be buying stocks and bonds (and losing all my money). Instead, I put my savings into a mutual fund and let someone else do the driving. This mutual fund resource provides useful, focused content and has original material with references to other valuable Internet resources.

Web:
> http://www.brill.com/

Real Estate Talk and General Discussion

It's just like a Monopoly game, except you use real money and the bail is higher if you end up in jail. Learn tips on acquiring real estate: how to choose a good agent, perks for first-time homebuyers, and how to avoid the rental property blues.

Usenet:
> alt.real-estate-agents
> misc.invest.real-estate

MONEY: PERSONAL FINANCE

Currency Converter

The currency converter is simple to use. You select the desired country and all the other countries' currencies will be converted relative to the one you selected. The name of the currency will appear as part of your selection.

Web:
> http://www.xe.net/currency/

Homebuyer's Fair

Buying a house is a little different than running to the corner market to pick up an extra package of hot dog buns. Get answers to questions about buying a home, learn information about mortgages and how to avoid "junk fees". You can even view images of homes for sale.

Web:
> http://www.homefair.com/

Mortgages

If you are contemplating a mortgage, find out lots of information about interest rates, mortgage companies, rate trends and loan programs from this web page. Not only will you learn interesting things that will help you make a better decision, but you can also utilize an online mortgage payment calculator, see historical interest rates and read consumer tips and information.

Web:
> http://www.dirs.com/mortgage/

Personal Finance Center

Create a good personal finance system for yourself or perfect the one you already have. On the Net, you can find newsletter excerpts, columns, and links to information relating to personal finance.

Web:
> http://webcrawler.com/select/bus.new.html

M

Selling by Owner

Have you decided you don't need a real estate agent? If so, check out the advice offered here about selling your house on your own. Topics cover hiring a lawyer, advertising and how to have a successful open house.

Web:
> http://www.fsboconnection.com/articles.html

MOTORCYCLES

Harley Owners Group

There's something so lovable about a Harley. Maybe it's because they are so sexy, powerful and have lots of thrust. Or maybe it's that air of exotic mystery and charisma. Or maybe they're just good motorcycles. If you're a Harley fan, check out this site, which has art, technical information, pictures and stolen bike information.

Web:
> http://www.harley-davidson.com/who/hog/

Motorcycle Online Magazine

While it's not as convenient as a paper magazine sitting in the bathroom, this electronic motorcycle magazine is spiffy and worth a look. It features news stories, video and photo archives, a virtual museum, a U.S. events database, sneak previews of next year's motorcycle models, and links to services offered by commercial parties and manufacturers.

Web:
> http://motorcycle.com/motorcycle.html

Motorcycle Talk and General Discussion

Anything named "Harley" is bound to be sexy. No doubt that is why so many people love their motorcycles. If you just can't live without something hard and powerful, these Usenet groups are the places to be.

Usenet:
    alt.motorcycles.harley
    rec.motorcycles
    rec.motorcycles.dirt
    rec.motorcycles.harley
    rec.motorcycles.racing

MOVIES

Cult Movies Talk and General Discussion

No matter how bad they get, no matter how outlandish they are or how far away from their origins they evolve, you will go see the hundredth remake of a film. There are a few movies that have a cult following and fans feel so strongly about these films that they will see them at all costs. These newsgroups cover cult movies in general and some in particular like the Evil Dead movies and Rocky Horror Picture Show.

Usenet:
    alt.cult-movies
    alt.cult-movies.evil-deads
    alt.cult-movies.rocky-horror

Internet Movie Database

It's a horrible feeling when you are trying to think of a movie title and you just can't remember it. That never has to be a problem if you connect to the Internet Movie Database. Now you can search for your favorite (or most hated) movie by the title, cast and crew names, cast character name, genre and other more obscure methods.

Web:
    http://ballet.cit.gu.edu.au/Movies/
    http://it.imdb.com/
    http://uk.imdb.com/
    http://us.imdb.com/

M

Movies and Filmmaking Talk and General Discussion

Movies are fun to watch from the audience, but don't you wonder what it would be like to be in on the action? You can at least get in on the talk. Discuss movies and the making of movies from a creative or technical point of view. Fans and filmmakers frequent these Usenet groups.

Usenet:
>   alt.movies.branagh-thmpsn
>   alt.movies.chaplin
>   alt.movies.hitchcock
>   alt.movies.independent
>   alt.movies.indian
>   alt.movies.joe-vs-volcano
>   alt.movies.kubrick
>   alt.movies.silent
>   alt.movies.spielberg
>   alt.movies.tim-burton
>   alt.movies.visual-effects
>   rec.arts.movies
>   rec.arts.movies.current-films
>   rec.arts.movies.lists+surveys
>   rec.arts.movies.local.indian
>   rec.arts.movies.misc
>   rec.arts.movies.movie-going
>   rec.arts.movies.past-films
>   rec.arts.movies.people
>   rec.arts.movies.production
>   rec.arts.movies.tech

MUDS: SPECIFIC TYPES

LambdaMoo

A large and popular virtual reality with more varied sections and interesting objects than you'll ever be able to explore. Players are allowed to program and create their own sections.

Telnet:
>   Address: **lambda.moo.mud.org**
>   Port: **8888**

Lua-uhane Mud

A wonderful Hawaiian mud with a fantasy theme. Populated by friendly folks who don't bother themselves with the politics and rules of player-killing. Morality rules on the player-killing issues. Killers become evil, which gives all good and neutral players license to gang up on them and kill them. Stealing is allowed, but so is revenge.

Telnet:
> Address: **linus.actioninc.com**
> Port: **4000**

Medievia Diku

Looking for a highly populated mud? Try this medieval-themed fantasy mud. Medievia allows for multi-classing and some player-killing in restricted areas. It's a heavily modified mud with ansi color. On Medievia you will encounter clan wars and a variety of environments, such as a watery zone called Atlantis and the catacombs with thousands of randomized rooms.

Web:
> http://www.medievia.com:8080/

Telnet:
> Address: **medievia.com**
> Port: **4000**

MUSEUMS

Exploratorium

Science is fun. You can blow things up, stick things together, make things float and create loud noises that will guarantee you a trip to the principal's office. The Exploratorium in San Francisco creates an environment of hands-on fun learning and you can visit their home on the Net.

Web:
> http://www.exploratorium.edu/

M

Museums, Exhibits and Special Collections

If you are not getting enough culture from television, try visiting some of the museums on the Net. You can hop around like a jet-setting socialite and visit museums all over the world. This web page has links to a diverse set of museums, exhibits and special collections that can be found on the Net.

Web:
> http://www.lam.mus.ca.us/webmuseums/

Museums on the Web

A collection of web links connecting museums and archives. This page offers pointers to such sights as the Hall of Dinosaurs, the Moscow Kremlin Online Excursion, the London Transport Museum, Native Vikings, and many other interesting destinations.

Web:
> http://www.icom.org/vlmp/

MUSIC

Discographies

When you have a blind date with a girl and you know she likes a certain band, go to one of these discographies sites, find the band and memorize every song and album they have ever released (along with the dates they were released). On the date, talk is bound to turn to music and you can wow her with your knowledge of her favorite musical groups. I always say, plan for success.

Web:
> http://www.cgrg.ohio-state.edu/folkbook/discographies.html
> http://www.teleport.com/~xeres/discog.shtml

Music Database

It's been on the tip of your tongue all morning, the name of that song running through your mind. It's driving you crazy. It has the word "grapefruit" in the title. Suddenly it hits you like a wet fish—search the online music database. They have thousands of albums you can search by artist, title, track, language, country, style, or submitter. If you have album information, you may enter it in the database, too.

Web:
> http://www.roadkill.com/~burnett/MDB/

Ultimate Band List

The Ultimate Band List offers the ultimate place to find out about your favorite band or musician. Find out where to look for information about thousands of different bands, as well as radio stations, record labels, clubs and concerts, record stores, and lots more. If you want any information about popular music, this is the place to start.

Web:
>   http://american.recordings.com/wwwofmusic/

MUSIC: PERFORMERS

Fan Favorites Talk and General Discussion

There are many discussion groups devoted to popular musicians and music groups. Tune in for the latest in concert appearances, reviews, opinions, and esoterica. Look for your favorites.

Usenet:
>   alt.fan.allman-brothers
>   alt.fan.barry-manilow
>   alt.fan.blues-brothers
>   alt.fan.david-bowie
>   alt.fan.debbie.gibson
>   alt.fan.devo
>   alt.fan.elton-john
>   alt.fan.elvis-costello
>   alt.fan.elvis-presley
>   alt.fan.enya
>   alt.fan.frank-zappa
>   alt.fan.jello-biafra
>   alt.fan.jimi-hendrix
>   alt.fan.jimmy-buffet
>   alt.fan.madonna
>   alt.fan.michael-bolton
>   alt.fan.oingo-boingo
>   alt.fan.run-dmc
>   alt.fan.spinal-tap
>   alt.fan.sting
>   alt.fan.u2
>   alt.fan.wang-chung
>   alt.music.amy-grant

M

alt.music.barenaked-ladies
alt.music.beastie-boys
alt.music.bela-fleck
alt.music.billy-joel
alt.music.blues-traveler
alt.music.brian-eno
alt.music.chapel-hill
alt.music.counting-crows
alt.music.danzig
alt.music.deep-purple
alt.music.def-leppard
alt.music.dio
alt.music.dream-theater
alt.music.ebm
alt.music.elo
alt.music.enya
alt.music.fates-warning
alt.music.fleetwood-mac
alt.music.genesis
alt.music.green-day
alt.music.gwar
alt.music.james-taylor
alt.music.jethro-tull
alt.music.jimi.hendrix
alt.music.kylie-minogue
alt.music.led-zeppelin
alt.music.leonard-cohen
alt.music.lor-mckennitt
alt.music.marillion
alt.music.monkees
alt.music.moody-blues
alt.music.nin
alt.music.nirvana
alt.music.pat-mccurdy
alt.music.paul-simon
alt.music.pearl-jam
alt.music.peter-gabriel
alt.music.pink-floyd
alt.music.primus
alt.music.prince
alt.music.queen
alt.music.roger-waters
alt.music.rush

alt.music.s-mclachlan
alt.music.seal
alt.music.smash-pumpkins
alt.music.smiths
alt.music.sonic-youth
alt.music.sophie-hawkins
alt.music.stone-temple
alt.music.the-doors
alt.music.the.police
alt.music.tlc
alt.music.tmbg
alt.music.todd-rundgren
alt.music.u2
alt.music.ween
alt.music.weird-al
alt.music.who
alt.music.yes
alt.rock-n-roll.acdc
alt.rock-n-roll.aerosmith
alt.rock-n-roll.stones
rec.music.artists.beach-boys
rec.music.artists.bruce-hornsby
rec.music.artists.queensryche
rec.music.artists.springsteen
rec.music.beatles
rec.music.dylan
rec.music.gdead
rec.music.phish
rec.music.rem
rec.music.tori-amos

Presley, Elvis

We have discovered where Elvis has been all along. He's really not dead. He has been living on the Internet. Take a tour of Graceland and learn all about the King. When you are not touring, you can talk to Elvis fans around the world on Usenet.

Web:
   http://sunsite.unc.edu/elvis/elvlinks.html

Usenet:
   alt.elvis.king
   alt.elvis.sighting
   alt.fan.elvis-presley

M

Rolling Stones

This band has endless energy and will probably outlive most of us and be recording their last albums from the wing of a hospital for the Geriatric Rich and Famous. This web page is the hot spot for all things Stones.

Web:
> http://www.stones.com/

NEW AGE

Aware Net

Clear your seventh chakra, open your third eye, expand your consciousness, control your breathing—it's a fitness program for your psyche. If you like to be aware of what is going on in the universe besides stuffy physics and science, go where the enlightened people keep their archives of discussion on cosmic happenings, paranormal occurrences and astrological data. Get a free astrological chart personalized just for you or someone you love. It makes a great gift.

Web:
> http://www.awarenet.com/

New Age Information

Once I was in a bookstore and this man came up to me and showed me a calendar with pictures of the Northern Lights on it. He began talking about Earth entering a photon belt and how certain unnamed lords of light and dark would be doing something or other. What do you say when this happens? If I had read this web site, I would have known, because there is a great deal of information on the photon belt as well as Nostradamus, Urantia, vegetarianism, Mayan prophesies and other New Age stuff. Oh, well.

Web:
> http://www1.tpgi.com.au/users/ron/newage.html

Spirit Web

Do you ever get the feeling that there is more going on around you than you realize? What is it with all these alien sightings and interactions with ghosts and people who say they channel voices from the great beyond? Do they know something you don't? You don't have to feel left out any longer. Get information on channeling, alternative healing, UFOs, light technology, Earth changes, out-of-body experiences, astrology and other subjects that really are out of this world.

Web:
> http://www.spiritweb.org/

NEWS

CNN Interactive

This is a great source of news information. CNN Interactive offers major news stories for the U.S. and the world, including sound clips and pictures. They also offer a compilation of articles for long-running stories and news events.

Web:
> http://www.cnn.com/

Daily Newspaper Email Addresses

Would you like to send email to a newspaper? Here is a large list of mail addresses of contacts and reporters for daily newspapers around the world. This list includes mail addresses in Canada, Czech Republic, Europe, Germany, Namibia, Poland, U.K., and a very large United States section. Send in your news tip today.

Web:
> http://www.acclaimed.com/helpful/new-add.htm

World News Sources

I'm warning you. Don't visit any of these sites unless you have plenty of time. There is so much news in the world of news that you will be distracted for hours. (And that's not news.)

Web:
> http://newo.com/news/
> http://users.deltanet.com/users/taxicat/e_papers.html
> http://www.discover.co.uk/NET/NEWS/news.html

N

OCCULT AND PARANORMAL

Astrology Talk and General Discussion

You've discovered that Uranus is in conjunction with your ascendant ruler, Jupiter. And as if that's not enough, Uranus also squares Mercury, your tenth house ruler, and you have four yods that are creating frustration and dissatisfaction in your life. What's a person to do? Besides calling the psychic hotline, you can post queries or hints to stargazers across the globe or even—depending on whom they know—across the universe.

Usenet:
> alt.astrology
> alt.astrology.asian
> alt.astrology.marketplace
> alt.astrology.metapsych

Paranormal Phenomena Talk and General Discussion

The weird, the unexplained, the things that go bump in the night. I love stories, especially ones that give me goose bumps and make the hair stand up on the back of my neck. Read stories and theories about paranormal phenomena.

Usenet:
> alt.paranet.paranormal
> alt.paranormal

Skepticism

It's not easy being the bad guy, but someone has to do it. Take a look into this debunker's paradise and read skeptics' opinions on topics like UFOs, the Shroud of Turin, firewalking, faith healing, and, yes, even home schooling.

Web:
> http://www.xnet.com/~blatura/skeptic.shtml

Usenet:
> sci.skeptic

ORGANIZATIONS

America's Charities

What can you do with all that extra money you have lying around? Why not give it to a charitable organization? You may not be able to use a tax deduction, but you can always use a few extra points with the Man (or Woman) Upstairs. Take a look at this web page, which has a list of charities that are just waiting for some free money.

Web:
> http://www.charitiesusa.com/

Nonprofit Organization Talk and General Discussion

Learn the ins and outs of running a nonprofit organization. Get ideas about raising money, hints on record keeping and how to start a nonprofit organization from scratch.

Usenet:
> soc.org.nonprofit

Service Organization Talk and General Discussion

Spending most of the day in front of the television is not the fastest way to feel fulfilled as a human being. Pull yourself out of the sofa and join a service organization. Check out this Usenet group to see which one would be right for you, or read the FAQ (frequently asked question list) at the web site.

Web:
> http://www.cis.ohio-state.edu/hypertext/faq/usenet/service-clubs/general-faq/faq.html

Usenet:
> soc.org.service-clubs.misc

OUTDOOR ACTIVITIES

Great Outdoor Recreation Pages

Get out into the sunshine and fresh air. When you want to know where to go and what to do, take a look at all this great information. You'll find loads of stuff to read about things to do and places to visit: national parks, forests, wilderness areas, hiking, biking, fishing and climbing.

Web:
> http://www.gorp.com/

Hiking

Articles and guides about hiking and the great outdoors. Includes hiking songs, a snakebite guide, campfire lore, water filtering information, and other topics of interest to campers.

Web:
> http://www.teleport.com/~walking/hiking.html

Spelunking

If you like crawling around in something that is cool, dark and wet, you are digging in the right place. Here you will find connections to speleological societies and servers around the world. If you just want to talk about caving, check out **alt.caving**.

Web:
> http://www.goodearth.com/virtcave.html
> http://www.gorp.com/gorp/activity/caving.htm
> http://www.infohub.com/TRAVEL/ADVENTURE/RECREATION/caving.html

Usenet:
> alt.caving

P

Court of Last Resort

The Court of Last Resort is a web site to which people submit their grievances against one another in the form of a court case. Then people from all over the Net read the complaints and vote on the verdict. It's a great way to help people decide their differences, and it actually works. And, I guess I don't have to tell you, it's a lot of fun to read about arguments between strangers.

Web:
> http://www.sandbox.net/court/pub-doc/home-x.html

Friends

Looking for some new friends? Try chatting on IRC. These channels are lively and always populated. It's the perfect place to start up a conversation and meet new people. These channels are not for the discussion of the television show Friends.

IRC:
> #Chatfriends
> #friend
> #friends

Shared Realities

Some days you just wake up and think to yourself, "Hey, I think I will be someone else today." It's easy when you participate in some of the shared realities of Usenet. In these groups, people assume a persona and write about their thoughts, feelings and actions as that character. Meet people, form bonds, make friends, entertain and be entertained. Even if you don't want to participate, these groups are fun to read because it's like seeing a story unfold before your eyes.

Usenet:
> alt.dragons-inn
> alt.kalbo
> alt.pub.cloven-shield
> alt.pub.coffeehouse.amethyst
> alt.pub.dragons-inn
> alt.pub.havens-rest
> alt.pub.kacees
> alt.shared-reality.sf-and-fantasy
> alt.shared-reality.startrek.klingon
> alt.shared-reality.x-files
> alt.world.taeis

PEOPLE: FAMOUS

Adams, Scott

Do you enjoy the Dilbert comic strip? Do you like Dogbert, the cute little dog that looks like a balloon with glasses? If so, tell the artist himself: Scott Adams. The web site takes you right to the heart of Dilbert Central, where you can look at an archive of comic strips. (Note, this site only works if you look at it when you should be working.)

Web:
> http://www.unitedmedia.com/comics/dilbert

Mail:
> scottadams@aol.com

Celebrity Talk and General Discussion

You've devoured every newspaper, magazine and tabloid in sight and you still want more news and information about celebrities. Here is a source that is available 24 hours a day, so you can always get a fix. Read stories, news and rumors of old and new famous people.

Usenet:
> alt.celebrities

President of the United States

Does anyone really believe that the President of the United States even sees any of his email? Just between us, the real truth is that nobody even reads it. Still, if you send in a letter you will get an automated response (which is more than you can say about writing to Bill Gates or the Pope). Actually, I don't really expect the President of the U.S. to drop everything just to respond to his email. After all, he has his hands full being Leader of the Free World, Commander-in-Chief of the U.S. Armed Forces, as well as Grand Poobah of the Illuminati. Still, if you drop him a note and tell him what is wrong with America, you will at least earn a few karma points. Couldn't hurt.

Mail:
> president@whitehouse.gov

Santa Claus

It's nice to know that as busy as Santa is, he always has time to stay up with the latest technology. Send your wish list to Santa by email or you can see what he, the elves and reindeer are doing on the Web. Maybe if you are especially good this year, Santa will bring you a high-speed Internet connection for the holidays.

Web:
> http://www.north-pole.org/
> http://www.santaclaus.com/

Mail:
> santa@north.pole.org

PERSONALS AND DATING

International Personals

Despite all appearances otherwise, this group is not for interplanetary dating. This Usenet group relates to dating immigrants to new countries or for people who are seeking to date people from foreign countries.

Usenet:
> alt.personals.aliens

> http://www.montagar.com/personals/

Singles Web

It's nice to have all the help you can get when you are on the dating scene. Singles Web offers tips for dating: things to do with your date, dating skills for men and women, a list of gifts you can give to your date, massage skills and novel trivia such as the meaning of various flowers and how to say "I love you" in many different languages.

Web:
> http://www.jjplaza.com/singles/

PHILOSOPHY

Ancient Philosophy

Do you ever get tired of the same old chit-chat at parties? Brush up on your ancient philosophy and you'll be able to discuss Hesiod over the clam dip and ponder Iamblichus while munching on meatballs.

Listproc Mailing List:
> List Name: **sophia**
> Subscribe to: **listproc@liverpool.ac.uk**

Extropians

It's not an alien life form, nor is it a variety of insectoid species. Extropians are people who are interested in anarchocapitalist politics, cryonics and other life extension techniques, the technological extension of human intelligence and perception, and nanotechnology. It's not just another little hobby. It's a way of life.

Listserv Mailing List:
> List Name: **xtropy-1**
> Subscribe to: **listserv@listserv.acsu.buffalo.edu**

Philosophy Archive

Before you draw your next hot bath, go look at the English Server's philosophy archive. It contains text by such notable thinkers as Nietzsche, Descartes, Kant, Aristotle, Bacon and Burke. Read a few of these while the tub is filling, so it will give you something to think about as you have a nice soak.

Web:
> http://english-www.hss.cmu.edu/philosophy/

PHOTOGRAPHY

Black and White Photography

I love black and white photography. It's so clean, basic and accessible. If you want to find good black and white photography on the Net, all you need to do is check this web site. You will find a monthly list of the top black and white photo web sites, as well as an archive of the past selections. They also have a great resource center for photographers, with some useful FAQs (frequently asked question lists).

Web:
> http://www.photogs.com/bwworld/

Darkroom Photography

Photographic creativity certainly doesn't stop with a click of the shutter. When you head to the darkroom you have to ask yourself all sorts of questions like "Should I print on warm or cold tone paper?" and "What kind of developer should I use?" Topics cover being creative in the darkroom as well as technical issues such as chemical usage, paper, tools, and equipment.

Web:
http://www.sound.net/~lanoue/

Usenet:
rec.photo.darkroom

Essential Links to Photography

Here's a great one-stop shop for photography resources on the Net: design and graphic resources, photography mailing lists and Usenet groups, galleries and exhibitions, and online photo zines.

Web:
http://he.net/~brumley/life/photography.htm

PHYSICS

Einstein in 3D

Experience Einstein's theory of relativity in a graphical, three-dimensional environment. Mathematical equations are turned into pictures for a much more visual physics experience.

Web:
http://jean-luc.ncsa.uiuc.edu/Exhibits/

Fusion

This web page offers links to fusion resources and pages at a number of institutions, including the University of Texas, MIT, U.C. Berkeley, the Office of Fusion Energy, an index of fusion research and links to related sites.

Web:
http://fusioned.gat.com/webstuff/FusionInfo.html

Usenet:
sci.physics.fusion

Physics Talk and General Discussion

Without physics, the world would be so much more dull and life would be much too easy to understand. Exercise your brain by getting in on some physics discussion.

Usenet:
> alt.sci.physics.acoustics
> alt.sci.physics.new-theories
> alt.sci.physics.plutonium
> alt.sci.physics.spam
> bionet.biophysics
> sci.astro.research
> sci.med.physics
> sci.physics
> sci.physics.accelerators
> sci.physics.computational.fluid-dynamics
> sci.physics.fusion
> sci.physics.particle
> sci.physics.plasma
> sci.physics.research

PICTURES AND CLIP ART

Clip Art

Need clip art for your books, publications, garage sale fliers, home pages, term papers or whatever? But just as soon not (shudder) pay for them? Okay, on the Net there are lots of public domain clip art sites ripe for the plucking. In these copious archives, you'll find all the royalty-free drawings, etchings, and whatnot that you could possibly use. If, as 'tis said by those who know such things, a picture is worth a thousand words, then these resources will increase your vocabulary by several million.

Web:
> http://www.barrysclipart.com/
> http://www.ist.net/clipart/

Usenet:
> alt.binaries.clip-art

Holography

This cool holographic pattern generator is something you have to see. Play around with the form to design a hologram to your specifications, make a million of them or fiddle with one to get it just perfect. You can save the images you make, too. At this site you will also be able to read news about the holography industry and a FAQ for those of you who are more technically inclined.

Web:
    http://www.holo.com/holo/gram.html

Kai's Power Tools Backgrounds Archive

Spiff up your graphics or your web page with these downloadable backgrounds for use with Photoshop. If you want to make your own backgrounds, read the tutorial on how it's done.

Web:
    http://the-tech.mit.edu/KPT/bgs.html

POETRY

Poetry Archives

There is a lot of poetry for you on the Net. Here are some collections that I think you will enjoy: lots and lots of well-known poems, as well as links to other poetry sites. These are good places to visit if you are looking for a particular poem or work from a particular author, or if you just feel like browsing for something to read.

Web:
    http://eng.hss.cmu.edu/poetry/
    http://etext.lib.virginia.edu/britpo.html
    http://www.hypersven.com/poets.corner/

Poetry Talk and General Discussion

Spirits soar free on the wings of poetry. Show your verses to like-minded, creative people. If you ask, you can get advice, but there are more poems posted than critiques.

Usenet:
   rec.arts.poems

Shiki Internet Haiku Salon

An introduction to haiku, including its history, information about Shiki Masaoka, the founder of modern haiku, and links to many haiku poems and resources, including mailing lists and poetry servers.

Web:
   http://mikan.cc.matsuyama-u.ac.jp/~shiki/

POLITICS

Democrats

The Democratic party was founded in 1792 by Thomas Jefferson. Originally, party members were called "Republicans" or "Democratic-Republicans" but in 1830, the name was shortened to "Democrats". This is the official web site of the Democratic party and, like the Republican site, there are no huge surprises. Visit the "Donkey Stomp" (a Republican bashing section) and the hilarious Quote-o-Rama page (which brings back memories of Dan Quayle). You can also read news and articles about the party and what you can do to help. The Usenet group is for the discussion of Democratic views and platforms.

Web:
   http://www.democrats.org/

Usenet:
   alt.politics.democrats.d

International Politics Talk and General Discussion

Usenet has a number of discussion groups specifically for the discussing of the politics of particular countries and regions: Britain, Europe, India, Italy, China, Middle East, Tibet and the former Soviet Union. As long as you stay more or less on topic, anything goes. However, please remember that if you are responding to an article written by someone in a foreign country, their first language may not be the same as yours. On the Net, irony and politics do not mix well. The world is a big place, and there is lots of room for two people to disagree and still both be right.

Usenet:
> alt.politics.british
> alt.politics.ec
> alt.politics.europe.misc
> alt.politics.india.communist
> alt.politics.india.progressive
> alt.politics.italy
> talk.politics.china
> talk.politics.european-union
> talk.politics.mideast
> talk.politics.soviet
> talk.politics.tibet

Republicans

The United States Republican Party was founded in 1854. The first Republican to be elected President was Abraham Lincoln (in 1860). This is the official Republican web site, and you pretty much get what you would expect. For instance, when I visited, I saw an opponent-bashing section in which I could view the "Outrage of the Day" (a hilarious animated picture of Bill Clinton as Pinocchio). There are also news releases, a chat room, some fun political stuff (games, crossword puzzles), email addresses of political people, information about GOP-TV, as well as background information on various governmental and political topics. Overall, there is lots and lots of pro-Republican, anti-Democrat stuff. For discussion of Republican views and platforms, you can participate in the Usenet group.

Web:
> http://www.rnc.org/

Usenet:
> alt.politics.usa.republican

Weird Politics and Conspiracies

Some days do you get the feeling there is a lot of stuff going on around you that you don't know about? It's probably true. Find out what sort of weird things the government is doing while you aren't looking. This site has lots of documents and archives from some of the more unusual political movements.

Web:
> http://www.physics.wisc.edu/~shalizi/hyper-weird/conspiracy.html

PRIVACY

Anonymous Remailers

It's embarrassing when your mom catches you posting to **alt.binaries.pictures. erotica.furry**. Avoid all the hassle of trying to explain by not getting caught in the first place. Try using an anonymous remailer. Here is information on what these services are and how they work.

Web:
> http://electron.rutgers.edu/~gambino/anon_servers/anon.html
> http://www.cs.berkeley.edu/~raph/remailer-faq.html

Electronic Privacy Information Center

The Electronic Privacy Information Center (EPIC) is a public interest research center based in Washington, D.C. EPIC concerns itself with all types of privacy issues: Internet privacy, medical records, proposals for national ID cards, and so on. The EPIC web site houses a large collection of privacy-related information and resources on many different topics. If you care at all about these issues, take a few minutes to look around. I guarantee you will find something useful or interesting.

Web:
> http://www.epic.org/

Privacy Resources

Privacy is everyone's business: you and you, and you there hiding behind your Macintosh thinking I won't notice you. Once the big boys (Netscape, Microsoft, AT&T, and so on) get into the "free software" act, it won't be long until you find that somewhere along the line, your personal interests were sold out for a handful of magic stock options and advertising revenues. I feel strongly that it is up to all of us to protect our privacy. The best way to start is by understanding the issues, and these sites are a good place to begin. Remember, once "they" control your browser, you will be able to run all over the Net, but you won't be able to hide.

Web:
> http://world.std.com/~franl/privacy/privacy.html
> http://www.vortex.com/privacy.html

PSYCHOLOGY

Creativity and Creative Problem Solving

That problem has really been nagging at you. It sits in the back of your mind taunting you, demanding attention, begging to be dealt with. No ordinary problem solving is going to take care of it. What's the difference between plain old problem solving and creative problem solving? Discover the answer to that question by examining stimulating factors for creativity in product development, strategic issues, and organizational settings.

Listserv Mailing List:
> List Name: **crea-cps**
> Subscribe to: **listserv@nic.surfnet.nl**

Optical Illusions

Optical illusions are really cool, even without the benefit of caffeine or other artificial substances. This site has a nice collection of images that make you think twice (or more) about what you are seeing.

Web:
> http://illusionworks.com/

Psychological Help

There are days when things seem overwhelming and unpleasant or you encounter a problem and you don't know exactly what to do with it. Check out the Usenet group that offers discussion about the problems people face. Maybe you will find an answer or just someone to talk to.

Usenet:
    alt.psychology.help

QUOTATIONS

Daily Quotations

There are a lot of people in the world and, every day, somebody says something interesting. This web site will show you a new quote every day, selected from a current event of some type. This site is a great place to visit every day, so you can have something to read while you take your daily vitamin. And when you have a little extra time, you can browse the collections of old quotations looking for some instant nostalgia.

Web:
    http://www.quotations.com/w_filter.htm

Quotation Talk and General Discussion

Here is the Usenet group devoted to a discussion of quotations. This is the place to ask if anyone knows who said "It isn't necessary to have relatives in Kansas City in order to be unhappy." Of course, questions like this only get answered if people participate, so if you like quotes, why don't you follow the discussion and see if you can help someone else.

Usenet:
    alt.quotations

Today's Fortune

If you are trying to cut down on sweets and you are bypassing the after-dinner fortune cookie, at least you don't have to feel deprived. Load up this page to get a nice fortune quote. And if you don't like it, you can reload to get another one.

Web:
    http://www.bsdi.com/fortune

RADIO

Amateur Radio

Radio is a great hobby and one day when you are an expert, you can have your own nationally syndicated talk show and screaming fans will throw themselves at your feet when you go out in public. Until then, you can spend time reading Usenet groups especially for amateur radio enthusiasts. Topics cover construction, packet and digital radio modes, transmission, regulations, repair and other general topics.

Web:
http://www.acs.ncsu.edu/HamRadio/

Usenet:
rec.radio.amateur.antenna
rec.radio.amateur.digital.misc
rec.radio.amateur.equipment
rec.radio.amateur.homebrew
rec.radio.amateur.misc
rec.radio.amateur.packet
rec.radio.amateur.policy
rec.radio.amateur.space
rec.radio.amateur.swap

Ham Radio

Do you want to be famous? Start practicing now by becoming a ham radio operator. After a while you will get a reputation around the neighborhood as that studly ham guy. Then you can start telling your opinions on the radio, build up your ego, put on a few pounds and eventually have your own conservative talk show on mainstream radio. Wouldn't that be fun? So get on the Net now and learn all about ham radio. The faster you learn, the faster you will be on your way to success.

Web:
http://www.cc.columbia.edu/~fuat/cuarc/callsign-servers.html
http://www.qrz.com/cgi-bin/webcall

Old-Time Radio

I love old radio shows like Jack Benny and Burns and Allen. This web site offers historical information about old radio shows and links to radio-related pages. Get a blast from the past.

Web:
http://www.old-time.com/

REFERENCE

Acronyms

Here is a resource that should be in everyone's bookmark list. You specify an acronym, and a program looks it up in the master list and tells you what the acronym means. You can also search the list of meanings for a particular word or expression. If you have a friend who thinks he knows everything, ask him what MOTSTJHTBHWIGH means.

Web:
> http://www.ucc.ie/info/net/acronyms/

Roget's Thesaurus

In 1852, Peter Mark Roget published the first edition of his "Thesaurus of English Words and Phrases", on which he had been working for 50 years. Throughout successive editions—which were supervised by Roget, his son, and later his grandson—what we now call the Roget's Thesaurus has become a standard reference work of the English language. The purpose of the Roget's Thesaurus is simply stated: you use it when you know the meaning of a word but do now know the word. Roget arranged all the words in the English language and their idiomatic combinations, not in alphabetical order as in a dictionary, but according to the ideas they express. If you care at all about writing, please take some time to become familiar with this classic reference and how to use it. Treating a Roget's Thesaurus as if it were nothing more than a dictionary of synonyms is like using a collection of Mozart CDs as a paperweight.

Web:
> http://humanities.uchicago.edu/forms_unrest/ROGET.html
> http://www.thesaurus.com/

Word Detective

Enjoy the online version of a column in which the writer answers about words and their origins. If you enjoy learning about language and words, you will like this site. Here are some examples. (1) One guy wrote a letter because he and his girlfriend had been having an argument about whether to say "have your cake and eat it too" or "eat your cake and have it too". (2) Another person asked if "busting someone's chop" and "busting someone's hump" is the same thing. (3) A third reader who mentioned the term "old fogey" wanted to know if there were such a thing as a "young fogey". (4) And finally, there is a link to an answer to the question "Aside from 'angry' and 'hungry', what well-known English word ends in 'gry'?" By the way, the answers to these questions are (1) It doesn't matter. (2) No. (3) Yes, but people don't use the expression. (4) There are no other common words that end in "gry". The whole thing is a hoax.

Web:
> http://www.users.interport.net/~words1/

Usenet:
> alt.fan.word-detective

RELIGION

Bibles Online

You can use these online Bibles to search and read specific passages. There are a variety of languages available as well as links to related reference material. On the Net, inspiration is never more than a few mouse clicks away.

Web:
> http://ccel.wheaton.edu/wwsb/
> http://www.gospelcom.net/bible

R

Christianity Talk and General Discussion

Discover important topics on Christianity. Fundamentalism, evangelism, interfaith marriages, the Trinity, biblical history, tithing, holidays, and the effects of the New Age movement are just a taste of what you will find.

Usenet:
> alt.christnet
> alt.christnet.christianlife
> alt.christnet.christnews
> alt.christnet.ethics
> alt.christnet.evangelical
> alt.christnet.hypocrisy
> alt.christnet.philosophy
> alt.christnet.prayer
> alt.christnet.theology
> alt.religion.christian
> soc.religion.christian
> soc.religion.christian.youth-work

Comparative Religion Reference

This is a table which organizes an enormous amount of useful and interesting information about many different religious faiths. I recommend this as a resource to anyone who needs to find out the basics of a particular religion or sect. What is especially insightful is you can see how various sects are related to their parent faiths. To help you use this site I have two suggestions. (1) Maximize your browser window, to make the table as large as possible. (2) Read the introduction before you start using the table.

Web:
> http://www.servtech.com/public/mcroghan/religion.htm

Religious Tolerance

Here's a refreshing change of pace from the hurry-scurry of everyone evangelizing on the Net or the eruptions of arguments between believers and non-believers. This web page promotes religious tolerance and makes an attempt to educate everyone about the various religions around the world. You can also read the United Nations Declarations on Religious Intolerance, articles on religious freedom, a glossary of terms, information on ritual abuse and cults, and find links to religious home pages.

Web:
> http://www.kosone.com/people/ocrt/ocrt_hp.htm

RELIGION: SECTS AND CULTS

Cyberculture Religions

The Internet is the new medium for enlightenment, according to some people. Join in the cyberevangelistic movement, by checking out some of these religions that have been spawned by the online culture.

Web:
> http://ourworld.compuserve.com/homepages/shadowcat/
> http://www.technosophy.com/
> http://www.tiac.net/users/ighf/

New Religious Movements

From what we have seen, there is big money and fame in the business of religion. In addition to that, you can get all the women you want. This academic group discusses new religious movements. If you are interested in becoming a deity in this lifetime, you might check in and see if you can get any helpful hints.

Listserv Mailing List:
> List Name: **nurel-l**
> Subscribe to: **listserv@listserv.ucalgary.ca**

Paganism

The nice thing about paganism is that you can pretty much do whatever you want. This is a nature-based religion with no central dogma. Pagans celebrate various gods and goddesses (one or many), nature and the cycles of the sun and moon. The best thing is that they don't have to wear uncomfortable clothes and sit in church. If any of this appeals to you, check out some of the pagan resources on the Net or talk to a friendly pagan at a Usenet group near you.

Web:
> http://www.cascade.net/arachne.html

Usenet:
> alt.pagan

ROLE PLAYING

Fantasy Role Playing Talk and General Discussion

Join up with the folks in Usenet and discuss your favorite or your most hated role-playing game and all the issues that come with it. Magic, mystery, and adventure await you once you step across the line that separates fantasy from reality.

Usenet:
> alt.dragons-inn
> rec.games.frp
> rec.games.frp.advocacy
> rec.games.frp.archives
> rec.games.frp.cyber
> rec.games.frp.dnd
> rec.games.frp.gurps
> rec.games.frp.storyteller
> rec.games.frp.super-heroes

Live-Action Role Playing

What a great way to spend the evening—dress up as someone else and take on a whole new life. Say goodbye to reality by doing some live-action role playing where you talk to other characters and solve a mystery or a problem the way your character would. You'll never be able to go back to ordinary board games again.

Web:
> http://www.coil.com/~zargonis/shade.html

Usenet:
> rec.games.frp.live-action

Miniatures

If you like to take the time to buy miniatures, paint them or role-play with miniatures, this is a great resource for you. This archive offers information and rules to games in a variety of categories such as ancient, medieval, Napoleonic, world wars, modern, science fiction and many other types of settings.

Web:
> http://www.cabm.rutgers.edu/~hooper/miniatures/bill/Miniatures_Rules.html

ROMANCE

Couples

It's the best of times, it's the worst of times. Relationships have their ups and downs, but like a roller coaster, it's fun and thrilling, makes you afraid, and makes you laugh. See what is going on in the lives of other couples. Get ideas for romantic outings, anniversaries, how to patch up a fuss, or what to do with in-laws.

Usenet:
> soc.couples
> soc.couples.intercultural

Listserv Mailing List:
> List Name: **couples-l**
> Subscribe to: **listserv@cornell.edu**

Love Letters

Every time you sit down to write a nice love letter to the person of your dreams, it never seems to come out sounding as wonderful as it does in your head. Don't let that stop you. Instead, get help from Cyrano de Bergerac, the notable romantic. Fill out a form with a few details and Cyrano will write the letter for you. Love was never so easy.

Web:
> **http://www.nando.net/toys/cyrano.html**

Romance Talk and General Discussion

Have you noticed life isn't quite like the covers of paperback romance novels (or the inside of the romance novels, for that matter)? Do something about that by generating a romantic fire with others who mourn the death of romance. Remember Cyrano de Bergerac and his words that could melt the hair off a moose? Where do you think he got his start?

Usenet:
> alt.romance
> alt.romance.chat
> alt.romance.mature-adult

Singles

Your mother probably said that anyone you can pick up in a bar is not someone with whom you want to develop a serious relationship. (What you probably didn't want to tell her was that you weren't looking for a serious relationship.) In the event that you change your mind, stop in at the nicest singles hangout in Usenet and the IRC and find that special someone just right for you. The web site has the **soc.singles** FAQ (frequently asked question list).

Web:
> http://www.csclub.uwaterloo.ca/u/rridge/ss/big/faq.html

Usenet:
> soc.singles

IRC:
> #singles

SCIENCE

Annals of Improbable Research

The Annals of Improbable Research (AIR) is a science humor magazine. It's hard to describe what you find here; suffice to say that, if you like science and you have a good sense of humor, you'll enjoy what you see. (Think of AIR as the National Lampoon for smart people.) Footnotes: (1) If you liked the old Journal of Irreproducible Results, you'll enjoy the AIR. (2) These same people also give out the annual Ig Nobel Awards to honor people whose achievements "cannot or should not be reproduced".

Web:
> http://www.improb.com/
> http://www.improb.com/airchives/mini-AIR/

Oceanography

The Earth has one large interconnected sea of water, covering 71 percent of the planet's surface. Traditionally, we divide all this water into four main oceans: the Pacific Ocean, the Indian Ocean, the Atlantic Ocean and the Arctic Ocean. Taken together, these oceans cover about 139,400,000 sq mi (361,000,000 sq km) and contain about 322,280,000 cu mi (1,347,000,000 cu km) of water. The average depth is about 12,230 ft (3,730 m). Oceanography is the study of the ocean and the life it supports. As such, oceanography integrates biology, chemistry, geography, geology, physics and meteorology into one marine-oriented field of study. There are a great many oceanography resources on the Net. Here are some web sites that contain particularly good collections. I have also included the web sites of two of the main oceanographical research organizations in the United States: Scripps Institution of Oceanography (California) and the Woods Hole Oceanographic Institution (Massachusetts).

Web:
http://scilib.ucsd.edu/sio/inst/
http://sio.ucsd.edu/
http://www.cms.udel.edu/
http://www.mth.uea.ac.uk/ocean/oceanography.html
http://www.whoi.edu/

Research Methods in Science

You need a certain kind of mind to be an organized and efficient researcher. Here is a list that helps researchers in classification, clustering, phylogeny estimation and related methods of data analysis to contact other researchers in the same fields. All professions are welcome to the list.

Listserv Mailing List:
List Name: **class-l**
Subscribe to: **listserv@ccvm.sunysb.edu**

Science Magazines

Here are links to a massive number of science-related magazines. This is a great way to check out a mag if you think you may want to subscribe, or to browse unfamiliar publications just to see what they are.

Web:
http://www.enews.com/monster/science/

SCIENCE FICTION, FANTASY AND HORROR

Science and Science Fiction

Stretch your mind by pushing your imagination to the limit. How real is the science in science fiction? A wide variety of topics are covered, such as the possibility of force fields, transcendental engineering, and Hawking radiation. Invent your own theories or pick apart someone else's.

Usenet:
>   rec.arts.sf.science

Science Fiction Resource Guide

This guide has everything under the sun about science fiction, including details on authors, awards, bibliographies, bookstores, fan clubs, movies, publishers, role-playing games, television, Usenet groups, and zines, as well as archives, reviews and criticism, fiction writing and more.

Web:
>   http://sflovers.rutgers.edu/Web/SFRG/sf-resource-guide.html

Science Fiction Writing

Allow yourself to linger on the words, your eyes playing gently back and forth across the pages of your latest sci-fi novel. There is something tangible about a book that you just can't get from television or movies. Discuss your favorite book, hear about someone else's. Find out what's new and what is hopelessly out of print.

Usenet:
>   rec.arts.sf.written

SECRET STUFF

Disney Secrets

Disney theme parks are very controlled. Try causing even a slight amount of trouble and see how fast the security people (materializing out of nowhere) will give you the bum's rush. When you visit a Disney park, everything you see and everything the employees do is planned carefully. For instance, you are never more than 25 paces away from a garbage can. Disney management goes to a great deal of trouble to sustain the illusion of "the happiest place on Earth". That is why people who work at Disney theme parks are called "cast members". (Repeat this often enough and even the employees think it's normal.) That is why I love to read about Disney secrets. None of these secrets are all that important. Nevertheless, they are intriguing because you just know that the pleasant folks who control the world of Disney would very much prefer that you didn't know anything about their behind-the-scenes management.

Web:
> http://musky.oitc.com/Disney/Secrets.html

Usenet:
> alt.disney.secrets

Phreaking

What to talk about phone phreaking: telephones, exchanges, toll fraud, kodez, signaling, and so on? Walk gently into that good night and talk to the people who love to phreak. To help you fit in, look at the web sites for help with phreaking terms and abbreviations. Or, if you would actually like to build a "box", you can get the plans. (However, now that phone companies use modern switching systems, most of these boxes don't work. Still, maybe you can find a red box somewhere.)

Web:
> http://arirang.miso.co.kr/~xter/phreak/

IRC:
> #phreak

Warez

Discussion of where and how to obtain the latest cracked and pirated software, much of it available through hidden sites on the Internet. Some of the channels are often by invitation only, so you will require contacts to get inside. There are lots of these channels. Start at the highest number you can find at any time and work your way down, seeing if they will let you in. (Unless you are a personal friend of God, you will never get in anything lower than **#warez5**.)

IRC:
>   #warez
>   #warez1
>   #warez2
>   #warez3
>   #warez4
>   #warez5
>   #warez6
>   #warez7

SEX

Complete Internet Sex Resource Guide

If you are looking for the latest sex resources on the Net, it's likely that you will find them here. Check out this index of mailing lists and Usenet groups.

Web:
>   http://sleepingbeauty.com/world/netsex.html

Pantyhose and Stockings

Soft, sleek, sensual... and more. Talk to the people who really appreciate what the well-dressed leg is wearing this season. Share your opinions and read provocative stories.

Usenet:
>   alt.pantyhose

Sex Stories

There's nothing like curling up with a provocative story and a hot cup of tea or a little classical music. You won't find tea or music here, but you will never want for a good, sexy story (or a bad one, for that matter). Stories range from mildly erotic mainstream to bold, raunchy kink. There's something for everyone. And if you'd like to hang around afterwards over coffee or a smoke and discuss the literary merit of the writing, check out **alt.sex.stories.d** for discussion.

Usenet:
> alt.sex.stories
> alt.sex.stories.d
> alt.sex.stories.gay
> alt.sex.stories.hetero
> alt.sex.stories.tg

SEXUALITY

Gender Collection

This web site offers a gigantic collection containing a wide variety of documents about women and men, gays and straights. There is history, politics and even some plain old fun. This is an excellent source of gender information.

Web:
> http://english-www.hss.cmu.edu/gender/

Purity Tests

Purity tests have long been a staple of Usenet humor groups. These tests consist of many sexually oriented questions designed to help you find out just how "pure" you are.

Web:
> http://www.bath.ac.uk/~ee3ken/purity/
> http://www.nmt.edu/~kscott/purity/
> http://www.sexkittyn.com/newsbrief.html

Sex Addiction Recovery

There are worse things than sex to which a person could be addicted; maybe that makes it even harder to recover from this addiction. This support group offers a way for recovering sex addicts to share feelings and get ideas on the recovery process.

Usenet:
> alt.recovery.addiction.sexual

SPACE

Electronic Universe Project

Space is cool because there is so much of it and it's just waiting to be filled with stuff. Get a closer look at our very own galaxy with all its stars and nebulae and planets. See movies of interacting galaxies and images and light curves of a recent supernova. If you want to impress your special loved one with your knowledge of the stars, but the sky happens to be cloudy, this site can be your backup plan.

Web:
> http://zebu.uoregon.edu/galaxy.html

Space Missions

Planning to go where no one has gone before? Check out the information on past or present space missions to make sure that nobody has been to your destination before you. You will find links to Apollo missions, the Cassini Mission, Clementine, Magellan and more.

Web:
> http://www.ksc.nasa.gov/history/history.html

Space Talk and General Discussion

Talk, talk, talk about everything under the sun (and the sun as well). Discuss all manner of space-oriented topics with aficionados around the world.

Usenet:
> sci.space
> sci.space.policy
> sci.space.science
> sci.space.tech

SPORTS AND ATHLETICS

Baseball

These sites are for baseball fans worldwide. Browse discussion groups, baseball collectible info, stats, rosters, team reports and fantasy leagues, and utilize the baseball search engine.

Web:
> http://www.justwright.com/sports/baseball.html
> http://www2.nando.net/SportServer/baseball/

Sports

There is more to sports than just the brawl of physical contact. Sportsters also come in the form of writers and newsmakers. Read articles and news stories about sports of all kinds.

Web:
> http://www.awa.com/arena
> http://www.sfgate.com/sports/
> http://www.tns.lcs.mit.edu/cgi-bin/sports

Sports: Women

Forget that chili cook-off. Get out of the kitchen and on to the playing field. Here are links to all sorts of women's sports, teams and sports clubs: baseball, skating, volleyball, gymnastics, basketball, golf, bicycling and many others.

Web:
> http://fiat.gslis.utexas.edu/~lewisa/womsprt.html

STAR TREK

Star Trek Stories and Parodies

If you can't get enough of Star Trek on television or in movies and books, check out this corner of the Internet universe. Creative and witty individuals post stories and parodies related to Star Trek in Usenet groups and on web sites. Often FAQs on submissions are posted containing tips for writing for Deep Space Nine and the Star Trek: Voyager series, where to send submissions, what to do, and what not to do when writing.

Web:
> http://www.netshop.net/Startrek/web/Stories.html

Usenet:
> alt.startrek.creative

S

Star Trek Talk and General Discussion

Light and lively debate volleys, occasionally turning warm, then hot as you defend your favorite episode or character. Talk turns to old shows, bloopers, insider information on actors' lives, and burning questions like, "Should the use of the Holodeck be restricted until the engineers eliminate the bugs (such as a malfunctioning mortality failsafe)?"

Usenet:

> rec.arts.startrek.misc

Star Trek Universe

This moderated group offers in-depth and accurate information on the universe as it relates to Star Trek. Read press releases, episode credits, synopses and factual articles. Since all posts are filtered through a moderator, you can be assured of the reliability of what you read. Queries are best moved to one of the other Star Trek groups.

Usenet:

> rec.arts.startrek.info

SUPPORT GROUPS

Divorce

Those who are going through a divorce can access a huge amount of resources that can help you through your trying times. Available resources include law and legal resources, information on recovery, support and child custody, resources for men and women and support group lists. You will also find resources on parenting as well as things to help you cope, such as links relating to religion and spirituality and some fun stuff to cheer you up.

Web:

> http://hughson.com/

Usenet:

> alt.support.divorce

Usenet Support Groups

It's great to know that when you have a problem, there are people who will be supportive of you. All over the world there are people who are willing to take the time to listen to the problems and try to meet the emotional needs of others. Get good information on nearly any subject like medical, emotional or psychological problems.

Usenet:

    alt.abuse-recovery
    alt.abuse.offender.recovery
    alt.abuse.recovery
    alt.abuse.transcendence
    alt.recovery
    alt.recovery.aa
    alt.recovery.adult-children
    alt.recovery.catholicism
    alt.recovery.codependency
    alt.recovery.compulsive-eat
    alt.recovery.mormonism
    alt.recovery.na
    alt.recovery.religion
    alt.support.abuse-partners
    alt.support.asthma
    alt.support.ataxia
    alt.support.big-folks
    alt.support.breast-implant
    alt.support.cancer
    alt.support.cancer.prostate
    alt.support.cerebral-palsy
    alt.support.childfree
    alt.support.chronic-pain
    alt.support.dev-delays
    alt.support.diabetes.kids
    alt.support.disabled.sexuality
    alt.support.dissociation
    alt.support.dwarfism
    alt.support.dystonia

S

alt.support.endometriosis
alt.support.epilepsy
alt.support.ex-cult
alt.support.food-allergies
alt.support.glaucoma
alt.support.headaches.migraine
alt.support.hearing-loss
alt.support.hemophilia
alt.support.herpes
alt.support.inter-cystitis
alt.support.jaw-disorders
alt.support.kidney-failure
alt.support.learning-disab
alt.support.loneliness
alt.support.marfan
alt.support.menopause
alt.support.mult-sclerosis
alt.support.musc-dystrophy
alt.support.myasthe-gravis
alt.support.obesity
alt.support.ocd
alt.support.ostomy
alt.support.personality
alt.support.post-polio
alt.support.prostate.prostatitis
alt.support.schizophrenia
alt.support.shyness
alt.support.sinusitis
alt.support.skin-diseases
alt.support.social-phobia
alt.support.spina-bifida
alt.support.stuttering
alt.support.survivors.prozac
alt.support.thyroid
alt.support.tinnitus
alt.support.tourette
alt.support.trauma-ptsd
alt.support.turner-syndrom

soc.support.fat-acceptance
soc.support.loneliness
soc.support.youth.gay-lesbian-bi

Widows and Widowers

Widows and widowers have a place to find support and friendship. This mailing list and web site are for widows and widowers to learn and talk about issues that affect their daily lives.

Web:
> http://www.fortnet.org/~goshorn/

Majordomo Mailing List:
> List Name: **widow**
> Subscribe to: **majordomo@fortnet.org**

TECHNOLOGY

Computer-Based Simulations

Computer-based simulations are good because you can do lots of terrible things on the computer and see what happens and chances are good that you won't kill or maim anyone. Here's a web site with various simulations such as defense modeling, fluid dynamics, oceanographic modeling and others. Go have fun.

Web:
> http://www.dataspace.com/WWW/vlib/comp-simulation.html

Technology Talk and General Discussion

As technology gets more advanced, we get more new toys to try. Explore the ideas and philosophy of technology as well as the more technical side of applying technology to real life. This Usenet group is good to read while waiting for someone to invent robots who will do all your cooking and cleaning for you.

Usenet:
> alt.technology.misc

Virtual Reality Resources

Here's a great collection of virtual reality resources available on the Net, including web sites, ftp archives, bibliographies, mailing lists, research and academic institutions, Usenet groups, FAQs, software, papers, and other material related to virtual worlds and virtual reality.

Web:
> http://www.hitl.washington.edu/projects/knowledge_base/onthenet.html

Usenet:
> sci.virtual-worlds

Listserv Mailing List:
> List Name: **virtu-l**
> Subscribe to: **listserv@postoffice.cso.uiuc.edu**

TELEPHONE AND TELECOM

Business and Toll-Free Directory Listings

Looking for a particular business? If the company or organization you want has a telephone, they are probably in here somewhere. These web sites allow you to search for the phone number of a business. Some of the sites are directories of toll-free numbers, the others help you find regular numbers.

Web:
> http://inter800.com/search.htm
> http://www.bigbook.com/
> http://www.tollfree.att.net/
> http://www.zip2.com/

Computers and Communications

This web page provides links to telecommunications companies, organizations, programs and projects, standards, and other computer communication-related resources. The page is intended to provide organization for the vast quantity of information available on the emerging global information economy.

Web:
> http://www.cmpcmm.com/content.html

Telecom Discussions and Digest

The Telecom Digest is an online digest posted regularly to Usenet. If you are interested in telecommunications, this is a source of information worth reading regularly. The **telecom** discussion groups are for all manner of telecommunications including—but not limited to—the telephone system. For more immediate gratification, check out the web site.

Web:
   http://hyperarchive.lcs.mit.edu/telecom-archives/

Usenet:
   alt.dcom.telecom
   comp.dcom.telecom

TELEVISION

Television Guide

This web page offers the ultimate TV list containing links for more than 30 television shows, a list of major TV-related sites, a place to post your favorite links and remove everybody else's boring links, and a TV poll where you can broadcast your opinions to a few hundred people.

Web:
   http://www.ultimatetv.com/

Television Talk and General Discussion

Don't waste your life in sitting in front of the computer. Instead, you can waste it in front of another electronic box which gives you a continuous feed of images that will lull you into a hypnotic daze and make you susceptible to the lure of home shopping channels. If you are so hooked that you like to talk about television when you are not actually watching it, check out these Usenet groups. The **alt.fan** group is for discussion of characters and actors on television. The **alt.tv** and **rec.arts.tv** are for discussion of specific television shows. The **rec.arts.sf.tv** is for discussion of particular science fiction shows.

Usenet:
   alt.fan.*
   alt.tv.*
   rec.arts.sf.tv.*
   rec.arts.tv.*

TV Episode Guides

This web site is a godsend to fanatics who need to know exactly when each episode of their favorite series aired. There are episode guides to many popular TV shows, including information about the individual episodes. After all, how many places can you turn to at three in the morning when you just have to know when Jerry put the Tweety Bird Pez dispenser on Elaine's knee? (It was episode #314 of Seinfeld, January 15, 1992, during a classical piano recital.)

Web:
> http://www.tardis.ed.ac.uk/~dave/guides/

TRAVEL

Money Abroad FAQ

This FAQ (frequently asked question list) offers information about dealing with money in just about every country you are likely to ever visit. Learn about banknotes and coins, traveler's checks, credit cards, and how and where to get cash when you need it. There is a guide to which form of payment is best for each country, with the black markets covered appropriately.

Web:
> http://www.inria.fr/robotvis/personnel/laveau/money-faq/money-abroad.html

Travel and Tourism Web Pages

There is no sense in keeping yourself closed off from the entire world. Check out all the places that you can travel and start planning your exciting world adventures. Even if you never go, it's certainly fun to dream.

Web:
> http://www.infohub.com/TRAVEL/traveller.html

Travel Health Advice

If you are planning a trip, you must take a look at some of the resources on the Net devoted to travel health advice. You can find information about particular countries you are going to visit, the hazards specific to that country, listings of immunizations you need and potential diseases you can bring home as unique souvenirs for you or your friends. While you are planning ahead, take a look at the tips on how to stay healthy while flying. You can learn about air quality on planes, what food to avoid during flights, how to prevent dehydration and much, much more. These sites will give you what you need to plan for a healthy vacation.

Web:

> http://www.flyana.com/index2.html
> http://www.tekamah.com/travelmed/

T

TRIVIA

Movie Trivia

If you like movies, you may be interested in trivia. For example, did you know that the working title for Annie Hall was "Anhedonia"? (It's a medical term referring to the inability to feel pleasure.) How about this? When Woody Allen was making The Purple Rose of Cairo, he originally case Michael Keaton in the male lead role. However, Allen wasn't satisfied with the first footage and replaced Keaton with Jeff Daniels. If you find factoids like this interesting, you may be a movie trivia person. Connect to these web sites and find out for sure. If you like to compete, you will find a great many movie trivia contests you can enter.

Web:

> http://www.cis.ohio-state.edu/hypertext/faq/usenet/movies/trivia-faq/faq.html
> http://www.primate.wisc.edu/people/hamel/movtriv.html

Today's Events in History

Do you ever feel like today is just like every other day? Well, I can tell you it's not. In fact, go right now and look up what happened on this day in history and I bet you will learn something wonderful. Just think, on this very day, something astounding happened. Watch what you do today. You might end up on this list.

Web:

> http://erebus.phys.cwru.edu/~copi/events.html

Trivia Page

When your favorite game show is over and already you are starting to have withdrawals, check out this site which has lots of links to various trivia sites all over the Net. There is enough trivia here to choke Alex Trebek.

Web:

> http://www.primate.wisc.edu/people/hamel/trivia.html

UFOS AND ALIENS

UFO Chatting

When it's late at night and you are afraid of the dark, you can find some companionship on IRC. The two X-Files channels are populated by people who are fans of the X-Files television show, but they also chat about aliens and UFOs. The **#ufo** channel is exclusively for talking about extraterrestrials and UFO-related subjects.

IRC:

> #ufo
> #x-files
> #xfiles

UFO Pictures

When you need some interesting pictures for your photo album, head straight to the Net and explore these archives of UFO snapshots. You can download them and put interesting captions on them like "last year's trip to England to make crop circles" or "Uncle Marty buzzes unsuspecting American farm workers". Pictures of alleged UFOs are divided by geographic locality and year.

Web:

> http://oasi.shiny.it/Homes/CISU/intphoto.htm
> http://ourworld.compuserve.com/homepages/AndyPage/ufopictu.htm

UFO Talk and General Discussion

Visit these Usenet groups for a cool, rational, scientific, intellectual, well-reasoned, plausible discussion about aliens visiting the Earth and swanking around like they own the place. Investigate, in person, the theory that man is really nature's last word. Just the place to spend your time when the TV is on the fritz.

Usenet:
    alt.alien.visitors
    alt.paranet.abduct
    alt.paranet.ufo
    alt.paranormal

USENET

U

Usenet Filtering Service

It's going to be an all-day job if you want to check every single Usenet group for reports of Elvis sightings, so why not let someone do it for you? Subscribe to this news filtering service, and they will send you postings on any keywords or phrases that you choose. So, if you're paranoid and you could just swear people are talking about you, this will be the proof you can finally show your therapist.

Web:
    http://www.reference.com/

Usenet Kooks

It used to be safe inside your home, but not anymore. The kooks are coming off the street and straight onto the Internet. Collected at this web site are the **alt.usenet.kooks** FAQ, the net.legends archives, information on Kibology, archives of the postings of various Usenet kooks, and the all-important Kook of the Month archive. Check to see if your name is there.

Web:
    http://www.wetware.com/mlegare/kotm/

Usenet:
    alt.usenet.kooks

Usenet Personalities

Just as there are people who gain notoriety in neighborhoods or in the news, there are faceless people who become equally notable in the Internet community and set tongues to wagging around the world. Read about these people and see samples of their posts and join the praise or cursing of them.

Usenet:

> alt.net.personalities

Weird Places to Hang Out on Usenet

Among the thousands of Usenet groups, there are a few strange places to hang out where anything goes. These are groups that were started as a joke, or real groups that have been abandoned by the original settlers. Check out one of these groups and meet the squatters. Sort of the free-trade zone of Usenet commerce. (In fact, there are some groups that are so secret, I can't even tell you about them.)

Usenet:

> alt.0d
> alt.1d
> alt.alien.vampire.flonk.flonk.flonk
> alt.alt.alt.alt.alt
> alt.art.theft.scream.scream.scream
> alt.basement.graveyard
> alt.bitch.pork
> alt.bogus.group
> alt.cuddle
> alt.dumpster
> alt.non.sequitur
> alt.religion.monica
> alt.rmgroup
> alt.silly-group.beable
> alt.test.my.new.group

VICES

Gambling and Oddsmaking

When you are not sitting in a smoke-filled room taking chances with your money, fill your urges with some great gambling and oddsmaking resources on the Net. The web sites will show you hints and tips about gambling and in the Usenet groups you can talk about various gambling games.

Web:
> http://www.rgtonline.com/
> http://www.vegas.com/vegascom/betbasc/bbtoc.html

Usenet:
> alt.gambling
> rec.gambling
> rec.gambling.blackjack
> rec.gambling.craps
> rec.gambling.misc
> rec.gambling.other-games
> rec.gambling.poker

Lotteries

Why work all your life and feel the satisfaction of successfully making your way in the world when you can buy a lottery ticket and have the chance to win your fortune all at once? Lottery fans, get together and discuss the lotteries on Usenet, or see all the lottery resources that are on the Web, such as number generators, lottery news and helpful software.

Web:
> http://www.aksi.net/lotto/lotlink.html

Usenet:
> rec.gambling.lottery

V

Sex Services Talk and General Discussion

Ah, the Modern Age. Overnight mail delivery, faxes, email, pizza in thirty minutes or less, home shopping networks and sex partners on demand. These are the things that make life worth living. Read about the going rates for services and where to find the various objects of your desire.

Usenet:
> alt.sex.erotica.marketplace
> alt.sex.services

WEATHER

Weather Reports: International

Here are weather reports for just about everywhere in the world. Once you have the Net access, no matter where are you or what you are planning, there is no excuse for letting the environment rain on your parade.

Web:
> http://www.intellicast.com/weather/intl/
> http://www.usatoday.com/weather/basemaps/wworld1.htm

Weather Reports: United States

As Mark Twain once said, "Everyone talks about putting up a good old American weather server on the Net, but nobody does anything about it"—until now, that is. When Mark Twain was alive, he had to get online weather information from an old gopher text-based system that was down a lot of the time. Today you have a choice of well-maintained, attractive web sites, all ready to show you current U.S. weather information whenever you want.

Web:
> http://www.intellicast.com/weather/usa/
> http://www.mit.edu/weather
> http://www.usatoday.com/weather/wfront.htm
> http://www.wunderground.com/

Weather World

The University of Illinois is making itself a Mecca of weather information. They provide current satellite images, weather maps and animations, as well as important meteorological information.

Web:
> http://ww2010.atmos.uiuc.edu/

WOMEN

Cybergrrl

Cybergrrl offers lots of great resources for women, covering domestic violence, family life, health and business resources and a gigantic listing of women's web pages.

Web:
> http://www.cybergrrl.com/

Feminism Talk and General Discussion

If it weren't for feminists, men wouldn't have anything to grumble about except the President's Address to the Nation interrupting the football game. It's been proven through history that women are good at organizing themselves and getting things done, and they've shown it once again in Usenet. Join one or all of these groups and discuss feminism in all its forms.

Usenet:
> alt.feminism
> alt.feminism.individualism
> soc.feminism

W

Notable Women

Everyone has heard of Susan B. Anthony. After all, her picture is on a piece of U.S. currency. Just because nobody happens to use that currency doesn't mean she's not popular. There are many other notable women who are not so famous, like Annie Jump Cannon, Blanche Ames, and Clara Adams-Ender, but they are among the many women who have done something remarkable during their lifetimes. Read these short biographies and become informed on women in history.

Web:
> http://mustang.coled.umn.edu/exploration/women.html

Web Weavers

Come explore the wonderful world of women by visiting Web Weavers, an annotated list of web pages by women. These pages will lead you down a rabbit hole of creativity, love, and whimsy. This is not a listing of every woman's home page. They have been selected for quality, not quantity.

Web:
> http://www.geocities.com/Heartland/Plains/1206/

WORLD CULTURES

Flags of the World

If you are looking for something unique and colorful with which to decorate your home, try downloading some of these flags of the world. Not only will they look nice hanging on your walls, but your visitors will be convinced that you have culture and good taste.

Web:
> http://www.adfa.oz.au/CS/flg/

Russian and American Friendship

Join this information system developed by Russians and Americans in an effort to form a bond between the two countries. There is information on almost anything you would want to know about Russia or the relationship between Russia and America—Cyrillic alphabet, news, history, music, art, medicine, economics, travel and tourism, and culture in general.

Web:
> http://alice.ibpm.serpukhov.su/friends/
> http://www.friends-partners.org/friends/

Listserv Mailing List:
> List Name: **friends**
> Subscribe to: **listserv@solar.rtd.utk.edu**

World Culture Talk and General Discussion

Usenet has many different discussion groups related to cultures. There are too many for me to list here, but all the names follow one of two patterns: either **alt.culture.***something* (for example, **alt.culture.hawaii**) or **soc.culture.***something* (for example **soc.culture.australia**).

Usenet:
>   alt.culture.*
>   soc.culture.*

WRITING

Electronic Publishing

Here's a great idea for a rejection-notice-free writing experience. Connect to this web site and read all about electronic publishing. Gather up all your writing and then publish it on the Net. Then write yourself a nice royalty check and treat yourself to some ice cream. The Net can make dreams come true.

Web:
>   http://www.iglou.com/hermit/epub/

Internet Directory of Published Writers

A database of published authors and literary agents who use the Internet. You can search the database by name or category or you can just browse the list. If you are a published author, enter yourself in the database.

Web:
>   http://www.writers.net/

Writer's Resources

Holy inkwell, Batman. The Net is loaded with resources for writers. Here are some links to useful references and fun material for all types of writers.

Web:
>   http://owl.english.purdue.edu/writing.html
>   http://www.arcana.com/shannon/writing.html
>   http://www.ceridwyn.com/motjuste/main.html

W

X-RATED RESOURCES

Erotic Resources

No bachelor party would be complete without a nice display of erotic links on your monitor. These sites will go well with any snack food you might be offering during the event except, perhaps, large, sloppy slices of pizza (which require your undivided attention). This list will take you to erotic places containing images and stories.

Web:
> http://naughty.com/
> http://web.cybercity.dk/clp/
> http://www.cyberporn.inter.net/indexg.html

Sex Magazines

When you are in the mood for a little culture or you want to read some informative articles, there are several big name magazines on the Net that you can browse. These magazines offer interesting excerpts of articles and columns from their print versions. For instance, while I was doing my research, I ran across an excerpt from an interview with G. Gordon Liddy in which the interviewer asked what Liddy thinks of group sex. (He likes it.) Oh, I almost forgot. These magazines have some pictures, too.

Web:
> http://www.hustler.com/
> http://www.penthousemag.com/
> http://www.playboy.com/

X-Rated Movies

Who needs gorgeous vistas, great soundtracks and good acting when you have a few naked people gyrating around in front of the camera? Get hard and fast information on X-rated movies, actors and actresses, and FAQs from related Usenet groups.

Web:
> http://alt.xmission.com/~legalize/asm/asm.html
> http://homepage.eznet.net/~rwilhelm/asm/dbsearch.html

Usenet:
> alt.sex.movies

IRC:
> #sexmovies

YOUNG ADULTS

Fishnet

Fishnet is an electronic magazine for academically gifted teens and their parents. It's packed with interesting news tidbits and has a college guide to assist a teen's move from high school to the higher education scene. Check out the collection of articles upd ited regularly and the teen jargon section.

Web:
> http://www.jayi.com/

Teen Chat Rooms

The great thing about working on the computer and saying it's a school project is that when you are grounded and you can't leave the house, you can still talk to kids your own age and have fun. There are lots of special chat areas just for people your age. Pick the one that is appropriate and talk all night long (or until you have to go back to doing your homework).

Web:
> http://pages.wbs.net/webchat3.so?cmd=cmd_doorway:Teen_13-15_Chat
> http://pages.wbs.net/webchat3.so?cmd=cmd_doorway:Teen_16-19_Chat

Teenagers

The nice thing about talking on the computer is that you don't have to worry about someone picking up the extension and listening to everything you say. Hop onto IRC and talk to teenagers around the world. They are waiting for you. (Don't forget to do your homework first.)

IRC:
> #teen
> #teens

Virtually React

For more fun than a barrel of teenaged monkeys, check out this great web site. It has an online version of React, a newspaper about teenagers. Read about teen-related news, sports features, entertainment topics, contests, jokes and lots of other stuff designed to make teenagers say, "Oh wow, Dude. That's so cool."

Web:
> http://www.react.com/

Y

ZINES

Netsurfer Digest

This is a cool zine. The fun folks at Netsurfer Digest troop around all week looking for interesting news and web sites just for you (and you, and you). I recommend you visit the site regularly, or even have the zine mailed to you, so there is always the guarantee that no matter what else happens in the chaos of day-to-day existence, at least you'll have something fun to look forward to this week. If you are new to Netsurfer Digest, check out all the back issues so you can see what you have been missing all this time.

Web:
   http://www.netsurf.com/nsd/

Urban Desires

If you are looking for a snazzy magazine to browse while sipping a cappuccino, you've found it. Urban Desires calls itself "an interactive magazine of metropolitan passions" and has a beautiful layout with book reviews, art, fiction, essays, regular columns and music reviews.

Web:
   http://desires.com/

Zine Lists

Making your own zine is the rage. In zine-land, nothing is sacred. Zines cover topics as mainstream as education, politics, and philosophy and as bizarre as hyperactive armadillos and free verse about plastic lawn ornaments.

Web:
   http://www.dominis.com/Zines/ByCategory/
   http://www.meer.net/~johnl/e-zine-list/

Zine Talk and General Discussion

Zines are cool, whether you are in the business of making them or just reading them. Learn about the latest releases, old zines making a comeback or calls for submissions. On this Usenet group, you can also participate in the discussion of publishing or submitting, copyright issues, and the production and distribution of electronic or print zines.

Usenet:
   alt.zines

ZOOLOGY

Frog Dissection Kit

Here's one of the hottest biology resources on the Net. The interactive web frog dissection kit is for use in high school biology classrooms. It uses photo images that allow you to perform a virtual dissection, including preparation, skin incisions, muscle incisions and examination of internal organs.

Web:
> http://george.lbl.gov/ITG.hm.pg.docs/dissect/
> http://teach.virginia.edu/go/frog/

Strange Animals

Scientists make mistakes, lots of them. This web site discusses the mistakes scientists have made in relation to animal life. Read about sea monsters, dragons, and dinosaurs, as well as forgeries and frauds perpetrated by scientists. There are also some fascinating drawings, made by scientists, that show various types of monsters.

Web:
> http://www.turnpike.net/~mscott/

Zoological Resources

Slippery, slimey, creepy, crawly, furry, or scaley, this site probably has it covered. This is a nice collection of resources such as web sites, databases, museums, databases, web servers, and image galleries related to zoology.

Web:
> http://www.york.biosis.org/zrdocs/zoolinfo/zoolinfo.htm

Z

Index

B

Categories from the catalog are printed in CAPITAL LETTERS.

browser, 166
    accessing anonymous ftp resources, 208, 354
    accessing gopher resources, 209
    accessing Usenet, 210
    initiating a telnet session, 212
    sending mail messages, 211
Bush, Vannevar, 165
BUYING AND SELLING, 634

C

Cailliau, Robert, 165
California, University of Southern, 389
ČANADA, 635
Čapek, Karel, 545
CARS AND TRUCKS, 636
cascade, 283
Cc header line, 109
CERN, 165
CGI script, 185
channels, 43
chat rooms, 492
CHEMISTRY, 637
client, 12
client programs
    shareware, 72
    where to get client programs, 72
client pull, 192
clients and servers, 12-14
clipboard, 108
COLLECTING, 638
COMICS, 639
common gateway interface, 185
compatible time sharing system, 292
compressed files, 426
COMPUTERS: CULTURE, 640
CONSUMER INFORMATION, 641
CONTESTS, 642
control message, 267
COOKING AND RECIPES, 643
Copenhagen, University of, 558
CPT, 435
CRAFTS, 644
CRYPTOGRAPHY, 645
CSO nameserver, 323
CTSS, 292
CYBERPUNK, 645
cyberspace, 180

D

D channel, 43
daemon, 95, 507
DANCE, 646
dark and stormy night, 412
data, 117
data channel, 43
data fork, 435
DCC, 543
de Morgan, Augustus, 195
DEC Network Systems Laboratory, 257
demodulation, 36
DIET AND NUTRITION, 647
digital, 36
Digital Equipment Corporation, 52
digital modem, 46
DikuMuds, 557
directories, ftp, 360
DISABILITIES, 648
distributed applications, 198
DNS, 70
DNS server, 70
document type definition, 222
domain name system, 70, 85
domain names, 70, 77
domains, 76
    list of top-level domains, 574-577
    pseudo domains, 91
dotfile, 104
downloading, 28, 350
DRUGS, 649
DTD, 222
Duke University, 255
dynamic IP address, 71

E

EARN, 455
ECONOMICS, 650
EDUCATION, 651
EDUCATION: COLLEGES AND UNIVERSITIES, 652
EDUCATION: K-12, 653
EDUCATION: TEACHING, 654
EFNet, 523
ELECTRONICS, 654
EMERGENCY AND DISASTER, 655
emulate, 51

Categories from the catalog are printed in CAPITAL LETTERS.

Categories from the catalog are printed in CAPITAL LETTERS.

Categories from the catalog are printed in CAPITAL LETTERS.

Categories from the catalog are printed in CAPITAL LETTERS.

Categories from the catalog are printed in CAPITAL LETTERS.

Categories from the catalog are printed in CAPITAL LETTERS.

Categories from the catalog are printed in CAPITAL LETTERS.

Categories from the catalog are printed in CAPITAL LETTERS.

Categories from the catalog are printed in CAPITAL LETTERS.

Categories from the catalog are printed in CAPITAL LETTERS.

U

Categories from the catalog are printed in CAPITAL LETTERS.

Categories from the catalog are printed in CAPITAL LETTERS.

Categories from the catalog are printed in CAPITAL LETTERS.

Categories from the catalog are printed in CAPITAL LETTERS.